German History in Modern Times
Four Lives of the Nation

This history of German-speaking central Europe offers an unusually wide perspective, emphasizing a succession of many-layered communal identities. It highlights the interplay of individual, society, culture, and political power, comparing German with other European patterns. Rather than treating "the Germans" as a collective whole whose national history amounts to a cumulative biography, these pages present the premodern age of the Holy Roman Empire; the nineteenth century; the years of war, dictatorship, and genocide between 1914 and 1945; and the Cold War and post–Cold War eras since 1945 as successive worlds of German life, thought, and mentality. The book sets forth the deep differences between them, even as it traces paths leading from one to the other. "Germany" here is polycentric and multicultural, including the many-peopled Austrian Habsburg Empire (and the post-1918 and post-1945 Austrian republics), the German Jews, and other minority groups. Women figure alongside men. Reinterpretation of National Socialism conveys here a new understanding of the Holocaust. A substantial final chapter appraises the post-1989 and present-day scene. Numerous illustrations reveal German self-presentations and styles of life, which often contrast with other cultures' ideas of Germany.

William W. Hagen is Professor of History at the University of California, Davis. He has held fellowships from the Alexander von Humboldt Foundation, the National Endowment for the Humanities, the Max-Planck Society, and the Institute for Advanced Study, Princeton. He is the author of *Germans, Poles, and Jews: The Nationality Conflict in the Prussian East, 1772–1914* and the prize-winning *Ordinary Prussians: Brandenburg Junkers and Villagers, 1500–1840* (Cambridge University Press). His wide-ranging research articles have appeared in many publications, including *The Journal of Modern History, Foreign Affairs, American Historical Review, Past & Present, Historische Zeitschrift,* and *Geschichte und Gesellschaft.*

"Bill Hagen has written a remarkable book that reconceptualizes the course of German history in several critical dimensions. Not only does Hagen take on and challenge several of the most conventional historiographical interpretations of the *longue durée* of German history (the Sonderweg thesis, etc.), but he shows in a very compelling way that one cannot understand German history in the twentieth century without a deep and profound knowledge of the history of the several competing German nations before 1866 and even before 1806. The result is an elegantly written book of great ambition and fascinating detail, particularly strong in social and political history and filled with surprising interpretive suggestions. The many illustrations, deeply integrated into the multiple, cascading narratives of the book, are also quite noteworthy."

   – John W. Boyer, University of Chicago

"Over a distinguished career William Hagen's histories have ranged masterfully across the fullest expanse of the German past, beginning in the long nineteenth century and continuing through the largest version of an early modern *longue durée*, before returning to the first half of the twentieth century. His themes have included the nationality conflicts of the Prussian east, early modern state formation and the character of absolutism, the relations of Junkers and villagers across four centuries, the transition from feudalism to capitalism, and the character of modern anti-Semitism. He now brings this extraordinary depth of knowledge to an ambitiously conceived general history, whose varying notations of 'Germany' between the premodern Holy Roman Empire and the successive states of modern times (his 'four lives of the nation') cast a familiar landscape in exciting new light. In its dethroning of His Majesty the nation-state, attentiveness to the many different Germanies, and attunement to the ethico-political challenge of writing German history after Nazism, this is truly a history for our times."

   – Geoff Eley, University of Michigan

"William Hagen's strikingly original book offers a rich picture of the history of German-speaking Central Europe since the Reformation. Hagen treats neither Nazism nor market capitalism as natural or inevitable results of the many-sided history of this diverse region, but emphasizes contingencies – and the reversibility of developments like liberalism, authoritarianism, communist dictatorship, and European integration. Hagen's concise text is accompanied by a thought-provoking visual history that offers a set of unusual and well-chosen images, and a fine bibliography. Both students and professional scholars will find this a fresh, clear, and fascinating introduction to the history of not one, but many Germanies over the last 500 years."

   – Suzanne Marchand, Louisiana State University

German History in Modern Times

Four Lives of the Nation

WILLIAM W. HAGEN
University of California, Davis

CAMBRIDGE
UNIVERSITY PRESS

CAMBRIDGE UNIVERSITY PRESS
Cambridge, New York, Melbourne, Madrid, Cape Town,
Singapore, São Paulo, Delhi, Mexico City

Cambridge University Press
32 Avenue of the Americas, New York, NY 10013-2473, USA

www.cambridge.org
Information on this title: www.cambridge.org/9780521175210

First published 2012

Printed in the United States of America

A catalog record for this publication is available from the British Library.

Library of Congress Cataloging in Publication Data

Hagen, William W.
German history in modern times : four lives of the nation / William W. Hagen.
    p.   cm.
Includes bibliographical references and index.
ISBN 978-0-521-19190-6
1. Germany – History.   2. Germans – Europe, Central – History.   3. Europe,
Central – History.   I. Title.
DD175.H35   2011
943–dc22   2011015743

ISBN 978-0-521-19190-6 Hardback
ISBN 978-0-521-17521-0 Paperback

Contents

Figures

Maps

Tables

Preface

From this the poem springs: that we live in a place
That is not our own and, much more, not ourselves
And hard it is in spite of blazoned days.

The major abstraction is the commonal,
The inanimate, difficult visage. Who is it?

How simply the fictive hero becomes the real;
How gladly with proper words the soldier dies,
If he must, or lives on the bread of faithful speech.

Wallace Stevens, *Notes Toward a Supreme Fiction* (1942)
(from *Collected Poems*, Vintage, 1982, pp. 383, 388, 408)

Wallace Stevens's words, penned at a dark hour of World War II, are polestars for the navigator of German history, as they are for all humanity. Their subjects – our precarious lifeline to time and place, collective identity's exultations and mysteries, the myths by which we animate the world and the roles we invent to enact – are central to the following pages. If these themes easily transmute into tragedy – and not only in the German lands! – Stevens evokes too the "blazoned days," inscribed with communal meaning and glory, when humanity experiences the reward of cultural belonging and confidence in its causes' triumphs.

I chart this book's course in the Introduction. It synthesizes more than a few decades of reading, writing, and teaching. Nowhere have I conveyed ideas encountered in the historical literature without reworking them to fit the arguments I have crafted and set forth here. I myself have spent long years in archival research and scholarly publication on widely differing themes in modern and early modern central European history. I believe it can be fairly claimed that this book's architecture of analysis and interpretation is new. So too are many of its sketches of the house of German history's separate rooms, and of their furnishings and inhabitants. My perspective emerged from lengthy dialogue with other historians, and I contrast it in the successive chapters to earlier and presently contending schools of thought. Citation in footnotes of the vast relevant literature would not brighten the light I aim to throw on a many-winged edifice, but would rather obscure it in scholarly thickets. In the bibliography, more far-ranging than most, the reader will find many roadmaps to further explorations.

The following pages' intent is illuminative, not encyclopedic. They do not convey dense narrative left to explain itself. For brevity's sake, and coherence, worthy themes remain unbroached. It is an undertaking wide in chronological and thematic compass, in which it would be improbable that no errors of fact should have sprouted here and there in the analytical garden. But I am confident they will not sap the strength of the interpretive tree, which has grown up thanks to insightful teachers and scholars of past generations, colleagues in the profession – including this volume's editor, Lewis Bateman – and innumerable classroom students whose search for clarity and comprehension reinvigorated my own. Shana Meyer expertly guided this book through production. David Cox authored its excellent maps.

To the guild – women and men – masters, journeymen, apprentices!
An die Zunft!

Introduction

I address this book to all readers curious to know the drama of modern German history. It assumes no prior acquaintance with the subject, but rather conveys what its author, in many years of teaching and writing, has learned to be the essential knowledge without which further exploration and inquiry are hardly possible. This includes a minimal familiarity with the principal broad-gauged interpretations and "master narratives" that have competed among historians and other scholars, and continue to do so today. All chronologically framed accounts are inescapably interpretive and theoretical. It is futile to suppose that German history – or any other history – can be compressed into a seemingly objective, self-explanatory narrative.

History, like all the human and natural sciences, happens in the global republic of letters. It is a form of human understanding, not a mirror-like reflection of events, which, after all, do not interpret themselves, nor are they laden with singular meanings obvious to all retrospective viewers. It accumulates documented, ascertainable knowledge, not only in response to controversies and riddles of life inherited from the past, but equally to questions rooted in contemporary dilemmas and strivings. The discipline of history is a space where inquiring minds, driven by multifarious and competing passions and interests, analyze facts of human experience – empirical knowledge – to gain structured understanding and guidelines for present judgment and action, and where they rigorously query the solidity of resulting claims to truth and meaning.

Yet such considerations must not deter the teacher and writer from fashioning a lucid and defensible, centuries-spanning analysis of even so complex a subject as German history – a perhaps deceivingly straightforward concept whose subtleties these pages will plumb. It is one of the historian's jobs to render multidimensional, long-range history coherent, and thus thinkable and debatable. I have often urged students to rise to the challenge of "creative simplification" so as to invest particularized phenomena with meaningful patterns. Did not Albert Einstein achieve this in the proposition $e = mc^2$?

The picture these pages present cannot be translated into a formula. But the reader will find that the separate chapters weave multicolored threads forming a larger tapestry. It is a pattern that emerges from the fundamental challenge that arises in thinking something anew: What is the first step toward comprehension, and what is the next? The answers amount to a burgeoning progression of arguments. The fundamental themes are, as they must be in an introductory work, the organization of power in state and economy; compelling visions of meaningful and desirable social and national life; and the interplay – ideologically and culturally coded – between these two realms of human life, material and intellectual.

National history, like the history of any other human collectivity, and even of single individuals, runs the risk of "naturalizing" its subject – that is, of treating it as an integrated phenomenon, with a "character" spanning the years and centuries, "evolving" or "unfolding" in time so as to "realize" itself or rise to the height of its "development." This book's subtitle, "Four Lives of the Nation," points not to the historical continuity of an organic whole – "the German nation" – but rather to four quite different epochs in the experience of the German-speaking peoples of central Europe. Between them, of course, were continuities, but also ruptures so great as to occasion the disappearance of social, political, and cultural identities and the death of worldviews and spirits of the age (terms derived from their now semi-English German originals, *Weltanschauung* and *Zeitgeist*).

The national lives I refer to, and discuss in the book's four subsections are (1) the era of the pre-nationalist German lands – the "Holy Roman Empire of the German Nation," as it came to be called – spanning the centuries before the world-changing French Revolution of 1789; (2) the years 1789–1914 – the "long nineteenth century" – during which new collective self-understandings emerged, distilled out of varying mixtures of modern nationalism, liberalism, and socialism; (3) the violent, traumatic, and tragic experience in the years between 1914 and 1945 of two world wars, crisis-rocked democracy, dictatorship and mass murder; and (4) the emergence from war, moral catastrophe, and national semi-extinction of new identities – in part imposed from outside, defensive, self-denying, but also self-generated, recuperative, and innovative – from the end of World War II to the present. The absorption in 1990 of defunct communist East Germany into the West German Federal Republic – an unprecedented fusion, yet also a reunification – raises the question whether dawn may now be breaking on a fifth German nation. It seems to be so – we will return to this question – but such a complex community's contours still lie in semi-shadow.

The emergence in their day of these four German-speaking life-worlds spelled the death or senescence of their precursors, accompanied by more or less violence, suffering, injustice, and crisis of meaning. Yet continuities abound, without whose emphasis long-range historical explanations pale.

After Chapter 1's sketch of influential twentieth-century interpretations of modern German history, the book unveils the geographical and regional settings in which German-speaking people – many-minded, socially variegated, politically and religiously centrifugal – have enacted their history. Another chapter addresses the legacy of the Middle Ages – the medieval millennium – and the struggles of the sixteenth and seventeenth centuries over the reformation of Christianity and the government of Christendom. On these great themes I offer the barest of what anyone pondering modern German history must understand.

With the emergence in the German lands in the seventeenth and eighteenth centuries of military-bureaucratic power-states, and the simultaneous impact of the European Enlightenment and a commercialized market economy moving toward industrialization, the book's plot thickens. It will be seen that the legacy of the early modern – that is, the pre-1789 or pre-French Revolution – era to the modern history of the nineteenth and twentieth centuries is of considerable and, in some interpreters' minds, fateful significance. It is important to gain confidence in one's ability to connect fundamental developments in the last three or four centuries, without succumbing to fallacious notions of inescapable predetermination.

This book proceeds more thematically than chronologically, although historical phenomena must be grasped in their passage through time. Human life displays an interaction between the search for power, material advantage, and self-interest on the one hand and cultural and ethical meaning and social community on the other. There is a *power-culture axis* around which human motives constitute themselves both by the pursuit of power (individual, communal, national) and of cultural values, so that power becomes meaningful and worthy of possession – that is, morally legitimate – in the eyes of its holders and (if wielded successfully) its subjects. Power shorn of legitimacy is, especially if it falters, ripe for repudiation and revolution.

In the history of the German lands, as in many other histories, the organization of government has been an explosive problem. Likewise, the state's cultural justification and mission, as well as the emotional and ethical benefits it promised its subjects, have been in Germany, as elsewhere, much contested. It is well known that in Hitler's National Socialist dictatorship of 1933–1945, history's most aggressive and bloody-handed nationalism held sway. Less often is it remembered that pre-1933 German society brought forth Europe's most formidable working-class socialist movement, much inspired by Marxism. Christian conservative monarchism, deep-rooted federalist-minded localism, populist political Catholicism, and ethnic and religious subcultures have all influentially walked German central Europe's stage.

The Holocaust – or Shoah (Hebrew for "catastrophe") – brought to a sudden and previously unimaginable end one of the world's most important Jewish communities. In the nineteenth century, most of the millions-strong central European Jews ardently embraced German culture and identity, making contributions of the highest importance both to Jewish and non-Jewish German life. In science and technology, and in art, literature, and music, the German lands have brought forth a fertile harvest of controversial and disruptive, but also enriching and horizon-widening modernity and modernism.

Alongside such themes, some of them neglected in broad-gauged histories, these pages will trace the earlier parliamentary and welfare-state developments on which the present-day German Federal Republic's political democracy and self-styled "socially responsible market economy" have built. Nor have I excluded Austria, and especially not the mighty Austrian Habsburg monarchy, from its crucial role in central European history. The attainment of a unified nation-state – born, as we will see, in 1866–1871 from Prussian-German armed might – could not sever the ties joining the two great German-speaking political and cultural spheres centered on Prussian Berlin and Austrian Vienna. Under Hitler they came together in a much desired reunion, although it proved to be a marriage of destruction.

The post-1945 years have witnessed great changes, as the homogeneity that nationalist intolerance and defeat in war imposed (despite deep regional differences among German-speakers themselves) gave way to large-scale immigration, especially from Christian and Muslim regions of the Mediterranean basin. Germany and Austria are today once again ethnically diverse societies, and their efforts to adjust to this condition against the background of earlier exclusionary nationalism are a crucial test.

A broadly conceived history of the German lands, like other accounts of whole societies, must appear as an interplay of cultural-intellectual, economic-technological, political, and social factors. The historian enjoys the freedom, more than the other human sciences' practitioners, of precisely *not* privileging any one of these life dimensions over the others, but rather of investigating each and all as the problem at hand dictates. Confidence must be gained to work knowledgeably at these four main desks of the historiographical command post, and to know when to shift from one to another. Causal primacy among the various spheres of human action and creativity will vary with the question raised. Panoramic historical interpretations are intellectual constructions – not rigid and unchanging verities, but rather ever-evolving. So long as their design does not recklessly fly in the face of empirical fact, they are true in – and, one could add, true to – their own day.

These pages trace the shifting interrelations of society, politics, and culture, but they also accept the "simultaneity of the dissimilar" in human affairs. Daily life in the countryside, small towns, and big cities moved to different rhythms. High intellectual and artistic culture, too, often followed its own paths. Family and gender relations display a certain self-generated dynamic, as was also true of the political history of the Austrian-ruled lands in comparison with other German states.

The tragic era of National Socialism shows that the optimistic concept of an ever-rising trajectory of historical progress must be countered by recognition that terrible breakdowns occur. In the time and place at which this book was written, and will be read, it is impossible not to contrast modern German history's configuration with the scenario for humanity written by liberal-minded thinkers of the eighteenth-century Enlightenment: advancing political enfranchisement and democratization, social equality, scientific mastery of nature, and the subjection of power to rationally grounded law and universal ethics. These ideals have long been the guiding stars for the western world's political cultures as they drift – or hurtle – forward into an unknown and undetermined future. These pages will reveal how this scenario took original shapes of its own in German central Europe, and how these fared over time.

A book's Introduction is not the place to deliver final judgments on such ventures' outcomes. Yet readers will appreciate that our own culture's concerns lend urgency to the question of the viability of the western democratic vision and its accompanying assumptions about human progress. At the same time, in science and philosophy, as in the writing of history, no beliefs – or hopes – are sacrosanct. We must test the strength of the liberal-democratic blueprint of rational progress to interpret the real world of human history, even at the cost of exposing it, in part or whole, as a powerful illusion. German history is one of its crucial testing grounds. Was Hitler's "Third Reich" a regressive and barbarous departure from the path of all-conquering Enlightenment, or was it an ominous embodiment of anti-liberal modernity? This is not the only question to pose, but it has absorbed powerful minds.

This book's many visual images translate into particular sites and individual personalities the historical structures, developments, and mentalities of which the successive chapters speak. They form a microconstellation illuminating the text's macrostructure. They aim, too, to evoke recognition of the humanity of the actors in this book's dramas, and in most cases sympathy for them as well, even if many of the German lands' inhabitants in the past several centuries were different from their Anglo-American counterparts and ourselves: more conservative-minded or more radical, or otherwise culturally distant.

National Socialism's shadow engulfed the lives of myriads of German-speaking people, morally crippling or destroying many of them through complicity in the deaths of millions of Jewish and non-German victims of Hitlerism's murderous machinery. Yet in the last three or four centuries a far greater number of them lived under the same moral firmament as overarched neighboring cultures in the past and ourselves today: clouded by present uncertainties and illusions and the past's irreparable missteps, illuminated by life's rewards, communal solidarities, and possibilities of freedom.

Between the late eighteenth century and the outbreak in 1914 of World War I, the German lands practiced less violence than other European Great Powers and the United States. The Federal Republic today, and Austria too, are democracies whose liberality, prosperity, and commitment to citizenly equality and universal human rights are, if imperfect, yet also second to none among the world's societies. A history of German central Europe must account for this outcome as well as the immense and tragic violence that the National Socialist regime – a dictatorship, although with much popular backing – inflicted on other peoples, on German-speakers themselves, and on the idea of Germany.

I

Historiographie

Interpreting German History

Historical knowledge, like scientific knowledge, is a many-dimensioned, accumulating but sometimes self-revolutionizing achievement of hypothesis-driven, empirical (evidence-based) research. It moves simultaneously in different directions, according to whether the problem under investigation is one of political, social, economic, or cultural history. Yet there has been, from the earliest human thinking about history, a powerful tendency to synthesize knowledge of the past into an all-encompassing single narrative, whether at the local level of the tribe or city-state, or at the higher levels of the kingdom or territorial state, religiously defined civilization, or the entire world. In present-day language, such integrated histories bear the name of "master narratives." However objectively they may be presented, as if there were no reasonable alternatives, it is important to realize that they are, at their best, intellectual constructions subject to revision in the light of new evidence and interpretation. At their worst they are ideologically distorted accounts serving the ends of seekers or holders of power.

Historical knowledge is not scholarship's exclusive preserve. Master narratives are memorized roadmaps by which individuals and whole societies attempt to guide themselves forward. They are learned in school, in political ritual, in the popular media, and in private life, passed – as is sometimes said, "at the supper table" – from one generation to the next. They are more often uncritically adopted, as if they were common sense, than consciously embraced after a process of critical appraisal, or of searching for alternatives to the popularly prevalent view. Yet it is also typical of modern societies that some aspects of widely shared historical narratives are controversial and even hotly contested, especially those on which conflicting political ideologies hinge.

In post-1945 thinking about modern German history, the disastrous era of National Socialist dictatorship, imperialism, and genocide, although it lasted but twelve years (1933–1945), has been the focal point of the broad interpretations contending for influence over people's minds and shaping German self-understanding. Because the war that Hitler launched was a traumatic

6

experience for all Europe, as well as for the United States and the world at large, any understanding of the twentieth century requires an explanation of National Socialism. Not surprisingly, there are many historians of Germany in foreign lands, especially in Britain and north America. Pre-1945 German history, although vital to German-speakers themselves, is important in a crucial – if in part ominous – way to the rest of the world.

Yet 1945 now lies several generations in the past. Post-World War II German history offers a dramatic story of recovery from crushing defeat amid conflicting tendencies to self-blindingly deny and constructively confront Hitlerism's agonizing legacy. In the end, repudiation of illiberalism prevailed, even if – as in all societies – authoritarian impulses survive. The vigor of West Germany's parliamentary democracy and "socially responsible market economy," which after 1990 successfully incoporated the lands of the former Soviet-aligned East Germany, has brought forth a contemporary state and society that other countries, especially in post-communist eastern Europe, are interested in emulating. Although it possesses one of the world's strongest economies, the Federal Republic of Germany is now struggling – like other western countries – to come to terms with economic globalization's destabilizing dynamics. Yet it acts more effectively than most nations in response to the challenges posed by social disparities and environmental degradation at home, and by North-South world inequality abroad.

How to connect the histories of the pre-1933 and post-1945 German lands with the National Socialist years is a challenging question, energetically debated among professional historians. Yet there is widespread agreement, especially in public education and popular culture (including the consciousness-molding film and television industries), about what seem to be the "central facts" of modern German history, even if controversy surrounds their interpretation. Here, summed up in ten widely shared propositions, is the "standard model" that competing broad-gauged narratives have, with varying emphases, conveyed and sought to explain. (Readers unfamiliar with the events and personalities mentioned here will learn of them in later pages.)

- Deploying the military power of the monarchical-aristocratic, Berlin-centered Kingdom of Prussia, "Iron Chancellor" Otto von Bismarck forged out of the scattered principalities of the premodern German lands (once quaintly called "the Germanies") a powerful united national state: the German Empire of 1871–1918.
- In 1914, Kaiser (emperor) William II's government – acting in concert with Austro-Hungarian emperor Franz Joseph's regime – unleashed (or co-ignited) World War I, aggressively seeking German preeminence among the Great Powers, overseas expansion, and large territorial gains in eastern Europe.
- Owing finally to American intervention in the war, the German-Austrian Central Powers in 1918 suffered defeat. The Kaiser's regime fell amid left-wing revolution on the home front. Moderate elements eventually gained

the upper hand, establishing a shaky liberal democracy: the Weimar Republic. But the 1919 Treaty of Versailles's punitive terms, imposed by the Great War's victor powers, weakened the new democracy's popular acceptance. In the 1920s, it suffered wrenching economic crises and international humiliation.

- In the worldwide Great Depression that gripped Germany in 1929–1933, radical mass movements on both the left (the German Communists) and the right (Hitler's National Socialists) grew mightily, paralyzing Weimar's parliamentary system. A similar fate befell the post-1918 Austrian republic. In 1933 Hitler, having assembled the strongest electoral base, assumed the chancellorship with the support of conservatives who had never reconciled themselves to their 1918 defeats.

- The National Socialists established a ruthless, police-state dictatorship. Economic recovery and rearmament followed. In 1939 Hitler's aggressive foreign policy sparked World War II, which his armies fought with seeming irresistibility. In 1941 he acted on a longstanding aim, launching an anti-communist crusade of destruction against Soviet ("Bolshevik") Russia, catalyzing an unprecedented program of mass murder against European Jews and a campaign of enslavement against other targeted peoples of eastern Europe.

- In 1943–1945, Germany suffered disastrous battlefield defeat at both Soviet and western hands. For the next forty-five years (1945–1990) the victorious Allies, after stripping the country of its eastern provinces, held it in division and subjection: the western Federal Republic of Germany opposing the eastern German Democratic Republic, subordinated respectively to the American-led NATO alliance and to the Soviet Union. Thus did the German nation suffer for having succumbed to fanatical, racist nationalism under Hitler's command.

- Under western – and especially American – tutelage, West Germany developed, after 1949, into a well-functioning liberal democracy. It bore responsibility, or was forced to bear responsibility, for National Socialism's crimes and for making reparations to its victims. When in 1989 the Soviet empire began to collapse, revolt stirred in communist East Germany. The peoples of the two German states seized the opportunity to incorporate the eastern lands into the western state, reunifying the country in 1990.

- Although reunification cost West German society some of its prosperity, there is wide consensus that it was desirable and has proved a success. Public opinion outside Germany largely accepts this judgment.

- Skeptical views surface occasionally among British, French, and north American critics, and among some Germans as well. They observe that, after 1990, reunification's burdens evoked embittered reactions, especially among former East Germans, but also in West Germany. Right-radical politics located the targets of resentment in the roughly 8 percent of the population who were born abroad, mostly in Turkey and other largely Muslim developing countries, and their German-born children. They suffered assault, on a few occasions lethal, as an alleged menace to the ethnic unity and cultural-political coherence of the nation. While acts of xenophobic violence, never numerous, dwindled in the new century, they occur intermittently, both in west and east.

- Yet in the present day an enlightened and liberal-minded electorate, favoring German integration in a united Europe (the European Union [EU]), steers public affairs. Although there exists in reunited Germany an anti-EU minority, sometimes nationalist-minded and prejudice-laden, it is smaller and less significant than similar right-radical movements elsewhere in western and central Europe. Meanwhile Germany – one of the world's leading trading nations – has built Europe's largest economy, inextricably bound up with its EU neighbors, controversial though their mutual relations and responsibilities sometimes are. The Federal Republic now figures on the world's landscape as a progressive and democratic land that has, in its public culture, confronted and largely disarmed the National Socialist past.

Contending Interpretations

If these points combine into a widely embraced scenario or narrative, the challenge remains to offer a causal explanation for it, including the tragic violence of Hitler's dictatorship. Among political writers and journalists, professional historians, and social scientists, four broad interpretive approaches have been especially influential.

There is, first, the "negative identity" argument. Raised to caricatured heights in the western Allies' anti-German propaganda in the two world wars, and fitfully perpetuated in the popular media today, this approach postulates a "German national character" stamped, before 1945, by authoritarianism toward outsiders and deference at home toward antidemocratic or dictatorial authority; by militarism and expansionary drives, particularly in eastern, Slavic directions; and by ethnic intolerance and anti-Semitism, readiness for violence, and related social-psychological disabilities.

This approach struggles to explain why the characteristics it targets were more prevalent among German-speakers than other peoples. The usual explanation (apart from emotion-driven, irrational notions of "inborn" or "inherent traits") concentrates on the historical effects of "Prussian militarism" (or the "legacy of the premodern military-bureaucratic state") paired – especially so far as anti-Jewish prejudice and political anti-Semitism are concerned – with "persecutory Christianity." Yet such influences bore down on most large European countries, so that it is not easy to explain why their effects were uniquely disastrous in the German lands.

Second, and dissenting from some of the previously listed ten propositions, there is the moderate-conservative view. This found influential expression in the writings of eminent German historians, notably Friedrich Meinecke (1862–1954) and Gerhard Ritter (1888–1967). They held that the ruling establishment of Imperial Germany (1871–1918), despite its conservative monarchism and

(a)

FIGURE I.I. STEREOTYPES OF GERMAN SOCIETY AND HISTORY
(a) Prussian reserve officers passing review, ca. 1900, quite likely on Imperial Germany's national holiday, which celebrated victory against France in the 1870–1871 war over German unification. Reserve officer status was a prized attribute among socially ascendant middle-class professionals of patriotic and nationalist temperament. Many critical eyes have detected in such pictures the "militarization of German society" and even the "feudalization of the bourgeoisie." But similar scenes might easily be documented from pre-1914 life in western Europe and the United States.

military ambitions, was politically responsible and mindful of the desirability of European peace. World War I was a catastrophe for which Germany and its Austrian partner were not more responsible than other Great Powers. Wartime defeat unleashed in German central Europe the radical forces of modern "mass society." Political democratization and waning popular religiosity weakened older social-cultural restraints and in the unstable conditions of the 1920s encouraged the rise of Communism and National Socialism. The 1919 Versailles Treaty gave fateful expression to French and Anglo-American opposition to Germany's rightful and necessary strong role in the international system, which in Bismarck's day had been, as this view holds, a stabilizing one.

A Madman's Dream—by Arthur Szyk

(b)

FIGURE 1.1 *(continued)*

(b) "A Madman's Dream," caricaturizing Adolf Hitler and accomplices, drawn by Polish-Jewish artist Arthur Szyk in his book, *The New Order*, published in 1941 in the United States, where he found wartime refuge. Italian dictator Benito Mussolini holds the standard above the National Socialist *Führer* (Leader), who is flanked by Japanese allies as well as National Socialist strongmen. Hitler sits enthroned on the prostrate figure of "the sub-human" (*Untermensch*), a racist concept the National Socialists applied with genocidal intent both to Jews and targeted Slavic peoples, and here embodied in the supreme bogeyman of the Russian Jewish communist or Bolshevik (who is inscribed with the NS sentiment "may the *Untermensch* croak"). Subservient Uncle Sam and British John Bull, defeated by German power, are led before Hitler in chains. Nazism deserved Szyk's ridicule, of course. Such propaganda built on anti-German imagery that took shape in the pre-1914 decades and during World War I, bequeathing stereotypes that persist today, as American popular culture still sometimes shows.

Source: (a) Landesbildstelle Berlin; (b) Reproduced with the cooperation of The Arthur Szyk Society, Burlingame, CA www.szyk.org.

Hitlerism was deplorable, but many German-speaking conservatives and moderate liberals (including many engaged Christians) opposed it, even at the cost of their lives. The furies of National Socialist racism and the Holocaust represent modern life's destructive potential when left unguided by political and social leadership firmly anchored in national tradition and western, Christianity-hued humanist culture.

This approach underplayed the problem of the early twentieth-century radicalization of conservatism, in which many among the propertied and educated classes eventually shifted their support to the National Socialists or became their fellow travelers. Moreover, it could not persuasively explain why "the masses" drifted away from the leadership of the long-established upper-class "responsible authorities" in church and state.

There is, thirdly, the mid-twentieth-century liberal-democratic view, representing still today the most influential of interpetations. Among its chief formulators were historian Hans Rosenberg (1904–1988), an emigré in America from National Socialist Germany, sociologist Ralf Dahrendorf, and West German historians Fritz Fischer and Hans-Ulrich Wehler. British and north American scholars also made vital contributions. This interpretation holds that the history of the German lands followed a (negatively judged) "separate path" (*Sonderweg*) because the strength of premodern institutions and power interests (especially in the kingdom of Prussia) prevented a revolutionary breakthrough of liberal democracy on the French or Anglo-American models. Instead, Bismarck's "authoritarian" and "pseudo-democratized" post-1871 Empire was the scene of a rapid industrialization that created powerful new economic elites siding with the imperial regime, while the burgeoning working class organized itself as a broad-based Marxism-inspired Social Democratic (Socialist) movement. In 1914 Kaiser William II's government, aiming to counter rising threats to his government's authority, provoked – or at any rate willingly plunged into – World War I, hoping for a resounding victory that would silence the Empire's internal critics. Liberal democracy could not flourish in this setting. Instead, mass-based right-radical nationalism arose among conservative-minded and resentment-laden sections of the population in opposition to the Socialists and (after World War I) the newly organized Communists.

Because, in this view, the pre-1914 Imperial regime and its backers had exploited German nationalism to legitimize its conservative-monarchical institutions, the National Socialists found it easier to manipulate this powerful sentiment in directing popular discontent over the Weimar Republic's economic misery against the West (held responsible for the hated Versailles Treaty), against the perceived threat of Russian Bolshevism, and against the domestic left, especially the Communists. Such National Socialist propaganda, paired with antidemocratic conservatives' active or passive support, opened the gates to Hitler's dictatorship.

"Separate path" analysis views the wartime Holocaust as the effect of German nationalism's extreme radicalization through pseudoscientific "racialization." It brought to murderous culmination a program of crude economic and cultural anti-Semitism accompanying Hitler's expansion into eastern Europe and anti-Soviet crusade. Even though effective internal domestic resistance against the National Socialist dictatorship was almost impossible, not all German-speakers supported Hitler's regime. Yet in 1945 infusion was required of imported Anglo-American ideas and institutions to buttress a fragile tradition of oft-defeated German liberalism and turn from the fateful "separate

FIGURE 1.2. DISTINGUISHED HISTORIANS OF MODERATE-CONSERVATIVE AND PRUSSIAN-GERMAN ORIENTATION

Pictured here is long-lived Friedrich Meinecke (1862–1954), prestigious and influential political-intellectual historian: liberal monarchist in his early career, supportive after 1918 of the Weimar Republic, associated with the post-1933 upper-class opposition to Hitler. In World War II's aftermath he authored *The German Catastrophe* (1946), which struggled to interpret Hitler's dictatorship without being able to explain the meanings it held for its followers or to confront its racism-driven crimes. Eminent also was Otto Hintze (1861–1940), progressive and innovative, sociologically oriented historian, but author nonetheless of an affirmative history of the Kingdom of Prussia (1915). Hintze withdrew after 1933 from professional life, in part because of persecution of his Jewish-born (and Protestant baptized) historian wife, Hedwig (1884–1942). She was driven to suicide in the German-occupied Netherlands, where she had earlier sought protection in exile from arrest and deportation to the concentration camps. Important as well was Gerhard Ritter (1888–1967), conservative nationalist historian and anti-National Socialist Christian also associated with the opposition to Hitler. After 1945 Ritter defended the Prussian legacy against charges of overweening militarism and interpreted National Socialism as a break with earlier German history. To Ritter, as to Meinecke and others of their persuasion, modernity's radical potentialities – including fascism and communism – seemed foreign to German culture, rather than figuring, as they should and must, as extremist elements within it.

Source: Bildarchiv Preussischer Kulturbesitz / Art Resource, NY.

path" onto a democratic highway. This was, initially, only possible in West Germany. In the Soviet-dominated German Democratic Republic communist dictatorship succeeded the vanquished National Socialist regime, one totalitarianism replacing the other.

This liberal-democratic perspective has overemphasized the weight of premodern institutions and mentalities, and underestimated modern society's susceptibility, apart from all "feudal-aristocratic tradition" and "manipulation from above," to the appeal of radical nationalism. Social groups that emerged with urban-industrial capitalism – and not only those rooted in the rural and small-town past, still deferential to "preindustrial elites" – showed themselves capable of yielding to a self-generated antidemocratic, anti-leftist, authoritarian-populist nationalism and in this way bringing forth Hitler's dictatorship.

Finally, a Marxist-Leninist master narrative flowed from the pens of Soviet-influenced historians, pre-1939 and post-1945 alike. They concentrated on the rise in Germany of an industrial capitalism that, in their view, aggressively sought imperialist expansion overseas and into eastern Europe. Big business used the Bismarckian Empire as its sword and shield, especially against the rise of socialism. There resulted a reactionary alliance of "Prussian militarism" and "monopoly capital." Defeated in World War I, and viscerally opposed to the Weimar Republic, these powerful forces patronized the National Socialists, building them up as a mass movement to overthrow the fragile democracy, "break the shackles" of the Versailles Treaty, and establish Hitler's dictatorship as a screen behind which right-wing power elites could continue on their destructive course.

Rejecting this Soviet approach, West German and Anglo-American neo-Marxists in the 1970s and 1980s fashioned a different analysis, arguing that liberal historians had idealized the democratic character of the French and Anglo-American paths to modernity. Instead, western society displays conflicting interactions between industrial-technological development and processes of democratization. Business entrepreneurs, and especially corporate capital, can coexist with various organizations of political power. In the past, they did not require liberal democracy alone to advance their interests and those of the social circles they represented. Meanwhile, industrialization gave rise to a city-based popular culture in which the pleasures of the entertainment media and the lure of affordable consumer wares, often patriotically packaged, accustomed ordinary people ever more to accept "high" or "late" capitalism as the "end of history." After the era of the world wars, while some supported moderate leftist programs at the polls, others drifted away to the center or the right.

This line of thinking emphasized that Hitler's dictatorship was the culmination of a grassroots right-wing mobilization in the German-speaking lands going back to the 1890s. It was stirred up by activists of mostly middle-class origin – in provincial towns and villages, but no less in the industrializing cities, including among conservative and nationalistic wage and salary workers – in hostile reaction (among other things) to Imperial German and Austro-German socialism. After the upheaval of World War I, many among the once well-situated educated and propertied classes, and much of big business, also supported National Socialism, which reaped the harvest of earlier right-wing movements.

The National Socialist seizure of power demonstrates, as historians generally agree, that modern liberal-democratic market societies are exposed to dictatorial mass movements from the right as much as (or more) than the left. The only guarantee against rightist totalitarianism, the neo-Marxist approach suggested, was to attain worldwide socialism – or, minimally, universal prevalence of a democratic and egalitarian social-welfare state that would be free of the aggressively competitive and nationalistic impulses of the capitalist system.

The Soviet approach suffered from the weakness of single-factor, crudely economic explanation exaggerating the causal agency of power elites. Western neo-Marxist analysis, in search of industrial capitalism's relation to democracy and dictatorship, underplayed the demonstrable importance of firmly anchored liberal democracy and its accompanying constitutional law and civil liberties as effective barriers to totalitarian radicalism and dictatorship. Germany alone, among advanced western industrial societies, fell under fascist rule, while other crisis-ridden capitalist polities upheld parliamentary democracy against the temptations of rightist authoritarianism. It remains today a crucial question how, in the midst of an ever more market-driven globalized world, rocked by deeply destabilizing social and cultural change, liberal-democratic political-legal institutions – and a fluid, evolving social order conducive to them – can be sustained and spread.

There is much to build on in the previously sketched interpretations. At any rate they pose challenging questions, including that of authoritarianism, as difficult as this may be to isolate and explain. Yet each approach is situated in an ideologically charged field that discourages more multidimensional analysis, such as these pages aim to offer. Moreover, as the alert reader will have observed, they all view the essential site of German history as the Berlin-centered Empire of 1871 and its successor states, the Weimar Republic and Hitler's dictatorship. This pushes offstage the Austrian Habsburg monarchy and many crucial developments of German political and cultural-intellectual history both within its boundaries and in other German-speaking lands.

If the Prussian-centered narrative, with its customary trajectory "from Bismarck to Hitler," is to be surmounted, the history of the German lands must be conceived in a wider chronological field. In these pages the legacies of the premodern German past to the nineteenth and twentieth centuries will prove more nuanced and civilizationally productive than "separate path" analysis holds. It will be seen that the deficits of modernity inhere to a high degree in modernity itself. It is important also to recast the drama, as these pages do, on the broad central European stage, highlighting especially German interactions with the non-German cultures of the region and points farther east.

FIGURE I.3. CLASHING PERSPECTIVES IN 1968
Pictured on the right is sociologist Ralf Dahrendorf (1929–2009), author of *Society and Democracy in Germany* (1965), influential in developing a social-historical approach to National Socialism (stressing the role of antidemocratic elites) and the emergence from its ruins (owing largely to the destruction or discrediting of those elites) of West Germany liberal democracy. He appears here, as spokesman for West Germany's middle-class liberal Free Democratic Party, in a January 1968 debate with Rudi Dutschke (1940–1979), leader of the German Socialist Student Federation (SDS). Dutschke voiced a neo-Marxist conception of German history, given sophisticated expression since the 1930s by emigré writers who highlighted political conflicts and authoritarian tendencies born of capitalist development, in contrast to liberal emphasis, such as Dahrendorf's, on persistence in pre-1945 Germany of an antidemocratic political culture upheld by conservative elites. Dutschke died of the lingering effects of a right-wing assassination attempt on his life in April 1968, a few months after this picture was taken.

Among pathbreaking early postwar historians was Fritz Fischer (1908–1999), who repudiated his own National Socialist past to advance stringently critical views. In his 1961 book, *Griff nach der Weltmacht* ("Grasping for World Power"), Fischer argued for the German government's provocation of World War I in pursuit of imperialistic ends – a position that ignited a turbulent but productive controversy over the "Fischer Thesis." Influential too, in a more measured spirit, was Karl-Dietrich Bracher (b. 1922), author of *The Dissolution of the Weimar Republic* (1955) and *The German Dictatorship* (1969), books fusing political narrative, theory of democracy, and social structural analysis. These and other historians prepared the ground for Hans-Ulrich Wehler (b. 1931), whose *German Empire, 1871–1918* (1973) controversially – and classically – synthesized the *Sonderweg* or German "separate path" approach and modern social-science history in an interpretation challenging both German conservatism and Marxist historiography. Wehler later magnified his analysis in a widely influential five-volume *History of German Society* from 1800 to the present (1987–2008).
Source: dpa Picture-Alliance GmbH.

German history is richer in meaning and insight into life than might be supposed from considering only the political narratives enshrined in historiographical tradition and popular memory. Germanophone philosophy and social thought have conveyed penetrating analyses of the human condition in the transition from premodernity to modernity and beyond, contributing much to the toolkit available now for understanding the contemporary world. These pages also offer an introduction to this legacy.

The challenge is to fashion a wide-angled interpretation appropriate to a twenty-first-century vantage point. Many historians are now in search of "transnational" analyses. This entails highlighting reciprocal international influences, whether intellectual-cultural or social-political, in the shaping of German life from outside and in the radiation outward of internal German developments. These pages interweave the transnational perspective, especially as it encompasses German-east European relations, with still-vital strands of earlier interpretation. A picture will emerge, not of a single Germany evolving through time, but of a succession of polycentric national existences constituted both by commonalities and contentions. In part born of their precursors, in part the progeny of new times, they unfolded in continuous dialogue – whether fraternal or rivalrous – with Europe, and eventually with America as well.

PART I

GERMAN CENTRAL EUROPE BEFORE
MODERN NATIONALISM

The first of this book's four German nations bestrides the stage in the following five chapters. The justification for imagining it in national dress arises partly from the custom, born in the late Middle Ages, of referring to the German-speaking and German-ruled lands of central Europe as the "Holy Roman Empire of the German Nation." Medieval civilization recognized nations, especially in the sense of the land of origin of educated elites: clergymen in training at medieval universities were registered and often lived together by nation, and councils of the Roman Catholic Church were sometimes similarly structured.

Premodern nations were *political* communities, not ethnic-linguistic or populist. Membership in them was the privilege of authority-wielding, governmentally privileged, socially empowered groups, made conscious of their identity by literature and other cultural forms, the glories and agonies of their collective history, possession (apart from Latin) of a common public language (although the tongues employed in private life might be several), and – usually, but not invariably – a shared form of Christianity. The thought was foreign to seek to join the masses of commoners to them in a single body abstractly conceived as "the nation," as modern nationalism aims – sometimes desperately and intolerantly, often unsuccessfully – to do.

Collective interests and identity might require defense, especially against invaders, or in the midst of internal strife or civil war. In that case social-political powerholders might well urge "the people" to rise in support of "the true faith" (against rival Christians, or Muslims) or to secure the government of the realm to a party or dynasty warring with competitors. But these were then cases of patriotic loyalty and sacrifice devoted to throne and altar, not "the nation" as a collective body or being – although ruler and priesthood might exaltedly claim to embody it.

A different book than this one, looking further back, would not neglect the pre-medieval, pre-Christian Germanic peoples of the centuries before Charlemagne's eighth-century empire, nor the subsequent forms of German medieval

Christian civilization. In these pages the first German nation appears in the early modern era (ca. 1500–1800), already in its robust middle years. And, like many historical formations, the Germany of the later Holy Roman Empire did not merely expire of weakness in old age. It was swept off the stage by revolutionary new forces – in part its own offspring – that had emerged in its midst. Their breakthrough to growth and domination spelled obsolescence for what, by the time of the French Revolution of 1789 and its turbulent aftermath, was little more than the German lands' brittle armature.

2

Herrschaft

Lordship and Power in the Germanies

In 1789 the German-speaking lands were, with few exceptions, encompassed within a sprawling geopolitical entity antiquatedly named the *Holy Roman Empire of the German Nation*. They were, strange as it may seem, divided into some three hundred and twenty-five separate principalities.

Comparing Germany with France, England, or Spain, the question arises: why did the medieval and early modern German lands not evolve, as these and many other European countries did, from the condition of a loosely strung together medieval feudal kingdom into a stoutly forged centralized "national monarchy," such as that of France's mighty Louis XIV, the seventeenth-century "Sun King"? Premodern monarchies on the French or British model created unitary frameworks for subsequent political democratization, such as preliminarily began in England with the Puritan and Glorious revolutions of the seventeenth century and in France with the revolution of 1789.

These cases are centerpieces of the old-established liberal (or "Whig") theory of European history, according to which internal political revolutions and reforms transformed premodern "national monarchies" into modern democratic nation-states. Thus in the French Revolution of 1789–1793, "the *people*," represented by the educated and propertied classes who took the lead in overthrowing the military-bureaucratic "absolutist" monarchy, conquered the *state*, eventually transforming it into the self-governing French *nation*.

Similarly, in the American Revolution of 1775–1783, "the people," represented largely by property-owning (and even slave-owning) English-speaking men, expelled the agents of British imperial power and converted the preexisting thirteen colonies – closely linked together by their common subjection to British rule – into a new "American nation," the United States of America. Those colonists who could not accept this change emigrated to Canada, whose evolution into a English-speaking nation encountered limits in the presence there of previously settled French-speaking Canadians who, unlike indigenous tribal peoples throughout north America, could not be ruthlessly dispersed or suppressed.

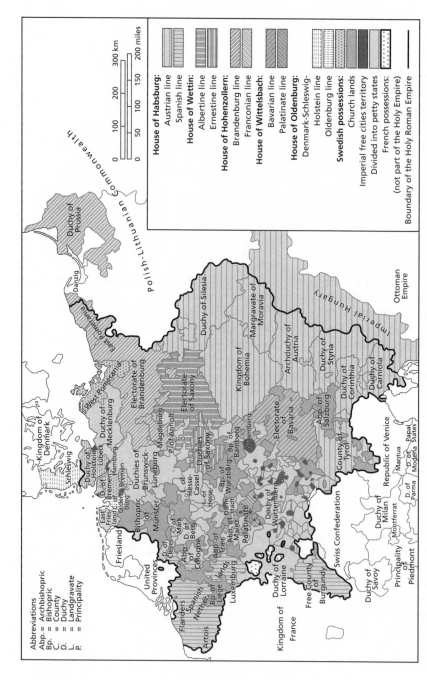

Abbreviations
Abp. = Archbishopric
Bp. = Bishopric
C. = County
D. = Duchy
L. = Landgravate
P. = Principality

House of Habsburg:
Austrian line
Spanish line
House of Wettin:
Albertine line
Ernestine line
House of Hohenzollern:
Brandenburg line
Franconian line
House of Wittelsbach:
Bavarian line
Palatinate line
House of Oldenburg:
Denmark-Schleswig-
Holstein line
Oldenburg line
Swedish possessions:
Church lands
Imperial free cities territory
Divided into petty states
French possessions:
(not part of the Holy Empire)
Boundary of the Holy Roman Empire

MAP 2.1. THE HOLY ROMAN EMPIRE OF THE GERMAN NATION, 1648

In Germany, the Holy Roman Empire did *not* figure as a "national monarchy" on whose political stage the passage to the modern nation-state was played out. Instead, it fragmented into a myriad of separate states. A basic understanding of why this occurred is vital to appreciate German history's distinctiveness. During what conventionally figures as the *age of absolutism* (1648–1789), the question narrows to how, among the hundreds of principalities into which the Holy Roman Empire disintegrated, two of them – the *Austrian* and *Prussian* monarchies – developed into military-bureaucratic states ranking among the European Great Powers. Austro-Prussian rivalry (or "dualism") stamped the German lands' political history in the nineteenth century, greatly complicating the problem after 1789 of finding a liberal path to German unity – that is, to the creation of a modern nation-state resting on liberal-democratic foundations.

Regionalism in German History

Apart from Russia, the German-speaking lands long formed, in a geographical sense, the largest and, in recent times, the most populous European country. Yet it was never, nor is it today, a uniform land. Historically, the following six distinctive regions have stood out (see Map 2.3 and, for the principal political territories, Map 2.1).

- The *Rhine river basin*, from the river's origins in Switzerland to its passage across the Netherlands to the North Sea.

In its early centuries the Roman Empire conquered and incorporated much of this region, which frames the Rhine's south-to-north flow. Roman villas and vineyards dotted the land. Later its ties to the French-speaking world were

---

MAP 2.1 *(continued)* The Empire appears here as it emerged from the Thirty Years War. The lands within the Empire ruled by the Austrian-based Habsburg dynasty ring the periphery, except in the Protestant north. The disconnected possessions of the Hohenzollern dynasty's Brandenburg-Prussian state cluster in the northeast, but also, in the form of small territories, extend westward to the Rhine. (The far eastern Duchy of Prussia, ruled from Berlin, lay outside the Empire.) Alongside such important regional principalities as Bavaria and Saxony, and the extensive lands ruled by high dignitaries of the Catholic Church, there existed a myriad of small and miniature principalities, not depicted here. The Swiss Confederation, housing a majority speaking a local form of German alongside speakers of French and Italian, was a bitter foe of its former Habsburg overlords. In 1648 it won independence from the German Empire. The Westphalian peace conference of 1648 also freed the northern Netherlands – that is, the Dutch Republic – from Spanish rule and formal subjection to the Empire, but the French- and Dutch-speaking southern Netherlands remained within it, under the Spanish Habsburg dynasty's scepter. Austrian-ruled Bohemia was predominantly Czech-speaking. Francophone enclaves, and Germanophone exclaves, underscore the point that the Empire made no claim to represent an ethnic nation.

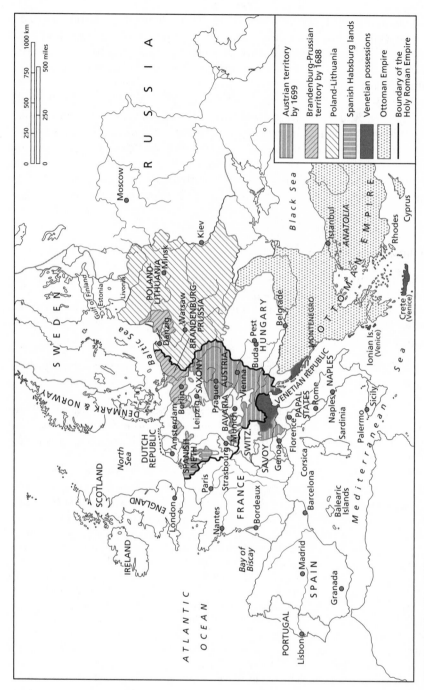

MAP 2.2. EUROPE, 1700

close. A complex Franco-German symbiosis emerged, especially in the lands of Alsace and Lorraine, the Saar river valley, the southern Netherlands, and western Switzerland. After the Germanic peoples' early medieval conversion to Christianity, the Rhineland became – and remains today – a stronghold of Roman Catholicism.

- *Alpine-Danubian* Germany

This region embraces the valleys and mountainous lands of Switzerland, Bavaria, and Austria, and the Danube river flowing from west to east out of and across them. It opened the German-speaking world to contacts across the alpine passes with Italy and down the Danube with Hungary and the Balkan countries.

- *Upland* Germany

Historically, this region comprised the mountainous fringes of Bohemia, Saxony, Silesia, and German settlements in the Carpathian mountain range extending southeastwardly across Slovakia into Transylvania and Romania. These areas, still rich in minerals (although not poor in farmland), lie below the high-mountain chains. In medieval times, German-speakers figured prominently in mining, smelting, and metalworking, helping establish eastward of their linguistic heartland important centers of town life and industry.

- *Maritime* Germany

Facing the North Sea and Atlantic Ocean, Germanophone settlements stretched from Schleswig on the Danish peninsula southwesterly across Friesland to the Dutch lands and the Rhine estuary. Here fishing flourished and seaborne commerce grew strong, particularly in the direction of Britain and Scandinavia. British cultural and political influences traveled through this region, especially by mediation of Hamburg, which emerged after 1648 as the Empire's greatest port.

- *Middle* Germany

MAP 2.2 *(continued)* The German and Italian polycentric state systems contrast with Europe's emergent "national monarchies," notably France, Spain, and the English-ruled British isles. The far-flung Polish-Lithuanian Commonwealth was, although nominally a monarchy, in reality a vast, decentralized aristocratic republic. The multinational Swedish monarchy stood at the high noon of its seventeenth-century Great Power status, soon to be lost in bruising war with ascendant Russia. The massive pressure the still-formidable Muslim Turkish-ruled Ottoman Empire exerted on Europe's southeastern and Mediterranean lands is evident in its huge extent: from Hungary and the Black Sea to Istanbul to Cairo and beyond toward the Atlantic. Although "national monarchies" shared the map both with empires and mini-principalities, their advantages in mobilizing power and motivating loyalties among the educated and propertied classes were considerable. Yet some states with nationally conscious ruling elites – the Dutch Republic, Poland, Sweden – suffered decline in power.

MAP 2.3. PHYSICAL MAP OF CENTRAL EUROPE

Flagged here are the six regions highlighted in the text above. The Rhine, Elbe, Oder, and Vistula rivers flow northward; the Danube flows toward the southeast. The militarily significant "Bohemian quadrilateral" is evident, surrounded by mountains. The wide Danubian basin, enclosed by the Bohemian, Carpathian, and Transylvanian mountains in the north and east and by the Balkan mountains in the south, forms a geographically well-defined region, organized politically as the medieval Kingdom of Hungary and later absorbed into the Austrian Habsburg monarchy, and thus into the world of German-ruled central Europe. Eastern Europe north of the central European east-west mountain ridge sits behind no unmistakable barriers, so that the lands of eastern Germany and western and central Poland, like those of Germany and the Baltic coastal lands, merge imperceptibly into each other.

This is a landlocked region, bordering in the west on the Rhineland, in the south on Bavaria, in the north on coastal lands, and in the east on the Elbe river. It encompassed numerous historic principalities, including those in Hessen, Franconia, Thuringia, and Lower Saxony (with Braunschweig and Hannover). Here village-scale farming and small-town manufactures long predominated.

- Eastern (or *East-Elbian*) Germany

The Baltic coastline harbored numerous and powerful German-speaking trading cities, such as Lübeck, Stettin, Danzig (or Gdańsk, long tied politically to Poland), and Königsberg. Inland a well-watered agrarian plain fanned out from the Elbe river across Brandenburg to Poland, including the predominantly Germanophone regions along the Baltic sea of Mecklenburg, Pomerania, and East Prussia. This whole wide region came to be a land of commercialized, mostly noble-owned large landed estates, producing grain and other agricultural products by the labor of subordinated villagers for the Empire's cities and western European and Scandinavian export markets. The towns here – including those inland, such as Saxony's Leipzig – served as a chain of communication eastward with the sprawling Polish-Lithuanian Commonwealth, the Baltic lands (where German-speaking commercial centers founded in the Middle Ages remained powerful), and Russia.

Each of these six regions possessed historically distinctive socioeconomic structures and political and cultural traditions that are still discernible today. Their existence underpinned a powerful centrifugal or federalist tendency that lives on in present-day Germany's decentralized structure. Partly because of such far-flung regionalism, unity or unification was never comprehensively achieved, as is evident now in the existence of the Federal Republic of Germany, German-speaking Austria (and Italian South Tyrol), Switzerland (where Swiss German most widely prevails), Liechtenstein (a tiny remnant-principality of the Holy Roman Empire, tied now to Switzerland), Luxemburg (largely speaking German in several forms), and the Dutch and Flemish lands (once also part of the linguistically variegated Germanophone world, as the connection "Dutch/*deutsch*" suggests).

Before 1933, an archipelago of important German-speaking settlements also stretched far beyond the linguistic heartland across both the northern and southern parts of east-central Europe, Russia, and the Balkans. But, disastrously, National Socialist-enforced population transfers and the consequences of the defeat of 1945 largely uprooted these outposts (while much of East-Elbia, from which its German inhabitants fled or were expelled, passed under Polish and Russian rule).

The Holy Roman Empire, 800–1806: Five Epochs of Its Thousand-Year History

Medieval Germany was a bastion of power and culture. Yet it splintered politically, exposing it to borderland losses and foreign incursions – painful

(a)

(b)

FIGURE 2.1. PREINDUSTRIAL LANDSCAPES

memories for modern nationalists. The distinctiveness of German history in later ages derives from the fading fortunes of the once-mighty Holy Roman Empire, whose development can be briefly sketched in five eras. These began in the year 800 with the Frankish king Charlemagne's (or, in the translation of his German name, Charles the Great's) coronation, at papal hands, as emperor of Latin Christendom. By this act, Charlemagne – as important in French history as in German – revived the imperial tradition that Rome had begun in Mediterranean and western Europe.

Under his successors, the medieval empire's center of gravity moved eastward into modern-day Germany, where powerful dynasties ruled in the tenth and eleventh centuries. These emperors – bearing the title *Kaiser* (from the word "Caesar") – extended their sway into Italy and over the Roman Papacy. Thus arose the "Holy Roman Empire," a name that signaled the revival and perpetuation of the ancient and glorious, once-pagan but eventually – and (in the medieval view) providentially – Christianized Latin imperium (see Map 2.4).

In the Empire's second epoch, beginning in the mid-eleventh century, the Kaisers suffered damaging blows in the revolt against their overlordship of the Roman popes, the heads of the Latin Christian church. The pontiffs, resentful of imperial tutelage, enlisted powerful European allies – notably the French kings – in their fight against the emperors, until by the mid-fourteenth century imperial control of lands and resources in Italy was broken for good. As the Kaisers struggled to retain their lucrative and prestigious positions in Italy, in Germany their great feudal vassals transformed themselves in their imperially granted fief-lands into hereditary territorial rulers in their own right. So too did the great churchly lords of Germany – archbishops, bishops, abbots and the like – break free of the emperors' domination and establish long-lasting ecclesiastical principalities, while the strongest German towns emerged as self-governing city-states, comparable to such Italian pioneers of urban liberty as Florence and Venice (see Map 2.5).

FIGURE 2.1 *(continued)* These photographs, taken around 1930, show, above, the city of Saarbrücken, near the German-French linguistic-cultural border, depicted in idyllic traditionalism. Would the eighteenth-century traveler – approaching by coach or foot – have encountered a similar view? Below is the rural landscape of the southwestern Palatinate region, showing the age-old agricultural field system, a patchwork of myriad small parcels. A typical farmstead possessed a number of such strips, whose dispersion corresponded to the customary annual three-field crop rotations and also minimized the risk that a poor harvest would strike all sowings equally. The upheavals of modern history transformed such sites from "life-worlds" of the population majority into nostalgia-laden and often mythologized counterpoint to urban-industrial existence. Yet the shift since the eighteenth century in social centers of gravity was revolutionary, inspiring widespread demand, as compensation for the loss of preindustrial folkways, for the elusive rewards of modernity: freedom and prosperity.
Source: 2.1A: Techno-Photographisches Archiv/Berlin; 2.1B: August Rupp.

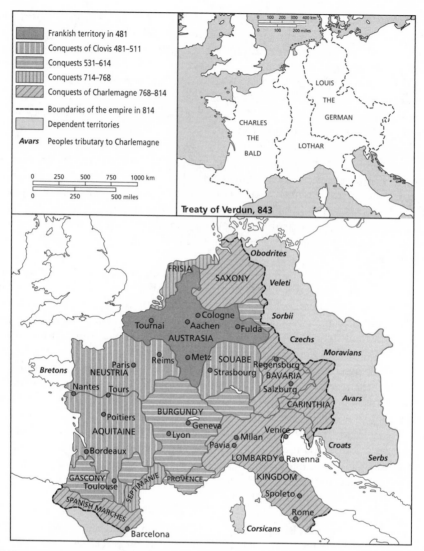

MAP 2.4. ORIGINS OF THE HOLY ROMAN EMPIRE IN THE CAROLINGIAN KINGDOM OF
CHARLEMAGNE

While after 843 a separate French kingdom began to develop, most of Charlemagne's
conquests remained within the German-centered Empire's field of power, although the
lands of Lothar (later remembered as Lothringen or Lorraine) came to be contested
between French and German (and other) rulers. The eastern tributary provinces eventually gained independence as the Christianized medieval kingdoms of Bohemia, Hungary
and Poland, with indigenous ruling dynasties and nobility. The western Slavs, wedged
between the German and Polish lands, mostly succumbed to expanding German feudal
power and the cultural influences it radiated. Nonetheless a 60,000-strong population
of Slavic-speaking but also Germanophone Sorbs has survived until today in Lusatia,
south of Berlin. The vital tie is evident in this map between the German lineages that
inherited the imperial office and the lands of Italy.

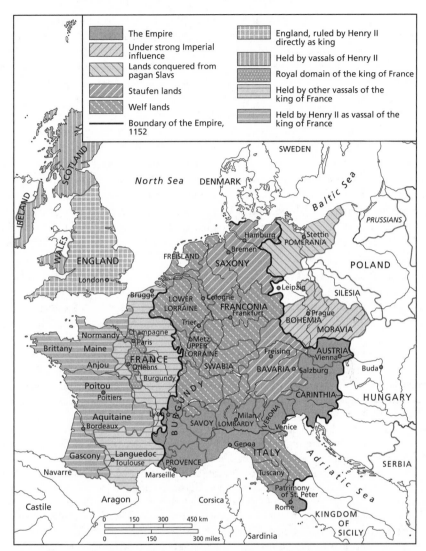

MAP 2.5. THE GERMAN EMPIRE AND WESTERN EUROPE IN THE TWELFTH CENTURY

Here depicted is the Empire at the accession of Kaiser Friedrich I "Barbarossa" or Red-Beard (r. 1152–1190). His considerable European power and prestige rested on control of provinces within the Empire directly ruled (in feudal fashion) by the imperial power, notably in south Germany and Italy, and on administrative units in Germany (duchies, counties) over which his lineage (the Staufen or Hohenstaufen) possessed the right of feudal rule or whose territorial overlords could be installed or dispossessed by imperial decision. The emperors' disposition over the extensive church-administered territories had been crippled, though not broken, in the eleventh-century Investiture Conflict with the Roman Popes, who in Barbarossa's time and thereafter further contested the Kaisers' rights to distribute ecclesiastical appointments and incomes. Secular opposition to imperial authority arose from the central German duchies in the hands

The Empire's third era saw the imperial power, now confined to predominantly German-speaking lands, redefined in a constitutional arrangement guaranteed by the "Golden Bull" (or Charter) of 1356. Henceforth an assembly of seven "electoral princes" (*Kurfürsten*) chose each successive emperor. It seated the dynastic rulers of four of the Empire's most powerful secular principalities (Bohemia, Brandenburg, the Rhenish Palatinate, and Saxony) and the three Catholic spiritual overlords of its most important ecclesiastical principalities (the archbishoprics of Cologne, Trier, and Mainz). This procedure broke the principle of hereditary succession to the imperial throne so as to ensure that, at each election, the new emperor would bind himself to respect the rights and powers of the Empire's myriad feudal rulers, each in his own territory, sometimes large but often small. The Kaiser, for his part, mediated between the territorial princes, duty-bound to protect the lesser from the greater. He also was responsible for defending from external dangers the borders of the "Holy Roman Empire of the German Nation," as it now (shorn of its Italian lands) came to be known.

In the mid-fifteenth century there began a succession of emperors elected from the Austrian Habsburg dynasty that lasted with no significant interruptions until the Empire's 1806 collapse following Napoleon's conquests in Germany. The Habsburgs were the Empire's richest secular territorial rulers,

---

MAP 2.5 *(continued)* of the Staufen rulers' rivals, the Welfen, as well as from dissident feudatories (such as Henry the Lion of Saxony), and the northern Italian states, which defeated Barbarossa on the battlefield (and where pro-imperial factions named themselves Ghibellines and anti-imperialists Guelphs – both titles rooted in German terms for Staufen and Welfen). The emperor looked for international backing to the Capetian dynasty, steadily hammering together the French monarchy, while the Welfen sought alliances with English Plantagenet king Henry II (r. 1154–1189).

Barbarossa's successful crusade to capture Jerusalem from Muslim hands gained him renown, but no institutional strengthening in Germany, and, on the return march, cost him his life through drowning. Late-medieval legends circulated of a mighty emperor of old, sleeping in a cave in the Kyffhäuser mountain while awaiting return to life to restore a worthy German Empire. These eventually focused on Friedrich Barbarossa, and underwent revival in the nineteenth century in literary works of romantic nationalism, which invoked Barbarossa's return in longings for a unified national state. Kaiser William II later associated the Kyffhäuser legend with Imperial Germany's military and imperialist program. While Barbarossa's crusading efforts focused on the Christian Holy Land, the National Socialists named their 1941 invasion of the Soviet Union "Operation Barbarossa" – imparting to it an epic, archaic, even redemptive aura.

The formation of national monarchies in late medieval and early modern Europe was, in the relatively few cases in which it successfully occurred, the unintended outcome of complex power-struggles, both within individual territories (between, variously, rulers, churchmen, nobility, and burghers) and between rival principalities. The Holy Roman Empire's great extent and many centers of power, as well as the emperors' self-understanding as champions of Latin Christendom, discouraged ambitions of German state-building.

possessing hereditary lands in Austria and elsewhere in south Germany, to which after 1526 were joined the once-independent kingdoms of prosperous, town-rich Bohemia and far-flung, agriculturally fertile Hungary. The Austrian Habsburgs could afford the expenditures associated with election to the Kaiser's throne, and could hope to heighten their power in Germany and Europe by adroit exercise of the imperial authority, weak though in essence it had become.

From 1356 to 1517, the possibility was real that a kind of federalized Germany would assume stable form, based on balance of power and interest between the emperors and the ecclesiastical and territorial principalities. But the outbreak of the Protestant Reformation, conventionally dated from Martin Luther's 1517 challenge to the Roman Catholic Church, severely polarized the Empire. The Habsburg emperors defended the Roman church. Most of the secular territorial rulers, whether princely dynasts or city-state magistrates, embraced Protestantism, mainly in Lutheran form but sometimes also as Swiss-born Calvinism (familiar in the Anglo-American world as Presbyterianism) (see Map 2.6).

In the Holy Roman Empire's fourth era, from 1517 to 1648, the Austrian Kaisers sought a triumph in the Reformation's religious contests that would also strengthen their hand as the highest powerholders in the land. In the climactic Thirty Years War of 1618–1648, a hugely destructive civil war that exploded into a far-ranging European conflagration, the emperors hoped, in their most ambitious moments, to break the territorial princes' power along with the Protestant cause, so as to centralize the Holy Roman Empire under a greatly expanded hereditary realm of their own, underpinned by Catholicism. The prospect of such a reinvigorated Germany was alarming to other European powers, particularly France, which fought successfully in support of the Protestant princes to defeat the Habsburgs' armies and hegemonial aspirations.

In the treaty of 1648 negotiated at the peace conference in Westphalia, ending the long war and ratified by virtually all European powers, the authority of the emperors suffered further diminution in favor of the now-proclaimed (if still partial) *sovereignty* of the more than three hundred principalities and city-states. And while the electoral princes continued to elevate them to the Kaiser's throne, the Austrian Habsburgs confronted a formidable obstacle in the Empire's reorganized central representative assembly, the Reichstag or Imperial Diet.

The Reichstag possessed three chambers: one for delegates of the seven (eventually eight) electoral principalities, one for the one hundred most important secular and ecclesiastical princes, and one seating the fifty-one imperial cities. New legislation encompassing the entire Empire required majorities in each body. On questions of the Christian religion, the deputies regrouped by confession, with any innovations – of which there later proved to be no important ones – requiring majority assent among both parties – Catholics, on the one hand, and Lutherans and Calvinists, on the other.

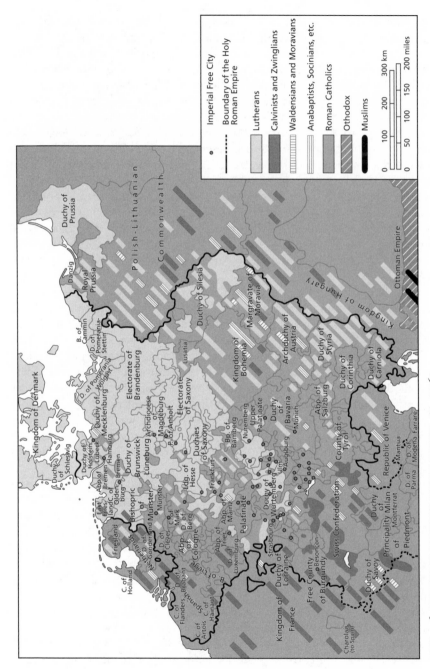

MAP 2.6. RELIGIOUS DIVISION IN THE EMPIRE, CA. 1560

Imperial Free City

Boundary of the Holy Roman Empire

Lutherans

Calvinists and Zwinglians

Waldensians and Moravians

Anabaptists, Socinians, etc.

Roman Catholics

Orthodox

Muslims

300 km / 200 miles

Duchy of Prussia

Polish-Lithuanian Commonwealth

Danzig

Royal Prussia

B. of Cammin

D. of Pomerania-Stettin

Duchy of Pomerania-Wolgast

Duchy of Mecklenburg

Kingdom of Denmark

Duchy of Schleswig

Duchy of Holstein

Abp. of Lübeck

Hamburg

Abp. of Bremen

East Friesland

C. of Oldenburg

Friesland

C. of Holland

Electorate of Brandenburg

Lusatia

Duchy of Silesia

Margravate of Moravia

Kingdom of Bohemia

Archduchy of Austria

Duchy of Styria

Duchy of Carinthia

Duchy of Carniola

Ottoman Empire

Kingdom of Hungary

Abp. of Magdeburg

P. of Anholt

Electorate of Saxony

Duchies of Saxony

Ldg. of Hesse

Duchy of Brunswick

Lüneburg

Bishopric of Münster

Sonderland

C. of Mark

D. of Cleves

D. of Berg

Abp. of Cologne

Nassau

Brabant

C. of Flanders

C. of Artois

C. of Hainaut

Frankfurt

Abp. of Mainz

Bp. of Bamberg

Nuremberg

Upper Palatinate

Duchy of Bavaria

Munich

Abp. of Salzburg

County of Tyrol

Republic of Venice

Mantua

D. of Modena Ferrare

D. of Parma

Principality of Montferrat

Duchy of Milan

Piedmont

Duchy of Savoy

Besançon

Free County of Burgundy

Charolais (to Spain)

Kingdom of France

Duchy of Lorraine

D. of Luxembourg

Abp. of Trier

Palatinate

Strasbourg

Duchy of Württemberg

Augsburg

Ulm

Swiss Confederation

34

One humane consequence of the Westphalian treaty was the establishment of a degree of religious toleration in Germany second only to Holland's and the Polish-Lithuanian Commonwealth's. The Empire's myriad rulers (after an initial period during which expulsions of unwanted religious confessions were possible) were bound to protect the existence within their borders of minorities professing one of the three major Christian faiths. Individual princes were free to extend toleration to other Christian sects and to Jews, if they wished (as sooner or later some did).

Not surprisingly, very little change occurred in the institutional and legal structure of this highly decentralized and complex power-system in its fifth and final era, embracing the 150 years prior to the Holy Roman Empire's dissolution in 1806. There were no significant imperial taxes, and hence no standing (that is, permanently mounted) imperial armed forces. An imperial supreme court (*Reichskammergericht*) served mainly to adjudicate disputes among the territorial principalities freely brought to it by the litigating parties, usually the minor rulers or, alongside them, the 1,500 "imperial knights" – noble possessors of postage-stamp lordships owing no allegiance other than to the far-distant emperor. For lack of a proper budget, in 1772 over 61,000 cases were thought to be backlogged in this court. The *Reichshofrat*, a tribunal in Vienna administered by the Kaiser's own officials, worked more efficiently as an Empire-wide court of appeals.

Even though for the many militarily weak small principalities the Kaiser's power served as a welcome guarantee of their existence, the Empire's political life came to be dominated by the larger territorial states: the Habsburg-ruled complex of Austria-Hungary-Bohemia; Brandenburg-Prussia; Saxony; Bavaria;

MAP 2.6 *(continued)* Protestantism in its early forms released several waves of social and civil war in post-1517 Germany. The Peace of Augsburg of 1555 wrung from the imperial power Lutheranism's right to exist, but only insofar as the territorial rulers of secular principalities chose to embrace or tolerate it. This reflected the agreed-on formula of "cuius religio, eius religio" ("religion is his who rules"), which left communal or individual dissenters beyond the law. The Augsburg settlement left undetermined the future both of Calvinism, a politically highly charged religion that surged ahead after 1555, and of the Catholic-ruled ecclesiastical principalities, in many of which nobility, burghers, and common people sought to embrace one or another form of Protestantism in the late sixteenth and early seventeenth centuries. These issues, alongside Protestantism's spread among the Austrian Habsburg emperors' Austrian and Czech subjects, triggered the Thirty Years War of 1618–1648.

This map highlights the triumphs of Lutheranism in central and north Germany. It prevailed too in Scandinavia and the eastern Baltic region. Calvinism was influential mainly in the vicinity of the Netherlands, on the Rhine, in Switzerland and also, although mainly among non-Germans, in Bohemia, Hungary, and Poland. The penetration of Catholic lands both by Lutheranism and Calvinism is evident, yet the Roman church defended its many strongholds in Germany. By 1648 Catholic rulers had, through their political and military gains during the Thirty Years War, recovered a considerable share of ground lost to Protestantism after the mid-sixteenth century.

Hannover; Hessen; and Württemberg. The Catholic ecclesiastical princes – led by the three electoral archbishops – tended to back the Austrian emperors. The strongest of the imperial cities – notably Augsburg, Bremen, Cologne, Frankfurt, Hamburg, Lübeck, and Nürnberg (Nuremberg) – tried to avoid dependency on the emperors or other territorial rulers.

At the French Revolution's outbreak in 1789 the Holy Roman Empire was, in practice, little more than an antiquated and immobilized confederation of myriad unequal states and statelets. Yet its thousand-year tradition, and the prestige still accorded throughout Europe to the emperors, sustained a lingering, if largely passive belief that the German lands should – somehow – possess overarching, integrating institutions. But now the Empire appeared in the eyes of ever more members of the educated and propertied, politically engaged elites as a bulwark of the status quo, an *impediment* to meaningful structure in its protection of the hundreds of "particularistic" miniature principalities. If the German-speaking lands were to attain common voice and purpose, the Holy Roman Empire would have to vanish so that the strongest among the territorial states might impose leadership on the rest – presumably within a federal system. The French Revolution also suggested, but only to a few radical minds, that the " people" could rise up, overthrow the existing states, and create republics, if not an entire nation, of their own.

In 1789 neither of the two dominant powers – Austria and Prussia – could prevail over the other, nor did these states, pursuing their own dynastic and "absolutist" goals, wish to champion a revitalized imperial order. The European Powers had long found the Empire's decentralization convenient and would oppose efforts to overcome it. Neither did the common people in 1789 possess the ideological vision to act on their own against their various princely overlords for the sake of a higher collectivity. Their identities reflected instead their local neighborhoods, the dynasties to which they as subjects owed allegiance, their religion, and their callings in life.

Among some intellectuals and members of the middle classes and nobility, a new organization of the German-speaking lands' institutional life seemed desirable but also – since both foreign and domestic power-states worked against it – unattainable. In 1797 the acclaimed poets and savants Johann Wolfgang von Goethe and Friedrich Schiller composed, under the heading "The German Empire," an epigram declaring: "Germany? Where is it? I cannot find this land." On the theme of "German national character" they wrote (addressing their fellow literati): "to form yourselves into a nation you hope, O Germans, in vain. Develop yourselves – this you can do – more freely into human beings." National identity resided in the realm of culture alone, as the literary, philosophical, and artistic expression of what the next generation of intellectuals would begin to celebrate as the "German Spirit."

3

Alltag

Contours of Daily Life in the Seventeenth and Eighteenth Centuries

Historians long distinguished this era for bringing forth the military-bureaucratic power-state, the Enlightenment's rationalist philosophy, and the cultural efflorescence of "the age of Goethe." Narratives of "modernization" link these commanding developments to the rise of bourgeois or middle-class society, including an emergent public sphere of liberal and nationalist political opinion, and new energies of the capitalist market economy propelling the German lands to the Industrial Revolution's portal.

In the eyes of successive generations of German-speakers who lived through it, the age appeared in different guises. Despite the ferocity and political duplicities of preceding religious conflicts, culminating in the disastrous Thirty Years War of 1618–1648, Germany remained an intensely Christian culture in which discovery of the soul's path to salvation far outweighed whatever contributions people unwittingly made to a future, self-styled, and (as it turned out) often self-deceiving secular modernity.

From the viewpoint of Germany's rulers – the emperors, the hundreds of territorial princes, the dozens of urban republics – the preservation of the far-flung Holy Roman Empire as a bulwark of international and domestic peace and as mediator and justiciar among its component principalities meant more, except to a few ambitious dynasts, than visions of sovereign independence of one or another German state. The "German nation" and "German unity" were concepts meaningful only as they might be embodied in the ancient Empire. "Glory" (*Ruhm*) was a fitting object of a German ruler's striving, but no more so than his subjects' "welfare" (*Wohl*) and "felicity" (*Glückseligkeit*).

As for those, whether high-born or low, who lived from their private property or labor, life's great aim was to evade untimely death from disease or warfare so as to marry well, bring forth heirs, and manage one's household as independently as was possible in a world structured inescapably by lordship (*Herrschaft*) and the obligations of "service" (*Dienst*) it imposed on upper and lower classes alike. "Freedoms" (*Freiheiten*) and "Rights" (*Rechte*) were historical, hereditary, and often individual or communal, not universal and

FIGURE 3.1. THE IMPERIAL POWER AND MYSTIQUE

Vienna's "Plague Column," unveiled in 1693, displays Leopold I, ruler of the Habsburg Austrian realm and German Emperor (ruled 1658–1705), giving thanks to God for the end of the 1679 epidemic, the last to torment the Habsburg capital, although plague struck again in central Germany in 1683 and in 1709–1711 in the northeast before its shadow finally departed the Holy Roman Empire. It was customary in Europe to commemorate such great afflictions – cruel expressions of life's transience – with monuments or specially minted medallions. Events, including the Ottoman Turks' strenuous 1683 siege of Vienna, conspired to delay the completion of the long-promised Viennese column, but it proved to be a masterpiece (still standing) of shining, ornate baroque magnificence. Imposing in elegant worldly dress, and with the military and symbolic attributes of kingly power prominently displayed, Leopold presents himself as the first and highest Christian of his land, responsible to his subjects for heavenly intercession on their behalf.

Source: Bill Barber.

egalitarian. They shielded and privileged those who could claim them, although without releasing them from subjection to churchly and earthly authority (*Obrigkeit*).

In a largely agrarian society, people's private fortunes hung on the bounty or miserliness of grain and other harvests. Dearth meant hunger, high food prices, and shrunken purchases of urban manufactures, spreading agrarian crisis into the towns. It meant, for landlords, rents in arrears. It could squeeze state tax receipts, churchly tithes, and feudal dues. Repeated harvest failure, while rare in peacetime, spelled starvation and death for the weak. In a world of villages and small towns remote from the few long-distance trade routes, salvation through agricultural imports at affordable prices was usually an illusory hope.

Before the late eighteenth century few people, even of the educated and propertied classes, aimed – or dared – to project their minds beyond the categories of Christian orthodoxy, folk mythology, and the romances of popular literature. Identities were mostly intensely local, tied to religion, social rank, occupation, sex and gender, kinship and age group. That one, by language or custom, was "German" entailed few, if any, consequences, especially in view of marked differences – spurring rivalries and reciprocal deprecation – among religious confessions, regional dialects, habits of dress, and social customs. Political loyalties were dynastic, not ethnic. Love of country was love of one's narrow historical-geographical homeland (*Heimat*), amplified sometimes by patriotic enthusiasm for one's ruling dynasty or religious or communal authorities.

Thoughts of cumulative mastery of nature through empiricist and experimental science had hardly entranced even savants' minds, which gravitated instead to philosophies founded on logical necessity. For most people, ancient usage and authority – such as that of the indestructible Aristotle – were the surest guides. Mysteries were better plumbed by clergymen or adepts of folk magic. Fate, although inscrutable, was often thought appeasable. Without God's grace (*Gnade*), body and soul would disappear into the abyss.

Such, in brief, was life deep into the eighteenth century. It was a multifarious German world, but the aspirations and values that ruled it were in no way self-consciously national. It was not a peculiarity of the Germans that, when the age of nationalism began to dawn after 1789, there was no easy answer to the question that the revolutionary musician-poet Richard Wagner posed in the title of his 1865 essay, "What is German?" For Wagner, as for most modern nationalists around the globe, national identity proved to be a self-exalting version of national history, bathed in universal significance and invested with a redemptive meaning that, in the now-fading premodern world, had belonged to religion alone.

Power: The Holy Roman Empire's Twilight

The Thirty Years War, as we saw, witnessed the culminatory struggle between the Catholic and centralization-minded emperors, long successively elected from the Austrian ruling house of Habsburg, and the secular territorial princes, mainly Lutheran Protestants but including Calvinists and certain Catholic rulers (as in Bavaria) jealous of their dynastic independence. The princes sought to protect from imperial encroachments their "liberty" (*Libertät*) and promote the devolution of governmental power within the Empire into their hands. This process had been occurring for centuries, but after the Protestant Reformation, the Austrian emperors attempted to reverse it in the name of Catholic orthodoxy and their own great-power interests, tied also to those of Spain, where

(a)

FIGURE 3.2. TERRITORIAL LORDSHIP IN THE AGE OF THE AMERICAN REVOLUTION
These handsome pictures, painted ca. 1765 by renowned portraitist Johann Ziesenis
(1716–1776), depict Friedrich Wilhelm Ernst, Count of Schaumburg-Lippe (1724–
1777) and his new wife, Marie Barbara Eleonore von Lippe-Biesterfeld, countess of
Schaumburg-Lippe (1744–1776). Their miniature Protestant north German realm was
one of the Holy Roman Empire's numerous petty principalities. The count poses with
instruments of command before a deceivingly far-flung landscape, while the countess
reposes amid the pleasures of peace and luxury. Both radiate mastery and satisfaction
in their respective roles, although neither lived a long life. They stand confidently in a
time-honored hierarchical eighteenth-century world that the French Revolution would
soon challenge, but whose deep-rooted social and political structures would prove difficult to dismantle.
Source: Reproduced in Ludwig Roselius, ed., *Deutsche Kunst* (Bremen: Angel-Sachsen
Verlag, 1935), I/22–23.

a collateral Habsburg lineage reigned. In the war of 1618–1648, Swedish and
French armed intervention on behalf of the German territorial princes defeated
the Austrian emperors' nearly attained project, whose realization would have
changed the face of German and European history.

(b)

FIGURE 3.2 *(continued)*

The 1648 peace of Westphalia had restructured the institutions of the Empire to definitively block unilateral imperial power. The emperors could attain no innovations without the Reichstag's consent. As of 1792, after various intervening changes, this body seated deputies of 8 electoral principalities, 63 deputies representing 299 other secular principalities, 35 delegates from the Empire's self-governing ecclesiastical territories, and 51 from the self-governing Imperial Cities. New legislation still required majorities in each of these three categories. When innovations touched on religion, the deputies regrouped, as we saw, as representatives of Roman Catholicism or Protestantism (whether Lutheranism or Calvinism): the three principal Christian religions whose practice the war's outcome had guaranteed (within some limits of toleration).

Before the Empire's demise in 1806, the Reichstag – meeting since 1663 in a standing committee of princely envoys on the Danube's banks in the mixed Protestant-Catholic Imperial City of Regensburg – promulgated exceedingly few important new laws. But the emperors dispensed rich patronage and exercised considerable judicial powers, important especially to the hundreds of

FIGURE 3.3. THE PAST IS A FOREIGN COUNTRY
Yet it is an intriguing question how mentally and emotionally distant from us its inhabitants were, despite all cultural differences. From the portraits here of a prosperous late eighteenth-century Bavarian farmer and his wife, faces peer out that well fit in the twenty-first century. The pair are warmly and comfortably dressed, appear healthy, and radiate self-confidence and intelligence. Yet it was common among urban artists to depict villagers in accord with long-established conventions emphasizing their naïve and uncultured qualities, the toll on them of labor and deprivation, and other stereotypical "peasant" characteristics. Subsequent generations, ever more urbanized and condescending in their view of the premodern agrarian past, came to regard the second mode of representation as more historically realistic than the view these portraits suggest, and which recent archivally based research ever more recommends.
Source: Heimatmuseum Trostberg, Bavaria.

minor territorial rulers and the nearly 1,500 Imperial Knights – landed nobility owing allegiance directly to the emperors alone – who frequently appealed to the Habsburg court in Vienna for resolution of internal and external conflicts. The stronger German states (notably Bavaria, Prussia, Saxony) resisted subordination to imperial jurisdiction.

In the late seventeenth century, in face of aggression by Louis XIV's France on the Empire's western borders, the threatened German lands sought to strengthen imperial military functions, organized since the year 1500 in "circles" (*Kreise*) encompassing multiple principalities. But the Austrian Kaisers now viewed such developments as curbs on their own military power, which was anchored in their hereditary lands, not in the Empire at large. While armed enforcement within the Empire of imperial law (*Reichsexekution*) was militarily allowable, it required a congruence between Habsburg and the territorial rulers' interests that rarely emerged. The Empire could not prevent locally crippling foreign invasions, notably by the armies of France under Louis XIV (ruled 1661–1715) and again in the era of the French Revolution and Napoleon

(1789–1815), but also on occasion by Swedish and Russian troops. Nor, as we will see, did it forestall internal war, especially the long and bloody confrontation of Prussia and Austria in the War of the Austrian Succession (1740–1748) and the Seven Years War (1756–1763).

The Holy Roman Empire could not develop into a modern state. It was rather a highly multipolar, decentralized national confederation, housing within itself at first embryonic, but then increasingly authentic German states alongside a mass of ever more militarily defenseless lordships and authority-structures (chiefly the Imperial Cities and Knights, and the Catholic ecclesiastical lands). These coexisted symbiotically with the Empire, and in the years 1803–1806 fell forever, together with it, under Napoleon's hammer blows. The Empire lived out its thousand-year history thanks to the post-1648 consensus of the European Great Powers that fragmentation of rule in German-speaking central Europe served their interests. But the European empire of Napoleon to which the French Revolution gave birth, short-lived though it was, rendered this perspective antiquated (without solving the resultant "German question").

Many modern German nationalists retrospectively condemned the Empire for failing to centralize power and advance on the path toward national unity. Post-1945 historiography has taken a more indulgent view, highlighting the benignity of life under the myriad princelings, and sometimes imagining the Empire as a precursor to the present-day European Union, which is also an assemblage of independent but confederated states. In the Holy Roman Empire, more than 300 rulers' courts resulted in an equal number of princely residence-towns, many with orchestras, theaters, libraries, museums, aristocratic colleges, and learned academies. Such conditions paid a cultural dividend – evident still today in Germany's rich musical and theatrical life – while also gratifyingly employing the intelligentsia. In the late eighteenth century an unaccustomed Imperial patriotism (*Reichspatriotismus*) flowed from some influential publicists' pens. They extolled a suddenly improved administration of imperial justice and the Empire's role in preserving German "liberties" against the rise, in one or another territorial principality, of "tyrannical" state power. Yet, simultaneously, absolutist Prussia's powerful king Frederick the Great basked in popularity among other (or even the same) Enlightenment literati.

Oppression of subjects, where it occurred, was no more tolerable under an urban republic, an archbishop, or a quasi-sovereign nobleman than under one of the handful of strong German states. Charges of "despotism" were typically rhetorical blows, even if class and political injustice was as familiar in Germany as in France or Britain. Yet appeal to courts of law was open to all Germans everywhere, including peasant serfs. The Empire afforded room to multiconfessional life in a Europe that otherwise mostly upheld single-faith Christian religious establishments. It lived by a conservatism that rewarded those with a stake in the status quo. It did not favor military aggression. It sustained in the German imagination a certain sense of national identity and dignity, although exceedingly far removed from most ordinary people's lives.

Power and Authority in the German Territorial Principality: The "Estates Polity"

The defeat and subsequent hobbling of the Austrian Habsburgs' imperial pow-ers caused responsibility for fulfillment of state functions to devolve onto the often frail shoulders of Germany's hundreds of territorial princes. It was they, not the emperors, who were obliged to oversee and maintain a system of local law courts and accompanying police institutions; to command militias and armies, whether miniature or great; and to cooperate with the Christian churches in supplying spiritual, charitable, and educational blessings.

These tasks they took in hand, not autocratically, but in cooperation with the urban-communal, aristocratic, and ecclesiastical bodies that had evolved in the millenium and more following the fifth-century fall of the Western Roman Empire: oligarchical, although often elective, councils and magistracies in vil-lages and towns, as well as regional assemblies seating landed nobility, high churchmen, prosperous burghers and, in a few regions, self-sufficient village farmers. These were the "estates of the realm" (*Stände*).

Social organization by estates was pervasive. The principalities and towns seated in the Imperial Reichstag were, in relation to the Kaiser's power, Empire-level estates. The thousand-plus Imperial Knights could boast of being "estates lords" (*Standesherren*). Correspondingly, within the myriad territorial prin-cipalities, rulers co-governed in partnership with the highest instances of the estates of their own lands, whether – in such large polities as Austria and Prussia – on a provincial level or – in smaller territories – in a single central assembly (*Landstände*). In Protestant territories, where the Reformation had transferred administration of the churches' worldly affairs into princely hands, the estates typically shrank to represent landed nobility and chief towns only. In Catholic ecclesiastical principalities, the worldly nobles seated in the power-sharing cathedral chapters embodied a variation on the estates concept. The church hierarchs recognized as well their subject towns' corporate liberties. In Catholic-ruled secular principalities, high churchmen survived as one of the three customary estates.

Historians often conceive the early modern territorial principality as an "estates polity" (*Ständestaat*), because rulers were bound to consult the estates in matters of new legislation, and war and peace as well. Tax levies usually gained passage on short terms requiring renewal, not always conceded. In many cases, estates proved stronger than princes, wresting control through their executive committees and influence on princely officials of domestic and foreign policy, so that a few German principalities – the Baltic-coast duchies of Mecklenburg are a good example – displayed into the nineteenth and even the early twentieth century an oligarchical parliamentarism with a dependent or figurehead dynast. Yet, so long as no insubordinate or revolutionary move-ments arose from below seeking abolition of estates-bound privilege and the common people's enfranchisement, the German *Ständestaat* embodied a work-able political constitution, comparable to many elsewhere in Europe (as in the

French and Spanish provinces, Scandinavia, the Low Countries, Hungary, and Poland).

All the Holy Roman Empire's ecclesiastical principalities, and nearly all its many secular principalities and urban republics, were estates polities of one kind or another. Yet it is common to envision the 1648–1789 period as the "age of absolutism," witnessing the rise of centralized military-bureaucratic states ruled by secular princes – the favored but rarely attained title was kingly – independent of the historic estates. Doubtless this view reflects the ascent, spectacular even in its own time, of the Kingdom of Prussia, which succeeded in the nineteenth century in crafting, through Chancellor Otto von Bismarck's diplomacy and the Prussian army's sinews, a single German national state, the Empire (*Reich*) of 1871, into which all other surviving German principalities entered under Prussian dominance. Imperial Austria, which also had trodden the absolutist path, suffered battlefield defeat in 1866 at Prussian hands, and as the lone still surviving German-ruled state outside the Bismarckian Empire's boundaries, followed a separate path from 1867 until its fall in 1918. In later chapters we will look more closely at absolutist Prussia's and Austria's rise and fall.

The Social Order

In the 1648–1815 era, sometimes expansively conceived as "the long eighteenth century," preindustrial society in Germany reached its fullest flowering, while it also put down roots of the industrialism that would later overshadow it. Rural life attained its peak of complexity, displaying a populous landscape of villages, manorial seats and hamlets serving them, market towns, pastoral and forest enterprises, and the many rural industries, notably milling of grain and many other raw materials, that depended on water power and wind. In such settings 80 or 90 percent of the population lived. Among town-dwellers, more inhabited medium-sized market and administrative centers counting a few thousands or tens of thousands of inhabitants than in the big cities, such as Berlin, Frankfurt, Hamburg, Leipzig, Munich, and Vienna, whose populations only slowly rose toward or beyond 100,000 souls.

Village farmers (*Bauern*, or "peasants") were either fullholders with lands wide enough to sustain their families from mixed cereal-livestock agriculture alone: on average soils, twenty to forty acres would have barely sufficed, and many peasant farms were much bigger. Or they were halfholders or small-holders, living partly from cultivating their fields and partly from wage-labor for others, sometimes including seasonal cottage industry, often spinning and weaving, but also woodworking and other handicrafts. Virtually all villagers were legal subjects of one or another old-established lordship (*Herrschaft*): seigneurial power exercised by the landed nobility or, in the case of villages bowing to the Catholic Church or a territorial ruler, by subofficials or tenant-farmers leasing ecclesiastical or princely estates. Lordship entailed responsibility for maintaining local courts and police services (including insalubrious but sometimes escapable jails), cooperating in upholding religious life and associated charitable works, and helping collect taxes and conscript soldiers.

Subject villagers typically held their lands in hereditary tenure, whether de facto or de jure. Often, but not always, they were free to sell their holdings among themselves, although rural culture greatly prized undiminished inheritance across the generations. Among commoners subject to seigneurial lordship, payment of rent – historians sometimes call it "feudal rent" – was universal. Such obligation might be met in natural payments (especially in valuable sacks of grain) or in cash. Widespread too was rent paid in labor-services: for example, minimally, a few days *yearly* of work on seigneurial land or, maximally, three days *weekly* or more of such labor, often employing – in the case of levies on largeholding farmers – two farmhands and a team of horses, both supplied by the subject farmer himself.

Wherever the seigneurial lords maintained large manor-farms of their own, producing crops for near or distant markets, labor services loomed large in peasant rent. Such conditions prevailed especially in northern and eastern (east-Elbian) Germany, most significantly in the Kingdom of Prussia, whose landed nobility long figured in the historical literature as "the Junkers" (a medieval word for young noblemen ["*junger Herr*"]). The Junkers' large estates often profitably shipped their grain surpluses from river and Baltic ports to Germany's burgeoning cities or western and Scandinavian Europe. Their subject villagers rendered heavy labor services and were, in some regions, tied to their natal villages as serfs (*Leibeigene*).

In west and south Germany, lordship rarely entailed large-estate enterprise on the east-Elbian model. Seigneurial authorities generally confined themselves to levying cash or natural rents on subject villagers, whose occasional servile legal status justified additional extractions, particularly death duties. Only along the North Sea coast did a freeholding peasantry, independent of seigneurialism, exist in significant and compact numbers.

Crucial to landed villagers were less the facts of lordship and legal subjection than the size and productivity of their landholdings, and the combined bite of rent, taxes, and – not only in Catholic regions – tithes or other churchly dues. Subjection and serfdom might hold farmers against their will, but more often the villagers' aim was to occupy desirable farms in their native regions and live well, by their own standards, from them. In west and south Germany, the impediment to this was population growth and fragmentation of peasant farms through partible inheritance (that is, division of farms among heirs). Here the number of marginal smallholdings proliferated over time, while numerous landless householders and renters dependent on wage-labor and seasonal cottage industry perched precariously on the land.

In east-Elbian Germany, the large-estate system – a form of "commercialized manorialism" – depended for its labor needs on fullholding peasants and their horsepower. Consequently, although a long-term expansion here of smallholders and cottagers also occurred, often onto marginal soils, the core of

(a)

FIGURE 3.4. VILLAGE LIFE

(a) A 1704 engraving depicts a "middle German" (Saxon) farmstead, standing alone in the countryside. This was untypical, because most farmhouses, then as now, stood alongside other farms of similar type in villages, sometimes strung along a main road, sometimes in clusters. But this picture accurately displays the common pattern of an enclosed set of buildings (farm house, barn and stalls, bake-house, a secondary dwelling for retired elders or, in their absence, lodgers or farm-servants). The picture evokes the ideal of self-sufficiency through possession of arable fields, pastures, gardens, orchards, and (for sugar's precursor) beehives.

the numerous large peasant farms remained intact. For their possessors, the great challenge was to minimize feudal rent, and especially weekly labor services. These became the source of interminable conflict, both in the fields, the seigneurial courts, and the princely or royal appeals courts.

(b)

FIGURE 3.4 *(continued)*

(b) Among the earliest photographic portraits of German country folk are these pictures, of unknown provenance, ca. 1860, of two villagers from the environs of Hamburg posing with baskets of wares – seemingly potatoes and fruit – which they sold on urban markets. Evidently healthy, they are well-dressed in folk costume signaling their social identity, clothes they would not have worn in their workaday rural world. Were these studio pictures intended for sale to a middle-class public inclined for reasons of cultural nationalism to idealize the rustic matrix of German identity? Even if so, country folk probably saw themselves in this photographic mirror as they themselves wished to be, and as – during trips to town or festive occasions – those among them not hounded by poverty actually were.

Source: (a) Reproduced in Adolf Bartels, *Der Bauer in der deutschen Vergangenheit* (1900), plate 36; (b) Reproduced in Franz Hubmann, *Das deutsche Familienalbum* (Vienna: Verlag Fritz Molden, 1972), p. 98.

Farming families' well-being thus depended less on legal status than on material assets, especially in land, and on the rents they paid. Peasant prosperity displayed itself in diet, clothing, dowries and marriage portions bestowed by parents on children marrying away from the farm, and in provisions for elders' retirement. A solid standard of farmstead living might just as well be encountered in East Prussia or Brandenburg as in Bavaria or the Rhineland. The Protestant freeholders of the North Sea coast, immune to feudal rent, collectively fared best of all (but their numbers were not great).

Virtually every village possessed its poverty-prone, land-poor or landless fringe population whose presence grew, especially as population mushroomed after 1763. For if recovery from the Thirty Years War's losses lingered into the 1720s, a generation or two later demographic pressure began building, especially in regions of partible inheritance. Even though premodern statistics must be compiled from disparate sources, and while the extent of losses in the great seventeenth-century war is controversial, the following approximations of the Holy Roman Empire's population (mainly German, but not including German communities to the east of the Empire's borders, nor excluding Czech speakers in Austria's Bohemian-Moravian lands) reflect wide consensus: 1618 – 21 million; 1650 – 16 million; 1700 – 21 million; 1750 – 23 million; 1800 – 31 million. By 1815, and in some regions well before then, self-sufficient farming families constituted, on average, only a minority of the village population (perhaps one-third, more or less). Alongside them, the marginal landtillers and landless villagers would have ranked, roughly, as equally large groups.

The nobility (*Adel*) embraced both rich and proud magnates and homespun country squires. The Holy Roman Empire's dissolution after 1803 reduced many previously sovereign rulers of miniscule principalities, along with the multitudinous Imperial Knights, to specially privileged noble subjects of the thirty-six territorial states that, together with three urban republics, survived on the post-1815 German landscape. Apart from these politically unhorsed aristocrats, each territorial principality had possessed for centuries a noble estate assembled from its own landed gentry, often descendants of medieval knights. They were customarily bound by kinship to a military and bureaucratic service nobility, whose ranks swelled over time by the addition of ennobled officials and other princely favorites.

In principle, noble families possessed property in land. Most noble lineages (allied families sharing a common ancestral name) held portfolios of palaces and manor houses, landed estates with forest and hunting reserves, and incomes from their tenants' and subject villagers' rents. But numerous individual nobles banked no incomes from agricultural sales or peasant dues, living instead from salaries, investments, and – sometimes – princely sinecures. In Catholic lands, unmarried nobles held most high church appointments, frequently endowed with ample incomes. In ecclesiastical principalities, favored families among the secular nobility enjoyed remunerative and hereditary Church patronage.

It befitted a nobleman to deal in wholesale trade of his landed estate's agrarian products, including beer and distilled liquor (*Branntwein* or *Schnaps*) made from seigneurial cereals or fruit. He might also have his alcoholic drinks sold at an inn or tavern under his lordship, but if he descended into retail trade or urban manufacture he would be obliged to forfeit his noble title and the privileges it carried. These encompassed, most prominently, shelter from most direct taxes, on the theory that nobles existed to share with the ruling princes the exercise of rule and lordship. The noble seigneur not only wielded local juridical and police powers, requiring him to employ and pay the officials who enforced them. Above all, he or others from his family, notably his sons, stood

(a)

FIGURE 3.5. EAST-ELBIAN ("JUNKER") LORDSHIP
(a) An idealized nineteenth-century depiction of the Reitwein lordship's manor house, near the Oder River east of Berlin. It stands before the local Lutheran church, displaying a tower modernized in the popular neo-Gothic style of the day. Noble lordships exercised patronage rights over ministerial appointments to the churches in their bailiwicks, although the pastors they nominated required confirmation by the state-supervised central religious administration (Consistory), while villagers and other parishioners submitted often highly opinionated views on their prospective clerical shepherds. Hidden from view, as is typical of such idyllic pictures, are the big barns and stables, laborers' quarters, and other structures indispensable to the workaday operation of east-Elbian estates, many of which spanned thousands of acres. Often such manor houses sat next to villages of subject farmers, although sometimes the noble lordships had earlier absorbed the villagers' lands into their own possession. The eighteenth-century Prussian monarchy worked against this practice – widespread in contemporary England, where it was known as "village enclosure."

under the obligation to serve the prince on the battlefield and at court, while his daughters too might be summoned to wait on their ruling mistresses at the princely residences. During their apprenticeship in these roles, the nobility paid much or all of their own way. For men in military or courtly service, only promotion to higher rank began to yield salaried dividends and other perquisites, allowing them also to marry.

(b)

FIGURE 3.5 *(continued)*
(b) An idealized engraving showing the reaping of a noble lordship's manorial fields, under the master's and mistress's watchful eyes. As was true everywhere, harvest time engaged all available hands in feverish labor, including those of children and the aged. Untimely bad weather – menacing here on the horizon – could ruin the ripened crops. Post-harvest fests followed, at which the well-worked villagers dined and amused themselves at lordship's expense. The custom was widespread for lord and lady to honor their field laborers' loyal service, bestowing on male and female leaders symbolic flowery crowns and, sometimes, a fleeting embrace. Musicians – some pictures show women among them – would accompany the proceedings from a platform stage. Such feudal outlays were (well into the twentieth century) an obligation of the manor house, which prospered by their village subjects' unpaid or underpaid labors (a form of feudal rent). *Source:* (1) Alexander Duncker, *Die ländlichen Wohnsitze, Schlösser und Residenzen der ritterschaftlichen Grundbesitzer in der preußischen Monarchie* (Berlin: Duncker 1857–1883); (2) reproduced in Sigrid and Wolfgang Jacobeit, *Illustrierte Alltagsgeschichte des deutschen Volkes 1550–1810* (Cologne: Pahl-Rugenstein Verlag, 1988), p. 43.

From the late seventeenth to early nineteenth century, the service nobility's numbers soared on the wings of the ascending military-bureaucratic "absolutist" state. Even though market forces and government-funded land reclamation programs enlarged the number of noble-owned large estates, the landed gentry as a class grew only slowly. Few among them were rich enough to measure themselves against the great aristocrats of England, France, Spain,

Hungary, Poland, and Russia. Some dozens of such magnate families bejeweled the Habsburg monarchy, but elsewhere most German noble landlords led prosperous or rich but not opulent lives, privileged yet also usually professionally engaged. Many died in battle, or in peacetime uniform. On the eve of the 1789 French Revolution, the number of aristocrats living in straitened circumstances – bereft of land and good salaries, sunk in debt, sometimes on the run and at daggers drawn with the law, sometimes behind bars – was not inconsiderable.

The German burgher class (*Bürgertum*) comprised wealthy merchants, often engaged in wholesale or long-distance trade. More numerous were master artisans or handicraftsmen, who were married, workshop-owning employers of journeymen and apprentice workers. The artisan trades, whose numbers in the bigger cities might exceed one hundred, were organized in craft-specific guilds – for example, carpenters, bakers, or shoemakers. These wielded powers, granted by ruling princes or urban governments, of regulating masters' numbers in a given town – for the artisan trades were mostly urban – so as to enable them all to earn a living deemed socially appropriate through service of a market monopolistically closed to "foreign" artisans, that is, from other towns. Likewise the guilds imposed standards of production (including allowable technology), set prices, and regulated the pay in cash and room and board that masters owed their unmarried workers (although many journeymen lived independently in rented quarters).

Like merchants, master guildsmen voted in town government, and might serve as mayors or aldermen. Important too among the burghers, although not so numerous, were the educated professionals: lawyers and judges, medical doctors, town officials, learned schoolmen and, especially in Protestant lands, the married, university-trained, often scholarly or literarily engaged clergy. Absolutism's rise swelled the ranks of bourgeois state servants, many of them graduates of newly founded or expanded universities specializing in the "administrative science" (cameralism [*Kameralwissenschaft*]) that boomed in eighteenth-century Germany. It offered training in state-centered, protectionism-oriented, bullion-hoarding "mercantilist" economics. This doctrine favored government foundation of monopolistic joint ventures of state officialdom and private entrepreneurs (the latter sometimes including so-called "court Jews" [*Hofjuden*]), especially to develop military provisioning and to manufacture armaments and uniforms.

By the late eighteenth century, growth of the state apparatus and private market economy had raised to prominence both a "bourgeoisie of education" (*Bildungsbürgertum*) and a "bourgeoisie of property" (*Besitzbürgertum*). They lived more in symbiosis than antagonism with the absolutist state and nobility, both of which depended in business, legal, and cultural affairs on bourgeois talent – and often paid well for it. But "feudal privilege" was increasingly a red flag in burgher eyes, especially when it entailed aristocratic monopolies on ownership of large landed properties (seigneurial lordships) and on high positions in public-sector employment, including the diplomatic and army officer corps.

FIGURE 3.6. THE EIGHTEENTH-CENTURY "BOURGEOISIE OF PROPERTY"
(*BESITZBÜRGERTUM*)
An early photograph (daguerreotype) from the 1840s displays Hamburg merchant
Johann Daniel Runge (1767–1856) and his wife Beata Katharina Wilhelmine née
Behrmann (1783–1862). Long-lived Runge, born on the Baltic coast in Mecklenburg-
Pomerania, grew to maturity in the eighteenth century. Here he presents himself as a
pious and frugal man, sharing life shoulder to shoulder with his wife, whose spinning
wheel symbolizes her industriousness. Other self-presentations of prosperous businessmen displayed them as office-holding urban patricians – luxuriously dressed, bewigged,
bejeweled, and trimmed in fur – or as proud and energetic men of affairs, seated in their
mercantile bureaus amid ledgers, legal papers, and drawings of their trading ships.
Source: Carl Friedrich Stelzner.

The military defeats and other humiliations that German territorial rulers
and their noble servitors suffered at French hands after 1792, and especially
after 1799 in Napoleon's day, encouraged (as we will see) middle-class critics
to raise their voices. Drawing inspiration from the philosophies of liberalism

(a)

FIGURE 3.7. ARTISANS (*HANDWERKER*)
These early photographs are reminders that the handicraft guilds, venerable communal
institutions born in the Middle Ages, housed sturdy self-confidence and a strong sense of
honor. Apprentices – boys in their mid-teens – depended on the paternal benevolence of
masters who taught, housed, and fed them. Journeymen formed a tradition-conscious,
literate, and well-organized preindustrial working class. Master craftsmen – collective
beneficiaries of market monopolies – claimed, and often enjoyed, the prestige of solid
householders with political voice in their communities. Here, (a), a mutton-chopped
young man memorializes his advance, perhaps already to master-status, as a fine-detail
smith (*Federschmied*) by posing in work clothes with his hammer and anvil in an 1860
Berlin photographer's shop. Such a scene (without camera) might well have occurred a
century before. Artisan masters posed also in their uniforms as members of independent
city-republics' militias, bearing symbolic or actual arms, and so demonstrating the connection between artisan-status and citizenship. The photograph (b), also from around
1860, assembles members of the city of Düsseldorf's Rhine river porters guild. These
mature and sturdy men, whose work clothes are of good quality and who sport jaunty
nautical caps, display a friendship doubtless celebrated with the jug of spirits sitting on
the table.

(b)

FIGURE 3.7 *(continued)*
Source: (a) W. Otto Hermann; (b) Reproduced in Franz Hubmann, *Das deutsche Familienalbum* (Vienna: Verlag Fritz Molden, 1972), p. 79.

and nationalism, they began to demand equality before the law, the "career open to talent," constitutional government, intellectual and academic freedom, an end to princely press censorship, and reorganization of common German institutions (if not "national unification").

Most townspeople could not claim the rights of citizen-burghers, but rather were town subjects without political voice. Many of these were journeymen artisans, typically young adult skilled crafts workers – unmarried, literate, and not averse to strikes and tumults. Numerous, too, were servants in burgher households, including boy apprentices living in their artisan masters' dwellings. Petty merchants, transport workers, and various salaried employees figured as well. On the margins there loomed the indigent poor, including widowed parents with young children, alongside the disgraced, the turbulent, the luckless, and the lawless. Journeymen artisans, heirs to old traditions of insubordination, would form a pioneering phalanx of the nineteenth-century labor movement. In town and village alike, charitable relief for the "deserving poor" depended principally on provisioning by secular authorities in the recipients' various birthplaces, although the Protestant churches also shepherded the indigent and needy. In Catholic lands, clerical ministrations and private individuals' almsgiving loomed larger still.

Social mobility raised and lowered people in all classes. For the common folk, marriages into landed farmsteads, apprenticeships in better-paid crafts, and the opportunity to study for the lower clergy were the most promising social escalators. For the bourgeois and noble classes, it was monied marriages and princely offices that led to higher things, sometimes aided by university study or entrepreneurial intrepidity and success. Among commoners, descent into the lower depths followed especially from untimely spousal deaths where small children were present, from bad harvests and debts, and from reckless living. For men, it sometimes ended in service among the socially scorned mercenary soldiery and for women in prostitution.

Economic Life

The Thirty Years War inundated the German lands with the greatest wave of crisis mortality between the bubonic plague ("Black Death") of the four-teenth century and World War II in the twentieth century. It left wide swaths of the Holy Roman Empire, town and village alike, in smoking ruins. Battle, famine, and plague killed millions and uprooted and dispersed millions more. The Empire's population in 1648 stood about 25 percent lower than in 1618. And while between the 1720s and the 1760s the worst seventeenth-century losses were surmounted, mid-eighteenth-century war mowed down new vic-tims. Multiyear harvest crises, accompanied by soaring mortality, occurred, with regional variations, in the early 1690s, around 1710, in the late 1730s, and again in the early 1770s. The subsequent years, down to 1815, witnessed brisk population growth, nourished by the transformation of the hitherto little relished potato – a seventeenth-century gift of South America – from livestock feed to staple garden crop and household food.

Recovery from war and famine – the one usually sporadic and localized, the other infrequent – usually gained momentum from falling marriage ages, reflecting opportunities for household formation opened to surviving youth by elders' death. Familiar economic structures – farmsteads, artisan workshops, town houses – were easily rebuilt, the technologies sustaining them, refined over the centuries, quickly reinstated. Agriculture's accustomed routines, including restoring requisite livestock, depended mainly – apart from wood for tools, harness leather, and blacksmith's iron – on human labor, skill, and time.

Early modern European international trade benefited Germany mostly through the commerce of Hamburg and other North Sea port cities, largely spared the Thirty Years War's ravages. Cottage-industrial networks supplied cheap flax-spun linens for export, including to overseas slave colonies. The Junker estates of north and east sent grain and forest products abroad. From south Germany and Habsburg-ruled Bohemia various manufactures – from luxury glass to wooden toys – traveled to eastern and Danubian Europe. But most of Germany's agricultural and industrial production circulated within the Empire's large, if toll-burdened, domestic market.

The absolutist state, apart from the war-related manufactures it subsi-dized and protected, followed an import-substitution policy, seeking espe-cially to raise up domestic luxury industries. Their products, it was hoped, would satisfy the propertied classes' hearty appetite for prestigious foreign manufactures of fine textiles, furniture, glassware, and decorative artworks, especially from Latin lands and the Low Countries. Frederick the Great's government strained to enable Prussian manufacturers to match Florence's silk and nearby Dresden's porcelain. It hectored its noble subjects (and prosperous Berlin Jews) to content themselves with these sometimes second-best goods, even as acrid local tobacco was officially mandated in place of the expensive, bullion-draining imported original. Unsurprisingly, smuggling flourished across the Empire's myriad borders.

Efficiency gains occurred through the spread of merchant-organized cottage-industrial production and rise of preindustrial factories or "manufactories," which emerged especially in textiles, as in the silkworks of west German Krefeld. They concentrated numerous workers outside the structures of the guild system (which favored an elaborate, disarticulated division of labor) in centralized workplaces, although without benefit of the steam-driven machinery that distinguished the British Industrial Revolution. Throughout Europe water power had long energized technologically sophisticated industrial processes in the milling of grain, lumber, and other raw materials.

By the early nineteenth century, the German lands counted manufactories by the thousands and had, in Prussian mining, begun to employ the steam engine for pumping. As the industrial revolution arrived from across the English Channel, entrepreneurs proved receptive and adaptive. Investment of capital in coal-driven industrialization, which in Germany pivoted on expensive railroad technology, required nineteenth-century innovations in banking and state policy. Masses of artisan producers depending on their own muscle power eventually came to ruin through mechanized competition, although others found jobs in the new factories. Labor recruitment into burgeoning industry required an end to peasant subjection. Governments began, hesitantly, to decree the subject farmers' personal legal emancipation and transformation of their feudal tenures into freehold farms, typically against compensation in cash or land to their former lordships.

Prussia pioneered this two-fold process, launching in the years between 1807 and 1816 a bureaucratically micromanaged freehold-conversion process that stretched to 1848 and beyond. Austria and the south German states found it easier to improve the peasantry's personal legal standing than to endow them with freehold farms, in whose absence the productivity gains of capitalist market agriculture, and the migration of emancipated labor from village to industrial site, were slower to materialize. Still, everywhere in the early nineteenth century redundant hands gravitated away from agriculture. As the technology of the Industrial Revolution came into reach, entrepreneurs seized it, confident of access to a cheap industrial labor force, although indispensable adult skilled workers commanded higher wages.

In the eighteenth century, the greatest innovations, alongside absolutist industries and middle-class entrepreneurs' manufactories, occurred in large-scale agriculture, especially on northern and eastern aristocratic estates and state-owned domain farms. Here widespread abandonment of traditional fallow-based cereal cultivation yielded a novel "convertible agriculture" (known earlier in the Low Countries and coastal Germany). Cereals now rotated with new fodder crops (turnips, potatoes, clover), while plowland alternated with pasture, significantly raising large-scale farming's output and profitability.

Such "agricultural capitalization," as it has been called, was often the work of leaseholders of middle-class origin managing the nobility's (and princely governments') large estates or domain farms. They, alongside many noble proprietors – "gentlemen farmers" – working with commoner bailiffs, took technological innovation's risks for the profits it promised. These and other agricultural investments, including arable expansion through wetland drainage funded by princely governments, helped moderate the rise of grain and other food prices accompanying population growth after the mid-eighteenth century. Favorable producer markets coined profits among agriculturalists, including millions of traditionalist village farmers selling their modest surpluses locally, thus invigorating rural demand – cumulatively great – for low-end manufactures.

It was long customary among historians and political writers to deplore miserly preindustrial living standards. This flowed in part from industrialization-friendly modern liberalism, and in part from class-conscious, anti-"feudal" Marxism. It reflected too a tendency to project the widespread poverty occasioned by urban proletarianization in the nineteenth century further back into the early modern era. Structural poverty did indeed afflict those at the bottom of the preindustrial social scale, but it was far from the common fate, even if it ballooned in times of war and food shortages. Only a small percentage of the population lived in want unrelieved by access to garden land, livestock-holding (if only a cow or a goat), occasional labor, and family or communal support.

Premodern average life expectancy within whole countries was low, but for the roughly three-quarters of the population who successfully ran the perilous gauntlet of infant and childhood diseases, longevity in later years improved notably. Epidemics – especially of smallpox and respiratory disease – and, for women, child-bearing dangers swept away many adults. Death lurked in anyone's shadow, but often he proved patient in claiming his harvest. There were numerous patriarchs and matriarchs.

Many people lived humbly, but not miserably. Many possessed claims on communal or seigneurial resources, such as grazing and firewood rights and jobs providing various payments *in natura* (including food), which modern social and economic history finds easier to overlook than laboriously translate into cash-value assets alongside what were often, for workers, modest money wages. Except in crisis years – which might affect the average individual once, twice, thrice in life (or never) – village farmers and urban craftsmen ate, dressed, slept, raised their children, celebrated their holidays, and passed the stations of life in a decency that does not deserve posterity's condescension.

To acknowledge this is not to exaggerate feudal benevolence, although this certainly manifested itself, if not always reliably. It recognizes, among other things, that ordinary people, while accustomed to bow to authority, understood something of self-defense, especially at the level of the village commune or guild corporation. This they staged through sometimes generations-long appeals to the law and, more summarily, through strikes, boycotts, or rougher forms of insubordination that, when collective, were much harder to quell through judicial or military punishment than individual rebelliousness.

4

Power States (*Machtstaaten*)

The Prussian and Austrian Military-Bureaucratic Monarchies

The Thirty Years War of 1618–1648 weakened German society, including the previously powerful landed nobility, to the advantage of ambitious rulers pursuing projects of military-bureaucratic state making. Contemporaries exaggeratedly described the end-result as "absolutism," a seemingly inescapable term modern historians have, to their disadvantage, kept alive. Following the Austrian Habsburg German emperors' defeat in the great war, the rulers of territorial principalities such as Brandenburg-Prussia no longer faced the threat of imperial blockage of their state-strengthening programs.

In the most successful cases, both in the Empire and across Europe, absolutist regimes overrode domestic opposition, whether from elites or commoners, and launched their lands on a path of state-directed economic development, propelled by wrenching tax increases and imposition of new political responsibilities on the various social classes: landed aristocracies now functioning as military-bureaucratic service nobilities; the propertied middle classes guided by the state toward larger-scale industry and trade and, through university education, toward key roles in the new, many-armed state bureaucracies; villagers and other unprivileged commoners burdened with new taxes and recruitment of one or more of their able-bodied sons into new standing armies.

Successful absolutisms were a kind of eighteenth-century "development dictatorship" under rationalist-minded ruling princes committed to schemes of power aggrandizement and economic self-strengthening. But these ambitious governments' freedom of action was far from unchecked. They could not escape the obligation to shield the inherited social order, acknowledging their subjects' ancient privileges and liberties even as they rearranged them on a new legal-institutional playing field.

In the mid-eighteenth century, a German form of the western European Enlightenment grew strong, with considerable state support, funneled especially into higher education. The absolutist regimes began to redefine themselves through an embrace of Enlightenment ideas of rational progress, thus giving birth in Germany to "Enlightened Absolutism." The educated middle class acquired profile and prestige as holders of important state offices, intellectuals and cultural producers, and technically adept businessmen. (Chapter 5 will unfold a roadmap of Enlightenment thought.)

By the eve of France's 1789 revolution, a tension had arisen in Germany between Enlightenment liberals – whether in state service or in the private sphere ("civil society") – and conservatives, whether aristocratic or non-aristocratic, state-employed or not. The question had emerged of how far the monarchical-bureaucratic absolutist state was capable of moving toward realization of Enlightenment ideas of individual freedom and the rule of law. Following the tremors the American colonies' liberal-nationalist revolt against British rule set off in Europe, the political earthquake of the French Revolution now rolled into Germany.

Brandenburg-Prussian Ascent

In the larger and most ambitious German principalities the trend in the 1648–1789 era was for rulers to strive for undivided executive power, based on unilaterally imposed new permanent taxation supporting a standing army and an expansive military-civil bureaucracy. Rulers sought with success to throw off earlier brakes on princely power applied by upper-class parliaments (generally dominated by the landed nobility), which had since medieval times shared power, in the previously discussed "estates polities," with the ruling dynasties. The new model was French absolutism as it developed under the "sun king" Louis XIV, to whom the proud claim was attributed: "l'état, c'est moi" ("The state? It's me").

The outstanding German case was Brandenburg-Prussia, one of the Holy Roman Empire's electoral principalities, embodied in the Hohenzollern dynasty. It was an archipelago of provinces stretching across north and central Germany from the lower Rhine to East Prussia on Russia's border (see Map 4.1). Its political capital was Berlin, in the medium-sized Electorate of Brandenburg. Its Hohenzollern rulers were (after 1613) Calvinists – in Germany called the "Reformed" Protestant faith – but most of their subjects were Lutherans. Eventually they comanded many Catholics as well, while, in the eighteenth century, Germany's largest Jewish population gradually congregated under their scepter. Prussia was both multiconfessional in its German-speaking population and, with its numerous French, Jewish, Polish and other Slavic subjects, pronouncedly multiethnic.

Frederick William, "the Great Elector" (ruled 1640–1688), fielded a standing army of 30,000 soldiers, financed by land taxes on village farmers and excise duties (effectively sales taxes) on urban consumers high and low. These levies the noble-dominated estates grudgingly approved, bending to the argument that a repetition of the Thirty Years War's ravages must be avoided at all costs. During that inferno Brandenburg-Prussia, like most other Protestant states, had stood largely defenseless between the warring Austrian-led Imperial and the anti-Imperial Swedish and French armies, in which German and

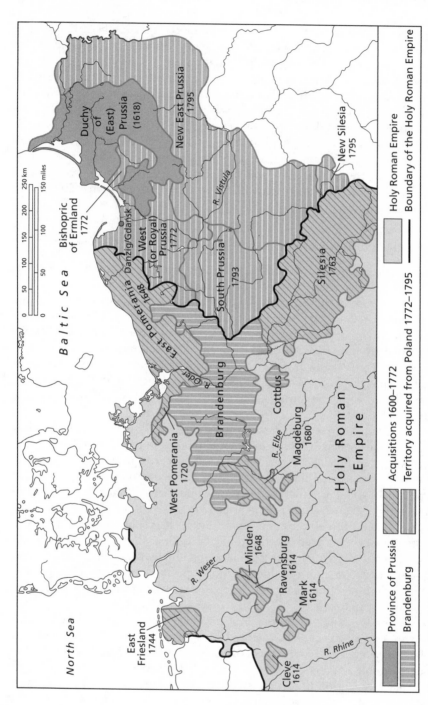

MAP 4.1. TERRITORIAL GROWTH OF BRANDENBURG-PRUSSIA TO 1795

non-German mercenaries fought in large numbers on both sides, spreading rapine and pillage.

The Brandenburg-Prussian nobility, although the Hohenzollerns ceased summoning their feudal assemblies, could hope to occupy preferred places in the new princely regime, especially as army officers and courtiers, but they received no monopoly on them. The Calvinist dynasty encouraged immigration of its co-religionists from France and west Germany, nobles and bourgeois alike. Provocatively, Frederick William favored them in state service over the local Lutheran aristocracy.

As a class, the landed nobility – known also, as we earlier saw, as Junkers – hoped the government would aid them in reassembling, by coercion and compulsion if necessary, their subject village farmers, scattered by war and hardship. These were obliged by their farm tenures to render unpaid labor services on the gentry's large estates, which profit-seeking, business-minded Junkers had organized in the sixteenth century to supply expanding domestic and foreign markets with grain cheaply produced on their broad acres by villagers' muscle. But post-1648 labor shortage was so severe that landlords were forced, much against their high-handed inclinations, to make many concessions over rent and labor services to repopulate their villages. Subject farmers frequently offset the burden of new state taxes by unilaterally reducing rents and services they tendered to their landlords. In this way, into the early eighteenth century, the nobility unwillingly shared in the new state-building project's costs.

The government soon embraced an activist program of repopulation through immigration: among others, many thousands of French Protestant refugees settled in Prussia after 1685. Mainly members of the French nobility and

---

MAP 4.1 *(continued)* A branch of the Hohenzollern lineage, whose roots lay in south Germany, ruled from 1415 as margraves in the Electoral Principality (*Kurfürstentum*) of Brandenburg Their seventeenth-century ambitions looked westward, to the commercially and industrially rich lower Rhine, where Calvinism thrived. Conversion to this faith helped them make small but profitable territorial gains there, but inheritance in 1618 of rule over Ducal Prussia created an eastern counterweight whose importance grew with Brandenburg's subsequent expansion into Pomerania, Silesia, and Poland. In Polish eyes, there were two Prussias: eastern or Ducal Prussia, self-governing but feudally subordinate to the Polish Commonwealth (which with its Lithuanian brothers had defeated the Teutonic Knights, medieval founders of Christian Prussia, in the fifteenth century); and Royal Prussia, lying between Ducal Prussia and German Pomerania, including the self-governing city-republic of Gdańsk (Danzig). In 1657, as the Polish Commonwealth was besieged by enemies, Brandenburg negotiated in Machiavellian manner Ducal Prussia's release from Polish overlordship. Berlin's acquisition in the first Polish partition of 1772 of Royal (renamed West) Prussia (and in 1793 of Gdańsk) crippled the remaining Polish-Lithuanian Commonwealth while initiating Prussia's fateful role as colonizer in non-German eastern Europe. This it played both in West Prussia and in the region known historically as Great Poland, acquired in the second partition of 1793, until the loss of these lands to the Polish state reborn in 1918. New East Prussia, gained in 1795, slipped after 1807 into Russian possession.

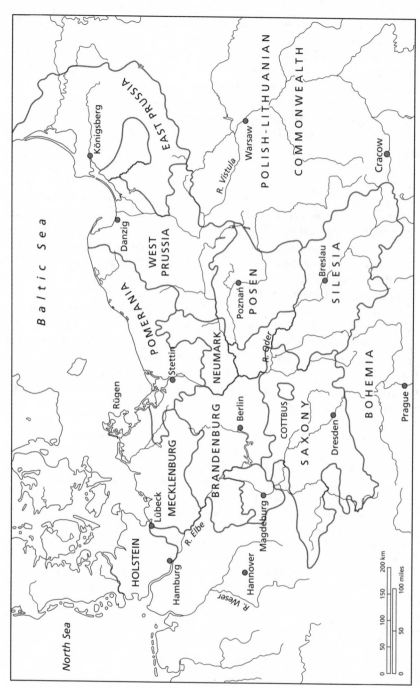

MAP 4.2. THE LANDS OF EAST-ELBIA IN THE EIGHTEENTH CENTURY

manufacturing-commercial classes, these Calvinists ("Huguenots"), whose descendants eventually assimilated completely into German society, figured importantly in eighteenth-century Prussia, both in state service and as private entrepreneurs.

The Great Elector's successor, Frederick I, parlayed his lands' gathering military and diplomatic muscle into acquisition in 1701, with Imperial consent, of the royal title ("king in Prussia"). His son, king Frederick William I (ruled 1713–1740) launched ambitious new state-administered military-industrial enterprises, alongside arms-enhancing joint ventures with industrial-commercial entrepreneurs, favored with royally dispensed subsidies and marketing monopolies. Even though the landed nobility exercised considerable powers in rural jurisdiction and tax-collection, his government insisted their sons serve at modest pay in the officer corps, while preferring non-nobles in the civil administration. Under his reign, the army's ranks swelled to 83,000 soldiers. Between 1688 and 1740, crown revenues increased fivefold, population nearly threefold.

Prussia acquired a European reputation as "Sparta of the North," its monarchs sternly devoted to the royal calling. Frederick William I, whose bureaucratic centralization and statist economics hardened Prussia's military muscle, is remembered as the "soldier-king" (although, frugally, he fought no wars). His government patronized the Lutheran lay revivalist movement known as Pietism, preaching Christianization of daily life and hard work in one's calling. Some scholars, their eye on Roman philosophy, describe the state's ideology as "neo-Stoic." After 1713 – exceptionally for the age – no lavish court was kept. Prussian baroque architecture was understated, often martial, if also comfortable and practical.

The Austrian Habsburg Monarchy

Most prestigious, richest, and long most powerful of the Empire's component states was the far-flung complex of lands comprising the hereditary possessions of the Austrian Habsburg dynasty. As the de facto lineage of German emperors, the Habsburgs suffered defeat in the Thirty Years War in their efforts to strengthen the imperial power within the Holy Roman Empire. After

---

MAP 4.2 *(continued)* The agrarian system of large estates worked by subject villagers ("commercialized manorialism") extended eastward from Holstein and Mecklenburg in the north and Bohemia-Moravia in the south, crossing Brandenburg-Prussia into Poland-Lithuania, the eastern Baltic littoral (modern Latvia and Estonia) and the Russian-ruled lands. Variations of it existed too in west-Elbian Magdeburg, in Saxony, and in Slovakia and Austria, Hungary, and the Romanian Danubian Principalities. Chapter 3 describes its workings in east-Elbian Germany. It is noteworthy that this form of the landlord-peasant relationship subsisted both under absolutist political systems (Prussia, Austria, Russia) as well as in noble-dominated states such as Poland-Lithuania, Mecklenburg, Hungary, and the Romanian lands.

(a)

FIGURE 4.1. ICONIC PRUSSIAN STATE BUILDERS

(a) Jan Mytens's 1660s painting depicts Frederick William, the Great Elector, posing contentedly with his wife, Luise Henriette, of the Dutch semi-regal House of Orange. Heaven, as the cherubs make clear, has blessed them with three sons, ensuring the all-important dynastic succession. Their marriage expressed not only religious solidarity between two Calvinist dynasties, but also Frederick William's hope to transform his largely land-bound and agrarian Brandenburg-Prussian realm into a seafaring and commercial-capitalist power. Like other European rulers (notably Russia's Peter the Great) he aimed to emulate the Dutch Republic, with its commanding fleet, overseas empire, rich trade, export industries, and internationally powerful banking system. Yet Frederick William's energies expended themselves mainly in domestic state building. On the battlefield, he won freedom from long-standing Polish influence over his East Prussian province, but – despite victories – could not break Sweden's post-1648 grip on the German Baltic coast. Emblematic of his ambition was a Brandenburg-Prussian colony, established in 1683 through the North Sea port of Emden, on West Africa's Gold Coast. But it languished for lack of naval power and capital investment until its final abandonment in 1720.

(b)

FIGURE 4.1 *(continued)*
(b) Polish-born Georg Lisiewski's painting, ca. 1737, memorializes Frederick William I and colleagues in the king's "Tabakskollegium," whose pleasures commenced following the ruler's regular weekly Friday work sessions with his ministers. The king sits at the table's near end, flanked on his right by son August Wilhelm. Younger sons Heinrich and Ferdinand appear diminutively at the lower left, bidding goodnight to their father. Crown Prince Frederick – subsequently Frederick the Great – was already married and grooming himself for the throne at a safe distance from his mercurial father. This naïve representation captures the austerity (and masculinism) of the "soldier king's" government, but also the good humor of such evenings of smoking and beer drinking. Seated at the rear opposite the king is a rabbit, symbolizing whimsicality, a quality given free rein on these evenings and embodied especially in the scholarly Jakob Paul von Gundling (1673–1731), the king's bibulous jester and verbal whipping boy, although also one of his close advisers. The king himself, while pious and anti-intellectual, was a creditable if blunt portrait painter.
Source: (a, b) Bildarchiv Preussischer Kulturbesitz/Art Resource, NY.

1648 they concentrated on ruling the territories they held hereditarily in their own dynastic right – the "power-base of their house" (*Hausmacht*): German-speaking Austria (with Slovenian-speaking southern districts) and nearby, scattered southwest German lands; the ethnically mostly non-German kingdoms of Bohemia and Hungary; and – later acquisitions – northern Italian provinces and sizeable Polish and Ukrainian lands. This patchwork state – the "Habsburg

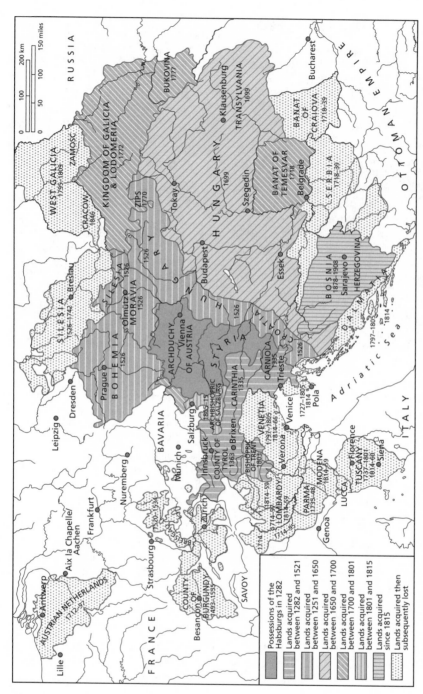

MAP 4.3. THE EXPANSION OF THE AUSTRIAN HABSBURG MONARCHY

monarchy" – was much larger than Prussia both in extent and population: in the early nineteenth century its subjects numbered around 20 million, in contrast to Prussia's roughly 7 million (excluding temporary gains from partitioned Poland). Yet Prussia defeated Austria on the eighteenth-century battlefield.

The multinational Austrian realm began to form in 1526, with its Habsburg rulers' inheritance of the crowns of Bohemia and Hungary. In the eighteenth century, Bohemia, adjoining Austria to the north, was – together with its constituent provinces Moravia and Silesia – a rich possession with a Slavic-speaking majority, but also with a powerful German-speaking minority entrenched in the landlordly-seigneurial, churchly, courtly-administrative, and urban upper classes. In acquiring the Hungarian crown, Austria assumed responsibility for expelling the Ottoman Turks from that large, multiethnic land, downstream on the Danube from Austria, which except for its western and northern parts the Sultan's armies conquered in the years 1526–1541.

The Habsburgs sought to consolidate their lands by enforcement of Catholic orthodoxy among their subjects. This entailed long battles with religious dissidents among the various nobilities they governed, but after 1648 they largely succeeded in imposing the Roman faith and corresponding schooling on all except scattered Christian nonconformists, who mostly withdrew from active political life (and sometimes into a crypto-Catholicism veiling clandestine Protestant practice). The Church acquired great wealth and power

---

MAP 4.3 *(continued)* The multinational monarchy's foundation was, as we have seen, the joining in 1526 of the Crowns of Bohemia and Hungary to the German Habsburgs' hereditary Austrian and southern Alpine lands. Wresting into Vienna's hands of the greater part of the kingdom of Hungary that the Ottoman Turks had conquered entailed prodigious military struggle, just as did the bitter loss of Silesia to Austria's Prussian rival. The Habsburg monarchy's early eighteenth-century efforts to push the Turks from northern Serbia and southwestern Romania failed, as Prussia's Frederick II duly noted on the eve of his assault against Austria. A century later, in 1878, Vienna's ill-fated acquisition of Bosnia and Herzegovina proved Balkan imperialism a trap. Similarly, Austria's occupation of Polish lands created a long and potentially dangerous border with Russia that had not previously existed. As in the nineteenth century Ukrainian political consciousness arose, the possibility emerged that Russia would exploit it to its own advantage, appealing to the large Ukrainian population of eastern Galicia. Had an assassin's bullet in Bosnia of 1914 not triggered the monarchy's fall, an act of terrorism in Habsburg-ruled Ukraine, sparking Austrian-Russian crisis, might conceivably have done so. Nor did Austria's impressive eighteenth- and early-nineteenth-century acquisitions in Italy long adorn its crown. In 1859-1866 Italian nationalism, in tactical alliance with France's Napoleon III, tore them from Habsburg hands, signaling Austrian weakness that, once again, Prussia was quick to exploit.

Despite the discontents of Czech and Hungarian nationalists, the mutual benefits deriving from the integration of the Habsburg heartlands of Austria, Bohemia-Moravia, and ethnographic Hungary were real and widely understood. World War I – a conflict of unprecedented material destructiveness and ideological radicalism – was required to tear them apart.

in the Austrian lands, but it inculcated dynastic loyalty in the nobility and other elites.

Between 1683 and 1711, Austria's armed forces drove the Turks from Hungary and subdued the rebellious Hungarian nobles the Viennese government acquired as new subjects. This came at the cost of tolerating Protestantism among a minority of them and promises to uphold the ancient Hungarian constitution, with its aristocratic parliament, noble freedom from taxation, and prohibition of army recruitment for service outside Hungarian borders. Such a crownland was to prove difficult to govern profitably.

In the eighteenth century, Austria gained possession, through the workings of the European Great Power system, of the southern Netherlands (modern Belgium). In Italy it acquired Milan-centered Lombardy and – to be ruled by a junior Habsburg dynastic line – Tuscany with Florence. As a cynical but eager participant, alongside Prussia and Russia, in the partitions of Poland (1772–1795), Austria captured the large province of Galicia, inhabited by Poles, Ukrainians, and Jews. Austria seized, too, the Romanian-Ukrainian province of Bukovina. Against these additions it suffered loss to Prussia of coveted Silesia, previously part of the Bohemian crown, and was rebuffed in its efforts in 1777 to trade the southern Netherlands for Bavaria, where the ruling dynasty had died out.

In Austria and Bohemia, some of the nobility were magnate aristocrats, loyal but too rich to depend on state service for economic well-being and prestige. With both Catholic Church and high nobility enjoying considerable wealth and autonomy, and having recently gained great military victories over the Turks, the Austrian government did not feel obliged, nor was it well-positioned, to embrace centralized, military-bureaucratic absolutism on the Prussian model. Austrian fiscal income stagnated, so that in the 1730s it was difficult to keep an army of 50,000 in the field for any length of time. Still, the late seventeenth and early eighteenth centuries were an age of political glory and cultural efflorescence, during which many of the regime's lavish baroque palaces and other state buildings arose, worthily matched by grand aristocratic urban residences. Imperial and noble patronage of orchestras and of the Italian – and, eventually, German-language – opera established the Habsburg lands' preeminence in central European musical and theatrical life.

The Austro-Prussian Rivalry, 1740–1789

The two emergent power-states decisively overshadowed the Empire's other secular principalities. The Electorate of Saxony, with its elegant capital in Dresden, possessed considerable economic muscle in mining and other industrial enterprises and in the profitable east-west commerce of the city of Leipzig. But its rulers' simultaneous occupancy in the years 1697–1763 of the throne of turbulence-beset Poland-Lithuania worked against absolutist state building at home, and Saxony's later alliance with Napoleon exposed it in 1815 to severe territorial losses, to Prussia's advantage.

FIGURE 4.2. HABSBURG AUSTRIA AT ITS MILITARY ZENITH

Jacob van Schuppen's portrait glorifies the Habsburg monarchy's greatest military commander, Prince Eugene of Savoy (1663–1736), conqueror of Ottoman-occupied Hungary. He crushes the Turkish army, here represented in orientalized and racialized figures, beneath his steed's feet. Catholicism's heavenly maidens, including – as it seems – the Savior's mother, hail and ratify his victory. In 1865 a monumental statue of Prince Eugene took its stand on Vienna's Heldenplatz ("Heroes' Square"), where it remains, framed by the Habsburg rulers' eighteenth-century urban palace, the Hofburg, and its adjunct, the magnificent National (formerly Court) Library. Thus was Prince Eugene's memory lodged at the Habsburg monarchy's public heart.

Absolutist army service appeared less glorious in ordinary recruits' eyes. Their missteps and infractions called forth canings or lashes, or even, as a torture reserved for desertion and other high crimes, running the gauntlet of blows, sometimes fatal, delivered by fellow soldiers. Such brutality was common across Europe in eighteenth-century armies. Soldiers in battle, driven forward to heavy casualties in massed formations, fortified themselves with Christian trust and – sometimes – monarchist enthusiasm, as well as with drink and hopes of triumphant survival.

Source: Portrait by Jacob van Schuppen, in possession of the Galleria Sabauda, Turin, Italy, reproduced in Helmut Günther Dahms, *Deutsche Geschichte im Bild* (Frankfurt: Ullstein, 1969), p. 131.

Similarly, the rulers of Electoral Hannover, in gaining the English crown in 1714, missed an opportunity to forge a stronger German state. Munich-centered Bavaria, long a powerful south German principality, faced in the eighteenth century the obstacles of relative urban-industrial decline, a small-scale noble class, and a rich and conservative Catholic Church. Its bitter rivalry with Austria, which lured it repeatedly into French alliances, exacted heavy military losses, compounded by local peasant revolts. Although Bavaria gained territory in the late eighteenth century, it did not bristle with arms. In Protestant Württemberg, the nobility, as Imperial Knights, stood directly under the emperor. This left the land to be ruled through a burgher-dominated estates-parliament in Stuttgart seeking jealously to block gains at their expense by the ruling dukes, whose conversion to Catholicism in 1733 deepened political antagonisms.

Crucial for German history was the war which Frederick II, in 1740 the ambitious new king of Prussia, launched against Austria, aiming to conquer the Habsburgs' rich Silesian province, abutting Brandenburg to the southeast. Hostilities raged intermittently after 1740, especially during the many-partied worldwide Seven Years War of 1756–1763, until in a comprehensive peace settlement European diplomacy awarded Silesia to Prussia. Having withstood French and Russian assaults while fighting the Austrians, Prussia had proven, at great cost to itself, that it was now one of the European Great Powers (the youngest and resource-weakest, alongside England, France, Austria, and Russia). For this steely deed, and his more peaceable talents, public opinion bestowed on Frederick in his own lifetime the sobriquet of "the Great" – the sole ruler in German history, apart from Charlemagne (and his now little-remembered tenth-century Saxon-dynasty successor Kaiser Otto I), to have won and retained in subsequent generations' estimation this title.

Frederick concentrated his post-1763 attention on centralizing and rationalizing the Brandenburg-Prussian legal system (also abolishing – for the first time in Europe – judicial torture). His reforms enabled humbler subjects, in accord with the Enlightenment's emphasis on the rule of law (but also to increase his state's central authority), to petition more easily against their immediate overlords to the higher appellate courts. He rewarded the nobility for their loyalty and grievous battlefield losses as army officers with preference in high civil appointments. Henceforth, until 1918 and beyond, a close alliance prevailed between Prussian Junkers and Hohenzollern dynasty.

To recover from war losses and fuel the economy, Frederick's regime ratcheted up indirect consumption taxes. He aimed to refill his coffers, among other things to subsidize new industries, particularly luxury production. He hoped, as we saw, that the propertied classes would cease purchasing expensive imports, thereby exporting gold and silver which, in contemporary cameralist (mercantilist) economic theory, ought to remain within the kingdom. The resultant state-steered silk and porcelain industries, although their products finally attained good quality, initially won only reluctant patronage of the monied classes. In Prussian mining and metallurgy, considerable gains were achieved, owing especially to Silesia's conquest.

Like his father, Frederick keenly pursued colonization – on uninhabited farmland and arable land newly gained through state-funded drainage and dyking projects – of tens of thousands of peasant families, especially solid fullholders (able to bear Frederick's tax burden) settled on good terms of tenure and rent. His officials pressured noble landlords to yield old-abandoned village lands to colonization. The strong property rights the colonists gained often spurred the nobility's long-settled village subjects to press for alleviation, through rent strikes and lawsuits, of their own legal disabilities and seigneurial obligations.

Altogether the kingdom grew richer in the late eighteenth century. Frederick's "fiscalism" earned the common people's resentment, but the masterful king's military prestige, judicial reforms, and improvements (some real, some only promised) in disadvantaged villagers' tenurial rights and legal freedoms stirred monarchist loyalism among many. There arose a certain Prussian mystique – if only an admiration for "old Fritz," as aging Frederick came to be known – that won adherents across the Empire. This was evident especially in Protestant lands whose princely regimes appeared undynamic and self-serving, unenlightened or unprogressive, inglorious and – an idea that began to arise after 1763 – indifferent to "Germany." In fact, Prussia, like other power-states, regularly put its own interests (its *raison d'état*) first, as its Machiavellian collusion in the partitions of Poland and self-aggrandizing policies during the French Revolution and Napoleonic period showed. Frederick himself was a Francophile who viewed German culture with condescension, if also with interest, but who saw no advantage to himself in the strengthening of the institutions of the Holy Roman Empire.

Nor does Prussia's success as a militarized power-state warrant exaggeration. In 1806 Napoleon's France dealt it a crushing battlefield defeat, imposing territorial, military, and economic losses that, had Napoleon's downfall in 1812–1815 not reversed them, would have extinguished the Prussian star. Yet, compared with other German states, Prussia exhibited decisive strength in its elites' cohesion and devotion to state service, and in marshaling its other human and material resources.

In Austria, the Prussian onslaught not only pried Silesia away, but also temporarily dislodged the Habsburgs from the Holy Roman Empire's throne. This was occupied, in 1740–1745, by the Duke of Bavaria, although without lasting advantage to his dynasty, until a lull in the Austro-Prussian rivalry enabled the husband of Austrian queen Maria Theresa, daughter of deceased (and son-bereft) Habsburg ruler Charles VI, to gain election. In the Austrian monarchy, the resolute and politically gifted queen and her ministers wielded power from 1740 until her death in 1780. After 1765, when her son Joseph II succeeded his expired father as emperor, Maria Theresa co-ruled with him in Austria. A turbulent decade of autocratic rule by Joseph alone ended in crisis in 1790.

(a)

FIGURE 4.3. PRUSSIAN LEGENDS

No dynastic state in German history has been more persistently mythologized – positively and negatively – than the kingdom of Prussia. This was the price of its success and the sometimes grudging admiration, as well as resentment (whether open or hidden), that it inspired. Such ambivalence also reflected the Janus-faced character of a modernizing state devoted both to military power and Enlightenment. (a) Johann Georg Ziesenis's benign and humane portrait of Frederick II, ca. 1763, depicting the king engaged, in the aftermath of exhausting wars (born of his own ambition), in a project of peace, probably the founding of villages on newly reclaimed land. The king's tunic, barren of all feudal distinctions and baroque grandeur, displays only the insignia of the Order of the Black (Prussian) Eagle, the reward for distinguished state service. (b) legendary battle-scarred cavalry General Hans-Joachim von Ziethen (1699–1786), portrayed by Anna Therbusch (1721–1782), daughter of painter Georg Lisiewski (see Figure 4.1). A leopard skin, associated with horseback officers, drapes his shoulder. Although a woman in a largely man's profession, Therbusch's reputation was high not only as prolific Prussian court painter but also in Parisian Enlightenment circles. From his teenage years Ziethen, Brandenburg nobleman and Frederick II's trusted friend and colleague, spent nearly the whole of his long life in military service, but through overseers and lessees he also profitably developed his landed property. He epitomizes the alliance of Junker nobility, Prussian army, and Hohenzollern dynasty.

(b)

FIGURE 4.3 *(continued)*
Nineteenth- and twentieth-century idealizations of frederickian rule were innumerable, both in high and popular art, eventually also in film. Robert Wartmüller's famous 1886 painting, "The King Everywhere," depicted the elderly Frederick II, bent but indefatigable, on one of his many inspection tours of his provinces. Villagers, shepherded by their Lutheran pastor, appear displaying to the king their sowing – as one of his blizzard of edicts had commanded – of the newly introduced potato, soon to become a vital staple food throughout Germany and Europe. Such celebrations of monarchist paternalism and the common people's gratitude for it reflect one of life's realities in the kingdom of Prussia. Familiar too were images of Frederick's visits to his state-subsidized manufactories where, in rough-and-ready uniform, he benevolently inquired into the male and female workers' well-being (and zeal for work), while elegantly dressed factory administrators obediently awaited his approval.
Source: (a) Erich Lessing/Art Resource, NY; (b) Bildarchiv Preussischer Kulturbesitz/Art Resource, NY.

Defeat by Prussian arms stung Maria Theresa, whose reign witnessed dramatic efforts to equip the Habsburg monarchy with a new military-bureaucratic armature. This program succeeded in Austria and Bohemia, but not in Hungary. In the two dynastic heartlands, a new provincial officialdom, drawn from the middle class or lesser nobility, assumed their posts, to the great nobility's irritation. The state confiscated the Catholic monasteries' extensive lands,

FIGURE 4.4. JOSEPH II, "REVOLUTIONARY EMPEROR"
Images of Joseph II behind the plough acquired iconic status during his lifetime and beyond. They derived from his working in 1769 an ordinary Moravian peasant's fields, as memorialized in this undated picture (which, reflecting eighteenth-century upper-class sensibilities, emphasizes the farmers' sun-beaten complexions, in contrast to Joseph's refined paleness). This incident epitomized Joseph's engagement in the common people's lives. He aimed (aside from his abolition of legal serfdom and plans for conversion of feudal dues into cash rents) to improve agricultural technology, raising his subjects' incomes and the Austrian government's tax revenues. Joseph rivalrously admired Prussia's Frederick the Great, whose pioneering innovations in the realm of "Enlightened Absolutism" the younger Austrian ruler hoped to overtrump with his own bold initiatives. But these left him more exposed to domestic political backlash than the more cautious and politically better-entrenched Frederick ever allowed to happen.

The Austrian state's national and cultural heterogeneity had long encouraged, within the slowly emerging public political culture, concentration on the Habsburg family dynasty as its ideal symbolization (although Austria's earlier role as Roman Catholicism's central and east European champion also focused loyalties among the devout). An especially powerful magnet for the Austrian Habsburgs' subjects' emotional identification was de facto German empress and Austro-Hungarian queen Maria Theresa who, with her husband, the titular emperor Franz I (d. 1765), raised sixteen children, including elder daughter and ill-fated future French queen Marie Antoinette and sons and successors, Joseph II and Leopold II (ruled 1790–1792).
Source: Engraving of unknown provenance (http://www.univie.ac.at/hypertextcreator/ferstel/site/browse.php).

devoting their often rich incomes in part to widening the network of public schools.

In 1781 Joseph II, with economic advantages especially in mind, introduced religious toleration for Protestants and Jews, enabling the former to emerge from the shadows of crypto-Catholicism and the latter to return from provincial or foreign exile to Vienna and other cities. He sought in 1787 to abolish the subject villagers' unpaid labor services and transform the peasant-landlord relationship into one of cash rents controlled by government statutes. He aimed after 1785 to introduce a German-language civil administration into Hungary, overriding the ancient noble-dominated constitution, while recruiting villagers as soldiers deployable outside Hungarian borders. He planned to expand the army's numbers to 300,000, so as to overshadow and overawe Frederick II's 200,000-man Prussian force.

Joseph II's ambitious reform program simultaneously stirred up against him, for divergent reasons, the Catholic Church, the German aristocrats of Austria and Bohemia, and the Hungarian nobility. As the 1789 French revolution erupted, he was forced to withdraw the controversial agrarian rent edict and backtrack to the *status quo ante* in Hungary (to avoid inciting turbulent elements of the Hungarian gentry into armed revolt). His reign showed that, in the Habsburg lands, the Church and the high aristocracy were too powerful to be reduced to mere tools of a centralized royal absolutism. Austria in the future would refrain from radical reform in Joseph II's manner, following instead a conservative line of upholding churchly and noble privilege as pillars of the dynasty's own power.

5

Aufklärung

The German Enlightenment and Other Spirits of the Age

Among ordinary people, the cultural bedrock of life was communally practiced religion intermixed with folk knowledge and wisdom. As society restabilized following the Thirty Years War, adult men and women increasingly displayed the elemental literacy that came with Protestantism, baroque-age Catholic Church reform, and the rise of the absolutist state. This accomplishment manifested itself minimally in an ability to decipher holy scripture and the hymnal, if not to sign one's name with confidence. Throughout the eighteenth century, many among the common folk displayed a robust appetite for reading devotional and inspirational tracts and broadsheets reporting recent news – especially sensations, catastrophes, and prophecies. Protestant piety encouraged introspective autobiography among those with a bent for writing, if only for the desk drawer. Eventually, at the eighteenth century's close, folk-savants appeared, publishing their gritty but hopeful life stories and religio-philosophical imaginings to the newly enlightened upper classes' applause.

The propertied upper classes' sons and daughters, both bourgeois and noble, moved beyond basic literacy to varying degrees of familiarity with their age's high culture. Until the mid-eighteenth century, this was framed within – and meant to express and reinforce – theologically orthodox Christianity in its prevalent German forms. Thereafter, among many university graduates active as officials and in the learned professions, as also among the intelligentsia of artists and writers, Christian orthodoxy weakened. Challenging it was metaphysical Deism, which conceived a nondenominational God common to all humanity as creator of the rational universe, but which also often perpetuated (sometimes unwittingly) Christian concepts and imagery from sacred history.

There arose as well an influential, religiously inflected philosophy of nature, expressed as pantheism and sometimes attacked by establishment theologians as "Spinozan atheism" (in reference to the seventeenth-century dissident thinker Baruch Spinoza, who found Reason and God coterminous in Nature).

Yet the German Enlightenment (*Aufklärung*), dawning in the late seventeenth century and reaching high noon a century later, retained a strong religious sensibility even as it increasingly turned away from baroque-age Christian orthodoxy. In France and England, by contrast, Enlightenment culture's embrace of secular-minded rationalism, empiricism, and (in varying degrees) materialism was more ardent. Many leading figures in German intellectual and cultural life were sons of Protestant divines. Many too had studied theology at university.

In Protestant Germany, Pietism's late seventeenth-century emergence represented a sea change. While guided by clergymen, this was a revitalization movement among laypeople, devoted to personalization and subjectivization of faith beyond mere rote observance, missionizing and inspirational publishing, and ministration to social needs for poor-relief and education of the common folk. As we saw, the Prussian monarchy patronized Pietism, both to its own advantage – through Pietism's reinforcement in public life of an ethic of work and duty – and that of the movement, whose institutions gained royal funding, although this ended after 1740 under the freethinking and skeptical Frederick II.

Such celebrated and brilliant Enlightenment and post-Enlightenment writers as Gottfried Ephraim Lessing, Immanuel Kant, Johann Gottfried Herder, Novalis (Friedrich Philipp von Hardenberg), Friedrich Schiller, Johann Gottlieb Fichte, and George Friedrich Wilhelm Hegel displayed a striking talent for imagining humanity's spiritual-cultural identity and destiny as unfolding toward (a perhaps never wholly to be attained) fulfillment in historical time. Conversion of Christianity's salvational narrative into a corresponding conception of earthly progress, whether cumulative or revolutionary, toward a final (that is, teleological) end – Reason, Freedom, Democracy, God-like Self-Knowledge – occurred wherever Enlightenment shone, but nowhere more brightly than in Germany. Doubtless the deep influence of Gottfried Wilhelm Leibniz (1646–1716) helps explain this characteristic. This many-talented luminary of philosophical and scientific rationalism – the first post-1648 German philosopher of European stature – strove after an understanding of the world, against Christian orthodoxy's preoccupation with the problem of sin, in which Divine Providence enabled humanity to attain, in historical time, moral and intellectual "fulfillment" (*Vervollkommnung*).

Pietism, although not unmindful of Man's fallen nature, also contributed to the emergent *Aufklärung*, especially through its orientation toward charitable and educational works. At the Pietist-influenced Prussian University of Halle, Christian Thomasius (d. 1728) and Christian Wolff (d. 1756) introduced the western European Enlightenment's foundational ideas, especially those of *natural law* and *natural rights*, to which German philosopher Samuel von Pufendorf (d. 1694) had earlier made contributions influential also in the Anglo-American world. Thomasius pioneered Latin's replacement as language of university lectures with German, advancing the process of associating the vernacular with a specifically German modern intellectual culture.

The Enlightenment in German Dress

It is customary to think of the European Enlightenment's ideas as seeds of revolution – 1776 in the thirteen American colonies, 1789 in France. Yet in Germany they first helped strengthen and legitimize the absolutist program, while only later did their liberal and democratic implications emerge.

The European Enlightenment's basic principles held that the Divine Creator structured the physical and human world according to inherent and invariable laws and endowed human beings with a developable faculty of reason, enabling them to perceive both laws of nature and humanity's path toward rationally structured earthly felicity. The Deity enabled them to discover and apply the liberating tools of scientific understanding, as Isaac Newton's much-celebrated formulation of universal laws of physics triumphantly demonstrated. Reason revealed to enlightened humanity their right (available first and foremost to rationally educated men) to individual freedom and self-determination, including through representative, parliamentary government, of which Englishman John Locke (1632–1704) was widely hailed as incontrovertible philosopher.

Enlightenment's progress was also aesthetic, making of art and literature paths to moral ennoblement and intellectual clarity. These were ideas brought to eloquent expression in Germany by the dramatist Lessing, the philosopher of art Johann Winckelmann, and the poet of genius, Johann Wolfgang Goethe, whose early works – notably the internationally acclaimed novel, *The Sorrows of Young Werther* (1774) – proclaimed an anti-authoritarian, socially critical message of cultured individualism and emotional liberation.

German political and social thought assigned pride of place, through most of the eighteenth century, to *Enlightened Absolutism*. Its theory, known in the Anglophone world from the seventeenth-century writings of Englishman Thomas Hobbes, held that human beings exited the primeval state of nature to enter into a social contract whereby, for the sake of peace and security, they created a sovereign power – typically, a monarchy – to rule irrevocably over them. Yet such authority was bound, both by reason and self-interest, to seek the social good rather than its own narrow self-aggrandizement. Frederick II, the intellectually gifted Prussian "philosopher-king," embraced such ideas, arguing that "the king is the first servant of the state." In his conception, "the state" figured as a power higher than the monarch, and one that, in *raison d'état* ("reason of state"), possessed its own rational necessity. This was to pursue only those diplomatic, military, economic, and social ends that would maximally strengthen it against rival powers and enrich it domestically.

There were, that is, *laws of statecraft* the ruler was bound to follow – on pain of his state's self-extinction. Frederick recognized the inequality prevailing among his subjects (nobles, burghers, villagers) but argued that greater rights imposed higher duties. It was the state's obligation to *rationalize* and *perfect* society by applying reason's principles to all public projects, including the Christian religion, whose precepts required reinterpretation so as to harmonize with Enlightenment ideas.

(a)

FIGURE 5.1. EARLY ENLIGHTENMENT AND PIETISM
(a) Gottfried Wilhelm Leibniz (1646–1716), philosopher, mathematician, and historian of European renown, appears here, richly bewigged, as an elegant and worldly savant-prince. He sought to transcend divisive Christian sectarianism by theorizing in terms of seventeenth-century Europe's new rationalist philosophy the relationship of Man and God, between whose (unequal) actions he postulated a "pre-established harmony." Leibniz served as co-founder – with the learned Prussian Queen Sophie Charlotte – and first president of Berlin's Academy of Sciences, launched in 1700. His far-sighted proposals for institutional and economic reforms within the Holy Roman Empire foundered on their dependence, characteristic of most of his endeavors, on imperial or other princely patronage.

It would be another half-century before there emerged in Germany an influential "civil society," grounded in a numerous educated middle class, whose support began to free artists and intellectuals from subservience to princely and aristocratic interests. Important in its emergence was professor-publicist Christian Thomasius (1665–1728), often depicted with a jaunty French moustache. An influential German pioneer of Natural Rights philosophy and co-founder of Halle University, he demolished witchcraft theory and authored satirical German-language journalism, helping advance the sphere of "public opinion," a concept he introduced into German terminology.

AVGVSTVS HERMANNVS FRANCKIVS,
S. THEOL. PROFESS. ORDIN. IN ACADEM. HALENSI,
IBIDEM AD D. VLR. PASTOR ET GYMNASII SCHOLARCHA,
ITEMQ. PAEDAGOGII REGII ET ORPHANOTROPHEI GLAVCHENS.
DIRECTOR I.
NATVS LVBECAE A. MDCLXIII. D. XXII MART. DENAT. HALAE. DVIII. IVN. MDCCXXVII.

(b)

FIGURE 5.1 *(continued)*
(b) August Hermann Francke (1663–1727), who piously eschewed bewigged finery in favor of his flowing natural curls. He was, with Philip Jacob Spener (1635-1705), the founding father of German Pietism, which aimed to deepen religiosity among adult laypersons by activating their subjective spiritual will and initative. Both were tireless preachers, authors, and institution builders, notably of the famous orphanage, school, and Christian publishing house at Halle, associated with an ambitious missionary program meant to bring forth Christian Reformation on a world scale.
Source: Bildarchiv Preussischer Kulturbesitz/Art Resource, NY.

It proved crucial that Frederick's Prussia patronized and even co-opted Enlightenment thought, which came to deeply stamp the state's political culture. Legions of mainly middle-class university graduates streamed into civil service and clergymen's posts, in which they preached the union of the Prussian kingdom and Enlightenment rationalism. In this view, heartily shared by Frederick II, the Prussian state figured as *an engine of rational progress and prosperity*. State power (*Macht*) served Reason (*Vernunft*). This is an

FIGURE 5.2. GOETHE AND OTHER ICONIC ENLIGHTENMENT-ERA INTELLECTUALS
This famous 1787 painting by Johann Heinrich Wilhelm Tischbein (1751–1829) depicts
Johann Wolfgang Goethe (1749–1832) underway on his long anticipated trip to Italy,
where he finally directly experienced the legacy of classical antiquity and the Mediterranean world's aesthetic and sensuous charms, much glorified in German thought of the
day (and thereafter). Italy mediated the Greek inheritance, the homeland of which lay
under Ottoman Turkish rule – difficult to reach in Goethe's day. As we have seen, Goethe
early attained European fame through his *Werther* (1774), attacking one-dimensional
rationalism (as well as aristocratic pretensions and religious bigotry) in the name of
Nature and individual freedom (both key concepts of the Enlightenment), and also in
the name of romantic love, unconstrained – if also often doomed – by social convention.
For the edification of the educated middle class, both during Goethe's lifetime and afterward, he appeared in commercially produced lithographs as a mature and respectable,
state-employed savant-poet – duly ennobled by his employer, the Duke of Weimar,
and so entitled to sign his name "von Goethe." Sometimes accompanying him in such
pictures were other intellectual titans of his day, including Johann Gottfried Herder
(1744–1803), Gotthold Ephraim Lessing (1729–1781), Friedrich Schiller (1759–1805),
and the then-lionized poets Friedrich Gottlieb Klopstock (1724–1803) and Christian
Martin Wieland (1733–1813). Lessing wrote celebrated stage-plays dramatizing
bourgeois-noble conflicts and, in *Nathan the Wise* (1781), proferring an iconoclas-
tic plea for Christian-Jewish-Muslim dialogue. His writings on religion and philosophy
of history, emphasizing the historical emergence among humanity of an understanding
of religious and moral principles of universal and not merely parochial scope, were
seminal for Enlightenment and post-Enlightenment thought in Germany.
Source: Bildarchiv Preussischer Kulturbesitz/Art Resource, NY.

equation that never acquired general assent in eighteenth-century France or England, however much the state there was respected (and feared) by its subjects. But by the later eighteenth century, largely because of the example of Frederickian Prussia, but also owing to Maria Theresa's and Joseph II's Austrian reforms, "Enlightened Monarchy" set the political standard throughout the Holy Roman Empire.

This trend heightened the self-confidence and actual importance in German society of the educated middle classes, who supplied many of the university graduates subsequently distinguishing themselves as Enlightenment intellectuals, skilled professionals, and state servants (although these ranks also counted numerous nobles' sons). Such middle-class graduates, as we saw, came to form a specific stratum: the "educated middle class" or "educated bourgeoisie" (*Bildungsbürgertum*). They increasingly set the intellectual and cultural tone, in contrast to the preceding era's aristocratic court society. They supplied the cultural producers who crafted the modern German language and a literature in it of European greatness. They joined courtly, aristocratic, and church circles to greatly enlarge the audience for eighteenth-century German music – famously that of Johann Sebastian Bach, Joseph Haydn, and Wolfgang Amadeus Mozart – as it ascended, inspired in part by Enlightenment philosophy, to European heights.

Prussian king Frederick II's preference for writing and speaking in French branded him increasingly in the educated middle class's eyes as a man of the past. It was they too who formed the greater part of the German reading and theatergoing public, including the intellectually most adventuresome who struggled to comprehend the thought of Immanuel Kant (1724–1804).

Kant's work constitutes perhaps the widest bridge into philosophical modernity. In three books of the 1770s and 1780s (the critiques of "pure reason" or rational knowledge, "practical reason" or morality, and aesthetic "judgment"), Kant set Enlightenment thought on new foundations. In response to eighteenth-century empiricism-driven philosophical skepticism – such as Scotsman David Hume's – questioning nature's rationality and man's freedom, Kant argued, in his self-described "Copernican revolution in philosophy," that it was not the realm of things outside human consciousness that was necessarily and ascertainably rational. It was, rather, the human mind itself, which was so structured as to organize all perceptions according to the categories of space, time, and causality. The human mind did not *mirror* a rational nature; it *constructed* it.

Human reason, Kant said, is nature's *lawgiver*. Nature may indeed be inherently rational. The mind cannot know this with certainty. Yet it must seek to comprehend the "thing-in-itself" outside human consciousness, including the entire physical universe, as if it did possess the attributes reason ascribes to it. As for human freedom, while reason may argue that all actions are causally explicable by preexisting conditions, and in that sense restrospectively predetermined, our possession of an unconstrained moral will – an idea Kant shared with the French philosopher Jean-Jacques Rousseau (d. 1778), whom he honored – enables us to act freely to the degree that we consciously choose to do so.

FIGURE 5.3. MUSICAL CRESCENDO IN GERMANY

German music brought forth genius in the work of the pictorially elusive Johann Sebastian Bach (1685–1750). While composing within a rich tradition of Christian religious music, Bach also raised Baroque contrapuntalism (or simultaneous interweaving of melodic lines) to unrivalled heights. He greatly expanded the possibilities of harmonically and rhythmically complex music as a wholly autonomous and infinitely developable art, later theorized as "absolute music." Eclipsing Bach in contemporary fame was the prolific and widely celebrated Joseph Haydn (1732–1809), pioneer of the modern orchestral symphony and string quartet. Haydn enjoyed life-long aristocratic patronage, whereas Bach lived from ecclesiastical salary supplemented by commissions. German-born Georg Friedrich Händel (1685–1759) followed the German Hanoverian rulers to their ascent in 1714 of the English throne, where his protean talent in baroque musical genres blossomed, rewarded by Britain's court, wealthy patrons, and middle-class public concertgoers.

Depicted here, in 1781, is Wolfgang Amadeus Mozart (1756–1791), at the keyboard with his affectionately named sister "Nannerl" (Maria Anna). Father Leopold poses with violin, while Mozart's deceased mother lives among them in spirit through her portrait. Such conventionalized paintings highlighted the well-established courtly functions of musician-lineages (from which Ludwig van Beethoven also emerged). Genial composer in many genres, Mozart also wrote the first great German-language operas, notably the inspired "Magic Flute" (1791). He introduced emotional and psychological dimensions into instrumental music that contemporaries sometimes found disturbing, but which also widened the path toward the conception, embraced later by Romanticism, of musical art as the poetry of the composer's turbulent soul, and as an individualized, often revolutionary commentary on the human and natural world.

Source: Erich Lessing / Art Resource, NY.

The moral law resides, not outside us, but within us, creating a potentiality – still far from fully realized – for ethical self-determination independent of divine power. As for aesthetics, the artist's mission is, similarly, not to bow to external authority, but to generate from within an independent and autonomous creative will.

Prussian censorship after 1789, during the period of the French Revolution, made it difficult for Kant to express his political philosophy with full freedom. It emphasized the primacy of government under the rule of law (the *Rechtsstaat*, or "state of law"). He insisted on the separation of executive and legislative powers but left parliamentary or representative government in theoretical shadow. His philosophy of history proposed that advancing trade (the sphere of the commercial and industrial middle classes) would work to unify the states of the world, bringing war into such disrepute – and making it so counterproductive economically – as finally to result in *perpetual peace*.

This was a vision of emancipatory progress in history emblematic of the Enlightenment. In his social and economic thought, Kant was an admirer of the Scotsman Adam Smith, another of the age's towering figures, who argued for the interplay in free markets of supply and demand undistorted as far as possible by political interference and government favoritism of some interests over others. Altogether, Kant stands as the philosophical godfather of nineteenth-century German liberalism.

Late-Enlightenment Tensions

Although the persistence of feudal-aristocratic social structures and absolutist state regulation of economic life may – as Adam Smith's followers held – have slowed industrial-commercial advance, economic growth both in this sphere and in agriculture in the pre-1806 decades was rapid, multiplying the numbers, wealth, and social-political influence of the entrepreneurial middle classes or "propertied bourgeoisie" (*Besitzbürgertum*). This important group increasingly took its cultural and political bearings from the Enlightenment intellectuals and artists setting the terms of debate within the educated middle class (or aforementioned *Bildungsbürgertum*).

In the late eighteenth century, many members of both groups, including civil servants, began advocating changes in the system of Enlightened Absolutism. They objected to the survival of both legally encoded and de facto aristocratic privileges, as in noble monopolies of possession of rural lordships and in privileged noble access to the highest military, diplomatic, and courtly posts. Enlightenment philosophy, after all, implied equality of rational beings. The music and literature of this cultural era, known today as German Classicism, questioned aristocratic pretension and exclusivity while indirectly pillorying, through allusions to the tyrants of old, unpopular contemporary rulers.

After the French Revolution's outbreak, Prussia followed Austria in drawing back from Enlightenment-inspired reforms, fearing that their egalitarian or "leveling" tendency would encourage political radicalization and revolt. In

FIGURE 5.4. THE GERMAN REVOLUTION IN PHILOSOPHY
An unknown artist's portrait depicts Immanuel Kant (1724–1806), son of a pious artisan family, who spent his life teaching and writing at the East Prussian University of
Königsberg. This picture, seemingly from the 1790s, projects Kant's gathering image
as paradigm-smashing and paradigm-setting philosopher. In his early career, Kant distinguished himself by arguing, in accordance (as he hoped) with Newtonian physics,
for the historical formation of planetary systems from nebulae – an early contribution
to evolutionary thinking about nature. He credited British philosopher David Hume's
work with awakening him later in life from his "dogmatic slumbers," challenging him
to formulate the innovative concepts of knowledge and human reason defended in his
Critique of Pure Reason (1781). In a 1784 essay, "Answer to the Question: What is
Enlightenment?" he urged his readers to "dare to know," and above all to act on their
natural right of freedom of thought, through which a public sphere of debate would
arise in which reasoned consensus would eventually prevail. Recognizing that many
intellectuals held official positions in the bureaucratic monarchical state, he argued that
they should bend, if necessary, to commands from on high in their "public roles," but as
private individuals they were free to criticize governmental policy in non-insurrectionary
published writings proposing more rational alternatives.
Source: unknown provenance. http://commons.wikimedia.org/wiki/File:Immanuel_
Kant_%28painted_portrait%29.jpg).

Prussia, the codification of state law begun in Frederick II's reign sparked a
controversy in 1791–1794 over the question whether such a legislative com-
pendium could, in quasi-constitutionalist manner, bind and limit the monarch's
will. The 1794 version of the General Law Code (*Allgemeines Landrecht*) eliminated any such possibilities. Meanwhile, it became evident that the absolutist

FIGURE 5.5. FRIEDRICH SCHILLER (1759–1805): POET OF REBELLION, PHILOSOPHER OF
MODERATION
The handsome but illness-plagued poet appears here in an 1804 portrait by Friedrich
Georg Weitsch. Often depicted was the iconic moment in the widely popular writer's
life when, in a secluded forest, he declaimed verses from his social-protest drama, "The
Robbers" (1781), to his fellow students at the hated princely military cadet school in
Stuttgart where he was unwillingly enrolled. Schiller's turbulent dramas – including
the famous "William Tell" (1804) – suggested a social and political radicalism his
philosophical writings did not uphold (his voice strengthening early German liberalism
instead).
    In his philosophical writings *On the Aesthetic Education of Humanity* and *On Naïve
and Sentimental Poetry* (1795) he argued, under the impression of the brutalities and
irrationalities of the French Revolution and its impassioned enemies, that humanity was
not yet ripe for self-rule, but required intellectual and emotional maturation and self-
mastery through art. Schiller was among the first European intellectuals to recognize
that the Enlightenment and the ensuing revolutionary era had torn society from its
previous anchorages and set it adrift on the stormy seas of a modernity that threatened
the individual and society with debilitating alienation and nostalgia.
Source: Bildarchiv Preussischer Kulturbesitz/Art Resource, NY.

system was not coping well with a spreading social crisis in the Empire, resulting from rapid population expansion (from some 23 million in 1750 to about
31 million in 1800). Rising numbers of uprooted and pauperized people
appeared on urban streets and country roads. The spread of capitalist-organized

cottage industry, and early forms of factory production, multiplied an ill-paid proletariat. Against the French Revolution's background, fears circulated among the propertied classes of lawless vagabonds and mob violence.

The sophisticated middle-class response was to call, in the spirit of Adam Smith, for *economic liberalism,* that is, a market economy freed of heavy government regulation and class privileges, allowing entrepreneurially energetic individuals of all stations in life access, as the contemporary phrase put it, to "careers open to talent." Militaristic monarchy's heavy expenses should be cut, and the antiquated system of guild-bound, monopolistic artisan handicraft production abolished, freeing such trades for all comers. Subject villagers should be released from feudal rents and given their farms in freehold, leaving noble landlords to adjust to an economy based on wage labor and free markets.

In the era of the French Revolution and Napoleon, monarchical or princely absolutism in Germany faced burgeoning objections on both philosophical-ideological and practical grounds, formulated mainly by middle-class intellectuals and members of the nobility whose university education and status as intellectuals drew them toward their commoner counterparts. Yet in Austria and other German states, and above all in the kingdom of Prussia, the absolutist system had created a centralized and militarized bureaucratic monarchy served by a self-confident and privileged elite of officials, many noble-born or ennobled, many of middle-class origins but loyal to the regime employing them. Such a system constituted a formidable obstacle to its critics. As the future would show, this configuration favored, not revolution, but *reform from above,* through compromises between middle-class liberalism and military-aristocratic monarchy. This would become the *Prussian path* to nineteenth-century political modernity.

Three Spirits of the Age

Before we step into the nineteenth century, a backward glance will be worthwhile at styles of thought and life that jostled one another on the late eighteenth-century German-speaking stage, at least among the educated, propertied, and empowered classes. Three distinctive worldviews, with corresponding "lifeworlds," are discernible, in part coexisting and competing with each other (as well as with a fourth, which began at the era's end to take shape). The chronologically oldest among them was the social and religious traditionalism that might be called the "Christian vision of an estates-bound world." Much in evidence after the Thirty Years War, its adherents clung to religious orthodoxy as it had crystallized in the conflicts leading up to the "great German war," as some then called it. Faith in one's creed and loyalty to its clerics and officials alone promised salvation. As for worldly life, a conservative and hierarchical mentality accompanied religious orthodoxy. It saw in the received traditions of the late medieval and Renaissance-era "estates polity" (*Ständestaat*) the promise of social equilibrium. Each collective interest in society, peasantry and

FIGURE 5.6. AN ABSOLUTIST "BERLIN WALL"
A contemporary engraving depicts the "Rondel," including the Hallesches Tor (or Halle Gate) in 1730s Berlin. Part of a structure encircling the heart of the eighteenth-century city, it channeled goods in transit into a state-controlled space where their owners could not escape paying excise tax on them. Here is the bureaucratically omniscient fiscal-military state in its architectural concreteness and police-backed action. In the foreground stand new apartment blocks, with workshops in their courtyards. For the lawless and undisciplined, work-house prisons stood ready.
Source: unknown provenance. http://commons.wikimedia.org/wiki/File:Mehringplatz_um1730.jpg).

the poor included, deserved – and would gain – just consideration under the joint rule of prince and corporately organized elites.

Throughout the Holy Roman Empire, the Westphalian treaty's modifications of the imperial constitution seemed to strengthen the longstanding ideal of harmonious power sharing between emperor and the Reich-level estates – particularly territorial rulers, both lay and ecclesiastical. Such a perspective on German life persisted into the Napoleonic era, when many of the political structures it valued – from the Empire itself to seigneurial and other small-scale forms of feudal lordship – collapsed or were abolished through conquest, impotence, and ideological delegitimization. Yet this mentality experienced *rebirth* in the form of nineteenth-century social and political *conservatism*, invoking the alliance of throne and altar and restamping the coin of old-regime lordship and liberties with the insignia of a patriarchally conceived modern market economy and sacred individual property rights.

FIGURE 5.7. ENLIGHTENMENT POLITICS OF RELIGION
This 1782 engraving by J.F. Beer celebrates Emperor Joseph II's Toleration Edict of 1781, which recognized the legality and right to public worship of the Habsburg monarchy's Lutheran, Calvinist, and Eastern Orthodox Christians (but not other Christian sects). Jews too gained official toleration, amplified by a 1782 edict freeing them from many civil and legal restrictions, including exclusion from settlement in Vienna. In the engraving an unidentified visitor, evidently representing the Enlightenment world, contemplates Joseph's image, accompanied by the grateful beneficiaries of his liberality, including an Orthodox Jew in typical eighteenth-century garb. In heaven above, lines from the Psalms place Joseph II under divine protection, while his mother, Maria Theresa – surrounded by the Pope, John Calvin, Martin Luther, and icons of Judaism and Eastern Orthodoxy – hails Joseph's legislation. Here Enlightenment and multi-confessional revealed religion peacefully stroll hand in hand under a benign Christian heaven.

Another of the emperor's religious reforms in 1782 closed monastic institutions so as to devote their incomes (and the remaining monks' energies) to social improvements, especially in public health and education, raising the people to greater civic reason and

A *second* worldview emerged in the mid-seventeenth century, associated with the rise of military-bureaucratic monarchy. It can be imagined as "state-building realism." Understanding itself to be, in its own time, bold and modern, it paid as much homage as inbred religiosity and self-interested appreciation of feudal privilege allowed to *raison d'état*, Machiavellian militarism and diplomacy, ruthless fiscalism, and bureaucratic and judicial rationalization. It redefined the subject population not by their prescriptive rights and liberties, but rather by their duties to the new and abstract "state" that was rising – or so this view's adherents hoped – into the human clouds. To many it seemed natural to ascribe this development to God's will. Religious conservatives who loudly opposed it – like aristocrats who doggedly fought against state aggrandizement – suffered the sting of princely disgrace and sometimes even sharper sanctions.

This mentality also persisted through the eighteenth century, as it does, in more modern dress, to the present day. It was shared, then as now, by business entrepreneurs, especially those working profitably with the power-state. In the mid-eighteenth century, however, it encountered a challenge in the form of a *third* worldview, which we may term "Enlightenment utopianism." This was the broader outlook of which adherence to "enlightened absolutism" was one influential expression. Fundamental was the ambition to remake the human world in the image of the rationality of Nature that Galileo, Newton, and other luminaries of the Scientific Revolution had discovered.

FIGURE 5.7 *(continued)* economic competence. The radical extension of state influence over Habsburg religious life came to be known as "Josephinism." Although sometimes rejected in Catholic circles, it actually anchored the monarchy more firmly in religious sentiment and loyalty.

Expressive too of Enlightenment religiosity was Freemasonry, highly influential in late eighteenth-century German intellectual and governmental circles. Born in Britain, it brought philosophically minded, Deism-inclined (but also mostly conventionally Christian) burghers and aristocrats together on common social and intellectual ground, devoting themselves to moral improvement and beneficial public works. Among its members were Austria's Joseph II (and Mozart) and Prussia's Frederick II. Historians have found it ironic that, before the 1789 French Revolution exposed the deadly stakes of Enlightenment politics, kings joined through Freemasonry in undermining the received Christian-feudal social-political order.

A characteristic image appeared in the frontispiece of a book published in 1791 in Vienna (where the leading Masonic lodge was suggestively named "Crowned Hope"). In it, a group of Freemasons – their dress signaling their social diversity – study the symbols of their association while peering into the mirror of Nature, from which emerges human understanding or Reason (imaged in freemasonry's triangled eye), accompanied by the caption "light from the shadows." Here, as in the earlier image celebrating Joseph's reforms, the time-honored Christian motif of light descending is put to the Enlightenment's ends. Not for nothing did American historian Carl Becker entitle his imaginative 1932 book *The Heavenly City of the Eighteenth-Century Philosophers*.
Source: Bildarchiv Preussischer Kulturbesitz/Art Resource, NY.

Ideal humanity found its reflection in Enlightenment culture's theoretical blueprints sketching out the rational organization of state, society, economy, and indeed of everything human. Fulfillment of such inspired imaginings might be attempted, top-down, through "enlightened despotism," but it could also be sought, bottom-up, through national and social-political revolution, as in the American colonies in 1776 and France in 1789. It was a view that, in conservative or moderate form, imagined an enlightened human elite managing the affairs of popular masses as yet (or perhaps forever) unqualified for self-determination. Ideologically dressed as democratic egalitarianism, it could envision the attainment by "all men," and perhaps by all people, of rationally informed voice and political participation.

Crucial was its pursuit of "enlightened reform" as emancipatory end in itself and as a snowballing venture cleansing and perfecting human life's every corner. Adam Smith's prescription of market freedom as people's entry-ticket to such shares of earthly felicity as their talents and energy justified found a strong echo in late eighteenth-century Germany, when the government-driven economic strategies of the "state-building realists" began to lose their transformative power and plausibility. Above all, this life-perspective assumed rational mastery of the world by enlightened individuals, whether the progeny of elites or not. Reason would dissolve all superstitious mysteries. All expressions of human life, including those of emotion and aesthetic response, would gain illumination through rational analysis. Art, given proper form, would enrich and edify the enlightened mind. Science and technology would switch on ever more real-life lights.

This mentality survived as nineteenth- and twentieth-century rationalist *liberalism* or progressivism – but only on condition it linked itself to one or another communalist doctrine. For even if rational individuals are the prime actors in life's drama, the question must arise in what social-political setting they find and exert themselves. In the eighteenth- and early nineteenth-century German lands the answer was, at first, the reforming power-*state*, guiding by enlightened genius (whether the ruler's or the ruling bureaucracy's). But *nationalism*'s emergence raised the possibility of "the German people" (or *Volk*) attaining collective freedom and felicity by its own actions within a self-determining *nation*. *This* worldview, following *fourth* upon those others sketched here, emerged simultaneously in time with what may be called the "Romantic-historicist" temperament. Yet, while Romanticism, historicism, and nationalism grew from Enlightenment roots, it took the storm of the French Revolution and the Napoleonic years for them to shoot up and tower over the German landscape.

PART II

GERMAN IDENTITIES BETWEEN LIBERALISM, NATIONALISM, AND SOCIALISM, 1789–1914

The following seven chapters trace the emergence and contentious trajectory of this book's *second* German nation. Seen through *nationalist* eyes, the long nineteenth century from 1789 to 1914 witnessed the struggle, partly triumphant, partly maddeningly frustrated and incomplete, to forge the *first* German nation from the shattered fragments of the ever more impotent and defenseless Holy Roman Empire, buried in Napoleonic avalanche. We, however, must concede the coherence, meaningfulness, and dignity of life before the French Revolution, recognizing that it represented an aristocratic-monarchical, agrarian/small-town, and Christian form of German identity that, certainly in the mind of the educated and propertied classes, was alive and self-aware.

The nineteenth century brought dramatic and revolutionary reordering to the German lands. The Enlightenment released energies of immense political and moral force in pursuit of "life, liberty, and the pursuit of happiness" and "*liberté, égalité, fraternité*." Industrial technology and the unprecedented new cities it stamped from the earth wrought epochal changes. Science and medicine were population explosion's midwives. "The nation," in the minds of nationalist intellectuals and – increasingly – most other educated people, became the ideal form of community to encompass such a newly structured social world, and to make possible the enactment in political life of the Enlightenment's ambitious principles and its many-visaged ideological projects.

The nineteenth century's new social formations required novel forms of legitimization, inspiration, and integration. Nationalism, understood as political mobilization and enfranchisement of the whole people (however defined) on the premise (however fictive) of their *kinship* through language, culture, and history, was the most indispensable and potentially the strongest, if also most explosive, social cement.

The nineteenth century did indeed bring forth a new German national state, in the form of the Berlin-centered empire of 1871–1918. Flanking it was an Austrian monarchy in which German nationalism, excluded from Bismarck's house, faced the challenge of subsisting on its own, and of seeking, as best it could, to impress the far-flung multinational empire with its own stamp. In each case a nationalism synthesizing elements of both Enlightenment liberalism and the absolutist monarchical tradition sought to take command of rapidly industrializing societies.

Yet, in a region with such a politically and religiously divided character as German-ruled central Europe, attaining consensus on *whose nationalism* should prevail was arduous and, before 1914, ultimately impossible. *Competing German nationalisms* had arisen, including that of new working-class movements speaking in the name of a revolutionary proletariat that, while international in theory, consisted in practice of nationally demarcated cadres. It some eyes it began to appear that a stable, powerful and successful German nation could only be built by suppressing alternative social and political visions. A contest of rival "utopias of modernity" began that would lead, across World War I's flaming trenches, to civil and ethnic war to the knife.

6

Liberté?

Facing the French Revolution, 1789–1815

The 1789 Revolution in France proclaimed principles of constitutional government, social justice, and national self-determination that stirred a positive response among many German-speakers, both in the educated and propertied classes and among the common people. But the French drift toward dictatorship and especially the wars that, beginning in 1792, erupted between revolutionary France and shifting coalitions of England, Russia, Austria, and Prussia eventually steered German opinion in mostly anti-revolutionary directions.

French territorial conquest in central Europe catalyzed German nationalism. Its apostles yearned for expulsion of the French from German soil and dramatic reorganization of state life, culminating in a new integrative structure to replace the defenseless, vanquished, and, after 1806, vanished Holy Roman Empire. In the kingdom of Prussia, military defeat at Napoleon's hands called forth dramatic and controversial political, socioeconomic, cultural, and military reforms. In west and south Germany, the Gallic conquerors' and overlords' hand was heavy, guiding their German vassals toward French models in refiguring political and social institutions.

Developments in these years set the agenda for the nineteenth-century German lands: national consolidation, self-government through representative, constitutionally-mandated parliaments, and free markets and entrepreneurship in agriculture and industry. Yet, even as by 1815 momentum toward these goals' realization had accelerated, so too had Prussian reforms in particular equipped existing state power anew for survival. In nineteenth-century Prussia, which was considerably larger and richer than Frederick the Great's state, liberalism would not face a monarchical-aristocratic "old regime" lurching toward political demise, as was the case in 1789 with the Bourbon monarchy in France, despite intelligent governmental reform efforts and the vitality of French civil society. It confronted instead a vigorous state displaying many elements of modernity.

The French Revolution in Germany, 1789–1807

Among the middle and upper classes, the early phase of the French Revolution met widespread approval. At its outset, the revolution found expression in the 1789 Declaration of the Rights of Man and Citizen, with its accompanying abolition of "feudalism" (principally the aristocracy's privileges), and in the moderate 1790 constitution, subordinating the monarchy of Louis XVI (now titled, in nationalist language, "king of the French") to an elected parliament representing educated professionals and property owners. The revolution's subjection of the French Catholic Church to stringent state control also elicited approval. German opinion widely condemned the prerevolutionary French monarchy for corrupt and inefficient despotism.

Yet there was little sentiment that similar revolution was required at home. In most eyes, monarchical-bureaucratic absolutism appeared, except in some minor principalities beset with irresponsible rulers, as a system possessing moral integrity and technical efficiency, capable – especially in the larger states – of piecemeal reform in a progressive direction. It was clear, too, that the secular German states possessed military and police power to repress any efforts at their violent overthrow. Nor was an insurrectionary tactic consistent with philosophical liberalism as understood in Germany, which emphasized the rule of law. Kant denied any "right of revolution," although he acknowledged that unjust regimes brought on their own downfall, and welcomed the revolution in France.

As in 1792–1794 the French Revolution transmuted into radical Jacobinism and terror-wielding dictatorship, German opinion largely recoiled in shock, concluding moralistically that the revolutionaries lacked requisite virtue and character to carry out beneficent, nonviolent transformation of state and society. Subsequent French politics, culminating in Napoleon's nationalistically high-charged military-bureaucratic and police-state regime (1799–1814), only deepened such negativism. There were scattered groups of pro-French radicals, drawn mainly from the ranks of anti-absolutist south and west German intellectuals gripped by visions of popular uprising and national renewal. But time was short to rally support among the common people for such an ideologically sophisticated program. At most, villagers and townspeople staged isolated small-scale rebellions against oppressive local overlords, especially in strikes and unruly lawsuits, some after 1789 voicing – if only through lawyers – revolutionary rhetoric.

The princely regimes' panicked reactions to the French Revolution and Napoleon's government, with which Prussia and Austria were sporadically at war – with intermittent truces – from 1792 to 1806 and from 1813 to 1815, strengthened conservative absolutist tendencies. This resulted in heightened censorship throughout the Empire (1791) and strengthened police surveillance, especially in the Habsburg monarchy. On the rise, too, was repudiation of Enlightenment rationalism as it had been applied to theological doctrines and religious practice, in favor of a sentimental-mystical ideology of "throne and altar," sometimes expressed in the budding language of Romanticism. Proponents of the Enlightenment and early liberalism objected to these trends but could not stop them, even though the censorship was relatively easy to evade, given the existence of more than three hundred principalities where writers could seek to publish their work.

The absolutist monarchies brought themselves down through their own military defeats. The French armies, reorganized along new ideological lines of "the career open to talent" and "the nation in arms," outmaneuvered on the battlefield the rigidly disciplined German armies. In 1795–1797, the French won a peace settlement surrendering to them the Rhineland – that is, the lands of the Holy Roman Empire west of the Rhine; in 1805 Austria suffered decisive defeat, leading to the Holy Roman Empire's 1806 dissolution and Vienna's submission to forced alliance with Napoleon. In 1806 Napoleonic policy also cajoled and corralled central Germany into the "Confederation of the Rhine," a clutch of satellite regimes under French control.

In that same year Prussia's turn came, as the army Frederick the Great made famous buckled under French onslaught. In the resultant 1807 Treaty of Tilsit, Berlin surrendered its Rhenish provinces and the wide lands annexed from Poland in the post-1772 partitions of Poland (1793, 1795). Tilsit reduced Prussia's army to 42,000 soldiers and saddled its government with draconian war reparations of 140 million gold francs. These terms toppled Prussia from its Great Power status, reducing it to a French-occupied dependency.

A "Beneficent Revolution from Above" – The Prussian Reform Era

The disasters of 1806–1807 enabled liberal-minded reformers in the Prussian monarchy's high ministerial bureaucracy and army to oust defeat-discredited prewar officeholders. After Frederick II's death in 1786, his successors (Frederick William II [ruled 1786–1797] and Frederick William III [d. 1840]) played weaker roles on the throne, while the high bureaucracy's authority escalated. But the kings and their courts – including various informal counselors, many recruited from among the conservative nobility – still commanded great influence. Above all, the monarch could dismiss ministers, appointing such new ones as he hoped would prove competent and respect-worthy in the eyes of high officialdom and "public opinion" embodied in the propertied and educated classes.

In the Reform Era, strong-willed ministers, led in 1807–1808 by Baron Karl vom Stein and in 1810–1822 by Prince Karl August von Hardenberg, steered the Prussian government forward, with the crown largely (but not entirely) acquiescing in their work. Among other notable participants were Wilhelm von Humboldt (educational and constitutional questions) and Carl von Clausewitz (military affairs). They undertook an ideologically moderate, self-styled "revolution from above," aiming (1) to reorganize the state as a power machine, so as to free it from French control and assist in Napoleon's military expulsion from Germany; (2) to accelerate economic growth through

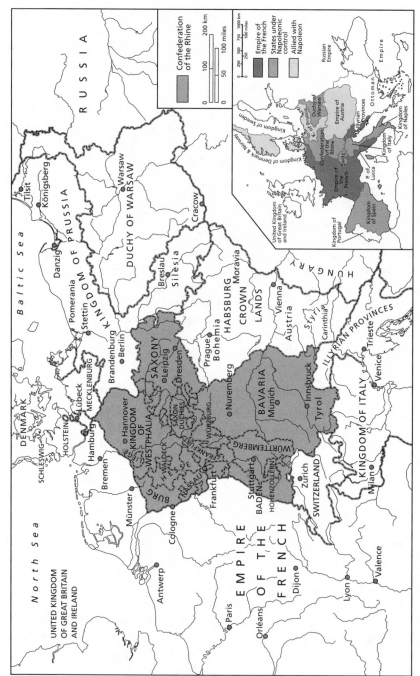

MAP 6.1. NAPOLEON'S CENTRAL EUROPEAN SATELLITES AND DEPENDENCIES

freeing of markets in land, labor, and capital; (3) to realize the Kantian ideal of the "state under law," or even to establish a parliamentary constitution in the kingdom of Prussia; and (4) to work with Austria and other German states to create new institutions in the vanished Holy Roman Empire's place.

Foremost was "emancipation of the peasantry" (*Bauernbefreiung*), a complex process of legislation and local regulation. It entailed both abolition (in 1807) of legal disabilities bearing personally on villagers living as subjects of the nobility or the crown and conversion (after 1811) of the farms such villagers had cultivated before 1806 into freehold property. This latter process the government, under pressure from aristocratic estateowners, largely confined to villagers with large, self-sufficient family farms; most smallholders found themselves excluded. Cultivators receiving freeholds compensated former noble lordships in land or money, becoming mostly medium-sized independent family farmers, although many managed to retain enough land to qualify as largeholders. The "unregulated" smallholders sometimes – but not always – saw their lands appropriated by the landlords, leaving them the option of working for the post-emancipation noble large estates as cottage-housed laborers or migrating away to the towns.

Later the 1848 revolution authorized numerous surviving smallholders to obtain freeholds, so that, from the mid-nineteenth century until communist land reform in World War II's aftermath, the wide Prussian east-Elbian countryside displayed new features. There remained its old-established large landed estates, occupying a third or in some provinces half of the cultivable land. Business-adept commoners bought many landed properties from economically faltering gentry (although virtually all well-to-do aristocratic east-Elbian families continued to own large and more or less profitable agricultural enterprises). Alongside these past or present Junker estates were holdings of some 20/40–100/200 acres

---

MAP 6.1 *(continued)* Absorbed into the borders of revolutionary France were, first, the Low Countries and, after 1797, the German Rhineland. French overlordship more or less discreetly steered the 1806-founded Confederation of the Rhine (*Rheinbund*), which assembled the numerous surviving principalities of middle and south Germany. Their governments worked – sometimes creatively and to lasting effect – to reshape institutions along French Revolutionary and Napoleonic lines. In particular, the civil and criminal legal statutes from 1804 known as the Napoleonic Code found wide adoption in west and south Germany, living on through the nineteenth century as "Rhenish law." A truncated Prussia and an Austrian Habsburg monarchy shorn of its Italian and Belgian lands stood defeated in Napoleon's shadow. From lands seized by Prussia in the final partitions of Poland Napoleon had in 1807 sanctioned creation of the "Duchy of Warsaw," hemming in Prussia on its eastern borders and serving as a launching ground for France's impending assault on Russia. As is the frequent fate of empires, that of Napoleon discredited itself among its conquered peoples, despite the prestige of the French revolutionary principles it proclaimed, through its fiscal extractions, dragooning of conscripts, and brutal assaults – as in Spain and Austrian Tyrol – against armed rebellions in the name of local liberty.

FIGURE 6.I. THE FRENCH REVOLUTION'S GERMAN FOES (AND FRIENDS)

H. A. Dähling's 1807 portrait of King Frederick William III with Queen Luise and their children captures a somber moment in Prussian history, following crushing 1806 battlefield defeat by Napoleon's armies. Yet, executed in the style of early German Romanticism (on which see Chapter 7), the picture also transmits a new sensitivity among the educated classes to children's individuality and existential blessedness (although the king's sons must educate themselves to leadership of the state, even to the point of reading political reports – as the two on the right seem to do). In a pathos-laden moment, Queen Louise of Prussia received Bonaparte at the site of the 1807 Tilsit negotiations, where, in a self-humbling private meeting, she entreated him not to dismember her husband's defeated realm. Louise (1776–1810), a daughter of the ruling house of Mecklenburg-Strelitz, was one of the few queens in modern German history, and the only Prussian consort, to fire widespread popular enthusiasm – in Louise's case, for her courageous patriotism in the face of her kingdom's humiliations, and for her engagement as her husband's adviser in Prussia's rebirth through reform. After her premature death, Queen Louise – celebrated also (as in this portrait) for her beauty – became an icon of conservative nineteenth-century Prussian-oriented nationalism. Her memory is alive still today.

(or 8/16–40/80 hectares) – the size depending on earlier settlement and soil fertility – belonging to independent family farmers (that is, landed peasantry). They cultivated a third or more of the land. Below them were smallholders, often called "cottagers," who needed to supplement incomes from cultivating their landholdings, often miniscule, with wages earned by working for independent farmers or large estates. Each of these three social groups was prominent in the northern and eastern countryside.

The introduction in 1811 of "freedom of the trades" (*Gewerbefreiheit*) abolished monopolies of guild corporations in the urban handicrafts. Artisan masters would need to adjust to free-market competition or abandon self-employment. Guilds continued to exist as voluntary associations of masters, with separate organizations for wage-earning journeymen. They served as social clubs, loan and burial societies, and interest group lobbies. The centuries-old communalities and solidarities of German handicraftsmen proved sturdy (surviving in some ways to the present day).

The manufacturing economy was now open to technological and organizational innovation, advancing the processes in the far-flung Prussian-ruled lands of the European industrial revolution. In 1819 the Berlin government launched the German Customs Union (*Zollverein*), which aimed to create a large free trade zone encompassing all Prussian provinces plus intervening non-Prussian territories. In 1829–1834 it succeeded in enlisting the main German principalities' membership, assuming supra-Prussian proportions (and foreshadowing a Berlin-centered German political unity). The Customs Union gave Prussia an economic leadership in industrializing Germany that the still largely agrarian and handicrafts-based Austrian monarchy could not successfully dispute, although capitalist development did not stand still there. Nor did Austria, despite Joseph II's abolition of juridical serfdom, move until 1848 to abolish seigneurial lordship and inaugurate village freehold conversion.

An 1812 edict initiated "emancipation" of Prussian Jews, a small group confined mainly to commercial-financial occupations in the towns. Those solid or wealthy property owners among them who were prepared to educate their children in public schools, adopt the German language in business accounting, assume "European dress," and allow their sons to serve in the armed

---

FIGURE 6.1 *(continued)* Another of the era's tragedy-stricken figures was Enlightenment savant, natural scientist, and world traveler Georg Forster (1754–1794), celebrated among the French Revolution's German partisans. He had sailed on James Cook's second world circumnavigation of 1772, and later published a scientifically important and internationally widely read account of it. Forster joined other German visionaries in attempting in 1793 to establish a democratic republic in the city of Mainz, in southwestern Germany, only to see it crushed by German armies. He fled to revolutionary Paris, where he fell ill and died. He differed from most other German progressive-minded intellectuals, not in supporting the revolution, but in dying for it.
Source: Bildarchiv Preussischer Kulturbesitz/Art Resource, NY.

FIGURE 6.2. PRUSSIAN REFORM LEADERS

Baron Karl vom und zum Stein (1757–1831) gazes with characteristic strength and dignity from Julius Schnorr von Carolsfeld's masterful drawing, executed in Rome in Stein's sixty-fourth year. Stein and his successor as chief minister, Karl August von Hardenberg (1750–1822), both stemmed from west German, non-Prussian aristocratic families. Stein championed local, elite-based self-government (as he imagined it in England) and, in his later years, valued German unity higher than Prussian state interests. Although his bold policies provoked both Napoleon's and Prussian Junkers' wrath, he advocated reform through rechanneling of organic historical development, not through theory-justified revolutionary breaks. Hardenberg, committed to restoring Prussia to its European Great Power status, combined political-diplomatic realism with a program of liberal institutional and social reform. Wilhelm von Humboldt (1757–1835) was a son of the Prussian service nobility and brother to celebrated natural scientist and South American explorer Alexander von Humboldt (1769–1859). The family's manor house near Berlin, including Wilhelm's study, abounded in images of classical antiquity. He distinguished himself as a scholar of language and culture, liberal political theorist (advocating diminution of state power in favor of individual freedoms), and educational reformer. Berlin University now bears his and his brother's name.

Source: Bildarchiv Preussischer Kulturbesitz/Art Resource, NY.

forces acquired citizenship and civil rights, including freedom of residence and occupation, with some limitations on state employment (from which Jewish converts to Christianity were formally exempt). In the Rhineland, acquired by Prussia in 1815, Jewish freedoms were broader, while in the once-Polish lands regained at the Vienna conference they were narrower. Laws of 1847-1848 widened the citizenly rights of poorer Jews, although full civil equality in Prussia, as elsewhere in the German lands, only arrived in legislation of 1869.

The Urban Ordinance of 1808 introduced municipal self-government through elected city councils in Prussian towns and cities. The franchise extended no further than to independently housed, tax-paying male burghers, while the central government retained control over urban police forces. Yet this was the beginning of middle-class parliamentary self-government in nineteenth-century Prussia.

Vital too were educational reforms, entrusted to eminent scholar and diplomat Wilhelm von Humboldt. These inaugurated a publicly funded network in all villages and towns of primary schools for both sexes, and likewise a government-financed system of secondary schools – intended mainly for the sons of the propertied classes, but not closed to talented children of humbler families – channeling young men into advanced studies. A new Berlin University (1810), its faculty bejeweled by such eminences as the philosopher Hegel, now arose as capstone institution. Among its distinctions was faculty self-governance in matters of research and curriculum, introducing "academic freedom" in the western world's higher education, although professorial appointments continued to require state authorization.

A network arose of new public secondary schools for boys (the *Gymnasium*), focused on humanistic learning anchored in study of Greek and Latin and devoted to the ideal of "self-cultivation" (*Bildung*). This prestigious education steered students toward university degrees leading to government services and learned professions rather than industry and commerce. But the Prussian economic bureaucracy distributed scholarships enabling small numbers of technologically minded youth to equip themselves as engineers and businessmen. By these reforms, Prussia assumed a widely acknowledged leadership in European higher education, while its primary schools largely eradicated illiteracy among both sexes by mid-century. The "Prussian schoolmaster" acquired a reputation for pedagogical competence, if not good-humored easygoingness.

Military reforms opened the Prussian officer corps to non-noble entry, although in practice aristocratic gentlemen set the political and social tone and continued to restrict membership to their own circles and to middle-class and other commoner candidates acceptable to them. The reforms also created the subsequently famous Prussian General Staff as a kind of collegial self-governing army leadership body. A new system of universal military service arose, involving two-year stints of active duty followed by inactive service and long-term reserve participation (*Landwehr*). Reserve officer appointments proved popular with educated professional men. In general, the middle classes saw the

FIGURE 6.3. CLAUSEWITZ AND THE PROBLEM OF PRUSSIAN MILITARISM
In this undated portrait by K. W. Wach, General Carl von Clausewitz (1780–1831)
meets the viewer's eye with friendly visage against a tranquil background of manor house
and church – pillars of the post-Napoleonic conservative restoration. Among his military
writings (which eclipsed those of Frederick the Great) was the posthumous treatise, *On
War* (1832–1834). Still classic today, it reflected his experiences in the Napoleonic wars,
whose unprecedented scale and tendency to escalate into all-consuming struggles of
states and societies found expression in his theories of "wars of exhaustion" and wars
seeking the enemy army's battlefield "destruction" (rather than momentary tactical
defeat).

Western European attributions to Prussia of a degree of militarism exceptional among
European states, although sometimes lodged against Frederick the Great's (and his
father's) regime, arose mainly after 1871, and especially under Kaiser William II and
during World War I. Eighteenth-century Prussia relied on conscription of its young
villagers for comparatively short terms of active duty, followed by longer years of reserve
duty – a system modernized in the post-1806 reforms. Other European states preferred
to maintain standing armies in which selected recruits remained under arms for much
longer terms than in Prussia, a circumstance that led Prussia's military rivals in the 1815–
1871 era to underestimate its war-making strength. Crucial to Prussian success was
drill, *esprit de corps*, and new technology – railroad, telegraph, and industrialized arms
production. Only slowly did the Prussian army adopt appeals to German nationalism in
disciplining its troops. In the century between 1815 and 1914, it waged little real war.
Source: Bildarchiv Preussischer Kulturbesitz/Art Resource, NY.

(a)

FIGURE 6.4. POPULAR ENGAGEMENT IN THE "WAR OF LIBERATION"
The first scene, a mid-nineteenth-century engraving by the popular artist Ludwig Richter (1803–1884), depicts in sentimental-melodramatic light a village patriarch and family members as they observe the 1813 fighting at Leipzig, in which 700,000 soldiers took part, making it the greatest battle, to its day, in European history. The picture suggests that the woman's husband – presumably the grandfather's son and child's father – is present in the fray, risking his life for Germany's freedom from French domination. That ordinary villagers should have begun to identify their fate and fortune with the larger fatherland was, apart from sometimes being true, a necessary postulate of nationalist thinking.

In the second picture – a painting of 1860 by Gustav Graef – middle-class civilian volunteer militiamen (*Landwehrmänner*) in Königsberg, East Prussia, emerge from church service, amid the jubilation of their families and neighbors, to march off in 1813 to the anti-French war. A Jewish soldier joins in, stepping out of the darkness in which the artist has enveloped his anxious and perhaps nationally aloof father. The picture epitomizes liberal nationalist idealism.
Source: (a) Ludwig Richter; (b) Bildarchiv Preussischer Kulturbesitz/Art Resource, NY.

reserve system as a liberal-democratic form of army organization preferable to the conservative, noble-dominated regular army.

Finally, an 1807 edict required the relevant responsible cabinet minister's co-signature, alongside the king's, for any new law to take legal force. This formally ended the era of monarchical absolutism; the ruler could still dismiss a recalcitrant minister and appoint a compliant one, but that was a disruption

(b)

FIGURE 6.4 *(continued)*

of government that kings needed to avoid if they were to recruit and retain able high officials. The threshold was thus crossed into an era of legally mandated joint rule of king and ministerial bureaucracy. Many of the reformers wished to proceed further to the establishment of some sort of Prussian-wide parliamentary assembly, although without investing it with legislative or fiscal powers robust enough to overshadow or veto the executive branch.

The Years of "National Liberation," 1813–1815

Napoleon's defeat in 1812 at Russian hands, in his armies' invasion of the vast tsarist realm, enabled zealous anti-Napoleonic elements in the Prussian government and army to take the initiative in defying French overlordship in Germany. In 1813 Prussia and Austria joined together to lead, with Russian participation, what came later to be known as the "War of Liberation" (*Befreiungskrieg*). King Frederick William III made a dramatic public appeal to his subjects to volunteer to fight in the reformed army. In return he promised a Prussian constitution (*Verfassung*) and establishment of an "honorable German Empire" (*Reich*). It was mainly the regular armies that in 1813 defeated Napoleon's forces, particularly at the climactic battle of Leipzig, and

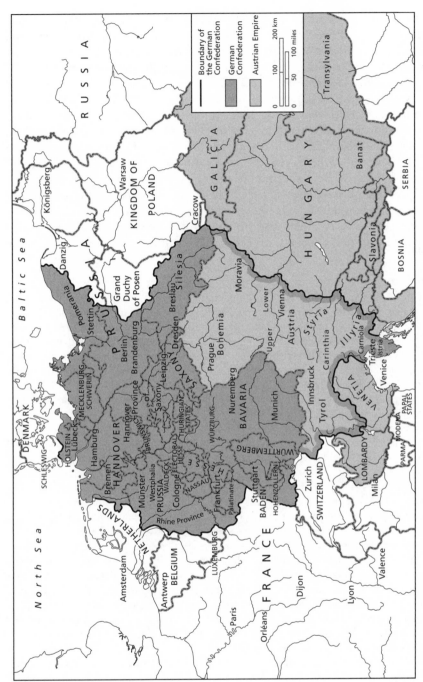

MAP 6.2. THE GERMAN CONFEDERATION OF 1815: NEITHER CHRISTIAN EMPIRE NOR NATIONAL STATE

again in 1815 at Waterloo in present-day Belgium. Yet many volunteers – particularly among university students and other patriotic youth from towns and villages – joined the struggle, which became a Prussian and German *nationalist* war, at least in the volunteers' and much of the civilian public's mind.

At the 1814–1815 Congress of Vienna, which assembled envoys of all surviving German and European governments to establish a lasting post-revolutionary, post-Napoleonic continental order, Austrian foreign minister Prince Klemens Wenzel von Metternich prevailed on the Prussian king and his ministers to backtrack on their wartime promises. The "honorable German Empire" proved to be merely the newly unveiled "German Confederation" (*Deutscher Bund*), an association of the remaining thirty-nine German states for defensive purposes that failed to create new national-level institutions of any significance and left its members' separate sovereignties undiminished.

The 1815 Vienna Treaty also stipulated that the German states were only empowered to grant constitutions for their territories that were based on the

---

MAP 6.2. *(continued)* Although in confederating "the Germanies" the Congress of Vienna paid faint lip-service to an ultra-conservative idea of national reorganization, the many ambiguities of the German central European scene could not be suppressed. By including Austria's German-, Czech-, and Slovenian-speaking lands in the new *Bund* while excluding but not releasing into their own national autonomy its Polish-Ukrainian, Hungarian, Slovakian, Romanian, and South Slavic provinces, the diplomats tacitly acknowledged Austria's, and so also the still non-existent "Germany's" – especially "Greater Germany's" (or *Grossdeutschland*'s) – claim to hegemony in non-German eastern and southeastern Europe.

In the province of Posen/Poznań that Prussia regained from its booty in the eighteenth-century partitions of the Polish-Lithuanian Commonwealth, the Hohenzollerns deigned to establish the "Grand Duchy of Posen," though the self-governing privileges extended to the Polish nobility there were modest. Prussian rule east of the German Confederation's borders – both in Posen, in 1772-seized West Prussia, and in East Prussia – implied a Prussian "mission in the east" that later would gain ominous weight.

Prussia emerged from the turmoil of the French Revolutionary and Napoleonic periods strengthened by the Vienna conference's conferral on it of the sizeable and, as was soon to be appreciated, coal-rich west German provinces of Rhineland and Westphalia, as well as lands of Saxony (which had in 1813 ill-fatedly fought on Napoleon's side). Some conservative Prussian officials and noblemen would have preferred that Berlin retain rule over the more easterly Polish lands it gained from the last partition of 1795. Such bastions of the large-estate/serf economy offered prospects of expansion of landownership to the Prussian nobility that appeared more enticing than having to guard the Rhine against future French onslaughts. Instead, Russia advanced its western borders beyond Warsaw to within a few hundred miles of Berlin. The "Kingdom of Poland" it established signaled Russian ambitions to control what was rapidly becoming known as the "Polish Question," whose resolution – in western European liberal (and Polish nationalist) eyes – would require establishment of an independent Polish state at the partitioning powers' expense. Against this eventuality Berlin, St Petersburg, and Vienna determinedly conspired until the outbreak of World War I.

pre-1789 "estates" principle, mandating that the traditional corporate bodies of clergy (in Catholic states), nobility, and burghers or commoners deliberate in separate quarters and vote as single groups, rather than by head. This was a formula guaranteeing the predominance of conservative elements, and especially landed nobility. Nor were such assemblies entitled to exercise more than deliberative powers over legislation – a provision assuring the princely regimes that such parliamentary representations as they authorized would not overpower them.

The Vienna settlement was deeply repugnant to German liberals and nationalists, many of whom occupied university posts from which they continued to advocate stronger measures of national unification and parliamentarization. In 1819 Metternich, adroitly reacting to the assassination of a well-known conservative publicist-playwright by a member of a clandestine student nationalist movement, persuaded the Prussian king and other German rulers to join in issuing the repressive Karlsbad Decrees, introducing throughout the German Confederation stringent political censorship and purging the universities of "radicals." These measures put a deep chill on political life in the 1820s, while further discrediting the Vienna settlement in oppositionists' eyes.

The 1789–1815 era ended in a tense stand-off between post-1815 throne-and-altar monarchical conservatism and burgeoning liberalism and nationalism. Reform had launched the Prussian lands into the main currents of the nineteenth century, but as a program – steered from above by crown, ministerial bureaucracy, and army – of reviving state power, rather than from below, by the middle classes and common people on their own behalf. The state, as embodied in the monarchy and its institutions, was *modernized* rather than broken by revolution (as had happened in France and, in the seventeenth century, in England) or discredited by its own increasingly antiquated and inefficient character (as was occurring in Russia and threatening the Austrian monarchy). Metternich and his friends employed police power to stifle dissonance between state power and its challengers, but only temporarily. In 1848, these political polarities, heightened by economic crisis, would spark revolution.

7

"Land of Poets and Thinkers" (*Dichter und Denker*)

From Enlightenment Universalism to German National Culture

The advance during the Enlightenment of the educated and professional middle class (*Bildungsbürgertum*) occurred during a great burst of cultural and intellectual innovation. It began around the mid-eighteenth century and reached an important point of transition, associated with the 1848 revolution, a century later. This era witnessed the culmination of the German Enlightenment, the maturation of Classicism in art and literature, and the rise of Romanticism, philosophical Idealism, the nationalist worldview, and historicism. These far-reaching movements transformed cultural and intellectual life from a considerable subordination in the early eighteenth century to external, especially French, influences, and to patronage within the Holy Roman Empire of Francophile rulers and aristocrats, to a condition of imagined national self-sufficiency and proud consciousness of German originality and accomplishment.

This cultural flowering represented the achievement primarily of middle-class Protestant intellectuals, although artists and thinkers of Catholic lineage distinguished themselves too. It encouraged the middle classes more broadly to raise claims to a greater degree of social and political equality with the courtly establishment. The absolutist state had long systematically trained talented commoners in its universities and recruited them into public-sector employment of one kind or another. This drew the aristocratic-monarchical ruling elites closer to the educated middle class's cultural achievements. Noble-born intellectuals themselves made important contributions. Eventually influential segments of the middle and upper classes joined in celebrating the German lands' exuberantly creative and ever more self-consciously national culture.

Yet the conservative tendencies of the Prussian monarchy and other German states, so evident in the Napoleonic wars' aftermath, worked against official embrace of constitutional, parliamentary government and national unification. Political and ideological tensions separating bureaucratic monarchy and civil society persisted. The revolution of 1848 sought empowerment of the middle classes, speaking in the name of the nation. Yet the cultural developments sketched here – taken together with the state-initiated reforms recounted in

(a)

FIGURE 7.1. THE EDUCATED MIDDLE CLASS (*BILDUNGSBÜRGERTUM*)
(a) an 1843 photograph (daguerreotype) of the Artists' Society (*Künstlerverein*) of
Hamburg. Such voluntary associations were the backbone of nineteenth-century civil
or bourgeois society. Liberal sentiments doubtless prevailed among these respectably
dressed, keen-looking young gentlemen, who included several architects. Were their
bank accounts as solid as their bourgeois appearance?

Chapter 6 – strengthened the educated and propertied middle classes' inclinations toward gradualism and cooperation with state power rather than
stiffening their resolve to seek swift, progressive change through revolutionary confrontation with the aristocratic-monarchical establishment. Historians
who extolled French and Anglo-American liberalism deplored such steps onto
a Prusso-German "separate path."

The Twilight of Enlightenment and Dawn of Romanticism

By the 1770s, dissatisfaction with Enlightenment rationalism was spreading
among the educated youth, who often saw it – however unfairly – as unemo-
tional and rosy-lensed. There were serious philosophical challenges facing
Enlightenment thought that Immanuel Kant, as we saw, sought to resolve in his

(b)

FIGURE 7.1 *(continued)*
(b) a mid-nineteenth-century portrait of two brothers, taken by their photography-enthusiast father. They appear in the jaunty dress and caps of university students, hands fraternally linked. Both lived to the eve of World War I. Altogether, the men portrayed in these pictures project personalities not far distant from those of their twentieth-century and even present-day counterparts. They radiate their own individuality, ambition, and self-confidence, and are free of "feudal-aristocratic" gestures and pretensions.
Source: (a) C.F. Stelzner; (b) unknown provenance.

critiques and treatises of the late eighteenth century. Yet, despite the profundity of his reconceptualization of reason and scientific knowledge, the younger generations, while they respected Kant's accomplishments and embraced his aesthetic and political principles, pressed beyond him into the new realms, of their own making, of Romanticism and philosophical Idealism.

This amounted to an intellectual sea change among the university-educated class. Some writers have explained it by pointing to an increasing scarcity of employment opportunities in state service, whether for officials, teachers, or clergymen. Public-sector appointments under Enlightened Absolutism usually presupposed embrace of confident, practical-minded Enlightenment rationalism. But educated youth, cut off from such jobs or forced to accept government posts below their expectations, felt less commitment to Enlightenment tradition. Moreover, the French Revolution shook German public life to its roots. Napoleonic conquest exposed the absolutist regime's limits while triggering an often vehement anti-French nationalism, particularly among educated youth. In the 1789–1815 era many of them felt themselves set free from the pre-1789 Old Regime's rigidities to explore internal and subjective experience and their own imagined worlds.

This is an interesting social and political account of Romanticism's emergence in Germany. But already in the Europe of the 1750s and 1760s challenges to Enlightenment rationalism in the name of subjective feeling and aesthetic sensibilities were arising, notably in the writings of Jean-Jacques Rousseau and the English and French novelists and painters whose work is often labeled Pre-Romantic. Earlier still, Protestant Pietism and baroque Catholicism had in different ways valorized emotionalism and psychological subjectivism.

In Germany, a pivotal figure was Johann Wolfgang von Goethe (1749–1832), prominent in his youth in the literary-aesthetic movement of the 1760s and 1770s known as *Sturm und Drang* ("Storm and Stress"). His 1774 novel, *The Sorrows of Young Werther*, not only (as we saw) attacked conventional society – both aristocratic courtiers and middle classes – for alleged soul-crushing conformism, social climbing, superficial rationalism, and burying of cultural originality under formulas copied from French courtly life. It also epitomized the newly fashionable cult of Homeric Greek poetry and other forms of epic literature reflecting the "youth" of European cultures, including hitherto neglected (or newly invented) traditions such as that of Celtic bardic verse. This reflected Romanticism's fusion of Art and Nature, in which nature was understood – including by exaltation-gripped Werther – as an endlessly varied, mystical, turbulent, and even sometimes demonic source of inspiration for each artist, whose mission was to find his – and increasingly also her – uniquely original voice. This vision repudiated Classicism's rules insisting on allegiance to the aesthetic forms and standards of Roman antiquity in poetry, drama, and art (as understood in Louis XIV's late seventeenth-century and Voltaire's early eighteenth-century France).

Goethe's youthful lyric poetry exhibited both literary genius and a maturation of the German language that fueled rebellion against the earlier prestige of French discourse and cultural models. Goethe himself moved on to more formalized modes of expression, although defined by rules of his own making ("subjective classicism"), adopting a skeptical or even critical attitude toward the younger generations of Romantics. Yet, while he sought to transcend it, Romanticism matured in him more than it paled. It coexisted in his consciousness with a reverence for the artistic attainments of Classical Greece (and their preservation in Roman art). These became, especially through the publications of pioneering art historian Johann Joachim Winckelmann (1717–1768), a virtual cult of the German intelligentsia. They were a mirror into which early German nationalists, imagining their historical affinities with the ancient

FIGURE 7.2. GOETHE'S SELF-REPRESENTATION
A 1953 photograph displays the "Juno Room" in Goethe's antiquities-graced house in central German (Thuringian) Weimar, where he spent the long years of his maturity, basking in ever greater international renown. Greco-Roman accents prevail in a setting, devoid of luxury but friendly to music and thought, such as subsequent generations of the German intelligentsia would favor, even today. Goethe's mind, like Hegel's, synthesized Greco-Roman, Christian, and Enlightenment traditions. He seriously pursued study of natural science, hoping to advance beyond materialistic and mathematicized empiricism to grasp Nature's underlying structures and dynamics. Although deeply German, he cultivated his subjective individuality while seeking to grasp the universal, and was not to be won for the German nationalism that inflamed many among the intelligentsia during the Napoleonic years. He possessed also a gift for graphic art. Striking was his drawing of Faust conjuring the "earth spirit" (*Erdgeist*), who appears as deified Man himself (and is reminiscent too of Jesus Christ). Faust, embodying the rational but power-hungry mortal, strove to assist humanity's worldly perfection, a theme central also to Leibniz's and Hegel's thought. Acting on God-given free will, human beings grope their way toward a fulfillment in history that Providence, by mitigating the effects of Man's self-destructive tendencies, may make possible.
Source: Deutsches Bundesarchiv.

Greeks, preferred to gaze instead of joining in the veneration of Rome characteristic of French and Anglo-American political culture.

Goethe's celebrated poetical drama *Faust* (published in various versions and parts between 1777 and 1832) genially synthesized Classicist with Christian, Enlightenment, and Romantic themes. Its hero's drive to transcend mere reasoned knowledge, plumb human experience's heights and depths and, through assertion of his political and technological will, transform social life gave birth in the western imagination to "Faustian man," a metaphor for modern individualism's (and rationalist "modernization's") grandeur as well as its perils.

Goethe's work inspired, both through emulation and opposition, much literary talent. Similarly influential, particularly as philosopher and dramatist, was Goethe's later-life friend, the previously discussed Friedrich Schiller (1759–1805), who communicated, in his celebrations of freedom in opposition to all tyrannies, a hopeful, early liberal message, but whose reflections on humanity's need of aesthetic-intellectual ennoblement in advance of political emancipation sounded a cautionary note. In music, Ludwig van Beethoven (1770–1827) exerted a similar influence, individualizing and emotionalizing the Classicism that Haydn and Mozart had raised to genial heights, while also infusing his art with a political credo of freedom and liberation. Although his works are prodigies of structure, built on a mastery of baroque and late eighteenth-century Classical forms, they surge into new spaces of emotional expression opened by Romanticism and by the revolutionary age in which it flourished.

From the 1790s to the 1820s, Romanticism in literature broke onto the German stage, exhibiting great creativity in the hands of many masterful writers, including Friedrich von Hardenberg ("Novalis"), E.T.A. Hoffmann, Friedrich Hölderlin, and Heinrich Heine. Romanticism's feelings and values exalted and spiritualized Nature, which was taking the place of receding Christian orthodoxy in many intellectuals' and artists' minds. Others turned to what they saw as an emotion- and mystery-laden Catholicism, romanticizing the Roman faith that to earlier generations of intellectuals had often appeared to stand opposed both to German Protestantism and Enlightenment reason and liberty.

Likewise central to Romanticism were a love of mystery and miracle and night over day, and a preference for emotion over cold reason, for sexual passion (or, alternatively, rarified and spiritualized love) as against socially sensible marriage, intuition over scientific knowledge, women's psychological sensitivities over traditional male authority, the (idealized) common people over privileged elites, children over adults, folk poetry and folk song over formalist high art.

Politically, Romanticism carried no clear charge, despite its frequent celebration and enactment of individual freedom. Its rebellious stance toward social convention (including bureaucratic routine and routinized marriage) made participation difficult in institutionalized reform or structured political movements. Its tendency to mystify the world left it susceptible to charismatic authority, whether royal or churchly. Its strong affinity for German nationalism could lead it to endorse existing "Germanic" institutions, including the ruling princely houses and historic elites. Yet no such correlations between Romanticism, conservatism, and nationalism were inevitable, and many romantics steered to the left or far left (as Heine did) or unsteadily moved from one political extreme to another. Some writers view romanticism as a largely unpolitical sensibility, at least in its relation to institutionalized politics, whether of right or left.

(a)

FIGURE 7.3. THE SYNTHESIS OF CLASSICISM AND ROMANTICISM
New branches grow from existing trunks. (a) a portrait of Wilhelmine Cotta (1802),
by Christian Gottlieb Schick (1776–1812). Schick's subject was the wife of Johann
Friedrich Cotta (1764–1832), celebrated publisher of Goethe and other distinguished
authors of the age (also, later in life, steamship entrepreneur and political advocate of
German economic unification). Her parasol (not insignificantly) cast aside, Schick fuses
her lightly clad beauty, reminiscent of Antique precursors, with Nature's warmth and
luxuriousness.

There was, however, a strong tendency to glorify an idealized social *community*, such as many imagined had existed in the Middle Ages, in contrast
to modern *alienation*, as exemplified in the misunderstood and lonely romantic artist, or even in modern society, whose members (as this view lamented)
led inauthentic, atomized, competitive, and perhaps ultimately meaningless
lives. This feeling likewise reinforced a romanticist inclination toward nationalism, promising gratifications of membership in an historical-cultural-linguistic
community transcending individual isolation. Alternatively, some Romantics
embraced post-1815 "throne and altar conservatism," which promised restoration of an "organic," hierarchical social world within the existing German
principalities' confines.

(b)

FIGURE 7.3 *(continued)*
(b) the oft-reproduced painting (ca. 1818) by Caspar David Friedrich (1774–1840) of a party inspecting the chalk cliffs of the Baltic island of Rügen. They seem to be plumbing the mysteries of God's shining, benign creation. This greatest of German Romantic painters infused nature, and humanity's everyday relation to it, with spiritual power and subjective epiphanies. Yet his works display a composure and tranquility prized in earlier painting, together with frequent invocations of a Christianity long central to European art.
Source: Reproduced in Werner Deutsch, *Malerei der deutschen Romantiker und ihrer Zeitgenossen* (Berlin: Kurt Wolf Verlag, 1937), plates 2 and 15.

Yet, perhaps most fundamentally, Romanticism embraced the Enlightenment's emphasis on the claims of the individual, unburdened by traditional Christianity's Original Sin, to "life, liberty, and the pursuit of happiness." But it also broadened the meaning of happiness to include acceptance of "irrational" passion and exaltation and the meaning to be discovered in emotional pain and even death. Beethoven's music, and that of his lyrical successors Franz Schubert (1797–1828), Robert Schumann (1810–1856), and Johannes Brahms (1833–1897), expresses this expansion of aesthetic-philosophical sensibility.

Although it was not difficult for Romantics to rediscover Christian faith, if only idiosyncratically, it is also true that Romanticism fit German nationalism like a glove. Indeed, Romanticism's susceptibility to fusion with *both* hyper-individualism and communitarianism qualifies it, alongside nineteenth- and twentieth-century social-political utopianism (of left, right, and center), as the modern imagination's commanding tendency.

The Birth of the Cultural Nation

German nationalism's rise accompanied middle-class intellectuals' rebellion, in the name of Germanophone culture's originality and freedom, against the western European Enlightenment's Francophile leanings. The modern concept of the nation, which had loomed small in Kant's thinking, began to spread its wings. As the communal or collective, cultural-historical counterpart to rationalism's individualist orientation, this idea had already preoccupied such French Enlightenment thinkers as Montesquieu, Voltaire, and Rousseau.

In Germany, Kant's friend and contemporary Johann Gottfried Herder (1744–1803) gained inspiration from Rousseau's idealization of the social solidarity and political virtue of historically evolved communities such as Rousseau's native Geneva in Switzerland. Herder won a broad readership expounding human history as a drama of national cultures or "peoples" (*Völker* [singular: *Volk*]), each possessing a unique individuality, expressed through folk poetry and music as a kind of "national soul" (*Volksseele*). This contrasted with the history, beloved of the western Enlightenment (and the liberal or Whig theory of history that flowed from it), of the progress of the universal human mind achieved by revolutionary individual thinkers, from Socrates to Newton.

In Herder's view, as in that of subsequent German Romanticism and histor-ically framed nationalism, identity flowed from culture (or from one's "peo-ple"). Nations were anthropological collectivities, traversing – in Herder's thought, at least – a centuries-long cycle of childhood, maturity, and senes-cence. The trend, on world-historical scale, was for now-existing nations to awaken to themselves, through the kiss of consciousness bestowed on them by nationally aware intellectuals and artists whom the *Volk* in time's fullness had brought forth.

Thus enlivened, the multifarious peoples would assume political forms appropriate to their individual genius and contribute through their cultural originality to the sum of human self-realization. Herder was son enough of the Enlightenment to believe that all peoples, although each was the fountainhead of unique social and political institutions and cultural forms, were all moving historically toward a democratic and pacifist-internationalist future. It was, he argued, military-bureaucratic absolutism and tyranny, and religious intol-erance, which plunged the world into war. Such a vision, harmonizing with Enlightenment ideas, inspired early German nationalism, even if the passions (and humiliations) of the Napoleonic wars infused in many of its apostles, such as the philosopher Johann Gottlieb Fichte (1762–1814), a warlike disposition foreign to the anti-absolutist, anti-militarist Herder.

Herder supplied a language in which national individuality could be imagined and expressed. This was of interest above all to the educated middle classes, to whom Germany as a broad cultural sphere transcending the myriad state borders was a far more meaningful concept than to either the historic aristocratic-princely courtly elites, wedded to their particular German states, or the common people, whose experiential realm did not usually extend very widely beyond their birthplace, and who rarely thought of themselves as participating in a larger political culture overarching their villages or home towns.

The French Revolution intensified nationalist sentiment among the German-speaking educated classes by holding out the example of a whole "people" that had, as it seemed, transformed a historic monarchy into a self-governing "nation-state." Unstable though this outcome was, French nationalism nonetheless underpinned Napoleon's empire, which held much or all of Germany in thrall in the years between 1799 and 1813. Many Germans concluded that their lands could only defend themselves against such foreign domination through national consolidation, although given Austro-Prussian rivalry it was difficult to see how both historic powers could be accommodated within a single framework.

Philosophical Idealism: The Hegelian Synthesis of Reason, Spirit, Nation, and State

Post-Kantian German philosophy, although dominated by Georg Wilhelm Friedrich Hegel (1770–1831), counted numerous figures of European stature, including Johann Gottlieb Fichte, Friedrich Wilhelm Joseph Schelling (1775–1854), and Arthur Schopenhauer (1788–1860). Common to them all was dissatisfaction with the limits on knowledge that Kant's philosophy imposed. Kant wished his thought to serve a cosmopolitan science and a politics of self-determination through constitutional government and market economy. He was German liberalism's first great figure. But the intellectuals who succeeded him after 1789 were inclined to take his emphasis on Reason's reality-ordering powers as a warrant to favor primacy of thought itself, or Spirit (*Geist*), over the material world. This tendency did not favor the science-friendly empiricist philosophy that in the nineteenth century conquered western Europe and North America.

There was an ambition, much influenced by Romanticism, to cast off the rationalist and empiricist fetters Kant had forged so as to plunge deeper into the heart of Being, even if by mystical or intuitional means. Fichte, philosophical hothead much favored in Romantic circles, entrusted to the thinking individual (or "ego") the power to construct the world so as to enable fulfillment of subjectively embraced ends or values. Schelling, a philosophical chameleon, gravitated toward a transcendental vision of Nature, which – in and through humanity – was in process of attaining self-consciousness. Schopenhauer, Hegel's

Das Original befindet sich im Besitze des Hofbauraths A. Schadow in Berlin.

„Das Bewusstsein: meine Streitkraft ist nur klein, wenn es auch ganz begründet wäre, könnte hierbei nicht beruhigen: denn, wie? wenn nicht sowohl auf die Streitkraft, als auf den durch das Ganze zu verbreitenden Geist gerechnet wäre, der hoffentlich aus den Schulen der Wissenschaft ausgehend, ein guter Geist sein wird; wie? wenn gerechnet wäre auf das grosse, den verbrüderten deutschen Stämmen zu gebende Beispiel Eines Stammes, der einmüthig und in allen seinen Ständen ohne Ausnahme sich erhebt, um sich zu befreien?"

(Aus Fichte's Rede an seine Zuhörer. Berlin, 19. Februar 1813.)

FIGURE 7.4. CULTURAL NATIONALISM, COSMOPOLITAN AND ETHNOCENTRIC

In this 1813 lithograph, philosopher Johann Gottlieb Fichte (1762–1814) appears outfitted for battle as a volunteer Prussian militia fighter in the anti-Napoleonic "War of Liberation." In its caption, an excerpt from a recent speech invokes the "good spirit," emanating from German schools, which would fuse the several German "tribes" (*Stämme*) – that is, regional cultures – and various "social ranks" (*Stände*) into one fraternal whole, capable of fighting for national freedom. In 1807–1808 Fichte had delivered in French-occupied Berlin his "Addresses to the German Nation." These glorified the German language for having survived without massive transformation since pre-Christian times, making of the Germans a more "primordial" (hence, "younger" philosophical foe, incorporated elements of Indian Vedic religion in his thought, which replaced Kant's hypothesized thing-in-itself with an impersonal cosmic Will – perceptible, Schopenhauer argued, in music. It was humanity's task to escape the cosmos's irrational power through art (and exposure to Schopenhauer's teachings) and thus to abandon futile pursuit of Enlightenment utopias against whose realization the turbulent forces of Being would ever conspire.

Hegel, by contrast, was the supreme philosophical synthesizer, whose dialectical method accustomed him to view ideas and history in their contradictoriness. He pushed forward radically Kant's argument that Reason lay, not in external things, but in the process of cognition itself. As Hegel said, with his penchant for oracular formulations: "the Real is the Rational, the Rational the Real." He developed a philosophy of thought itself, showing it to possess an inner dynamic that drove it to overcome its one-sidedness through conceptual formation of ever greater scope and complexity. The mind aimed to exhaust its own possibilities, to know itself completely.

In a move that can only be understood as a reflection (or sublimation) of Christian religiosity, in which Hegel like most other German intellectuals had been raised and educated, he equated thought with Spirit (*Geist*). Like God, Spirit created and, like Jesus Christ, entered the world to realize itself in and through the cultural creativity of humanity, and especially through human achievements in philosophy, religion, and art. Thus Hegel saw a divine force working toward its own fulfillment in humanity's history, but also inseparable

---

FIGURE 7.4 *(continued)* and more "original") people, especially in contrast to the French, whose culture, Fichte truculently held, was a now-tired amalgam of Roman and medieval Christian legacies. In the later nineteenth century such national contrasts underwent, in some quarters, an ominous pseudo-scientization and racialization. Fichte invoked the high intellectual and material culture of the late medieval German city-states – such as Nürnberg and Augsburg – as models for the middle-class German society of his own day, struggling to break free of "Latin" and also German monarchical-aristocratic domination. He avoided more directly provoking the French (under whose bayonets he was speaking), and laid out no concrete program of German national or constitutional reorganization.

Fichte built on the foundation Johann Gottfried Herder laid down before him. As befitted a man whose theories of folk and national cultures later won him honor as one of the intellectual fathers of modern anthropology, Herder had striven to avoid invidious comparisons between more and less prestigious or powerful peoples, even if he naively or unwittingly clothed in scholarly dress not a few popular stereotypes about "national character." His interest in eastern Europe encouraged nationalist-minded Slavic and other non-German intellectuals there. In pondering the German "*Volk*," Herder dwelt on its warlike propensities, which he derived partly from traditions of Renaissance scholarship contrasting "barbarian" Germanic peoples with the "civilized" Latin peoples, and in part from the proliferation of states, many with not inconsiderable military forces, within the Holy Roman Empire.

Source: Bildarchiv Preussischer Kulturbesitz/Art Resource, NY.

from humanity itself. The Spirit's self-perfection in the course of human history would also be humanity's self-perfection, leading through a conceivable, if perhaps historically never reachable, perfect knowledge to perfect freedom. Reality is driven forward, as is the mind itself, by the endless clash and resolution (or dialectical self-transcendence) of contradictions – a process that generates much tragic conflict and destruction, as history attests. Yet Hegel preserved a Leibnizian (and quasi-Christian) serenity about the world's meaningfulness, both in its present moment and in its overall trajectory.

In an appropriation of cultural nationalism's newly emergent categories, available in Herder's philosophy, Hegel held that the Spirit moves through history by inhabiting one leading culture after another: from Ancient Near East to Greece and Rome, thence to Latin Christendom, and eventually to the modern nations. What the future holds is unknowable: "the owl of Minerva" – symbolizing wisdom – "flies at dusk," that is, at the end of the day, when that which has actually occurred can be grasped retrospectively in thought. In the present, after having been lodged among the western European cultures, the Spirit – as Hegel believed, impressed with the greatness of his country's cultural efflorescence – had moved to Germany.

Culture cannot exist without institutionalized forms, and it is the State's task to provide these. Here Hegel embraced the tradition of Enlightened Absolutism. The State gives form to religion by neutrally protecting and supporting the confessional communities within its bounds. It elevates ethical and cultural life – the medium through which, alongside religion, the Spirit moves – by maintaining schools and artistic institutions. Altogether, the State orders *civil society* (*bürgerliche Gesellschaft*), which otherwise, left to itself, is a shortsighted and conflictual scene of class egotism and subjective, private interest. The State sustains and protects the ethical and cultural life through which the Spirit moves.

The State – and here Hegel addressed a basic Romantic issue – alone creates the possibility of individual identities that are not merely subjective, arbitrary, and prone to debilitating feelings of isolation and alienation. The State is the Fatherland (*Vaterland*), toward which its inhabitants feel natural and instinctive ties. People acquire their social and *national* identities through the states of which they are citizen-subjects.

Because the world of humanity is the scene of the Spirit's self-realization, each culture – although all appear historically on a hierarchical scale ranging from primordialism to high civilization – embodies ethical values that its inhabitants can live by, even if these are more fully developed and morally sophisticated in modern cultures than in archaic ones. In any case, modern Europeans, and Germans in particular, can safely cleave to the values embodied in their own traditions, without feeling obliged to search for a world-encompassing culture in which all national differences are eliminated. Here Hegel broke with Enlightenment universalism in favor of national uniqueness, while assuring himself and his readers that each culture is ethically and politically worthy of its members' loyalty and trust.

Hegel's politics inclined toward the existing order's acceptance, which meant acquiescence in the political disunity embodied in the thirty-nine states coexisting after 1815 in the German Confederation. Yet he advocated constitutional monarchy, including parliamentary representation of the educated and propertied classes, although this could only be rightly attained through compromises with existing authorities, not their overthrow. Like Kant, he recognized that the World Spirit, in its passage through history, often took violent and revolutionary form, destroying antiquated ideas and defenseless structures. Napoleon, in the young Hegel's admiring eyes, was a world-historical figure embodying the Spirit's often ruthless march.

Hegel's legacy to German nationalism is ambiguous, considering his inclination to glorify the Prussian state. But it was the Prussian state as associated with Reason's progress that he had in mind, exemplified by the Stein-Hardenberg reforms. Some modern writers have faulted him for exaltation of state power, in the sense of military-bureaucratic authoritarianism. The more plausible charge, from state-skeptical liberalism's perspective, is that he viewed the state's role in ethical-cultural life with excessive optimism.

Yet, considering the indispensability after the Thirty Years War of effective state power for economic reconstruction, religious-cultural well-being, and self-defense within war-ridden Europe – and the Prussian kingdom's imperfect but relative success in these tasks – Hegel's attitude is comprehensible, especially in a Christian tradition preaching the secular authorities' ethical-religious responsibilities in the divine plan's fulfillment. Civilization has ever been dependent on political power's protection and patronage.

Historicism

Hegel's ideas constituted a formidable synthesis of Enlightenment and post-Enlightenment ideas and sensibility. His philosophy possessed great appeal to intellectuals in part because of its quasi-religious emphasis on Spirit, and also because of the bridge it constructed over the gulf between Romantic temper and state-governed, economically driven bourgeois or civil society. It further offered a grandiose philosophy of history in which contemporary Germany, whose achievements in art and philosophy were so imposing (and, in nationalist eyes, so gratifying), could rightfully claim a place of its own, without having to emulate the political or social institutions of England or France (although Hegel admired both countries).

In the historian Leopold von Ranke (1795–1886) a writer emerged who could present German, European, and world history in less abstract and spiritualized terms than Hegel's, while yet conveying an essentially Hegelian understanding of the world-historical process and Germany's role in it. Ranke pioneered modern methods of archivally based scholarship, lending his work a quality of empirical solidity everywhere earning it great trust and respect in the scientifically and scholarly minded nineteenth century. He proclaimed that "all historical eras are equally near to God," meaning – in Hegelian fashion –

FIGURE 7.5. HEGEL
Here the master lectures to his young gentlemen students at Berlin University, as depicted
from direct experience in artist-historian Franz Kugler's 1828 drawing, later popularized as a lithograph. After the philosopher's death in 1831, Hegelianism divided into
rival schools – a conservative doctrine of state authority, establishment culture, and
gradualist, top-down change and a left-oriented Hegelianism, eventually dominated by
Hegel student Karl Marx, emphasizing "dialectical contradictions" within any historically given social formation, which eventually would bring forth revolutionary change
(see Chapter 9). Coming to terms with Hegel's thought was German philosophy's principal challenge in the 1830s and 1840s.
Source: Franz Kugler.

that all cultures possess their own ethical justification and value in the World
Spirit's progress. Ranke wrote histories of the major European states in what he
judged their most influential epochs, when they were, so to speak, the Spirit's
prime vessels.

Ranke epitomized a mode of thinking about the world that *historicized* it
in such a way that the explanation for all things, whether spiritual-intellectual
or material, became an account of their emergence in time. There was no
clear-cut border in human history between that which was rational and that
which was not. It was, as this historicist way of thinking held, the Enlightenment's error to assume such a black-white boundary between itself and what
had gone before. Rather, things evolved in time, and it was the task of the
historically attuned mind to understand the logic animating previous social-
cultural-political-economic formations, and their contribution to the Spirit's
progress. Value-relativity as between different cultures was not a profound
threat, because all cultures embodied positive ethical values (though some more

FIGURE 7.6. HEROES OF SCIENTIFIC HISTORY

Photographed here is long-lived Leopold von Ranke (1795–1886), at age eighty-two, posing with one of his fifty-four books. He rose to a professorship at Berlin University, receiving numerous state honors for his accomplishments, including in 1865 a title of nobility. Ranke brought to full expression a conception of the history of the Prussian monarchy and state as vehicles of beneficent progress in German history – a view legitimizing the Prussian-created German Empire of 1871. Critics dubbed such an approach to German history – the positively valorized "Prussian road to German unity" – "Borussian" (from the Latin term for "Prussia"). Although blind, the elderly Ranke continued work, dictating his (ultimately incomplete) *World History*.

Rivaling Ranke in fame and accomplishment was Theodor Mommsen (1817–1903), whose engagement in the 1848 revolution provoked judicial sanctions and loss of academic positions during the conservative Reaction that followed. But Mommsen's three-volume history of the Roman Republic, published in the 1850s, raised him, alongside Ranke, to a Berlin professorship and, eventually (in 1902) to the Nobel Prize for Literature. Mommsen wedded vivid prose to exhaustive empirical scholarship and a liberal temperament that did not hesitate to conjure up disunited Germany's dilemmas in the expiring Roman Republic's history. He refused, however, to see in Bismarck Julius Caesar's counterpart. In the 1860s and 1870s, he clashed, as a prominent left-liberal parliamentarian and publicist, with the Bismarckian political establishment. In old age he distinguished himself as sharp and prominent critic of rising anti-Semitism, although he took a German nationalist view of the Habsburg Empire's accumulating tensions.

Source: unknown provenance.

than others). As Ranke wrote, in a sentence emblematic of early, liberal-minded nationalism: "The nations are the thoughts of God."

Practitioners of historicism achieved brilliant results in nineteenth-century Germany, both in the writing of history itself and in all the social sciences and humanities. Its claim to scientific soundness – that is, that its epistemological status was as philosophically firm as that of the natural sciences – gained assent and confirmation from its sophisticated approach to gathering, evaluating, and synthesizing primary-source evidence. Moreover, the German language identifies what in English figures as "science" as "scholarly knowledge" (*Wissenschaft*) – a word that may apply no less appropriately to the English "humanities" than to the natural sciences.

The publication in 1859 of Charles Darwin's epochal work, *On the Origin of Species by Means of Natural Selection, or the Preservation of Favoured Races in the Struggle for Life*, crowned a century-long European development of evolutionary – that is, historical – thinking in biology. Complementary works appeared in geology and cosmology. Thus German historicism gained further underpinning from the natural sciences' historical turn. In the later nineteenth century, influential writers – led by zoologist Ernst Haeckel (1834–1919) – developed Darwinian science in Germany into a materialistic worldview that won much backing, especially among the educated and liberal-minded middle classes.

And, even though it tended to favor a gradualist approach to social and political change, German historicism could be harnessed to a program of radical change. This famously occurred in the thought of Karl Marx (1818–1883) who, in wrestling with Hegel's philosophy, broke through to a view of the world anchored in dialectically driven revolutionary cycles rather than the universalist principles of the Enlightenment's Natural Law to which earlier western liberals and democrats had appealed. Marxists welcomed evolutionary science as a mighty ally. Historicism was, similarly, compatible with liberalism to the degree that it could persuasively argue that, as a historically evolved civilizational form, liberalism was a higher expression of the human spirit than its ideological-institutional precursors, notably monarchical-aristocratic absolutism and, before it, feudalism. Thus did historical thinking fan across the nineteenth-century field, throwing static, universalist modes of thought on the defensive, or even into the moat.

Yet historicism's tendency, congenial to most members of the educated and propertied classes, to look to the existing state to help bring forth new fruits of the Spirit reflected a Hegelian optimism rooted in Enlightened Absolutism's accomplishments. The 1848 revolution would put Germany's existing states, and especially the kingdom of Prussia, to a test of such optimism that they would not robustly pass. Doubt would seep into German consciousness about the extent to which historic state power could be entrusted with human progress – and with the nation's fate as well.

8

Freedom and Voice, "Iron and Blood" (*Eisen und Blut*)

Liberalism and Nationalism, 1815–1914

The victors of 1815 could banish Napoleon to island exile, but they could not stop the momentum of early industrialization and other capitalist development. Nor could they halt swelling sentiment in Germany for constitutions and national unity (to achieve which blueprints proliferated). Neither could the Prussian and Austrian monarchies disengage themselves from competition for leadership in Germany, or from restless rivalry for power within the European state system. In 1848 the interplay of these historical dynamics triggered revolution.

Although the boldest programs then suffered defeat, the urgency only increased of the issues contested. Between 1849 and 1871, a *second* phase of the struggle ensued, in which compromise between moderate liberals and the Prussian government and its partisans seemed to attain both camps' basic goals: national unity (at Austria's expense), economic liberalism, constitutional and parliamentary government constraining but not nullifying the executive powers of the Prussian (or, after 1870, the Prussian-German) monarchy.

Because the outcome was a partial victory for *both* sides, historians have long been tempted to emphasize the triumph of one or the other. Marxists, and some liberals too, have seen the 1871 German Empire's creation as the middle classes' ascension to power sharing, and even as "bourgeois revolution." Prime Minister Bismarck's nationalist partisans celebrated his rebaptism of the Prussian state in popular enthusiasm's water and its fusion with non-Habsburg Germany, greatly amplifying the Prussian monarchy's power and – as it seemed – its capacity to survive in the modern world. Anti-Bismarckian liberals and democrats lamented the failure to achieve full-scale parliamentary sovereignty. Catholics and national minorities criticized the rising tide of Protestant-hued German nationalism in the new Empire. Austrian Germans found themselves bereft of the nation-state that many among them had yearned to join, and stung by Bismarck's overthrow of the Habsburg monarchy's symbolic primacy among the German lands.

Judgment of the German Empire cannot rest on analysis of its origins before 1871, but depends mainly on an understanding of the years that followed, ending in World War I and the 1918 revolution. In the framework of the years after 1815, the 1871 outcome suggests interpretation as contentious but hopeful compromise between the two strongest forces of the time: the Prussian state, with its tradition both of military power and enlightened reform, and the educated and propertied middle classes of Protestant faith or heritage.

The "Restoration" and "Pre-March" Years, 1815–1848

The post-1815 conservative reaction left the Prussian reforms inaugurated in 1807 unfulfilled. No written constitution was promulgated, no kingdom-wide parliament of even limited, consultative scope was convened. The old-fashioned provincial assemblies established in 1822 were no substitute for liberal self-government. Nor did the German Confederation of 1815, joining in a loose organization the still-sovereign thirty-nine princely states and urban republics, satisfy demands – voiced most ardently within the younger generations, but also by the intelligentsia and business classes – for national unity.

The south German states of Bavaria, Württemberg, and Baden had been much enlarged by absorption during the Napoleonic years of smaller principalities and ecclesiastical jurisdictions. Their post-1806 governments, deploying French-inspired legal and institutional reforms to centralize state power, issued constitutions establishing countrywide parliaments. Here forums of middle-class liberalism arose whose influence radiated across Germany. Still, the constitutions did not allow ministerial control by parliamentary majority, and the franchise remained the middle and upper classes' privilege. Many deputies occupied state posts in their professional lives and were inclined to compromise with royal or princely regimes. Nor did south Germany adopt market-enlivening reforms to the same extent as Prussia, so that it remained a stronghold of village farmers and small-town artisans. For these reasons, despite their progressive features, the south German states did not lead the drive for national unification. Yet from their institutions and political culture many figures emerged who played leading roles on the stage of nineteenth-century German public life.

We have seen how the German Confederation's Karlsbad decrees of 1819 tightened press and literary censorship and initiated police surveillance of liberal-nationalist university student organizations and professors suspected of radical tendencies. Nonetheless, their enthusiasms grew more popular, manifesting themselves spectacularly in the southwest German Hambach Fest of 1832. Here, inspired by the July 1830 liberal revolution in nearby France, some 30,000 men and women from across the German lands demonstrated (in what many hoped was prerevolutionary fashion) for constitutional government and national unification.

The executive committee of the German Confederation struck back with harsher repression, driving numerous liberals, democrats, and workers' tribunes into foreign exile, mainly in Paris. There a popular literary-political trend

FIGURE 8.1. SOUTH AND WEST GERMAN LIBERALS AND DEMOCRATS
Left: Heinrich von Gagern (1799–1880, here depicted in an 1848 daguerreotype) was a Bavarian-born scholar-official's son and wandering law student at several universities (a typical and often intellectually stimulating practice among nineteenth-century German students). Gagern fought as a volunteer soldier against the French at Waterloo. After 1815 he was a leader in the liberal nationalist student fraternity movement (*Burschenschaften*) and later an official and parliamentarian in Hessen. Forced out of political life under conservative pressure after 1832, he devoted himself to advocacy of parliamentary power and national unification. In the 1848 revolution he attained popularity and influence as president of the Frankfurt National Assembly (on which see more later in this chapter). Gagern personified the liberal program advocating German unification under Prussian leadership.
Right: Cologne-born Jacob Venedey (1805–1871), lawyer, publicist, and parliamentarian, whose participation in liberal nationalist demonstrations in 1832 drove him into Parisian exile, where he was active among radical German émigrés. In the 1848 revolution he stood on the left, advocating German unification in the form of a democratic republic. His self-representation in this picture, like Gagern's in his, reflects his political stance.

Other notable pre-1848 liberals were Carl Theodor Welcker (1790–1867), professor of law and politics and (like Gagern) a volunteer in the 1813–1815 war, supporter of student nationalism and German unification, and parliamentary activist in the 1848 revolution on the moderate-liberal side. With fellow Badener Carl von Rotteck (1775–1840) he co-edited the *Staatslexikon: Encyclopedia of the Political Sciences* (1834–1866), a widely influential mid-nineteenth-century mirror of liberal philosophy that, in contrast to historicist trends in German political thought, invoked Enlightenment concepts of Natural Rights. Also influential was Hannoverian historian Friedrich Christoph Dahlmann (1785–1860), who sacrificed a professorship in the cause of constitutional government, which he defended as a high achievement of European historical development rather than a postulate of universal Enlightenment principles. Dahlmann, and Welcker and Rotteck too – like Gagern – backed Prussian-led German unification.
Source: Left: Jacob Seib; Right: Hermann Biow.

FIGURE 8.2. IMAGINERS OF THE NATION
Here, depicted in an 1842 daguerreotype, are the Grimm brothers – Wilhelm (1786–1859) and, standing behind him, Jakob (1785–1863). Born in west German Hessen and educated in German historicism's spirit – and having absorbed Herder's interest in language and folk poetry as mirrors of evolving national culture – they devoted themselves, among myriad other scholarly labors, to the collection and enormously popular publication of German folk tales and myths. They crowned their work with a thirty-three-volume historical and literary dictionary of the German language (published in 1854–1860), a towering monument of cultural nationalism. Both numbered (with Dahlmann) among the Göttingen Seven – professors dismissed in 1837 for their advocacy of constitutional government in the Kingdom of Hannover. They found refuge and work in Prussia. Jakob Grimm later served as deputy in the Frankfurt Assembly. Thus they combined construction of national literary and linguistic identity with German liberalism.

Celebrated too among the nationalist intelligentsia was Ernst Moritz Arndt (1769–1860). Son of a upward-striving north German landed estate administrator who had bought himself free of juridical serfdom, Arndt – a poet who rose to a literary professorship and eventually the chancellorship at Bonn University – combined sharp criticism of social injustices with a robust German nationalism filled with undisguised hate and scorn for the Napoleonic occupiers, but also for Poles and Jews, particularly Jewish immigrants from eastern Europe. Arndt's poetry and other writings invested German emerged, which, as "Young Germany," stood alongside other similarly named nationalist opposition movements among Italian, Irish, and Polish émigrés in western Europe. It came to be associated with the widely read political journalist and literary critic, Ludwig Börne, and especially with the virtuoso poet and satirist, Heinrich Heine (1797–1856), whose works, smuggled into Germany alongside those of many other writers, the censors could only imperfectly suppress.

Scion of a family of west German Jewish businessmen, the university-educated Heine converted *pro forma* to Lutheran Christianity to escape discrimination in academic and public life. But his partisanship for French-style liberalism and biting criticism of German bureaucratic monarchy exposed him to censorship and other reprisals that drove him into permanent exile in Paris, where he moved further to the political left. Yet his poetry – whether lyric, comic, Romantic, or tinged with national feeling – won him a large readership in Germany, still intact today. Heine embodied the acculturation-minded German-Jewish intellectual who sympathized with popular democracy but viewed with reserve the rise of ethnically assertive German nationalism, which sometimes, driven by old and deep-rooted anti-Jewish prejudice, displayed anti-Semitic colors.

Heine's and other political exiles' message to the homeland was withering criticism and ridicule of the prevailing regime of bureaucratic "despotism," aristocratic "feudalism," and Christian-conservative "obscurantism." The path forward led toward "bourgeois" – or even "proletarian" – revolution. In Germany, many advocates of moderate reform made their voices heard. In 1837 Friedrich Christoph Dahlmann, distinguished historian and political theorist, stood together with six colleagues at the Hannoverian university of Göttingen in protesting royal arbitrariness. Their dismissal made of these "Göttingen Seven" martyrs to constitutionalism. Yet in Prussia, the ascent in 1840 of Frederick William IV to the throne initiated a political thaw inspiring hope in compromise-ready liberals such as Dahlmann.

FIGURE 8.2 *(continued)* nationalism with a widely popular voice and diction. He was among the most prominent of German liberal nationalists hounded from his university post under the Karlsbad Decrees of 1819, although he outlived his persecutors.

Famous too was Friedrich Ludwig Jahn (1778–1852), leader of the nationalist gymnastic clubs (*Turnvereine*) that arose among youthful volunteers in the 1813 War of Liberation. In his early years Jahn – or "Exercise-Father (*Turnvater*) Jahn," as he came to be colloquially known – was a wayward long-haired student, keen soldier, and gymnast. In 1810 he published his innovatively titled "German Folk-Identity" (*Deutsches Volkstum*), which (like Arndt's work of the time) xenophobically inveighed against French, Poles, and Jews. He later suffered imprisonment and long police surveillance for his gymnastic movement's brotherhood with the student nationalist fraternities. He gained pardon and rehabilitation after 1840 and conservatively supported Prussian-led German unification in the 1848 revolution.

Source: Hermann Biow.

In Austria, Prince Metternich's influence was, while not uncontested, dominant during his long tenure from 1809 to 1848 as foreign minister and chancellor. Son of a high official in Habsburg service, Metternich (1773–1859) descended from the Rhineland's Catholic nobility. He distinguished himself by an intellectualism that employed the Enlightenment's rationalist toolkit to defend conservative monarchical interests along with the aristocracy and Christian religion underpinning them. Heir to a tradition of realist diplomacy, Metternich flexibly steered the Habsburg monarchy through the ebbing Napoleonic era's turbulent waters, attaining seniority among European diplomatists reinforcing the authority his cool-minded, illusion-averse political talents had won him. But with his roots in eighteenth-century politics, he was ill-fitted for the age of parliaments and popular ideologies.

Already in the 1790s a stringent Austrian regime of police surveillance and censorship sought to stifle unwanted stirrings in an awakening public sphere, confining political discourse and power to government circles. The profound problem the regime faced was that liberalism's spread through civil society threatened to spark not only demand for constitutional, parliamentary government, weakening the monarchy's executive power. It would also encourage centrifugal nationalism among the non-German peoples, notably the Habsburgs' Hungarian, Italian, Czech, and Polish subjects, whose advancing nationalist consciousness, even if presently confined to the upper classes, would likely spread among the common people.

Especially significant was Czech nationalists' self-mobilization. This nascent movement would eventually militantly challenge political control of the Czechs' Bohemian homeland (contiguous with Germany on three sides) by the Germans settled within it. This Germanophone minority, although but a third of the whole population, predominated (without possessing – before 1848 – a pronounced German national consciousness) in the educated and propertied middle classes and among the landed nobility.

Metternich and colleagues preferred to clamp the repressive lid down tight, while pursuing Austria's cooperation with conservative governments in Russia and Prussia, and also in post-Waterloo Britain and France. In the 1830s, following middle-class revolution in France and liberal parliamentary reform in Britain (1832), the Habsburg chancellor's political-diplomatic system slowly broke down. But at home the conservative regime ruled unchallenged into the 1840s. Nor did it rush forward with liberal free-market economic reform, for fear of its political effects. Noble landlordism and subject village farmers' feudal rents and farm tenures persisted until 1848, as did the artisan guilds' authority (and internal customs barriers within the monarchy).

Early Industrialization and Social Turmoil

By contrast with Austria, Prussia's "peasant emancipation" and abolition of guild monopolies accelerated economic growth within a free-market setting. Annexation in 1815 of the formerly politically splintered Rhineland and

Westphalia, sanctioned by the European powers to induce Prussia to assume a frontline military position against anticipated future French aggression, added strong new bourgeois influence to the Hohenzollern kingdom's political life. This was a region whose unexpectedly rich coal and iron deposits nineteenth-century steam-driven technology now began to exploit. Here was one of the Industrial Revolution's main sites in Germany, although before the 1850s it was still in its early stages. An increasingly strong Rhenish-Westphalian industrial-commercial middle class, headquartered in west German Cologne and the Ruhr Valley mining and metallurgical region, grew prosperous and influential.

Other sites of Prussian industry were Berlin, strong in machine-building and the railroad industry, and, in the southeast, the large province of Silesia, whose old-established textile and mining and metallurgical concerns were making profitable technological advances. Outside Prussia, industrialization progressed most rapidly in the adjacent kingdom of Saxony, like Silesia a site of well-developed early modern industry and trade. In 1831 a populist-proletarian uprising inspired by the 1830 Parisian revolution, though repressed by arms, elicited issuance of a Saxon constitution and other liberal, bourgeoisie-empowering reforms.

The Prussian government continued after 1815 to spur industrial growth by various state investment agencies. As we earlier saw, it initiated in 1818–1819 a customs union (*Zollverein*) among the far-flung, disconnected Prussian provinces that eventually, in 1828–1834, drew in most of the other German states, apart from Austria. This created a near-unified German internal market, with common tariff policies, open internal borders among member states, and an integrated currency system, all greatly advancing the profitability of investments in transportation and interregional trade. The *Zollverein* helped launch German railroad building, which accelerated from the late 1830s through the 1840s. By the 1850s, the railroads' demand for metal track and locomotives had ignited the Industrial Revolution on a rapidly advancing, self-sustaining basis, with forward and backward linkages – notably, demand for steel and steam engines – that reverberated throughout the economy.

Before 1848, industrial development did not keep pace with the birth rate. Within the lands of the German Confederation (including Austria's western provinces), together with Prussia's eastern, previously Polish (but ethnically mixed) lands, population rose – vertiginously, by preindustrial standards – between 1816 and 1865 from 33 million to 52 million. Peasant emancipation and abolition of guild monopolies, where they occurred, lowered marriage ages and so (although contraceptive practices were not unknown) raised fertility, causing population to surge, particularly among the poorer classes. By the 1830s and 1840s, there was lively discussion in the middle-class press of the rise of the "proletariat" (a newly coined word, referring to ancient Rome's lower depths) and the "pauperism" accompanying it.

Village land fragmentation or landlessness compounded dissatisfaction with old-regime noble landlordism's lingering survivals. Artisan trades, now open (where guild abolition had occurred) to all comers, grew overcrowded, with

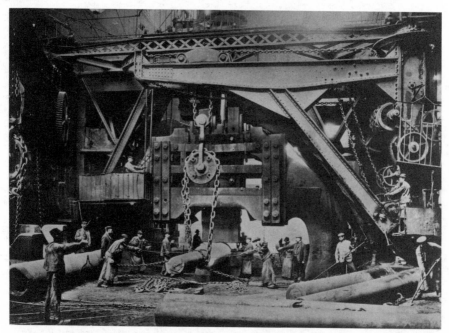

FIGURE 8.3. EARLY INDUSTRIAL IMAGERY
Industrialist Alfred Krupp's iron and steel works in Essen, in the Rhenish-Westphalian Ruhr valley, designed and cast the huge steam-driven hammer depicted in this 1861 photograph – the epitome of hitherto unimaginable, humanity-dwarfing industrial technology. Yet the sense of mastery the workers project reflects pride in technical competence characteristic of the preindustrial artisan world. The structures of industrialization, both physical and mental, were in part embedded in the preindustrial past and in part radically new. The oft-pictured neo-Gothic architecture of – among numerous similar sites – August Borsig's cutting-edge machine-building works in Berlin-Moabit appealed to the age's taste for Romanticist evocations of the medieval past. But, as the above-pictured massive artillery gun barrels rolling off the Krupp production line ominously suggest, a new form of military-industrial complex was arising whose inventions would call European civilization in question. Krupp's capitalist empire, in later alliance with the Bismarckian and Hitlerian regimes, ultimately brought itself to ruin.
Source: Bildarchiv Preussischer Kulturbesitz/Art Resource, NY.

poor masters operating with few or no journeymen or apprentices. Industrialization's pace was too slow to generate sufficient new factory-based jobs to rescue such marginalized sinking artisans.

Overseas emigration, mainly to the United States, began to boom in these decades: some 450,000 left the country in the 1840s, generally with some assets in their wallets, many of them seeking farms on the expanding American frontier. Emigration to the United States soared again – after the 1848 revolution – in the 1850s, and again from the 1880s to World War I. Altogether, from 1820 to 1917 some 5.5 million inhabitants of the German lands crossed the Atlantic – alongside some hundreds of thousands of post-1867 Austrian German emigrants.

In the textile branches, mechanized factory competition depressed hand-laboring cottage industry's wages, leading to protests such as Silesian workers' tumultuous but fruitless 1844 demonstrations against flint-hearted merchants and middlemen. Harvest crises multiplied in the 1840s, especially with the arrival of the potato blight (as in Ireland) in 1845–1846, potatoes having become, since the late eighteenth century, the staple food of the poor. In 1844–1847, food price increases averaging 50 percent were widespread. In 1847 bread riots erupted in Berlin and other cities.

On the revolution's eve, crisis was boiling: widespread rural land hunger, industrial competition both foreign and domestic weighing down on artisanry and cottage workers, oversupply of university-educated young men in the public-sector employment market, an industrial-commercial recession since 1845, state policies caught between old-regime impulses and hesitation to press forward determinedly into the industrial capitalist future.

The 1848 Revolution

At the *social* and *economic* level, several fundamentally conflicting questions came into play during the revolution. In view of "immiseration" and "proletarianization" of many landless or smallholding villagers and struggling, self-employed artisans, was it possible to take state action to better their lot – for example, by strengthening (or returning to) guild-organized production, or by setting up publicly funded cooperative enterprises? Or was it necessary to proceed by revolutionary means to the "liberation of labor" and to "socialism"? Alternatively, should the principles prevail of the free-market economics favored by liberals, whose voices were now most influential within civil society, and should hope for new jobs and better pay concentrate on the spread of factory-organized, steam- and coal-driven industry – that is, on the Industrial Revolution?

At the level of the thirty-nine *individual states* comprising the German Confederation of 1815, the *basic political question* was whether middle-class liberals, backed by "the people," could in each land (or city-state) come to power and, acting through popularly elected constitution-drafting ("constituent") assemblies, impose written charters on the preexisting, now deeply unpopular systems of bureaucratic monarchy or urban oligarchy (or, alternatively, democratize the preexisting constitutions in south Germany and Saxony)? In fact, in local revolutions throughout Germany of March 1848, shaken conservative regimes, as in Prussia and Austria, bowed to the installation of liberal "March ministries," which proceeded to hold, for the first time, elections to constituent assemblies in their respective states.

Such regimes cooperated among themselves in repudiating the authority of the long immobilized, institutionally feeble German Confederation and in organizing elections throughout Germany in April 1848 to the unprecedented

FIGURE 8.4. "PRE-MARCH" MISERIES

Carl Wilhelm Hübner's 1844 painting depicts Silesian cottage-based hand-weavers, their wives and children in despair, meeting rejection of their wares by the almighty merchant-middlemen. In the same year, cotton-weavers stormed the premises of merchants whose payrates were exceptionally low, or who patronized "foreign" – that is, non-local – workers. In fact, the Silesian linen-weavers, demoralized by their advancing impoverishment, held aloof from this "Silesian Weavers' Revolt," which the Prussian military crushed amid bloodshed. Hübner's rendition of the drama appeals to middle-class sensibilities: the weavers appear as respectable if modest burghers or "little people" (*kleine Leute*), threatened with ruin by merchant hardheartedness. The painting provoked considerable public interest and contributed to the conceptualization of the Silesian "revolt" – which had no political agenda – as the 1848 revolution's precursor. Heinrich Heine memorialized it in a powerful poem conjuring up proletarian revolution, a vision the socially critical realist playwright Gerhart Hauptmann later revived in his influential drama, "The Weavers" (1894).
Source: Bildarchiv Preussischer Kulturbesitz/Art Resource, NY.

"National Assembly" (*Nationalversammlung*). This body convened in the urban republic of Frankfurt, charged with the mission of promulgating a constitution uniting *all the German states* into a single nation. Thus, or so the revolutionaries hoped, constitutional government would come to *each* of the thirty-nine states, *as well as* to a newly united Germany *as a whole*.

In the kingdom of Prussia, conservatives clustered about the throne of Frederick William IV to resist revolutionary pressure. They found backing among estate-owning aristocrats, other intransigent nobles in bureaucracy and army officer corps, monarchist-conservative religious authorities and antirevolutionary middle-class property owners and intellectuals. Could the liberals hold the common people on their side in this confrontation?

In the Habsburg lands, the liberal agenda was complicated by the existence, simultaneously, of insurgent nationalist movements among the various non-German subject populations (especially the Italians, Hungarians, and Czechs). These sought, if not secession, then at least home rule in their areas of settlement under Habsburg rule, including use of their languages in public administration and education. Could the Austrian monarchy be converted to a constitutionalized and federalized state, satisfying the demands of liberals and democrats not only among German-speakers, but among non-Germans as well?

The outcome after much internal turmoil and struggle, both in Prussia and Austria, was the triumph in the fall of 1848 of a pro-monarchical *counterrevolution*, led by loyal royalist armies over which liberals had failed to gain command, or to replace with citizen militias. In Prussia, the monarchist court party expelled liberals from ministerial office and tore up the progressive democratic draft constitution the Prussian Constituent Assembly had hammered out in summer and fall. In November 1848 Berlin's counterrevolutionary aristocratic-military-bureaucratic government unilaterally promulgated a conservative constitution that would remain in force until 1918.

It established a central parliament, seated in Berlin, elected on an oligarchical franchise that weighted adult males' votes differentially, according to whether they were to be found among the relatively few payers of the top one-third of the Prussian income tax, the fairly numerous middle third, or the multitudinous lower third. Each one-third of the electorate chose, by individual voice vote before an electoral commission (that is, without advantage of secret balloting), an equal number of deputies. The wealthy upper and middle classes easily dominated the new assembly, though appointment of the cabinet of ministers remained a royal prerogative. The lower classes (subject to reprisals for their votes from employers) either followed cues given them by the conservative and liberal parties or absented themselves from the polls. The Prussian Crown had shown it would use military force to prevent imposition on the country of institutions too liberal for its liking, even if public opinion supported them.

In Austria, the conservative court party repudiated a promising federalized constitution drafted by moderate liberals and nationalists, both German and non-German. The government unleashed the army, which ruthlessly crushed the liberals and democrats in their Viennese stronghold and vanquished on the battlefield the nationalist breakaway movements in Hungary and the Italian provinces. By the fall of 1849 a regime of centralized "neo-absolutism" had battened itself on the far-flung Habsburg realm.

Meanwhile, the prime question of *national unification at the all-German level* was whether the democratically elected Frankfurt Assembly would succeed in calling forth a German national state endowed with a workable constitution. Debate soon focused on the alternative between "small Germany"

(*Kleindeutschland*), encompassing Prussia and the other states but excluding the Austrian lands, and "big Germany" (*Grossdeutschland*), incorporating also those Habsburg lands considered German – that is, the Austrian, Bohemian, and Slovenian provinces. Despite Bohemia-Moravia's Czech-speaking majority, German nationalists contested Czech claims to home rule, while sometimes promising observance of Czech linguistic and cultural rights. They took a similar view of the Slovenian-settled southernmost districts of the Austrian heartland.

To shield its centralized monarchical-bureaucratic-military powers, the Habsburg regime brusquely spurned cooperation with the Frankfurt Assembly. Having then drawn up a liberal-democratic constitution tailored to a "small German" solution, the Frankfurt deputies suffered the rebuff of the Prussian king's haughty refusal, on conservative-monarchist ideological grounds, to wear the newly crafted imperial crown they offered him.

Militants who continued to support the Frankfurt constitution organized themselves and their followers in spring 1849 to force it on the existing governments through revolutionary protests and armed mobilizations, but were defeated in pitched battles in southwestern Germany and Saxony with the Prussian army. Meanwhile, the Berlin government strove to craft in negotiations with other princely regimes a conservative and federalist *Kleindeutschland*, but encountered opposition threatening war from Austria, and dropped its "Prussian Union" plan in 1850. In 1851, the once-again conservatively ruled, counterrevolutionary German governments restored the German Confederation of 1815, greatly unpopular in civil society, as it had existed on the eve of 1848.

Judging 1848

The claim persists – often couched in "separate path" discourse – that the revolutions were a failure, proving the middle classes' incapacity to take command of German history. Bismarck, in his later duels with liberals, accused them of having no appreciation for power – of failing to see that national unification would require "iron and blood" (as he drastically put it), not parliamentary speeches and votes. Left-leaning historians have argued that in 1848 the liberal middle classes put their own interests before those of villagers, artisans, and industrial workers, who might have acted more effectively as popular mass base. With such backing, the revolutionaries might have better resisted with guns in hand the monarchical counterrevolution and imposed the Frankfurt Constitution on the Prussian king and the various liberal federal-state constitutions on recalcitrant rulers. Instead of seeking a peaceful compromise with Germany's crowned heads, the 1848ers should have stirred agrarian revolt with promises of land reform at big landlords' expense. They should have stilled the suffering workers' complaints with social programs rather than preaching that only through free-market capitalism could society prosper.

FIGURE 8.5. REVOLUTIONARY ACTION, 1848

This lithograph – from a widely popular periodical published in provincial Brandenburg's Neuruppin (*Der Neuruppiner Bilderbogen*) – dramatized the March revolution
in Berlin with scenes of barricade fighting between civilians and military. Highlighted
too is King Frederick William IV's proclamation of March 21, 1848, "To the German
People (*Volk*)," in which he proclaimed a new era of political freedom and vowed to
champion national unity, saying "Prussia will be absorbed into Germany." The young
revolutionary depicted here, dressed in an artisan worker's blouse and cap, displays
the "black, red, and gold," that is, the flag – a tricolor, on the French revolutionary
model – representing a united Germany (in contrast to the feudal-heraldic character of
the existing principalities' dynastic flags – black eagle on white field, in Prussia's case).
The banner displays a revolutionary text extolling the sovereignty, "by the grace of
God," of "the people" (*das Volk*).

In the National Assembly in St. Paul's Church in Frankfurt, the national tricolor also
overhung the podium, above which loomed a representation in beauteous female form
of mythical-metaphorical "Germania." The public, including many women, filled the
upper galleries. The Assembly's draft constitution for the future united Germany – with
bill of rights, federalist structure, and universal adult male suffrage – was admirable for
its day, but the deputies were unable to create a strong interim revolutionary executive
power and citizen army to impose their will on the existing German states. They counted
instead on the states, having themselves introduced liberal parliamentary constitutions,
to embrace Frankfurt's majority will.

Source: Bildarchiv Preussischer Kulturbesitz/Art Resource, NY.

The revolution's leaders were indeed often too trusting in their dealing with the monarchical regimes and too fearful of popular radicalism. Yet it was embedded in their program and mentality that they should seek their goals without violence and by legal means, so as to bring to pass the rule of law – the Kantian *Rechtsstaat*. Many artisan masters felt such deep opposition to free markets and such a hankering for the perpetuation or restoration of guild monopolies that compromise was impossible with advocates of minimal government intervention in the economy – that is, in a word coined in these years, of laissez-faire economic policies. Nor was it likely that a united front of middle-class liberals, peasants, artisans, and workers could have overawed the Prussian and Austrian military machines and the kings and aristocrats commanding them. Army discipline held firm in 1848, which witnessed authentic political crisis of the German states, but not their institutional collapse.

Most liberals instead wagered on the monarchical regimes' willingness to undertake reform, as occurred in Prussia in 1807–1819. There was also widespread belief that established military power would be necessary to face external challenges to German unification arising from likely French and Russian opposition. The liberal nationalist middle classes had a motive to conserve the existing armies, especially Prussia's, so as to turn them to their own purposes, rather than undermine them.

The conservative Prussian constitution imposed by royal fiat in November 1848 and the abortive Prussian Union plan of 1849–1850 witnessed the royal regime's recognition that introduction of parliamentary government and attainment of German unification under Prussian leadership were unavoidable challenges. The 1848 revolution forced this understanding on it, just as the Prussian government's broadening of freehold conversion legislation to formerly excluded village smallholders, and its extension of citizenship and civil emancipation to the entire Jewish population, were revolutionary gains.

The liberal-democratic revolution *partially* realized its agenda, while keeping central issues alive and in play. The Prussian state showed itself still capable of incorporating, although in conservative form, central demands of the day into its own program. But now, for the first time, Prussia also engaged in forcible repression of broad movements challenging its power from the liberal and left-wing sides. There was now reason to suspect that, in the future, repression might again prevail over reform.

The Politics of German Unification (1850–1871) and the German Empire (1871–1914)

Since the 1807–1819 reform era, the Prussian government had been divided between advocates of moderate reform and conservative resistance to liberalism (except in the economic realm, where most conservatives came to support free-market policies). In the 1848 revolution, Berlin continued to display this Janus-face. But in the following ten-year "Era of Reaction," Hohenzollerns joined Habsburgs in seeking social-conservative and Christian-conservative alternatives to political liberalism and laissez-faire economics, while hounding regime critics with police repression.

Dramatic international events – the Crimean War of 1853–1856 (pitting Britain and France successfully against Russia) and the war of Italian independence of 1859 (in which France joined with Italy's kingdom of Piedmont-Savoy to defeat Austria) – ushered in the Prussian "Constitutional Conflict" of 1858–1866, breaking the post-1848 logjam. Elections in 1858, left unmanipulated by officialdom, returned a liberal majority to the Prussian parliament in Berlin. Conflict ensued between assembly and government over control of the army budget, leading to the crown's appointment of Otto von Bismarck in 1862 as Minister-President (Prime Minister).

This redoubtable figure, born in provincial Brandenburg in 1815, was a conservative noble landowner with close family ties to the Prussian civil service. After 1848 he rose high in diplomatic service. His university education had awakened him to German nationalism's broad popular appeal, to which he was not himself indifferent, even as he clung to Prussian identity and interests. Bismarck had absorbed the historicist mentality in a tough-minded realist sense: state interests (or *raison d'état*) could only be perceived and pursued in relation to contemporary history's grand currents. Conservatism must change with the times. Prussia must bend modern nationalism to its own purposes as a power-state. For this "iron and blood" were necessary, and not just – as he supposed liberals believed – ideologically attractive blueprints of a benign future.

In 1847–1848 he distinguished himself in parliamentary debate and court politics as the liberals' aggressive and eloquent foe. At his 1862 appointment as prime minister, his objectives were economic and fiscal growth and corresponding strengthening of state and army; cooperation with business-oriented and nationalist-minded liberals in pursuit of a Prussian-dominated unified Germany (*Kleindeutschland*), which would entail, probably through war, the exclusion of Austria; and marginalization of the oppositionist Progressive liberals who sought subordination of Prussian monarchical government (symbolized by Bismarck himself) to a parliamentary regime under their own influence.

Bismarck maneuvered Prussia into three wars. The first erupted in 1864 against Denmark, goading Austria into later conflict over control of the largely German-inhabited duchy of Holstein and the mixed Danish-German duchy of Schleswig, both now conquered from Denmark (and in 1867 annexed by Prussia). This led, secondly, to the Austro-Prussian War of 1866 – the final showdown in the rival powers' duel (begun in 1740) for mastery in German central Europe. Prussia's victory was the battlefield's positive verdict on skillful deployment of modern military technology, including railroads, telegraph, and new weapons forged in industrialization's workshops, foremost among them Alfred Krupp's.

Bismarck now wielded a free hand in creating the new "North German Confederation" of 1867, joining Prussia in a federalized union with those remaining principalities of north and west Germany that, unlike such hapless "middle

FIGURE 8.6. BISMARCK (1815–1898): FROM JUNKER SQUIRE TO "IRON CHANCELLOR"
Bismarck's marriage to Joanna von Puttkamer (1824–1894) connected him to pious circles among the landed nobility. His combative opposition to the 1848 revolution encouraged Christian-conservative elements – whose mouthpiece was the Berlin-published
New Prussian Newspaper or *Kreuzzeitung* – to view him as paladin of their interests.
They especially hoped that he would help maintain the Junker landlords' privileges
and preeminence, support the revivalism-gripped Evangelical Protestant Church (the
product in Prussia of a controversial, royally decreed fusion in 1817 of Lutheranism
and Calvinism), and hold tradition-trampling capitalism and all-German nationalism
at bay. Such a conservative program (shorn of its doubts about the market economy)
found institutionalization in 1876 in the German Conservative Party, which – like the
Kreuzzeitung – spoke with a powerful voice until the National Socialist dictatorship
disarmed them both. But Bismarck strayed from ultraconservative orthodoxy, allying
with liberal nationalists to establish the 1871 German Empire.
  Bismarck's imposing successes after 1862 persuaded many conservatives, especially
those outside Prussia, to support him in the new Reich. In the picture above he poses in
1889 in the imperial legislature (Reichstag) with several of them. He wears the bureaucratic uniform in which he always appeared in parliament (showing his independence
of political parties and electoral process, and signaling his subordination to the monarchical power that sustained him in office – on his terms – for nearly thirty years). The
inscription on the Reichstag wall conveys the new Empire's fragile self-identity: "A
nation's holiest right is to exist and be recognized as such."
Source: Julius Braatz.

states" as the Kingdom of Hannover and the city-republic of Frankfurt, escaped
outright Prussian annexation. This big step toward German national consolidation won support of moderate and nationalist liberals in Prussia who, dramatically, made peace with Bismarck in 1866 by passage of an "Indemnity Bill."

This settled the constitutional conflict of 1862–1866 between prime minister and parliamentary majority. The liberals forgave Bismarck his fiscal breaches – chiefly unauthorized spending on a military buildup – while he acknowledged the unconstitutionality of his defiance of parliament's budgetary oversight. This brought about a firmer anchoring of constitutional parliamentary government in Prussia, but it also broadened Bismarck's popularity. In Austria – as Chapter 11 will show – battlefield defeat triggered the Habsburg monarchy's restructuring in 1867 as the "Austro-Hungarian" monarchy, standing separately as a diminished European Great Power in ascendant Prussian-led Germany's shadow.

There followed the war of 1870–1871, a result of French diplomatic miscalculations allowing Bismarck to unleash a Prussian-led army against France, which since Napoleon's time had figured as Europe's most formidable land-based military power. The 1870 war's outbreak, amid nationalist exaltation, forced the south German states (Baden, Bavaria, Württemberg) to side with victorious Prussia and enter the new, enlarged united German state, proclaimed under Bismarck's orchestration in Versailles outside Paris in January 1871 as the German Empire (*Deutsches Reich*). The Holy Roman Empire had found a *kleindeutsch* successor.

In its formal structure, the 1871 Empire was a federal union encompassing the twenty-five surviving German principalities, notably the south German states and Saxony. Dominating it was now much enlarged Prussia, holding some two-thirds of the new Empire's territory. The federal state constitutions remained in force but were subordinate to the new imperial government, anchored in the office of Emperor (Kaiser). This title the lesser dynasts bestowed on the Prussian king, William I (1797–1888), who had ruled in Berlin as regent for the disabled Frederick William IV from 1858, and as successor king from 1861. He wielded independent authority to appoint the Imperial Chancellor (*Reichskanzler*), from 1871 to 1890 the resourceful Bismarck, whose military-diplomatic triumphs lent him great European-wide prestige. At the same time, Bismarck retained his powers as Prussian Minister President.

Imperial chancellors were obliged to negotiate budgets and new laws with a national parliament (Reichstag), elected – disarmingly, from Bismarck's opponents' viewpoint – by universal male suffrage. In drafting the new Reich's constitution, he had risked the democratic enfranchisement of men (at age twenty-five) in the belief that more voters, including among workers and the lower middle classes, were inclined to support paternalist monarchical government than free-market liberals. Though Bismarck's calculation proved wrong, critical historians have labeled its consequences "pseudo-democratization" or "negative integration." The imperial government could not legislate without the Reichstag majority, but the parliament, although democratically elected, could not unilaterally impose its will on the government, nor force the chancellor from office so long as he maintained the Kaiser's backing. Neither did majority party or parties possess the right to appoint chancellor and cabinet (as was the rule in the British House of Commons).

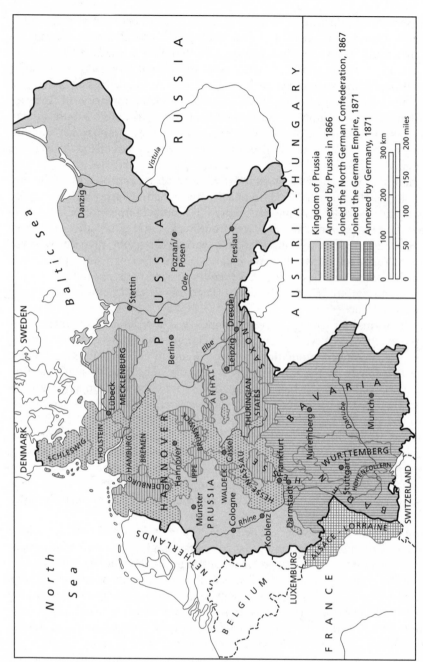

MAP 8.1. IMPERIAL GERMANY: FORGED IN WAR'S CRUCIBLE

During the new empire's Bismarckian years (1871–1890), the "Iron Chancellor" – as admirers misleadingly hailed this canny negotiator and striker of compromises – struggled to create a stable, pro-government coalition of Reichstag parties. This was meant to consist, firstly, of two closely allied Conservative Parties, strongholds, respectively, of Prussian conservatives led by the landed nobility and of upper-class conservatives from elsewhere in Germany, both joined with monarchist and religious-minded middle classes. The Prussian conservatives, championing agrarian interests, gained widespread backing among the Empire's numerous Protestant village farmers. The second partner in Bismarck's pro-government coalition was the National Liberal Party, representing business interests and nationalist sentiment among the middle classes, both within and outside of Prussia, and their mainly Protestant followers among ordinary citizens. These two camps remained the chief pro-government forces in Imperial Germany to its fall in 1918, although often at loggerheads with one another.

Opposition to the Bismarckian regime embraced, first, the middle-class liberal Progressive Party, which accepted the government's free-market economic policies of the 1860s and 1870s, but criticized the privileges of the landed gentry, now stigmatized as "Junkers." It aimed – against militant conservative objections – to subject executive power to parliamentary control both at the Reich level and in the kingdom of Prussia, where the oligarchical-monarchical constitution of 1848-1850 continued to decide over vital matters (including

---

MAP 8.1. *(continued)*

The Prussian-ignited war of 1864 against Denmark and the German civil war of 1866, in which Bismarck provoked the Austrians – who were backed by most of the other states comprising the German Confederation of 1815 – into a battle they haplessly lost, swelled the Kingdom of Prussia, as this map shows, with annexations of lands of its subdued foes. Had the war of 1870 not ushered the south German states into the Bismarckian house, the outcome as of 1867 would have been yet another historic magnification of Prussia within Germany, even if concealed behind the façade of the North German Confederation, which Bismarck constructed to fuse Prussian self-aggrandizement with *kleindeutsch* nationalism and to assuage the surviving non-Prussian member states' wounded dignity. Bismarck displayed no misgivings about unseating historic dynasties, dismissing the minor German states' claims to sovereignty as a "swindle."

Acquisition in 1871 of Alsace-Lorraine resolved a contentious discussion between Bismarck, Prussian king William I, and the Prussian General Staff. The crown and army pressed for annexation both from thirst for glory and to strengthen Prussian defenses against future French designs. Bismarck aimed rather to harden France's enmity so as limit its options within the international diplomatic system and to gratify German nationalists, who thought of the new provinces as former lands of the Holy Roman Empire unjustly torn from it by French aggression, particularly under Louis XIV. Though German-speakers predominated in Alsace and were numerous in Lorraine, they widely saw themselves as members of a French political culture and resisted Germanization in a pro-Prussian sense.

income and property taxes, and educational and religious policy) outside the imperial government's purview.

Secondly, there was the newly founded Center Party (*Zentrumspartei*), representing Catholics of all classes, who accounted for one-third or more of the new nation-state's citizenry, including large majorities in various principalities and provinces of west and south Germany. Provoking them into action was Bismarck's and the Protestant liberals' largely successful 1870s campaign (staged in the arena of Prussian state politics) to bring the Catholic priesthood and their role in public education under rigorous state regulation (the so-called *Kulturkampf* or "struggle over culture").

Allied with the Center Party were the deputies of the large Catholic Polish minority, resident mainly in the eastern provinces and amounting to some 10 percent of the Kingdom of Prussia's population. Against them, Bismarck and his backers in the Prussian state parliament (*Landtag*) launched an increasingly many-pronged legislative campaign to repress the Polish-Catholic clergy's influence in the schools, suppress Polish-language instruction, and so to "Germanize" the Poles through public schooling. "Germanization" of the historically Polish regions was also to result from tax-funded settlement there, after 1886, of German-speaking family farmers, and through other costly government programs favoring the German and German-Jewish middle classes at urban Poles' expense. As in the anti-Catholic *Kulturkampf*, so too in official *Polenpolitik* the Protestant German political elites – whether conservative or liberal – assigned to themselves a nationalist mission to remake "backward" or "disloyal" Catholics in their own image. In other European lands secular-minded liberals mainly strove, often very zealously, to trim the Catholic Church's powers in education.

The third oppositional force comprised the Social Democrats (SPD), on whom Chapter 9 will focus. Their constituency was mainly the burgeoning industrial working class, including many artisan craft workers cut adrift from the preindustrial economy, along with middle-class sympathizers. They aimed at gaining a Reichstag majority and establishing the parliament's constitutional right to appoint chancellor and cabinet, so as to use their power (if revolution were to be avoided) to legislate socialism. By this they understood publicly administered and funded social welfare programs, step-by-step nationalization of private industry and large-scale commerce, and land reform eliminating large estates, especially those of the Prussian Junkers. This was an economic program that made conservative and middle-class liberal blood run cold.

The Wilhelmian era (1890–1914) comprised the years before World War I under the leadership of Kaiser William II (1859–1941), who in 1888 ascended the throne at the age of twenty-eight, self-confidently divesting himself of the elderly Bismarck's services two years later. In frustrated search for pro-governmental consensus and majority backing, the Kaiser's government proclaimed in 1897 a program of overseas imperialism (*Weltpolitik*), which entailed – riskily – the building of a new high-seas navy. The mighty ships duly sailed, to German heavy industry's considerable profit and amid great patriotic, often chauvinist, fanfare. But this did not enable the government to gain impressive and prestigious overseas colonies and thereby (as the Kaiser's ministers hoped) broaden its base of popular domestic support.

Germany entered the competition for overseas colonies later than England and France, and was obliged to content itself between 1884 and 1914 with secondary though not inconsiderable prizes in the European "scramble for Africa," together with scattered islands in the western Pacific and a precarious coastal toehold and "sphere of influence" in China's Kiao-Tschau (as Germans called it). As elsewhere in the empire-keen West, imperialist ideology robustly trumpeted the colonial drive. Picture books featured splendid German-style villas in the colonial administrative centers, indigenous servants in the foreground. To inhabit such structures in the colonizer's crisp white uniform possessed great appeal to the ambitious professional classes in pre-1914 Germany. But the German overseas empire, although geographically extensive, was too short-lived to allow heavy colonial settlement and exploitation such as occurred in the principal lands of the British, French, Dutch, and Portuguese empires. Yet the sometimes bombastic and belligerent Kaiser's championship of German "world-power" (*Weltmacht*), seconded by such prestigious middle-class nationalist advocacy groups as the Pan-German League, created expectations in public opinion that the government found itself under heavy pressure to fulfill.

Colonial violence flared in 1904 when the army in German Southwest Africa (today's Namibia) cruelly defeated the rebellious Herero people, decimating their numbers by as much as one-half. Some 50,000–80,000 Herero died in battle or after having been driven into arid desert. This colonial war, like the repression of indigenous resistance in the 1905 Maji-Maji rising in German East Africa (today's Tanzania), revealed the murderous potential of mobilizing the Prusso-German army, schooled on Clausewitz's theories of battlefield "destruction" of the enemy, against militarily inferior opponents ideologically stigmatized in racial terms. The tendentially genocidal dynamic driving such armed repression, justified by policies of agricultural development through European settlement, found apologists in Berlin. Yet colonial violence was a contentious issue in the 1907 Reichstag elections, compelling the government to repudiate the local commanders' brutalities. Subsequent reforms of the overseas administration forestalled further bloodshed.

In home politics, the Conservatives and National Liberals could only uneasily stand together in upholding the Wilhelmian regime. The Conservatives were tied to east-Elbian agrarian interests, and to Bismarck's post-1879 system of protective tariffs shielding the German market from competitive agricultural imports from Russia and the New World. The National Liberals spoke for more western-oriented industry and trade – in 1914 Anglo-German commerce overshadowed Germany's other economic partnerships. They were also fitfully resentful of the aristocratic conservatives' conspicuous privileges in Imperial German society and government.

FIGURE 8.7. KAISER WILLIAM II: HEIR TO THE PRUSSIAN ARMY, VISIONARY FOUNDER OF
THE GERMAN NAVY, BENEVOLENT PATRON OF THE PEOPLE

This pre-1914 postcard, proclaiming that "our future lies on the water," displays the
Kaiser with his grandson (and presumptive eventual successor) against the backdrop of
the high-seas fleet, built after 1897 to support the German Empire's bid for world-power
status. The navy embodied technological modernity, while its officer corps was a field of
ambition and glory popular among the Wilhelmian middle classes. The publicity-keen
emperor frequently appeared in public, including in yearly New Year's Day marches
in Berlin, flanked by his six sons, sworded and plumed. This spectacle on Unter den
Linden, Berlin's chief political boulevard, reasserted the ruling establishment's Prussian
character, upheld by the noble-officered land army. The Kaiser also patriarchally con-
sorted with his subjects as they studied in school and vacationed at the seashore. He
was the first (and last) Hohenzollern ruler to cultivate his image and popularity through
the emergent mass media, especially the photo-illustrated press.
Source: provenance unknown.

TABLE 8.1. *Deputies Elected to the Reichstag, 1871–1912*

	Conservatives	Catholic Party	National Liberals	Progressive Liberals	Social Democrats	Others
1871	124	63	125	47	2	36
1890	93	106	42	76	35	45
1912	57	91	45	42	110	52

Meanwhile, the number of parliamentary seats falling in elections to the mass-based Social Democrats and Catholic Center Party was rising steeply, while that of the pro-government parties was declining (see Table 8.1). After 1890 the Conservative-National Liberal bloc needed backing, not easily gained, from the Center Party or Progressives to wield a majority. Redistricting the Reichstag's electoral constituencies to reflect Germany's fast-paced urbanization and population growth was overdue in 1914, and would have only accelerated the oppositional trend. A mood of pessimism and alarm spread in conservative and nationalist circles.

Yet their opponents were ideologically, if not always tactically, divided among themselves. Although sometimes compromise prevailed, polarization could emerge, in varying combinations, between anticlerical and antiliberal Social Democrats, antiliberal and antisocialist Catholics, and antisocialist and anti-Catholic (or anticlerical) liberals. In any case, the Bismarckian constitution blocked their accession to executive power in a coalition of their own, whatever their strength at the polls.

German Reich-level politics in 1914 were deadlocked. This tempted some in the government to take advantage of the 1914 crisis triggered, as we will see, by a Habsburg subject's assassination for Serbian nationalist ends of the heir to the Austrian crown. As the government in Vienna sought reprisals against the independent Serbian state (Russia's Balkan client), the post-1904 European alliance system – pitting England, France and Russia against Germany and Austria – triggered armed confrontation across the continent. The German Kaiser, the imperial chancellor, and the Prussian army commanders could not resist the temptation to seek victory in what they conceived (thinking of the 1864, 1866, and 1870 wars) would be sharp but brief conflict. This, they hoped, would both break Germany's (largely self-inflicted, but perhaps unavoidable) military-diplomatic encirclement and relegitimize the imperial regime, strengthening the pro-government parties and weakening oppositional forces, especially the Social Democrats.

By pursuing a moderate course in the July 1914 crisis, the Berlin government could likely have prevented the European Powers' hurtling into war – an observation that applies to the other combatants as well. Instead, hoping for domestic gains from a successfully fought and delusively imagined "short war," and concerned not to allow its only reliable ally, the Austro-Hungarian monarchy, to sustain further weakening by internal ethnic conflicts, Kaiser

FIGURE 8.8. POLITICIZATION OF THE COUNTRYSIDE

In this work of 1877, entitled – patronizingly, perhaps – "The Village Politicans," realist-school painter Wilhelm Leibl (1844–1900) presents comfortably dressed Bavarian villagers reading the news to their neighbors, some of whom may have been less practiced in the art. The press, alongside activist local clergy and schoolteachers and itinerant party organizers, was crucial to the country-folk's integration into supraregional politics. Newspapers were commonly organs of political parties, such as – in this case – the Bavarian People's Party, which championed agrarian interests, Bavarian federalist state rights, and populist Catholicism. Protestant farmers gained representation through the National Liberal Party and the German Conservative Party, which also spoke for the Junker landlords – the east-Elbian village farmers' mighty and overbearing neighbors.
Source: Reproduced in Richard Hamann, *Deutsche Malerei: Von Rokoko bis zum Expressionismus* (Leipzig: Teubner, 1925), p. 370.

William II's regime marched into war. This led, unimaginably in 1914, to the disastrous defeat and downfall both of the Austro-Hungarian monarchy and Imperial Germany, and to the abdication amid revolution of the Habsburg and Hohenzollern dynasties.

9

Sozialdemokratie

Workers and Politics in the Age of Industrialization

Socialism's rocketing ascent in Imperial Germany, borne by the seemingly ever accelerating German Social Democratic Party (SPD) and its myriad associated trade unions and social-cultural organizations, has long sparked vigorous debate. There were writers and historians, including embittered left-leaning liberals, who attributed socialism's growing strength among the working class – spreading too into the lower-middle and middle classes – to an excess of free-market orthodoxy among Bismarckian-era bourgeois liberals. Because German liberalism could not gain and hold the laboring classes' support, they fell under the control of a socialism dominated by radical-populist intellectuals and other activists opposed to the industrial-capitalist system's stabilization. Social Democracy's rising strength alarmed the propertied and conservative-minded middle and upper classes, driving them to the right, away from liberal-democratic political reforms and in some cases into the arms of extreme nationalists, antidemocratic right-wing radicals and even, eventually, the National Socialists.

Such a view faults nineteenth-century liberals for not taking stances that would have won the laboring classes' support, and especially for having made peace after 1866 with Bismarck. In 1878, as we will see, liberal parliamentarians supported the Iron Chancellor's law banning socialist organizations. The liberal parties defended the capitalist order, sometimes opposing, in their laissez-faire zeal, social reforms beneficial to workers, especially the social insurance programs Bismarck promoted to stem socialist advances. Liberals also voiced Protestant-hued nationalist patriotism celebrating Imperial Germany and its Prussian dynasty, and pushed navy construction and overseas expansion even as the Social Democrats voiced an ever more radical critique of what, in their eyes, were feudal-aristocratic militarism and capitalist imperialism.

Thus the Marx-inspired Social Democrats found themselves in opposition *both* to liberals and conservatives marching under Bismarck's and the Kaiser's banners. Responsibility for strengthening parliamentary authority, widening of civil liberties and women's and religious-ethnic minorities' rights, and the struggle for social justice and against militarism fell heavily on Social Democrats' shoulders. The liberal middle classes, who should – as many argue – have more determinedly championed these goals, too often allied themselves with Imperial Germany's monarchist regime. The charge of "self-feudalization" has targeted them.

Doubtless these circumstances burdened the Social Democrats, but there is little profit in belaboring the liberals for the stands they took, which require instead retrospective understanding and explication. In any case, historians have more recently preferred to debate whether the non-revolutionary course the socialist movement followed in the period 1890–1914 was justifiable and politically promising. Some see it as a derailment in which Social Democracy succumbed to bureaucratization, co-optation into the existing electoral-constitutional system, and bread-and-butter trade unionism tacitly upholding the capitalist order and seeking only better conditions for workers within it. Was the SPD, even against consciousness and will, "negatively integrated" into Imperial Germany, losing its ability to project a revolutionary challenge while suffering confinement to a largely powerless opposition? Or was it courageously working to transform the land into a more democratic and socially just society? The one question assumes that the SPD existed for revolutionary purposes, the other that it was liberalism's successor in a long-term democratization process within the capitalist order.

The Emergence of Industrial Society

We saw that the Industrial Revolution – sparked by widespread steam-powering of machinery – dates in Germany from the 1830s, but with railroad building it entered a rapid-growth stage in the 1840s and 1850s. Capital-intensive railroad investments gave a decisive boost to the iron and coal industries, whose development spurred many technological innovations and new industries. From the mid-nineteenth century the German industrial economy assumed a shape that in some respects lingers today, characterized by vigorous engagement in foreign trade from a highly organized home market, in which the leading industrial firms, often quite large, frequently distributed market shares among themselves through legal contracts – or cartels – enforceable in German courts (a practice abandoned after World War II). Well-funded private investment banks helped funnel venture capital into new industries. These rode successive waves of innovative technology set in motion by a network of public universities and laboratories of private companies and public technical institutes, as well as state-funded research centers such as Prussia's Kaiser-Wilhelm-Institute (now the Max-Planck Society).

From the 1860s, national-level pressure groups closely tied to the liberal parties organized and disciplined competing industrial and business interests. The imperial government administered the unprecedented social insurance and workers' pension programs that Bismarck launched in the 1880s in the hope,

FIGURE 9.1. SCIENTIFIC SOCIALISM
This 1897 postcard celebrates the socialist movement's self-appointed annual holiday of May 1 (observed with parades on the nearest Sunday, rather than with work-stoppages that could lead to pay cuts or other employers' reprisals). It proclaims that "Knowledge is Power." A cross-section of workers, occupationally and generationally mixed, some urban, some rural, receive enlightenment's sword from a revolutionary goddess, who supports herself on tomes by Karl Marx, Charles Darwin (whose theory socialists prized, among other things, for replacing religious explanations of biological life with a naturalistic-materialist account), and the German pioneering socialist Ferdinand Lassalle. A cleaning woman clears away rubble symbolizing damage that reactionary politicians of the 1890s sought to inflict on social welfare programs and other workers' interests. In the background, well-dressed workers and their families hear socialist speeches, march in parades, and enjoy the holiday leisure. Marxism drew strength from its claim to offer a historically and empirically – that is, scientifically – verifiable account of the rise and future fall, due to internal contradictions, of the industrial capitalist system.
Source: Provenance unknown.

largely unfulfilled, that such state paternalism would turn the tide against rising socialism. The reforms were milestones in the early development of the European welfare state. Opposed by most liberals because of their state-expanding effect, they offered benefits (mainly worker- and employer-funded) providing, over time, successively more categories of wage and salary earners some significant protection, absent in other western countries before World War I, against sickness, disability, and old age.

FIGURE 9.2. INDUSTRIAL BARONS
This 1890 photograph depicts the heart, in the Ruhr Valley's city of Essen, of the
vast empire of iron, steel, machinery, and armaments manufacturing built by Alfred
Krupp (1812–1887), which his heirs extended (and eventually squandered through
criminal complicity in National Socialism, especially murderous exploitation of captive
labor). An icon too of German industrialization was Werner Siemens (1816–1892),
pioneer with his brother-partners of electrotechnology, including electrified urban trams.
Both the Krupps and Siemens, like many other German industrialists, offered their
numerous work forces – apart from extensive company-built housing (not pictured
here) – paternalistic (and advantageous) fringe benefits, foreshadowing Bismarck's social
insurance system. The Krupps paired their industrial patriarchalism, successfully, with
militant resistance to socialist unionization of their employees (a pattern familiar also to
then-contemporary American industrial workers). Alfred Krupp, proud of his bourgeois
accomplishments and independence, refused governmental offers of ennoblement, but
Werner Siemens, despite his scientific-technological progressiveness and association with
liberal interests, accepted a royally bestowed aristocratic title.
Source: Stadtbildstelle Essen.

There were also state-funded continuation schools for youth not bound
for bourgeois glory, paired with the survival of (non-monopolistic and voluntary) artisan guilds as sites where youth received apprenticeship training
in handicrafts and commercial employment. A powerful, multi-branched but
increasingly centralized labor union movement arose, mainly allied with the

Social Democratic Party. Although these unions were ideologically scornful of laissez-faire, free-market capitalism, they were interested, so long as the socialist millennium had not yet arrived, in cooperating with state and private business management to gain, not just bread and butter advantages, but representation – as was eventually achieved during World War I – in state institutions regulating industrial labor conditions.

This pattern of German industrialization and social policy is different from pre-World War I Anglo-American development, with its libertarian stress on "free enterprise" and "rugged individualism" and its tendency to assign state power (at least within national borders) a modest "night watchman" role. It needs to be understood against the background of the widely respected German absolutist tradition of state-initiated and state-guided economic growth, and with the great historic strength in Germany of guild organization of handicrafts and manufactures in mind.

The social change accompanying nineteenth-century industrialization and adaptation of economic life to free-market principles is evident, in rough measure, in the following figures.

TABLE 9.1. *Approximate Total Employment, 1843 and 1907 (Employers and Employees) in Various Occupational Sectors (%)*

	Kingdom of Prussia, 1843	German Empire, 1907
Agriculture and Forestry	61.0%	34.0%
Industry and Handicrafts	23.0	39.5
Commerce and Communications	2.0	13.5
Public Service and Professions	5.0	7.0
Domestic Servants and Occasional Day Laborers	9.0	6.0
	100.0%	100.0%

TABLE 9.2. *Population Growth in the German Empire of 1871*

total population	1871–41 million	1910–68 million
urban-rural ratio:	1871–36:64	1910–60:40.
number of cities over 100,000:	1870–5	1900–41.

These data show that, amid booming population growth, Imperial Germany rapidly made the transition from a largely rural and small-town society to an increasingly urbanized, industrial way of life. Yet around 1910, some 34–40 percent of the population still lived in villages or small market towns, working in agriculture or closely related fields. In industry, artisans and handicraftsmen did not disappear from the scene, but increased absolutely in number, as skilled and independently employed specialists proved essential to the factory-dominated landscape. Nevertheless, they stood in the shadow of the burgeoning

(a)

FIGURE 9.3. WORKERS (*ARBEITER*)
(a) mechanics at the Carl Benz automobile factory, Mannheim 1896. The company advertises "horseless carriages." These men, skilled in new technology and relatively well paid, were young, and presented themselves as proud and self-confident.

blue-collar, semi-skilled or unskilled industrial labor force, often recruited in overcrowded villages and settled as new in-migrants in mining and metallurgical districts and the big cities.

The industrial-commercial ownership and managerial class – or "bourgeoisie of property" (*Besitzbürgertum*) – rose to ever higher prominence by virtue of its numerical expansion and often ostentatious wealth. The prestige and numbers of the educated, professional middle class (*Bildungsbürgertum*) likewise rose with increasing demand for their services as officials, lawyers, medical doctors, scholars and scientists, journalists, engineers, and cultural producers of all sorts. Ranged below these groups were many middle-class and petty bourgeois elements – small manufacturers and merchants, shopkeepers, schoolteachers, lesser officials, white-collar workers, and similar types – who prospered (or hoped to prosper) and imagined the future as open to them and their children.

But, especially in economically hard times, these middling classes also often felt squeezed by competition and frustrated by blockage of upward mobility. Such dissatisfactions could grip the working class and the middle classes' upper ranks as well. German society was learning that life under modern capitalism

(b)

FIGURE 9.3 *(continued)*
(b) a family-run business of shoemakers and shoe repairers, working (with child labor)
in their cramped living quarters, Berlin ca. 1900. Although they offered custom-made
shoes, they doubtless also – and probably mainly – supplied simple wares to tightfisted
wholesaler buyers. Their photographer was Heinrich Zille (1858–1929), medical doctor
to Berlin's proletarian poor and (still today) much esteemed cartoonist and humorous
artist of everyday life among ordinary Berliners, whose distinctive tough-talking dialect
he captured to perfection.
Source: (a) Provenance unknown. (b) Heinrich Zille.

was often a roller-coaster ride in which, during the rapid-growth cycles (1848–
1873, 1893–1914), exhilarating social and material gains were possible, but in
which also, during the slow-growth cycles (before 1848, and 1873–1896), the
weakest or unluckiest flew from their seats.

Populist Democracy and Socialism

In the pre-1848 years, disintegration of the artisans' accustomed world and rise
of the early industrial working class inspired ideological ferment among radical intellectuals, resulting in pioneering theories of socialism. In the 1830s and
1840s Wilhelm Weitling (1808–1873), a self-educated, Christian-minded tai-
lor, organized in French exile a "League of the Just." It posited an unbridgeable
gulf between bourgeois and proletarian, and steered toward social revolution.

(a)

FIGURE 9.4. THE GERMAN EMPIRE'S *GRANDE BOURGEOISIE*
(a) A "gilded-age villa" in fashionable Babelsberg, between Potsdam and Berlin, such
as the newly rich favored, and one of many that arose to grace Germany's commercial-
industrial centers and their suburbs in the 1880s and 1890s. Allusions, as in this case,
to late medieval styles were widespread in Imperial German architecture, reflecting the
nationalist absorption in the life and culture of the Middle Ages (evident, for example,
in Richard Wagner's operatic dramas). Ornate and dense interior furnishings were the
rule.

There were other forms of Christian socialism and theories aiming to revitalize
the artisan guild system.

The young Karl Marx (1818–1883) criticized these as he began to formulate his own philosophically sophisticated, Hegel-indebted socialism. At its
heart was a historical analysis of the rise, out of the "feudal mode of production," of modern capitalism, whose inner (dialectical) social contradictions
found expression in class struggle that would eventually distill into a contest
between bourgeoisie and wage-dependent industrial proletariat. Marx held
that the "capitalist mode of production" would culminate in crises of overpro-
duction (occasioned by increasingly sophisticated mechanized technology) and

(b)

FIGURE 9.4 *(continued)*
(b) Emil Weyerbusch (1846–1909, depicted here in an 1890 painting by Paul Gerhart Vowe), textile manufacturer, Protestant philanthropist, Prussian reserve officer, Reichstag deputy of the Free Conservative Party, and exemplar of the prosperous bourgeoisie comfortably integrated into the Bismarckian-Wilhelmian governing system.
Source: (a) Bildarchiv Preussischer Kulturbesitz/Art Resource, NY; (b) Von der Heydt-Museum, Wuppertal.

underconsumption (resulting from capitalist profit extraction, wage squeezing, and replacement of workers by machines). Accordingly, working-class political strength would grow in self-defense organizations and militant protest until socialism (the society-wide ownership of the means of production) could be introduced following the revolutionary breakdown of the "bourgeois-capitalist state." Crucial to this scenario was human consciousness and will, which – Marx held – would have to be enlightened by a revolutionary intelligentsia, drawn both from the educated middle classes (as were Marx and his lifelong ally Friedrich Engels) and from the ranks of politically alert and ambitious workers.

The 1848 revolution witnessed the formation, under the leadership of print-
ing worker Stephan Born, of the "General German Workers' Brotherhood"
(*Arbeiterverbrüderung*). Its goals were the attainment of political democracy,
workplace rights, and cooperatively organized industrial production as a supplement to laissez-faire capitalism. This mass-based movement, which grew
out of the educated artisanry's traditions, sought alliance rather than conflict
with middle-class liberals. Many of its members opposed the 1849 counterrevolution with gun in hand, but their cause, and the Brotherhood, suffered
defeat.

In 1862–1864 the charismatic lawyer and writer-publicist Ferdinand Lassalle (1825–1864) cooperated with other activists in founding the "General
German Workers Association," organizing wage laborers, including among
the new industrial proletariat, across the kingdom of Prussia. In harmony with
Born's ideas, but in opposition to many liberals wary of popular democracy,
it sought universal male suffrage, to gain political muscle to achieve state
funding for cooperative, worker-owned industry, thus – it was hoped – allowing escape from capitalist "wage slavery." Lassalle held conversations with
Bismarck, seeking common anti-liberal tactical ground, but without success.
He died prematurely as a result of a duel occasioned by romantic entangle-
ments, but his combative personality and militant writings and speeches won
him great and lasting popularity among workers and their supporters.

Marxian socialism began to sink deeper roots after artisan-trained worker
August Bebel and teacher-journalist Wilhelm Liebknecht, inspired by Marx's
writings and encouragement, in 1869 organized in Saxony the Social Democratic Workers Party (SDAP). It was both anti-Bismarckian and antiliberal,
favoring instead plebeian or working-class democracy in a republican (anti-
monarchical and antiaristocratic) Germany, including also German Austria.
They embraced Marx's critique of capitalism and affirmation of class struggle. In politics, the working class would need to avoid debilitating political
compromises and stand alone.

The foundation of the Social Democratic Party of Germany (SDAP, later
SPD) followed in 1875 at a congress in Gotha, where Lassalleans and Bebel-
Liebknecht forces united. They ratified Marx's "labor theory of value," which
held that workers alone lent the commodities they produced (under exploitative conditions) their intrinsic (as opposed to marketable) worth. They paired
Marxian class struggle with Lassallean state-funded producers' cooperatives
(and with Lassalle's "iron law of wages," predicting that workers' pay would
hover around the culturally defined, existence-reproducing minimum). The SPD
announced it would fight "by all legal means" for a "free state." The Gotha
Program's reticence about revolutionary activism and retention of the cooperative ideal drew Marx's characteristically biting, but only privately expressed
criticism.

Bismarck's antisocialist "Socialist Law" of 1878, ratified by the votes of
Conservatives, a majority of the National Liberals, and a minority of Progressive liberals, radicalized but also energized the budding socialist movement.

This discriminatory statute outlawed the Social Democrats' organizations and press, driving the movement underground. But it did not annul their right to participate in Reichstag elections, a provision that reflected liberals' concern not to jeopardize parliamentary powers in the new empire. Thus, paradoxically, the proscribed movement continued to defend itself and project its appeal from the Reichstag floor and during imperial election campaigns. Yet, not surprisingly, in the 1880s the new discriminatory law reinforced revolutionary and anarchist tendencies in SPD ranks. Clandestine operatives smuggled socialist literature into Germany from Switzerland and other neighboring countries, and socialist cells operated in the shadows.

Following the Socialist Law's expiration, when in 1890 a Reichstag majority recognized that it had failed to throttle socialism in its cradle, the Social Democratic movement reemerged into public life, formulating a new platform under the guidance of theoretician Karl Kautsky. The SPD's 1891 Erfurt Program represented triumph of then-orthodox Marxism, with its theories of working-class "immiseration" and inevitable economic breakdown. Capitalist crisis would, as Marx predicted, emerge from human labor's replacement with non-exploitable machines and resultant contradiction between rising productive capacity and declining employment and consumption. The working class should organize itself as what has been termed an "inheritor party," avoiding any but occasional, tactically justified collaboration with the "bourgeois parties." Yet the Erfurt Program also counseled that, in the short run, the SPD should strive for incremental, progressive democratic reforms through electoral politics and trade-union action.

In 1899, theoretician and journalist Eduard Bernstein challenged the capitalist breakdown theory. He argued that, despite Marx's forecast, industrialization was neither eliminating the small-scale property-owning middle classes ("petty bourgeoisie") nor, despite injustices and inequalities, "immiserating" the working class, whose real living standards, in the economically bustling pre-1914 decades, were actually rising as industrial society matured. Socialists should therefore abandon ideas of utopian collectivism beyond capitalism – that is, in a future socialism or communism – and ally with village farmers and small businessmen, and with the educated middle class, to seek realizable ends gradually by nonrevolutionary means. In Bernstein's British-influenced view, socialism would amount in practice to a modern welfare state with nationalized big industry and finance, but preserving property rights in smaller enterprises and family farms.

A left-wing opposition soon emerged to combat Bernstein's views, which were not unpopular among Social Democrats and even sympathetically viewed by some middle-class liberals. Under Rosa Luxemburg's leadership, Bernstein's critics attacked him and his friends as antirevolutionary "revisionists." Luxemburg argued (with some prophetic accuracy) that European imperialism in Asia, Africa, and Latin America was reenergizing the capitalist mode of production, delaying its terminal crisis through exploitation of foreign markets and resources and through the rise of new armaments industries. But, she held,

(a)

FIGURE 9.5. GERMAN SOCIALISM'S FOUNDING FATHERS

As a student in the 1830s at Berlin University, Karl Marx (1818–1883) began fashioning his left-Hegelian critique of liberal ("bourgeois") economic and political theory. Marx argued that liberalism concealed working humanity's alienation from the product of its labor, and thus of its creativity, by treating the capitalist market economy's (politically steered) mechanisms as universal and inescapable necessity. Later he claimed scientific validity for his analysis of capitalism's "laws of motion," which, he predicted, would lead dialectically to crisis-bearing contradictions igniting socialist revolution. Marx's lifelong collaborator in socialist theory and practice was politically perceptive Friedrich Engels (1820–95), who – ironically – inherited and managed (but for revolutionary ends) his capitalist family's textile manufacturing firm. Realist-minded, he knew industrial workers' often miserable plight firsthand, and expounded Marx's class-struggle analysis in writings of his own that proved immensely popular among proletarians and leftist intellectuals. Pictured here are (a) Wilhelm Liebknecht (1826–1900) and (b) August Bebel (1840–1913), who poses in a photographer's studio in 1884 with his wife Julie and daughter Frieda. These two long-serving cofounders of the German Social Democratic Party, widely revered in its ranks, suffered imprisonment in 1872–1874 for their opposition to the Franco-Prussian war and German annexation of Alsace-Lorraine. Although capable of fiery denunciations of injustice to workers, they steered the SPD toward organizational discipline and electoral success.

Source: (a) Provenance unknown; (b) Bildarchiv Preussischer Kulturbesitz/Art Resource, NY.

(b)

FIGURE 9.5 *(continued)*

imperialism would lead to war, while international markets would eventually become saturated, leading to a final great worldwide economic depression. In present-day bourgeois liberal society, she claimed, only socialists had a necessary interest in political democracy, while other parties would turn, in extremity, to right-wing reaction or authoritarianism to rescue their sinking fortunes. Democracy's only guarantee would be revolution, leading to the overthrow of the presently ruling aristocratic-bourgeois condominium and private industry's conversion into socialist enterprises.

Luxemburg argued that the SPD needed to deepen the workers' class consciousness and revolutionary will and spontaneity. The best means would be the "mass strike," targeting not bread-and-butter but rather political gains (such as replacement by universal suffrage of the oligarchical three-class voting law regulating Prussian state-level elections, or women's enfranchisement, or even "overthrow of the bourgeois state"). Luxemburg and her allies strongly criticized "bureaucratic" – that is, nonrevolutionary – tendencies within the SPD and its allied trade union movement.

FIGURE 9.6. IDEOLOGICAL DEBATES IN GERMAN SOCIAL DEMOCRACY
Here Rosa Luxemburg (1871–1919), apostle of the politically focused "mass strike,"
speaks at the SPD party convention in Stuttgart, 1907. She is flanked by iconic images
of Lassalle and Marx. Among her targets, apart from the Socialist trade unions and SPD
journalist Eduard Bernstein (1850–1932), exponent of the parliamentary and gradualist
path to socialism, was Prague-born journalist and chief SPD theoretician Karl Kautsky
(1854–1938). Although he was a doughty defender of Marxist revolutionary orthodoxy, the 1891 SPD program Kautsky had penned strove, so long as Marx's grand
structural crisis of capitalism had not yet arisen, for liberal democratic reforms that, in
Luxemburg's view, could neither ward off the proletariat's "immiseration" nor fan its
revolutionary ardor.
Source: Bildarchiv Preussischer Kulturbesitz/Art Resource, NY.

Such "bureaucratization" slowly emerged during the years between 1890
and 1914, with a crucial moment coming in 1905–1907, when (while revolution stormed in the neighboring Russian Empire) party congresses effectively
rejected the Luxemburgists' "mass strike" strategy. Instead, the SPD party
organization increasingly focused its efforts, machine-like, on winning elections. This strategy triumphed in the 1912 Reichstag election, when the SPD
won 34.8 percent of the vote, more than twice the number polled by its nearest competitor, the Catholic Center Party. But, as it turned out, a "one-third"
electoral barrier within German society had been reached, beyond which the
Social Democratic vote could not easily surge. The ideological rift separating working-class and middle-class parties impeded parliamentary cooperation

(a)

FIGURE 9.7. TWO FACES OF SOCIAL DEMOCRACY: QUEST FOR LIVING WAGE AND CIVIC EQUALITY, AND FOR REDEMPTION THROUGH JUSTICE

(a) Friedrich Ebert (1871–1925) and family (photographed in 1898). A wage worker and SPD organizer, Ebert rose from 1906 Party Secretary to Co-Chairman in 1913 (and to the Weimar Republic's presidency, 1919–1925). The three children display dress and toys typical of lower-middle-class Imperial Germany. Allied with Ebert was flamboyantly mustachioed Carl Legien (1861–1920), minor eastern Prussian tax official's son, worker and trade-union organizer, and head (1892–1919) of the SPD-linked Free Trade Unions. Legien and his unionist colleagues suffered the SPD left wing's charges of neglecting revolutionary goals for bread-and-butter pursuits, but no Social Democrat favored abandonment of the often bitter struggle with business owners for better pay and collective bargaining rights.

that might have achieved further liberalization of Empire-level political institutions and the electoral systems that, in most German states and municipalities, privileged propertied interests and blocked women's participation.

At the same time, the self-designated Free Trade Unions – that is, the SPD's socialist trade unions independent of the employers (as opposed to pro-management company unions) – grew spectacularly (or, from their opponents' viewpoint, ominously). In 1912 they counted 2.5 million members (in contrast

(b)

FIGURE 9.7 *(continued)*
(b) "The Evangelist of the Poor," a painting of 1900 by Danish-born longtime Berlin resident Jens Birkholm (1869–1915), in which the figure of the speaker is the artist's self-portrait. Depicted is an SPD meeting, dignified by Marx's bust but conducted under the gimlet eyes of Prussian police officials (as the pre-1908 law on associations prescribed), who were authorized to dissolve the assembly should seditious statements be uttered. The picture conveys the popular association, strong among those still emotionally connected to Christianity, of socialism's message with Jesus's Sermon on the Mount.
Source: (a) Provenance unknown. (b) Bildarchiv Preussischer Kulturbesitz/Art Resource, NY.

to 1 million SPD party members and 4.3 million SPD voters). These unions constituted a giant workers' self-help system, thanks to numerous social and financial services they offered their members, including savings-and-loan societies and burial funds. Mindful of not squandering accumulated assets, they opposed political strikes (including the "mass strike") and what they stigmatized as "revolutionary actionism" or "chaos." But the unions could not break employers' power to block their penetration of many important branches of heavy industry, to lock out nonstriking workers during strike actions targeting selected individual firms or branches, or to refuse to negotiate the end of strikes. Nor did state-administered unemployment insurance yet exist.

After 1890, an extensive SPD-organized working-class subculture thrived, animated by social and cultural-educational clubs and musical groups, high-circulation socialist print media, workers' libraries, socialist pubs for party faithful, and sports and hiking-excursion societies. These absorbed SPD members' current interests from cradle to grave, while socialist ideology promised deliverance from capitalist exploitation in the indistinct future, giving voice also to workers' resentment over maltreatment at the propertied and ruling classes' hands.

Perhaps clearer to SPD members than the socialist ideal was hope of attaining a democratic republic (entailing the end to the Hohenzollern and other ruling dynasties) and a more egalitarian society. Yet many workers also sought social integration and upward mobility, admiring middle-class values and accomplishments, and not immune to German patriotism and nationalism's appeal. Most male workers had passed through peacetime army induction and training. Yet the zeal in combating Social Democracy of the widely popular, government-backed Wilhelmian-era army veterans' social clubs (*Kriegervereine*) dampened SPD members' enthusiasm for maintaining army ties. The SPD reciprocated conservative antagonism, routinely denouncing militarism's repressive functions.

The balance between revolutionary and "revisionist/integrationist" tendencies would undergo agonizing test in World War I and its turbulent aftermath. It was not a signal of working-class intransigence that, as war flared, the SPD's Reichstag parliamentary delegation cast its votes, despite the party's longstanding pacifism, in favor of the August 4, 1914 army funding bill, supporting the exploding conflict. The war proved to be an unprecedented cataclysm, hurtling what in socialist theory figured as bourgeois capitalist society into a crisis the Social Democrats alone could not master, and which eventually claimed them among its victims.

10

Frauen

Women, Family, Feminism, 1789–1914

Women's Lives in the Eighteenth Century

Young unmarried women, like young men, lived under the economic and disciplinary authority of elders, whether parents or – if the youths had left home and begun working for wages – mistresses or masters on farms, in artisan workshops, shops or other establishments. Many young unmarried women were domestic servants in bourgeois or upper-class households. Marriage enabled women to become mistresses of their own domicile, but to enter into it they needed accumulated assets in cash and household goods – that is, a dowry. Propertied families' daughters received dowries from parents as marriage portions, often more valuable to them than later inheritances. Poorer young women saved their wages to improve whatever meager marriage portions their families might bestow on them. They might only manage to bring into their newlyweds' cottage a trunk of clothes and linen, a milk-cow, and a month or two of wages in cash. Noblewomen, by contrast, could lavish on their husbands – who often grandly reciprocated – fortunes in cash and jewelry, with future prospects of rich inheritances, including town houses and country estates.

Once married, women lived under their husbands' authority, and often suffered from it. Yet husbands were in principle only stewards of their wives' marital assets on behalf of their children. A substantial dowry strengthened a woman's position in her household, and reserved for her, if things went tolerably well, lifelong support in widowhood or old age. High mortality made remarriage common, and German law was accustomed to meticulously recording and enforcing people's inheritance and dowry rights, especially those of widows and children. It was also characteristic of farm and artisan households that retiring elders should receive separate lodging and food, and often also garden-land and horse and cart, from younger couples taking their places – typically, one of their children and a spouse. Provision of such "elders' portions" (*Altenteil*) was also enforceable in court.

Aristocratic women's property rights in their dowries and inheritances were well protected, especially because marriages were commonly understood as actions undertaken in noble lineages' interest, and not only (or necessarily) as fulfillment of personal wishes. Such wives needed also to retain control over assets allowing them to contract advantageous remarriages, should their husbands – as might happen quite suddenly – die prematurely. Not a few people in their prime left home on trips never to return, having fallen victim to unexpected illness while traveling. Prosperous middle-class or bourgeois families' married daughters enjoyed similar protection.

Before 1789, nearly all women lived confined to society's private sphere, bereft of public voice. Exceptions were widows managing landed estates, aided by bailiffs and lawyers. Widows occasionally also headed their deceased husbands' urban businesses, sometimes temporarily taking their husbands' seats in guild organizations or other economic corporations. Often prominent and influential (alongside female members of ruling houses) were rich upper-class women, possessed of skills to represent successfully a political point of view – or to charmingly represent themselves – at one or another of the myriad German courts. There was, too, a small number of women whose intellectual, literary, and artistic talents gave them public recognition and influence.

Women, the Enlightenment, and Romanticism

If in Enlightenment philosophy it was sometimes granted that women possess the same potential for rational thought as men, it followed that they could claim the same rights as men to "education to reason" and self-determination in the public sphere. Highly educated women who were active in scholarly and artistic life were not unknown. Yet men, including Enlightenment enthusiasts, widely believed that Nature destined women primarily to be wives and mothers. Among the educated classes, the view prevailed that there was usually little or no time to qualify them for the professions men exercised. Upper-class women should indeed possess sufficient education to make them intelligent and agreeable partners of their husbands. Among common folk, women performed – alongside mothering – household and field work which everyone recognized as indispensable and valuable. But the division of labor was stringently gendered, and women's work within it did not liberate them from their husbands' higher powers.

Pre-Romantic and Romantic tendencies in upper-class culture in the late eighteenth and early nineteenth century attributed to women a separate sensibility and consciousness, in which positively judged emotionalism and intuitive understanding loomed large. These qualities were seen to balance men's rationalism and ambitious purposefulness in public life. With the coming of the French Revolution and nineteenth-century liberalism and nationalism, women's responsibilities in the private sphere took on the added importance of preparing sons for schooling and socialization as citizens and patriots.

(a)

FIGURE 10.1. MARRIAGE AND MOTHERHOOD
The first of these two pictures, both made in 1847 by the pioneering photographer
Carl Ferdinand Stelzner (1805–1894), displays a Hamburg merchant and wife with
seven well-dressed children – mostly still young. Frequent childbearing's physical toll
on women sometimes seems detectable in such pictures, but the survival of mother
and children was a socially honorable triumph. Fatherly engagement and devotion are
evident, while the children express more intimacy with each other and their parents
than subordination to a hierarchy of authority. In the second picture, a Hamburg
widow (1771–1851) poses with a portrait of her departed husband (1764–1840), an
old-regime man of distinguished and prosperous appearance. Such a scene highlights
the conjugal bond independent of parenting.
Source: C. F. Stelzner.

    As first tentative claims arose, both in western Europe and the German lands,
for women's legal-political equality in the public realm, it seemed to people of
moderate or conservative views that women – long entitled, in the middle and
upper classes, to basic and sometimes intermediate education – already played
crucial social roles in their own separate sphere and were destined to do so
in the foreseeable future. As for unmarried women among the educated and
propertied classes, if they could not find a marriage partner, their best hope to

(b)

FIGURE 10.1 *(continued)*

avoid social descent was to assist in married kinfolk's household management in exchange for lodging and board. Alternatively, they became governesses of children in upper-class families, although this entailed some loss in social status. A more or less cloistered life in one or another religious order also remained possible.

Nineteenth-Century Movements for Women's Rights

The middle-class ideal blossomed of a newly emotionalized "companionate" – although still patriarchal – marriage. It was meant, however, to coexist with a social world anchored psychologically and materially in family alliances. In some German lands, women in the nineteenth-century propertied classes found their economic rights within marriage weakened, in comparison with the "aristocratic-feudal" eighteenth century, through civil-law reforms favoring husbands' power of disposition over family capital. Yet prenuptial contracts often preserved women's interests in dowries and other assets brought into marriage. As, later, married women's possibilities of working for wages and salaries

(a)

FIGURE 10.2. WOMEN INTELLECTUALS AND ARTISTS

(a) An elegant, calm and reflective self-portrait of 1781 by Angelika Kauffmann (1741–1807), wearing the regional costume of her homeland of Bregenz, in alpine Austria. She was a gifted and well-schooled Swiss-Austrian painter of considerable productivity and European and British renown, counting Goethe among her many distinguished friends. Notable among her contemporaries for their literary achievements was Sophie von La Roche (1730–1807), who rescued her collapsing aristocratic fortunes by crafting a career as a popular novelist. Earlier pioneers of women's writing were Louise Gottsched (1713–1762), popular playwright and wife and intellectual partner of J. C. Gottsched, influential author and critic. Although uncelebrated in her own time, Glikl bas Judah Leib ("Glückel of Hameln") (1646–1724) was a successful businesswoman and the first modern German female autobiographer, whose memoirs, authored in Judeo-German (see Chapter 12), came to be widely read in modern translation.

slowly materialized, husbands' legal power to condone such employment and dispose of wives' incomes became contentious issues.

Divorce, too, although never easy to obtain, grew more difficult for women who wished to initiate one. In the kingdom of Prussia, the Enlightenment-inspired General Law Code (Allgemeines Landrecht) of 1794, which with modifications remained in force through the nineteenth century, tolerantly viewed

(b)

FIGURE 10.2 *(continued)*

(b) An 1843 daguerreotype of Caroline Stelzner, painter of miniatures, taken by her husband, C. F. Stelzner. She epitomized the infrequent type of a mid-nineteenth-century woman who combined middle-class marriage with an artistic calling (although many such women excelled at the piano and in letter writing). Her self-presentation here, not unlike that of other contemporary women from the artistic and literary milieu, ignores strait-laced Victorianism, and makes no reference to maternity or conventional piety. The book she holds signals poetry, probably in a Romantic vein.

Source: (a) Tiroler Landesmuseum Ferdinandeum, Innsbruck; (b) C. F. Stelzner.

divorce as a practical matter of ending unsustainable marriages. In the early nineteenth century, however, sentiment among Protestant clergy turned against approval of new marriages among divorced adults.

There was certainly a German equivalent of morally self-righteous English and American Victorianism, if perhaps not so stringent and militant. Among the common folk and working class, economic need dictated that women should perform productive labor required by their husbands' occupations and fortunes. Proletarian women could expect that, outside family and neighborhood circles, little or no respect would be paid to their feminine honor and sensitivities.

FIGURE 10.3. THE GERMAN INTELLIGENTSIA'S ROMANTIC-ERA MUSES
A portrait of 1798 by Johann Friedrich August Tischbein (1750–1812) depicts Caroline
Schlegel-Schelling (1763–1809), neé Michaelis, professor's daughter and then young
widow, among whose unconventional experiences was her arrest in the Rhineland
as French revolutionary partisan. She was friend to Goethe and, remarried to virtuoso translator of Shakespeare and literary-linguistic scholar August Wilhelm Schlegel,
an influential figure in Romanticism's emergence. Later, divorced from Schlegel,
she married celebrated Romantic philosopher Friedrich Wilhelm Schelling. Caroline
Schlegel-Schelling was sister-in-law to Dorothea Veit (1763–1839), daughter of Moses
Mendelssohn, the father of the Jewish Haskalah or Enlightenment (on which, see Chapter 12). As wife to August Wilhelm Schlegel's brother, the critic and publicist Friedrich
Schlegel, Dorothea later converted with her husband to Romanticism-tinged Catholicism. Prestigious salons, hosted by these and other women of intellect and wealth,
gathered the German intelligentsia, particularly in the decades from the 1790s to the
1820s. Such women as Caroline and Dorothea Schlegel were intellectually influential
more through letters than publications, and through aid and inspiration they gave their
husbands.
Source: Bildarchiv Preussischer Kulturbesitz/Art Resource, NY.

(a)

FIGURE 10.4. EMOTION IN THE BOURGEOIS FAMILY

(a) An idyllic 1835 painting of a provincial Austrian lawyer and family, by renowned and – in his time – aesthetically progressive, today still much-admired Austrian painter Georg Waldmüller (1793–1865). The husband with the couple's three sons and wife with their five daughters form a vital and happy totality. Although not depicted as organically rooted in Nature (as Romanticism supposed the common people to be), this large family of the educated bourgeoisie is comfortably at home in a magnificent but benign alpine landscape. Compare this with the anonymously authored photograph, (b), of the internationally renowned research chemist Justus Liebig (1803–1873) and his family, ca. 1844: a picture radiating dignified self-awareness, family solidarity, and perhaps also ambition, but lacking any touches of Romanticism.

In another genre, a mid-nineteenth-century photograph – doubtless not unique – memorialized a bourgeois father's birthday, on which (under ancestral eyes peering from portraits on the wall) his six children, guided by their young mother, pay him – seated in his living-room chair – their respects: the epitome of Victorian-era patriarchalism.

Source: (a) Reproduced in Werner R. Deusch, *Malerei der deutschen Romantiker und ihrer Zeitgenossen* (Berlin: K. Wolff, 1937), pl. 100; (b) Provenance unknown.

(b)

FIGURE 10.4 *(continued)*

The pursuit of women's rights in the public sphere crystallized in the movement for middle-class women's higher education. Its argument was that, unless
women could educate themselves to earn a living, they faced the ethically
indefensible choice of accepting an unwanted marriage partner or a life of
spinsterhood, which the diminishing size and complexity of bourgeois households was reducing to ever greater economic precariousness. New patterns
of consumption arose, notably purchase of ready-made food (some industrially preserved in metal containers) and acquisition of labor-saving household
devices, eventually electrically powered. This, alongside urban housing's rising
cost, made it harder for relatives to justify provision of room and board to
unmarried kinswomen. As good-quality private and public primary education
spread, governesses' opportunities shrank.

Early activists made the case for women's higher education and access to
white-collar jobs in (present-day) terms of a "feminism of difference" or "separate spheres." Orthodoxies of gender difference stood unchallenged. Instead,
stress fell on advantages women would gain within their own social-cultural
realm from education and salaried employment. Such "separate-spheres feminists" conceded that women's highest fulfillment came in marriage and motherhood (*Mütterlichkeit*). Yet they insisted that unmarried women and women
who could find no satisfactory husband should play socially beneficial and

self-supportive roles that higher education made newly possible – as teachers, office workers, nurses, writers, shopkeepers, and other small-business owners or managers.

Slowly, after 1848, academically rigorous secondary education grew more available to women from the propertied classes, although the poor lacked both time and money to qualify for education beyond primary school. By the 1880s and 1890s, some German-language universities in Switzerland and south Germany were admitting women students. In 1908, universities in the kingdom of Prussia opened their doors to them. But women's access to work as educated professionals – such as physicians, lawyers, academics, and officials – would require long struggle in the twentieth century, with drastic setbacks under National Socialism.

Conservative men feared for male authority at home and in public life should women gain political voice (and the vote). Many liberals, averse to churchly influence in society, suspected that women – especially Catholics – would vote as clergymen signaled. Women's engagement in 1848's radical politics, although largely confined to intellectual circles, gave the Prussian government a pretext, in its 1850 Law on Political Associations, to forbid women's membership and participation in pressure groups and parties. Not until 1908 was this statute abolished, finally permitting women in Prussia – that is, in the greater part of Imperial Germany – to legally join in public political discussion. Other states were more liberal, but nowhere in Germany (or elsewhere in Europe, except for Scandinavia) did women gain the vote before World War I's end.

German women invested much energy in nominally nonpartisan but politically significant organizations, beginning (after stirrings in 1848) with the General German Women's Association (Allgemeiner Deutscher Frauenverein), founded in 1865. In 1894, the many (by then) existent women's organizations combined in the Union of German Women's Associations (Bund deutscher Frauenvereine), whose membership, in several thousand local organizations, by 1913 numbered some half-million.

This "bourgeois women's movement," as it was known, concerned itself especially with legal, educational, and employment issues, and breathed moderate liberalism's spirit. It could claim considerable credit for improvements in women's rights registered in the German Empire's new Civil Law Code (Bürgerliches Gesetzbuch) of 1899–1900. These included, among others, acknowledgment of married women's powers, via attorneys, of self-representation before the law (in place of their husbands' former prerogative of speaking for them). Wives' disposition over their wages and salary-earnings also gained legal defense. In other respects – for example, in husbands' continuing right (should they wish to exercise it) to forbid their wives to work outside the home – the new law code left women activists unsatisfied.

The German Protestant Women's Union (Deutsch-Evangelischer Frauenbund) and the Patriotic Women's Association (Vaterländischer Frauenverein) expressed their numerous members' conservative-nationalist views and philanthropic energies. In general, women from Protestant and Jewish backgrounds

FIGURE 10.5. CHAMPIONS OF WOMEN'S RIGHTS AND FEMINISM
German activists assemble – in a typically furnished middle-class home – in 1914 Berlin
during the International Women's Congress. At the table's far end sits Helene Lange
(1848–1930), successful advocate of women's education and longstanding leader of the
major German women's organization (ADV/BDF). Second from right is Gertrud Bäumer
(1873–1954), popular author, BDF leader from 1910 to 1919, and subsequently deeply
engaged in the Weimar Republic's social policy administration. The National Socialist
dictatorship sidelined her, even though – like many bourgeois liberals – she initially
imagined she might continue work and writing in harmony with it. Second from left
is Alice Salomon (1872–1948), left-liberal activist for women's education and social
work – and, later, refugee from the National Socialist regime, which objected to her
Jewish parentage. She converted to Protestantism in 1914.

   Controversial in the pre-1914 years were Clara Zetkin (1857–1933), left-wing Social
Democrat, editor 1891–1917 of the SPD's women's journal, *Gleichheit* ("Equality"),
and after 1919 leading German Communist, and Helene Stöcker (1869–1943), advocate of birth control and other forms of sexual liberation, and of pacifism too. The
liberal women's suffrage movement (*Verein für Frauenstimmrecht*) projected a jaunty
image. An 1896 photo of its youthful leaders showed them in thoughtful poses, pressing
pencils – symbols of voting – to their chins.
Source: Bildarchiv Preussischer Kulturbesitz/Art Resource, NY.

FIGURE 10.6. WORKING WOMEN IN THE EARLY TWENTIETH CENTURY
Characteristic were such scenes as this, which shows women workers, under male and female supervisors, in the Imperial German Postal Service's long-distance telephone bureau. Then-current women's images also included fashion models, exhibiting prestigious styles from the Vienna Workshops, outposts of pre-1914 artistic modernism. Women found depiction as high-spirited country girls in regional holiday costume and – less often – as bare-armed farm wives, in bandanas and wooden clogs, baking hefty loaves of bread for their households. Hidden from public view, but familiar to social consciousness, were homebound women workers earning piece-rates – for example, an elderly dressmaker at her sewing table, a caged songbird in the window.
Source: Deutsches Bundesarchiv.

took the lead in nineteenth-century feminist mobilizations. Some Catholic women joined them, but more found entry in religiously defined Catholic charitable and social-work movements an easier step to take into the public sphere.

In Imperial Germany's wide Social Democratic subculture, many women's groups sprang up. Most activists were SPD members' wives, the more zealous of them viewing the family as a kind of "socialist cell." In the labor force, working women gained only narrow footing in heavy industry, but they were numerous in textiles and light industry. While the middle-class women's movement equivocated over winning the vote, or even spurned the prospect (fearing "politicization of women's interests"), Social Democrats advocated women's suffrage straightforwardly.

In the pre-1914 decades, women's employment surged, especially among unmarried youth. The industrial economy's maturation, along with proliferation of big cities, created a myriad of new women's jobs, both in white-collar office work and service-economy positions. Women began finding work in the governmental sector – for example, as telephone operators. A young women's subculture emerged, based on apartment sharing, economic independence, membership in professional self-help organizations performing some of the functions of labor unions – such as the Association of White-Collar Women Workers (Verein weiblicher Angestellter) – and willingness to postpone marriage until an appropriate and desirable partner appeared.

To conservative critics, such new manifestations of women's life portended weakening of customary male authority and loosening of sexual behavior in women's favor, as well as widening of support for big-city popular culture that seemed irreverent and even subversive. Women's emancipation had progressed far enough to fuel the fires of right-wing ideological reaction against modernity's "corrosive effects."

11

State of Many Peoples (*Vielvölkerstaat*)

The Habsburg Austrian Monarchy

Austria dominated the Holy Roman Empire of the German Nation until that labyrinthine-roomed house's collapse in 1806. Not before Prussia's eighteenth-century ascent did any single German state possess the strength to defy the Habsburg monarchy. Even after its armed struggle with Austria ended victoriously in 1763, absolutist Prussia was content to share influence in the Empire with the Habsburgs, and defer symbolically to their greater prestige. But when, after the turmoil of 1848, national unification's challenge became a life-and-death matter for the Hohenzollern monarchy, Bismarck and King William I did not shrink in 1866 from aggressive war against Austria. Prussia's victory led to mastery of the 1871 Reich, representing itself as the new national home. Austria stood defeated and "expelled from Germany."

Anticipating Prussia's 1871 triumph, many German histories peripheralize the Habsburg monarchy even before the Austro-Prussian showdown of 1866, and abandon it altogether thereafter. Yet it was not until 1945 that Austria ceased to be part of – and play a crucial role in – German history. It is still today a major site of German-language culture and German historical memory and so also of one of several historically constituted German identities, even if it is now understood as autonomously – and even exclusively – Austrian. In the Prusso-German Empire's 1871–1918 lifetime, Austria was its closest ally. Political and ideological developments in the Habsburg monarchy crucially shaped Imperial Germany's destiny. It is important, then, to observe the Austrian-ruled state's historical trajectory, especially in its decisive 1867–1914 end-phase. It is not amiss to recall that, in 1889, Adolf Hitler was born on the German-Austrian border, a Habsburg official's son and soon-to-be ardent pan-German nationalist.

In the aftermath of the twentieth century's terrible violence, nostalgia for the vanished Habsburg realm lingered. It was a feeling born not only of memories of a brilliant Viennese society and culture, but also of pre–World War I civility and cosmopolitanism. Certainly, the monarchy was far from being, in any

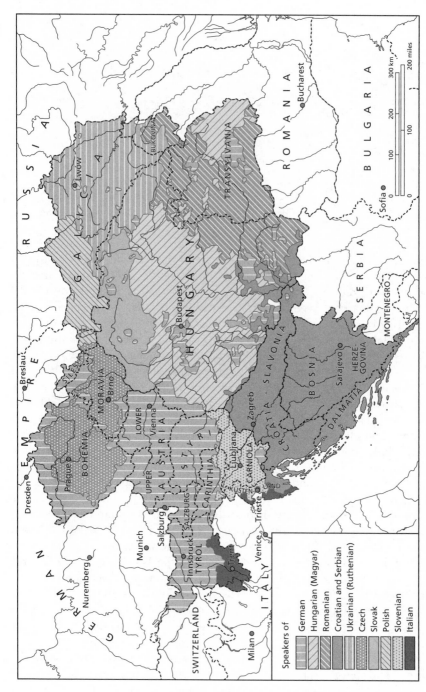

MAP 11.1. MAJORITY LINGUISTIC GROUPS, ACCORDING TO THE AUSTRO-HUNGARIAN CENSUS OF 1910

totalitarian sense, the "prison-house of nations" that breakaway-minded anti-Habsburg nationalists sometimes called it. Still, although the far-flung state was assembled in part through diplomacy and marriage alliances, it was also forged in prolonged warfare. The challenge is to understand it *both* as a product of power-driven state building and as a multinational structure that sought to reconcile its many peoples to coexistence under a common government and through mutual cultural and political sympathies.

Modern historians struggle to explain the Austrian monarchy's failure to become a confederation of nationalities enjoying civic equality. Perhaps it did not entirely fail, collapsing only because of defeat in World War I. The conclusion seems nevertheless unavoidable that only more resolute pursuit of political and social equality in the post-1867 decades could have preserved the multinational state. Yet neither did the Habsburg regime, captive of its own historical legacy, press such a program to conclusion, nor is it clear that, under more fully democratized conditions, the monarchy's many nationalities would have wished and sought to live together peacefully.

Austria's Transformation into Empire, 1526–1815

Another look at the earlier drawn picture of premodern German history is necessary to highlight Austria's angle of political vision, its ambitions and dilemmas. The inheritance of the Crowns of Bohemia and Hungary dramatically widened the Habsburgs' medieval power base in ducal Austria. In the late fifteenth century, central European dynastic politics had joined the Bohemian and Hungarian kingdoms together under a single ruler to face the challenge of the Ottoman Turks' drive up the Balkan peninsula and Danube valley. The great Turkish victory in 1526 over Bohemian-Hungarian arms at the battle of Mohács then delivered, through the workings of prior diplomacy, royal power in the kingdom of Bohemia to the Austrian-German branch of the Habsburg

---

MAP 11.1 *(continued)* Here displayed are the areas of settlement, as the 1910 census defined them, in which a majority prevailed of speakers of one or another of the monarchy's recognized languages. An English-language mapping of these data, published in 1911, bore the title of "Distribution of Races in Austria-Hungary," reflecting the tendency of the age (still alive in popular culture today) to equate linguistic-cultural attributes with "race" and to suppose that linguistically-marked populations – often also labeled as "nationalities" – possessed homogeneous national-political consciousness. Such populations were indeed available for political mobilization by nationalist movements, but other identities competed for their loyalty, based on religion, social class, devotion to the Habsburg dynasty, and deference to local elites speaking languages other than those of their subjects. Maps such as this, like the censuses they derived from, were politically biased, favoring some nationalist causes over others. They also underplayed or screened out the prevalence of linguistically mixed regions and "ethnic islands."

dynasty (other members of which, as we know, sat in the sixteenth and seventeenth centuries on Spain's throne). This was an extremely valuable acquisition in view of Bohemia's wealth, flowing from mining and urban manufactures as well as fertile agriculture. But the Habsburgs' inheritance of rule in the kingdom of Hungary long remained confined to the west and northwest of that large land, the rest of which the Turks occupied after their 1526 victory there.

In this way, one empire, that of the Ottomans, indirectly created another, that of the Austrian Habsburgs. The Turks became the Austrians' great enemy, terrifyingly – if unsuccessfully – laying siege to Vienna twice, in 1529 and 1683. Finally, in the years between 1699 and 1718, Austria brilliantly reconquered all the lands of the Hungarian Crown, including in southeastern Croatia and Transylvania. In the Polish partitions of 1772–1795, Austria acquired the large province of Galicia, inhabited primarily by Poles in the west and Ukrainians in the east, with a large Jewish population throughout. In 1815, the Congress of Vienna, redrawing the European map following Napoleonic France's defeat, bestowed Venice and its Italian hinterland on Austria, together with the former Venetian-controlled eastern Adriatic coastland of Dalmatia. Austria ruled as well in northern Italian Lombardy, centered on Milan. As a European Great Power engaged in absolutist state building, the Habsburg monarchy looked on these various far-flung lands as a power-base, to be profitably managed in the service of dynastic stability, military-bureaucratic discipline, and further territorial expansion, especially in the Balkans, at the Turks' (and, later, the Russians') expense.

"Absolutism" and "absolutist monarchy" are, as we recall, time-honored terms for the process in early modern Europe in which executive power in monarchical or other princely governed states was centralized at the ruler's court, while earlier-established parliamentary bodies representing feudal elites (high churchmen, landed nobility, privileged burghers) suffered reduction in power and competence. It was a process aimed at making the hereditary dynastic rulers' authority within their own realm "absolute," especially by introducing salaried bureaucracies and new permanent taxation allowing the maintenance of large standing armies of soldiers recruited among the common people and foreign mercenaries. Absolutist policy aimed too at state-guided economic development, in part to create a military-industrial complex to serve expansionist foreign-policy ambitions.

Absolutist regimes recruited landed aristocrats or their sons into the army officer corps, and the civilian bureaucratic and diplomatic service as well, although in these latter two branches many among the educated middle class or bourgeoisie also served, often rewarded – particularly by the Austrian Habsburgs – for rising up the promotional ladder with ennoblement by the ruler. Absolutist regimes sought also to bring Christianity into state service. Characteristic of Catholic lands, including Austria, were elite academies maintained by the church (especially the Jesuit order) for the nobility's education. Except fitfully in Russia, absolutism did not actually endow dynastic rulers with irresistible authority, but this stage of European state building did indeed witness considerable centralization and expansion of state power, and subordination of formerly autonomous and powerful social elites to it.

In 1740, the Habsburg monarchy's principal institutions were the imperial court and executive cabinet in Vienna; the standing army, with its many garrisons and militarized border with the Ottoman state, settled with Christian soldier-farmer colonists; the high bureaucracy and judiciary in Vienna and its extensions in the provincial governorships; and (though not part of the bureaucratic apparatus) the state-supportive Catholic Church, with handsome incomes from tithes and rents on lands in its direct possession. The leading posts in the empire rested largely in the wealthy and high-ranking (magnate) aristocracy's hands. They were Catholic and Habsburg in mentality, rather than Germans in any nationalist sense, even though most spoke German as a native tongue. Many others were non-Germans, especially (apart from Italians) among the numerous Hungarian and Polish aristocracy.

The Czech-speaking nobility of medieval origins had dwindled greatly, owing to reprisals and other consequences they suffered at Habsburg hands for their rebellion of 1618. Many among them having been executed, dispossessed and dispersed, the remainder were overshadowed in the lands of the Bohemian crown after the Thirty Years War by German noble immigrants and marginalized by politically and religiously induced Germanization in their own ranks.

The monarchy as a whole was supra-national, yet also German (although French and Italian culture commanded high prestige). To the mid-eighteenth century, the monarchy depended on the loyalty of the various regional nobilities, inculcated through education in the Jesuit academies, more than it did on integration by means of bureaucratic centralization.

Austria fought desperately against Prussia's challenge to Habsburg rule in the rich Bohemian province of Silesia (1740–1742, 1745–1748, 1756–1763), which – as we know – ended in Vienna's loss of that land to the oft near-vanquished but finally victorious Frederick the Great. This prestige-diminishing catastrophe triggered a long era of centralizing and rationalizing reform by queen/empress Maria Theresa (ruled 1740–1780) and her son, Joseph II (co-ruler 1765–1780, emperor 1780–1790). The half-century spanning their reigns figures conventionally as Habsburg Austria's era of Enlightened Absolutism.

Their innovations included the merger of the Austrian and Bohemian lands into a single administrative unity and economic free-trade zone; curtailment of noble local self-government in favor of new levels of centralized bureaucratic administration, carried out mainly by middle-class German functionaries; new taxes, imposed also on the landed nobility; and closure of Catholic monasteries and seizure of their rent-yielding estate land, with the aim, among other things, of funding expanded elementary education, including in the pupils' mother tongue, whether German or not.

Joseph II, as sole ruler, banned juridical serfdom and attempted to abolish the nobility's seigneurial labor rents drawn from the villages by converting them into fixed cash payments – both actions beneficial to the peasantry, although

Joseph aimed also to raise the state taxes they paid. He sought to expand his army, so as to challenge Prussia and regain Silesia or equivalent new territories in the future. Joseph also proclaimed religious toleration of Protestants and Jews where previously they had been excluded from habitation, as in the Austrian-German heartland.

Most importantly, he tried to overturn the kingdom of Hungary's ancient constitution, seeking to divide the land into provinces ruled directly from Vienna by German officials. His objective was to override the Hungarian nobility's fulsome privileges, preventing his government from satisfactorily exploiting Hungary's potential for yielding tax revenues and military recruits for monarchy-wide purposes. This outraged the Hungarian gentry, while Joseph's agrarian and religious reforms soured German-speaking elites in Austria and Bohemia against him. At the 1789 French revolution's outbreak, and following Joseph's premature death in 1790, the Habsburg government under his brother Leopold II saw no alternative to rescinding Joseph's more radical agrarian reforms. Leopold restored as well the former status quo in Hungary, where revolutionary ferment aimed at rebellion against Vienna was brewing in insurgent circles of noble-born intellectuals and gentry.

Liberalism, Nationalism, and the Problem of German Unity

The French Revolution and Napoleonic Empire succeeding it (1789–1815) raised ideological issues of explosive force in the Habsburg lands, and in eastern Europe and the Balkans too. One of these, as we know, was *liberalism*. This was, in twentieth-century terms, the philosophical-ideological expression of the right of *individual self-determination*, defended in Enlightenment thought by such luminaries as John Locke and Immanuel Kant. This right legitimized the claim, for the rationally educated and propertied middle classes if not for "the people" as a whole, to self-government, as opposed to the subject status to which longstanding religiously sanctioned social-political hierarchies of the pre-1789 Old Regime relegated them.

Divine-right monarchy had invoked the Christian doctrine of original sin to justify benevolent Christian monarchy ruling uncontested over imperfect and potentially unruly society. Liberalism viewed humanity, endowed by nature with reason and an inclination to moral benevolence, as potentially perfectible, given institutions necessary to restrain the inborn, but not indomitable, instinct for aggression and self-aggrandizement. Advanced liberals accepted that *democracy* would eventually arise as enlightened education fitted the common people for the rights and duties of self-government. But many other liberals preferred a political constitution confining parliamentary power to their own propertied ranks, seeing democracy as a turbulent and irrational challenge to ordered progress and the rule of law.

The other force that the French Revolution raised to previously unimagined potency in central and eastern Europe was *nationalism*. This was the philosophical-ideological expression of the right, as it was later known, of

FIGURE 11.1. THE MAGNATES' STRONGHOLDS
Pictured here, in the present day, is the provincial settlement of Telč, in the Czech Republic's Bohemian heartland, centered on a grand northern Renaissance palace (visible on the right) with architecturally matching churches and subordinate town. It was a sixteenth-century foundation of Czech aristocrats, seigneurial masters of a surrounding countryside that yielded them rich feudal rents. Although villagers and townspeople, like local churchmen, possessed chartered rights, their magnatial overlords exerted near-irresistible power over local judiciary and police. The lake was one of the commercial fisheries for which Bohemia was renowned. Among many churchly counterparts to such aristocratic bastions as Telč was the still-today resplendent Benedictine Abbey of Melk, on the Danube upstream from Vienna, a jewel of Baroque architecture and religiosity, and of centuries-old ecclesiastical wealth.
Source: http://commons.wikimedia.org/wiki/File:Tel%C4%8D.jpg.

national self-determination. It was to be exercised by the *nation* or *ethno-cultural community* exhibiting collective will to political self-determination (ideally, in a sovereign state of its own), based on *consciousness* of communal or *national identity* and on common interests and solidarity. It was usually a highly contentious question how such nations could and should be defined. Did they, in 1789 or even in 1815, really exist? Or would nationalists, inspired by such ideas, need to "create" or even "invent" them through nationalist propaganda and mass mobilization?

Habsburg Austria was both a far-flung multinational monarchy and, with Prussia, one of the two dominant German power-states. Its fate would prove to be inextricably entwined with – indeed tragically ensnarled in – German nationalism. We have seen how, after Napoleon's final defeat in 1815, the Habsburg monarchy, under the leadership of Austrian Chancellor Klemens

FIGURE 11.2. ALLEGORIZING, "AWAKENING," AND "INVENTING" THE NATION

Friedrich Overbeck (1789–1869) painted this allegory of "Italia and Germania" in 1828. Chief among the prominent German artists comprising the "Nazarene school" – who like the British pre-Raphaelites venerated both medieval Christianity and Renaissance art – Overbeck sought here not to exemplify emergent nationalism, but rather to honor friendship. Yet his picture offers one of the finest embodiments of female Germania, an inspiring symbol for nationalists, while also evoking national greatness in the past.

Contemporary with the conservative Overbeck, and influential on European scale, was the Genoese Italian Giuseppe Mazzini (1805–1872), advocate from the 1830s, in west European exile, of a revolutionary-democratic "Europe of Its Peoples," including "Young Italy," "Young Germany," and other nationally divided or conquered peoples, easily imaginable in such images as Overbeck's. In Bohemia, František Pálacký (1798–1876) fathered the master narrative of Czech national history as an epic struggle of a culturally and linguistically subjugated, democratically minded small Slavic people against Habsburg German imperialist-absolutist domination. His countryman Karel Havlíček (1821–1856) popularized the Czech cause in journalism, invoking the contemporary Catholic Irish nationalist movement against Protestant England as model. Sándor Petöfi (1821–1849), a gifted Hungarian poet, democratic idealist, and critic of conservative and Habsburg loyalist tendencies among the Hungarian nobility, died in 1849 fighting Austrians and Russians for Hungarian independence. Thus did intellectuals construct, sometimes at the cost of their lives, the nineteenth century's new politically conscious nations and strive to mobilize common folk in their name.

Source: Bildarchiv Preussischer Kulturbesitz/Art Resource, NY.

von Metternich (in high office between 1809 and 1848), set its face against both liberalism and nationalism.

Instead, Metternich's regime championed ultraconservative restoration and rigid upholding of aristocratic privilege and religiously sanctioned dynastic rights. Modern European conservatism arose in these years, in dialectical opposition to liberalism and populist-hued nationalism. It championed "organically evolved" social and political structures so as to perpetuate monarchical and aristocratic power, invoking Christianity's blessings. In 1815 contemporaries spoke of restoration of the "alliance of throne and altar." Yet equally important were conservative reassertion of the nobility's political and social privileges and opposition to bourgeois empowerment and the liberal causes accompanying it.

But as public education – along with early industrialism and advance of capitalist commerce and finance – strengthened the Habsburg monarchy's middle classes, pressure arose, especially among German-speakers, to replace bureaucratic absolutism with constitutional and parliamentary government. Even many among the German-speaking landed nobility grew critical of repressive "Metternichean" bureaucracy, reinforced by policemen and soldiers. Similarly, the emergent educated and propertied elements among the *non-German* subject peoples began embracing nationalist and liberal doctrines to reduce the weight on them of the Viennese regime and to gain *home rule* through the establishment of decentralized regional structures of more or less democratic self-government.

In 1848, revolution erupted in the Austrian monarchy. Although eventually crushed by the Habsburg army, with some help in Hungary from the Russian Tsar's soldiers, this convulsion's aftershocks reverberated throughout imperial Austria's final era. From 1848 to 1918 the crucial question was how the monarchy's continuation as a dynastically based Great Power could be reconciled with its subject nationalities' increasingly vocal and broad-based demands for individual and communal voice.

The Revolution of 1848

German Austrians precipitated this revolt against the Metternichean regime, forcing the aged chancellor to flee into exile. In the forefront were educated professionals, intellectuals and students, and politicized artisans and villagers seeking constitutional parliamentary government and Austrian engagement in German national unification. Influential too were early industrialists, other businessmen, and modernizing, market-engaged large estate owners, who sought a scaled-down, less bureaucratic government more responsive to their interests, and who too were interested in national unification. The 1848 revolution also inspired nationalist elements among the non-German peoples in the empire to advance demands (at minimum) for local self-government and use of their language in education and public life.

Revolutionary outbreaks in France and Italy sparked the Viennese revolution of March 1848. As it spread through the Habsburg lands, five issues came to the fore:

- the movement among German liberals and democrats for constitutional government within the Habsburg monarchy;
- the Habsburg lands' participation in the movement for national unification, led by the newly elected all-German National Assembly in the city of Frankfurt;
- the non-Germans' drive for home rule within the Habsburg Empire;
- rebellion in Austria's Italian provinces, seeking breakaway to join a newly projected united Italian national state;
- revolt in Hungary, ending in war against Habsburg rule, aiming to establish an independent, politically liberalized (but nationally exclusive) Hungarian state.

Although the monarchical regime reluctantly took initial steps toward adopting constitutional government and granting autonomy to the non-German peoples, it bridled at the Germany-wide national movement, despite its many Austrian German supporters. Its success would have established a "large Germany" (*Grossdeutschland*), including the Habsburg German (and Czech and Slovenian) lands, subject, even if within a federal system, to a central government outside Austria in Frankfurt.

In Hungary the gentry-born lawyer-politican Lajos Kossuth (1804–1892) emerged as liberal-nationalist leader. He rallied the Hungarian intelligentsia and lower nobility against conservative, pro-Habsburg loyalists. He sought also backing among propertied commoners, but shied away from land reform favoring the multitudinous rural laborers, and championed Hungarian rule against the non-Hungarian minorities in the historic Hungarian kingdom. (In post-revolutionary exile, he embraced a more democratic and multiethnic program for a hoped-for independent Hungary of the future.)

The Italian and Hungarian revolts seemed to demonstrate that nationalism among the Habsburgs' non-German subjects, given free rein, would necessarily lead to separatist movements for national independence. In September–October 1848, the monarchical regime in Vienna turned its army against the revolutionaries, and by summer 1849 had defeated all challenges, including the Italian and Hungarian insurrections. The various rebellions and reform movements in the Habsburg lands could not combine to defeat the monarchical counterrevolution.

Meanwhile, moderate nationalists and liberals had drafted, at a newly elected Austrian Constituent Assembly seated at Kremsier/Kroměříž (in Bohemian Moravia), a monarchy-wide charter (the "Kremsier Constitution"). This aimed to provide federally delineated local home rule for the various nationalities, together with a central parliament for the whole Austrian Habsburg realm. But this did not satisfy exclusivist nationalists in any camp, while it decentralized and weakened monarchical power too much for the crown to

FIGURE 11.3. 1848 REVOLUTION: STUDENTS IN ARMS
The 1848 revolution in varying degrees mobilized all social classes, but students and other politicized intellectuals figured more prominently in it than in earlier European revolutions. Vienna especially witnessed bloody fighting, in which the popular Frankfurt Assembly Democrat Robert Blum took part, suffering execution at counterrevolutionary hands – a fate that also befell prominent leaders of the Hungarian revolt of 1848–1849.
  This photograph displays Italian (Lombard) nationalist revolutionaries in 1848, celebrating (some in captured caps) a victory over Habsburg troops. Their self-presentation marks them as middle-class students, evidently under a teacher's leadership. Austrian painter Franz Scham's 1848 depiction of the well-dressed, pipe-smoking, arms-bearing student legion at Vienna University presents a similar scene.
Source: provenance unknown.

accept. Nor were delegates from Hungary – not even moderates willing to see Hungary remain within the Habsburg state – engaged in its drafting.

The 1867 Compromise

The imperial government's conservative and bureaucratic "neo-absolutism" of the 1850s broke down because of (1) military weakness, evident in Austrian defeats in the 1859 war for Italian unification and in the Austro-Prussian war of 1866; (2) the rising influence in the monarchy of oppositional liberalism among the Austrian German educated and propertied classes; and (3) the impossibility of governing the kingdom of Hungary against the landed gentry's militant and concerted, if now nonviolent, resistance.

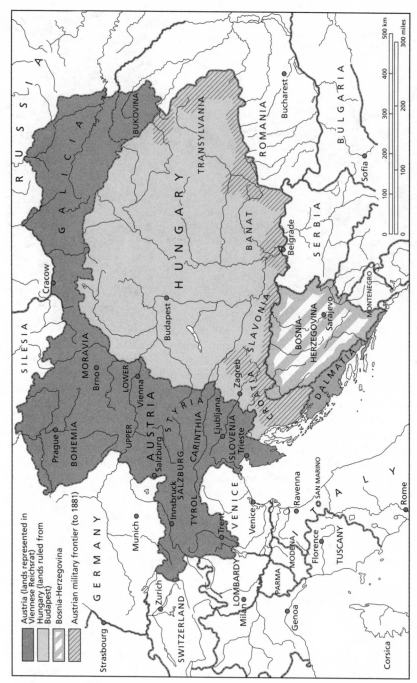

Austria (lands represented in Viennese Reichsrat)

Hungary (lands ruled from Budapest)

Bosnia-Herzegovina

Austrian military frontier (to 1881)

RUSSIA

GERMANY

SWITZERLAND

Strasbourg

Zurich

Munich

Innsbruck
TYROL

SALZBURG
Salzburg

UPPER

LOWER

Vienna

AUSTRIA

Brno
MORAVIA

Prague
BOHEMIA

SILESIA

Cracow
GALICIA

BUKOVINA

HUNGARY

Budapest

TRANSYLVANIA

BANAT

ROMANIA

Bucharest

STYRIA

CARINTHIA

Ljubljana

SLOVENIA

Trieste

Zagreb

CROATIA SLAVONIA

Belgrade

SERBIA

BULGARIA

Sofia

BOSNIA-HERZEGOVINA

Sarajevo

MONTENEGRO

DALMATIA

Trent

VENICE

Venice

Ravenna

SAN MARINO

MODENA

PARMA

LOMBARDY

Milan

Genoa

Florence

TUSCANY

ITALY

Rome

Corsica

500 km

300 miles

400

300

200

200

100

100

0

0

MAP 11.2. AUSTRIA-HUNGARY IN 1914

Seeking escape from these dilemmas, the regime in 1867 negotiated a compromise (*Ausgleich*) with the two strongest forces in the monarchy: the German liberals in the western half ("Austria"), and the Hungarian nobility in the eastern half ("Hungary"). This dramatic and fateful constitutional restructuring established parliamentary systems in both halves while retaining several common imperial institutions. These comprised – apart from the Habsburg dynasty itself, embodied since 1848 in Emperor Franz Joseph (1830–1916) – the army, the imperially directed diplomatic apparatus as single foreign-policy source, and a council formulating common, periodically renegotiated tariffs regulating both the Austrian and Hungarian economies. Thus emerged the Habsburg state in its final character as the "Austro-Hungarian monarchy" or, in shorthand, "Austria-Hungary."

The Monarchy's "Austrian Half," 1867–1914

Here the crucial trend was toward widening the socially elitist, middle-class liberal political system created in 1867, centered on the parliament in Vienna (*Reichsrat*), so as to give political voice to the German lower middle classes,

---

MAP 11.2. *(continued)* Spanning 676,615 square kilometers (261,242 square miles), the Habsburg monarchy in 1914 was Europe's second largest state (after the Russian empire) and, with some 52 million inhabitants, the third most populous (after Imperial Russia and Germany). The "Austrian half," as it emerged from the 1867 Compromise, had – apart from representation of its component parts in the Viennese parliament – no common territorial identity. From the Austrian German viewpoint, it figured sometimes as "*Cisleithania*," or "the lands on this side of the Leitha river" (forming part of the historic boundary between Austria and Hungary). The "Hungarian half" was seldom known, even in German, as *Transleithania*, but figured officially instead as the "lands of the crown of St. Stephen," royal medieval founder of Christian Hungary. The Habsburg army long administered the lengthy military frontier zone running from Croatia to Transylvania, in which Christian peasant colonists of many nationalities served as soldiers guarding against incursions of the Ottoman armies. Despite its predominantly non-Hungarian ethnic-linguistic character, it passed under Hungarian rule in 1881. In 1867 Transylvania – historically autonomous from the Hungarian kingdom – joined the new self-governing Hungarian state at the will of the Magyar (i.e., Hungarian) nobility that had for long centuries dominated the land, in which Romanian villagers formed the demographic majority, alongside a considerable German ("Saxon") minority, strong especially in the towns. Bosnia and its sub-component Herzegovina, since their occupation in 1878 by the Habsburg army, were administered as a joint Austro-Hungarian "condominium" under the empire's Finance Ministry until, after formal annexation in 1908, the province received a civilian governor and representative assembly. Here Orthodox Serbs and Slavic-speaking Muslims lived in roughly equal numbers, with Catholic Croats comprising an additional 20 percent. The imperial authorities, while pursuing Bosnia's economic modernization with some success, favored the historically dominant Muslim landowning elite, preserving a rent-based agrarian structure to the Christian villagers' disadvantage and sanctioning – alone among European states – the teaching of Islam in public schools to Muslim children.

FIGURE 11.4. FRANZ JOSEPH (1830–1916), THE LATE HABSBURG MONARCHY'S EMBOD-
IMENT

Here, in 1889 Berlin, the Austrian Kaiser (on the right), crisply saluting, meets his
Imperial German counterpart, the newly regnant William II. In this photograph, the
young German Kaiser seems not yet to have mastered the rigid protocol to which Franz
Joseph religiously adhered. Feather- and eagle-helmeted Guards officers surround them.
Enthroned in 1848 at age eighteen by the revolution-beleaguered government, Franz
Joseph – disciplined, pious, unimaginative – ruled so long (sixty-eight years) that many
came to believe (not, as it happened, altogether wrongly) that his life and the monarchy's
would be coterminous. Later, wits nostalgic for the vanished monarchy said of him: he
made but one mistake – to die.

The emperor cultivated the dynasty's close association with Catholicism, sturdily
parading even in old age with his military entourage in annual Corpus Christi proces-
sions: a 1908 photograph showed him accompanied by a dashing Hungarian guard officer feudally shouldering a panther-skin. He had long stood at the center of a widespread

villagers, and industrial workers as well as to non-German peoples (principally Czechs, Slovenes, Italians, Ukrainians, and Poles), most of whose populations were also commoners (although a numerous and influential Polish nobility dominated the province of Galicia). By stages, notably in 1882 and 1905–1907, such enfranchisement (for male citizens only) occurred, although parliamentary majorities still faced imperially appointed Austrian-half cabinets with strong executive powers. But, as in Bismarck's Germany, these could not effectively govern without majority backing in parliament.

These steps toward the monarchy's institutional democratization led also to a rapid, post-1867 political and nationalist mobilization among all the various peoples of the "Austrian half." Above all, this pitted the Germans in Czech-majority Bohemia and Moravia and in the Slovene-majority southeastern Alpine provinces, who were previously the politically most influential, best educated, and wealthiest linguistic group, against their Slavic-speaking neighbors' superior numbers and heightening national zeal.

In the self-governing Crownland of Galicia, also represented in the Viennese Reichsrat, the Polish nobility ruled to their own advantage in an oligarchical, semi-parliamentarized system over a large, disadvantaged, and increasingly dissatisfied and restive population of Polish and Ukrainian villagers, while a numerous Jewish population swayed between Austrian German loyalties, alliances with the Polish upper classes, religious separatism, and Zionism. Lacking a powerful local German presence, the monarchy's control in Galicia, based on military garrisons and the protection it offered the Polish nobility, would in wartime prove precarious.

This state of affairs in the "Austrian half" triggered, beginning in the 1880s, the spread of aggressive-defensive, populist, right-wing and antiliberal nationalism among many Austro-Germans. It found expression in the Christian Social Party: patronized by the Catholic Church, anti-socialist, loyal to the monarchy, anti-Semitic, and advocate – especially in multiethnic Vienna – of primacy of the Germans and their language. Under Vienna's charismatic mayor Karl Lueger (in office between 1897 and 1910) the Christian Socials gained imposing strength.

Their rivals, organized in the German-National/Pan-German (*Alldeutsche*) movement, were disillusioned with the multinational monarchy and, at their

---

FIGURE 11.4 *(continued)* culture of popular royalism, among whose manifestations were family portraits sold as popular lithographs, along with such naive paintings, suitable for hanging in farmhouse parlors, as one of the emperor and his consort Elisabeth of Bavaria in folk costume, enjoying an outing on an alpine lake. Tragedy slowly enveloped him: in 1889 his only son and heir died with his wife in a double-suicide, while in 1898 Franz Joseph's own consort, empress Elisabeth, perished by an anarchist assassin's dagger. In June 1914 his nephew and designated successor Franz Ferdinand fell, with his wife, in the Bosnian capital Sarajevo to an anti-Habsburg Serbian nationalist's bullets.
Source: Bildarchiv Preussischer Kulturbesitz/Art Resource, NY.

most embittered, interested in somehow fusing its western half with Berlin-centered Imperial Germany. In day-to-day Austrian politics they came to stand for noisy and harsh anti-Semitism, anti-Slavism, and (to their disadvantage) anticlericalism directed against the Catholic Church. Meanwhile, among German industrial workers a socialist movement – the Social Democratic Workers Party – arose that strove to empower the lower classes at the propertied elites' expense, further dividing the Austrian German population and provoking middle-class nationalist antagonism. In 1911 the Socialists commanded the largest Reichsrat delegation, prefiguring the German Social Democrats' attainment in 1912 of the same honor in Berlin's Reichstag.

For Franz Joseph's government, the great question after the 1870s was whether to relegate the Austro-German liberals to minority status, so as to patch together a coalition within the monarchy's western half of pro-government support from among the non-German parties. These, as the emperor's advisers reckoned, would be joined by reliably cooperative German-speaking Catholic conservatives. The socially prominent and culturally influential liberals – the government's partners in the 1867 Compromise – found themselves, to their embitterment, driven after 1879 into ever-weakening opposition.

Such a post-liberal, multinational governing strategy entailed accepting the German language's reduction in the public sphere and educational system outside German-majority areas to near-equal status with the locally prevalent non-German language. The government's attempts to move in this direction, especially in the years of Prime Minister Eduard Taaffe's "Iron Ring" coalition (1879–1893), provoked powerful German nationalist protests, forcing Taaffe to retreat. This in turn embittered the non-Germans, especially Czech nationalists, among whom faith faltered in the idea that the Habsburg regime could become a nationally neutral system in which non-Germans might attain equal rights with Germans.

The "Hungarian Half," 1867–1914

The basic problem in this far-flung assemblage of lands was that the constitutional system created in 1867, centered on a separate parliament in Budapest, was ultraoligarchical, representing only 6.5 percent of the multinational Hungarian kingdom's population. This was the result of an electoral property qualification that effectively confined the vote to ethnic Hungarian – that is, to employ the Hungarians' word for themselves, Magyar – noble landowners and wealthy professionals. The Magyar commoners, along with the vast majority of the demographically numerous non-Hungarian peoples (Romanians, Slovaks, Croats and Serbs), found themselves excluded from political life. Political crisis rocked the years between 1905 and 1910, when Franz Joseph's ministers threatened, against elemental Magyar upper-class interests, to introduce universal male suffrage in the "Hungarian half" (as occurred in 1905 in the "Austrian half"). This chastened hardline anti-Viennese nationalists and

(a)

FIGURE 11.5. HABSBURG GERMANS: RULING NATIONALITY, OR BELEAGURED MINORITY?
(a) A contemporary photograph of unknown provenance, capturing a pre-1914 scene
from Prague's fashionable Kuchelbad racecourse. The foregrounded men are members
of the Bohemian magnate noble family, the Lobkowitzes, in whom Czech and German
identity swam together. The women include a Habsburg archduchess. On such a plane
of social and political privilege, nationalist exclusivity – both in these circles and among
German Austria's aristocracy (and conservative nobles in Polish Galicia as well) – yielded
to solidarity in defense of upper-class interests and the Habsburg monarchy's survival.
(b) Artist Wilhelm Gause's 1904 celebratory painting of Karl Lueger (1844–1910),
leader of the German nationalist, anti-Semitic but also Habsburg-loyal Christian Social
Party and powerful mayor of Vienna (1897–1910). Sunday-garbed members of Vienna's
lower middle-class – the Christian Socials' main constituency – cheer Lueger as he
rides through Prater Park. Modestly clothed workers also pay their respects. Gause
insightfully presents Lueger as a bourgeois counter-emperor. His followers had shifted
their psychological attachment away from feudal-aristocratic Habsburg tradition to
a representative of contemporary urbanized middle-class society sworn to defend his
constituents against proletarian and multicultural democracy. Franz Joseph, recognizing

(b)

FIGURE 11.5 *(continued)* Lueger's symbolic challenge, had initially vetoed the Christian Social leader's installation as Viennese mayor, but in face of Lueger's popularity he was obliged to give way. (c) A well-dressed farmer from Austria's Waldviertel district, signaling his discontent with Habsburg rule, smokes a pipe bearing the likeness of Georg Ritter von Schönerer (1842–1921). Lueger's rival in Austrian German politics, Schönerer was leader of the antiliberal, anti-Semitic, and anti-Catholic German-Nationalist (Pan-German) movement. Political posters showed him straddling the Imperial German and Austrian border, signaling his advocacy of a united *Grossdeutschland*.

Emblematic too of the late Habsburg monarchy was Victor Adler (1852–1918), of German-Jewish parentage, who embraced and led Austrian Social Democracy from its 1889 foundation in the belief that it could overcome class and nationality conflict through a program of political democratization and cultural ennoblement in the spirit of nineteenth-century German high culture. It came as a shock to him and like-minded German-speaking colleagues when, after the turn of the century, Czech and other non-German socialists embraced nationally self-centered programs of their own.

Source: (a) provenance unknown; (b) Artothek; (c) Österreichische Nationalbibliothek.

returned the oligarchical system in Budapest to Habsburg-loyalist hands until the monarchy's fall in 1918.

The dilemmas were that, first, the Magyar-speakers were a minority in the Hungarian kingdom as a whole and, second, the Hungarian elite faced a population of common people among whom, as time passed, interest sparked in worker unionization and land reform at the great estate-owners' expense. To democratize the franchise would likely lead to overthrow of the Magyar elites'

(c)

FIGURE 11.5 *(continued)*

privileges, as well as to defeat of the upper-class Hungarian nationalists' project of linguistic and ideological Magyarization (that is, Hungarianization) of the entire kingdom.

While, among the Hungarian elite, the Liberal Party advocated continued union with the Habsburg monarchy, the more radical Magyar nationalists gathered in the Independence Party dreamed of recovering national sovereignty. Meanwhile, the non-Hungarian national movements, especially among Serbs, Croats, and Romanians, reacted with alienation and hostility to policies of linguistic Magyarization in the schools and public administration, and to their exclusion from parliamentary representation. Extremists among them veered ever more toward ideas of national breakaway, taking with them the lands in which they formed an ethnographic majority – even if along their borders such lands, densely populated by national minorities, were hotly disputed.

The Habsburg monarchy's *South Slavs* (Serbs, Croatians, Slovenes) lived divided between the Austrian lands, the kingdom of Hungary, and Bosnia-Herzegovina (a formerly Ottoman Turkish Balkan province which Austria occupied in 1878 and annexed in 1908). It seemed that the 1867 Austro-Hungarian compromise doomed them to disunity and voicelessness (although Slovene prospects for local home rule in the "Austrian half" were not hopeless and the Croatian upper classes enjoyed relatively privileged status in Hungary and Austrian-administered Dalmatia). Some strenuous nationalists advocated breakaway from the multinational monarchy and formation of an independent South Slavic (that is, "Yugoslav") state, although how interests of Serbs, Croats, Slovenes, Montenegrins, and other Balkan Slavic people could be balanced within it remained murky and contentious.

The prospective heir to Franz Joseph's throne, Crown Prince Archduke Franz Ferdinand, associated himself with the idea of reorganizing the monarchy on a "trialist" (as opposed to German-Hungarian "dualist") basis, so as to bring his future South Slavic subjects together in a new and separate crownland. This scheme, which aimed to win South Slavic minds and hearts for the Habsburgs, only hardened the determination of advocates of resistance and revolt, including the Bosnian Serb nationalist whose assassination in June 1914 of the Archduke and his consort in Bosnia's capital city of Sarajevo plunged the monarchy into terminal crisis.

On War's Eve

In the "Austrian half," the imperial government ruled from 1893 to 1914 ever more often by emergency decree independent of the parliamentary Reichsrat, which was paralyzed by bitter quarrels among German and non-German delegations, and by deepening disunity among Germans themselves. Franz Joseph's ministers could neither abandon German interests nor militantly uphold them. The Austro-German Socialists, along with most other populist and democratic parties among the non-German peoples, favored equal rights for all national groups. Whether they could have lived amicably under greater egalitarianism, despite various knotty linguistic questions as well as socioeconomic and cultural disparities and resentments, was never put to reality's test, and is doubtful.

In the "Hungarian half" the imperial authorities, wary of Magyar nationalism, supported the conservative Hungarian elite (the Liberals) in their oligarchical domination, even though this alienated all other parties there. But taking real steps toward political democratization risked provoking nationalist rebellion and social revolution.

Franz Joseph's imperial regime was reluctant to relax its sovereign grip on the monarchy's lands. His dynasty was closely tied to the interests of conservative aristocrats and landowners throughout his realm, as well as to the far-flung and multiethnic Catholic Church. His government could not break out of its circle of privilege to carry political and social reform through to a point that might possibly have satisfied the non-German peoples. Yet the forces favoring monarchy-wide plebeian democracy were neither sufficiently strong nor united to impose their demands.

In July 1914 political deadlock and rising nationalist agitation gripped Austria-Hungary. To blame the neighboring independent Serbian state's government in Belgrade for the assassinations in Sarajevo and punish it diplomatically or militarily seemed likely, in the regime's eyes, to restore its wounded credibility and demonstrate to radical nationalists throughout the Habsburg lands that it would not tolerate moves toward political violence or territorial dissolution. Owing to Imperial Germany's support of Vienna's policy (for reasons of its own), Franz Joseph's ministers took the risk of goading Russia into coming to its Serbian ally's rescue. Germany countered with army mobilization, activating French and English commitments, sealed in 1904–1907, to join Russia should Germany appear to provoke war. By this chain-reaction the European-wide inferno exploded, so weakening the Habsburg monarchy that by 1918 its non-German subject nationalities could break away into the idealized freedom of national self-determination extolled, among others, by American President Woodrow Wilson. What remained was an Austria that did not recognize itself.

Appendix: Linguistic Communities in the Habsburg Monarchy, According to the Censuses of 1910

These censuses were not without political bias. The following figures are only approximate. Language did not rigidly determine national consciousness or political loyalty. Yet distinctive language groups widely figured in the nationalist imagination as existing or potential nations.

TABLE 11.1. *Linguistic Groups, 1910: the "Austrian Half" of the Habsburg monarchy (i.e., the lands represented in the Viennese parliament* [Reichsrat], *as determined by the Compromise of 1867)*

1.	Christian German-speakers	8.5 million	29.7%
2.	Jews (mainly German-speakers)	1.5	5.2
3.	Czech	6.4	22.5
4.	Polish	5.0	17.5
5.	Ukrainian	3.5	12.2
6.	Slovene	1.3	4.5
7.	Croatian (mainly in Dalmatia)	0.8	2.8
8.	Italian	0.8	2.8
9.	Others, including Sinti/Roma (Gypsies)	0.8	2.8
Sub-Total		*28.6 million*	*100.0%*

TABLE 11.2. *Linguistic Groups, 1910: The "Hungarian Half" of the Habsburg monarchy (i.e., the lands of the Kingdom of Hungary, as defined in the Compromise of 1867)*

1. Christian Hungarian-speakers	9.4 million	46.5%
2. Hungarian-speaking Jews	0.5	2.5
3. German	1.9	9.4
4. Romanian	3.1	15.3
5. Slovak	1.9	9.4
6. Croatian	1.8	8.9
7. Serbian	1.1	5.5
8. Ukrainian	0.5	2.5
Sub-Total	20.2 *million*	100.0%

III. Bosnia-Herzegovina (occupied, 1878; annexed, 1908)

1. Christian and Muslim speakers of Slavic languages	1.7 million	95.0
2. Others	0.1	5.0
Sub-Total	1.8 *million*	100.0%

IV. Total, I-III, above: 50.5 million

among whom were speakers of:		
a. German (Christians and Jews)	11.9	23.5%
b. Hungarian (Christians and Jews)	9.9	19.6
c. Czech	6.4	12.7
d. South Slavic (Croatian, Serbian, Slovenian)	6.7	13.3
e. Polish	5.0	9.9
f. Ukrainian	4.0	7.9
g. Romanian	3.0	5.9
h. Slovak	1.9	3.7
i. Other languages	1.7	3.5
Total	50.5 million	100.0

12

"German Citizens of Jewish Faith" (*deutsche Staatsbürger jüdischen Glaubens*)

Jews, Germans, German Jews, 1789–1914

Jewish Life and Christian-Jewish Relations Before the Modern Era

After conquest by Rome, the ancient Hebrews lived in dispersion in their rulers' empire. The earliest Jewish settlements in the German lands followed Roman expansion to the Rhine frontier. From Christianized medieval Germany, Jewish migrants moved eastward into Bohemia and Poland. Long residence in Germany led to the local language's adoption in daily life. It developed, under the sacred and scholarly Hebrew language's influence and in conditions of social segregation, into a distinctive form of German known among modern scholars as Judeo-German or western Yiddish (from the German word for "Jewish"). This in turn, once transplanted to eastern Europe, metamorphosed into Slavic-influenced eastern Yiddish, eventually spoken by the millionfold Jewish population there. When printed, Yiddish employed the Hebrew alphabet, making it inaccessible to Christian readers. Because of their language and northern residence, the Jews of medieval and early modern central Europe figured on the larger Jewish landscape as Ashkenazic ("German"), distinct from Mediterranean Sephardic ("Spanish") Jews, who spoke Ladino, a form of Spanish, and from other Jewish cultures of the Middle East and north Africa.

Before 1789, Jews could legally reside in the German lands only in religious communities possessing chartered privileges issued by Christian princely or ecclesiastical authorities. In return, Jewish communities paid additional, separate taxes. The German Jewish population was numerous in a few regions, but overall it was small. By the late eighteenth century, it probably numbered around 50,000. The partitions of Poland (1772–1795) bequeathed to Prussia and Austria sizeable and largely unwanted Jewish populations. Frederick the Great's government sought, with some success, to chase the poorest Jews away, but nonetheless annexation of the once-Polish provinces expanded Germany's Jewish population greatly.

In 1914, after rapid nineteenth-century population growth, the German Jews (self-defined by religion) still amounted to only about 1 percent of the Imperial

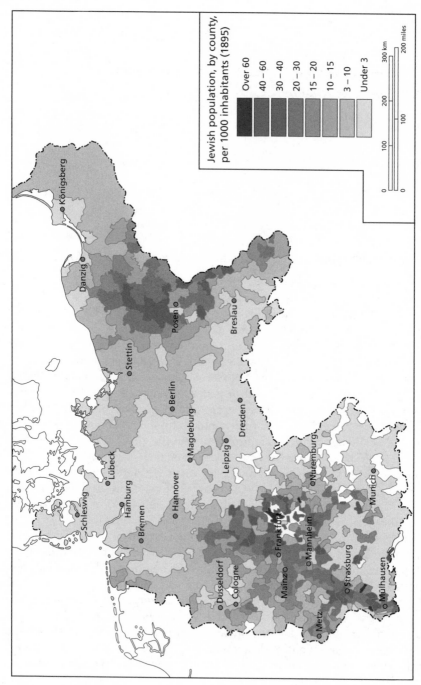

MAP 12.1. DISTRIBUTION OF THE JEWISH POPULATION, DEFINED BY RELIGIOUS SELF-IDENTIFICATION, IN IMPERIAL GERMANY, 1895

Jewish population, by county,
per 1000 inhabitants (1895)

Over 60
40 – 60
30 – 40
20 – 30
15 – 20
10 – 15
3 – 10
Under 3

German population, or about 600,000 people. The Habsburg monarchy was home to two million and more Jews speaking various vernaculars, mainly German, Hungarian, Polish, Czech, and Yiddish. In Austrian Galicia and in the Russian-annexed lands of the historic Polish Commonwealth there resided Europe's absolutely and relatively largest Jewish population. When Poland reemerged in 1918 as an independent state, every tenth inhabitant was Jewish: altogether, nearly three million people, with millions more living farther east in Lithuania, Belarus, Ukraine and other formerly or still Russian-ruled lands, as well as in Russia itself. In these lands, Yiddish predominated, although many also spoke Russian or Polish, or both, while German commanded high esteem as a language of advanced western culture.

Premodern Jewish settlements – sometimes rural, but mainly urban (if only in small towns) – possessed their own communal organs and leadership. A gulf separated these, as in other countries, from their Christian coresidents' institutions. Jews were absent from Christian town councils and guilds. In Christian-Jewish conflicts and other serious matters, the Jews' official for external affairs, the *shtadlan*, dealt directly with the Christian authorities. Among Jews themselves, rabbis – men learned in Jewish theology and law – conducted courts, led councils of elders upholding Judaic law, and presided over religious services.

The Jewish and Christian worlds, while bordering each other, possessed no institutional integration. Nor were Jews supposed, in economic life, to compete directly with Christian neighbors. They were confined to the commercial-financial sector: pawn-brokering and other money-lending operations; currency exchange and, sometimes, minting of money; urban-rural, wholesale, and long-distance trade. Barred from Christian artisan guilds and merchant corporations, they possessed only the craftsmen their own communities needed and could support. Barred from landownership, they engaged in agriculture – mostly livestock raising and dairying – only to the degree justified by their dietary practices.

Jewish communities supported a narrow *economic* elite of well-to-do merchants and financiers; a modest middle class of artisans and shopkeepers serving

---

MAP 12.1 *(continued)* This map, mirroring official county-level census data, highlights the widespread prevalence of Jewish settlement in two broad regions. In western Germany, Jewish communities, often with medieval roots, were numerous in the lands of Hessen, the Rhineland, the southwestern states, and Alsace-Lorraine. In the east, Jewish life was still vigorous, despite emigration westward in the course of the nineteenth century, in the provinces deriving from or bordering on vanished Poland, that is, in Poznania, West Prussia, and eastern and southern ("Upper") Silesia. Yet by 1895 the largest settlements were in the big cities, including Berlin. While a map such as this cannot properly display large urban populations, it usefully recalls that the Jewish presence was relatively widespread in certain broad regions but not in others. If a map displaying the National Socialist vote at its mid-1932 height were superimposed on this one, it would be evident that Hitlerite sentiment sometimes – as in middle Germany – soared where Jewish settlement was sparse, while it could be relatively weak – as in Catholic south and west Germany – where Jewish communities were well-established.

the internal Jewish market; a numerous lower class of wage workers, peddlers, and folk artists; and an underclass of occasional laborers, smugglers, and beggars. Many men immersed themselves in religious study, and others drifted through life as socially stymied, otherworldly and impractical *Luftmenschen* ("people of the air"), dependent on other people's provisions for them, including – if they were fortunate – industrious and business-like wives.

The Jewish *social-cultural* hierarchy reflected the degree of men's Hebrew-language education in the Judaic Bible and the many-branched literature expounding Jewish law. The most learned became rabbis. The wealthy often patronized and married their daughters into scholarly and rabbinical circles, and gave charitably to sustain the community.

Such a world was self-enclosed and, apart from slow changes in economic life and religious practice, self-replicating. In relations with the outer Christian sphere, Jewish communities depended critically on territorial rulers' goodwill to protect them from sporadic economic and religious hostility of their Christian urban neighbors and creditors among landed nobility and villagers. But Christian princes, sometimes themselves indebted to Jewish financiers, might support movements to expel Jews from their territories. This happened widely in Germany (and elsewhere in western and southern Europe) in the late medieval era, and in the sixteenth century in such lands as Brandenburg. These expulsions, while they might be only temporary, at times (as in the fourteenth century) considerably thinned the German Jewish population, propelling flight eastward to Poland.

After the Thirty Years War, Jewish settlements reconstituted themselves and began again to grow. Absolutist rulers were interested in services of "court Jews" (*Hofjuden*), wealthy businessmen and financiers who often stewarded the early military-bureaucratic states' fiscal and monetary affairs and brokered loans during wartime. Such men might be unpopular among Christians, but they sometimes succeeded in trading their accomplishments for princely protection of humbler co-religionists. Yet so long as Jews lived – in the larger towns – in prescribed and restricted quarters (ghettos), friction arose between them and Christian townspeople over settlement expansion driven by population growth. The ghettos were often cramped and overcrowded, prey to fires that sometimes spread into Christian districts, on occasion igniting anti-Jewish tumults.

In theory, the Christian churches preached toleration of Jewish "error" and rejection of the New Testament. They interpreted the Jews' suffering presence as testimony to Jesus's historical reality. Yet in practice the Christian clergy often denounced Jews as eternally guilty "betrayers of Christ." They supported such popular superstitions as belief in Jewish desecration, especially – as it was alleged – during the Passover holy days, of the Christian Host (communion wafer), or religiously mandated "ritual murder" of Christian children, rumors of which might trigger (and justify) anti-Jewish violence.

Murderous assaults on German Jewish communities accompanied the European-wide crisis climaxing in the bubonic plague of the mid- and later

|פב רב החסיב האון הרב תוינת|
|עין רבי| בין הגדולה בן לכ לכ צל|
|"ל איגר עקיבא|

Rabbi Akiba Eger s. A.

Oberrabbiner, Posen.

(a)

FIGURE 12.1. EARLY MODERN GERMAN (ASHKENAZIC) JEWRY

(a) In this commercially distributed portrait, aimed at pious purchasers, Akiva Eger (1761–1837), eminent and influential Orthodox rabbi, appears in furred finery. Born in Hungary, he held various appointments in Prussia's eastern provinces after 1791 and distinguished himself as one of the Jewish Enlightenment's (or *Haskalah*'s) major opponents. Here he appears as chief rabbi of Poznań/Posen. The inscription reads: "Image of the Great and Pious Rabbi, Master of the Entire Diaspora, Master and Our Teacher, Akiva Eger, May His Memory Be a Blessing."

(b)

FIGURE 12.1 *(continued)*
(b) A photograph, ca. 1865, from the Mohr brothers' studio, displays the recently
built Reform synagogue in the main street of Frankfurt am Main's Jewish quarter,
formerly known as "Jews' Lane" *(Judengasse)* but renamed in honor of the popular
liberal-democratic German-Jewish political writer Ludwig Börne (1786–1837). Before
the 1796 abolition of laws confining Jews to this area, Frankfurt's ghetto had been
one of Europe's most densely populated places. But the Jewish community's advancing
well-being is evident in the bourgeois solidity of the architecture this picture displays.
The synagogue incorporates elements of the Moorish style, recalling Jewish life in
late-medieval Iberia, which nineteenth-century Jewish romanticism celebrated as a
Golden Age. By contrast, Prague's "Old-New" Gothic-style (and Europe's oldest
surviving) synagogue, built ca. 1270, was – and remains – a small and architecturally
undistinguished, peak-roofed, brick-walled and narrow-windowed building (although
the nearby Jewish town hall, built in the 1760s, is a stylish high-towered structure,
whose clock displays Hebrew numbers).

(c)

FIGURE 12.1 *(continued)*
(c) An evocation of 1869 by German-Jewish artist Daniel Oppenheim (1800–1882) of a bar-mitzvah (boy's religious confirmation) ceremony in a west German Jewish household, ca. 1800. The youthful initiate expounds a religious point, while elders listen respectfully and thoughtfully. Literacy in Hebrew and basic understanding of Jewish religious law and literature were expected of reputable males – a tradition favorable, after nineteenth-century Jewish civic emancipation, to launching studious young men into the secular sciences and professions. Oppenheim's scene displays, in the participants' clothing and in house and furnishings, great similarity to German Christian middle-class everyday life.
Source: (a) provenance unknown; (b) Mohr Brothers; (c) The Jewish Museum, NY/Art Resource, NY.

fourteenth century. The religious wars of the fifteenth and sixteen centuries sometimes rained violence down on German Jews, whether individually or communally. The last serious premodern urban riot driven by anti-Jewish animosity occurred in Frankfurt am Main in 1614, but was suppressed, to embittered Jewish satisfaction, by the imperial authorities. Thereafter, through the eighteenth century, communal violence against Jews alone waned in extent and significance, although they might be caught, as civilian Christians also were, in the rapine and plunder of war.

Jews and the Enlightenment

Apart from all conflict, Christians rarely understood or admired Jewish religiosity and learning, even though Calvinists and Protestant sectarians might celebrate the Jews of the Old Testament, as Rembrandt did in many paintings, and as north American colonists sometimes did in their theology and religious self-image. Conversely, the Jews' learned tradition forbade them to take any serious interest in Christian literature or culture, as seventeenth-century Jewish philosopher Baruch Spinoza – expelled from Amsterdam's Jewish community – learned to his dismay.

The European Enlightenment popularized rational humanism and a generalized, universal Deism, regarding all earthly religions as imperfect efforts to grasp the one Supreme Being and his Creation. The idea of religious toleration followed, urging that Jews, especially, should be released from the bonds of discrimination that Christianity had fastened on them. Jewish "emancipation" and civic equality figured among the Enlightenment's battle-cries (mixed with rationalist philosophers' sometimes aggressive criticism of pious traditionalist Jews' alleged "medieval benightedness").

In Germany, the Jewish response found voice in Berlin's Moses Mendelssohn (1729–1786), eminent scholar-philosopher-theologian who fathered the Jewish Enlightenment or, in Hebrew, *Haskalah*. He and his followers advocated that Jews integrate themselves culturally, socially, and politically into the larger German civil society that the Enlightenment was bringing into existence. Jews should educate themselves in contemporary European learning and culture, abandoning Yiddish for the newly refined High German literary language. They should adopt modern European dress and manners. Judaism would remain their religion, practiced among themselves in their own private sphere.

Most German Jews subsequently accepted that Judaism could be regarded as a theological-ethical realm independent of many traditional practices of ritual law, whose abandonment would make integration into German society easier. This perspective gave birth in the early nineteenth century to modern *Reform Judaism*, which gained predominance in the German lands (and in the United States, brought there by German Jewish immigrants). Other, more conservative religious Jews retained observance of much or all of the venerable ritual law, but otherwise integrated themselves into the German social-cultural-political world.

Many historians prefer to describe these changes as Jewish *acculturation* rather than *assimilation*. They did not entail the loss of specifically Jewish identity, but rather its modification so as to enable Jews living in Germany to regard themselves, and to hope that Christians would also view them (in the language of their principal political interest group, founded in 1893), as "German citizens of Jewish faith" (*deutsche Staatsbürger jüdischen Glaubens*).

FIGURE 12.2. EARLY MODERN ANTI-JEWISH TENSIONS AND VIOLENCE

Matthäus Merian's 1628 engraving depicts plundering in Frankfurt's "Jews' Lane" during the Fettmilch Uprising of 1614, in which Christian burghers, acting on religious prejudice, political resentments, and economic rivalry, drove the Jewish community from the city. This was an incident in a larger drama among Christians for power in the city. With backing from Frankfurt's commercial patricians, the German emperor and nearby territorial princes, the Jews gained readmission to Frankfurt, but on terms narrowing the scope of their economic activities.

In the eighteenth century, anti-Jewish animosity often targeted the "court Jews" of the day. "Jud Süss" (Joseph Süss Oppenheimer, 1698–1738) appeared in widely sold broadsheets, depicted in captivity (sometimes seemingly comfortable), at his trial, and at his public execution (with the brutality early modern judicial practice commonly meted out to non-privileged offenders). He was a financier drawn into the high-handed policies of Duke Karl Alexander of Württemberg, whose absolutist-style defiance of the Württemberg Estates delivered Oppenheimer over to anti-Semitism-drenched judicial murder following the duke's death. The case, in which sexual charges figured luridly, was reenacted in a lavishly produced National Socialist film of 1940, propagandizing the idea of centuries-old continuity in German-Jewish antagonism. An earlier "Court Jew," Samuel Oppenheimer (1630–1703), unrelated to the unfortunate Joseph Süss, ably assisted Austrian army commander Prince Eugene of Savoy in financing the Habsburgs' anti-Turkish campaigns. Yet upon his death, the Austrian government repudiated its considerable monetary debt to him.

Source: Matthäus Merian.

Christian Germans were, after all, divided between Catholics and Protestants. German identity should not – indeed, could not – be religion-bound.

Nineteenth-Century "Jewish Emancipation" and Social and Political Integration

Jews' release from discriminatory and oppressive legal restrictions – in other words, proclamation by legislative decree of Jewish citizenship rights and civil equality – occurred first in revolutionary France. It followed in Germany through the Napoleonic Law Code's adoption in the Confederation of the Rhine, the French satellite state organized after 1806 in western Germany. The Prussian Reform Era also launched Jewish emancipation in the 1812 law that conferred citizenship and civil equality on Prussian Jews, provided they educated their children in German, adopted European dress, submitted to military conscription, and otherwise met expectations of bourgeois respectability and acculturation into German society.

These were conditions – regionally varying, as we earlier saw – that restricted Prussian emancipation before 1848 to the Jewish population's higher classes, but between 1848 and 1869 the remaining legal barriers to Jewish civil equality throughout the German and Austrian lands fell away through legislative action. Emancipation figured everywhere as a postulate of political liberalism, which won support from most German Jews. Yet many Jewish religious conservatives had misgivings, accustomed to old-fashioned trust in benevolent Christian monarchs and fearing that liberalism would sap religious zeal.

Emancipation freed Jews to settle where they liked. This led to heavy migration into the burgeoning metropolises: Berlin, Vienna, Frankfurt, Hamburg, Breslau, Prague, Budapest. In 1933, half of Germany's religious Jews and other citizens of Jewish heritage lived in Berlin. The universities likewise opened their doors, and Jewish students qualified for admission in large numbers. Many were attracted to the learned professions: medicine, law, natural science, and humanistic scholarship. By the 1860s and 1870s, public opinion had approvingly learned of numerous notable accomplishments attributable to Jewish-born practitioners in these fields, as also in journalism, theater, and music.

Government, particularly in Prussia, continued to display de facto reluctance to appoint unconverted Jews to positions in the bureaucracy and judiciary, although exceptions were numerous in the south German states and even in Bismarck's Prussia. Many Jews rose in the civil and also military hierarchy of the post-1867 Habsburg monarchy, where their co-religionists figured, in the "Austrian half," as a regime-upholding, loyal pro-German element. In the Hungarian kingdom, the linguistically Magyarized (but commonly also German-speaking) Jewish population supported the pro-Habsburg Hungarian ruling oligarchy.

Frustration over barriers to state employment contributed to a wave of Jewish conversions to Christianity in the pre-1848 years, enabling more than a

FIGURE 12.3. HASKALAH

This popular lithograph reproduces an 1856 painting by German-Jewish artist Daniel Oppenheim. It depicts Moses Mendelssohn (1729–1786 [seated, left]), confronted in 1770 by celebrated Swiss pastor-psychologist J. C. Lavater's aggressive demand that he refute Christianity or convert to it. At Mendelssohn's side, upholding the Jewish thinker's unyielding resistance, is his friend, the philosopher-playwright Lessing, who modeled on Mendelssohn the hero of his 1779 drama, *Nathan the Wise*. Lessing's play treats Christianity, Islam, and Judaism as equal in God's eyes, but also as human creations striving and evolving toward a higher and more universal spiritual truth. Important in advancing Jewish emancipation was scholar and long-time Prussian official Christian Wilhelm Dohm (1751–1820), author, with Mendelssohn's encouragement, of the politically influential work, *On the Civil Improvement of the Jews* (1781), the European Enlightenment's first sustained plea for ending by state action laws and social practices discriminatory to Jews. Dohm argued that the disabilities Christian society imposed by law on Jews sowed prejudice against them. Civil equality (if only achieved in stages) would morally improve both parties and draw them together in civic cooperation. Religion would retreat into the sphere of private social-cultural practice.

few to successfully climb the bureaucratic ladder. Still, the expectation among most Jews, before and after civic emancipation's end in the 1860s, was that advancement in the civil service, even as academics, was difficult, making private-sector careers more attractive. After 1848, conversion slowed, even as religiosity cooled among some of the secularly educated who remained nominally and formally within the Jewish faith's fold.

In the half-century before 1914, Reform Judaism flourished as the principal expression of communal identity and religiosity. Many architecturally impressive synagogues arose embodying it, often built in the neo-Romanesque style, popular in the day, which conjured up the great age of early medieval Germany. Other synagogues displayed a neo-Moorish style, reflecting nineteenth-century Christian and Jewish Romanticism's celebration of Jewish civilization and the coexistence of religious cultures in Muslim-ruled medieval Iberia.

In business, the tendency was to capitalize on centuries-long experience in commerce and banking, including investment banking. There were fewer Jewish industrialists, although some registered successes in light-industrial fields, especially textiles. In heavy industry Jews were more active as financiers and members of boards of directors than as entrepreneurs. Many persisted in retail trade, both as owners and employees.

In Imperial German politics, the Jewish majority voted either for the mostly middle-class National Liberals or Progressives, although in the post-1890 years increasingly large numbers of the Jewish-born, especially among younger salary-earners and educated professionals, backed the rising Social Democratic Party (which recruited a certain middle-class following). Jewish politicians, including parliamentary deputies, were prominent, if not numerous, in all three parties. A similar pattern prevailed in the Austrian lands. Because of their small numbers, Jews never figured as a major collective interest group or political player in Austria-Hungary or in Imperial Germany and its federal states. Yet in urban government, in the kingdom of Prussia and other federal states where political representation was weighted according to taxes paid, the Jewish electorate's well-to-do members wielded much influence and their mostly liberal leaders figured prominently, particularly in the Berlin city government and other major cities. Here they compiled an impressive record of political activism and public service, for which many reaped the reward of local and even regal distinctions, among them honorific official titles and accompanying, proudly worn medals.

FIGURE 12.3 *(continued)*

Enlightenment Reform did not sweep the entire German Jewish community. Samson Raphael Hirsch (1808–1888), chief rabbi of Frankfurt, was father of a vigorous Jewish neo-Orthodoxy, reformed in its liturgy and doctrinal emphases through embrace of nineteenth-century German and European scholarship and culture, including the High German language.

Source: Daniel Oppenheim.

In the late 1890s interest began spreading, especially among restless and discontented middle-class youth, in the secular Zionist movement launched by Austrian journalist Theodor Herzl with his 1896 book, *The Jewish State*. Herzl held that European Jews, considered apart from religion, were a distinct nationality or nation. They needed and deserved a state of their own, preferably in once-biblical Palestine. But it might be found elsewhere (British-ruled Uganda came under discussion), if only to halt the fulsome stream of Jewish emigration from east-central Europe and the Russian Empire to north America and other non-European regions, where secularizing and assimilative forces worked, as it seemed, against Jewish identity's preservation.

The Zionist program was unwelcome and even scandalous to the majority of German-speaking Jews, who clung to the notion they were "German (or Austrian) citizens of Jewish faith," that is, Germans in the same sense as Catholic or Protestant Germans. Before 1914, Zionism in Germany and the Austrian German lands remained a numerically small movement, but it attracted many talented activists, created a high-quality press of its own, and introduced a challenging and unsettling perspective into the Jewish community. In ethnically mixed regions, such as the German-Polish borderlands and Bohemia-Moravia, Zionism's embrace could spare Jews the dilemma of choosing between antagonistic non-Jewish nationalisms, although at the cost of forfeiting the national belonging among Christians that civic emancipation and acculturation promised.

The Dawn of Modern Anti-Semitism

Anti-Semitism, a term referring to modern political ideologies and movements, must be distinguished from centuries-old religiously based *anti-Judaism*, even if this latter attitude usually went hand in glove with harsh anti-Jewish social prejudices and stereotypes. Nevertheless, anti-Judaism drew its strength from Christian antagonism toward the Jewish religion's practice, and often preached love and forgiveness toward Jews, if only they would convert to Christianity. By contrast, anti-Semitism, although many of its nineteenth- and early twentieth-century enthusiasts were conventional (and occasionally fervent) Christians, steered toward *secularization* and even, so far as it merged with newly arising anthropological theories of race, toward would-be or pseudo-*scientization* of anti-Jewish prejudice and antagonism. It aimed to halt or at any rate subordinate religious criticism of Judaism's adherents, which increasingly appeared to the science-minded nineteenth century as parochial and arbitrary, to its own new program opposing the roles in which it cast Jews in modern society. Any worldview stigmatizing an entire ethnic or cultural group as a pernicious actor in human history conjures irrationally with distinctions of essential good and evil that earlier found expression in religious notions of the diabolical and the redemptive. Yet modern anti-Semites have commonly striven to represent their anti-Jewish prejudices as justified by empirical fact.

FIGURE 12.4. JEWISH-BORN NINETEENTH-CENTURY POLITICAL NOTABLES
Pictured here, in a popularly distributed photograph by Ephraim Moses Lilien (recalling
the earlier displayed Akiba Eger's portrait [Figure 12.1]), is short-lived Theodor Herzl
(1860–1904). The Budapest-born Viennese journalist was driven by the sensational,
anti-Semitism-fueled Dreyfus Affair in France, rising ethnic conflict in Austria-Hungary,
and ideological anti-Semitism in Germany to devise a secular-political Zionist program
seeking an independent Jewish national state. He appears here as visionary leader at the
Fifth World Zionist Conference in Basel, 1902. In many Jewish minds his charismatic
figure rekindled the fires of religious messianism, but he also drew heavy criticism from
assimilation-minded German and Austrian Jews and from the rabbinate, many of whom
viewed Jewish return to the Land of Israel as a matter for the divine will alone to decide.
Among notable earlier Jewish-born figures in German politics were Friedrich Julius Stahl
(1802–1861), who converted to Christianity and became a stalwart conservative writer
and Prussian politician, opposing the Enlightenment's Natural Rights philosophy and
defending "Christian monarchy." Eduard Lasker (1829–1884) led Imperial Germany's
National Liberal Party's left wing as legal and constitutional reformer, opposed in

After 1933, National Socialist anti-Semitism assumed increasingly violent form, culminating in mass murder on unprecedented scale. In the Holocaust's aftermath, all pre-1933 anti-Jewish doctrines and movements, both in the German lands and elsewhere in Christendom, stand suspect of having contributed to the enormous tragedy of the National Socialist genocide. Yet large-scale anti-Jewish violence in Germany was, as we have seen, a rarity after the Thirty Years War. The year 1819 witnessed in south Germany the "Hep-Hep" riots (so named after an anti-Jewish battle-cry in mob attacks). These protested Jewish civic emancipation, which in townspeople's eyes portended incursion in their political and economic lives of unwelcome Jewish co-burghers.

Property damage and personal injuries were serious, but these events, suppressed eventually by the authorities, were not murderous. The same holds for anti-Jewish protests of a similar type accompanying the various German revolutions of 1848–1849, although in the eastern provinces the German-Polish nationality conflict of those years triggered anti-Jewish plundering with some loss of Jewish life. In the 1880s and 1890s anti-Jewish demonstrations, including charges of "ritual murder," exploded in a few small towns in the Prussian east and the Rhineland (and in Hungary and Bohemia). But the state police and courts squelched them, and even the right-wing nationalist press, inclined to anti-Semitism, condemned anti-Jewish violence, as did some – but not all – leading anti-Semites.

Ominous violence, when it came, appeared first in eastern Europe. Destructive pogroms, inspired in part by new anti-Semitic ideology linking Jews and anti-tsarist revolutionism, flared locally and sporadically in Ukraine and Russia in 1881–1884, and again in 1903–1906. The number of murdered victims rose into the dozens and hundreds, with the curve peaking in Russia's western and southern provinces during the revolution of 1905. But Germany and Austria before 1914 did not harbor such plunder and bloodshed.

Instead, modern anti-Semitism in the German lands emerged as a diffuse ideology of social and political resentments. The worldwide stock-market crash of 1873 and ensuing economic crisis initiated a wave of business failures and a long era of reduced profits and economic belt-tightening lasting, despite simultaneous if slow cumulative growth, to the mid-1890s. It triggered an anti-Semitic backlash in Germany and Austria, as well as in France and elsewhere, among economically injured or frustrated members of the non-Jewish intelligentsia and middle classes. Industrialization and the laissez-faire economy, which for so long had seemed to promise rapid upward social mobility, now appeared as unpredictable and threatening forces. Business scandals conjured an image

---

FIGURE 12.4 *(continued)* later years by Bismarck. Ludwig Bamberger (1823–1899), National Liberal architect of major banking and currency reforms, broke with Bismarck after 1878. Austrian liberalism counted influential Jewish-born leaders, as did Austrian Social Democracy (notably Victor Adler).
Source: Ephraim Moses Lilien.

FIGURE 12.5. LATE NINETEENTH-CENTURY ANTI-SEMITISM

In 1879 Heinrich von Treitschke (1834–1896), influential historian of the pro-Prussian ("Borussian") and pro-Bismarckian school, ignited a major debate on anti-Semitism. He insisted on German Jews' full assimilation (arguing that assertion of Jewish social and cultural individuality or distinctiveness was undesirable and even harmful). Like other anti-Semites, and many others (including even German Jews), Treitschke objected to the immigration into Germany of "eastern" (or "Polish") Jews, who were commonly contrasted negatively with acculturated German Jews.

The combative philosopher and renegade socialist Eugen Dühring (1833–1921) pioneered and popularized a secularist and materialist, self-styled scientific anti-Semitism based on biological "race theory." In 1878 Adolf Stoecker (1835–1909), Evangelical Protestant minister and longtime Hohenzollern court preacher, launched the Imperial German Christian Social movement. This sought populist mobilization of the laboring classes through anti-Semitic attacks on "big capital" and socialism, but Stoecker's message resonated better in lower-middle-class circles (although electoral success eluded his of capitalism as a murky world of adventurers, swindlers, and manipulators of public trust.

Jewish businessmen and entrepreneurs had, in previous decades, often reaped praise in the non-Jewish press as *benefactors* of society, creating new jobs and wealth by their investments and activities. They now came under fire from anti-Semitic propagandists as scapegoats for the injuries the 1873 crash and its aftermath inflicted, and more generally for the widespread social uprooting of economically weak small property owners – merchants, farmers, craftsmen – that accompanied the industrial revolution. Among university students and graduates, heightened post-1873 competition for jobs in the educated professions and intellectual life fueled anti-Jewish antagonism. In the rapidly expanding ranks of salaried white-collar workers in industry and commerce, and especially in retailing, similar competition, organized by rival employees' unions, arose between Jewish and non-Jewish workers.

In German and Austrian politics, particularly from the 1870s, ideologically inflamed conservatives and nationalists associated both liberalism and socialism with "Jewish interests." Although there were outstanding Jewish or Jewish-born leaders in these camps, the great mass of supporters and activists were of Christian background. Similarly, while the Jewish majority expressed the same cultural preferences as other middle-class Germans, critics and propagandists opposed to the breakthrough of cultural modernism – in art (as in "reality-blurring" Impressionism), music ("dissonant" Atonalism), in literature and the theater (socially "subversive" Realism, or "dreamlike" Symbolism) – sometimes sought to brand it, pointing to various prominent artists and impresarios, as "Jewish."

In Imperial Germany, specifically anti-Semitic political movements and parties – appealing especially to discontented farmers, tradesmen, and workers – displayed some regional strength in the 1880s and 1890s, although in Reichstag elections they never gained more than a few percentage points of all votes casts. More significant was the powerful German Conservative Party's selective incorporation in coded terms – as in attacks on stock exchanges, and on "cultural commercialization" – of anti-Semitic planks into its platform, so

---

FIGURE 12.5 *(continued)* movement). He rose to prominence as the embodiment of traditional Christian-Prussian conservatism fused with an anti-Semitism aiming to deter worker abandonment of the church in favor of socialism, and expressing anti-capitalist resentments. Chapter 15 expands on these themes.

Pictured here is Theodor Mommsen (1817–1903), renowned ancient historian (see Chapter 7), activist liberal, and eloquent opponent of anti-Semitism, photographed in 1848 with historian colleagues (before a bust of Goethe). In 1890 Mommsen joined other non-Jewish notables, mostly liberals of various stripes, in founding the "Association for Defense Against Anti-Semitism" (*Verein zur Abwehr des Antisemitismus*) devoted especially to discrediting anti-Jewish calumnies and ideologies. Mommsen wore long hair – a symbol of his Romantic-era youth – into old age.
Source: Bildarchiv Preussischer Kulturbesitz/Art Resource, NY.

FIGURE 12.6. EMINENT JEWISH BUSINESSMEN IN THE GERMAN EMPIRE

Pictured here in a pre-1914 photograph of unknown provenance is Walter Rathenau (b. 1867), chief entrepreneur in the German electrical industry (head of the technologically advanced, powerful company AEG), influential political adviser to the imperial government, author of widely noticed pessimistic musings on modernity and, after World War I, German foreign minister (assassinated in 1922 by rightist nationalists).

Prominent in an earlier generation was Bethel Henry Strousberg (1823–1884), railway magnate and socially minded entrepreneur of humble social origins, in later life ensnarled in business and political conflicts. Like other newly rich industrialists and financiers, he purchased an elegant country estate, against the backdrop of which he commissioned a painting of himself and his numerous family, posing as capitalist gentry. A literary theme that stirred many German (and other European) readers' resentments and disapproval was marriage between the Jewish business elite's daughters and self-seeking, often cynical-minded sons of financially wobbly but prestigious Christian noble families. A notable peer of Rathenau was Albert Ballin (1857–1918), founder and master of the mighty Hamburg-Amerika (HAPAG) shipping line. He was a frequent guest aboard Kaiser William II's yacht, where he was wont to raise toasts on the Kaiser's birthday. Anti-Semites objected to the ruler's friendship with Ballin, who – shattered by Germany's loss of World War I (and the ruin it portended for himself) – in 1918 took his own life.

These three captains of industry, although targets of anti-Semitic opinion, enjoyed wide respect for their accomplishments.

Source: United States Library of Congress.

FIGURE 12.7. JEWISH-BORN INTELLECTUAL-CULTURAL MODERNISTS
Pictured here in a 1904 photograph by Jacob Hilsdorf is Max Liebermann (1847–1935), influential, wealthy, and fashionable Berlin painter, liberal-minded pioneer of the then-controversial styles of Impressionism and early Expressionism. From 1920 he was president of the Prussian Academy of Arts, but in 1933 he resigned in protest against National Socialist persecution of Jewish-born and other artists, particularly of the various modernist schools.

Internationally celebrated was Sigmund Freud (1856–1939), bold and outrage-eliciting Viennese theorist of the human psyche (housing an "unconscious" inhabited by instinctual drives), of sexuality (passing through life-stages, and unruly), and of religion (interpreted as human self-projection). Arnold Schönberg (1875–1951), Austrian composer, developed in the pre-1914 years an "atonal" style shocking the public and posing a revolutionary challenge to classical music. The work of Liebermann, Freud, Schönberg, and many other artists and intellectuals of Jewish heritage scandalized cultural conservatives and adherents of nineteenth-century orthodoxies of Judeo-Christian morality, philosophical rationalism, and aesthetic realism.

None of these three was a religiously observant Jew. Schönberg converted to Lutheranism (until the National Socialists' coming to power in 1933 moved him to as, in part, to deflect public criticism from its very partisan support of tariff protection for agriculture and of east-Elbian large landowners in general.

Although at the Imperial court in Berlin and in conservative upper-class and upper middle-class circles "vulgar anti-Semitism," with or without pseudo-scientific, racialized and Social Darwinist accents, often figured as "bad form," a snobbish and supercilious, prejudice-laden attitude toward Jews was common. Despite fervent embrace of German culture and self-identification with the nation, Jews in 1914, both in Imperial Germany and German Austria, lived apart to a significant degree. Intermarriage was not uncommon among the intelligentsia (and working class), but was otherwise rare. Many middle-class Jewish families had no close non-Jewish friends, even when they maintained good collegial relations with Christians and belonged to common public-sphere organizations.

Still, in 1914 the arrival of anything remotely like severe anti-Semitic violence was unimaginable. The strongest forces governing German-Jewish relations were Jewish acculturation and mutual coexistence on a basis of civic equality. Liberal humanism among Christians, and secularist distancing from religion in other circles, were drying up old theological animosities. Respectable science scorned religious or crypto-religious superstitions (such as "ritual murder" or "blood-libel" charges). The Center Party, although it defended Catholicism and maintained reservations about Judaism, was committed, in its own interest as the representative of Imperial Germany's Catholic minority, to religious toleration toward Jews. The Austrian Christian Socials, however, yielded – as we saw – to anti-Semitic temptations (while Pan-German nationalists trumpeted denunciations of Austrian Jews as pillars of the Habsburg monarchy). Social Democrats, despite some naïve and populist anticapitalist/anti-Jewish stereotyping in their ranks, condemned anti-Semitism, as did the liberal parties.

If the future belonged to the friendly or tolerant social forces, German Jewry had little to fear and much to hope for. But if the liberal, Catholic Center, and Social Democratic parties were to decline or be muzzled – as happened after 1930 – the central European German Jews' legal-political defenses would fall. A space would open into which anti-Semitic radicalism could unrestrainedly rush. In 1914 there were in Imperial Germany no powerful vehicles of such radicalism (even if – both there and in Austria – disgruntled nationalists were often anti-Semites). But soon, forged in war, they would ominously roll into view.

FIGURE 12.7 *(continued)* reassert his Jewishness). Gustav Mahler, the celebrated late-Romantic Austrian composer (1860–1911), embraced Catholicism so as, among other things, to qualify for appointment in 1897 as director of the Vienna State Opera. In 1943 Liebermann's widow Martha committed suicide in Berlin to escape deportation to Theresienstadt concentration camp.
Source: Jacob Hilsdorf.

PART III

DUELS OF IDENTITY AND THE DEATH OF NATIONS, 1914–1945

In the next six chapters German-speakers will be at war with themselves and much of the world. Both Imperial Germany and the Austro-Hungarian monarchy will vanish as sovereign states embodying those forms of German national identity (conflicted though they were) that had prevailed in the late nineteenth century – that is, the Germans housed in Bismarck's empire, and the Habsburg monarchy's Austro-Germans, imagining themselves the vast and polyglot empire's dominant people. Startlingly, defeat in World War I inflicted mortal wounds on the self-understandings these two great states had sustained. After 1918, millions who had lived to maturity in them found themselves in an unrecognizable political landscape where they often figured in younger people's vision as ghosts of the past.

Like the Holy Roman Empire of the German Nation in 1806, Imperial Germany and Habsburg Austria receded in 1918 into history's shadows without having exhausted the creative life they harbored. These embodiments of German life might have endured much longer, adjusting without further recourse to "iron and blood" to the twentieth-century world. The political, social, and cultural forms in which they were cast might have attained greater articulation, and engendered different offspring.

Instead, the problem of national identity and political structure – the "German question" so imperfectly resolved in 1871 – boiled again to the surface. In the 1920s, democratic republics vitally dependent on Social Democratic backing struggled in Germany and Austria to make themselves into attractive homes for new and modern nations, but vast numbers of citizens rejected the new lodgings. In the 1930s, under the turbulent skies of unprecedented worldwide economic depression, right-wing authoritarian dictatorships strove, to much domestic applause, to breathe life into new militant, intolerant, more or less racialized identities. In 1938 the mightier National Socialist dictatorship swallowed up its feeble Austrian counterpart in a "Greater Germany" reminiscent of nineteenth-century *Grossdeutschland* before 1871's Prussian-dominated *Kleindeutschland* eclipsed it.

In 1939, as World War II commenced, Germany was again, like the long-vanished Holy Roman Empire, a wide central European realm, but committed now, under warlord Hitler, to self-magnification through armed conquest into a continent-spanning world power. A new, grandiosely self-styled "thousand-year" Third Reich had succeeded the short-lived "Second Reich" (never in its time so called) of 1871–1918, aiming to outshine the "First Reich" Charlemagne founded in 800 A.D. A less aggressive vision of *Weltmacht* had driven Kaiser William II's Germany forward to disaster in World War I. But the ruin wrought by Hitler's twelve-year Reich was incomparably greater, both for its aggression's victims – foremost among them millions of Jews, Poles, Belarusians, Ukrainians, and Russians – and for Germans themselves, whether they had embraced a National Socialist identity or not.

At the 1914–1945 era's smoldering end, the German nation's institutional framework and self-consciousness had disintegrated to a point where its survival was shrouded in doubt. Did it, except in a linguistic sense, and as an object of its conquerors' administrative and punitive will, still exist? These thirty years present the spectacle of a twofold or – considering the German and Austrian republics' violent deaths in the early 1930s – even a fourfold national self-destruction. It was a drama, not of modern nationalism's triumphant forward march, but of its terrifying power, gun in hand, to destroy collective identities, to grind them into bone and ash.

13

Krieg

The Prussian-German Monarchy's Sudden Death in War and Revolution, 1914–1920

Was the German government involuntarily swept into a great European war, or did it boldly – and recklessly – seize an opportunity to break out of "hostile encirclement" and win continental hegemony through vanquishment of France and Russia? This question long sharply divided historians, but the dichotomy it rests on misleads. The Kaiser's generals hoped to avoid protracted war on two fronts, if necessary by successfully operationalizing the Schlieffen Plan, which called for immediate invasion of France through neutral Belgium to produce quick victory in the west, after which a longer eastern campaign could be fought to defeat Russia or force it to sue for peace.

Germany's leaders, including Kaiser William II, would also have settled for resounding diplomatic victory, allowing Austria-Hungary to win its points against the Serbian government (charged with collusion in the Habsburg crown prince's June 1914 assassination) and so also against rebellious south Slavic nationalists within the monarchy's own borders, one of whom had pulled the trigger. Vienna and Berlin both hoped, vainly, that Russia and France's reluctance to enter a war with mighty Germany would restrain them from attempting to stop Austria's campaign of punishment against Serbia.

As it happened, by 1914's end it was evident the war would be a grinding process of attrition, requiring total mobilization of labor and resources. The army command soon concluded that, because workers were crucial participants both in war industries and at the fighting fronts, the war could not be won against their opposition. The government could not avoid making wartime concessions to working-class interests and political demands. Yet these did not compensate for popular suffering and alienation, which at war's end sparked monarchy-toppling revolution.

The imperial regime's home-front compromises with its political foes, and its wartime creation of a state-dominated command economy, antagonized conservative groups that had been the Bismarckian-Wilhelmian system's pillars: Prussian Junker landlords, big business, and even the high bureaucracy. When, in the fall of 1918, the war's loss was inescapable, these power elites did not rally determinedly around William II's throne. Instead, as revolution flared, they sought to shape the successor system by striking bargains with the Social Democratic Party's moderate leaders. Conservatives sought isolation and defeat of the SPD's radical left-wing rivals – the "German Bolsheviks" – to ensure both the capitalist market economy's and the upper- and middle-class parties' survival.

The paradoxical outcome was that, if in 1914 the government had hoped to exploit the war crisis to strengthen itself at home and fend off internal pressures for democratic reform, the war's prolongation forced it to make significant concessions to the Social Democrats. Thus it repelled the very interests whose domestic authority the government leaned on and wished to uphold. In its hour of defeat, the Prussian-German monarchical state died ill-defended and little mourned. Not for the first time in history did war, instead of averting revolution, provoke it.

War

In the summer and fall of 1914, the imperial government presented the war to the public as one of defense against Russian aggression, the tsarist army having mobilized before the German army. Proclaiming cessation of party politics and ideological polarization – the Kaiser melodramatically announced a domestic *Burgfrieden* or "peace within the castle walls" – the government succeeded on August 4, 1914 in gaining near-unanimous Reichstag support for fiscal war credits. A great wave of patriotic national solidarity swept the land, later enshrined and exaggerated in memory, especially by the nationalist right, as the "spirit of 1914." Simultaneously, martial law and military-controlled censorship clamped down on public life and politics.

The Schlieffen Plan's fall 1914 battlefield failure – German attack through Belgium failed to sweep forward to Paris – led to stalemate on the western front. In 1915 the Reichstag, back in session, voted new war credits and countenanced food rationing. In December 1916 the Reichstag passed the Auxiliary Service Law, which authorized government officials to allocate all strategic raw materials and requisition adult laborers for war industry. For their support of this sweeping law Social Democrats gained government and business management's agreement to compulsory arbitration of wage disputes in war industries, appointment of workers' councils in larger private firms, trade-union participation in the Auxiliary Service Law's administration, and creation of a new Imperial Labor Ministry. These dramatic gains in the Socialists' political influence locked them more tightly into the war's support.

Winter 1916–1917 witnessed severe food shortages, as Britain's naval blockade of seaborne imports into Germany took a deadly toll. People called it the "turnip winter," when grain and potato scarcity forced many to eat the lowly vegetable (scorned as livestock fodder). April 1917 witnessed wildcat strikes in war-related industry, ominously signaling working-class insubordination (the SPD's trade union leaders having earlier agreed to a policy of no strikes for the

FIGURE 13.1. THE "SPIRIT OF 1914"
In this photograph, taken at war's August 1914 outbreak, well-dressed men and women of the middle and upper classes – doubtless including students of adjacent Berlin University – hail a military display on Unter den Linden, the capital's central governmental boulevard. In these days, civilians joined recruits marching through city streets to war, enthusiastic women – wives, girlfriends, strangers – embracing them. Exalted welcome of the war occurred widely throughout the country, although the pervasiveness nationalists later wishfully claimed for it was exaggerated. Only a short time elapsed before massive transports of the dead began arriving from the fronts, raising shadows of relentless slaughter.

Most intellectuals rallied to the cause, elevating – as they thought – depth-plumbing German *Kultur* over rationalist Anglo-French *Zivilisation*. They blamed the western powers for refusing to grant Germany its "place in the sun," and specifically the right it claimed to colonial empire overseas and military-diplomatic hegemony in eastern and Balkan Europe. Their self-exaltation encountered a barrage of rude anti-German propaganda in western countries, which the German army's brutal invasion of neutral Belgium, entailing many civilian deaths, only redoubled.
Source: provenance unknown.

war's duration). Unpopularity in working-class and leftist circles of the SPD's cooperation in the war effort led, ominously, to a party split and formation of the "Independent Social Democratic Party" (USPD). Under influence of this breakaway socialist movement's antiwar agitation, sailors' mutinies erupted in German ports in the fall of 1917.

In 1916–1917 an extensive war-aims debate took place in parliament, press, and the political parties. It pitted annexationists, advocating "peace of victory" (*Siegfrieden*), especially including the creation of a large sphere of

FIGURE 13.2. WOMEN AND THE WAR
In this picture, women and their children queue for milk and other dairy products in 1917 Berlin. Fodder shortages undercut domestic meat and dairy production, while the Allied blockade of shipping cut Germany off from many vital imports, including fats and other food staples. Malnutrition claimed hundreds of thousands of victims, especially among children. Masses of women found employment as munitions workers, subject to strict discipline. Emblematic was Heinrich Zille's famous 1916 drawing, "The Iron Cross," depicting a proletarian widow sitting in her tenement room (with four small children) resignedly contemplating the ominous letter announcing her medal-decorated husband's battlefield death.
Source: Deutsches Bundesarchiv.

German influence at Russia's expense in eastern Europe and the Balkans (the "Mitteleuropa" strategy), against anti-annexationists, advocating a "peace of understanding" (*Verständigungsfrieden*) restoring the prewar configuration. In 1917 there emerged in the Reichstag the future postwar governing majority grouping (later called the "Weimar Coalition"), joining SPD, liberal Progressives, and Catholic Center Party in a bloc favoring peace without annexations and democratic reform of the Imperial German and Prussian state constitutions. In July 1917 these parties passed the Reichstag's "Peace Resolution" in response to the United States' April 1917 declaration of war against Germany and its allies. It expressed, too, widespread war-weariness in the aftermath of the colossal losses suffered both by Germany and the French and English on the western front, notably at the 1916 German-French battle of Verdun, which alone claimed a million lives.

Striking back, German conservatives and annexationists formed an aggressive nationalist political front – the *Vaterlandspartei*. These forces, cooperating with the army, engineered the fall of Chancellor (since 1909) Theobald von Bethmann-Hollweg, who had acquiesced in the Peace Resolution. Behind a new chancellorship's facade there emerged what many regarded as a "military dictatorship" of army leaders Field-Marshal Paul von Hindenburg and Quartermaster-General Erich Ludendorff.

Following the Russian revolution of October 1917, in which V. I. Lenin's antiwar Bolsheviks rose precariously to power in Moscow and St. Petersburg, the German army and government imposed on its near-prostrate eastern antagonist the Treaty of Brest-Litovsk, ratified by the Reichstag in March 1918. It handed over to German annexation or domination vast regions along the former western borders of the now toppled Russian Empire, stretching from the Baltic coastlands to the oil-rich Caucasus and including fertile Ukraine. In protest against the Reichstag's acceptance of Brest-Litovsk – even the Social Democrats passively acquiesced, only abstaining from voting – German antiwar, anti-annexationist elements, especially numerous among leftist activists and industrial workers, staged big strikes in early 1918.

Spring and summer of 1918 witnessed a desperate German offensive on the western front, seeking victory before United States power decisively tilted the scales of war. But American soldiers' appearance alongside the French and British armies, combined with shortages of oil and other raw materials resulting from ever tighter blockade of German access to neutral countries' products – and, not least, the burden on the German army of its occupation of eastern Europe – weakened and finally halted the attack. The western allies' punishing counteroffensive in July 1918 provoked Hindenburg and Ludendorff – wishing to avoid further battlefield defeats and impending invasion of Germany – to advise William II to sue for peace. Austria-Hungary, crumbling from within, was already maneuvering to withdraw unilaterally from the war.

In October 1918, the Kaiser appointed as new chancellor liberal-minded Prince Max of Baden, who began peace negotiations while simultaneously proposing that the Reichstag convert the Imperial and Prussian governments into western-style parliamentary democracies. This entailed scrapping Prussia's oligarchical voting system while granting majority coalitions in parliament the power to unilaterally select Reich-level chancellors and Prussian prime ministers and their respective cabinets. This "revolution from above" the "Weimar coalition" parties – SPD, Catholics, Progressives – had been advocating since 1917.

Germany, fighting on two fronts, suffered the heaviest battlefield losses among all combatants: 2.4 million men dead and more than 3 million wounded, encompassing altogether some one-third of the male adult population. On the home front, official food rations shrank, driving civilians onto the black market, or into undernourishment. The British-enforced wartime blockade is reckoned to have inflicted some 700,000 deaths from food shortages and resultant maladies.

MAP 13.1. THE EASTERN FRONT, 1917–1918: *MITTELEUROPA* IN THE MAKING

War-related business and large-scale farming gained economically from the strife. The government, while regulating prices, could not effectively police profits, and farmers with adequate labor to work their land often advantageously sold their products illegally to hungry townspeople. Still, the war dramatically impoverished German society: in 1918 the index of industrial production was 40 percent lower than in 1914. Industrial workers' real (inflation-adjusted) wages had fallen in war-related industry by 23 percent and in other branches by 46 percent. Income levels for white-collar workers and civil servants similarly plunged.

Revolution

War's turmoil radicalized politics, particularly among urban workers. SPD membership fell by three-quarters, partly because economic hardship halted dues payment, partly because of battlefield death or injury. The socialist trade unions' ranks thinned by one-third. Membership in the breakaway leftist and antiwar Independent Socialist Party (USPD) rose by war's end to some 100,000. Yet the majority SPD's moderate prewar leadership remained intact, although increasingly out of grassroots touch with embittered and hotheaded proletarian youth.

Amid Prince Max's government's October 1918 armistice negotiations, and rumors the navy would stage a bloody suicidal high-seas battle rather than countenance Allied confiscation of the fleet, the Social Democrats put themselves at the head of popular demonstrations culminating on November 9 in a

---

MAP 13.1 (*continued*) Although in 1914 and 1915 the Russian army forced Germany to defend its East Prussian soil and captured Austria's eastern Galicia for a prolonged period, by 1916 the Central Powers had turned the tables, occupying the heartland of Russian Poland, where in November they announced the establishment of a future "Kingdom of Poland," to be ruled under German military overlordship by a junior Habsburg lineage in cooperation with Polish conservatives and anti-Russian nationalists. This scheme foundered on its own inner contradictions – not least the Central Powers' attempt to raise a Polish army with promises of semi-statehood – and under the impact of president Wilson's 1917 advocacy of an independent Poland and the February and October revolutions of 1917 in the Russian Empire. The Central Powers exploited the circumstance of emerging civil war in Russia to impose the Treaty of Brest-Litovsk on the Bolsheviks. Here displayed are the vast territorial losses it imposed, mainly of ethnically non-Russian lands (although the Ukrainian-speaking population's relationship to Russian identity remained unsettled). Romania, though a prewar ally of the Central Powers, in 1916 joined the French and British side. Though it suffered temporary defeat and occupation at the German powers' hands, Romania gained rich territorial rewards at the 1919 Paris peace conference. In the Lithuanian and Belarusian lands, the German military occupation authority (*Ober-Ost*) projected grandiose Germanization projects, clothed in the rhetoric of modernization. But the exploitative character of the day-to-day German regime drove the occupied populations into sullen opposition or active resistance.

FIGURE 13.3. THE DRIVE FOR EASTERN EMPIRE

This anonymously authored picture of 1917 presents, on the right, Quartermaster General Erich Ludendorff (1865–1937), from 1916 chief of army operations, with General Field Marshal Paul von Hindenburg (1847–1934), supreme army commander, in consultation with Kaiser William II. After war's outbreak the militarily untested emperor acquiesced ever more in his generals' strategic and tactical decisions. From 1916 Hindenburg and Ludendorff gained unchallengeable supremacy. Both were sons of estate-owning, military-minded families in Prussia's Polish-German borderlands. In Vienna, the war's powerful advocate was Conrad von Hötzendorf (1852–1925), Habsburg army Chief of Staff. Austrian losses at Russian hands, and the gradual erosion of the Austro-Hungarian monarchy's war-making strength, reduced Hötzendorf to dependency on German decisions before his 1917 fall from power.

In April 1917 German officials, seizing a chance to deepen Russian turmoil, permitted Lenin and colleagues to escape Swiss exile and travel by train across Germany to take command of the Bolshevik movement in St. Petersburg. In the winter 1917–1918 negotiations at Brest-Litovsk, in the Polish-Russian borderlands, Field Marshal Leopold, Prince of Bavaria – embodying German aristocratic-monarchical conservatism – eventually signed for Germany. The Soviet delegation included revolutionary Bolshevik notables Lev Kamenev and Adolf Joffe. This was a temporary truce between irreconcilable foes. Russia's collapse enabled German power to surge eastward, staking out future inner-European empire. German public opinion applauded or tolerated this, relieved to see "tsarist despotism" fall, patronizingly believing the east European peoples would gratefully accept German overlordship, and fearful of Russian-born "Bolshevism" – which to its myriad opponents seemed little more than anarchist overthrow of Christian European civilization.

Source: Deutsches Bundesarchiv.

democratic republic's proclamation in Berlin. The army abandoned the Kaiser, who fled into Dutch exile. As the Prussian and other German dynasties toppled, SPD leader Friedrich Ebert signed an agreement with General Wilhelm Groener, the army's political negotiator. Groener promised support for an SPD-led provisional government, provided it proceeded rapidly to a national assembly's election and promulgation of a constitution for a pluralist (that is, in his view, "non-Bolshevik") parliamentary democracy. Resembling this arrangement was the November 15 agreement between heavy industry's spokesman and socialist trade union leaders (the Stinnes-Legien pact). Here German industry traded the eight-hour workday and agreement to binding state arbitration in collective bargaining conflicts – weighty concessions, unthinkable before the war – in return for assurances the trade unions would not push for socialization of industry.

A "second revolution" followed, spanning November 1918 and January 1919. In November, locally elected workers and soldiers councils sprang up across the land, while in Berlin a central assembly representing them all emerged. Would these bodies transform themselves into "German Soviets," that is, into revolutionary structures on the Russian Bolshevik model, representing only far-left elements to the exclusion of others? Would they press for "democratization" of the new republic's armed forces and for socialization of the means of production?

In December, radical leftists, led by Rosa Luxemburg and Karl Liebknecht, founded the German Communist Party (KPD). Revolt followed in Berlin, subsequently known as the "Spartacus Uprising," aiming to wrest the city's control from SPD hands and guarantee primacy of the workers and soldiers councils over the impending new national parliament. In crushing the Spartacists, the SPD-led provisional government accepted armed aid from right-wing nationalist paramilitary forces (*Freikorps*), who brutally murdered – among other victims – Luxemburg and Liebknecht. These events opened a gulf of resentment and distrust between communists and socialists never later wholly bridged.

On January 19, 1919, the elections to the new National Assembly, convening in the city of Weimar – tied to Goethe's and Schiller's memory, and thus to the peaceful and enlightened Germany of "poets and thinkers" – gave the SPD 38 percent of the 30 million votes cast (which now included, for the first time in German history, women's ballots). The Catholic Center Party won 20 percent and the liberal Progressives, now renamed the German Democratic Party, gained 18 percent. On the left, the USPD won nearly 8 percent, while the Communists – uncertain of broad popular backing and hostile to "bourgeois democracy" – abstained. On the right, nationalist liberals and prewar conservatives gained but 15 percent between them.

Seemingly, a sizeable electoral majority did not wish to see revolution move left of Social Democratic positions: acceptance of a politically pluralist republic and state-regulated capitalist market economy, and confinement of "socialism" to whatever might be attainable through coalition-based legislation. Cooperating with Catholics and liberal Democrats, Social Democrats led the new

Paul Hoffmann & Co.
Berlin-Schöneberg.

1982.

Truppeneinzug in Berlin.
Auf der Rednertribüne Unter den Linden: Ebert, Kriegsminister
Scheuch, General Lequis, Oberbürgermeister Wermuth.

(a)

FIGURE 13.4. TRIBUNES OF RIVAL REVOLUTIONS
The first of these two picture postcards – enterprisingly sold during the German Empire's tumultuous breakup – displays, on a podium, the alliance of moderate revolutionaries and pragmatists. From left to right: Friedrich Ebert, SPD leader and first president of the Weimar Republic; representatives of the army, now supportive of the Republic; and Adolf Wermuth, Progressive liberal mayor of Berlin. Ebert's colleague, SPD leader Philipp Scheidemann, had on November 9, 1918 eloquently proclaimed from a Reichstag window the Empire's downfall and the birth of a republic – an unscripted act meant (unsuccessfully) to forestall a more radical ("Bolshevik") turn of events. In the second picture, sturdy and confident soldiers, sailors, and civilians guard the Reichstag building in a machine-gun-bearing truck, while well-dressed onlookers (including women) mill about. Many such revolutionists soon came to oppose the new SPD-led republic, supporting instead workers and soldiers councils and the German Communist Party, born in January 1919.
Source: Bildarchiv Preussischer Kulturbesitz/Art Resource, NY.

republic's government, for which the National Assembly later promulgated an advanced democratic constitution.

A "third revolution" occurred in February–May 1919, when local Marxist revolutionary regimes, representing the USPD and KPD, emerged in Bavaria, in Prussia's Ruhr industrial district, and in Saxony. Right-wing nationalist, anticommunist counterrevolutions soon toppled them, amid considerable bloodshed. In March-April 1920, in a fourth revolutionary crisis, the Social Democrats headed a successful nationwide general strike against an attempted

(b)

FIGURE 13.4 *(continued)*

right-wing power seizure in Berlin – the Kapp Putsch, the latter a newly fashionable word describing violent and conspiratorial government takeovers, whether successful or only attempted. Ruhr workers, prominent in the anti-Kapp resistance, formed a "Red Army" and tried to establish local autonomy as prelude to new left-wing revolution throughout Germany. The SPD-led government dispatched the Weimar Republic's newly organized army to defeat the Ruhr district rebels. Right-wing paramilitaries joined in, inflicting "white terror" on bloodied workers.

In June 1920 the second national election since war's end occurred. On the moderate left, the SPD polled 6.1 million votes (22 percent). The farther-left, anti-government Independent Socialists (USPD) robustly won 5 million (18 percent), while 600,000 votes (2 percent) fell to the Communists (KPD) who, defeated at the barricades, now reaped a meager but not insignificant reward in electoral politics. The German left, united in 1914, now stood divided into two roughly equal but bitterly opposed camps.

The Catholic vote fell to 18 percent and the liberal democrats (DDP) tumbled below 9 percent, while the antirepublican right-wing parties expanded to around one-third of the electorate. In other words, the "Weimar coalition" parties had, fatefully, lost their majority, while a process of polarization to the far left and far right began to undermine the new state's political center. The revolution had resulted in a bitter split within German socialism, and considerable radicalization on right and left.

FIGURE 13.5. REVOLUTIONARY POLARIZATION

Karl Liebknecht, the soon-to-be-murdered co-leader of the January 1919 Communist ("Spartacist") uprising, addresses a December 1918 rally in Berlin's central park, the Tiergarten. Note the socially mixed, respectably dressed audience. In the background a Prussian military hero's statue looms, ghostly and symbolic. Social Democrat Gustav Noske, the Provisional Government's Minister of Defense, engaged nationalist *Freikorps* troops to combat the communists. Such fighters belonged to conservative or right-wing nationalist irregular postwar forces battling Polish separatists on Germany's crumbling eastern borders and Russian Bolsheviks and local nationalists in the Baltic lands, where influential German minorities resided. In this and subsequent crises the new republican regime sought but did not always gain the regular army's backing.

Source: Deutsches Bundesarchiv.

Another "Failed German Revolution"?

In 1918 revolutionary enthusiasm gripped the working class more than it did Social Democratic leaders. The SPD-steered provisional government fulfilled some Socialist or populist hopes: adoption of the eight-hour industrial work-day, binding state arbitration of labor conflicts, creation of workers' councils in large industrial firms, opening the path to rural laborers' unionization, pro-mulgation of the progressive Weimar national constitution, which also man-dated women's enfranchisement. But in SPD leaders' eyes, "nationalization" or "socialization" of industry (opposed by the western Allies) seemed unworkable and suicidal amid war's-end economic crisis.

Many ordinary Germans wanted *social* democracy, humbling the former privileged elites' power and purging and restructuring the German army. What stayed the Social Democrats' hands? The SPD, like the parties to its right,

FIGURE 13.6. REVOLUTIONARY AFTERSHOCKS, RIGHT AND LEFT
This picture displays rebellious soldiers in the course of the March 1920 Kapp Putsch, distributing broadsheets in Berlin to passers-by in middle-class dress. The rebels' helmets are inscribed with the swastika (*Hakenkreuz*), "Aryan" symbol (since the late nineteenth century) of the ultranationalist and now antirepublican right. Wolfgang Kapp (1858–1922), the attempted coup's co-leader, was well known as a right-wing, anti-Semitic defender of maximalist war aims and conservative-nationalist interests. He was, as well, director of the East Prussian large landowners' credit bank.

Following Kapp's defeat, the Ruhr-based revolutionary "Red Army" fought to establish a socialist workers' regime. Many on the radical left hoped the Soviet army would break through the lines of its war with renascent Poland to come to the German Communists' aid, but the newly arisen Polish army, aided materially by the Western Allies, defeated the Soviet offensive in the summer of 1920 outside Warsaw.
Source: Bildarchiv Preussischer Kulturbesitz/Art Resource, NY.

feared Russian-backed Bolshevism might engulf the land, bringing to power the SPD's leftist rivals – the USPD and the newly founded German Communists. This apprehension inhibited radical social reform. It was, too, a heavy responsibility to represent defeated Germany in face of vengeful victors, and to defend borders east and west against annexation-hungry Poles and French. The Social Democrats did not wish to appear, at the moment they came to power, as the "unpatriotic rascals" William II had in the 1890s once contemptuously and publicly labeled them. Such anxiety over their national standing was a legacy of the SPD's (unsought) ghettoization under the prewar Bismarckian system.

The conservative elites proved politically astute in binding the SPD's hands in the unsteady republic's early days through the aforementioned November pacts, and in saddling the SPD with the thankless task of heading the government that signed the 1919 Versailles Treaty at the Paris Peace Conference. Yet the January 1919 middle-class swing to the pro-republican liberal Democrats and the absence of significant right-wing opposition to the republic's foundation led SPD leaders to think that history was on their side: they aimed, first, to establish parliamentary democracy, then escape the Allies' clutches as best they could and, finally, to establish moderate socialism gradually through parliamentary action.

Historians still argue that the Social Democrats' failure to unhorse the old political-military elites later helped crucially to bring National Socialism to power. Yet war and revolution had already weakened Imperial Germany's power holders – discredited by the war's loss and Kaiser's flight – and thrown them on the defensive. It is doubtful whether their political defeat could have been made more decisive amid the turbulent currents roiling the country at World War I's calamitous end. The Versailles Treaty's disarmament provisions dislodged many conservative aristocrats from the army officer corps. Others fell from their civilian posts, or resigned rather than collaborate with the new republic. Land reform stripping them of their agricultural incomes, had it been attempted, would not have quieted them politically. If, in 1932–1933, military-aristocratic conservatives had not held Hitler's stirrup, bourgeois rightists were prepared to claim the honor. It was war and its dire consequences, not Social Democrats' deficit of revolutionary zeal, that watered – in blood, impoverishment, and visceral nationalist resentments – the seeds of National Socialism.

14

Weimarer Republik

Democracy's Bitter Fruits, 1918–1933

Germany of the Weimar Republic – "Weimar Germany" – was in some ways one of the post-1918 world's most modern societies. The political constitution stood on the cutting-edge of progressive liberal democracy as the western public then understood it. In economic life, the country attained new heights of technological innovation and organizational rationalization, while its social welfare system and labor rights regime stood in advance of those of other large western societies. In the cultural field, film-making distinguished itself both as popular and high art, while in music, literature, philosophy, and the natural and social sciences German achievements, often crowned with Nobel prizes, matched or set world standards.

Yet Weimar's modernity was unsettling, volatile, precarious, even – in many eyes – threatening. The contrast, especially in the middle and upper classes' experience, between life in the turbulent Weimar Republic and the now-vanished "golden age of the Kaiser" (*goldene Kaiserzeit*) evoked much nostalgia for the prewar world. It bred resentment over losses suffered since then – commonly, if unfairly, blamed on the Republic itself rather than on the imperial regime's war from which Weimar had emerged.

In political life, modernity meant not only compromise-ridden and unglamorous middle-of-the-road liberal democracy, but powerful drumbeats on the far left of the militant Communist Party and on the far right of irreconcilable antirepublicans, of both conservative-monarchist and – more ominously – radical rightist coloration. Could German society endure such antagonistic political tensions without falling into deadlock or civil war?

"Weimar conditions" led many people to view the present as unstable and unlikely to persist, and to accustom themselves to the idea that a new social and political system would or should emerge to eclipse the controversial republic, bringing longed-for harmony and certainty. Some saw this coming from the revolutionary left, others from the revolutionary right. Even Weimar's defenders eventually came to feel that the republic's political constitution required major revision – in favor of stronger state power – if it were not to succumb to the menaces facing it from opposing extremes.

Northern Schleswig
voted to join Denmark

Southern Schleswig
voted to remain German

Danzig
declared a Free City
administered by
League of Nations

Memel Land
occupied by
Lithuania 1923

Eupen-Malmedy
transferred to
Belgium

Allenstein
voted to
remain German

Marienwerder
voted to remain German

Posen and West Prussia
transferred to Poland
without a plebiscite

Upper Silesia
divided into two
after plebiscite
to remain German

Saarland
administered by France under the League of
Nations until a plebiscite to be held in 1935

Alsace-Lorraine
ceded to France without a plebiscite
after 47 years of German rule

Germany

Territory lost by
Germany

Territory retained
by Germay
following a
plebiscite

Territory retained
by Germany, but
within which no
fortifications could
be built or soldiers
stationed

MAP 14.1. WEIMAR GERMANY'S INGLORIOUS POST–WORLD WAR I BORDERS

Here displayed are the territorial losses the 1919 Versailles Treaty imposed on defeated Germany, notably the cession of Alsace-Lorraine to France and of Posen/Poznań, West Prussia (known in circles unfriendly to Poland as the "Polish corridor") and eastern Upper Silesia to the newly reborn Polish state. Danzig's conversion into a Free City under League of Nations authority, but also joined in a customs union with Poland, met widespread rejection in Germany. Poles were not wrong to point out that, historically, West Prussia and Danzig – with prosperous German burghers and villagers (and Polonized German nobility) – had loyally belonged to the Polish-Lithuanian Commonwealth from the mid-fifteenth century to the eighteenth-century partitions.

Versailles-mandated plebiscites in southern East Prussia and a corner of West Prussia (1920) and in Upper Silesia (1921) proved disappointing to Polish nationalists. The numerous Polish-speaking but Lutheran Protestant population of East Prussian Masuria voted massively against their inclusion in newborn Poland. Here, as happens not infrequently, political and cultural affinities overtrumped language and ethnicity. In Upper Silesia, the numerous Catholic Slavic-speakers had long cultivated a local identity enabling coexistence with Germanophone neighbors and acceptance of life under Prussian rule. Many of them viewed Polish nationalism skeptically, Silesia having gravitated away from the kingdom of Poland in the Middle Ages. Polish nationalists nevertheless staged three armed risings between 1919 and 1921, aimed at maximizing Poland's acquisitions in Upper Silesia. In the end, the Allies awarded Poland districts rich in mining and metallurgical enterprises.

In many contemporary people's thinking, Weimar figured less as a desirable destination that German history had reached than as a transitional zone through which it was passing to attain a higher and grander condition. Such future visions commonly possessed the dangerous quality that they *excluded*, often in rhetoric and ideology laden with violence and aggression, the forces and tendencies that made life in the Weimar Republic seem, to discontented people, unsatisfactory and menacing. Weimar was steering toward a showdown between antagonistic forms of *intolerant modernity*, with peaceful acceptance of interest group democracy and industrial society's perpetually unresolved tensions losing ground.

The Weimar Economy

The war years witnessed a steep decline of industrial output and real wages. The currency inflation that plagued the early Weimar Republic was likewise

---

MAP 14.1 *(continued)* In 1920 Belgium took possession of the largely German-populated Eupen-Malmédy region, previously ruled by Prussia. In Schleswig-Holstein, a 1920 plebescite favored the Danish side, though Germanophile Danes and Danophile Germans were not unknown. Protestant Lithuanian-speakers in former East Prussia leaned to Germany, yet in 1923 the Allies permitted the newborn Lithuanian state to occupy and incorporate the Memel district where they lived. The German land west of the Rhine river stood until 1929 under occupation by France, which in 1923 temporarily seized the industrial Ruhr District as well. The Rhineland was, on its recovery by Germany, to be permanently demilitarized.

In Alsace-Lorraine the anciently settled German-speaking urban population had embraced French liberalism and bourgeois culture before the region's annexation in 1871 into the new Empire. The following forty-seven years of German administration failed to win their hearts, so that Berlin was obliged to rely on settlement of in-migrants – especially public-sector workers and garrisoned soldiers – to create the impression these lands were embracing a German identity. After their recovery by the French government the recent German immigrants were in effect officially expelled (as also happened at the new Polish administration's hand to former German officials and peasant-colonists in Poznania).

As for Imperial Germany's overseas colonies, the Versailles treaty assigned their administration to the victor powers, including Japan. Although the treaty's economic consequences proved less crushing than feared, its punitive intent was unfeigned and German resentment correspondingly deep.

The postwar formation of a separate German Austria violated widespread wishes on both sides of the former Habsburg-Hohenzollern border, but the western Allies vetoed fusion of the Austrian and German lands in a single new republic. Anticipating the realization of this form of *Grossdeutschland*, the Austrian-German national assembly of 1918 designated the land they represented as *Deutschösterreich* ("German Austria"). They and their Weimar German allies appealed – self-righteously, perhaps, but not illogically – to the right of national self-determination that President Wilson had elevated to the world's governing principle.

(a)

FIGURE 14.1. "WEIMAR CULTURE"
These words conjure up various manifestations of cultural and intellectual modernism in the pre-Hitler years. It is a prized legacy in the present-day world, but was highly controversial in its day, and generally condemned by cultural conservatives and people on the right.
(a) Marlene Dietrich (1901–1992) in her internationally acclaimed role in *The Blue Angel* (1930), a film ambiguously dramatizing sexually charged modernity's triumph over bourgeois convention and metaphorically depicting, in the figure of the blue angel Lola Lola's self-destructive admirer, Professor Rath, Imperial Germany's ignominious demise.

a wartime product, traceable to the imperial government's expansion of the money supply to cover war costs in excess of revenue collected from taxation and war-bond borrowing. The gold-backed German mark declined against the U.S. dollar from a 1914 exchange rate of 4:1 to a 1919 rate of 9:1. The 1919 Versailles Treaty's imposition on Germany of a (initially unspecified but vast) war reparations liability then caused international flight from the German mark.

The early Weimar Republic's coalition governments preferred to print money rather than levy new taxes. Expanding the money supply also worked to uphold postwar employment and counteract joblessness's politically radicalizing effects, which would otherwise result from following economic orthodoxy's dictates to deflate the mark through money supply reduction. From this there

(b)

FIGURE 14.1 *(continued)*

(b) Max Beckmann's painting, "The King," completed in 1937 in Dutch exile. Beckmann (1884–1950) rose to fame and honors in the Weimar Republic as a preeminent modernist painter of Expressionist sensibility. The National Socialists banned his work, vilifying it in their notorious 1937 traveling exhibit of modern art as "degenerate" (see Chapter 16). Not a political artist, but contemptuous of war and state violence, he conjured much with dream-like visions in which eroticism and brutality often intermingled. One of Beckmann's many self-portraits, "The King" invites multiple interpretations. Its regal subject's darkened vision may signal the artist's blindness, self-admitted in exile, to the historical forces engulfing him. Not a straightforward allusion to contemporary dictators, the image of the king appears nonetheless to embody irresistible, paternalist, emotionally and sexually inviting power, while his female subject – one face turned toward the king, the other toward the viewer – figures as ambivalent but helpless unfreedom. An oracular figure behind the king seems admonitory, warning perhaps against his veneration.

(c)

FIGURE 14.1 *(continued)*
(c) Max Weber (1864–1920), social scientist and political writer of genius. He was a robust nationalist liberal in prewar years, but disillusionment with the ineptitude of the Kaiser's government led him to embrace the postwar republic, despite his misgivings about the Social Democrats' power to rally the nation. He developed a realist defense of modern democracy (paired with enduring theories of political legitimacy and charisma) and forged theoretical and methodological tools for nineteenth-century historicism to refashion itself in a post-Hegelian, post-Rankean sense. He talks here in 1917 with students, including (on his left) Ernst Toller (1893–1939), who, after a prison term for revolutionary leftism in the 1919 Munich revolution, became a notable Expressionist playwright, authoring among other works the symptomatically entitled "Mass Man." He later fled the National Socialists to despairing New York exile. This picture evokes the intensity surrounding Weber and the young intellectuals who were both drawn to him and driven to challenge his pessimism about political utopias.

Perhaps most emblematic today of Weimar culture is Berthold Brecht (1898–1956), poet-playwright of genius, willful and wayward communist, self-ironizing celebrant of big-city modernity. Actress Lotte Lenya (1898–1981) and husband-composer Kurt Weil (1900–1950) enacted Brecht's dramas in revolutionary stage triumphs, notably the widely applauded *Threepenny Opera* (1928) and *Rise and Fall of the City Mahagonny* (1930) – musically and poetically brilliant, biting satires on modern capitalist society.

Celebrated too in the Weimar years was Thomas Mann (1875–1955), modern Germany's greatest novelist. He broke with prewar aestheticist elitism and Romanticism-driven loyalties to Schopenhauer and Wagner to delicately embrace Enlightenment liberalism and so also Weimar democracy, a transition dramatized in his novel *The Magic Mountain* (1924), for which, among other works, he received the Nobel Prize for literature in 1929. His brother Heinrich Mann (1871–1950) was also a widely read novelist, projecting leftist and anti-Establishment views. It was his prewar novel, *Professor Unrat*, that supplied the text for "The Blue Angel."

Source: (a) and (c): Bildarchiv Preussischer Kulturbesitz/Art Resource, NY; (b) Bildarchiv Preussischer Kulturbesitz/Art Resource, NY; © 2010 Artists Rights Society (ARS), New York/VG Bild-Kunst, Bonn.

followed the infamous and unprecedented "Great Inflation," which peaked in 1923 when the German mark (DM) stood, absurdly, at 4.2 billion to the dollar.

Among inflation's grim consequences was the loss – through shrinkage of face value – of laboriously accumulated personal savings, especially among the middle and lower middle classes, but also among frugal workers. The same fate befell other savings, notably commercial banks' reserves and the funds that trade unions had assembled over long years. Conversely – and highly welcome to all debtors – the inflation reduced to triviality prewar and wartime debt, notably in agriculture, but also in industry and government.

Strategies for surviving the inflation existed, and most employed wage and salary earners stayed afloat. But there was widespread feeling that the middle classes, bereft of savings and formerly reliable financial investments, were paying for Germany's defeat and the 1918–1920 revolution's consequences. Conversely, many among the monied classes had the foresight early on to convert liquid capital into ownership of such assets as farmland, houses, commercial-industrial real estate, and physical stocks of raw materials and capital goods. These were hedges against inflation, and – when prices were right – steppingstones to greater wealth. Those who emerged enriched from the inflation reaped losers' embittered resentment.

The years from 1924 to 1929 were brighter, following diplomatic regulation in 1924 of Germany's war debt and attendant currency restabilization. In 1921 the Allies fixed German reparations, payable mainly to France and Britain, at 132 billion prewar gold marks (equivalent to the then giant sum of $33 billion). The 1924 Dawes Plan prescribed open-ended annual payments on a rising scale of DM 1–2.5 billion. Later, in 1929–1930, the internationally negotiated Young Plan reduced Germany's total debt to DM 37 billion, payable at some DM 2 billion annually until 1988. Despite this considerable scalingdown, German public opinion almost unanimously regarded war reparations – which presupposed the imperial regime's sole "war-guilt" in unleashing the 1914–1918 carnage – as the victorious western powers' self-serving, cynically righteous, and punitive imposition on a scapegoated and defeated enemy.

Still, between 1924 and 1929 the German domestic economy regained 1913 gross national product (GNP) and average per capita income levels. Big industry again grew robust. Cleansed of old debt, it borrowed money (especially in America) to finance new technologies and organizational methods (e.g., "Fordist" assembly-line production). Banks and trade unions, obliged to build up new reserves, were relatively weaker. Farmers, especially small landholders, fell back into debt because of the international commodity price slump of the 1920s, occasioned by wartime expansion in many countries of planted acreage.

The international Great Depression lasted in Germany from 1929 to 1934–1935. It followed the Wall Street stock market crash of October 1929, which eventually caused a drastic shrinkage worldwide of bank credit. U.S. banks recalled the short-term loans they had liberally extended to Germany after 1924 (including to the Weimar government, so that it might more easily pay its reparations installments). The resultant contraction of available capital slowed

(a)

FIGURE 14.2. ECONOMIC UPHEAVAL

(a) Black-bearded Hugo Stinnes (1870–1924), mining, smelting, and electricity magnate and Weimar Germany's most powerful industrialist. He profited greatly from munitions and other war production, and from accumulation during the inflation of coal and other raw materials reserves, drawing much criticism, especially from the inflation's victims. In November 1918 he brokered a compromise with the trade unions, offering concessions from industrial management to block socialist radicalism. He later served as Reichstag deputy for the right-leaning liberals (DVP – the prewar National Liberals). With him is Friedrich Carl Duisberg (1861–1935), who rose to power and influence in the burgeoning chemical industry, captaining the mighty Bayer firm and collaborating in the 1925 launching of the huge chemical trust I.G. Farben, of which he was board chairman until his death. His nationalist and Pan-German inclinations later smoothed cooperation with Hitler's regime.

(b)

FIGURE 14.2 *(continued)*
(b) An iconic picture of postwar impoverishment: a numerous and roughly clad family, in seemingly underheated quarters, glumly sharing a loaf of bread and a sausage.
Source: (a) Bildarchiv Preussischer Kulturbesitz/Art Resource, NY; (b) Deutsches Bundesarchiv.

investment, ruined firms dependent on credit, and initiated a downward spiral of unemployment, causing a fall in consumer spending. This shrank industrial markets, spurring further layoffs and weakening demand both for consumer and capital goods.

A severe crisis of central European banking followed the powerful Viennese Kreditanstalt's 1931 failure. Unemployment in Germany rose, precipitously and terrifyingly, from 1.4 million in 1928 to 3.1 million in 1930 and 5.6 million in 1932, when it amounted, among wage- and salary-earning men, to about one-third of the workforce. Many who remained at work suffered more or less drastic pay cuts. Industrial output contracted from a 1929 level of 100 to 52 in August 1932. But that was the depression's trough. In 1933, the ranks of the jobless shrank by 900,000. By November 1933 industrial production's index had risen – before National Socialist recovery programs had much time to take effect – to 72. Changing levels of businessmen's confidence and consumer expectations following the establishment in early 1933 of Hitler's dictatorship played an unquantifiable but doubtless weighty part in this upturn.

Long-term social trends, as reflected in the 1907 and 1925 censuses, included the agricultural sector's slow shrinkage (to 31 percent of all employed in 1925); continued expansion, especially in medium and large industry, of blue-collar and skilled craftsmen's jobs (to 41 percent); and more rapid growth, especially among white-collar workers, of the commercial sector (from 14 to 17 percent). The bureaucratic/professional field remained stable (7 percent), while domestic servants and occasional laborers declined (to 5 percent). It was a profile of a maturing industrial society with a burgeoning urban white-collar class, but also with a still large agricultural hinterland.

Power Elites

The Versailles Treaty drastically reduced the German army, now named *Reichswehr* (Reich Defense Force), to a corps of 100,000 soldiers, stripped of heavy weaponry and unsupported by air force and navy. This did not prevent active-duty retention of many members of the prewar, strongly Prussian upper-class officer corps. Army policy was to train as many men as possible in the rank-and-file to function as noncommissioned officers in a restored, full-sized army of the hoped-for future. Reichswehr leaders cultivated an ethic of political self-sufficiency. They recognized the Weimar state's authority, but often only reluctantly, and mostly coolly. Should the republic collapse, the army was capable of shifting allegiance.

It was fateful that the Kaiser's forces surrendered in 1918 without having suffered catastrophic battlefield defeat, and with its far-flung wartime conquests in eastern Europe seemingly intact. It was hard for the public, for many professional soldiers, and especially for militarist-minded political rightists to see the roots of the war's loss in inadequate resources – food, fuel, manpower, sea power, allies – to sustain the two-front fight. On the right, it became an article of faith that the vanquishing of German arms followed from a "stab in the back" that defeatist or traitorous German leftist revolutionaries delivered to an idealized heroic, self-sacrificing, and well-disciplined frontline army. Desire for revenge, both against the victors in the world war and the German left, burned hot in many a civilian and Weimar officer's heart.

The civil bureaucracy retained largely unpurged its middle and lower-ranking corps of pre-1918 officials, most of whom had been conservative monarchists. The new republic's constitution, liberally extending the citizenry's civil rights, allowed public officials to form their own interest group and

(a)

FIGURE 14.3. FROM FARM AND FACTORY TO APARTMENT HOUSE
(a) A late-Weimar-era photograph by Albert Renger-Patzsch, an exponent of the post-Expressionist artistic movement known as "the New Objectivity" (*neue Sachlichkeit*). It is a masterful depiction of a widespread social-cultural juxtaposition, evoking ominous transition from rural rootedness and nearness to nature to industrialism's sooty and anonymous asphalt, or – in the sociological terminology of the day – from "community" (*Gemeinschaft*) to "society" (*Gesellschaft*).

lobbying organizations. Although they swore a loyalty oath to Weimar, many were vehemently critical of it and flaunted monarchist views. The government viewed the defiantly antirepublican Communists and National Socialists as beyond the pale, and banned them from civil service employment.

Civil officials hired after 1918, especially in the big, republic-spanning, SPD-ruled federal state of Prussia, mostly felt ideologically committed to Weimar. Still, in 1933 it was not difficult for masses of long-employed public servants, in an atmosphere of fear and coercion, to shift their loyalties – or at least to bow – to Hitler's regime. In the judiciary, prewar judges retained their posts on condition they professed allegiance to the republic, as most of them did. But, like some other public officials, many judges (now with lifetime tenure) displayed open partisanship against the Weimar state, particularly in trials for political offenses (including, sensationally, right-wing violence, sometimes lethal, against the republic's high functionaries).

(b)

FIGURE 14.3 *(continued)*
(b) Stuttgart's Weissenhof housing development, completed in 1927, designed by
the internationally renowned German architect Mies van der Rohe in the modernist
"Bauhaus style" aiming to pragmatically and coolly aestheticize everyday life (and
famously pioneered by Walter Gropius and colleagues at their Bauhaus Institute,
founded in 1919). The Weimar years witnessed many other such municipally subsi-
dized housing projects, which especially favored and appealed to better-paid white- and
blue-collar families. Here, as also in new office buildings and department stores, was
the breakthrough into daily experience of architectural modernism's "functional," flat-
roofed, unornamented, ever-higher (and sometimes curvilinear) glass-and-steel structures.
Source: (a) © Albert-Renger Patzsch Archiv/Ann und Jürgen Wilde, Zülpich/Artists
Rights Society (ARS), New York; (b) Bildarchiv Preussischer Kulturbesitz/Art Resource,
NY.

Among teachers and professors, many who remained psychologically and
intellectually tied to the Kaisers' era stayed at their posts, prejudicing students
against the new government. Recruitment of democratically minded educators
proceeded only slowly. Many intellectuals were "republicans of the head"
(rather than "of the heart"). University students – as a numerically small and
proud upper-class social-intellectual elite, as entrants into overfilled job markets
for degree holders, and also as mostly young men whose older brothers, fathers,
and other elder relatives had (unlike them) fought and often died in the world
war – inclined strongly to right-wing nationalism and right-radical politics.

A 1931 opinion poll at the republic's eighteen universities showed that, at fourteen of these, 40 percent and more of the students favored the National Socialists. At eight universities, more than 50 percent were pro-Hitler. These were proportions much higher than in the country at large.

Parliamentary Politics

Was Weimar a "republic without republicans"? This was almost the case, for by the early 1930s the only sizeable party that positively favored Weimar's existence over any other alternative was Social Democracy. Moreover, the seemingly ultraprogressive constitution possessed features that facilitated right-wing political agitation and success. These included an electoral system based on proportional representation, enabling radical fringe parties to gain Reichstag representation without winning majorities in election districts. After awarding of parliamentary seats to the candidates of the larger parties who had won them directly, further mandates were assigned according to the number of votes cast on the national level. If requisite minimum numbers were achieved, otherwise unelectable small parties gained seats, proportionally reflecting the will of those – some of them extremist-minded antirepublicans – who had voted for them. In this manner the National Socialist Party (NSDAP) first gained voice in the Reichstag.

The Weimar constitution mandated direct popular election of the republic's president, authorizing him (under Article 48) to unilaterally appoint chancellors with emergency-decree powers should no parliamentary coalition exist to form a majority government (although the tenure of such emergency cabinets was limited, and their legislative actions required parliament's subsequent ratification). In 1925, following pro-republican Social Democrat Friedrich Ebert's stormy presidency, staunch conservative monarchist and wartime hero Field-Marshal Paul von Hindenburg took office. In 1933, following his 1932 reelection, Hindenburg disastrously employed his article 48 authority to appoint Hitler as Reich chancellor.

From 1919 to 1923, the Social Democrats, middle-class liberal German Democratic Party, and Catholic Center Party were Weimar government's pillars. This was a period of severe instability and frequent crises, including armed violence. In the years between 1924 and 1929, the right-leaning liberals under Gustav Stresemann' leadership embraced the republic, signaling the newly stabilized regime's advancing acceptance in the business class and among moderate middle-class nationalists. Bourgeois coalitions tended to rule, while the SPD stood in sometimes vehement opposition. Yet a workable domestic parliamentary order emerged, solidified by foreign minister and sometimes Prime Minister Stresemann's guiding of Germany back into the international diplomatic system. The Nationalist (prewar Conservative) party, alongside numerous small-scale but vociferous right-wing radical splinter parties (including National Socialists), scorned Weimar, and so too did the Communists. (For electoral data and analysis, see this chapter's appendix.)

FIGURE 14.4. WEIMAR'S BOURGEOIS DEFENDERS
Gustav Stresemann (1878–1929), prewar National Liberal politician and advocate of business interests and overseas expansion (and World War I annexations), postwar leader of the right-leaning middle-class liberal German People's Party, chancellor (1923) and foreign minister (1923–1929), co-recipient with his French counterpart, Aristide Briand, of the 1926 Nobel Peace Prize for diplomatic rapprochement between Germany and France. Here he speaks to the League of Nations in Geneva on Germany's 1926 admission: an important measure of the Weimar Republic's advancing integration into the postwar international system.

Succeeding Stresemann as leading bourgeois defender of the Weimar Republic was Heinrich Brüning (1885–1970), Catholic Center Party deputy and Reich chancellor, 1930–1932. Despite diplomatic success in gaining suspension of German reparations payments imposed by the Versailles Treaty, Brüning lost political authority by rigid commitment to ineffective antistatist economic orthodoxy and by his dependence on President Hindenburg's backing and Social Democratic parliamentary toleration. As after 1930 the Weimar Republic's political system grew increasingly dysfunctional, Brüning would likely have supported modifying the constitution in a conservative-monarchical direction, but he did not seek to subvert the republic to that end.
Source: Deutsches Bundesarchiv.

The Great Depression joltingly signaled its political effects in the 1930 Reichstag elections, in which the National Socialists – previously a small if noisy presence – made spectacular gains while Communists surged forward at SPD expense. Thereafter neither a pro-republican bourgeois party coalition nor an SPD-led government could command a parliamentary majority. A presidentially empowered emergency-decree regime muddled along into 1932 under conservative chancellor Heinrich Brüning, of the Catholic Center Party, with liberal middle-class backing and toleration from the opposition by the SPD (which feared worse things should this cabinet fall). Brüning initiated no effective anti-Depression policies, but leaned toward the western world's business-class orthodoxy (embodied in the United States' Herbert Hoover) of cutting taxes and government spending so as to encourage reinvigorated private-sector investment. But this, in face of consumer demand's collapse, failed before 1933 to materialize.

After the National Socialists doubled their vaulting strength in the July 1932 Reichstag elections, President Hindenburg dropped Brüning in favor of other right-wing chancellors who might better – or so Hindenburg's friends argued – hold the line against further Hitlerite gains, while moving the country toward a stronger presidential regime or even (as old-fashioned conservatives wished) restoration of the Hohenzollern monarchy. Although unable to form a cabinet among themselves, an SPD-led Reichstag majority drawn from the moderate parties was prepared to continue backing Brüning's emergency chancellorship, suggesting that Hindenburg acted unconstitutionally, and certainly unwisely, in dismissing Brüning.

Later, despite significant ebbing of the National Socialist tide in the November 1932 elections, Hindenburg's advisers counseled him to appoint Hitler as chancellor, in order – as some argued – to "force the NSDAP to take responsibility" rather than continue to undermine the national government through relentless opposition and agitation. To lessen Hindenburg's and his advisers' qualms, and soften the blow to public opinion at home and abroad, Hitler's cabinet, installed January 30, 1933, included a majority of right-wing conservative non-National Socialists. Yet high-ranking NS leader Hermann Göring assumed key powers as Minister of Interior and Minister-President of the federal state of Prussia (whose SPD-led government Brüning's successor as chancellor had ominously, and unconstitutionally, sacked in July 1932). Hitler aimed to hold elections soon in which his party would, as he was confident, gain majority backing in parliament. Otherwise, he would be obliged – or so others thought – to leave office.

Hitler was *not* – as is still today widely believed (even in Germany) – voted into office by electoral majority. But the National Socialists' great strength at the polls (peaking, in unintimidated voting, at 37.4 percent in July 1932) created an oppositional phalanx that, when reinforced by the advancing Communists (whose electoral share rose to 17 percent in the November 1932 elections), all but prevented any combination of parties excluding both NSDAP and KPD from governing the country with a majority. A sufficient number voted against Hitler to block formation of a National Socialist majority government. Yet his shadow on the landscape was so pervasive that President Hindenburg yielded the chancellorship to him and, with it, access to levers of power that could help achieve a majority.

Even then, in the final pre-dictatorship elections of March 5, 1933, staged under extreme political duress and police repression of the left-wing parties, the NSDAP's 43.9 percent fell short of a majority, which only Hitler's conservative

(a)

FIGURE 14.5. EVE OF CIVIL WAR?

Among Hitler's voters, many feared the Communists would attempt to seize power, plunging the land into civil war. The Communists themselves anticipated the republic's political breakdown, opening an insurrectionary window. They expected a National Socialist dictatorship, should it emerge, to be unstable and short-lived, conjuring up hope of a future power-seizure from the left. Yet, in the end, it was Hitler's party that staged the revolution.

(a) KPD leader Ernst Thälmann (1886–1944) as messianic revolutionist, addressing a 1925 audience in both working-class and bourgeois dress. Symbolically, he clasps hands with both a worker and a man of the middle class. Thälmann's and most other German Communists' style and self-presentation were unmistakably Bolshevik – a message about their inspiration lost on no one, especially not anticommunists. In Weimar's end-phase, after 1929, Thälmann tirelessly marched with his party followers through Berlin's proletarian districts, hard-fought-over between Communists and Nazis. Under Hitler's dictatorship Thälmann suffered imprisonment and, finally, execution – a fate endured by thousands of other communists.

(b)

FIGURE 14.5 *(continued)*
(b) a glimpse into everyday National Socialist agitation, showing Adolf Hitler in 1930 at Munich's massive beer-hall, the Hofbräuhaus, much frequented by National Socialists. He sits – abstaining from alcohol as was his custom – with "party comrades" (*Parteigenossen*, a word nazifying a time-honored Socialist term of address) after having delivered one of his innumerable speeches, not seldom of two or three hours' duration. Second to Hitler's right sits Gregor Strasser, who with his brother Otto organized the NS Party's crucial advance after the mid-1920s into north German industrial cities. Breaking with Hitler in 1932, Gregor fell to bullets in the Hitler-ordered political purge of June 1934 (see Chapter 16). Second from the right sits Max Amann, Hitler's World War I comrade, financial manager, and NSDAP press mogul.
Source: Bildarchiv Preussischer Kulturbesitz/Art Resource, NY.

Nationalist allies' additional 8 percent gave them. The National Socialists now possessed sufficient executive and police power, and enough popular support or fear-ridden toleration, to fasten a populist dictatorship on the country.

Appendix: Electoral Politics, 1919–1933

Row 10 (see Table 14.1) depicts the fortunes of the pro-republican Weimar Coalition parties. Although they soon lost their majority, they fared well as a group until 1930. After 1924 they sometimes gained reinforcement in support of the Weimar Republic from the bourgeois center-right People's Party (DVP) and even the nationalist-monarchist DNVP. Row 12 dramatizes the deepening split on the left between SPD and KPD, with Communists gaining fast at Social Democrats' expense after 1928. The political parties' relative strength does not directly reflect behavior of their own previous voters alone, but also the actions of other voters abandoning former allegiances. Among other possibilities, some voters switched from left to right, and vice versa.

Yet, aggregate changes indicate broad trends of support for – or resistance to – the rising NSDAP. The combined vote on the left (SPD and KPD) stood at 37.3 percent in November 1932, showing that National Socialism could not conquer this front in the political battle, although it wore it down somewhat. Above all, as row 11 shows, the NSDAP gained by swallowing up the right-leaning splinter parties and the constituencies of the former bourgeois parties – DDP, DVP, DNVP. The National Socialists gained too at Catholics' expense. Yet in November 1932 the Catholic parties held three-quarters (15 percent) of the strong position they had occupied in 1919 (20 percent).

The National Socialists' rise was meteoric. Yet in November 1932, more than 53 percent of the German electorate opposed them and other right-wing antirepublican forces. Within this majority, however, the Communists (17 percent) stood bitterly opposed to the strongly anticommunist Social Democrats and Catholics (with combined strength of 36 percent).

The March 1933 polling reflected the emergent dictatorship's preelection repression of the left parties – especially the Communists. The KPD could not campaign freely, and its deputies could not take their seats in the new Reichstag. The parliament's composition thus favored the National Socialists and their Nationalist Party (DNVP) allies, who together claimed a thin majority of 52 percent in this last Weimar election.

Big business did not especially favor the NSDAP with financial aid before establishment of Hitler's dictatorship. National Socialist radicalism, with its talk of "German socialism," alarmed some businessmen. Yet, from the 1930 election's aftermath to the end of 1932, the various business lobbies judiciously funded the NSDAP alongside other parties and groups. And when, after Hitler's appointment as Chancellor in January 1933, his impending triumph appeared increasingly likely, big business jumped on the bandwagon, massively contributing to the NSDAP's electoral success in March 1933.

The *presidential* elections of 1925 and 1932 were important events. In the 1925 polling, six parties presented candidates in the first round. In the decisive runoff, Paul von Hindenburg, the candidate of the right, defeated the combined center/moderate left parties' candidate, the Catholic Center's Wilhelm Marx. The Communists ran their leader, Ernst Thälmann, in both pollings, gaining nearly 2 million votes in the runoff. The charge has been raised against them of having lifted Hindenburg into office (even though had they abstained from voting, Hindenburg would have also won). The Communists saw no advantage to themselves in strengthening a liberal-democratic republic of Social Democrats and bourgeois moderates. What requires explanation is the Communists' appeal to the people who chose to support them.

TABLE 14.1. *Parliamentary Elections, 1919–1933*

PARTY a. seats b. percent of vote	1919 National Assembly	1920 Reichstag	1924 (May) Reichstag	1924 (Dec.) Reichstag	1928 Reichstag	1930 Reichstag	1932 (July) Reichstag	1932 (Nov.) Reichstag	1933 (March) Reichstag
Eligible Voters (millions) Percent Voting	36.8 83.0	35.9 79.2	38.4 77.4	39.0 78.8	41.2 75.6	43.0 82.0	44.2 84.1	44.4 80.6	44.7 88.7
1. Social Democrats SPD	a. 165 b. 37.9	a. 103 b. 21.9	a. 100 b. 20.5	a. 131 b. 26.0	a. 153 b. 29.8	a. 143 b. 24.5	a. 133 b. 21.6	a. 121 b. 20.4	a. 120 b. 18.3
2. Catholic Party Zentrum/BVP	a. 91 b. 19.7	a. 84 b. 18.0	a. 81 b. 16.6	a. 88 b. 17.3	a. 78 b. 15.1	a. 87 b. 14.8	a. 97 b. 15.7	a. 90 b. 15.0	a. 92 b. 14.0
3. Bourgeois Democrats DDP	a. 75 b. 18.6	a. 39 b. 8.3	a. 28 b. 5.7	a. 32 b. 6.3	a. 25 b. 4.9	a. 20 b. 3.8	a. 4 b. 1.0	a. 2 b. 1.0	a. 5 b. 0.9
4. Liberal-Nationalists DVP	a. 19 b. 4.4	a. 65 b. 13.9	a. 45 b. 9.2	a. 51 b. 10.1	a. 45 b. 8.7	a. 30 b. 4.8	a. 7 b. 1.2	a. 11 b. 1.9	a. 2 b. 1.1
5. Conserv.-Nationalists DNVP	a. 44 b. 10.3	a. 71 b. 15.1	a. 95 b. 19.5	a. 103 b. 20.5	a. 73 b. 14.3	a. 41 b. 7.0	a. 37 b. 5.9	a. 52 b. 8.7	a. 52 b. 8.0
6. Right/Center "Splinter Parties"	a. 7 b. 1.6	a. 10 b. 3.1	a. 29 b. 8.7	a. 29 b. 8.5	a. 51 b. 13.1	a. 72 b. 11.1	a. 11 b. 2.7	a. 12 b. 3.1	a. 7 b. 1.7
7. Independent SPD = USPD	a. 22 b. 7.6	a. 83 b. 17.6							
8. Communists DKP	a. – b. –	a. 4 b. 2.1	a. 62 b. 12.6	a. 45 b. 8.9	a. 54 b. 10.6	a. 77 b. 13.1	a. 89 b. 14.6	a. 100 b. 16.9	a. [81] b.[12.3]
9. National Socialists NSDAP	a. – b. –	a. – b. –	a. 32 b. 6.6	a. 14 b. 3.0	a. 12 b. 3.5	a. 107 b. 18.3	a. 230 b. 37.4	a. 196 b. 33.1	a. 288 b. 43.9
10. Total 1–3 = Weimar Coalition	a. 331 b. 76.2	a. 226 b. 48.2	a. 207 b. 42.8	a. 251 b. 49.6	a. 256 b. 49.8	a. 250 b. 43.1	a. 234 b. 38.3	a. 213 b. 36.4	a. 217 b. 33.2
11. Total 4–6,9 = Right Parties	a. 70 b. 16.3	a. 146 b. 32.1	a. 201 b. 44.0	a. 197 b. 42.1	a. 181 b. 39.6	a. 250 b. 41.2	a. 285 b. 47.2	a. 271 b. 46.8	a. 349 b. 54.7
12. Total 1,7,8 = Left Parties	a. 187 b. 45.5	a. 190 b. 40.8	a. 162 b. 33.1	a. 176 b. 34.9	a. 207 b. 40.4	a. 220 b. 37.6	a. 222 b. 36.2	a. 221 b. 37.3	a. [201] b.[30.6]

Source: data from http://www.gonschior.de/weimar/Deutschland/Uebersicht.RTW.html.

259

In 1932, Hitler's presidential candidacy failed in the face of a rally behind Hindenburg of all anti-National Socialist forces, except – once more – for the Communists, who again voted for Thälmann. Communist separatism had no effect on this election's outcome. Even though he lost the presidential bid, Hitler gained twice the votes his party had reaped in 1930, imparting to the National Socialist movement a juggernaut quality that vaulted it still higher in the July Reichstag elections.

In the November 1932 Reichstag elections, the NSDAP's vote slumped considerably – by more than four percentage points – from its July peak. Many NSDAP opponents, and even some influential National Socialists, reckoned that Hitler's wave had crested. Yet Hindenburg and his advisers declined to play a waiting game, especially as Communist strength was rising. In retrospect, especially considering the 1933 upturn in employment and industrial output, a strategy of excluding Hitler from office at all costs might well have blocked the National Socialist dictatorship. But the question whether the Weimar Republic could have been restored to working order as a parliamentary democracy raises many doubts.

15

A People without a State? *Volk ohne Staat?*
Middle-Class Discontent and Populist Utopia

Interwar Europe witnessed wide rejection of pre-1914 liberalism's reigning hopes. Popular disillusionment was keen with parliamentary rule steered by privileged elites with often only tenuous popular consent. Had the aristocrats and bourgeois gentlemen not led Europe into its greatest bloodletting? There was widespread dissatisfaction, too, with the capitalist economy that, during World War I, fell conspicuously under the domination of the militarist state and great industrialists, while ordinary consumers went hungry. After the onset in 1929 of unprecedentedly severe world-spanning depression, the western free-market system appeared in many eyes in terminal crisis.

In noisy harmony with these crises and doubts was the emergence of militant and even revolutionary nationalist movements. They aimed, in the name of "the people," "the nation," or "the race," to silence political parties and social or ethnic groups thought to menace the collective destiny. The violence-prone among them, when they could boast a mass base, embodied the new and ominous phenomenon of fascism. This term derived, by distant etymology, from the symbols of judicial power in ancient Rome, but entered the early twentieth-century vocabulary as a designation in Italian politics for extra-parliamentary opposition groups. It appeared in the name of Italian dictator Benito Mussolini's political movement, the *Partito Nazionale Fascista*, which came to power in 1922 through collusion with the once-liberal monarchy against a leftist populism whose strength, while real, Mussolini exaggerated to heighten his own self-proclaimed role as Italian national savior.

Mussolini's was the first successful right-wing nationalist revolt against the liberal-democratic (would-be "Wilsonian") world order that the western Allies' World War I victory had aimed to establish and uphold. Others followed in the 1930s, above all in Hitler's Germany, but also in Austria, Spain and Portugal, Romania and Greece and other eastern European and Balkan countries, and even, finally, after its 1940 defeat by German arms, in previously stalwartly – if not calmly – democratic France.

Important differences distinguished the various fascist movements, particularly in the practice of murderous violence, but also in the salience in theory and practice of racist ideology, and of the Christian religion too. They were conscious of their mutual affinities, especially in marking them off from Communists, whose followers – inspired by Bolshevik victory in Russia – were proliferating (whether at home or in neighboring countries) wherever fascist or semi-fascist regimes came to power.

Fascist movements looked to charismatic leaders of extra-parliamentary mass movements to seize power from the despised democratic (or self-styled democratic) state. They branded the Soviet Union and allied western communist parties as arch-enemies, to be destroyed root and branch. They preached class conflict's end through attainment of new forms of national community, invigorated by mobilization of youth and women, alongside the male-dominated fascist party and paramilitary formations glorifying the martial virtues that had justified World War I's sacrifices. Rival political parties, however conservative and fascism-friendly, usually faced – and eventually suffered – suppression or disbandment.

To sharpen national community's boundaries, fascist movements stigmatized opposing ideological movements – and groups they branded as ethnically or racially hostile – as enemies to be silenced, whether with threatened, exemplary, or comprehensive violence. To resuscitate and ennoble the capitalist market-economy, they preached transcendence of individual egotism and greed, while pouring government spending into industrial recovery, social welfare, and armaments production. To restore shaken or fallen national power, they advocated belligerent foreign policies and territorial expansion, whether at European neighbors' expense or in colonial conquest overseas, or both. The grandest destiny was empire.

To reinvigorate the national body, they championed programs of physical fitness and public health, sometimes informed by then-fashionable eugenic theories aiming to separate out and prevent from biological reproduction people or groups stigmatized as degenerate or inferior. Paired with ideological racism, eugenics steered toward physical domination and bureaucratically administered violence, if not worse things. In power, fascist movements mounted dictatorships of the charismatic leader, stringently policed to terrorize the unwilling and lukewarm into conformity. They ruthlessly repressed enemies, whether or not engaged in active resistance (as they often were).

National Socialist Germany, under Adolf Hitler's dictatorship, was the most repressive and destructive of Europe's fascist powers. It was the product of a national crisis that, in the years between 1914 and 1933, shook society, economy, and political system more severely than in any other large European country, with the exception of Russia, which under the communist regime after 1917 also succumbed to an increasingly brutal single-party, police-state dictatorship.

National Socialism's roots reach into the pre-1914 world in which Adolf Hitler grew to early maturity. But it was Imperial Germany's unforeseen revolutionary breakdown at war's end, and the Weimar Republic's turbulent instability and contested legitimacy, that gave him a nation-wide stage for his demagogic talents, as well as – more importantly – an interested audience. Without a German society susceptible to National Socialism's appeals, even if only among a large minority, Hitler would have remained the obscure and powerless figure he was when World War I broke out.

To accept National Socialist propaganda proclaiming Hitler an irresistible man of destiny and power – or the post-1945 popular media's reversals of this image, casting Hitler as the German nation's uncanny hypnotizer (or embodiment of the "dark side" of the "national character," or of cosmic Evil itself) – is to lose sight of the diverse interests and anxieties impelling some, but not all, people to look to the National Socialists for solutions. Millions turned to the political left, while still others clung to the Weimar Republic or dreamed of the Kaiser's return.

The "Folkish Ideology"

Despite pre-1914 Imperial Germany's strength and growing prosperity, there were many who viewed the rapidly moving trajectories of society and culture with dissatisfaction or alarm. A group of conservative, mainly Protestant intellectuals gave voice to various protests that, taken together, came to be known as "folkish thinking" (*völkisch*, from the word *Volk*). This was right-wing populism and nationalism, radical and intolerant. Hitler himself, in his 1925 book *Mein Kampf* ("*My Struggle*") employed the word liberally, especially to describe the goal his movement aimed to actualize – the "folkish state." National Socialism's authoritative newspaper was the "Folkish Observer" (*Völkischer Beobachter*), whose circulation soared above one million after 1933.

The folkish publicists' audience counted many schoolteachers, clergymen, and others of the educated middle class. Here too were many male white-collar workers, lower officials, self-employed craftsmen, and family farmers. Those who saw themselves as vulnerable to personal loss resulting from social change, or as suffering from insufficient social recognition, were most likely to interest themselves in folkish ideology and its social-political prescriptions.

The movement's principal message was that the *Volk* – that is, the nation, understood in its populist, grassroots ethnic sense as "the German-speaking people" – was in danger. Underlying this thought was the belief that the *Volk* did – or should – constitute an organic whole (although it is common experience that modern societies grow socially and culturally more complex, and are seriously and often durably divided along various internal fault lines). Folkish voices arose against the danger of democratic mass politics trending, as alarmists claimed, toward "materialist liberalism" and "godless, collectivist socialism." They railed against the parliamentarized "political party-state," dominated by monied lobbies and other powerful interests.

They denounced the political self-mobilization of non-German nationalities or national minorities against German interests, especially in the Habsburg monarchy. But also in Imperial Germany the millions-strong Polish population in Prussia's eastern provinces resisted Germanization pressures and built up a linguistically demarcated subculture that many nationalists found as threatening as German Social Democracy. Were Prussia's eastern provinces succumbing to "Polonization"? Would Polish-speaking citizen-subjects seize a moment of German preoccupation – in a future war, perhaps – to rebel and break away, taking their formerly German-ruled provinces with them in founding, together with their ethnic brethren under Russian and Austrian rule, a resurrected Polish state?

Folkish eyes commonly perceived industrial capitalism as a menace, overshadowing rural and small-town society with burgeoning big-city culture and celebrating secularism and sexual permissiveness. Industrialization threatened social declassing or proletarianization, while enabling ascent of a new German (and German-Jewish) capitalist elite or "plutocracy." Rising living standards and improved public health favored population growth among eastern European peoples, alarming German nationalists in Bismarck's empire, the Habsburg monarchy, and in Germanophone minority communities elsewhere. The folkish image was of a "rising Slavic tide" engulfing German "outposts in the East."

There was, further, the challenge of cultural modernism, displayed in the aforementioned artistic and literary avant-gardes (such as Social Realism, Impressionism, Symbolism) and defying the earlier nineteenth century's often sentimentalized middle-brow culture. "Soulless materialism" loomed in the rise of modern science, especially Darwinism, with its challenges to religious tradition. Compounding the dilemma was presumed elite indifference to folkish concerns, stoking suspicion that aristocracy and ruling dynasties, basking in wealth and comfortable privileges, would float with the treacherous currents rather than steer the *Volk* against them.

Resentment also simmered at seeming self-satisfaction among prosperous and powerful business leaders. Women's emergence into the public sphere rattled folkish nerves as well: the rise of feminist politics, male competition with women for white-collar jobs, threats posed by novel secular or bohemian subcultures to Victorian-style morality and sexual practices, convention-defying, scandalously erotic depictions of women in art.

Pre-1914 folkish writers' prescriptions for action in face of the daunting and manifold challenges they conjured up called, first and foremost, for unifying and strengthening the *Volk* by subordinating class and other sectional interests to national solidarity and community (*Gemeinschaft*). The nation seemed riven by conflict, which sapped its will to power and even survival. The chief forces promoting inner division were socialism, with its doctrine of class struggle; liberalism, with its emphasis on individual self-interest and worldly comfort; "Manchester capitalism," that is, the free-enterprise, laissez-faire economy, defended both by liberals and business-minded conservatives, benefiting the strong against the weak to the disadvantage of national solidarity and idealism; and cultural modernism, with its flight from reassuring realism in visual art and

FIGURE 15.1. VIENNESE MODERNISM

Gustav Klimt (1862–1918) was the preeminent painter in the late Habsburg Empire – controversial, but also celebrated and fashionable. In the graphic arts, his work epitomizes the turn-of-the-century *Jugendstil* ("Youth Style"), familiar in the West as Art Nouveau. Pictured here is one of a pair of 1904–1907 paintings known as *Freundinnen* ("Women Friends") or *Wasserschlangen* ("Water Snakes"). In these, as in many of his other numerous depictions of women, a powerful erotic and emotionalized atmosphere, often (as here) presented in a dream-like setting, prevails. In the pre-1914 years, psychological and sexual themes – profoundly explored not only by Sigmund Freud, but also such widely read authors as novelist-playwright Arthur Schnitzler (1862–1931) – loomed large in avant-garde cultural life. Klimt's symbolist and subjectivist art outraged defenders of the nineteenth-century conservative tradition of artistic verisimilitude to nature in service of bourgeois morality.

Architectural modernism also flourished in pre-1914 Vienna, notably in the work of Joseph Hoffmann (1870–1956), which in its rejection of nineteenth-century historicism and ornamentation anticipated post-1918 Bauhaus architecture. He and Klimt cooperated on pathbreaking projects. Other great figures in late Habsburg cultural life were the pioneering musical modernists Arnold Schönberg (1874–1951) and Anton Webern (1883–1945), and the writers Robert Musil (1880–1942) and Franz Kafka (1883–1924), who like Klimt cast aside bourgeois pieties and illusions of life's order and stability. Folkish and, later, National Socialist opinion condemned such art as antisocial and decadent.

Source: Artothek.

literature, and its dissonant or atonal musical innovations – all, seemingly, anti-bourgeois provocations and betrayals of middle-brow taste and morality.

Folkish thinking could not accept that these developments had emerged from a conflict-laden Germany and Europe as expressions, variously, of self-interest, opposition to injustice, or the modern world's new aesthetic energies.

(a)

FIGURE 15.2. PHILOSOPHERS AND ARTISTS OF ANTILIBERAL TRANSCENDENCE

Crucial to both composer-poet Richard Wagner (1813–1883) and philosopher-poet Friedrich Nietzsche (1844–1900) was the thought of philosopher Arthur Schopenhauer (1788–1860), particularly his *World as Will and Idea* (1819). This post-Kantian, post-Hegelian masterpiece interpreted material and biological life as an irrational, passion-driven realm which the wise would seek to selflessly transcend in art, and especially music, Being's highest expression, where human subjectivity merged with cosmic totality.

(a) Wagner, here photographed in 1870 with his wife Cosima, daughter of celebrated Romantic pianist and composer Franz Liszt. Wagner reinterpreted operatic theater as the "total art work" (*Gesamtkunstwerk*), and sought to harmoniously integrate in his "musical dramas" – as he fervently believed ancient Greek tragedy had once done – continuous song, poetry, and narrative (all genially authored by himself). The result would inspire humanity, he hoped, to transcend middle-class hypocrisy and the blinders of materialistic common-sense philosophy and rise into a culturally ennobled community.

Wagner, a self-willed student of Schopenhauer, fused this aesthetics with romantic German nationalism in his four-part opera *The Ring of the Nibelung*. This is a work of Shakespearean depth and complexity that charted humanity's victory, through love both carnal and emotional, over the gods. Yet it was a triumph compromised by human lust for power and domination, leaving the question open whether, in the future, love

(b)

FIGURE 15.2 *(continued)* and selflessness would ever again prevail. In notorious essays Wagner propagated an anti-Semitism based on hostility to commercialization of culture (although this was far from a "Jewish invention"). In his later years, he preached an eccentric spiritualized biological racism that imagined purification and regeneration of humanity through post-Christian religion, art, and vegetarianism.

(b) An undated photograph of the young Friedrich Nietzsche (1844–1900), whose philosophy denounced Christian humility ("slave morality"), middle-class conformism, political democracy, and mass nationalism. This it did in the name of the heroic individual (*Übermensch*) who – driven by an inner and subjective "Will to Power" – would formulate his own morality and rise to domination of Being, bringing forth the high-cultural creations that alone justify human life. A Darwinist strain in Nietzsche's thought left "the weak" and "ungifted" with no claims, although their services to cultural and political elites were indispensable.

Important for this chapter's theme is less these towering figures' contribution to "folkish thinking," even though Wagner's anti-Semitism was influential among sect-like followers and Nietzsche's later disciples unfaithfully bent his philosophy into intolerant nationalism's tool. More significant was the legitimacy their work and ideas lent to rejection of Enlightenment rationalism and principles of democratic liberty and equality in favor of a "higher" or "deeper" Being, where the "superior" branches of humanity would flourish. Such cultural elitism was, in the dawning age of democratic mass politics, easily transmuted into nationalist fantasy and arrogance, however vulgar it might have seemed to these refined aesthetes.

Source: (a) Bildarchiv Preussischer Kulturbesitz/Art Resource, NY; (b) provenance unknown.

FIGURE 15.3. INTELLECTUAL HEROES OF "FOLKISH THOUGHT"

Pictured here in 1895 is English-born Houston Stewart Chamberlain (1855–1927), Richard Wagner's son-in-law and zealous disciple, whose cloudy 1899 tome, *The Foundations of the Nineteenth Century*, advocated a racialized and imperialistic (but also Christian) vision of world dominance by "Aryan Germanic peoples" that found wide readership and respectful acceptance well outside radical right-wing circles.

Another author conveying grand "historiosophic" vision was Oswald Spengler (1880–1936), whose best-selling *Decline of the West* (1918–1922), conceiving civilizations as mystical organic collectivities, pronounced western liberalism's exhaustion. His political writings exalted antidemocratic "Prussian virtues" but without embracing biological racism. Stylistically innovative and critically lionized modernist poet Stefan George (1868–1933) fashioned around himself a prestigious and influential cult of aristocratic aestheticism, whose membership imagined a Nietzsche-inspired "new Reich" transcending vulgar middle-class society. Although courted by the National Socialists, neither George nor Spengler supported them. Yet their worldviews were adaptable to National Socialist purposes.

Earlier influential folkish writers included Paul de Lagarde (1827–1891), scholar of languages and religion whose widely read political writings offered an antiliberal,

Instead, folkish ideologists and their followers preferred to stigmatize them as "un-German" and harmful invasions of a once-harmonious German world by English, French, and eastern European "corruption" and "radicalism." As late nineteenth-century anti-Semitism revealed, people in the folkish camp were quick to brand contemporary life's unwelcome and disquieting aspects as "Jewish," regardless that the large majority of German (and European) Jews clung to inward-turned religious traditions or had adopted, along with Enlightenment liberalism, conventional European middle-class tastes and values.

Folkish Politics

The strongest impulse was to harness robust state power to the folkish chariot. Parliament, with its parties and interest groups, seemed a site of national weakness. Strong national leadership should subdue if not silence it, while pursuing programs of national renewal and expansion. In Imperial Germany, the Pan-German League, formed in 1893, advocated in Social Darwinist terms overseas territorial expansion and political alliance between all Germans in central and eastern Europe, whether Imperial German citizens or subjects of the Habsburg or Russian Empires. A drive toward German hegemony if not direct rule in eastern Europe coursed through folkish veins.

Political unity of central Europe's Germans, harkening back to 1848's enthusiasm for *Grossdeutschland*, grew more popular as German predominance in the Habsburg monarchy tottered. Georg Ritter von Schönerer's Austrian Pan-German movement condemned the Habsburg monarchy as a debilitated structure incapable of championing German interests, and dreamed of future union with the Bismarckian-Wilhelmian empire.

In the 1890s, as we also earlier saw, many Austrian Germans found a political home in the Christian Social Party, led by Vienna's demagogic (but also respectably bourgeois) mayor Karl Lueger. While asserting their Catholic religious identity and dynastic loyalty, the Christian Socials aggressively demanded conformity of non-Germans settling in German-majority areas (such as the many Czechs in Vienna) to a pro-Habsburg, pro-German mentality. Lueger voiced a demagogic anti-Semitism, aimed against the numerous Jewish immigrants into Vienna and the Habsburg monarchy's western half who brought with them their east European religious orthodoxy and Yiddish-language folkways (although most aimed to embrace Germanophone culture). The Christian Social Party was also a powerful political machine fighting Austrian Social

FIGURE 15.3 *(continued)* anti-Semitic exhortation to the German *Volk*'s expansion through programs of settlement deep into eastern and southeastern Europe. Celebrated, especially among restless middle-class youth, was Julius Langbehn (1851–1907), writer on art and "life-philosophy" (*Lebensphilosophie*), whose book *Rembrandt as Educator* (1890) – with its Nietzsche-flavored, anti-Semitism-tinged message of revolt against modern urban-technological society's aridity – found a wide audience.
Source: provenance unknown.

FIGURE 15.4. FOLKISH (AND LIBERAL) IMPERIALISTS
Depicted here around 1912 – in unstarched bourgeois democratic dress – is Friedrich
Naumann (1860–1919), Protestant pastor, founder in 1895 of the "National-Social
Club," an influential middle-class social-reform movement, and a leading journalist
and politician in the era of William II. Enthusiast for German imperialism, he valorized
Weltpolitik in liberal terms. He urged embracing the 1908 "Young Turk" revolution in the Ottoman Empire in the hope that a modernized and democratized Turkey
would expand German influence and economic opportunities in the Middle East. In
his widely read wartime book, *Mitteleuropa* (1915), he blueprinted a vast sphere of
German hegemony in eastern and southern Europe, cemented by convergence of economic self-interest among German and non-German peoples and resting on widespread
self-administration (but not full sovereignty) of the Russian and Habsburg monarchies'
various hitherto "unliberated" or subject nations. He fundamentally misunderstood
contemporary nationalism in non-German central and east Europe, while his enthusiasm for Ottoman modernization blinded him to the Turkish government's genocidal
campaign of 1915 against its Armenian subjects. Yet Naumann helped transform liberalism into a movement friendlier to state-led reform projects, inspiring such younger
talents as Max Weber and Gertrud Bäumer, and helped craft the progressive 1919

Democracy in the Habsburg state's German-speaking urban-industrial spaces. Together with Schönerer's movement, it framed the young and unknown Adolf Hitler's emergent worldview.

In Imperial Germany, the folkish camp looked to Kaiser William II to back its program, and enthusiastically supported overseas imperialism and government programs to "Germanize" Polish, French, and Danish minorities. It called for legislation favoring family farmers and small businessmen, preference of male white-collar interests over female, state patronage of antimodernist cultural programs, and – among other discriminatory measures – explicit legal exclusion of unbaptized Jews from public-sector employment. The small single-issue anti-Semitic parties that arose in the 1880s failed to take root and survive in parliamentary life for long. Still, the powerful German Conservative Party, together with influential right-wing interest groups promoting big agriculture, the armed forces, and overseas expansion, selectively – in part cynically, in part credulously – employed folkish and anti-Semitic rhetoric.

Despite income inequalities and intermittent recessions, pre-1914 Imperial Germany was a society rapidly gaining in economic strength and wealth. It was difficult for folkish activists to persuade the larger population that the nation was so beset by crisis and danger as they imagined. The nineteenth-century gospel of scientific and social progress – popularized Enlightenment thinking – pervaded the atmosphere, despite cross-cutting ideological conflicts. The persistence in power of old-established, aristocratic-monarchical elites, underpinned by conservative Christianity, worked against the folkish movement's radical aspirations. In the Habsburg realm, most Germans – whatever their misgivings

---

FIGURE 15.4 *(continued)* Weimar constitution. Publicist Paul Rohrbach (1869–1956) also purveyed a liberal and Christian conception of German imperialism. Born in the German ethnic minority in Russia's Baltic provinces, he advocated the Tsarist Empire's dismantling to make way for a system of pro-German successor states in eastern Europe. Simultaneously, Rohrbach defended Germany's "colonial mission" in Africa. Unlike Naumann, he championed the Christian Armenians against Ottoman Turkish violence. His book, *The German Idea in the World* (1912), argued in nonracist, ethical-cultural terms for German "world power."

Bitterly opposed to his liberal counterparts was Heinrich Class (1868–1953), chairman from 1908 of the Pan-German League, cofounder in 1917 of the reactionary Vaterlandspartei, after 1918 anti-Weimar right-radical nationalist and, after 1933, NSDAP advocate. His widely read book, *If I Were Kaiser* (1912), called for the Reichstag's abolition and establishment of an executive dictatorship, repression of Social Democracy, cancellation of citizenship rights for Germany's Jewish-born inhabitants, aggressive Germanization policies on Germany's and Austria's eastern ethnic frontiers, and acquisition of overseas colonies through defiance of Britain and France, backed by redoubled German arms. During World War I he spoke prominently for arch-annexationists. His program darkly foreshadowed that of the National Socialists. Altogether, he embodied the folkish movement, yet – and this difference from the National Socialists is crucial – in a form limited in practice to bourgeois membership.

Source: Bildarchiv Preussischer Kulturbesitz/Art Resource, NY.

about the future – bowed to the elderly and widely respected Kaiser Franz Joseph's rule.

In 1914, folkish thinking represented more an oppositional and subcultural mentality than a powerful movement (despite the many organizations that had arisen espousing one or another of its ideas). It had not succeeded in imposing any program that was not – like the overseas imperialist movement – already widely popular outside folkish circles. Nonetheless, in the future, when stability and confidence in the world of 1914 had been shaken or shattered, it would be a decisive National Socialist accomplishment to absorb virtually the entire constituency for folkish ideas throughout German-speaking central and eastern Europe.

Adolf Hitler's Early Life

Hitler's father was Alois Schickelgruber (1837–1903), a man of humble extramarital birth who adopted the name Hitler from his foster father and whose third wife, Adolf's mother Klara Poelzl (1860–1907), was his niece, twenty-three years his junior. Hitler's father made a career in the Habsburg customs service's lower ranks, achieving a salary comparable to an elementary school principal's and enjoying the respectability that came with wearing the Imperial uniform. Adolf Hitler, born in Austrian Braunau in 1889, grew up in modest middle-class comfort, principally in the Austrian provincial capital of Linz, where in 1895 his father, at age fifty-eight, retired.

Adolf was baptized in the Catholic Church and later briefly served as altarboy. He successfully attended elementary school and at age twelve moved on to the (nonobligatory) secondary-level *Realschule*, with its curriculum of modern languages and sciences, rather than to the more scholarly *Gymnasium*, which trained future scholars, lawyers, and civil servants. Following his father's death he fell into difficulties, having to repeat one year's studies and faltering at social integration. In 1905 he quit school, staying home to prepare himself as a candidate in painting for admission to the Viennese Academy of Art. He spent his free time with friend August Kubizek, a young pianist also aiming to study in Vienna. The two were aspiring artists, with conventional rather than radical aesthetic or social ideals. In these years Hitler became an enthusiast for Richard Wagner's operas, redolent of Germanic romanticism, but also posing revolutionary challenges to worldly and spiritual authorities and pointing to dramatic new dawns for humanity (and twilights of the gods).

In 1907 he and Kubizek moved to Vienna, sharing an apartment. Kubizek gained entry to the music conservatory, but Hitler's application as art student met rejection on grounds that his portfolio, although displaying some technical competence, only weakly represented the human figure and, altogether, lacked originality. He then sought to gain admission in architecture, but this application likewise failed. Meanwhile, his mother had died. As recipient of a civil servant's orphaned child's pension, he possessed modest economic self-sufficiency. But, seemingly, he could not face Kubizek following his second rejection at the Academy of Art, and moved without notice in 1908 to lodgings of his own.

In winter 1909–1910, his pension having expired, he landed on the streets, spending nights in a municipal men's shelter. From 1910 to 1913 he lived in a publicly funded men's home, where he supported himself by painting oils and watercolors – often from picture-postcards – for sale to tourists and other shoppers. In this minor artistic role he succeeded in making an exiguous living. He committed himself to radical nationalism, with its Pan-German hostility to the Habsburg dynasty and wish for fusion of German Austria with Germany. Evading Habsburg army service, he moved in 1913 to the Bavarian capital of Munich, where he continued to work as a street artist.

At World War I's outbreak he volunteered for the Imperial German army. The Habsburg authorities having assented, he served on the western front, mainly as a runner between command posts and the front trenches. He earned two decorations, including the Iron Cross, and rose to corporal rank. In 1918 his zeal for political discussion drew the army's political officers' attention. They recruited him as a speaker who proved capable of addressing common soldiers in defense of army policies and against revolutionary socialist antiwar agitation.

In his Viennese years Hitler had become an anti-Semite, attracted to crude forms that interwove anti-Jewish antagonism with doctrines of "Aryan race purity" and calls to battle against "inferior races," among which in Hitler's mind Jews figured alongside east Europeans and peoples of color. For the half-educated and socially humiliated Hitler, racism in general, and anti-Semitism in particular, appealed on grounds that to be an "Aryan" was not to be a "nobody." Virtue, in other words, lay "in the blood," not in birth or social standing. Such a mentality often stamps lower-class ethnic prejudice. In Vienna, Hitler regularly read a racist and anti-Semitic publication entitled *Ostara*, which – alongside higher intellectual pretensions – warned against the violation of "Aryan" women by "racial inferiors."

As a bourgeois social failure, Hitler – ardent German nationalist from youth – accumulated massive social and political resentments that, under post-World War I influences, he channeled into comprehensive anti-Semitism, eventually anchored in a conspiracy theory that located Jewish power and influence behind everything Hitler hated and feared. This included, notably, the cultural elites who rejected him (as at the Academy of Art), and the Socialists, with whom he brushed shoulders on Vienna's streets and whose emphasis on class struggle, as he thought, divided the German *Volk*, exposing it to subversion by foreign nationalists east and west. At a deeper level, Hitler's anti-Semitism projected hostility he felt toward the social-political establishment onto Jews. This psychological move justified him, in turn, in his own aggressions.

Hitler appears to have had no sustained relations with women until the mid-1920s, when he was in his thirties. Yet it is not necessary to assume any pathologies to account for his obsessions with "racial purity" and combating of prostitution and sexually transmitted diseases. These were commonplace

FIGURE 15.5. HITLER IN OBSCURITY
This photograph, in improbable coincidence, displays a jubilant Hitler on August 2, 1914 in a crowd on Munich's Odeonsplatz, celebrating the war's outbreak. As would-be artist, he was a lifelong partisan of traditionalist, sentimentalized realism, prizing painterly skill while rejecting social criticism or existential doubt. As dictator he amassed through purchase and seizure a vast art collection exemplifying his aesthetic preferences. This he intended to display in a new museum in Austrian Linz, his youthful home, which he planned to rebuild according to his own design as a new cultural Athens in opposition to the Habsburg capital of Vienna, the hated multiethnic scene of his early humiliations. After 1933 he acquired the manuscripts of the (deeply religious) Austrian symphonic composer Anton Bruckner (1824–1896), whom he wished to champion as Beethoven's worthy successor. Of Hitler the soldier his comrades later recalled his earnest self-identification with the war's politics and strategy.
Source: Bildarchiv Preussischer Kulturbesitz/Art Resource, NY.

phobic concerns in his day, particularly among single men on big-city streets and in wartime trenches. In Hitler's view, anti-Semitism and other racial theories seemed to be expressions of modern science, on the same level with eugenics, which advocated "scientifically" guided policies of human reproduction, including sterilization of the "unfit," so as to maximize social health and happiness. As an ill-educated man disoriented by the world's complexity, Hitler like millions of others gravitated to single-factor or monocausal theories – in his case, of race-centered biological determinism – to gain illusory intellectual certainty.

Why Hitler fixated on Jews is in part explicable by the association that right-wing German nationalism and folkish ideology proposed between liberalism, capitalism, and socialism on the one hand and "the Jews" on the other. Yet despite the connection of various notable Jewish-born individuals with them, liberalism, capitalism, and socialism did not depend on Jewish influences for their existence, but rather were largely or wholly inventions of non-Jewish Europeans. Tracing them to Jewish sources was a refusal to understand them on their own terms, while reformulating ancient anti-Jewish prejudices and antagonisms in modern, secularized terms. Hitler, raised a Catholic, had been socialized to accept a dichotomous and apocalyptic view of the world pitting God against Satan, light against darkness, Good against Evil. For those, like him, inclined to embrace it, anti-Semitism perpetuated and politicized this deep-seated drama in the western (and human) imagination.

World War I was crucial in exposing Hitler to mass murder on a vast, industrially based and technologically sophisticated scale, legitimized by nationalist struggle for survival. Participation in the war solved his own life's dilemmas, enabling him to move beyond obscure and directionless life in Munich. He discovered his capacity for steadfastness under fire, his affinity for a male-dominated world of hierarchy, discipline, and justifiable violence, his loyalty to Germany rather than Habsburg Austria, and his talent for political speech. Together with millions of other soldiers and civilians, he saw the war as a cleansing fire, out of which, it could be hoped, new and purer forms of social and political life would emerge.

Hitler was beset by repressed psychological furies. Yet scholars competent in psychiatric diagnosis have generally declined to judge him clinically disordered, at least before the end-phase of World War II, when megalomania and hyper-paranoia, heightened by drugs administered for Parkinson's disease, gained the upper hand. Before then, he was a dangerously self-confident, indefatigable and politically canny man. He was intoxicated by ideology channeling embitterment and aggression, but also by utopian hopes transmuted from early religious socialization into racist nationalism casting the "German Aryan *Volk*" as history's chosen people. His example shows that an individual's social experience and political reaction to the historically given world can well bring forth an ideologically self-justifying response of greatest aggressiveness. Hitler's actions were, as is retrospectively clear, sociopathic and eventually psychopathic. Yet he was also, in his social-cultural environment, a persuasive and charismatic man. The challenge to understanding is less Hitler's uniqueness – real enough, but impossible to plumb to its depths – than humanity's susceptibility to such aggressions and formulas for worldly redemption as he self-righteously championed.

The National Socialists' Ascent

At war's end, the German army retained Hitler's services as speaker combating political unrest and leftism during troop demobilization. Later the army commissioned him to observe the activities in Munich of a minor right-radical party, which sought to win local workers away from Social Democrats and Communists. Dropped from the army's payroll in 1919, Hitler took control of this small party, renaming it in 1920 the German National Socialist Workers Party (NSDAP).

Its twenty-point program railed against the Versailles Treaty and otherwise voiced extremist folkish complaints, including calls to strip those it labeled as Jews of citizenship. Hitler's party, like right-wing nationalists generally, blamed the war's loss on a treacherous "stab in the back" that "Jewish-led" left-wing parties on the home front had delivered against an army undefeated in the field. Yet Hitler also denounced Imperial Germany's power elites for military incompetence, conservative political timidity, and war-profiteering, while also vilifying "international Jewish capitalist conspiracy" against German national interests.

From 1920 to November 1923 Hitler honed his speaker's skills in noisy meetings in Munich beer-halls, rising to local celebrity. His followers, especially men organized in the NSDAP's brown-shirted paramilitary organization, the SA (*Sturmabteilung* or "Storm Division"), aggressively plunged into brawls and street fights with leftist opponents. Local army commanders and conservative politicians governing the federal state of Bavaria viewed National Socialists with benevolence. In 1922 the media-lionized and socially prestigious World War I flying ace Hermann Göring (1893–1946) joined the NSDAP, opening new doors among well-heeled political patrons to Hitler, who astutely widened his upper-class backing.

In 1923 these circumstances led Hitler, emulating Mussolini's 1922 "March on Rome," to stage an uprising in Munich as a first step toward seizing power over the inflation-torn and politically unstable Weimar Republic. Hitler and co-conspirators – including the projected new regime's titular leader, renowned retired war commander Erich Ludendorff – reckoned that, if they took the initiative, Bavaria's rightist officialdom and local Reichswehr commanders would readily join in. On November 9, 1923, the National Socialists attempted their putsch. To Hitler's surprise, the army opposed him in a blaze of bullets that left a number of his partisans dead and led to his and his accomplices' arrest.

Standing trial for sedition, Hitler used the defendant's platform to preach the National Socialist program to the nation-wide public, which through the press now took a keen interest in the failed revolution. He was found guilty and imprisoned, but this incident won him many new followers outside Bavaria, especially in industrial north Germany and Berlin. After thirteen (comfortable) months in prison, Hitler emerged in 1925 to resume the NSDAP's leadership. In prison he had written his book *Mein Kampf*, now published (but, on his editor's insistence, without the intended subtitle, "Four and a Half Years of Struggle Against Lies, Stupidity, and Cowardice").

This rambling tome was rarely carefully read, but in it Hitler laid out his notion, couched in rhetoric of Social Darwinist "racial science" and eugenics, of the future "folkish state" that his government would erect. It was a

FIGURE 15.6. EARLY NATIONAL SOCIALISM

This postcard photograph displays Hitler at the NSDAP's annual meeting in Nürnberg (Nuremberg), September 1923. Outfitted in up-to-date civilian style, he strikes a Mussolini-like pose. On his left, the crude and incendiary anti-Semitic journalist Julius Streicher; on his right, old-school conservative-nationalists, some in Prussian helmets, some in frock coats. Among Hitler's valuable allies in the NSDAP's early years was aforementioned Hermann Göring, who was wont to display his prime war decoration, the prestigious *pour le mérite*, paired with the National Socialist swastika on arm and helmet. Alfred Rosenberg (1893–1946), a German émigré from Tsarist Russia, was editor from 1923 of the National Socialists' principal newspaper, *Völkischer Beobachter* (*Folkish Observer*). His anti-Semitic interpretation of Bolshevism impressed the young Hitler. Rosenberg conceived his murky historico-philosophical treatise, *The Myth of the Twentieth Century* (1930), as a sequel to H. S. Chamberlain's earlier-mentioned work. Dietrich Eckart (1868–1923), *Völkischer Beobachter*'s first editor, minor *littérateur* and anti-Semitic theoretician (eccentrically deriving Bolshevism from biblical Judaism), encouraged Hitler's developing conviction that he was a man of destiny, a compliment Hitler repaid by dedicating *Mein Kampf* to this early mentor.

Source: Bildarchiv Preussischer Kulturbesitz/Art Resource, NY.

blueprint for a ruthlessly racialized society, as well as for power expansion aimed at continental European empire, especially through the Soviet Union's defeat and occupation by its National Socialist conquerors. Germany's destiny lay in acquisition of "living space" (*Lebensraum*) in "the East," where future generations of colonists would settle, building the *Volk* into a vastly larger and more populous nation. A continental-size National Socialist Germany would rank alongside the United States and the British Empire in ruling the earth. *Mein Kampf* did not predict mass murder of Jews, but it aggressively announced that they would be excluded from the German *Volk* and stripped of citizenship, security, and well-being wherever National Socialist power prevailed.

Between 1925 and the its great gains in the 1930 Reichstag elections, the NSDAP figured as a right-wing political sect, largely self-financed by its lower-middle-class and right-wing working-class members. In Joseph Goebbels (1897–1945), a failed playwright with a doctorate in German literature, Hitler possessed a talented propaganda chief and speaker to mass audiences, particularly in northern industrial cities that Hitler, a south German, at first found difficult to sway. Mindful of the army and upper-class conservatives' 1923 betrayal, Hitler aimed, when economic and political instability returned, to come to power by formally legal means.

He and his associates built the NSDAP into an efficient electoral machine while organizing shadow ministries poised to enact National Socialist programs. Under Goebbels's direction a cult of Hitler as "Leader" (*Führer*) arose, culminating from 1927 in yearly multiday mass rallies in tradition-rich Nuremberg. Contemplating such theatrics, scholars have inclined to characterize National Socialism as a quasi-religious movement. But despite the millenialist or redemptionist longings it conjured up, its resolute, often crudely materialist this-worldliness made it unfit as religion in any real sense. Yet it was a charisma-gripped sect eliciting fervent faith – Hitler did not shrink from invoking "the Lord" and "Providence" in his speeches – and readiness for activism and sacrifice among followers.

Between 1930 and Hitler's 1933 appointment as Reich chancellor, the NSDAP won a mass following approaching 40 percent of the electorate. As we saw, it captured the votes of most upper-middle-class, middle-class, and lower-middle-class Germans who previously had supported liberals, left and right, and the conservative parties, as well as the many small splinter or protest movements that sprang up in the 1920s. The National Socialists proved especially attractive to youth from these social circles. Numerous nationalist-minded blue-collar workers, generally without trade-union loyalties, also backed the NSDAP. Women, after initial hesitations over National Socialist belittling of the traditional Christian churches, eventually joined men in roughly equal proportions in voting for Hitler.

The crux of the NSDAP's appeal, spread across the country by Hitler's hyper-energetic campaigning (including innovative use of airplanes and radio addresses), was that National Socialism would restore Germany's fallen strength and greatness by defying the pro-Versailles powers, and even more importantly by uniting the people, presently divided by class conflict, into a great national community – the "community of the *Volk*" (*Volksgemeinschaft*). This Hitler proposed to do by defeating and silencing the "Reds" – Social Democrats, accused of causing the war's loss and misgoverning Weimar Germany, and Communists, denounced for aiming to "bolshevize" the land through bloody revolution. Hitler's vision promised to join the united middle class (*Mittelstand*) with a working class freed of Marxist domination, all following Hitler's appeal to "embrace the fatherland" in confidence that he and the NSDAP would govern in their collective interest.

Hitler attacked conservative upper-class elitism and self-centeredness, evoking a future in which big business, armed forces, universities, and high civil service would be the *Volk*'s servants, not its masters, and access to whose ranks would be widened for lower-class talent. The economic depression would be ended – details were vague – through National Socialist deployment of state fiscal and monetary power.

The NSDAP exhorted women to become activists. In the National Socialist future, they would no longer need to work at wage-earning jobs they disliked, but would follow their biologically driven deepest inclinations and marry to raise families, supported by well-paid husbands and state-funded pro-children (pro-natalist) programs. If necessary, single women would continue to work at "gender-appropriate" salaried jobs. Such appeals to women were quite successful, especially in light of the National Socialists' fervent, idealistically expressed German patriotism, which many Weimar women shared.

As for Christianity, Hitler and colleagues privately professed Nietzschean contempt for its "slave morality." Yet they left committed Protestants and Catholics to suppose that Hitlerism would not oppose their religion's practice and its teaching in the schools. The National Socialists proclaimed themselves, vaguely, "believers in God" (*gottgläubig*). In the Protestant Church, a numerous movement arose – the "German Christian Faith Movement" – advocating the Old Testament's abandonment, recognition of Jesus as "Aryan," and stripping Christianity of its "Jewish elements" (notably the Pauline gospel).

National Socialism's harsh anti-Semitism was self-evident. Yet in the non-stop electioneering of 1930-1932, NSDAP propaganda tended to leave the public to its own imaginings of the Jews' future, rather than placing anti-Semitic threats and tirades at center-stage. Many voters for Hitler rated anti-Semitism high in importance, but others did not, viewing it as a vulgar eccentricity of the folkish right, although not without utility in winning votes in unsophisticated circles. An analogy to the politics of white racism in the American South could be pursued.

The National Socialists presented their "racial program's" positive side as prompt creation of a eugenics-based society in which the "Aryan German" *Volk* would enjoy better health through improved medical care and physical culture. Hitler himself was a vegetarian and strongly condemned smoking and alcohol abuse. Voting for Hitler, people did not feel obliged to believe they were advocating anti-Jewish violence, let alone genocide, a course of action never promoted in pre-1939 official discourse. Nor were NSDAP enthusiasts consciously steering toward renewed world war, for Hitler loftily promised recovery of German equality among the nations by peaceful and diplomatic means. The press and organizations speaking for German Jews bitterly opposed National Socialism but did not imagine the Jewish community's physical life was at stake.

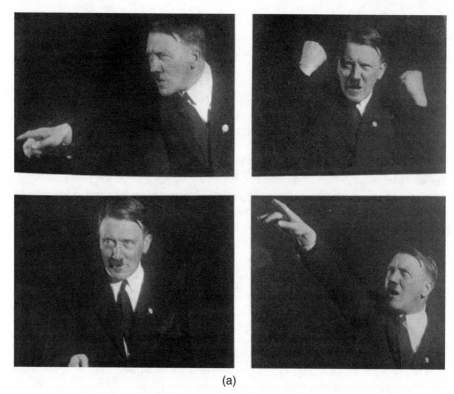

(a)

FIGURE 15.7. NATIONAL SOCIALIST SELF-PRESENTATION: CHARISMA, CALCULATED MEN-
ACE

(a) Widely distributed pictures of September 1930, taken by Heinrich Hoffman, Hitler's
photography czar, demonstrating the future dictator's characteristic rhetorical gestures
and moods. Since 1927 the NSDAP leadership had been groping at annual Nuremberg party rallies toward what eventually became propaganda triumphs, presenting
Hitler in mass-orchestrated settings as messiah-like Führer. (b) Joseph Goebbels. Of
humble Rhineland origins and revolutionary temperament, educated as literary scholar,
he devoted his propagandist's talents to winning National Socialist support in Berlin,
where he aggressively challenged the Communists, emphasizing National Socialism's
revolutionary promises to the urban lower classes.

Future National Socialist police chief and master of concentration and death camps
Heinrich Himmler (1900–1945) was of middle-class Bavarian background, and trained
in agronomy. He organized Hitler's blackshirted bodyguard, the *Schutz-Staffel* (SS),
whose pre-1933 political purpose, successfully realized, was to project Nazism's hard
menace toward its chosen enemies. Ernst Röhm (1887–1934), soldier and post-1918
paramilitary professional, headed the *Sturm-Abteilung* (Storm Troopers), whose anti-
leftist street-fighting and huge numbers prefigured a future, ideologically radicalized
German army. Röhm, Himmler, and Hitler occasionally marched together with their
various uniformed myrmidons, intimidating opponents and projecting an image of
ineluctable, unstoppable triumph.

Source: (1) Deutsches Bundesarchiv; (2) Bildarchiv Preussischer Kulturbesitz/Art
Resource, NY.

(b)

FIGURE 15.7 *(continued)*

Power elites viewed the NSDAP's ambition to govern with nervous ambivalence. The army feared National Socialists would replace the still largely upper-
class officer corps with their own more or less plebeian representatives. Yet the
brownshirted SA, numbering nearly half a million at the end of 1932, seemed
a perfect core of an army liberated from Versailles's shackles. Big business dis-
trusted the National Socialists' talk of "German socialism" but welcomed their
promises to defeat Social Democrats and Communists, whom business owners
and corporate managers widely viewed as their worst enemies. The Protestant
clergy – divided over the issue – in part feared the National Socialists but also
widely saw them as the healthy embodiment of idealism and patriotism, preferable to the liberal secularism they associated with the Weimar Republic. The
Catholic episcopate resolutely forbade its parishioners to join or support the
NSDAP, reinforcing loyalty to the Center Party. But Catholics – or Germans

FIGURE 15.8. INTELLECTUALS: NATIONAL SOCIALIST FRIENDS AND FELLOW TRAVELERS
German intellectual history's vanguard moved from the mid-nineteenth century away
from Enlightenment and romanticist-historicist traditions, following a three-forked path
toward various expressions of Marxism, non-Marxist modernist social theory and science (exemplified in Max Weber), and the previously discussed anti-liberal, more or less
folkish right. Some artists and thinkers in the rightist camp enjoyed great prestige in the
Weimar Republic. Even when they stood aloof from National Socialism, their messages
often ran parallel to its worldview and, in many eyes, legitimized it. Prominent among
them was long-lived Ernst Jünger (1895–1998), pictured here at upper right, leaning on
the podium after having delivered a speech in 1953 West Berlin. He authored a powerful
World War I memoir and other post-1918 works projecting a welcoming vision of a
militarized and war-beset, collectivized, desentimentalized, hard and illiberal world. He
refused NS party membership but did not oppose the regime.

In this picture, Jünger speaks with Werner Heisenberg (1901–1976), Nobel Prize-
winning physicist and pioneer of quantum theory. Although not a NSDAP member,
Heisenberg's nationalist mentality permitted him to collaborate easily with Hitler's
regime, accepting its commission to develop nuclear weapons. Whether he and his
colleagues deliberately delayed production of the bomb their researches had made prac-
tically feasible, as he later claimed, remains controversial. The regime did not, in any
case, assign the weapon top priority, unlike Franklin Roosevelt's government.

Foregrounded in this picture is Martin Heidegger (1889–1976), philosopher whose
Being and Time (1927) initiated a career of (still contested) intellectual greatness.
His Romanticism-rooted critique of modern rationalized, technologized existence in
favor of recovery of Being's immediacy, in part through reunion with Nature, led him,
as rector (president) of Freiburg University, to enthusiastically endorse the National
Socialist "revolution" and attempt its implementation among students and faculty.

of Catholic parentage – more distant from the church frequently yielded to Hitlerism's call.

Prussian Junkers worried about National Socialist talk of settling landless villagers "in the East," thinking their own estates might be carved up. But the NSDAP's aggressive nationalism otherwise appealed to them, especially among younger generations. Similar ambivalence prevailed in the high bureaucracy and judiciary and among university professors, who saw so many of their students waving the Hitlerian flag. There was a strong tendency, as among aristocratic landowners, for the younger generation to trust the National Socialists to champion their interests, while conservative or liberal scruples held many of their elders back in skepticism.

It was not difficult for people attracted to National Socialism, if only because of disaffection from the Weimar Republic or suffering they were enduring – or feared enduring – in the economic depression, to project their wishes onto it, failing to recognize Hitlerism's ominous elements. Many others adamantly opposed Nazism, whether from loyalty to left-wing parties, parliamentary democracy and pluralistic liberalism, cultural modernity, or a Christianity that recognized National Socialism's essentially secular, biologically driven and aggressive worldview. Hitler's accession to power was not inescapable. It resulted from collusion in the NSDAP's 1933 "seizure of power" of conservative elites – both aristocratic and bourgeois – that had never reconciled themselves to Weimar democracy, and from divisions among National Socialism's opponents.

FIGURE 15.8. *(continued)*
Defeated in this project by his political ineptitude, he resigned the rectorship and withdrew, reputation forever damaged, into the would-be unpolitical National Socialist-era "inner emigration" that harbored many intellectuals of conservative disposition.

Undepicted here, Carl Schmitt (1888–1985) was a much-respected post–World War I Catholic conservative legal and political philosopher who charged Weimar liberalism with ethically hollow formalism and incomprehension of power. He advocated a constitutional shift toward executive dictatorship (not necessarily Hitler's) and, after 1933, joined the NSDAP, serving as the regime's most prestigious juridical theorist. His National Socialist enthusiasms, like Heidegger's (but deeper), sidelined him in post-1945 Germany, although scholars still engage with his self-styled hard-boiled, power-centered analysis of modern democracy.

Hans F. K. Günther (1891–1968) authored racial and eugenic textbooks that, while claiming scientific objectivity and validity, glorified "Nordic Aryan" cultures. He served the NS regime as a professorial mouthpiece, and remained after 1945 an unrepentant savant of "racial science," with a following including American apologists for racial segregation in the United States.
Source: Bildarchiv Preussischer Kulturbesitz/Art Resource, NY.

16

Volksgemeinschaft

The "People's Community" at Hitler's Command, 1933–1945

National Socialism in power evokes two fundamental interpretive visions. One emphasize its ruthless efficiency and clear blueprints for action. The other stresses its improvised, disorderly structure, its reckless policies' dependence on unpredictable dilemmas and crises, and a resultant "cumulative radicalization" that was murderous to the groups it proscribed and eventually fatal to itself. In retrospect, clear tendencies, corresponding to Hitlerian ideological prescriptions, are certainly discernible in the regime's institutional development. But expediency, internal power struggles, external pressures, and unanticipated logics left their imprint too.

National Socialist zeal for industrial recovery and rearmament, and for a continentally proportioned "folkish state" structured by racialist and eugenic ideology, set German society's trajectory. Broad objectives were clearer to Hitler's government than the precise form of their realization and the paths leading to them. In National Socialism's aftermath, interpretation must contend with the ominous implications of the fact that enormous violence prevailed over lesser.

The National Socialist "Seizure of Power," 1933–1934

President Hindenburg's appointment of Hitler as chancellor in January 1933 was technically legal. The Weimar constitution had lost coherence and moral force during the period since 1930 of "presidial" cabinets lacking majority parliamentary support and governing instead by emergency powers under Article 48. As we saw, most of Hitler's cabinet members were rightist conservatives rather than National Socialists. Hitler aimed to broaden his freedom of action soon by holding and winning elections securing the NSDAP a strong majority.

But then there occurred the Reichstag fire of February 1933. Denouncing this act of an unbalanced individual's arson as attempted revolt, Hitler charged the Communist Party with sedition and persuaded Hindenburg to approve suspension of habeas corpus guarantees, permitting arrests of suspects without evidence of wrongdoing. Nazi Storm Troopers were – lawlessly – sworn in as auxiliary policemen. With their help, the police agencies – undergoing rapid nazification – smashed the Communist Party, imprisoning its leaders in a newly established detention facility at Oranienburg, outside Berlin: National Socialism's first concentration camp.

In the March 5 Reichstag election, with Communist organizations broken and Social Democrats threatened with similar fate, the pro-Hitler vote rose, as we saw, to 44 percent, while its rightist partners won 8 percent. In the "Enabling Act," passed on March 23, 1933, the Reichstag – crucially – granted Hitler blanket decree powers for four years. It was but an unenforceable concession to lingering reservations (or wishful thinking) about Hitler's impending dictatorship that this law shielded basic features of the Weimar constitution – notably the elected Reichstag and the federal states' self-governing rights – and that the parliament after four years might rescind any of Hitler's intervening decrees.

The Enabling Act won Reichstag assent, with a two-thirds majority, in an atmosphere heavy with threats of National Socialist reprisals against dissenters. It was pivotal that the Catholic Center Party, following Pope Pius XI's lead, supported it in exchange for Hitler's duplicitous promise, formalized in his government's July 1933 Concordat or treaty with the Vatican, not to diminish Catholic religious and educational rights in Germany. Only the Social Democrats dared speak and vote against the Enabling Act, although they were certain to suffer for their defiance.

In a terror-laden process known as "synchronization" (*Gleichschaltung*), beginning in spring and summer 1933, National Socialist officials took control of the trade unions, whether Social Democratic or not, and most other previously independent social organizations of any importance. The bourgeois political parties and SPD, menaced by police terror and stricken with defeatism, dissolved themselves. The government imposed press censorship and declared the previously nonofficial National Socialist Party a state institution. Police violence raged in 1933, catching in its clutches some 100,000 regime opponents, mostly leftists. Many suffered beatings, torture, and death. Others were permanently jailed, while lesser offenders only gained release following physical abuse, sometimes crippling. The press, whether under NSDAP control or undergoing more or less heartfelt self-nazification, widely publicized arrests and newly built concentration camps – Dachau, near Munich, was the biggest and best-known – as admonitions to loyalty, self-improvement, and conformism.

The following year, on June 30, 1934, Hitler directed Himmler's SS-men to attack and purge the Storm Trooper (SA) leadership so as to eliminate alleged National Socialist "radicals" and "social revolutionaries." Doubtless SA commanders had hoped to put themselves at the head of a future nazified army, while the (by then) millions of SA rank-and-file waited restively for rewards the new regime was unable to promptly bestow. Some one hundred SA officers and sundry other regime opponents, including prominent anti-NSDAP

(a)

(b)

FIGURE 16.1. PRETENSIONS OF LEGALITY, MAILED FIST OF TERROR

rightists, died in the June 1934 hail of bullets. In return, the conservative-led army assented to Hitler's assumption of the Reich president's powers on Hindenburg's long-anticipated, soon ensuing (natural) death. By this means, Hitler, in a crucial step, became the armed forces' commander-in-chief, capping his authority as Reich chancellor and charismatic Leader (*Führer*) of the NSDAP and German *Volk*.

The National Socialists' step-by-step consolidation of dictatorship took place *following* formally legal attainment of their (initially limited and revocable) executive power. This process starkly illustrates the dangers modern democracies face from antidemocratic movements, not only *outside* legal government's boundaries, but also *within* them.

FIGURE 16.1 *(continued)* Photograph (a) depicts, in a seemingly unguarded moment, Hitler's newly unveiled cabinet of January 30, 1933. Flanking him are Göring (left) and (right) the politically defeated ex-chancellor Franz von Papen (1879–1969), loosely and contentiously connected to the Catholic Center Party's right wing and now symbolizing conservative-nationalists' hopes of upholding their interests under the National Socialists. Standing on far right: Alfred Hugenberg (1865–1951), former Krupp manager, Weimar press mogul, and powerful Conservative Party (DNVP) chief, like Papen soon to be outmaneuvered and driven into political retirement. On March 21, 1933 Hitler's government staged a widely publicized media event, "The Day of Potsdam," when the newly elected, NSDAP-subservient Reichstag assembled in the Prussian garrison city and Hohenzollern summer residence. Hitler, in civilian dress, famously bowed to President Hindenburg, outfitted in pre-Weimar fashion as national military chief, conveying a duplicitous promise that his regime would respect conservative tradition.

(b) In August 1933 SA men induct arrestees into the Oranienburg concentration camp, outside Berlin. The prisoners – anti-Nazi Social Democratic politicians, parliamentarians, and state-run radio managers – include Friedrich Ebert, the Weimar Republic's deceased first president's son, municipal officeholder, and SPD activist (fifth from left), and Ernst Heilmann, long-serving and widely respected SPD parliamentary leader (first from left). Heilmann remained imprisoned until his 1940 judicial murder, but Ebert later gained release and survived as a worker under police surveillance. The National Socialists' brutal methods found depiction on one of 1933's locally produced political postcards documenting the tumultuous regime change. Its inscription dripping with malevolent irony, it showed National Socialists in northwest Germany carting off to imprisonment a former Social Democratic provincial governor, against whom revenge for involvement in the November 1918 revolution was being exacted. Similarly, in Munich in March 1933 SA men paraded a humiliated German Jewish lawyer through the streets, having hung around his neck a placard saying "I will never again complain to the police." Many such acts of ritual degradation and symbolic violence – centuries-old elements of popular culture – occurred in and after 1933, aimed at the regime's designated enemies, both Jewish and non-Jewish.
Source: Deutsches Bundesarchiv.

The National Socialist State's Structural Development, 1934–1945

In short order, "synchronization" subjected virtually all public institutions to National Socialist control or overlordship. Hitler practiced divide-and-rule to prevent the emergence of overweening bureaucratic or executive agencies that might impair his freedom of action. The various ministries and other state organs fought hard battles among themselves for influence and access to Hitler and his patronage. A concept influential in the historical literature is "polycracy" (*Polykratie*), ascribing to the National Socialist regime many power-centers. Hitler countenanced independent pursuit of their several agendas, inspiring them to seek – by their own efforts (in another widely employed phrase) at "working toward the Führer" – to anticipate his hidden or unannounced (or still unformulated) preferences, gain his backing, and raise their standing in the NS hierarchy. He intervened as he saw fit to favor one over the other, without attempting himself to specify and guide all state policy. Yet Hitler was certainly a "strong dictator" in his unassailable power, which he readily asserted, to set the regime's agenda, especially in the direction of forced-draft rearmament, foreign-policy aggression, war and "racial revolution."

Over the twelve-year arc of the regime's history, NS Party functionaries (notably the provincial NSDAP party leaders, or *Gauleiter*) ascended in executive authority and influence over the populations under their power at the preexisting civil bureaucracy's expense. A similar rise occurred, overshadowing older criminal courts, of the nazified "people's court" (*Volksgerichtshof*) in Berlin, established in 1934. It worked with political police and SS, handing down drastic sentences, increasingly entailing the death penalty, for an ever-expanding list of alleged political crimes. A tension-ridden, near-chaotic "dual state" emerged, with party organizations paralleling state agencies, but with neither one in command of various other powerful institutions, whether the army, the expanding SS-police empire, or semi-public, semi-private economic task forces conjured up by the Führer's will.

Still more important was steady expansion of police and coercive power, delivered into SS leader Heinrich Himmler's ambitious hands. Crucial was the assemblage after 1936 under Himmler's immediate command of regular police, secret political police (*Gestapo*), and SS. It was the latter, black-uniformed force that, among other repressive functions, brutally administered the handful of dreaded post-1933 concentration camps. These multiplied rapidly after 1939, including from 1942 the Holocaust death camps.

Police power ominously widened, both at home and, later, in German-occupied conquered lands. In the fall of 1939 Hitler appointed Himmler "Reich Commissar for the Strengthening of German Nationality" (*RKFDV*), granting him control of all measures concerning "racial policy" in Germany and, especially, in occupied eastern Europe (and, later, in conquered France and the Low Countries). After 1941 Himmler built up, in the *Waffen-SS*, a formidable, ideologically high-charged, nazified battlefield soldiery challenging the future existence of the regular armed forces (*Wehrmacht*), still rooted after 1933, if ever more tenuously, in Prussian military-aristocratic tradition. In 1943 Himmler further expanded his reach, assuming the office of Minister of Interior commanding most of the civil bureaucracy.

The NS state's inner dynamic drove toward consolidation of a Führer-led, militarized police state, working in tandem (but sometimes also at odds) with a powerful and ideologically radical NSDAP hierarchy. Yet various elite-led institutions and interest groups continued to possess some autonomy: private business, although highly cartelized and ever more dependent on state patronage; churches, although anti-Nazi dissidents could expect imprisonment; regular army, although younger officers were increasingly zealous National Socialists. Academic and public intellectual life fell under the NSDAP's control, and succumbed to its spirit, at the cost – outside certain precincts of natural science and technology – of advancing ideological cultism and careerist mediocrity.

To individuals and groups it condemned as "enemies of the *Volk*" Hitler's regime presented a bloody-handed authoritarian police state's face. But in relation to the "German Aryan" people's "biologically worthy" members, it ceaselessly sought assent and enthusiastic engagement. Where historians once saw a dictatorship over the German people, most now highlight its dual character, arguing that, from the viewpoint of the majority who eventually embraced – or at any rate accepted – the regime and conformed to its rules, it was a "consensual dictatorship." There was, certainly, widespread consent but, as we shall later see, its extent remains controversial. It was to a considerable degree consent of the kind that modern techniques – sometimes only charades – of popular legitimization (as in occasional plebiscites eliciting mass approval of Hitler's steps) confer on governments whose actions "the people," unable effectively to control or repudiate them, and wanting to live comfortably and believe in themselves, are inclined to accept as necessary and just.

The National Socialist Economy

In 1933 Hitler's government purged from public-sector employment those they marked as Jews (with grudging and short-lived exceptions for World War I battlefield veterans). In the following six years, German Jews suffered progressive expropriation of their private-sector business assets, especially after the immense, nationwide "Crystal Night" pogrom (that is, the riotous and murderous, NS Party-led assault on Jewish property and persons) of November 9, 1938. Such dispossession, brutally termed "Aryanization," bestowed into the hands of National Socialist activists and the regime's cynical and opportunistic fellow travelers a mass of Jewish-owned shops, businesses, and – in the wake of a huge Jewish emigration exodus after Crystal Night – thousands of much sought-after apartments and dwelling houses. The state, under the industrial overlord Hermann Göring's command, seized expropriated Jewish financial fortunes and large-scale economic enterprises.

In November 1933 the "German Labor Front" (*Deutsche Arbeitsfront*) went to work. This massive organization replaced independent, mainly Social

FIGURE 16.2. THE NATIONAL SOCIALIST POLITICAL ELITE

On the podium at a 1939 Hitler Youth organization congress (from left): Gertrud Scholz-Klink, leader (*Führerin*) of the NS women's organization (on which, see more later in the chapter); Heinrich Himmler, SS and police chief; Rudolf Hess, deputy chief, behind Hitler, of the NS Party; Baldur von Schirach, NS youth leader and NS governor (*Gauleiter*) of (German-annexed) Vienna. Such NS notables were not uniformly powerful, although any such functionary's enmity toward individual subjects could prove deadly. But to the faithful and to conformists they aimed to project benevolence, if also to spur them to self-sacrifice and "hardness" (an oft-invoked NS "virtue"). A much advertised exemplar was Reinhard Heydrich (1904–1942). He rapidly rose from Bavarian police chief to second-in-command under Himmler in the criminal and secret police system, also becoming chief administrator of "racial policy," including Holocaust planning. In his personal self-presentation the ideal (if not typical) "Aryan Nazi," and embodiment too of bureaucratized terror and mass murder, he fell – as the occupied Czech lands' brutal governor – to Czech resistance fighters' bullets. Widely dreaded and hated was Roland Freisler (1893–1945), who symbolized the judicial system's ruthless subjection to Hitlerism. From 1942 Freisler headed the Supreme People's Court (*Volksgerichthof*), escalating drastically death sentences handed down against non-Jewish German citizens charged before it. He perished in the Allied bombing of Berlin.

Source: Deutsches Bundesarchiv.

Democratic trade unions, but also drew private business's interest groups under its roof. Thereafter, state-appointed Labor Front Trustees administered government-dictated wage and price controls throughout the economy. This launched a program of state-funded industrial recovery, driven by clandestine rearmament, without danger of serious resistance by workers or employers.

The regime entrusted economic policy to well-known private-sector bankers and technocrats. They assembled public investment funds by suspending the German mark's international convertibility, levying import and export duties, taxing business profits, holding wages low, and deficit spending to prime the business investment pump. In 1935–1936, after recovery from the Great Depression had begun and as Hitler moved openly to expand the army to maximum strength, rearmament overshadowed other economic objectives.

The regime promised "worthy" Germans higher living standards, including an affordable family automobile (the *Volkswagen* or "people's car"). But military priorities took precedence and the VW never rolled onto the sales floor. Still, by 1939, per capita real incomes had returned to 1928 levels. Unemployment gradually vanished under the impact of a state-funded "Labor Service's" public-works programs and of industrial expansion accompanying rearmament. By 1938, labor shortages had arisen, leading to illicit competition to hire workers away from employers and compulsory recruitment of youth into seasonal farm labor.

Social Life Under "Consensual Dictatorship"

Between 1925 and 1939, the occupational census registered decline in the agricultural work force (to 27 percent of all employed persons), together with expansion of the commercial and services sector (to 32 percent) and stability in industry and crafts (41 percent). The proportion of self-employed persons declined from 21 to 18 percent. White-collar salary earners increased from 19 to 20 percent, while wage-earners and family members employed on farms and in small businesses rose from 60 to 62 percent. Thus Hitler's regime, despite nostalgia-laden pre-1933 propaganda promising resuscitation of the tradition-imbued self-employed middle classes (*Mittelstand*), did not halt social trends typical of the modern urban-industrial, service-oriented economy. Instead, Hitler demanded its recovery and growth, to achieve an "American-style" social modernity and establish the German hegemony in eastern Europe that he saw as its precondition.

National Socialist policies to shore up family farms were frequently unpopular, especially because – above a certain size of landholding – they enforced impartible land inheritance in wide regions where partibility earlier prevailed. National Socialist regulations shielded farmers from foreclosure, but at the cost of limiting borrowing of money against land. They also entailed compulsory participation in government marketing programs that inhibited cultivators' farming strategies. Yet, in town and country alike, economic recovery was

FIGURE 16.3. NATIONAL SOCIALISM AND CAPITALISM

Here Hitler and Hjalmar Schacht (1877–1970) march in May 1934 to the groundbreaking ceremony in Berlin for a new Reichsbank. Schacht was an internationally respected financier of liberal background, whose policies as central bank president in 1923–1930 had helped lift the economy out of inflation and into renewed growth. As Hitler's banking chief in 1933–1939, he was architect by means of ingenious deficit spending schemes and foreign-trade diplomacy of an industrial and commercial recovery widely seen, at home and abroad, as spectacular. His misgivings about Hitler's overheated rearmament drive pushed him onto the sidelines, but he never broke decisively with the regime.

Deficit-financed public-works programs, especially automobile freeway (*Autobahn*) construction, also recharged the depression-stricken economy. Hitler himself knowledgeably wielded a shovel alongside a humble worker, to the propaganda-works' fanfare, at highway-building's start in September 1933. Managing the giant project was private entrepreneur Fritz Todt (1891–1942), an able engineer who rose to preside over a vast National Socialist construction complex, including military installations.

Seizure of property designated as Jewish escalated in the 1930s. Characteristic was an advertisement of November 22, 1938 in a newspaper in Karlsruhe, Baden, announcing a local Jewish-labeled department store's passage into "Aryan possession." This real and correspondingly popular. National Socialism built on German traditions – which these pages earlier highlighted – of the strong interventionist state, large-scale and interlocked industrial firms under government patronage, and a tightly organized labor movement, although now under despotic state control.

Raising Hitler's regime's popularity in ordinary people's eyes were the low-cost sea cruises and other leisure activities available in the 1933–1939 prewar years through the Labor Front's program of "Strength Through Joy" (*Kraft durch Freude*). Boat trips to friendly Mediterranean dictatorships (notably in Iberia and Italy) and to Scandinavia, along with group outings in Germany and membership in KdF-sponsored sports clubs, aimed to overtrump and eclipse the now-banned Socialists' and other social-political organizations' earlier, widely popular recreational programs. It was through the KdF organization, too, that the public was given the opportunity to make advance payments on Volks-wagen automobiles. Yet the nearly 400,000 buyers who entered the savings program before 1941 never drove a VW on the modern freeways the NS regime built across the German landscape. These were happily traveled, however, by better-off families of the middle and upper classes owning automobiles bought from older-established German producers, including the widely sold Opel, a firm in which the U.S. General Motors company held a controlling interest from 1929 until 1941 (and then again after the war).

In its policy toward women and family, the regime's main concern was to raise birthrates (pro-natalism) and subject the population to "racial" and eugenic discipline. It favored early marriage, large numbers of children, and husband-dominated families. Exceptionally in economically stricken Europe of the 1930s, the German birthrate rose – by about one-third – between 1933 and 1939, owing largely to higher marriage frequency. Propaganda exhortations to raise more than one or two children went largely unheeded.

At the same time, by 1939 the ideologically zealous medical authorities sterilized some 200,000 non-Jewish German women judged "biologically unfit" to be mothers. A roughly equal number of German "Aryan" men, found on physical or social grounds to be "degenerate," suffered the same fate. This sterilization program proceeded in step with a murderous euthanasia program directed against non-Jewish Germans labeled as physically or mentally severely impaired. In putting during its initial 1939–1941 years some 70,000 victims to death, the euthanasia administrators devised lethal techniques, especially death by poison gas, later employed in the Jewish mass murder.

FIGURE 16.3 *(continued)* was "Aryanization"'s end-stage in the aftermath of 1938's "Reich Crystal Night." The advertisement promised that the store would henceforth be managed according to (unspecified) "authentic German business principles." Jewish expropriation was a huge transfer of fixed and liquid assets, mostly into state hands. Such plunder fueled the war machine that delivered eastern Europe into Hitler's hands and so, eventually, helped make Jewish mass murder possible.
Source: Bildarchiv Preussischer Kulturbesitz/Art Resource, NY.

National Socialism aimed to mobilize and politicize women in its support, whether as party members (some 200,000 at their peak) or through the
NSDAP's women's auxiliary organization (*NS-Frauenschaft*, with two million
members). The regime did not discourage *single* women from extra-domestic
work, but it initially reduced women's enrollment at universities and steered
them away from "men's occupations." Later in the war, men's high battlefield
mortality forced policy reversal. Women were more likely in the middle than
the working class to embrace NS gender concepts, but so long as acceptable
living standards prevailed – that is, until the later war years – the regime's
approach to women and family proved widely acceptable.

National Socialist Culture

Public education's "synchronization" entailed introduction of "racial science"
into the curriculum at all levels, along with compulsory membership after 1936
in the "Hitler Youth" (*Hitlerjugend*) for adolescent boys and the "League of
German Girls" (*Bund deutscher Mädel*). These organizations' several subdivi-
sions at their height amassed some nine million boys and more than four million
girls from ten to eighteen years of age. Stringent indoctrination in racism and
militarism accompanied outdoors activities and propagation of patriotism and
class harmony in devotion to the *Volk*.

Many – perhaps most – German young people proved susceptible to such
propaganda, combined as it was with opportunities to develop sporting and
other physical talents and to prepare for an adult career in the NS Party. But the
youth organizations' collectivized rigors, anti-intellectualism, group tyranny,
and conformism repelled others. As for youths beyond age eighteen, prewar
secondary school graduates bound for university, like other young people,
were liable to spend six compulsory months in the Labor Service, working in
agriculture or industry. This aimed to prepare them for military service and to
counteract "bourgeois aloofness" from the *Volk*.

During the war, disaffected youthful subcultures appeared, even though
police persecuted them: middle-class, Anglophile, jazz-loving "swing youth,"
and working-class "gangs." Students in the 1942–1943 White Rose movement
at Munich University staged clandestine protests, of Catholic Christian inspiration, against National Socialist mass murder and international aggression.
Arrests led to brutal executions of student leaders, notably siblings Sophie and
Hans Scholl and Professor Kurt Huber.

National Socialism violated traditions of autonomous culture and bourgeois self-cultivation (*Bildung*). This alienated many among the middle and
upper classes, especially those who found the biologized and racialized National
Socialist worldview crude, fanatical, and immoral. The National Socialists had
celebrated their "seizure of power" with public burnings of works of German
literature, both classic and modern, objectionable in National Socialist eyes,
whether for liberalism, avant-gardism, or Jewish authorship. Stifling censorship

FIGURE 16.4. IMAGES OF *VOLKSGEMEINSCHAFT* AND THE NATIONAL SOCIALIST GOOD LIFE

This 1938 picture of middle-class campers – young woman in unbourgeois shorts – advertised the Volkswagen or "people's car," developed by the tradition-rich Porsche firm. Many people subscribed to the saving program for the modestly priced vehicle, but war's outbreak blocked its production. The regime high-handedly diverted the investors' millions to military expenditures. Such pictures as this conjured up the National Socialist ideal of harmony – not only at the workplace between workers and managers, but also of men and women in private life – which the Labor Front and its leisure-time organization, "Strength Through Joy" (KdF), continually and, in many eyes, compellingly propagated.

The regime also strove with some success to make factories and other workplaces more beautiful and healthful (through modernistic lighting and decoration, and by offering break-time classes – for example, in chorus-line dancing for women workers). Hitler readily visited shop-floors, posing benevolently with workers. Yet the VW advertisement photograph displayed here unintentionally suggests tension between social ideals of a collectivist "people's community" on the one hand and the privatized world of family autos and other high-consumption activities on the other – a tension KdF's low-cost mass tourist programs (since they reached only a small minority) could not resolve.

Source: Deutsches Bundesarchiv.

of artists and writers occurred through NSDAP-controlled professional guilds, membership in which was obligatory to publish, perform, or exhibit.

National Socialist threats and provocations drove hundreds of leading representatives of non-Jewish German literary and artistic culture – many of them, such as Thomas Mann, world-famous – to join Jewish-born colleagues (Albert

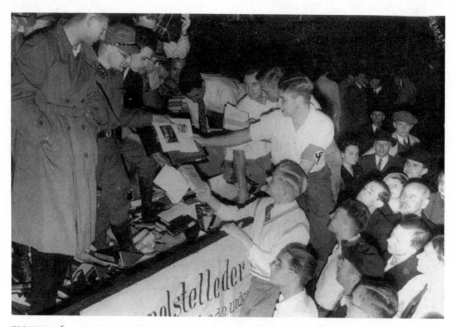

FIGURE 16.5. NATIONAL SOCIALIST INDOCTRINATION OF YOUTH
In this May 1933 scene, university and high-school students in Berlin, evidently of mainly middle-class background, collect for public burning books authored in an allegedly "un-German spirit" by such writers as Karl Marx and Heinrich Heine, but also by contemporary novelists without Jewish roots such as Erich Maria Remarque (famous for his antiwar novel *All Quiet on the Western Front* [1929]) and Thomas and Heinrich Mann. Such Nazi-organized book burnings spread a chilling message across the country.

After 1933 the regime marched Hitler Youth units in massive numbers to the annual NSDAP Nuremberg rallies. Official photographs cannot conceal that fanatical enthusiasm and military precision were not ubiquitous among them. Yet regimentation of youthful bodies and minds advanced ominously, foreshadowing the wartime ruthlessness in which young men displayed the "hardness" that National Socialist socialization had encouraged in them.
Source: Deutsches Bundesarchiv.

Einstein was emblematic) in abandoning the country for exile abroad. In a cultural regression unprecedented in modern western society, Germany fell in a few short years from its worldwide prominence and prestige in the humanities and social sciences, literature, music, and art to a land largely bereft – apart from science and technology – of significant innovation.

Nazified substitutes for proscribed art and scholarship found little echo abroad and left a barren legacy to post-1945 German life. Conservative-minded artists and scholars under Hitler's rule cultivated the memory of past cultural greatness. Some attempted to deepen cultural and social-anthropological study of the *Volk* but racist assumptions crippled many such projects. Cultural notables who cooperated with the National Socialists, such as philosopher

Martin Heidegger or composer Richard Strauss, sometimes – if later rather than sooner – recognized National Socialism's incompatibility with their philosophy or genius, or suffered marginalization at NS hands for lack of comprehension or zeal for the cause.

Many millions, young and old, submitted to the pressures to conform and embrace the National Socialist program that the government-dominated mass media exerted in intensive and unremitting propaganda, including over the new, affordable, and highly popular home radio. Joseph Goebbels worked zealously to deepen National Socialist sentiments and sensibility through regime-controlled film production. Offerings ranged from unvarnished glorifications of Hitler's Germany – as in the gifted filmmaker Leni Riefenstahl's alluring photography of the 1934 annual NSDAP rally ("Triumph of the Will") and the 1936 Berlin-staged Olympic Games – to loudly trumpeted, widely viewed, lavishly produced costume dramas, such as the anti-Semitic film "Jud Süss" (1940).

Most influential were numerous movies and radio programs offering Hollywood-style light entertainment, spiced by slightly jazz-inflected pop music, "normalizing" and glamorizing everyday life under National Socialism. The aim was to channel the viewers' emotions and desires in the direction of the NS "people's community," with its promises of proliferating consumer goods, leisure pleasures, and conflict-free social advancement. Propaganda encouraged the "biologically fit Aryan German" people to regard themselves as entitled to physical fulfillment in all senses. This included sexuality, which in the *Volk*'s eugenic interest was to be liberated from old-fashioned Christian disapprobation. Like all modern dictatorships, Hitler's regime sought to screen out alternative worldviews, especially by closing unauthorized windows on the outside world. Rebelliously – or only curiously – listening to foreign radio broadcasts (notably Britain's widely respected BBC) became an offense punishable by imprisonment or even death. But many people furtively defied this ban in domestic privacy.

The judicial system's degradation, spread of uncontrolled police power, and introduction of concentration camps offended deep-rooted traditions of the rule of law (the *Rechtsstaat*) and frightened and alienated many people in all classes. As for religion, National Socialist ideology, grounded in racialized and biologized concepts, was implicitly although not overtly anti-Christian. The regime's long-term objective was to eliminate the Christian churches' influence from education and public sphere as much as possible (as was evident during the war in its anti-Christian policies in annexed and officially "Germanized" western Poland).

Among Protestants, many wished to fuse National Socialism and Christianity, which had led before 1933 to emergence of the "German Christian Faith movement," proclaiming Jesus an "Aryan." By 1932 it encompassed about one-third of active Protestant Church members. In 1933 pro-Hitlerite pressure won the appointment of a Christian Faith movement member as head (Reich Bishop) of the nationwide German Protestant Church, but conservative

FIGURE 16.6. NATIONAL SOCIALIST CULTURE: "AESTHETICIZATION" OF POLITICS, BIOL-
OGIZATION OF ART

The "cathedral of light" rises in 1936 above the vast site of the 1934–1940 Nuremberg
party rallies, where as many as one million participants massed together facing the
huge stadium, built in the oversized neo-Roman architecture favored by Hitler and his
trusted architect and adviser on art and propaganda Albert Speer (1905–1981). Speer
designed the Nuremberg site and orchestrated its events, including this display of powerful anti-aircraft spotlights, anticipating their deployment in a coming war. Director
Leni Riefenstahl recorded the 1934 rally for mass viewing throughout the land in her
cinematographically celebrated propaganda film, *Triumph of the Will*.

Regime-favored prolific sculptor, Austrian Josef Thorak (1889–1952), crafted gar-
gantuan representations of warriors and workers, their muscles bulging, some intended
to grace NS freeways. Officially patronized art glorified the physical body, often without reference to the subject's emotional or psychological interior. Art that extolled the
Volksgemeinschaft displayed many commonalities with Soviet-style "socialist realism":
joyous workers; awakening of the passive citizenry to the new order's moral-political
clarion calls; mobilized activists, often with gun in hand. Adolf Ziegler (1892–1959),
president of the Reich Chamber of Visual Arts, organized the notorious 1937 traveling
exhibition of "degenerate arts," pillorying artistic modernism as a cultural and political
affliction that National Socialist art would blot out and eclipse. His own paintings of
female nudes provoked clandestine mockery among fellow artists and the public alike.

Premier National Socialist portrait-sculptor Arno Breker (1900–1991) depicted
National Socialist luminaries, such as Speer, as heroic, lockjawed and psychologically veiled power-wielders. The regime hoped such artists, together with collabora-
tionist (although not always NSDAP card-carrying) composers (Richard Strauss, Hans
Pfitzner), musicians (Wilhelm Furtwängler, Herbert von Karajan), filmmakers (Veit Har-
lan, Leni Riefenstahl) and actors and entertainers (Emil Jannings, Gustav Gründgens,

opposition within the church unseated him in 1934. Evidently, determined assertion of non-National Socialist cultural-ideological concerns could, at least in the dictatorship's early years, put brakes on the regime in some spheres. On the Protestant fringes, a dissenting movement arose (the "Confessing Church"). Resistant to state "synchronization" of religion and tending toward condemnation of National Socialism, the police persecuted it with increasing zeal.

Despite Hitler's 1933 Concordat with the Vatican, guaranteeing Catholic religious rights in Germany, the regime whittled down Catholic education, prompting Pope Pius XI in 1937 to issue a strong public denunciation of National Socialist ideology and anti-Catholic discrimination. However enthusiastic many or most German Christians felt about Hitler's regime, the pious and faithful among them had good reason to mistrust and even oppose it.

Consensualism's Limits

The National Socialists' educational, cultural, and religious policies evoked disquiet in wide circles. Working-class resentment at the regime's smothering and smashing of pre-1933 Social Democratic and Communist Party subcultures simmered, although such feelings rankled less among youth than elders. At war with such attitudes was the fervent appreciation felt among all non-persecuted Germans for restoration of full employment, together with nationalist gratification at Hitler's uncanny string of foreign-policy triumphs, chief among them rearmament and the 1938 ushering of the Austrians into the Greater German house. Yet popular opinion is hard to measure under a regime that had, since 1933, criminalized even private verbal criticism of it, and unleashed against opponents state violence of a brutality never before experienced in German history. It would be rash to suppose that, even at the 1938–1939 height of its success, Hitler's regime enjoyed untroubled mass support of "the German nation," as its propaganda claimed and as many people, scholars and non-scholars, have subsequently thought.

Still, before Hitler's armies began in 1942–1943 to suffer ominous battlefield setbacks, his regime basked in wide, sometimes euphoric domestic support. Comparisons of Hitler with Frederick the Great and Bismarck swelled many patriotic hearts. The media hailed him as the "greatest military commander of

---

FIGURE 16.6 *(continued)* Zara Leander) would establish National Socialist Germany's credibility as a robust alternative to the cultural modernism it had smashed and proscribed. Yet association with National Socialism degraded instead of heightening these gifted artists' talents. And the emigration abroad – or "inner emigration" – of a great mass of Germany's most celebrated cultural producers struck a crippling blow against the country's creativity as well as its Romanticism-era reputation as "land of poets and thinkers."
Source: Deutsches Bundesarchiv.

FIGURE 16.7. PRO- AND ANTI-NATIONAL SOCIALIST CHRISTIANS

In this picture, a summer 1933 Prussian Evangelical (that is, predominantly Lutheran) Protestant open-air religious service honors the Berlin SA chief, Count Helldorf. Such events characterized the pro-National Socialist German Christian Faith Movement, advocate of a "heroic Jesus" within a "dejudaized" Christianity. Even though this current was strong among church members in the dictatorship's first years, countervailing conservative forces persisted. The two camps remained divided.

In October 1933 Count Clemens von Galen (1876–1946) took office as Bishop of Münster. His 1940 sermons against the NS euthanasia program dramatically, if only partially, halted it. The German Catholic hierarchy cooperated with Pope Pius XI in the issuance of his 1937 encyclical, "With Burning Concern," a condemnation of National Socialist racist doctrines and repression of Christianity read from pulpits throughout Germany. Yet the Catholic clergy, burdened with a legacy of defensiveness toward state power reaching back to the Bismarck-era *Kulturkampf*, inclined to retreat into their confessional subculture in hope the National Socialist storm would blow over – if they did not, as often occurred, embrace the regime as an alternative preferable to secular liberalism or militantly atheistic bolshevism.

all times." Yet the high noon of Hitler's popularity reflected no less his government's success, in the course of but a few years, in propagandizing – in the shadow of a police power whose lethal potential was clear to all – a population whose older age-cohorts were led to believe that "the Führer" had rescued them from social breakdown and international humiliation. The younger generations found intoxicating the prospects of the National Socialist future – consumerist modernity, greater egalitarianism and social mobility among the "Aryan" majority, and an enrichment-promising German-dominated Europe. Like some other "utopias of modernity," that of the National Socialists, inculcated in society with ominous speed, proved a cruel and destructive illusion.

The regime was aware of popular backing's potential brittleness, and did not press the public hard for sacrifices. Facing labor shortages in the late 1930s, it refused to lengthen the industrial workweek. It continued to pay out family subsidies encouraging early marriages and women's withdrawal from paid jobs into motherhood and housekeeping. After 1939 it refused to compulsorily draft women into war industries, although necessity drew many into factories and offices. German women, because of the country's numerous family farms and craftsmen's shops, were already in 1939 working in higher proportions than British or American women.

The government wanted both guns and butter. To have them, Hitler in 1938 accelerated foreign-policy aggression, aiming – among other things – to gain control of the industrially strong Czechoslovak economy. After unleashing war in 1939 against Poland, National Socialism ruthlessly exploited captive labor in eastern Europe and plundered the region for its food supply, raw materials, and manufacturing resources. In this way, racially justified barbarism in the

---

FIGURE 16.7 *(continued)* Conversely, lay activists in the ill-fated 1942–1943 White Rose antiwar protest movement distributed flyers at Munich University condemning the government's crimes, including the Jewish mass murder (and also widespread killing of Polish Catholics) as violations of Christian ethics, dishonoring the German nation and prefiguring its own imminent destruction.

Among Protestants, theologian Dietrich Bonhoeffer (1906–1945) figured prominently in the "Confessing Church," which opposed the German Christian Faith Movement, but was more concerned with Christian autonomy within the state than defending the regime's non-Christian and non-German victims. In 1938 Bonhoeffer – himself a critic of National Socialist racism – entered the clandestine conservative anti-Hitler political opposition. In 1943 the regime arrested and later executed him among those condemned for the failed assassination attempt against Hitler of July 20, 1944. Pastor Martin Niemöller (1892–1984) – World War I submarine commander, supporter of National Socialism to 1933 and beyond – also figured importantly in the Confessing Church's leadership. He suffered concentration-camp internment from 1937 to 1945 for criticizing the regime's efforts at "synchronization" and "Aryanization" of Christianity. After 1945 he helped lead German Protestantism away from its traditions of partnership with conservative state power and steer the West German peace movement.

Source: Bildarchiv Preussischer Kulturbesitz/Art Resource, NY.

east cushioned the hardships the home population faced, at least until in 1943 British and American bombs began falling ruinously on German cities.

In the end, with millions dead and more millions wounded, captured, and disappeared, and having been bombed in huge numbers out of their homes, uprooted in the eastern German provinces from their settlements, with savings, public finances and currency ruined, dependent on the victorious occupiers' food and fuel, burdened with guilt for the National Socialists' (that is, often their own) previously unimaginable crimes, Germans found themselves, not in a *Volksgemeinschaft* or "community of the people," but in a *Notgemeinschaft* – a "community of hardship and suffering."

17

Lebensraum

War for Empire in Eastern Europe

Germany's invasion of Poland on September 1, 1939 escalated into European war, grimly reprising the 1914–1918 struggle. Interlocking with Japan's Asian-Pacific aggression, which goaded the previously isolationism-inclined United States to arms, Germany's European venture became a bid for world power. Succumbing to megalomania, Hitler and accomplices imagined that, in the war's aftermath, the surviving imperial powers – victorious Japan, defeated and chastened Britain and the United States – would bend their knee to Berlin's overlordship (or, as the artist-architect Führer intended to rename the capital city, after rebuilding it on gigantomanic scale, "Germania").

National Socialism's European and world hegemony would rest on conquest in eastern Europe. It was there that the German "folkish state" would expand into folkish empire, projecting National Socialist racial revolution onto a space vastly greater even than the *Grossdeutschland* that Hitler's belligerent diplomacy achieved in 1938. He aimed indeed also to subjugate France and subordinate Britain, but Germany's 1940 war with these powers was one of necessity more than design, aiming mainly to neutralize their opposition to its eastward expansion.

This chapter focuses on the eastern war for *Lebensraum* and empire. Germany's assault on western Europe was fierce and inhumane; its campaign in north Africa to defeat the British, capture Suez, and reach Middle Eastern oilfields was integral to final success. Yet these aggressions served the goal less of a generalized National Socialist European or world dominion than of a vast, Germanized land empire in central and eastern Europe, in whose conquest they were necessary thrusts. The drive for east European empire was also the crucial precondition of the European Jews' mass murder, National Socialism's definitive act.

The International Security System in Eastern Europe

How after 1919 would the newly created east-central European and Balkan states born of the Paris Peace Conference – that is, the three Baltic states

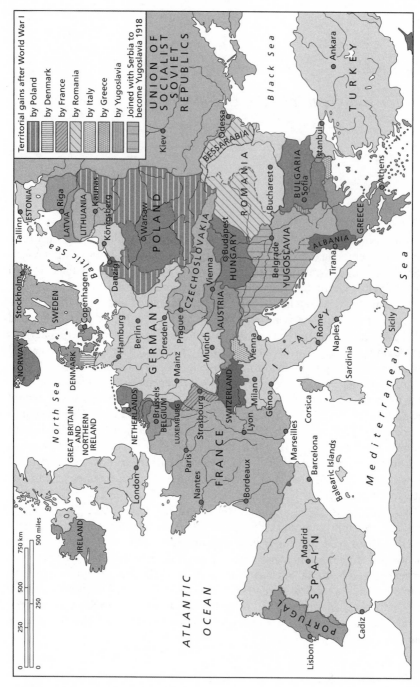

MAP 17.1. INTERWAR CENTRAL AND EASTERN EUROPE (TO 1938): NATION-STATES IN PLACE OF FALLEN EMPIRES

of Estonia, Latvia, and Lithuania, together with Czechoslovakia, Poland, Yugoslavia (which absorbed prewar Serbia), and barely-nascent Albania – safely sail the seas of independence? Would the east European and Balkan states that had existed already before 1914 – Bulgaria, Greece, Hungary, Romania – join the flotilla, and would the western victor powers send well-armed escort ships?

After the U.S. Congress's refusal – on anti-Wilsonian and isolationist grounds – to ratify the Paris treaties, and England's post-1918 withdrawal into preoccupation with the British Empire and Commonwealth, responsibility for east European security weighed heavily on French shoulders. In the years between 1921 and 1926 Paris mediated a set of treaties, commonly termed the "Locarno system" (1925), joining France to the Versailles settlement's principal east European beneficiaries – Poland, Czechoslovakia, Romania, Yugoslavia, and Greece – and the latter three among themselves.

So long as Germany remained effectively disarmed, as the Versailles treaty required, and so long as the newborn Soviet Union was weak and isolated, such a French-steered security system could function. In central and Balkan Europe it could block moves toward border revision ("irredentism") from Austria, Hungary, or Bulgaria, whose nationalists felt pain from World War I's territorial losses. Mussolini's Italy gestured toward upheaval in southeastern Europe, but did not threaten war.

MAP 17.1 *(continued)*

The revolutionary transformation of eastern and Balkan Europe into a realm of newly minted or territorially restructured nation-states forced Russia into a major retreat from Finland, the Baltic lands, Bessarabia, and above all Poland and the historic Polish-Russian borderlands. Yet the Soviet communists retained under their rule a vast empire. From the vantage-points of Berlin and Vienna, the new order in the east and southeast appeared as unmitigated disaster, entailing an immense loss of German influence and power. The temptation among German nationalists to cooperate with Russia to reestablish German co-hegemony in eastern Europe – a policy stemming from the practice of Frederick the Great and Bismarck – seemed unworkable in the face of the ideological gulf separating them from Lenin's revolutionary Marxist regime. Yet Stalin and Hitler found their Machiavellian way to tacit and, in 1939–1941, unconcealed partnership to the mortal disadvantage of the new eastern Europe.

The map cannot display the ethnic complexity of the new post-1918 states that gained territory from the Paris Peace Conference. Poland, Czechoslovakia, Romania, and Yugoslavia in particular counted numerous minorities, most of them politically restive under the rule of the majority peoples whose nationalist leaders were keen to infuse their states with their own national narratives and self-understanding.

To the list of German nationalists' postwar grievances must be added loss by Austria to Italy of the largely German-speaking alpine South Tyrol. After Mussolini's accession to power in 1922, it strained the patience of many of Hitler's followers and sympathizers that he refrained from demanding its return to German rule, reckoning – at least until undisputed National Socialist hegemony in Europe was attained – fascist solidarity higher than German ethnic unification.

Poland was the largest and most populous of east European states. Following Hitler's 1933 accession to power, the government in Warsaw, aware of its precarious situation, sought refuge in a policy of balance, signing identical nonaggression treaties with Germany and Stalin's Russia. Hitler's agreement to the 1934 Polish treaty was, in the European public's eyes, surprising in light of the Weimar Republic's bitter grievances against its eastern neighbor for having recovered statehood at German territorial expense (however much the lost lands were inhabited by Polish-speakers, or had been acquired in the eighteenth-century Polish partitions).

Fatal to the French-anchored east European security system was Hitler's 1935 restoration of universal army conscription and the German military reoccupation in 1936 of the western Rhineland province, since 1919 a demilitarized zone buffering France and Belgium from renewed German assaults. These bold steps, shredding the Versailles treaty's disarmament clauses, pushed France militarily on the defensive. The Parisian response was to sign in 1935 an alliance with the Soviet Union, now gaining international stature as it underwent rapid industrialization and military modernization under Stalin's autocratic rule. Czechoslovakia made a similar pact with Russia. Stalin set a new course for the international communist movement (Comintern): "united front" with "progressive bourgeois democratic forces and states," such as France or Czechoslovakia. This signaled the USSR's search for allies against the threat of National Socialist aggression against its western borders.

German foreign policy from 1934 sought to reduce the east European countries to economic dependency on German trade, scoring successes especially with Hungary and in the Balkans. Hitler's broader eastern strategy – indeed his highest goal – was to achieve a much radicalized, racialized version of the World War I *Mitteleuropa* concept of eastern empire, including massive German colonization and cultural-political obliteration of east European peoples standing in its way. This imperialist scenario's enactment entailed the overthrow of Soviet communism, a revolutionary and totalitarian system that Hitler and other National Socialists, like anti-Semites worldwide, delusively attributed to Jewish inspiration and direction. Bereft of its Bolshevik leaders, conquered Russia would become, Hitler said – alluding to the British Empire he admiringly took as a model – "Germany's India." As for the east European and Balkan states, their fate within this imagined National Socialist empire – at least in the near future – hung on events as they unfolded in 1938 and 1939, when Hitler strove to subvert and bend to his purposes the Czechoslovak and Polish states, thereby clearing the path to a showdown with the Soviet Union.

German Conquest in Eastern Europe, 1938–1945

In Hitler's view, there was but one inevitable serious war – that with the Soviet Union. His other aims he meant to achieve through diplomacy and swift applications of irresistible force (later known as "lightning war" or *Blitzkrieg*). An exemplary Hitlerian action was Austria's occupation and annexation in

March 1938, which the National Socialists termed "fusion" or *Anschluss*. Pro-NS propaganda represented this subversion as Austria's welcome liberation from uninspired right-wing government and allegedly unwanted independent statehood, in favor of the "Greater Germany" dreamed of in 1848 and 1918. Among many Austrian nationalists and conservatives, including a strong faction of outright National Socialists, union with Hitler's Germany was extremely popular.

Hitler celebrated his next foreign policy triumph in October 1938 at the ill-famed Munich conference. Here Britain and France sanctioned his demand, buttressed by self-righteous invocation of the German right to self-determination, for annexation of Czechoslovakia's heavily industrialized, ethnically mixed western and northern Sudetenland district. This blow would cripple Czechoslovakia, both economically and militarily. Yet western appeasement sentiment had risen to full flood, its representatives arguing that Hitler was essentially a pan-German nationalist whose goals, although radical, were limited. In their view, his demands were also, from an ethnic viewpoint, not wholly unjustified and could be peaceably realized through the Munich concessions.

Military defense of Czechoslovakia was still at that moment possible. Prague possessed an army rivaling Hitler's, and could appeal to alliances with France and the Soviet Union. But antiwar sentiment soared in France, while neither Poland nor Romania would risk allowing the Soviet army to march across their borders, for fear of Soviet-inspired breakaway movements among national minorities. The USSR itself had descended ever deeper into Stalin's fearsome internal purges, including that of the Soviet army, sowing doubt abroad about the USSR's value as an ally. Multinational Czechoslovakia was hobbled by cross-cutting, ethically inflected internal politics. Hitler overeagerly wanted war but settled for the annexation that Mussolini brokered for him with Britain and France.

Abandoning pretences of pursuing limited, German nationalist goals, Hitler unleashed his soldiers in March 1939 to invade and occupy the remainder of independent Czechoslovakia, thereafter erecting a Slovakian satellite state in its eastern half under Catholic priest Joseph Tiso, Slovak ultranationalist and clerical fascist. The new German-governed "Protectorate" in the formerly Czech lands of Bohemia-Moravia represented the first direct incorporation into Hitler's Reich of ethnically non-German territory.

In spring and summer 1939, Hitler pressured Poland to surrender the League of Nations-administered "free city" of Danzig and the Polish land surrounding it – known outside Poland as the "Polish Corridor" – separating the German province of East Prussia from Germany farther west. Compliance would have spelled Poland's reduction to National Socialist satellite state. The Warsaw regime balked, trusting in its armed forces and in English and French resolve to observe treaty commitments and defend Poland's independence. But Germany persuaded the Soviet Union – in the "Hitler-Stalin Pact" of August 23 – to stand aside in the looming German-Polish war in return for Soviet annexation

(a)

(b)

FIGURE 17.1. INTERWAR AUSTRIA AND THE *ANSCHLUSS*

FIGURE 17.1 *(continued)*

(a) Engelbert Dollfuss (1892–1934) rose from humble origins through activism in the Austrian Farmers League to the chancellorship in crisis-gripped 1932. In 1933, parrying Hitler's accession to power, he embarked on the Austrian right's long-anticipated "clerico-fascist" dictatorship, with affinities to Mussolini's Italy. This led Dollfuss to unleash the army in February 1934 to suppress Austria's Social Democratic and Communist parties. Austria's National Socialists, fearing Dollfuss's authoritarianism would eclipse their own, chaotically murdered him in an unsuccessful putsch attempt of July 1934. In the picture here, he rallies support, alongside glum-faced backers, soon before his assassination. The Austrian Republic came into existence in 1918 against many of its own citizens' misgivings. The 1919 constitution called for fusion with Weimar Germany, but the victorious Allies forbade it. The small and war-impoverished new country fractured politically along prewar lines between Social Democrats, Christian Social conservatives, and Pan-German nationalists. Its first chancellor, Social Democrat and internationally respected jurist Karl Renner (1870–1950), found backing outside the politically divided army and police in the *Schutzbund*, a pro-republican paramilitary force facing the antagonism of increasingly robust right-wing paramilitary units (the *Heimwehr*).

Elections soon obliged the Social Democrats to yield parliamentary power to the right under Ignaz Seipel (1876–1932), Catholic priest, Christian Social leader, and Austrian chancellor, 1922–1924 and 1926–1929. Seipel bitterly opposed the Austrian left, which his party denounced in accustomed anti-Marxist and anti-Semitic rhetoric. He wished to steer the country toward a clericalist authoritarian constitution. In 1927, he stood behind police repression of leftist demonstrations in Vienna, resulting in the Justice Ministry's burning and deaths of eighty-nine protesters – an explosion of violence that gravely and permanently weakened the democratic republic's stability and legitimacy. Chief (1930–1936) of the *Heimwehr* was Prince Ernst Starhemberg (1899–1956), whose fascist colors shone ever more brightly. Like many on the Austrian right, Starhemberg aimed – if fusion with a right-radical Germany proved impossible – at a police-state regime in which repression would foil the perceived (and exaggerated) threat of Marxist revolution. After Dollfuss's assassination, authoritarian chancellor Kurt Schuschnigg (1898–1977) fell ever more on the defensive, under pressure from Austrian National Socialists to coordinate if not merge the state with Hitler's Germany.

(b) Hitler's address of March 15, 1938, following Germany's invasion of Austria, which had foiled Schuschnigg's plan to buttress Austria's independence by plebiscite. Hitler speaks from the former Habsburg palace (Prince Eugene's statue at his feet) to a vast Viennese crowd assembled on the Heldenplatz. He depicted himself, once Austria's obscure son, as Providence's instrument in uniting the German *Volk*.

Anschluss evoked wide approval in the economically weak and politically fragile land. Hitler installed Austrian National Socialist Arthur Seyss-Inquart (1892–1946) as plenipotentiary before Austria's seamless incorporation into Hitler's Germany in 1939. Seyss-Inquart later headed the NS occupation regime in the Netherlands, suffering condemnation at the postwar Nuremberg trials and subsequent execution. While individual Austrians' participation in the National Socialist regime was very high, public opinion came to believe, not altogether wrongly, that the land had been marginalized and subordinated to Berlin. This increasingly widespread perception, coupled with the Third Reich's calamitous defeat, initiated a retreat from German nationalism which slowly led to post-1945 emergence of a specifically Austrian identity.

Source: (a) Bildarchiv Preussischer Kulturbesitz/Art Resource, NY; (b) Deutsches Bundesarchiv.

FIGURE 17.2. CZECHOSLOVAKIA'S SUBJUGATION
Here, on March 15, 1939, the German army enters the important industrial city of
Brno (Brünn), greeted with NS salute by Germans among its mixed Czech-German-
Jewish population. A different scene unfolded the same day in predominantly Czech
Prague, where the German soldiers' presence elicited massive embitterment and tears
of rage. Under National Socialist rule such ethnic polarization – disastrous radicaliza-
tion of nineteenth-century nationalist mobilization in multiethnic central and eastern
Europe – spelled cultural and even physical doom for numerous non-German populations. Among Czechoslovakia's many rich economic assets whose seizure strengthened
National Socialist war-making muscle were the huge Škoda machinery and armaments
works in Plzeň (Pilsen). Exploitation of conquered and colonialized east-central Europe
and lands beyond enabled Hitler's regime to sustain in wartime Germany living standards and working conditions far more favorable than would have been possible through
reliance on domestic resources alone.
Source: Deutsches Bundesarchiv.

of eastern Poland and a free hand in the Baltic states. Stalin was acquiescing
in dangerous expansion of German power to the east, but he shrank from
immediate hostilities. Although England and France declared war, they were
not logistically prepared to fight. In three weeks' time the German armies
defeated Poland, amid ruthless bombing of Warsaw and other cities and towns.
The Soviet Union joined in Poland's dismantling, seizing its eastern half, and
later – in mid-1940 – brutally annexed Estonia, Latvia, and Lithuania.

Two years later, in June 1941, Hitler's armies attacked Stalin's vast land
empire, convinced this most colossal invasion in military history could topple
the communist state in the few months before winter began. Although the

Reichswehr had rapidly defeated and occupied France in the spring of 1940, Germany had failed to break British resistance in the desperate 1940–1941 air war (or "Blitz"). Hitler concluded that Britain would only surrender when hope paled that Russia would eventually challenge Germany. The United States, even though it was aiding Britain, would not be able to bring its military power to bear, Hitler assumed, before his armies had subjugated Moscow and Leningrad. But Russia withstood National Socialism's punishing and cruel onslaught (see Map 18.1). Three years of murderous war followed before the Red Army pushed Hitler's troops back across the 1939 German eastern frontier.

In the Danubian-Balkan region, a conference of late 1940 (the "Vienna Awards") partially dismembered Romania. Here Hitler bowed to Stalin's pressure for territorial rewards for previous neutrality, while tying other participants in the Romanian spoils (Hungary and Bulgaria) to Germany. Italy, after occupying Albania in 1939, invaded Greece in 1940, but faltered on the battlefield, forcing the German army to intervene to secure the region against Greece's longstanding ally, England. This provoked a crisis in Yugoslavia over Hitler's demand for passage through the country and military alliance. Yugoslav refusal drew a brutal German attack on Belgrade in June 1941, followed by the country's occupation and partition. A pro-Hitler fascist Croatian state arose. Serbia fell under German occupation, while Bulgaria, Hungary, and Albania seized the remaining Yugoslav land. German conquest of Greece followed.

By mid-1941 the Versailles order in southeastern Europe lay in ruins, replaced by German-Italian condominium. But in 1943, Mussolini's weakening regime buckled and collapsed, forcing Italian withdrawal from the Balkans. There followed bloody and implacable anti-German and internecine guerilla war, concentrated in the Serbian-Bosnian-Albanian-Macedonian lands, until in the fall of 1944 the advancing Soviet Army drove Hitler's troops into retreat and occupied the regional capitals (Athens excepted), ending the war on the Danube and in the Balkans.

Building the Folkish Empire, 1939–1945

Poland and neighboring Belarus and western Ukraine suffered National Socialist Germany's harshest occupation policies. In Russia itself, even though many millions tragically died, military operations dominated German action. The emergence of a mighty world war, engaging all the great powers, led Hitler – at the latest, in December 1941 – to abandon all hesitation in pursuing imperialist-racist goals. The fighting's outcome could only be total victory or total defeat.

The basic National Socialist objective in those parts of eastern Europe marked as future German *Lebensraum* ("living space") was Germanization – but, as Hitler declared in *Mein Kampf*, "of the soil, not the people." German minorities scattered throughout eastern and Balkan Europe were in their hundreds of thousands to be "brought home to the Reich" and settled as farmer-colonists – a process that began in the fall of 1939 in annexed western

FIGURE 17.3. WAR IN THE EAST
Hitler's eastern European military strategy applied maximal force deliverable by modern technology, combined with measureless, unrestrained brutality toward opposing troops and civilian masses. This triggered grim, revenge-hungry and finally triumphant resistance. In 1939, Blitzkrieg methods – aerial bombings inflicting heavy civilian losses, motorized attacks spearheaded by tanks, and rapid advance of huge troop forces – inexorably overwhelmed Poland. The June 1941 invasion by over 3 million soldiers of the Soviet Union, based on the same tactics, foundered on vast distances, harsh weather, and Soviet resistance, provoked by murderous German treatment of civilians and captive soldiers alike.

In this photograph, Waffen-SS troops, with both motorcycle and horse-power, move through a village in Soviet Belorussia/Belarus, torched to break resistance. In this Soviet republic alone, some 20 percent of all villages suffered such a fate. In the southern Russian industrial city of Stalingrad, a prolonged battle in the fall and winter of 1942–1943 inflicted huge losses, ending in Germany's demoralizing defeat, costing upward of 300,000 German lives lost on the battlefield and in subsequent epidemics among captive survivors.
Source: Bildarchiv Preussischer Kulturbesitz/Art Resource, NY.

Poland. East European large estate-owners faced eviction from their lands by SS farm managers. The politically suspect non-German intelligentsias were to be "liquidated" (murdered). On the eve of the 1939 attack, Hitler spoke to his generals of the forthcoming "destruction" and "extermination" (*Vernichtung, Ausrottung*) of the Polish nation altogether, although it was to be the European Jews (against whom he had earlier in 1939 publicly uttered the same threat) who principally suffered this fate. Hans Frank, the Hitler-appointed governor of occupied Poland, boasted that soon the Vistula river basin – ethnic Poland's heartland – would be as German as the Rhine valley.

SS chief Heinrich Himmler's "General Plan for the East" (*Generalplan-Ost*), drafted to Hitler's satisfaction in 1941–1942, looked forward thirty years beyond the war's end. It forecast the diminution of the targeted east European peoples' populations by the following measures: Poles – 85 percent; Belarusians – 75 percent; Ukrainians – 65 percent; Czechs – 50 percent. These enormous reductions would result from "extermination through labor" or decimation through malnutrition, disease, and controls on reproduction. National Socialist policy would simultaneously impose far-reaching Germanization of public life and repression of east European languages, religions, and cultures. Himmler's agencies would comb the occupied lands to seize biologically suitable Germanization candidates, especially among young children. Non-Germans surviving thirty years of such policy would live as culturally disarmed, humble colonialized subjects, some among them amenable (as National Socialist planners imagined especially of Czechs) to Germanization through schooling and intermarriage.

The Russian people, once subjugated in war, would join the four Slavic-speaking nations whose fate *Generalplan-Ost* foreshadowed. They all faced long-term linguistic-cultural extinction, together with a high degree of abuse-engendered short-term death under police-state domination. Such outcomes qualify under the 1948 United Nations Convention as genocide, although the term ethnocide may be preferable. There is a difference, in comparison with the Jewish mass murder, between immediate death by firing squads and gas chambers and gradual death by overwork and neglect. Yet masses of civilian non-Jewish east Europeans also died by the bullet, while a million or more Jews died as ghetto and economic slaves.

Generalplan-Ost blueprinted the most extreme outcome. That the targeted Slavic peoples did not suffer the fate Himmler prescribed for them resulted from the Jewish "Final Solution's" higher priority, wartime exigencies, and 1945 defeat. Nevertheless east European losses were colossal. Hitler, Himmler, and their myriad servitors in various agencies building the *Lebensraum* empire envisioned Germanized eastern Europe as a technologically advanced but still heavily agrarian realm, anchored in a numerous German family-farming population, with medium-sized cities connected by great east-west freeways.

War's Toll in Eastern Europe

German policy conceded the Czechs a relatively tolerable standard of living in hope that Bohemian industry could be efficiently exploited. Still, 38,000 Czechs, active or implicated in resistance, suffered execution during the war. In Poland, during the fall 1939 conquest, the German army and police, aided by local ethnic German vigilantes, executed between 45,000 and 65,000 Polish citizens, some 7,000 of them marked as Jewish, the rest political activists and nationalist intellectuals, soldiers and ordinary people. Many thousands

(a)

(b)

FIGURE 17.4. GERMANIZING OCCUPIED POLAND

of prisoners of war classified as Jewish died in the winter of 1939–1940 from a deliberate maltreatment that was the harbinger of worse things to come. These were World War II's first mass killings, venting the pressure for murderous violence at all levels of government and armed forces which six

←

FIGURE 17.4 *(continued)*
(a) Upper Silesian Gauleiter Fritz Bracht with SS officers and other administrators, several of them quite young, at a 1941 Berlin exhibit, "Development in the East" (*Aufbau im Osten*). They contemplate a model of a colonization village for new German settlers in territory annexed from defeated Poland, from which its Polish population would be expelled, if that had not already occurred. Thus was the National Socialist "General Plan for the East" concretely enacted, radicalizing with great brutality German colonization programs in historically Polish regions launched in Bismarck's time, and reaching back to the age of Frederick the Great, who – although without nationalist inspiration – settled lands he seized in the Polish partitions with thousands of mostly German families. In Imperial Germany, the Prussian Colonization Commission between 1886 and 1914 implanted, mainly in Poznania and at considerable governmental cost, more than 14,000 German "farmer-colonists" and their families on medium-sized farms. Although policy decreed such land should be purchased from Polish landowners, Polish resistance forced the Colonization Commission to buy from German estateowners. The National Socialists looked back scornfully on such reliance on capitalist market mechanisms and respect for property rights to achieve Germanization ends (although, ominously, in 1912 the Prussian government began expropriating – if, hesitantly, on a small scale – Polish estate land for colonization purchases).
(b) Poles expelled in the fall of 1939 from their homes in western Poland (Germany's new "Wartheland" province). They march, carrying minimal possessions, under armed guard to stations that will transfer them to occupied central and southern Poland (the opaquely named "General-Government"), where they will be obliged to fend for themselves. The picture shows that such Poles were little different in appearance and self-presentation than Germans. Yet "racial theory" condemned them, like the other east European ethnicities targeted in the "General Plan for the East," to social-cultural extinction. In the 1939 campaign, regular German army units publicly executed Polish civilians on a large scale. By such terroristic means, ensnaring the army in NS policies of mass murder, the pacification of conquered Poland was attempted. Paired with such shootings were mass executions out of public sight of tens of thousands of Poles identified as "intelligentsia" and "nationalist leaders," including many civilian politicians and social activists.

SS-administered Germanization was ruthlessly swift. In March 1944 Wartheland Gauleiter Arthur Greiser received thanks from a German farmer from Ukraine, the propagandistically acclaimed millionth new settler in German-annexed western Poland. The speaker recounted to attendant National Socialist dignitaries – army and SS alike – and an audience of fellow emigrant-colonists the terrors of life in Stalin's Soviet Union. In 1946 a Polish court ordered Greiser's execution for war crimes. Many of the millions of ethnic Germans the National Socialists removed from long-settled homelands in eastern Europe, the Soviet Union, and the Danubian-Balkan region were grateful to escape local discrimination or uncertainty and receive property plundered from non-Germans (initially, mainly from Poles). Yet they had no choice, and many privately mourned their uprooting, while others were loath to receive stolen property.
Source: Deutsches Bundesarchiv.

years of National Socialist dictatorship had pumped into public life (and many Nazi psyches). Hitler's regime promptly annexed Poland's western provinces into the "old Reich," ghettoizing their Jewish inhabitants and expelling much of the Christian Slavic population to central Poland, where under the name of "General-Government" a ruthless and lawless National Socialist occupation regime emerged aiming to avoid all associations with Polish nationality or former statehood.

The "General-Government" became a vast hunting ground for coerced labor and site of the major SS death camps – principally Bełżec, Treblinka, and Majdanek. Auschwitz, the iconic site of mass murder, stood on land annexed directly from Poland into Hitler's Germany. The prewar eastern Polish lands, captured in 1941 from the retreating Soviets who had seized them in September 1939, were integrated into new National Socialist administrative units in Ukraine, Belarus, and the Baltic region. In the "General-Government," amid deepening hardships and social disintegration that German occupation fostered, the underground "Home Army" (AK), subordinated to the pro-western Polish government-in-exile in London, eventually grew to large numbers, forming a resistance movement second only in military participants to the Yugoslav communist partisans, and in civilian engagement Europe's largest.

The Home Army was active in anti-German sabotage, espionage, and occasional assassinations and armed actions, but long abstained – for lack of firepower, and to minimize terroristic National Socialist reprisals – from outright partisan war. In August 1944 it launched an uprising to liberate Warsaw in advance of the Red Army's arrival – spurred on by Moscow's encouragement but, in the end, cynically abandoned to their fate by nearby Soviet forces. German counterattack against Polish insurgents killed and wounded some 40,000, decimating the Home Army's strength, while 150,000 or more civilians perished, trapped in the city's destruction.

Polish resistance was unable to prevent massive losses through dragooning of forced laborers for work in German industry and agriculture, ruthless German requisitioning of food, and deliberately neglected public health. Upward of three million non-Jewish Poles died during the war. A similar number of Polish Jews were inhumanly murdered. These losses together amounted to 20 percent of the state's 1939 population. Defeated Warsaw sank in rubble.

In the German-occupied lands east of Poland, and in the occupied USSR, comparably high or even higher losses occurred. Göring and other top National Socialist planners reckoned coldly with death through starvation, occasioned by requisitioning of east European foodstocks for the German population, of 30 million people. The German armed forces' struggle against numerous forest-based, pro-Soviet partisan fighters reduced much of Belarus and northwestern Ukraine to depopulated and smoking ruins. The occupiers burned more than 600 Belarusian villages and left the country's population – like Poland's – reduced by 20 percent. Everywhere the National Socialists plundered local industry and private assets.

Among Soviet citizens – speakers mainly of Russian, Ukrainian, Belarusian – some three million soldiers starved to death or succumbed to disease as

FIGURE 17.5. PARTISAN WAR AND CIVILIAN RESISTANCE
This superb undated photograph of unknown provenance depicts partisans attacking Germans in a flame-engulfed Ukrainian village. A boy fights among them. National Socialist ferocity toward the occupied Soviet population – expressed in arson and property expropriations, labor enslavement, and mass hangings and shootings of innocents as punishment for German losses to resistance fighters – drove many Soviet subjects into partisan units, over which Stalin's government exercised final control, commanding their formation where they did not spontaneously arise. Losses on all sides – especially in western Ukraine, Belarus, and eastern Poland – were immense.
Source: Deutsches Bundesarchiv.

prisoners of war, while battlefield casualties were cumulatively colossal. A million civilians perished in the 1941-1944 German siege of Leningrad. Others were dragooned elsewhere in NS-occupied Soviet territory in great numbers as slave laborers in German industry. The Jewish inhabitants of the western USSR, apart from those who succeeded in fleeing eastward or in surviving as members of partisan fighting units, perished in the Holocaust.

In German-occupied eastern Europe, severe economic crisis, food shortages, and epidemic disease struck everywhere. In the Danubian-Balkan lands, German direct rule confined itself largely to Serbia and some adjacent parts of dismembered Yugoslavia, and to hunger-plagued Greece. Losses in pitiless fighting between German and non-German pro-Hitler forces and anti-German partisans were high on all sides. Fascist or semi-fascist regimes arose, apart from Croatia, in Romania and finally, in 1944, in Hungary as well. In Croatia and Romania especially, local state-organized violence against Jewish residents reached genocidal proportions, while National Socialist pressure in 1944 forced deportation to death camps with local government's ready assistance of much of Hungary's large Jewish population.

German domination of western Europe – notably the Low Countries and northern France – exacted a heavy price in economic plunder, food and labor requisitioning, and brutal transport to concentration and death camps of Communists, Jews, resistance fighters, and other persecuted groups. Yet the ferocity of National Socialist actions in the east was incomparably greater.

Eastern Europe was, alongside Hitler's Germany itself, a nightmarish laboratory of National Socialist racism. Although professional history and popular memory in the West often fail at the task, the full measure of National Socialist inhumanity and ideological extremism requires a vision that takes in the disastrous blows Hitlerism rained down both on the (predominantly eastern) European Jews, other east Europeans targeted for extinction, and those inhabitants of Germany itself – and western Europe too – for whom there was no place in Hitler's boastfully trumpeted "Thousand-Year Reich."

National Socialism's designs on eastern Europe generated war, mass murder, interethnic fighting, and social and cultural trauma more colossal and inhumane than had ever been witnessed in European history, and seemingly – measured in numerical terms – in all human history. This resulted from the importation in technologically intensified form onto European soil of methods of European overseas imperialism, for which the early modern Atlantic slave economy or ruthless exploitation of Belgian Congo's indigenous population stand as examples, among many other terrible cases. Where Spain and Portugal, Britain and France, the United States and Canada, as well as Russia and other states had gained expansive overseas colonies or huge inland frontier-zones, Imperial Germany – which had risen before 1914 to one of the world's industrially and militarily strongest lands – failed in competition for world-scale empire.

Hitler – the baleful son of both Habsburg and German history and the murderous executor of the "folkish movement's" most extreme potentialities – aimed with crystal clarity and utter ruthlessness to reverse this historical verdict. At the same time, he sought to bring to life the reveries of nineteenth-century "greater German" (*grossdeutsch*) nationalism, claiming for itself all German-speakers scattered across central Europe and the tsarist Russian empire's western reaches. The National Socialist project in eastern Europe pursued the chimera of a single, vast, ethnically homogeneous German nation-state that, through ethnocidal elimination of Germany's eastern Slavic neighbors, would rapidly expand into a "German Aryan" Eurasian empire rivaling and finally overshadowing the world's other imperial giants. This was a German nationalism, locked in a Faustian pact with "scientific racism" and drunk on military-industrial-technological overconfidence, that destroyed the German nation as it had taken shape since Bismarck's day.

18

Shoah

Banned from Nation and Earth
German Jews after 1914, National Socialist
"Jewish Policy," and the Holocaust

Two interpretive traditions have, since Hitler's day, commanded scholarly efforts to understand the Holocaust. One emphasizes *ideas*, recounting the intellectual history of anti-Semitism and the aims and political actions of those gripped by its poisoned talons. Its motto might be the poet Heinrich Heine's dictum: "thought precedes act as lightning thunder." Paired with this approach is the conviction that history is made by human beings' conscious choice: beliefs inspire purposive behavior seeking their realization. Historical actors are aware of their actions and responsible for them.

In Holocaust historiography, this widespread understanding of history and human behavior has yielded the "intentionalist" argument. This holds that (1) anti-Semitic ideology of a uniquely aggressive type flourished in late nineteenth- and early twentieth-century Germany; (2) Adolf Hitler and other National Socialist leaders embraced it and crafted it into a political program; and (3) the anti-Jewish policies (*Judenpolitik*) of Hitler's "Third Reich" led, if perhaps by a "twisted path," to a mass murder that the National Socialists' anti-Semitic ideas, and the dictator Hitler's in particular, authorized and even commanded.

The second interpretive approach, no less venerable than intentionalism, figures in historians' debates as "functionalism" or "structuralism." It sees complex historical phenomena such as the Holocaust as the outcome of intersecting supra-personal political and social developments, of which individuals – including the dictator Hitler – are both creations and embodiments. Actors' intentions are important, but they must be understood as responses to configurations of power and culture over which no one exercises guiding control.

Where intentionalists have stressed Hitler's self-expressed beliefs and commanding will, and other National Socialist perpetrators' clear-eyed, cold-hearted purposefulness, "functionalists" have sought to grasp the Holocaust as the expression in Germany of mighty – if ominous and often pitiless – trends in modern history: the formation of ethnically and culturally homogenized nation-states, imperialism, political mass mobilization (driven by utopian, sometimes biologized, visions of modernity), and the emergence of amoral, bureaucratized and militarized states, especially totalitarian states, warring among themselves and riddled internally with self-aggrandizing political factions and other institutional struggles. From the interaction of such developments events crystallize, such as the Holocaust, which, even though they result from the aggregation of individual thoughts and actions, are only comprehensible in their multicausal, supra-individual complexity.

The historical literature on the Holocaust, whether intentionalist or functionalist, has in recent decades focused relentlessly on the origins of the comprehensive mass murder of which Auschwitz, as the largest and deadliest of National Socialist death camps, is the terrifying symbol. How did the NS leadership arrive at the *decision* to "annihilate" (*vernichten*) or, in an even more inhuman idiom, "exterminate" (*ausrotten*) the millions of Jews it held captive? Slowly a historiographic consensus has emerged that the *implementation* of *policies* of comprehensive mass murder arose, not from Hitler's unilateral decree, but from the dictator's interaction with high police and NS party functionaries and their on-the-ground agents, particularly in occupied eastern Europe, under the military and economic circumstances prevailing after the invasion of the Soviet Union in June 1941. Though intentionalist analysis chafes against it, the conclusion has established itself among leading Holocaust scholars that the "Final Solution," as the mass murder came to be known, did not depend on a *final decision*, but rather entailed an ongoing series of decisions, only brought to an end by Germany's 1945 defeat.

Yet the genocide's *causes* remain controversial. Many historians of intentionalist bent view the initiation of mass murder in 1941-1942 as the triumph of Hitler's will, breaking – in the midst of apocalyptic war – through the shackles of restraint that prewar circumstances had forged. Other, structuralist-inclined historians emphasize the unpredictable, step-by-step unfolding of a process of "cumulative radicalization," driven by "bureaucratic Darwinism," among National Socialists high and low seeking support of a dictator who contented himself with conjuring up desired outcomes – the "removal" (*Entfernung*) of Jews from the folkish state, or their "annihilation" – without specifying precisely how to achieve them.

This debate is necessary and productive. It forces both intentionalists and structuralists to marshal the concrete empirical evidence and to construct the chronologically framed narratives without which their approaches remain philosophical-methodological manifestos. This chapter aims, however, to focus explanation of the Holocaust and its origins not so much on the wartime decision-making process as on a wider-ranging interplay of factors. The first of these is the ideology and political program of anti-Semitism, especially in its National Socialist form. The second is Germany's drive to establish in conquered eastern Europe a "Greater German Racial Empire" ("*Grossdeutsches Rassereich*," in historian Hans-Ulrich Wehler's unusual but apt phrase). The third is the National Socialist project of building, among the racially designated "Aryan" German population – and on an imperial scale – a prosperous, socially mobile, harmonious, and politically alive "people's or folk community"

(*Volksgemeinschaft*). The argument here is that only by a linked analysis of these three dimensions can the Holocaust, both as a National Socialist project and as an object of our own present-day knowledge, begin to come adequately into focus.

National Socialist anti-Semitism aggressively demanded the "exclusion" of Jews from German society, and often even – if seemingly only rhetorically, and by unspecified means – from life itself. Yet in the absence of German conquest and attempted empire building in eastern Europe, the Holocaust could never have occurred. The great majority of its victims were east European Jews: among a total of some 6 million dead, there were roughly 2.7 million Polish Jews, 2.1 million Soviet Jews (mostly inhabitants of the historic Polish-Lithuanian-Ukrainian borderlands), 500,000 Hungarian Jews, and about 150,000 Jewish citizens of Czechoslovakia. Those who were German or Austrian inhabitants numbered, respectively, some 165,000 and 65,000. In western Europe the genocidal machinery engulfed 200,000 people, not a few of them refugees from the German lands and eastern Europe.

To radically simplify: no anti-Semitism, no Holocaust. But also: no east European National Socialist empire, no Holocaust. Yet anti-Semitism as ideology did not unswervingly mandate German empire, nor did empire in eastern Europe inescapably unleash lethal anti-Semitism, as German practice in World War I shows. *It is the convergence of these two projects, neither necessarily entailed by the other, that generated the Holocaust.* As for the "people's community" or *Volksgemeinschaft*: its creation was the National Socialist regime's *foremost promise* to its "Aryan" German subjects. The degree of its realization was the decisive test of Hitlerism's legitimacy, in the eyes both of National Socialism's rulers and Nazi-inclined "Aryan" subjects.

Crucially, however, *Volksgemeinschaft* at the Germanic center depended, in the theory and practice of Hitler and the National Socialist governing elite, on the extension of racially exclusivist empire into its eastern periphery. The "American-style" prosperity and modernity the National Socialists sought for their favored German subjects could only, they believed, be attained through ruthless, colonial exploitation of conquered eastern Europe. Thus *Volksgemeinschaft* presupposed eastern empire which, as projected by its anti-Semitic conquerors, demanded the "removal" of its Jewish population, eventually by means of mass murder. In this way, the three factors this chapter highlights – anti-Semitism, eastern imperialism, and the promise of social modernization at home in Germany – interlocked to bring forth the Holocaust.

Anti-Semitism in World War I and the Weimar Republic

Germany's loss of World War I and experience of the revolutionary upheavals of 1918–1923 stirred up turbulent new waves of anti-Jewish animosity. The bloodier the war's fighting and the more distant the prospects of definitive victory at the front, especially in the west, the more resonance – amid growing home-front suffering – folkish and anti-Jewish propaganda found in public opinion. Yet this reaction was mostly confined to center-right and ultranation-alist circles, while among other Germans antiwar appeals and leftist insubor-dination won wide assent. Under the radical right's pressure, the army agreed in 1916 to conduct a census of Jewish soldiers, so as to show – as army spokesmen put it – that Jewish men were not avoiding conscription or evading frontline action by desk service behind the lines. The inquiry bore out these contentions, but agreement that the question needed investigation was a con-cession to right-wing prejudice that outraged and disheartened anti-Semitism's foes.

The 1918 revolution's rightist opponents frequently highlighted the promi-nence of various Jewish-born leaders and activists, and anchored the stab-in-the-back theory in anti-Semitism. The right-wing paramilitary forces (Freikorps) active during the early republic, like the still diminutive National Socialist movement, were anti-Semitic strongholds, and much inclined to stig-matize Weimar in anti-Jewish terms. In 1922 Jewish-born foreign minister and highly respected industrialist, Walter Rathenau, perished in a hail of right-wing assassins' bullets, cutting him down as the embodiment both of the republic's attempt to "fulfill" the Versailles Treaty and of "Jewishness" illegitimately arrived in positions of state power.

Jewish Germans' civic and personal security depended on the postwar order's stabilization under the Weimar Coalition's auspices: Social Democrats, Catholic Center Party, and liberals (that is, Democrats, joined after 1923 by Gustav Stresemann's center-right People's Party). In the years between 1924 and 1929, these forces dominated the political scene, while the radical right, including the National Socialists, lost ground. The Communists, although menacing the mainstream German Jewish community in their antagonism to middle-class property, culture, and religion, fumed in their proletarian subcul-ture. They were, in any case, enemies of anti-Semitism, which they scorned as a reactionary tool to distract ordinary people from capitalist exploitation's true sources.

Had this state of affairs persisted, German anti-Semitism likely would have grown gradually weaker. It was, however, undergoing a vital change, as its eugenic significance – evident in Hitler's concept of the "folkish state" – loomed ever larger. Ultimately, the eugenic-racist stigmatization of Jews could only have occurred because of the earlier existence of religious anti-Judaism and social-cultural anti-Semitism (which had defined Jews as menacing outsiders). Yet many National Socialists, especially degree-holding SS and NSDAP plan-ners and functionaries – but also Hitler and Goebbels – scorned and ridiculed old-fashioned "bourgeois" anti-Semitism in favor of the "racial science" fueling their vision of eugenic modernity.

To the considerable extent that the Holocaust served the realization of this social Darwinist dream, the emergence of modern right-wing radical national-ism underpinned by racist eugenics was a fundamental cause of the Jewish mass murder. Its triggering power was, arguably, more potent than that of the older anti-Semitism that, had it not undergone "scientization," likely would have gradually disappeared (as has happened in western Europe and north America) in the interstices of religious obsession and crank politics.

Like other largely middle-class groups, German Jews suffered great economic losses through wartime and postwar inflation. In their occupational profile, Germany's half-million self-declared Jews (comprising only about 1 percent of the entire population) increasingly resembled middle-class Germany in general. An additional population of acculturated Germans of Jewish heritage – of uncertain, but not small number – had found, through religiously mixed parentage, conversion to Christianity or abandonment of religion, non-Jewish German identities that the National Socialists would later seek to ruthlessly annul, although some in this class (notably the pejoratively branded people of "mixed race" or *Mischlinge*) managed to remain in Germany and survive.

As a group, the German Jews numbered ever more private-sector salaried white-collar workers. The Weimar Republic's creation ended earlier obstacles to Jewish entry into civil service jobs, teaching, and other public employment. The Jewish-born were still numerous in the educated professions, but their salience in banking and other business was declining as ever more non-Jewish entrepreneurs and firms arose. The bonds of religiosity were loosening among all faiths, and intermarriage was rising accordingly. The German-Jewish birthrate was falling toward the point of demographic reproduction only.

Jewish immigration from eastern Europe remained, as before the war, unpopular among both German Christians and Jews, because such migrants were pejoratively seen as "Polish" or "Russian" or otherwise "un-German." Britain's pledge, expressed in the 1917 Balfour Declaration, to advance the cause of Zionism in Palestine, where territorial control was slipping from the Ottoman Turks' government into British hands, encouraged Zionist enthusiasms in Weimar Germany. Heightened Jewish national-cultural self-awareness expressed itself also in deepening interest among intellectuals in mysticism-tinged Judaism and Judaic philosophy.

Still, the Jewish majority remained wedded to German national identity. In the burgeoning new mass-media of the 1920s, especially film and radio, Jewish-born writers and other cultural producers figured prominently, winning popularity among the public at large. The Great Depression conceivably might have reinforced integrative or assimilative social-cultural trends among German Jews. The salaried and wage-earning majority among them faced the same future as their non-Jewish counterparts. But the political conflicts the Depression raised to boiling point broke the German Jews' political defenses.

National Socialist Violence in Its Twentieth-Century Setting

The National Socialist regime combined ferocity and bureaucratic coldness with unprecedented ruthlessness. The twentieth-century mind unwillingly grew accustomed to the existence of right-wing militaristic police-states devoted to cruel repression, through executions and concentration camps, of democrats

(a)

FIGURE 18.1. JEWISH-BORN GERMANS AND GERMAN JEWS

(a) Theodor Wolff (1868–1943), chief editor (1906–1933) of the influential and widely read German newspaper, *Berliner Tageblatt*. Wolff was a liberal democrat, advocate of German-Jewish assimilation, and target of National Socialists and others on the folkish right. Arrested in southern French exile by Mussolini's police, he died in a German concentration camp in 1943.

(b) Hannah Arendt (1906–1975), secular-minded political philosopher and historian. She was a close friend and professional colleague before her emigration in 1933 to both Martin Heidegger and philosopher Karl Jaspers. After 1945 she gained world-renown as an analyst of totalitarianism and the Holocaust. As political thinker, she emphasized civic rights and duties over ethnic-cultural identities. Photographed here in 1935 in exile, in a Parisian cafe, she was exemplary of the early twentieth-century emergence of a high scholarly-philosophical intelligentsia among women of Jewish heritage.

Eminent during the Weimar years was epoch-making physicist Albert Einstein (1879-1955). In 1919 he supported the liberal German Democratic Party but – gripped with concern over rising anti-Semitism and crises facing east European Jewry – also supported Zionism. In 1921 he joined the delegation to the United States of the World Zionist Organization, headed by Russian-born, German-educated Chaim Weizmann (1874–1952), WZO chairman and, in 1948, Israel's first president. Einstein later moved leftward, joining other prominent intellectuals in denouncing Hitlerism's rise. As a émigré in America, he abandoned further engagement with Germany.

Walter Benjamin (1892–1940) was a modernist literary scholar and philosophical essayist who engaged idiosyncratically with Marxism and Zionism and has risen to great posthumous influence. He was a major figure in the circle of the 1920s Frankfurt Institute for Social Research (including also Theodor Adorno and Max Horkheimer), whose project – as will be seen in Chapter 20 – was to analyze modern society and popular culture, building on Hegel, Marx, and Freud. Jewish-born Victor Klemperer (1881–1960) was a convert to Protestantism, World War I soldier, and professor of Romance philology. He married a Christian wife together with whom, and with whose help, he survived

(b)

FIGURE 18.1 *(continued)* (just barely) under National Socialism. Klemperer authored a pioneering and influential analysis, published after the war, of National Socialist discourse, demonstrating how it constructed totalitarian reality. He also penned one of the most important and vivid secret diaries compiled under Hitler's dictatorship. As was true of other Germans of Jewish heritage, indeed of all Jews, National Socialist racism imposed an ideology-derived identity on him which in no way accorded with his own self-understanding.

Emblematic also of the Weimar years were Martin Buber (1878–1965), Polish Galician-born, Austrian-educated resident (until 1938) of Germany, philosopher and scholar of east European mystical Judaism (Chasidism); Gershom Sholem (1897–1982), Berlin-born scholar of Jewish history, especially of cabbalist mysticism, and champion of modern Hebrew as a scholarly and philosophical language, 1923 emigrant to Zionist Palestine; Franz Rosenzweig (1886–1929), Hegel scholar and key figure in the post–World War I renewal of German-Jewish religious philosophy. Characteristic of militantly nationalist German Jews was Ernst Kantorowicz (1895–1963), born in Poznań/Posen in the German-Polish borderlands, wartime soldier and postwar fighter in the Freikorps, eminent medieval German historian, émigré after 1933 to America. *Source:* provenance unknown.

and Marxists. Exemplary were Mussolini's Italy, Franco's Spain, Pinochet's Chile, and *apartheid*-ruled South Africa. On the left, brutal dictatorships, such as Stalin's in the Soviet Union, Mao Zedong's in China, or Pol Pot's in Cambodia, caused the deaths of millions – even tens of millions – of "class enemies."

Hitler's goal of overthrowing the Soviet Union, if necessary in large-scale war, was an expression of ideological anticommunism, common throughout the western world. It was also a reaction, within the unstable post-1918 international system, to the Soviet Union's perceived weakness, which invited Machiavellian exploitation by a strong Germany, particularly in light of the precedent of German conquests at Russia's expense ratified in the 1918 Brest-Litovsk treaty. Soviet Russia's defeat was also, together with German subjugation of

Poland, a precondition for the establishment of the *Lebensraum* empire which alone, in the National Socialist view, could raise the middle-sized European German nation-state to a global power.

The National Socialists' enactment of Jewish mass murder occurred amid a life-and-death struggle with still undefeated Russia and Britain, with the United States poised to intervene on the anti-German side. Many have asked why Hitler's regime diverted scarce resources of money, manpower, and transport to methodically murder a vast Jewish population who posed no threat and were willing, if necessary, to serve Germany as a labor force possessing many useful skills. Why follow a policy of murder and terror against Slavic Poles, Ukrainians, Belarusians, and Russians, when creation of a German-dominated empire in eastern Europe, raised on the ruins of the widely – although not universally – hated Soviet Union, was imaginable without such a policy? Achievement of German hegemony in eastern Europe was, or so it would seem, much more likely without it. The National Socialists might have gained numerous allies among these peoples, while avoiding the cumulatively painful losses they actually suffered in fighting the Soviet, Polish, and other central and east European resistance forces that their murderous policies provoked into existence.

The National Socialist regime was not only an imperialistic and anticommunist right-wing or fascist dictatorship. It was also an engine of utopian racism. In Hitler's and other National Socialist leaders' minds, the most rapid progress possible toward "German-Aryan racial rebirth," within a "people's community" vastly expanded to the east and free of the Soviet menace, was the *one* great positive goal whose pursuit was *unconditionally* necessary at all costs. *How* those they labeled as Jews and other "enemies of the *Volk*" would be disarmed and removed from the scene was a matter of tactical options, but not *whether* they would be eliminated.

Ideologically, Hitler and his colleagues justified the territorially expansionist "racial revolution" in Social Darwinist terms: before 1933 Germany had been falling behind the world's imperial nations – Hitler thought of Britain, Japan, and especially the continent-wide United States – because of the German Empire's defeat in World War I and postwar revolution and disarray, which he ascribed largely to "Jewish Bolsheviks" and "international Jewish capital." Germany's survival as Great Power required remilitarization and racial-eugenic renewal. To defeat the mortal threat the National Socialist leadership imagined the country faced justified, in their minds, other peoples' and nations' ruin.

Historians and other scholars, especially those who have concentrated on tracing the intellectual and cultural roots of anti-Semitism in German and western Christian society, have not always appreciated the connection between the National Socialists' imperialist expansion into eastern Europe, construction there of an "Aryan" German racial utopia at the expense of Jews and other eastern European peoples, and genocidal action.

Yet, once again: the Jewish Holocaust was primarily mass murder of *east* European Jewry, above all the defenseless Jews of Poland, the Baltic states, Belarus, Ukraine, Hungary, and the prewar Czechoslovak lands. Catastrophe struck also away from the primary eastern war theater, in Danubian and Balkan Europe. The Jews of Romania and Romanian-occupied southern Ukraine suffered varying degrees of genocidal violence under Marshal Ion Antonescu's militarist-fascist government in Bucharest. The German army's own occupation forces murdered the Serbian Jews, while the Croatian fascist satellite state extinguished its Jewish subjects in a dreaded death camp of its own. German occupiers deported most of the Greek Jews to Auschwitz. Bulgaria surrendered Jews living on formerly Yugoslav and Greek territories, but not (so as to shield national sovereignty) its own prewar Jewish citizens.

In the absence of German conquest in eastern Europe, the extent of Jewish losses – confined to German-speaking Jews and such western and southern European Jews as may have fallen into National Socialist hands – would have been vastly smaller than was ultimately the case. The tragedy would have remained, but on a very different scale. After the National Socialist regime's 1945 defeat and overthrow, the linguistically and culturally assimilated Jewish communities of western Europe had a chance at demographic and social recovery. But in the Holocaust, as it actually happened, the millions-strong and widely Yiddish-speaking Jewish societies and cultures of eastern Europe suffered extinction.

German Jews under National Socialist Dictatorship, 1933–1939

Action on Hitler's racialist program first required neutralization of opposition in Germany itself. This occurred through concentration in 1933–1936 in Himmler's hands of all police powers and diversion of jurisdiction over political crimes to draconic new "special" and "people's" courts, cooperating with the SS and Gestapo and funneling their victims into concentration camps.

In the years between 1933 and 1938 most members of the previously influential bourgeois-liberal and conservative elites in the army, diplomatic corps, and high economic bureaucracy who were inclined to oppose radical National Socialist measures, including against Jews, were dismissed from office and replaced by pliable NSDAP members or fellow travelers. Hitler's creation of numerous powerful new ministries and state-supervised development programs – Goering's rearmament-oriented Four-Year Plan Office, the building projects giant *Organisation Todt*, Himmler's "Reich Commissariat for the Strengthening of German Nationality" – further fragmented governmental authority, creating avenues for unimpeded radical action. The Christian churches, when they did not make their peace with the NS regime, found themselves on the defensive, struggling to uphold religious instruction of a youth ever more drawn into National Socialist organizations and psychology.

We have seen how in 1933 Hitler's regime began purging Jewish Germans from the civil service and fitfully dispossessing Jewish property owners through the "Aryanization" program. Jews suffered exclusion from the legal, medical, and academic professions, as well as from cultural life. Against Jewish retailers the National Socialists preached an April 1933 boycott, although its shrillness, occasional wildcat violence, and assault on accustomed shopping locales proved widely – but certainly not universally – unpopular in German public opinion. Protests in Britain and the United States against the boycott, and against German anti-Semitism in general, counseled the National Socialists, vulnerable to foreign economic and political reprisals, to call it off. The boycott had made its point, and briefly gratified the NSDAP's anti-Semitic enthusiasts.

In 1935 the regime promulgated the notorious "Nuremberg Laws," stripping Jews of German citizenship, reducing them to merely tolerated subjects of the state, and forbidding Jewish-Christian sexual relations and intermarriage. Despite their racial theories, the National Socialists knew of no other way to define those they labeled Jewish except as descendants of one or more grandparents who had practiced the Jewish religion, or as its current practitioners. In September 1941 the regime required German Jews to wear yellow-starred armbands, previously imposed in 1939 in occupied Poland.

By 1935 many Jews had already emigrated from Germany, but most remained. Many believed, like other opposition-minded Germans, that Hitler's regime could not long survive. Others resignedly thought the Nuremberg Laws might establish a lasting basis for Jewish life, comparable to the state of affairs that had prevailed before nineteenth-century Jewish civil emancipation. Many German Jews took a new view of themselves as racially and nationally Jewish and embraced Zionism, hoping for a chance to emigrate to British-ruled Palestine and join there in building the Hebrew-speaking Jewish national community. Under a 1933 agreement between Hitler's regime and Zionist leaders in Palestine some 50,000 German Jews, after surrendering most of their property, escaped to the future Israel, but British willingness to protect additional Jewish immigrants flagged in the late 1930s in face of Palestinian Arab protests.

Many Jews lost hope for the future, particularly in the aftermath of the regime-staged "Crystal Night" pogrom of November 9, 1938. In this two-day explosion of violence, SA bands, abetted and applauded by large crowds of hate-inflamed ordinary citizens, damaged or destroyed upward of 7,000 Jewish businesses, especially glass-fronted shops; irreparably burned some 200 of Germany's synagogues, vandalizing 1,000 more; murdered some 100 persons; and brutally rounded up and imprisoned 25,000 or more, causing still more deaths through cruel abuse. Coming soon after Hitler's menacing diplomatic triumph at the Munich Conference, this represented a decisive, coldly deliberate escalation of anti-Jewish policy, aimed at seizing remaining Jewish assets and terrorizing those Jews who could do so (after robbing them of their assets) to emigrate from Germany. In Austria, Jewish dispossession by plunder and bureaucratic chicanery, accompanied by cruel and unruly street violence, followed the *Anschluss* of March 1938, triggering mass Jewish emigration.

By the eve of war in 1939, three-fifths of Weimar Germany's half-million Jews had found refuge abroad, mainly – apart from Palestine – in France, Britain, and the United States. Some 200,000 German Jews remained, and about a third as many in Austria, where exodus after 1938 shrank a Jewish population numbering some 250,000 in 1933. Those trapped in the wartime

Reich comprised in large measure impoverished, often elderly people, living in a condition approaching "social death," and condemned, if no worse fate befell them, to die away by natural mortality in the future. Those who were young faced insuperable obstacles in marrying and raising children. Thus, *before* the Holocaust, National Socialist policy, not yet having crossed the mass murder threshold, effectively destroyed German-speaking central Europe's Jewish communities.

This was an astonishingly rapid process, viewed by most Germans who inclined to a favorable view of Hitler's regime with varying degrees of compassion, distance, intimidation, indifference, and coldheartedness. As recognition spread of the regime's unchallengeable determination to exclude Jewish Germans – as a group "alien to the *Volk*" – from national life, people seemed to prefer that this occur in an "orderly" fashion, implemented from top down. Many non-Jewish Germans thought the Nuremberg Laws had settled matters, leading their economically crushed Jewish neighbors into a ghetto existence, but one in which physical survival would offer an alibi for inhumanity and indifference.

Publicly defending victimized Jews and criticizing anti-Semitic abuses were criminally punishable acts. Although many Germans clandestinely helped Jewish friends and neighbors, if only to assist their emigration from the country, few were prepared to challenge official "Jewish policy." They knew of the regime's carceral rigors and increasingly understood the deadly seriousness of the assault on the Jews.

Zealous Hitlerites, especially among youth and brownshirted SA, often displayed sadistic taste for cruel physical abuse and public humiliation of defenseless Jews. This manifested itself in the arrests, torture, and murders carried out during the NSDAP's 1933 assault on the German left, which counted many Jews, and in the aforementioned April 1933 boycott of Jewish businesses. In 1934–1935, widespread grassroots anti-Jewish coercion and intimidation occurred, especially in small towns and villages, where National Socialist organizations vied with each other to render their communities – in the harsh phrase – "cleansed [or free] of Jews" (*judenrein/judenfrei*).

The alarmingly violent 1938 "Crystal Night" pogrom, although by many contemporary accounts widely and nervously condemned outside Party ranks, put a chilling readiness for anti-Semitic mayhem and murder on display. Yet the regime did not intend to let "Jewish policy" slip from its fingers, tactically useful though popular violence might be at certain junctures. Crucial to Hitler and his lieutenants was propagandization of the public, especially youth, in the "folkish worldview," so that an appropriately "hard" attitude developed sanctioning Jewish Germans' disappearance from the "people's community." In this brutal mission they could claim considerable success. Psychologically, and beyond the threshold of conscious morality, the persecuted victims inspired guilt and anxiety among non-Jewish onlookers. The impulse spread to flee the presence of people so rapidly and ruthlessly reduced to doom-laden pariahs or even, sadistically, to join in attacking them.

(a)

FIGURE 18.2. TORMENT AND TERROR UNLEASHED AGAINST JEWS OF GERMANY AND AUSTRIA, 1933–1939

In the NS Party's nation-wide boycott against German Jewish businesses, on April 1, 1933, SA men affixed posters to shop windows with the exhortation: "Germans! Defend yourselves. Don't patronize Jews." Contemporary photographs sometimes show the public reacting warily, and even often ignoring the boycott injunction. Protests abroad, especially in the United States, persuaded Hitler's regime not to persist. Instead, the dictatorship squeezed Jewish businesses out through its "Aryanization" campaign and, finally, in the property confiscations that followed the November 1938 pogrom.

(a) A 1934 sitting in Berlin of the board of directors of the Reich Association of German Jews, a fusion of the leading interest groups representing assimilationist German Jews and separatist Zionists. At the podium is Association president Leo Baeck (1873–1956), scholar of German Reform Judaism, field chaplain in World War I, and social activist. He bravely remained in National Socialist Germany, shepherding the ever more beleaguered Jewish community, before suffering internment in Theresienstadt concentration camp, where captured German Jewish notables were imprisoned, dying en masse. Having survived the war, Baeck emigrated to the Anglo-American world, where he founded the leading institute (later named after him) for German-Jewish history. Second from the left in this picture sits Siegfried Moses, German Zionist president. The countenances of both leaders reveal the extremity of the Jewish predicament.

(b)

FIGURE 18.2 *(continued)*
(b) In March 1938, in the midst of the German annexation (*Anschluss*), local National Socialists – young men – in Linz, Austria (Hitler's boyhood home) publicly shave the heads of three equally young Austrian Jewish women, who bear signs saying "I have been ejected from the people's community (*Volksgemeinschaft*)." Like boycotting and sexual stigmatization, such public shaming delegitimized Jewish presence and enacted metaphorical violence that signaled great danger. Following the installation of Hitler's government, as we saw, many such cruel anti-Jewish actions occurred. In July 1933 National Socialists mockingly paraded a young couple – a German-Jewish man and a non-Jewish German woman – through the streets of North Sea port Cuxhafen, before displaying them at the local NSDAP headquarters. Placards hung around their necks confessed, in self-derogatory rhyme, their violation of Nazi-mandated sexual boundaries. Such grassroots violence was sporadic in the prewar years, but familiar and menacing enough to drive most provincial Jewish families to Berlin and other big cities. Following the 1938 "Crystal Night Pogrom" great columns of arrested victims were marched through the streets to punitive imprisonment, in which many died or were disabled by maltreatment. Following this traumatic assault, most German and Austrian Jews who possessed the means to do so emigrated. But many others were trapped.
Source: Bildarchiv Preussischer Kulturbesitz/Art Resource, NY.

War and the Holocaust, 1939–1945

The National Socialist regime inaugurated systematic mass killing during Poland's conquest. Here, in the fall of 1939, political murder exploded on a scale previously unknown to central Europe, although it also manifested itself in the Spanish civil war of 1936–1939 and, on an ominously large scale, in the Russian revolution and civil wars of 1917–1920 (and in earlier European-inflicted colonial violence). Simultaneously, in Germany there began the afore-mentioned medical murder ("euthanasia") of non-Jews condemned as mentally defective. Some 70,000 died, mostly killed by lethal gas, before in 1941 the Catholic Bishop of Münster, Clemens von Galen, voiced public protest. These killings stirred public opinion, particularly in Christian religious circles, often responsible through their charitable institutions for handicapped and disabled people. The regime publicly halted the euthanasia program, but it was clandes-tinely pursued to war's end, claiming upward of 300,000 victims, among them many non-German captives.

National Socialist anti-Jewish policy following the war's outbreak on September 1, 1939 consisted primarily of the effort to expel Polish Jews from the "incorporated eastern territories." These were the western regions of defeated Poland annexed directly into what had officially become (since the absorption of Austria and the Czech lands) the "Greater German Reich" (*Grossdeutsches Reich*). We saw that Polish citizens, Jews alongside non-Jews, died in 1939–1940 in massive numbers before firing squads and from mal-treatment in military captivity. In the large German-annexed industrial city of Lodz/Łódź and in occupied central and eastern Poland – that is, in the colo-nially conceived and administered "General-Government" – National Socialist policy began forcing the millions of Polish Jews into ghettos, sealed in 1940, where rampant death through malnutrition and disease set in.

In Holocaust historiography, the next two years in conquered Poland, prior to the German invasion of the Soviet Union in June 1941, have sometimes figured as a "holding pattern" on the "Reich model." The National Socialist occupation of Poland is better conceived as the *beginning* of the Holocaust, understood as mass death induced by violence and abuse. Yet National Socialist *Judenpolitik* in 1939–1941 displayed an ominously blocked, negative charac-ter. German authorities, above all SS leaders Heinrich Himmler and Rein-hard Heydrich, Himmler's second-in-command responsible for implementing anti-Jewish policy, sought feverishly to deport Poles and Jews from the newly acquired "incorporated eastern territories" so as to settle in their place ethnic Germans from east European minority communities, especially those under Soviet control (whose emigration Stalin had agreed with Hitler to allow).

The German-Polish ethnic frontier had, since the late nineteenth century, been a site of embittered nationalist competition for predominance in popu-lation and landholding. As we have seen, the National Socialists now inaugu-rated what they intended to be a "final solution" to this "nationality struggle" (*Nationalitätenkampf*) by ruthless decimation of the Polish political leader-ship class, uprooting of Polish farmers, and rapid-fire settlement of German colonists, pushing the ethnic boundary far eastward in but a few years. National Socialist policy in occupied Poland meant cultural death for the Poles. After the fall 1939 wave of political murders – violence that had shocked many among the German authorities, and had led to resignations and sackings of the faint-hearted in high places – 3,000 more Polish political leaders, among 30,000 fresh arrestees, were shot in May 1940. SS death squads, army units, and local ethnic German militias plundered and murdered individual Poles and Jews at will.

Meanwhile, it intensely frustrated National Socialist authorities that captive Polish Jews especially, but also German, Austrian, and Czech Jews, could not be successfully "removed" through deportation to somewhere in occupied eastern Poland, as foreseen in the abortive 1939 "Lublin Reserve" plan to create a large Polish Jewish-settled district. The alternative of urban ghettoization in Poland amounted to human warehousing pending shipment to a still-unknown destination. After Germany's military defeat of France in the spring of 1940, hopes arose among National Socialist leaders, Hitler included, that the large east African island of Madagascar (today's Malagasy Republic), hitherto ruled by France, could be acquired as a destination for deported Jews (who would languish if not perish there under SS rule). But Britain's refusal to capitulate and its continued naval domination of the high seas doomed this idea.

After 1939, NS *Judenpolitik* depended on a course of events driven by Hitler's pursuit of *Lebensraum* through war and *Volksgemeinschaft*-expansion through German colonization in "the East." If, in occupied Poland, Jewish mass death was commencing, this was the consequence of the National Socialist effort to build an east European German-populated empire while plundering a shattered Poland for food and other assets with which to offset the cost of war and maintain or raise living standards in Germany. If such a deathly outcome gratified Hitler and other anti-Semites, it nevertheless represented "collateral damage" to the captive Jews more than achievement of *Judenpolitik*'s objectives, which still focused on mass removal through deportation.

Instead, the burden of policing and minimally sustaining several million Jewish hostages appeared to National Socialist planners as a deficit whose continued weight "German society" – that is, Hitler's wartime regime – could not be expected to bear. It had been clear to NS officials responsible for food supply that war would require replacement of lost overseas imports at eastern Europe's expense, where crops and livestock would be seized for German consumption. There was no place in this calculus for captive Jews. In Germany itself, the question whether the residual Jewish community there should continue to have a beggarly claim on now scarcer food and other consumer goods grew ominous.

Germany's June 1941 invasion of the USSR promised Hitler world power, perhaps world domination, through extension of *Lebensraum* thousands of miles eastward to the Ural Mountains and beyond. The dictator foresaw the German population soon swelling to 125 million and more, the German language conquering Europe. British resistance would buckle, and a German imperium from Atlantic and Mediterranean to Black Sea and Arctic would begin its thousand-year sway. This was, too, a "war against the Jews," for Hitler understood the Bolshevik political class as "racially Jewish" or "Jewish-controlled."

His "commissar order," issued on invasion's eve, mandated summary execution of captured Communist political-administrative functionaries. To this end, and to murderously suppress anti-German subversion and partisan resistance which Soviet Jews were, according to anti-Semitic formulas, expected to launch wherever possible, SS-commanded "Task Forces" (*Einsatzgruppen*), which had earlier performed execution duty in Poland, were greatly expanded and sent into action on Soviet soil. Mass shootings commenced. In August 1941 more than 25,000 Jews – many expelled into German-occupied Ukraine by Hungarian authorities – fell to the SS Task Forces' bullets in a single action. By the end of 1941, they had shot a half-million Jews, eliminating, in the occupied Lithuanian-Baltic region, virtually the entire Jewish population – man, woman, and child.

In the summer and fall of 1941, National Socialist Party regional administrators and SS police chiefs in occupied eastern Europe (and in the German heartland too) began competing with one another to render their districts, by means of murder or deportation, "cleansed of Jews" (*judenrein*). In this they imagined themselves, not wrongly, to be "working toward the Führer," who – without having (so far as the evidence shows) explicitly ordered them to eliminate Jewish populations – was informed of SS shooting tallies, and could be expected to reward his servitors' bloody-handed zealotry with advancements in the power hierarchy.

On July 31, 1941, Hermann Göring commissioned Reinhard Heydrich to draft a plan for "the Final Solution of the Jewish Question in Europe." Historians debate whether this amounted to an "overall extermination plan of all European Jews," but certainly it registered the deadly escalation that the anti-Soviet war inaugurated. Food-supply planners, led by the SS's Herbert Backe, intended systematic starvation of captured or besieged Russian cities and in plundered Soviet, mainly Ukrainian, agricultural districts. The National Socialist elite accepted that the victims would number in the tens of millions: the greatest mass death, Göring cynically observed, since the seventeenth-century Thirty Years War.

As we saw, Himmler's "General Plan for the East" forecast, in its several drafts, the reduction, in thirty or even twenty years, of the mainly Slavic population, from the Polish General-Government eastward into Russia, by between 30 to 50 million people. Hitler, who in July 1942 approved the document – "the happiest day of my life," as Himmler reported – favored an analogy between *Lebensraum* colonization in eastern Europe and nineteenth-century white settlers' conquest of the north American West. As he lectured his dinner guests in October 1941, "we eat Canadian corn [i.e., wheat] and don't think of the Indians."

After mid-1941, particularly as the Polish Jewish ghettos faced conditions (created by German policy) of worsening famine and epidemics, and as food grew scarce throughout the National Socialists' vast and burgeoning European empire, ideas favoring mass-scale, euthanasia-style killing found support among "racial experts" and other occupation officials. These ranks counted many youthful, ambitious and upwardly mobile graduate-degree holders in such modern social science disciplines as sociology, demography, urban planning, and public health. But there were others – sometimes today labeled

FIGURE 18.3. MASS DEATH AMONG SOVIET PRISONERS OF WAR

The German army's victories and advances in 1941–1942 delivered four million Soviet POWs into its hands. In this tragic photograph of July 1941, seemingly a German soldier's illicit work, the meagerness of bread rations in the Ukrainian camp of Vinnytsia provokes panic among starving prisoners and apprehension among their captors. This region of the historic Polish-Russian-Ukrainian-Jewish borderlands was the eye of twentieth-century east European violence's apocalyptic storm: scene of bitter interethnic and ideologically driven violence during the revolutionary years 1917–1920; site in 1937–1938 of mass shootings of Soviet citizens by the Soviet political police (NKVD); site too of National Socialist mass killing of the local Jewish population. Nearby stood Hitler's wartime command center, named "Wehrwolf." Here too Himmler undertook to settle some 10,000 German colonists in a model outpost of Teutonic expansion – dubbed "Hegewald" ("Forest Stockade") – at Slavic expense. As the German grip loosened, Ukrainian nationalists ruthlessly fought the local presence of Russians, Poles, and Jews, eliciting lethal counter-attacks from their Slavic neighbors. In this picture, victims and tormentors alike are young men, enacting a script written by elders. In the end, more than three million Soviet POWs perished.
Source: Deutsches Bundesarchiv.

"productivists" or "attritionists" – who believed the captive Jews should be left to dwindle through undernourishment and other maltreatment while continuing to perform work (such as making military clothing) useful to the war effort. In some ghettos, as in Łódź (renamed Litzmannstadt), attritionist policy prevailed into 1944.

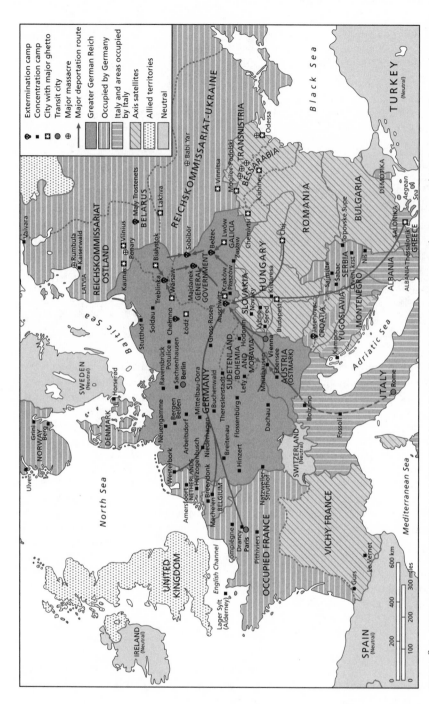

MAP 18.1. EUROPE UNDER NATIONAL SOCIALIST OCCUPATION AT ITS GREATEST EXTENT (1942–1943), INCLUDING THE DEATH CAMPS, MAJOR CONCENTRATION CAMPS AND GHETTOS, AND SELECTED SITES OF MASS SHOOTINGS

In Berlin, where most of the remaining German and many Austrian Jews had huddled together, some 40,000 young adults were dragooned into munitions and other war industries. This violated Hitler's and other high-ranking National Socialists' conviction that Jews embodied subversive revolt in the making, on analogy with what they remembered as the "Jewish-Bolshevik"-led strikes and antiwar demonstrations – the "stab in the back" – which in 1917–1918 had, as they vainly believed, undermined an otherwise triumphant Germany.

Jews in German hands had seemed politically useful to National Socialist leaders as pawns in gaining the western powers' – especially the United States' – toleration of Hitler's empire building. But as President Roosevelt deepened his commitment to British resistance and to German defeat, such considerations – in fact delusional, considering National Socialist abuse of the captive Jews – faded. Yet the idea of deportation persisted. In February 1941 Goebbels recorded that Hitler, speaking confidentially to his associates, said that "originally he had only thought of breaking the power of the Jews in Germany, but now his goal had to be the exclusion of Jewish influence in the entire Axis sphere... If only he knew where to put several million Jews, there were not so many after all." But he would not risk German ships to deliver them to Madagascar. "He was thinking of many things in a different way, and not exactly more friendly." Ominously, in mid-October 1941 Heydrich blocked further Jewish emigration from German-occupied Europe, even when foreign entry visas and economic support were on offer.

Doubtless the National Socialist death camps' shadow arose out of the anti-Soviet war's violence. By fall 1941 regionally confined genocidal killing was issuing from barrels of SS guns, already broken in to mass executions earlier in Poland. The technique of gas-chamber murder had been employed since the summer of 1939 in the "T-4" euthanasia program to kill tens of thousands of German and, later, also Polish mental hospital inmates. SS agents now began adapting it for use against east European Jews. Concentration camps equipped with or convertible to facilities for mass murder began to be constructed in

---

MAP 18.1 *(continued)* Evident here is National Socialist *Grossdeutschland*'s rapid mushrooming into a semi-continental giant through the absorption of Poland, whose Germanization by methods of radical murderousness and social neglect began in fall 1939. Clear too are the Holocaust's vast scale and the great distances involved in its execution. Crucial to the mass murder were railroads, not only in Germany and occupied eastern Europe, but also those administered by its satellites and allies in western and southern Europe. Death while underway in the crowded railway cars was massive. The Auschwitz-Birkenau camp on the fringe of the old Polish town of Oświęcim (known to its many prewar Jewish inhabitants in [Latinized] Yiddish as Oshpitzin) burgeoned from its 1940 origin as a prison for non-Jewish Polish political prisoners into the principal site of death for Jews deported from western European and the Danubian and Balkan lands. The millions of Polish and east European Jews perished in the death camps of the German-administered General-Government and in mass executions farther east.

the fall of 1941. These would eventually include Auschwitz, Bełżec, Chełmno, Majdanek, and Treblinka.

National Socialist policy's murderous drift accelerated in the aftermath of the United States' entry into the war. It was on December 12, 1941, one day after his declaration of war – in solidarity with his Japanese ally – against the United States that Hitler, addressing a large audience of top National Socialist leaders and regional NS-Party Gauleiters, announced that now that "the world war is here, the extermination" – that is, destruction (*Vernichtung*) – "of the Jews must be its necessary consequence." This was a reference to his oft-cited Reichstag speech of January 30, 1939, in which he had threatened "destruction" of the European Jews should "international finance Jewry" – from their supposed British and American bastions of influence – provoke a new world war. On December 18 Himmler noted of a private meeting with Hitler: "Jewish Question[:] exterminate as partisans." In other words, Soviet Jews, at least, were to be murdered on the pretext of eliminating underground armed resistance.

In January 1942 the Wannsee Conference near Berlin gathered, at Heydrich's invitation, a wide array of key German government ministerial officials who readily agreed to commit resources, including the railroad system, to Jewish "deportations to the East." There the able-bodied would be put to hard labor that, if it did not do them to death, would be followed by "special treatment." It was understood but left unspoken that for the Jewish masses unable to "build roads," death awaited. The previous smooth operation of the T-4 euthanasia program had proven that German officialdom was prepared to cooperate in the dictatorship's murderous programs, if only so as not to appear indifferent to the regime's bureaucratic imperative of "working toward the Führer" – attempting to anticipate Hitler's will and satisfy its expectations by means of maximally radical measures. Mass death was, by winter 1941–1942, becoming National Socialism's familiar accompaniment: as the Wannsee participants toasted each other, millions of Soviet prisoners of war were already dead or dying, while the guns of the SS *Einsatzgruppen* continued to blaze.

Poor harvests and food shortages in 1941–1942 prompted SS officials, backed by Himmler, to mandate "liquidation" by the end of 1942 of the Polish General-Government's ghettos. The productivization strategy saved a core population of workers in the Białystok ghetto until the fall of 1943 and in the larger Łódź ghetto until 1944. Otherwise, however, the German regime, reassured by fulsome harvests in the summer and fall of 1942, undertook to nourish better its *non-Jewish* slave laborers from east Europe and elsewhere (notably France), so as to consign captive Jews – including the politically suspect German Jews – to death camps. This was a process largely completed in 1943. With the tightening in 1944 of National Socialist control over the satellite government of Hungary, on-the-spot murder of Hungarian Jews and other victims and mass deportations to Auschwitz accelerated the genocidal process anew.

Only the Soviet army's driving of German armed forces from eastern Europe ended the far-advanced but still not completed mass murder. To the fall of

Hitler's regime in May 1945, surviving imprisoned Jews, along with other captives, were done to death in concentration and work camps, and through death-march retreats westward. Both in public addresses to the nation and confidential speeches to military and civil officials, from 1939 to 1944, Hitler and other leading National Socialists, notably Joseph Goebbels, had frequently threatened, predicted, or advocated the Jews' "destruction" as Germany's necessary self-defense and revenge for "world Jewry's" instigation of global war. In a speech of January 30, 1942 at the Berlin Sportpalast, Hitler exulted that "the hour will strike when the most evil world enemy of all time will have ended his role at least for a thousand years." And in his political testament, dictated shortly before his suicide on April 29, 1945, Hitler blamed "international Jewry" for the war and the sufferings it imposed on Germany, justified his fight ("by humane methods") with the Jewish archenemy, and called for "the strictest keeping of the race laws" and "merciless struggle" in the future "against the universal poisoner of all people." Thus did perpetrator project murderous impulses onto victim.

We have seen that the "path to Auschwitz" did not proceed directly from *Mein Kampf*, but rather that it opened up on the roads to Warsaw and Moscow, especially once Hitler had burned his bridges to the West. In retrospect, the Holocaust looms as the fulfillment of an ideological program entailing belief that world salvation required "removal" of "the Jews." Yet it appeared in this light more clearly *after* its occurrence than before. Prior to the Wannsee Conference and the subsequent inauguration of the death-camps, *Judenpolitik* figured in contemporaries' minds, as the empirical record requires us to see it too, as a function or entailment of objectives independent of anti-Semitic postulates alone. And how far, after Wannsee, the chemicalized murder would extend was unknown to the perpetrators themselves, and depended on the vagaries of war. Yet, as it happened, the National Socialists seized every opportunity to escalate genocidal violence.

The Greater German East European Empire and its corresponding *Volksgemeinschaft* were the goals for which Hitler's Reich fought and died. If their realization called for Jewish exclusion, and even eventually mass murder, it was nonetheless these objectives that beckoned to National Socialist enthusiasts as the great positive destinations lying on the far side of the "Jewish question's" solution (and also of the "questions" posed by biologically "unworthy" existences at home and in non-German eastern Europe). It was in large measure because National Socialists could view the world in this racialized and self-referential manner that they accepted with so vanishingly few moral scruples the human destruction their actions wrought.

Among individual Germans (and non-Germans) pressured – or tempted by psychic derangement – to participate personally in the mass murder, as executioners or other perpetrators dealing face to face with the doomed victims, anti-Semitic beliefs and prejudices were frequently a sufficient, but not always a necessary motive. Research has demonstrated that many killers were neither NSDAP members nor ideologically inflamed anti-Semites. Their brutal acts flowed from fear of peer pressure threatening exclusion, should they refuse to collaborate in a murderous assignment, from the military or police unit to which they belonged. Others shrank from the consequences of refusal to carry out death-dealing orders. Yet, despite widespread postwar opinion, this seldom entailed a death sentence or imprisonment, although transfer to the fighting front might occur. Careerism, conformism, and subservience to higher authority – to "the Führer's will," or even merely to "the government" – sufficed to motivate beatings, torture, and killing on unprecedented scale. Murder, when it occurs, will usually not be hard to justify, if only as cruel necessity, in the self-righteous or self-pitying executioner's mind. It was crucial, nevertheless, that perpetrators could invoke official racial doctrine to legitimize their actions.

Had Europe and America managed to halt German expansion in the borders of the summer of 1939, the Holocaust in the sense of Jewish mass murder would never have occurred, even if central European Jewry could not have avoided disappearance through forced emigration and brutal maltreatment. A *grossdeutsche Volksgemeinschaft* would have absorbed National Socialist energies, including such murderous eugenic impulses as propelled the T-4 euthanasia program. The fate of the east European Jewish millions, had they escaped National Socialist domination, would perhaps have been hard – depending on ethnic politics in the various eastern countries. Yet it would not have been mass death under the auspices of pseudo-scientific anti-Semitism.

But could Hitler's state have survived without external war? Would it have consumed itself in mad internal "cleansings" and purges? Might it have ossified into an inward-turned authoritarianism? Would domestic rebellion have upended it? These questions are unanswerable, but point to possibilities, had ways been found to block the National Socialist assault on eastern Europe.

Perpetrators, Resisters, Bystanders

Intentionalist analysis justly holds that National Socialist genocide and murder, directed against both Jews and non-Jews, occurred because, under wartime circumstances enabling ruthless elimination of politically suspect and other unwanted populations, Hitler and his lieutenants *willed* them. There is no more forceful demonstration that ideologically saturated ideas may have the worst of consequences. The murders could, in practice, be carried out because Hitler's regime had supplied itself with police and bureaucratic structures facilitating their commission. From the beginning in 1933 the German Jews themselves had been powerless to resist. An unknown but sufficient number of German soldiers and SS men, policemen and officials – several hundred thousand or possibly many more – were willing to follow or devise murderous commands in the "Final Solution's" physical implementation. National Socialist supervisors, while ever present on the scene, delegated much of the cruel handiwork to non-German east European collaborators, not always willingly recruited, and to victims themselves and other captives.

(a)

FIGURE 18.4. THE PASSAGE TO MASS MURDER

(a) In September 1939 the National Socialist occupiers, indifferent to their captives' physical capacities, round up Jewish laborers in Lublin, Poland, one of eastern Europe's most important Jewish communities. The captives' dress signals proletarian, bourgeois, and religious identities. Humiliation of ritually observant Jews was deep-rooted in anti-Semitic violence, which the National Socialists practiced unrestrainedly in eastern Europe and against Orthodox Jews elsewhere. In Germany, where assimilation and acculturation had widely erased outward differences between Jews and non-Jews, the yellow star's obligatory display from fall 1941 identified those officially labeled as Jewish. Many wore this badge with dignity. The police reported that the ominous star's appearance on the streets was unwelcome to the public, and not only for anti-Semitic reasons. The regime soon began deporting remaining German Jews to murder stations in the east.

The enormity of the murder raises the question of the German population's knowledge of the regime's genocidal actions, the degree of their active complicity, and the depth of their assent. On one side stand those who underscore the National Socialist regime's "consensualist" nature. They argue that support for Hitler's regime skyrocketed from a near majority in 1932 to massive acclamation by war's eve in 1939 of its – in certain respects, stunningly successful – accomplishments. Whether for reasons of material self-interest, political conviction, or quasi-religious self-immersion in the sea of collective belief, most Germans – so this view holds – accepted the National Socialist regime, regarding iron-fisted repression of Communists and Social Democrats, antagonism to the Catholic Church and liberal Protestantism, advancement of the NS eugenic program (including sterilizations and, from 1939, euthanasia), and persecution

(b)

FIGURE 18.4 *(continued)*
(b) arrival of a transport of victims at Auschwitz-Birkenau, 1943. Uniformed Jewish prisoners, doomed themselves, were compelled to assist in these operations, during which most of the new arrivals, including nearly all women and children, along with the elderly and infirm, suffered "selection" for immediate murder in gas chambers. A crematorium smokestack looms in the distance. Jews in the Warsaw Ghetto revolted against their German tormentors in April–May 1943, a deliberately suicidal gesture of resistance among the remnant of the huge ghetto population of a half-million which death-camp transports in 1942 had decimated by nine-tenths. Among the Jewish fighters were many leftists and Zionists. Thousands of Jews died fighting or were executed. Further transports emptied the ghetto completely.
Source: (a) Deutsches Bundesarchiv; (b) Bildarchiv Preussischer Kulturbesitz/Art Resource, NY.

of Jewish Germans as justifiable and necessary to attainment of the yearned-for *Volksgemeinschaft*.

Consensualist historians point to absence of effective resistance to Hitler's rule (while underestimating resistance *attempts*, which – in group form, leaving individual actions aside – numbered in the hundreds, some of them not inconsequential). They cite, too, the regime's own confidential soundings of public opinion in concluding, about official "Jewish policy," that most Germans either actively embraced the anti-Semitic program or viewed it with the indifference of bystanders for whom everything else was more important. National Socialist indoctrination of youth was widely effective, so that numerous young NSDAP activists and recruits into armed forces and SS showed little hesitation in acting – in one intentionalist writer's phrase (meant to apply widely to the German population) – as "Hitler's willing executioners." The regime and zealous youth alike contemptuously dismissed the scruples of those fellow Germans, especially among the older generations, who were still bound to the seemingly fading subcultures of liberalism and Christian morality.

Two clouds trouble these consensualist skies. One is cast by the ultrarepressive power of the NS Party and the dictatorship's judicial-administrative and police organs. Opposition and regime criticism were from the start serious crimes, commonly punished by imprisonment or death. *Monthly* Gestapo arrests of non-Jewish Germans as late as October 1941 numbered 544 for "Communism and Marxism," 1,518 for "opposition," 531 for "prohibited association" – frequently sexual – "with Poles or prisoners of war," and 7,729 for "stopping work." This amounted to some 65 arrests *daily* throughout the Reich for often severely penalized political offenses. During the war, the German armed forces staged 3 million courts-martial, including 400,000 against civilians and prisoners of war. Thirty thousand German soldiers received death sentences, of which two-thirds were carried out (in contrast to the forty-eight condemned soldiers put to death during World War I).

During the war the civil criminal courts imposed on German citizens 16,000 death penalties, three-quarters actually carried out (amounting to six executions daily in a six-year period, commonly reported in the press as warnings to others). In 1944 the Justice Ministry began drafting a law empowering the courts and police to eliminate "community aliens" (*Gemeinschaftsfremde*), an omnibus term encompassing defeatists, critics, misfits, outsiders, "failures" (*Versager*), and "folk-pests" (*Volksschädlinge*). Of jailed Germans deemed physically unsightly a 1944 Justice Ministry conference concluded: "they look like miscarriages of hell . . . It is planned that they too shall be eliminated. Crime and punishment are irrelevant."

Under such circumstances, Germans – as much evidence testifies – widely enacted the script attributed to them by a clandestine informant of the exiled Social Democratic Party in March 1940: "The comprehensive terror compels 'national comrades' (*Volksgenossen*) to conceal their real mood, to hold back from expressing their real opinions, and instead to feign optimism and approval. Indeed, it is obviously forcing ever more people to conform to the demands of the regime even in their thinking; they no longer dare to bring themselves to account. The outer shell of loyalty that forms in this way can last a long time yet."

This psychologically insightful report points to the second cloud casting shadows on consensualism. In the fullest and most sophisticated study of German attitudes on anti-Jewish policy, German historian Peter Longerich has shown that the dictatorship suppressed "public opinion" in any meaningful sense. It was instead official propaganda's task, notably in press and radio, but also even by means of the regime's own confidential internal reports on the public mood, to *create* and *mold* opinion. This was vital to imposing assent to anti-Jewish policy both within NS officialdom and on a population widely suspected by political authorities of inclining against it – for example, in deploring the November 1938 pogrom's violence and cruelty, or in observing with disquiet and alarm the German Jews' fatal deportation beginning in October 1941, or in (rightly) fearing, as war turned toward defeat, that mass murder in eastern Europe would spell profound disaster for German society. National Socialist opinion formation figured also as a step in the implementation of successively more radical stages of official anti-Jewish policy. It simulated – through periodic blaring press campaigns, distribution of posters and other advertisements, and release of anti-Semitic films – public support for new steps, aiming simultaneously to forestall and repress any dissent they might elicit.

Local-level anti-Semitic violence in pre-1939 Germany, and even such important events as adoption of the 1935 Nuremberg Laws or the November 1938 pogrom, went unmentioned or found only minimalist treatment in the official media. After the war began, concrete information on violence against Jews in eastern Europe rarely came officially into view. When in late 1941 and 1942 the regime turned to systematic genocide, loud media proclamations of the "final solution," or of the Jews' "total destruction" or "extermination," were accompanied, ominously, by news blackouts of factual details of Holocaust murder.

In spring 1943, Goebbels's Propaganda Ministry undertook a two-month campaign in which, while attacking the Soviet Union for mass murder of captive Poles, it brazenly acknowledged that Jewish populations under National Socialist command had largely ceased to exist. This revelation aimed to stiffen German resistance to the Soviet offensive by making it clear that the entire society must stand behind the Holocaust. Grim warning of Soviet reprisals, often (self-projectively) depicted as "Jewish death squads," induced unnerved and fear-ridden reaction in the German population, encouraging denial of knowledge and complicity. Already in October 1942 Göring employed this tactic in a nationwide radio broadcast: "This war is not the Second World War, it is the Great Racial War (_grosser Rassenkrieg_)." It was a life-and-death struggle between "German and Aryan and Jew.... Let no one fool himself into believing he can come forward later on and say: I was always a good democrat among those terrible Nazis."

The effect of National Socialist opinion molding was to destroy alternative public spheres at home from which the German population could gain information and understanding about _Judenpolitik_ and the unfolding Holocaust. Although many grasped that the deported Jews were going to their doom, and rumors of death by gas circulated, the scale of the death-camp slaughter was rarely understood. This was also true even in the West, despite arrival there from Polish resistance sources of credible eyewitness reports on the genocide. Locked in private isolation, many Germans continued anachronistically and deludedly to conceptualize the "Jewish question" in pre-1933 terms. Among National Socialist true believers, the regime's messages concerning anti-Jewish policies doubtless encountered complacent acceptance or welcome. Yet there is also evidence that well-educated and serious-minded NSDAP members preferred to block information and rumors about the nightmarish mass murder from their minds. So too did many ordinary people, for whom *Judenpolitik* and anti-Semitism *troubled* rather than solidified their relationship with the National Socialist regime.

After Hitler's fall, sociologist Michael Müller-Claudius published evidence he had earlier furtively gathered from a small number of NSDAP members indicating that, in the aftermath of the November 1938 pogrom, 63 percent were indignant over the anti-Jewish violence, while 5 percent thought it justified. His soundings in 1942, when awareness of the "final solution" – however interpreted – was widespread, revealed that some 5 percent accepted the Jews' destruction, while 21 percent expressed opposition or reservations. The rest – the large majority – concealed their views, whether (as Müller-Claudius thought) from "indifference" or owing to reluctance, driven by fear or anxiety, to confront the subject.

Such figures are at most suggestive, not conclusive. In any case, civilian Germans were forbidden under threat of arrest and death to resist the genocidal program, or even to take notice of it. Not a few paid with their lives for transgressing these rules. Most people, sensing the murderous reality or knowing something of it through whispered conversations with one or another of the millions of soldiers on leave from the eastern front, where the Jews' murder – at least by bullet, fire, and starvation – was common knowledge, anxiously but willingly looked away. Anti-Semitic propaganda and socialization, indifference, fear, and fixation on their own grievances and tribulations coarsened or silenced their moral sensibilities.

The security police's confidential reports on public opinion during the war often noted that ordinary people dreaded the consequences, should Germany lose the war, of Hitler's regime's anti-Jewish persecution. Some worried, in anti-Semitic terms, of "Jewish revenge." Anxiety that Nazism's exterminatory crimes would be requited, in the event of defeat, with the country's ruination, and even the mass death of the German people themselves, stiffened some people's resolve to fight to the bitter end. The British and American thousand-plane raids on Germany's cities gave a foretaste of national extinction. On the Allied side, National Socialist murderousness justified the bombings and all other countermeasures, whatever their toll on innocents and the regime's opponents.

German Resistance to Hitlerism

Before the war's outbreak, organized defiance of National Socialism found expression, after the crushing of the Communist and Social Democratic parties, in scattered and small-scale, leftist-oriented underground groups. These often sought Soviet support, and gained some strength after the eastern war started in 1941. Imagining them, under the name *Rote Kapelle* ("Red Choir"), to be a unified movement, the police succeeded in 1942 in entrapping and executing many of them. Additionally, many small and isolated plots to murder Hitler were conceived, but the difficulty of weaving broader networks under pressure of Gestapo surveillance and brutal torture of arrested suspects foiled them. A lone man – south German cabinet maker and factory worker Georg Elser – set a powerful bomb in the National Socialists' Munich beer-hall on November 9, 1939, but Hitler unexpectedly delivered his speech and departed before it exploded.

More effectual was anti-Hitler opposition that arose during the war in elite circles of upper-class conservatives and bourgeois moderates. The riskiness of the dictator's diplomacy, and the growing evidence of his determination to plunge into war to realize his grand designs, had already in the mid-1930s inspired apprehension among some highly placed military and diplomatic officials, who feared another German debacle such as the 1914–1918 war had generated. Yet the unbroken string of Hitler's successes, culminating in France's stunning 1940 Blitzkrieg defeat, silenced those critics who had, unlike others of similar temperament, evaded removal from their posts under suspicion of lukewarmness or defeatism.

When the 1941 invasion of the Soviet Union failed to deliver the early knockout blow Hitler had promised, realization spread among senior military officers and civil officials that the war's loss was likely, if not certain. Combined with growing knowledge in such circles of the horrifying extent of anti-Jewish mass murder and other great crimes on the eastern front, networks of resistance grew denser. Yet, among others in positions of power and influence, awareness of the unfolding Holocaust had the opposite effect of hardening determination to persevere in the war, so as to avoid the catastrophe for themselves, the regime, and the country which its loss would entail.

A conspiracy crystallized to assassinate Hitler in the course of a military coup establishing a provisional government that would seek to negotiate the war's end in the west while attempting somehow to halt the Soviet Union's formidable counterattack in the east. The key actors were army officers, many of them – including the ill-fated 1944 assassination bomb deliverer General Claus Schenk von Stauffenberg – from conservative aristocratic families. But civilian politicians representing both the bourgeois and Social Democratic camp were also involved. On July 20, 1944, Stauffenberg's planted bomb exploded beneath a conference table, but failed to kill Hitler, who was presiding at it. The Gestapo arrested some 5,000 conspirators and sympathizers, of whom about 1,000 were executed or committed suicide.

Goebbels's propaganda machinery, like Hitler himself, hailed the coup's failure as another proof of the Führer's miraculous powers and providential calling. Not surprisingly, in view of the government's control of the incident's reportage, the conspirators' association with the widely resented privileged aristocracy, and existence-threatening dangers besetting Germany – devastating bombing raids, impending Soviet conquest of pre-1939 German provinces – the population in large measure rallied around Hitler, greeting the oppositionists' ruthless execution with satisfaction.

The July 20 conspirators risked and lost their lives to rid Germany finally of Hitler. Few among them had acted only to halt the Jewish genocide, although this was a fundamental consideration, even if their minds were rarely free of anti-Jewish prejudice. Nor did many wish to return to Weimar-style democracy, preferring one or another kind of conservative-nationalist elite-guided rule. In their blueprints for a postwar Germany there was little or no place for a reintegrated or reassimilated body of Jewish citizens. Nazism had rendered the once-flourishing German-Jewish coexistence no longer easily thinkable. Such loss of intercultural imagination and trust occurred, for obvious reasons, also on the Jewish side. Even though after the war some surviving German Jews remained in or returned to the country, this was from Zionist and other specifically Jewish perspectives for many years unjustifiable.

Resistance to Hitler's regime within the Christian churches was weak and ineffectual. Pius XI's 1933 Concordat with Hitler's regime discouraged domestic Catholic insubordination. But, as we have seen, tensions nevertheless accumulated, and in 1938 the pope publicly condemned Hitlerism's anti-Christian dynamic. Pius XII, whose reign began in 1939, spoke out publicly during the war on behalf of the suffering Catholic Poles, but remained silent on the Jewish Holocaust. Not a political anti-Semite, and cognizant of the Holocaust, he doubted that public condemnation would halt National Socialist policy, and feared reprisals injurious to Catholic interests. Later in the war, anxious over anti-Catholic Soviet communism's accumulating strength, and of its many post-fascist Italian partisans, he conjured vainly with thoughts of brokering peace between Germany and the western powers in hope of halting the Red Army's advance.

In Germany, high churchmen both Protestant and Catholic eventually formulated protests against wartime mass murder which, although they did not speak concretely of Jewish victims, condemned violence against those of "foreign race." Bishops' proclamations to this effect were read in September 1943 from Catholic pulpits. The German Protestant clergy, divided between NS enthusiasts, regime conformists, and the oppositional Confessing Church, did not go so far, but a 1943 denunciation of mass murder penned by Württemberg bishop Theophilus Wurm circulated in the church hierarchy.

Many individual Christians sought to oppose or hinder mass murder. But the regime was in no way deterred by efforts at Christian protest or resistance. Troublesome persons among the laity could expect brutal persecution or death. The Confessing Church leader Dietrich Bonhoeffer, eminent theologian and clandestine participant in the conservative-moderate resistance effort, suffered imprisonment and later execution following the July 20, 1944 assassination attempt. Bishop Wurm received an icy warning to desist. Arrest and, for the leaders, the guillotine silenced the aforementioned non-violent Catholic-inspired White Rose movement among university students and faculty in Munich.

National Socialism proved a mortal danger to traditional Christianity. In German-occupied Poland the Catholic Church faced the threat of extinction, as did the Christian churches farther east, already menaced by the Soviet shadow. Thousands of priests and other clergymen, including Germans, perished at

(a)

FIGURE 18.5. LEADERS OF THE MODERATE-CONSERVATIVE OPPOSITION AND PARTICI-
PANTS IN THE ATTEMPTED ASSASSINATION OF HITLER, JULY 20, 1944
(a) Count Claus Schenk von Stauffenberg (1907–1944), elitist-minded south German
Catholic aristocrat and initially pro-NS officer who, finally convinced of Hitlerism's disastrous character, volunteered to set the July 20 bomb. He was shot in Berlin without
trial in the failed plot's aftermath. Here he appears at Hitler's East Prussian headquarters ("Wolf's Lair") a week before the assassination attempt – others earlier having gone
awry. Hitler is flanked to his left by General Field Marshal Wilhelm Keitel (1882–1946),
Chief of Army High Command and the Führer's compliant tool.

National Socialist hands. Yet centuries of theologically inspired Christian hostility to Judaism, coupled with widespread indifference to persecuted Jews'
worldly fate and inability to regard them as deserving objects of Christian moral
obligation, lamed the churches' will to speak out and act in their defense. More
courageous protests would hardly have deflected the all-powerful National

(b)

FIGURE 18.5 *(continued)*
(b) Carl Goerdeler (1884–1945), confronting – before a rapt but doubtless hostile audience – chief judge Roland Freisler of the Berlin "People's Court," which condemned him and the others here named to death (except for the already perished Stauffenberg and General Ludwig Beck). Goerdeler, of bourgeois conservative-nationalist background, was Leipzig's mayor in 1930–1935, and nationally prominent as economic-fiscal expert. The NS regime's political-diplomatic radicalism drove him into opposition. The designated post-coup chancellor, Geordeler clandestinely sought foreign support for the anti-Hitler opposition, but in vain. Among other conspirators was Ludwig Beck (1880–1944), who rose to army chief of staff in 1935, but was dismissed in 1938 for criticism of Hitler's war aims. He was a principal mediator between the disparate circles of the conservative and military opposition. Beck accepted the regime's offer to commit suicide rather than stand trial. Count Helmut James von Moltke (1907–1945), although tried before the Berlin court, was not a July 20 conspirator, but rather was active in seeking support from Britain for the anti-Hitler opposition. He stood at the center of the Kreisau Circle, a clandestine Christian conservative group that sought to plan a post-Hitler Germany. Among those prominent in the Kreisau Circle who participated in the July 20 plot, many of them scions of the Prussian nobility, were Peter Graf Yorck von Wartenburg (1904–1944), a cousin of Stauffenberg, and Albrecht von Hagen (1904–1944), both lawyers. Field Marshal Erwin von Witzleben (1880–1944) had agreed to command the post-coup armed forces. Julius Leber (1891–1945), Social Democrat, was peripheral to the military conspiracy, some of whose members viewed him as standing too far to the left. He was nevertheless designated to join the post-Hitler government.
Source: Deutsche Bundesarchiv.

Socialist leaders' iron resolve to carry out the "Final Solution." From that not even impending battlefield defeat could deter them.

Nor, in declarations of war aims or in military strategy, did the British or American governments highlight the Holocaust, about whose systematic, bureaucratic, and terrifying nature they were definitively informed at the latest by the fall of 1942 – even if incredulity took some time to overcome. There was reluctance to encourage the National Socialist idea that the war – understood in the West as liberty's self-defense of all humanity against Hitlerite tyranny – centrally involved Judaism and its adherents. Western military commanders refused Jewish pleas, delivered to the West through the Polish underground, for Allied bombing of the death camps, preferring instead to defeat the German armies in the field by conventional military means as the swiftest way to end National Socialist crimes.

For individuals in Germany and German-occupied Europe, danger-fraught opportunities arose for assistance to beleaguered Jews and other fugitives. Countless acts of courage and compassion occurred, saving Jewish lives on a scale of perhaps 100,000 and more. But the chances of collective action to halt National Socialist violence and inhumanity dissolved almost immediately after the establishment of Hitler's power, both in Germany and the occupied countries. The National Socialists' deathly grip proved unbreakable until cataclysmic defeat unlocked it. The challenge humanity faces in the contemporary world is to hold totalitarian impulses at bay, for once the ramparts of power are breached, the executioner's sword is set free.

PART IV

THE COLD WAR GERMANIES AND THEIR POST-1989 FUSION

A Nation Reforged from Its Remnants?

With the destruction of Hitler's empire, the German nation – as distinct from German-speakers – ceased to exist. This happened, paradoxically, just as in 1945 the newly established United Nations Organization proclaimed the nation-state the normative political structure in the brave new post-imperialist world that was arising across the globe out of world war's ashes. But the defeated Germans, instead of taking their place on one of the UN General Assembly's benches, found themselves under the victorious Allies' lock and key.

Nationalists prefer talk of blood and soil, but nations are communities of political will, brought to life through collective institutions, constitutions, and, most fully, through statehood. However vibrant a population's linguistically coded culture may be, however unique its social forms, it cannot articulate itself as a nation without developing political consciousness and crafting structures giving it political voice. Nationally minded German were, at modernity's dawn, uneasily aware there was no certainty that the *Kulturnation* would become a *Staatsnation*. In fact, except in the minds of those who equated German identity with the culture of the Protestant educated middle class or *Bildungsbürgertum*, modern history has never witnessed a unitary German "cultural nation." There were, instead, multiple subcultures, heavily stamped by religion and regionalism.

These pages have shown how political nations may perish by anachronism, as happened in 1806 to the Holy Roman Empire of the German Nation, or by battlefield defeat, as happened in 1918 to Imperial Germany – a nation in the making – and the Habsburg monarchy – a would-be house (with self-styled benevolent German and Hungarian landlords) of nations in the making. New projects of nation building may fail to mature, or self-destruct, as the fates of Weimar, the post-1918 Austrian republic, and National Socialist Germany reveal. After 1945, the victor powers decreed that German-speakers should assume new identities within the dual framework of a soon-to-be communist state, in what remained of the historic German east, and an "Atlantic"-style liberal democratic and capitalist state in the west. The Germans of Austria should renew, in a revived (but victor-occupied) Austrian state, an identity that most of them had repudiated in 1938 in welcoming incorporation in Hitler's Greater Germany.

Did determination exist in the bombed-out, demoralized, and disoriented ruins of National Socialism to enact these new identities, or would they be but masks hiding repudiation, or incomprehension, or lack of collective civic will of any kind? This was the shape the postwar German national question assumed. The following chapters will display the answers given by the forty-year histories of the western German Federal Republic and the eastern German Democratic Republic, and by the first two decades of the reunited Germany that emerged in 1989 into the dawn of the post–Cold War world. This was the fourth Germany of which this book's title speaks. First traumatized, fragmented, walled off and walled in, then unexpectedly joined under a single roof: *this* Germany was something new under the central European sun, and still is today. Yet it is an intriguing question whether, two decades after East Germany was enveloped by West Germany, a fifth political nation is gestating within its chrysalis.

Nations in the present-day urban-industrial (or suburban/post-industrial) world are communities of citizens, not expressions of uniform ethnicity, even when a common language is usually necessary to enable communication within them. Large-scale modern societies are many-chambered houses, honeycombs of subcultures, congeries of inequalities and incongruities. A single language will express many, often conflicting worldviews. Warring nations may share the same tongue. Imaginings of unitary and homogeneous, conflict-free nations, bound by a "single will," are formulas for disaster (as are, in the lives of the great powers, analogous thoughts about the entire world). As we will see, the present-day Federal Republic of Germany, one of the world's leading states, has come close to embodying a post-ethnic or post-nationalist understanding of modern nationhood.

Many people are inclined to think that this outcome represents a triumph within German history of the culture's better self, and arrival at a preordained but long-elusive goal of History. But we will see that, like all great events, Germany's attainment of a (imperfect) liberal democratic consensus and free-market prosperity was contingent on the unforeseeable. Like other modern political nations, today's Germany is fraught with conflict and contradictions. Like them, the life span of its present collective existence is unknowable.

19

Beyond "Zero Hour" (*Stunde Null*)

*Defeated Germany and the West German
Federal Republic, 1945–1989*

Hitlerism's Nightmarish End

The racially framed war that Hitler's Germany inflicted on eastern Europe and the Soviet Union was one of history's grimmest pages. Some 20 million Soviet subjects died, a third of them civilians. Six million Jews perished, including the vast majority of Yiddish-speaking east Europeans. Much of the landscape – human and physical – of Poland, Belarus, Ukraine, and western Russia was cinder and ash. The National Socialists and their allies and servitors perpetrated murder of utmost cruelty on a colossal scale. Civilians and captured soldiers and slave laborers – at war's end there were some 700 foreign-worker labor camps in the German heartland alone – died in huge numbers of starvation and abuse. By the present-day German Ministry of Justice's count, concentration camps and their outlying penal colonies altogether numbered 1,634 throughout the "Greater German Reich."

Never was there a greater military defeat of a once-powerful nation, nor a more complete political and moral bankruptcy. Lacking only were atomic bombs. These the United States invented to drop on Germany, but they were not yet ready when on April 29, 1945 Hitler, surrounded by the Red Army, committed suicide in his Berlin bunker, allowing the European slaughter to end soon afterward. Yet for more than three years British and American aircraft had fire-bombed Germany from the air, decimating historic cities (among many others, Lübeck, Cologne, Hamburg, Dresden, Nuremberg, Berlin), killing some 500,000 and leaving 8 million homeless. Nor had Austria's Vienna escaped the wreckage.

At the July 1945 Potsdam conference, Joseph Stalin, Winston Churchill, and Harry Truman decreed that the German-speaking inhabitants of the pre-1939 provinces of Silesia, eastern Brandenburg, Pomerania, and East Prussia, together with German communities in the prewar Czechoslovak and Hungarian lands, should be "resettled" in the German heartland – that is, expelled to it. But already, months earlier, millions of Germans in the east had begun to flee westward in terror before the advancing, often undisciplined and revenge-hungry Soviet army. They fled, too, before Poles, Czechs, and other peoples who rose in fury inflamed by wartime suffering to drive out German occupiers and German-speaking minorities – stigmatized, in part unfairly, as National Socialist enthusiasts – and seize their possessions for themselves.

In the end, this "expulsion of the Germans from the east" amounted to the greatest ethnic cleansing in modern world history: some 12 million or more were uprooted and driven westward, a million or more dying on the way. Soviet troops murdered countless innocents and committed an enormous mass rape, victimizing perhaps 2 million German women. It was mainly Poles who resettled Germany's lost eastern provinces (themselves often refugees from a now Soviet-annexed prewar eastern Poland), although part of East Prussia fell to Russia, which still rules it today as Kaliningrad. These lands, predominantly German in language and culture since the high Middle Ages, had accounted for one-quarter of the pre-1938 state's territory.

Germany's wartime population losses were proportionally as high as the Soviet Union's: between 6 million and 7 million dead, the greater part soldiers, whether killed in action or victims of Soviet captivity. The wounded, disabled, and psychically deranged numbered millions more, in a population that in 1933 had encompassed 65 million, but which in 1946 counted just 64 million. Occupied Germany's postwar reparations were as high as the Allies could ratchet them: coal and other industrial deliveries to western Europe, industrial plants dismantled in the eastern Soviet occupation zone and shipped to Russia, seizure of German assets and patent rights in the United States.

At conferences in Paris (1946) and London (1953), German state debt deriving from unpaid reparations under the 1919 Versailles Treaty as well as the enormous damages inflicted on Germany's neighbors and other countries in World War II was recomputed, eventually to the fledgling and still feeble early Federal Republic's advantage, which in subsequent decades nevertheless paid the weighty sum of DM 14 billion to its various creditors. To this must be added the considerable value of German foreign assets of all descriptions seized after 1945, for which the Allies allowed no compensation. After 1989 further reparations payments, especially to surviving victims of the Holocaust and National Socialist slave labor, were settled with east European countries whose enclosure in the Soviet empire prevented their participation in the 1946-1953 agreements. A notable instance was the "Polish-German Reconciliation Foundation," established in 1992, which to 2006 disbursed to Polish claimants some $2 billion.

The war's last months, when the Soviet army fought its way across pre-1938 German soil to costly victory in Berlin, witnessed a paroxysm of violence: concentration camps abandoned, their inmates decimated by death-marches; mass sacrifice of boys and older men, serving as cannon fodder in last-ditch auxiliary armed forces; lynchings by SS forces on German streets of army deserters, along with soldiers separated from their units and suspected war shirkers and "defeatists"; massacres among the millions of enslaved foreign workers scattered across town and country – including many from western Europe and even Italy, Germany's former fascist friend; napalm-like firebombs falling on cities and industrial works; economic collapse, driving people – among them, millions of homeless and uprooted – to comb the land for food and fuel, or to die for their lack; Gestapo arrests striking or menacing surviving conservative and liberal oppositionists, real and imagined; youth bands living anarchically; epidemics of hunger, typhus, tuberculosis, venereal disease. In February 1945, British and American bombers, with little more intent than to break German morale and exact revenge, destroyed the city of Dresden, a baroque jewel, killing outright upward of 25,000 of its inhabitants.

Such was the stage on which postwar German history unfolded. In an important sense, as these pages have proposed, National Socialism and war destroyed the preexisting, crisis-gripped German nation. The historic configuration of Prussia had all but disappeared, its lands to the east of the Oder-Neisse river line emptied of Germans, the landed nobility who remained in east Germany (if they had not taken flight – or their own lives) on the verge of dispossession through communist land reform, the Hohenzollern kingdom's very name abolished from official usage by a 1947 decree of the joint occupation powers. In Austria, enthusiasm for *Anschluss* with Hitler's Germany had backfired disastrously: masses of Austrian National Socialists stood among the war-crimes perpetrators; the Soviet-invaded, impoverished, and war-blighted land lay like Germany under Allied occupation.

German Christianity, especially Protestantism, bore scars of complicity with National Socialism, which hastened postwar decline of faith and churchly engagement, especially among the educated middle class. The expulsions from beyond the Oder river and the communist collectivization of agriculture uprooted traditional village culture in east-Elbian Germany, where it had constituted one of Protestantism's mass bases and underpinned a robust and long-lived Prussian-centered political conservatism, whose Faustian pact with Hitler sent it to its grave.

The pre-Hitler political left also never recovered its earlier strength. Stalinism and post-1945 Cold War dictatorship in East Germany corroded German communism. The working-class subcultures that before 1933 had lent Social Democracy its characteristic militancy, authenticity, and self-confidence were bombed and then, after the war, urban-renewed and modernized out of existence. Finally, the middle-class culture whose roots reached back to Goethe and Kant and forward to Thomas Mann and Karl Jaspers had lost its commanding grip on intellectual life. In part it suffered the fate of German Protestantism, to which its cultural if not theological bond had always been vital. Its adherents stood all too often guilty, if not of compromise with Hitlerism, then of inability to resist it or, in the aftermath of defeat, to explain it.

Germany's Jews had emigrated or lay murdered. Its relations with Poland, once familiar and meaningful, if contentious, were ruined. Its bridges to virtually all European lands were burned. Moral and intellectual confusion and rudderlessness were rampant. The depths were measureless of individual shame,

(a)

FIGURE 19.1. DEFEAT, DESTRUCTION, DISGRACE, DISPLACEMENT

Many are the harrowing war's-end scenes that burn or flicker in German historical memory.

(a) In April 1945 a Soviet prisoner in liberated Buchenwald concentration camp, near Weimar, denounces a disarmed German camp guard while a member of an Allied inspection team looks on. Germans (and others) guilty of concentration camp brutalities often faced judicial tribunals and imprisonment, but incontrovertible proofs were sometimes elusive and many perpetrators escaped judgment.

(b) Soviet soldiers escort a German woman, very probably a captive of their desires – in effect, enslaved, if (as it usually turned out) temporarily. Many women subjected themselves to specific soldiers' attentions to avoid exposure to all. If in their shame they later could not conceal such misfortune, they often suffered blame hurled on them by German survivors unable to accept the full extent of national defeat and disgrace.

Iconic also were images of the bombed and skeletalized city of Dresden, destroyed by Allied firebombing, and of the innumerable "rubble women" (*Trümmerfrauen*) – survivors, often widowed or elderly – who cleared away the immense ruins in Germany's cities. Captured in collective memory too were refugees from the prewar eastern provinces, from which the German population was ethnically cleansed and expelled, moving by foot or horse-drawn wagon with the remnants of their possessions across country roads, or clinging to overcrowded trains, or waiting stranded for assistance, their mood stricken or despairing, haunted by rampant deadly diseases. Many too were the pictures of captured German soldiers – wounded, exhausted, demoralized – together with traumatized boys who had been impressed at war's end into the "People's Storm" (*Volkssturm*): poorly equipped last-ditch, casualty-decimated units of youth and elderly men.

Source: (a) Deutsches Bundesarchiv; (b) Bildarchiv Preussischer Kulturbesitz/Art Resource, NY.

(b)

FIGURE 19.1 *(continued)*

defensiveness, defeatedness, and psychological self-repression in the face of Hitlerism's bankruptcy and National Socialism's crimes, whose full extent would take decades to compile, but whose genocidal nature was immediately indisputable. Some fell silent, while others sought escape in self-denial and self-victimization or, after 1948–1949, in manic material reconstruction and self-enrichment.

Intellectual luminaries of the older generation lamely counseled, as historian Friedrich Meinecke urged, return to the culture of the "age of Goethe." In his influential lectures on *The Question of Guilt* (published in 1946), philosopher Karl Jaspers conjured with degrees of moral fallenness that German survivors of Hitlerism faced in themselves. No one in what he termed the "pariah nation" could claim innocence. At the same time, the Allies' 1945–1946 International Military Tribunal at Nuremberg condemned the National Socialist regime as a criminal conspiracy, and tried and executed many surviving NS leaders, military men, and high functionaries, with long-lasting resonance in national memory.

Public-opinion surveys reported into the mid-1950s that many Germans clung to the notion that National Socialism had been, in principle, a "good idea," and even that Hitler was betrayed by unworthy brownshirted underlings. Nevertheless, the realization that Hitlerism had practiced genocide, to Germany's ruination, and that, in postwar West Germany, responsibility if not guilt for National Socialism's disastrous outcome could not be evaded, but must be stoically borne, sank ever deeper into the population, painful – or numbing – though the psychological effects might be.

In Europe outside Germany, World War II generated a renewal of utopian hope in the idea of socialism and – under the dazzling (and stage-managed) impression of the Soviet Union's great military victory – of communism too. Postwar leftist parties surged forward at the polls. European conservatives regrouped around the idea of Christian Democracy, which fused pro-capitalist political liberalism with affirmations of a Christianity now seen as compatible with democracy and the welfare-state. These were also, amid Nazism's rubble, the only promising political paths leading beyond the immediate postwar horizon in Germany. But many Germans, intellectuals or not, mistrusted renewed ideological enthusiasms, the more so as Hitlerism had virulently propagandized both against European leftism and Anglo-American liberalism. Many retreated into silent conformism, single-minded pursuit of economic recovery, and the sentimentalism and narcissism that formed one side (not the best) of postwar "Americanized" popular culture.

The German future depended in any case on the victorious Allies, who had promptly carved out for themselves military occupation zones monopolizing all public and political power, under which the conquered Germans could only bow their heads. In the German west, south, and north, the Americans and British held sway, although in a gesture to Charles de Gaulle's Free French forces' participation in the war's victory, a French occupation zone stretched along Germany's southwestern border. In what remained of the German east, including industrialized Saxony, the Soviets held sway. Berlin too was carved into four zones, where the western powers found themselves surrounded by East Germany's Soviet tanks.

Neither the British and Americans nor the Russians strove deliberately to divide Germany into the two hostile states born in 1949: the pro-Soviet German Democratic Republic and the pro-western Federal Republic of Germany. Yet this outcome lay in the logic of emergent Cold War polarization of West and East. The western powers soon committed themselves in their occupation zones to restoration of the privately owned industrial economy, for otherwise the cost to them of feeding and caring for their German subjects would hollow out their military victory. The Soviet Union could not allow its German dependency, or its other central and eastern European satellites, to enter the revived capitalist world economy (which the Americans championed) without seeing

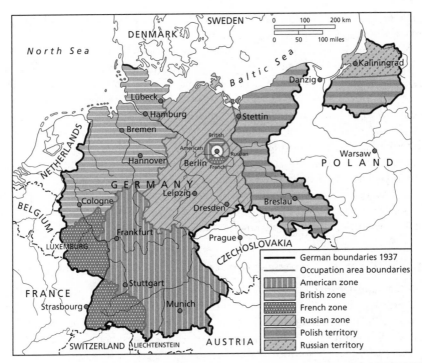

MAP 19.1. THE DISMEMBERMENT OF BISMARCKIAN GERMANY AND THE END OF PRUSSIA: TERRITORIAL LOSSES AND PARTITION AFTER 1945

Although division of the occupied country into two Cold War states was unforeseen in 1945, Germany's loss of its trans-Oder provinces and the evacuation from them of their German-speaking inhabitants were Allied war aims settled by Hitler's defeat. They amounted to the dismantling of historic Prussia, which both western and Soviet opinion held responsible for supplying National Socialism with its military muscle and the inspiration to project German power into eastern Europe (though Habsburg Austria had for centuries proven more successful in this venture). Paradoxically, National Socialism was unfriendly to Prussianism, effectively stripping Weimar's federal state of Prussia of its powers of self-administration and marginalizing the historic Prussian elites within the Hitlerian power structure, except to the extent that their members embraced National Socialist priorities. Embittered German public opinion only slowly accepted the eastern losses, though in international law the Oder-Neisse border gained recognition by East Germany in 1951, by West Germany in 1970, and by reunited Germany in 1990. West German maps long routinely designated the lost eastern provinces as "under Polish administration," while public television through the 1960s included them in its domestic weather reports.

Among the Allied occupation zones west of the Oder-Neisse line, those of the Americans and British found more toleration in German eyes than the regions administered by the Russians and the French. Apart from its economic extractions, the French government conjured with the idea of detaching the industrialized, German-inhabited Saar District, located within its occupation zone, from any future German state. This kindled resentful memories of French support after World War I for the creation of a freestanding German Rhineland.

the prospects for "building socialism" to their own advantage in their hugely enlarged European empire dissolve before their eyes.

Not surprisingly, each side patronized the formation after 1945 of friendly German political movements with familiar roots in pre-1933 history: communists in the east; bourgeois conservatives, liberals, and Social Democrats in the west. The new states of 1949, fitted out with appropriate constitutions, were the handiwork of political elites, appointed from above rather than democratically elected, trusted and steered by the occupiers, not the expressions of the "liberated and self-governing German people." Left to their own devices in an undivided land, the postwar Germans, acting on a field of mass-based politics, would perhaps have fallen into deadlocked political incoherence and fragmentation, or revenge-driven civil strife. It is unlikely they would have surprised themselves and the world by constructing a democracy better than the western Federal Republic that actually emerged in 1949.

Framing Postwar West German History

Among mainstream German and Anglo-American historians, and in journalism and politics, the central question about the Federal Republic was long whether it was a "stable democracy." Would "Weimar conditions" arise again? And if they did, would the Federal Republic prevail against them? The answer, in the *skeptical view* (widespread among Germany's recent foes and victims, but also – and to this day – among some Germans), proceeded from the assumption that history since the seventeenth-century Thirty Years War had accustomed German society to expect and accept, especially in crisis conditions, authoritarian or semi-authoritarian leadership and institutions. After 1945 the western allies lifted into power in their three occupation zones, fused in 1949 into the Federal Republic, German politicians of the moderate left, center, and right, untainted – or only faintly tainted – by Nazism. In the skeptics' view, this amounted to yet another "revolution from above" in German history.

Nevertheless, after 1949 the West German state prospered mightily, and its citizens played by democratic rules. In the treaties of 1970–1972, negotiated with the Soviet Union, Poland, and communist East Germany, the Federal Republic – by then well integrated into the American-dominated North Atlantic Treaty Organization (NATO) military system and the evolving western European political-economic community – proved it was a state capable of breaking with aggressive tendencies toward the east. Still, could the Federal Republic stand the test of deep economic crisis? Can it avoid the temptations of great-power politics that the German unification of 1990 might place before it?

In the now widely accepted *hopeful view*, associated in the 1950s and 1960s with such West German liberal thinkers as aforementioned sociologist Ralf Dahrendorf, National Socialism resulted more from the authoritarianism of Prussian-German elites and the "old middle classes" than of the entire society or culture. The 1945 defeat sounded the death knell for the social and political patterns that had earlier supported conservative-nationalist institutions. In the post-1945 decades a modern German social structure arose, similar to that of western Europe and the United States, providing a stable and positive base for liberal democracy. Since 1989–1990, the crucial question in most observers' eyes has been whether people in the former *East* Germany (the German Democratic Republic), who were socialized into more or less grudging acceptance of Soviet-style socialism, can in a positive spirit adapt themselves, together with younger cohorts of East Germans, to the Federal Republic's institutions and values.

In the eyes of pre-1989 East German ideologues, and not a few leftists in West Germany, the Federal Republic figured as a creation of "U.S. imperialism." In this view, revivified post-1945 German capitalism, joined to a deep-rooted militarism restored in 1955 through rearmament and entry into the NATO alliance, served American policy aiming at economic domination of Europe and the Soviet empire's containment or rollback. The Federal Republic was not, allegedly, an authentic democracy, because economic and political elites steered or manipulated popular opinion from above, especially by inculcation of anticommunism and consumerism, which carried antidemocratic (if not neofascist) potential.

Such critics believed that when working people finally threw off their blinders, they would embrace socialism and anti-American neutralism. After the Soviet Union's dissolution on January 1, 1992, this view grew antiquated, but did not entirely die away. The unfriendly critique of consumer capitalism, of electoral democracy dominated by pressure-group-driven political parties, and of a Germany allegedly subservient to United States and NATO interests keeps a militant leftist mentality alive in a few quarters.

These several perspectives were varying approaches to the overarching question of whether the Cold War–era Federal Republic displayed a deepening commitment to conflict resolution by peaceful and democratic means, and whether the pre-1933 "folkish mentality" animating and energizing National Socialism had vanished as a significant presence in society and political culture. Since the 1989 fall of the Berlin Wall, these questions, while they have not lost all relevance, have yielded salience to the present age's urgent challenges facing all industrial/post-industrial societies.

The Occupation and Adenauer Years, 1945–1963

The victorious Allies, including the Soviet Union, pressed a program of *denazification* on a German population shattered by defeat and, although shamed by the revelation of National Socialist atrocities and inhumanities, widely uncertain about how – or even whether – to face them. The Allies' International Military Tribunals at Nuremberg, addressing between 1945 and 1949 twelve separate sets of defendants, forced a confrontation with National Socialist war crimes. In the end, Allied courts found 5,025 defendants guilty, pronouncing on those not imprisoned 806 death sentences, of which 486 were carried out.

Such stringent externally imposed retribution was unprecedented in modern European history. Despite many complaints of "victors' justice" (*Siegerjustiz*), there was little effort in German society to defend National Socialist criminals, who bore the stigma, not only of shocking deeds, but of having dragged the country into the abyss of unprecedented defeat, dismemberment, and disgrace.

Subsequently, West German courts took responsibility for prosecuting National Socialist war crimes. To 2007, they directed nearly 107,000 investigations of charges against individual defendants, some 30,000 of them before 1960, the rest in the following several decades (after which death summoned the remaining perpetrators). The number of guilty verdicts, generally accompanied by imprisonment (the death penalty having been abolished), was – at 6,498 – proportionally small. This reflected in part the legal problem of establishing individual guilt, for which modern criminal law is designed, in the unprecedented case of state-mandated and collectively implemented mass murder.

Nevertheless, specific cases riveted the West German public's nervous attention, notably the three Auschwitz trials of 1963–1968 in Frankfurt, where high-ranking National Socialist administrators of the dreaded camp and an array of their murderous myrmidons faced the court, with surviving victims present as witnesses. Denazification in the Soviet occupation zone – the later German Democratic Republic – combined populist confrontation and authoritarian-bureaucratic methods familiar from Russian practice to bring nearly 34,000 cases to trial, yielding 13,000 guilty verdicts, most of them pronounced before 1952, a date officially – and prematurely – marking the end of such "reckoning with the past" in the burgeoning communist state. As Cold War polarization widened, the western Allies' desire to win West German backing weakened their zeal for denazification, bringing relief to many politically compromised people. Retribution had mainly targeted public-sector employees, many of whom after 1945 were initially sacked for joining or serving the National Socialists, although many too were later rehired or evaded punishment altogether for complicity as "desk-bound perpetrators" (*Schreibtischtäter*). Business elites and private-sector employees in general got off lightly. One result, which was hardly avoidable, was that throughout the Federal Republic's history, questions of prominent individuals' role under Hitlerism continuously arose, keeping the subject uncomfortably alive. The effect of this on West German political identity was – by prolonging the National Socialist legacy's discussion – positive, if painful.

As the western Allies sanctioned the renewal of German political life, pre-1933 pragmatic Catholic politicians, such as Weimar-era Cologne mayor Konrad Adenauer (1876–1967), joined with Catholic and Protestant religious conservatives to found the Christian Democratic Union (CDU). Allied with the much smaller Christian Social Union (CSU), its more right-leaning, largely Bavarian sister party, the CDU rose to West German predominance. The Social Democrats (SPD), the pre-1933 working-class powerhouse, reemerged as main

FIGURE 19.2. DENAZIFICATION AND COLLECTIVE GUILT
In this picture, West German citizens read of the Nuremberg War Crimes Tribunal's sentences in the liberal-democratic "South German News" (*Süddeutsche Zeitung*), successor to a venerable Munich newspaper that the Allies authorized to resume publication under a new name, distancing it from its semi-coerced, semi-willing subservience to Hitler's regime. (Today it is Germany's largest national-distribution daily paper.) The Allies, who in 1943 had already publicly warned the National Socialist leadership of legal retribution, framed the tribunal's proceedings in international law on war crimes, particularly as it had emerged in the early twentieth century. Despite this body of law's controversial status, and Soviet-western dissonance in interpreting it, the Nuremberg prosecutors' charges, findings of guilt, and sentences provoked no serious challenges among legal thinkers or in public opinion. The flagrancy and extremism of National Socialist crimes were unchallengeable.

In 1946 Karl Jaspers (1883–1969), professor of philosophy at Heidelberg University, delivered lectures immediately published as *The Question of Guilt*, in which, while rejecting the German people's collective guilt for National Socialism, he asserted that all citizens of a state are responsible for its actions (whether they know of them or not). Those who supported or tolerated Hitler's regime bore a "political guilt," over whose consequences the victorious Allies wielded power to decide. Jaspers denied that "following orders" absolved NS subalterns of personal responsibility, even if they were not judicially prosecuted for it ("moral guilt"). Those who might have acted to resist Hitlerism and protect its victims, but who did not, bore – "before God" – a "metaphysical guilt." But "criminal guilt" could rightly be charged only against individuals responsible for specifiable and demonstrable offenses.

No more profound or influential formulation of the "guilt question" appeared in the postwar years. Into the 1960s Jaspers was an influential voice for liberal democracy and antiwar sentiment. Alarmed by political developments, including the election of an opposition party. (See Table 19.1 for election statistics in the Federal Republic, 1949–2009.)

This configuration reversed the pattern of the early Weimar Republic, which had been widely understood as the Social Democrats' creation and responsibility. Allying itself with Adenauer's CDU, which had fused the pre-Nazi Catholic Center Party with the salvageable remnants of the old Protestant German Conservative Party, was the new Free Democratic Party (FDP), which – resuscitating pre-1933 liberal traditions – appealed both to the more secular-minded (and nationalistic) middle classes and to free-market business interests from whose libertarianism the CDU withheld its full blessing.

Adenauer, unsympathetic to pre-1933 Prussian-oriented German nationalism and concerned to gain maximum American protection against the Soviet Union, was prepared to join the three occupation zones in western hands into a single Federal Republic, even at the cost of countenancing Stalin's establishment of a separate East German state. The Social Democrats found it impossible to turn away from former SPD strongholds in the Soviet occupation zone (such as Berlin and Saxony), nor did they wish to appear indifferent to German unity. For these reasons, they opposed the Federal Republic's 1949 founding.

The new West German constitution, the 1949 Basic Law (*Grundgesetz*), mandated a democracy buttressed by extensive civil liberties, anti-militarism, and what came to be called the "socially responsible market economy" (*soziale Marktwirtschaft*), in contrast both to hyper-individualistic laissez-faire capitalism, never greatly popular in Germany, and to Marxist and Leninist socialism. Eastablishing the new republic's governmental seat in Bonn, Beethoven's birthplace on the banks of the Rhine, signaled – as Weimar had done – abjuration of power-state ambitions and orientation toward the West. But the Basic Law mandated the Federal Republic to strive peacefully for a German reunification that – if ever achieved – would crown Berlin anew as capital city.

Reconstruction in the 1950s benefited from the 1948 U.S. European Recovery Program (or Marshall Plan), which offered credits for purchase of American goods and favorable access of German exports to the American domestic market. There followed in the 1950s such an "economic miracle" (*Wirtschaftswunder*) of rebuilding and rising living standards that in 1959 the Social Democrats formally demoted Marxism as their principal theoretical tradition, highlighting their identity as a labor-oriented "people's party" (*Volkspartei*) striving for a just welfare state under liberal capitalism.

FIGURE 19.2 *(continued)* ex-NSDAP member as federal president, he later moved to Switzerland, abandoning German citizenship. Thomas Mann, whose wartime radio broadcasts – illegal listening in Germany – had knowledgeably demolished Hitlerism and spoken eloquently to the German conscience, declined to return after the war from America to Germany, but in 1952 chose Switzerland instead, dying there three years later.

Source: Deutsches Bundesarchiv.

Meanwhile, West Germany in the 1950s successfully absorbed most of the 12 million expellees from the lost eastern provinces and non-German central Europe. Joining them in their westward trek, until the Berlin Wall went up in 1961, were some 3 million refugees from communist East Germany. Their presence in the west reinforced the already strong conviction there, including among Social Democrats, that Soviet-style state socialism under communist party dictatorship was an unhappy fate to be strenuously avoided.

In 1955, it was not difficult for the United States, seeking military reinforcement against the Soviet Union, to persuade Adenauer's government to introduce troop conscription, form a German army, and enter into the anti-Soviet North Atlantic Treaty Organization (NATO) military pact, founded in 1949 and anchored in Europe in Britain and France. Yet strong post-1945 German pacifist sentiment inspired laws placing the armed forces under civilian ministerial command and making alternative national service available to conscientious objectors to military draft. Soldiers gained the right to protest military injustices to an Ombudsman (or neutral parliamentary investigator), and remained subject to civilian courts alone. Abjuring nuclear weapons and operationally integrated with non-German NATO forces, the Federal Republic's army subsequently showed vanishingly few signs of reviving militaristic traditions. The impulse was widespread in West Germany to absolve the regular pre-1945 army (*Wehrmacht*) of complicity in National Socialism's crimes, but postwar trials and historical research inexorably dissipated this comfortable illusion. The army's festive evening ceremony with musical accompaniment (*grosser Zapfenstreich*), marking the end of presidential terms and other political occasions, long triggered pacifist and leftist protest against the perpetuation of premodern military culture.

A 1952 law on "Equalization of Burdens" taxed the propertied classes to compensate those who had lost their assets in war. This – and the "economic miracle" – helped the expellees from the east merge into West German society successfully enough that in 1969 the Ministry for Refugees closed its doors. In 1952 Adenauer's government proposed a Reparations Treaty with Israel, whose government, amid understandable domestic political controversy, eventually ratified it, gaining DM 3.5 billion together with long-term military aid. This led to establishment of formal diplomatic relations in 1965. The Federal Republic's economic and political support of Israel has remained unwavering.

These various laws and measures expressed a liberality contrasting with the 1951 law compensating Hitler-era civil servants (except those found guilty of criminal charges) for salaries and pensions lost through denazification in the years after 1945. This action, and the Adenauer government's employment in public service of ex-NSDAP members, doubtless helped wavering partisans of Hitlerism shift their loyalties to the postwar order, but left victims and other critics embittered.

Between 1953 and 1965 legislation provided monetary compensation to survivors of National Socialist persecution. DM 1 billion was distributed already by 1955. In that year, too, the federal parliament designated anti-National Socialist resistance activities (previously often stigmatized as traitorous) as meritorious, establishing eligibility for reparations of survivors or heirs. In 1951–1952 Adenauer's government passed legislation mandating participation of workers' representatives in heavy industrial boards of overseers and creation of workers' councils in most sizeable industrial firms in all branches. Such measures met central demands of the once again large and well-organized trade-union movement which, as before 1933, continued to regard itself as the Social Democratic Party's close ally.

In 1952 the West German Supreme Court upheld, on grounds of democracy's defense, a government ban on National Socialist or neo-Nazi party organizations, propaganda, and speech, and corresponding restrictions on Communists. Whether either tendency could have satisfied the new constitution's provision seating in the federal parliament (or *Bundestag*) only parties gaining at least 5 percent of the national vote – to prevent proliferation of small extremist parties such as had plagued the Weimar Republic – is uncertain, if not unlikely. As Table 19.1 shows, between 1949 and 1961, the pro-Adenauer CDU/CSU's vote rose from 31 to 45 percent (exceeding even 50 percent in 1957), revealing that neither this strong anti-NS measure nor the conciliatoriness Adenauer had shown to Jewish and German victims of Hitlerism diminished his government's popularity. Still, these years favored the economically strong over the weak, while in many minds anticommunism overshadowed reflection on National Socialism and its legacy.

Turbulent Transition, 1963–1969

In the 1960s a new generation of youth stepped forward on the political stage, especially among the rapidly widening ranks of university students. Many rejected Cold War conservatism and demanded franker confrontation with the National Socialist past. Widely viewed German films of the late 1940s and early 1950s addressed, among other themes, German anti-Semitism and Nazi-era mass murder. Yet public debate on the National Socialist genocide only began to swell with the publication in 1955 of young Jewish Holocaust victim Anne Frank's poignant wartime diary, which stirred widespread empathy. At the level of West Germany's federal states, responsible for public education, a joint decision of 1962, following disturbing incidents of anti-Semitic vandalism, introduced instruction in elementary and secondary schools in the history of National Socialism and the Holocaust. In the same year the West German Catholic bishops, following cues from a reformist Vatican, formally condemned Hitlerism. In 1965 a twenty-month trial ended in Frankfurt with many convictions against German personnel at Auschwitz. Here the Holocaust moved toward center stage in West German public life. Other such trials followed, stretching into the 1970s and beyond.

Adenauer retired in 1963 in favor of new CDU chancellor Ludwig Erhard, the "economic miracle's" economist mastermind. In the mid-1960s mild

(a)

FIGURE 19.3. THE ADENAUER YEARS: POLITICAL DECOMPRESSION, "ECONOMIC MIRA-
CLE"

(a) Chancellor Konrad Adenauer returning from Moscow, September 1955, where he
had negotiated the release of some 15,000 remaining German war prisoners, one of
whose mothers here shows her gratitude, while the chancellor radiates an aura of
protective, suffering-inured benevolence. The pathos of the moment does not escape
the onlookers. (b) An advertising photograph of the late 1950s celebrates a modestly
dressed, iconic four-member family's accumulation of consumer goods, laid out on a
minimalist modernist table – mainly canned or prepackaged food, but with a few toys
and children's sweets.

Characteristic of German memory of the postwar years are images of housewives
admiring (sometimes with incredulity) the unaccustomed appearance, following the
1948 currency reform and end of black-marketeering, of everyday groceries, including
familiar but long-scarce *Wurst*. Embodying the "economic miracle" was portly, jolly,
cigar-chewing Ludwig Erhard (1897–1977) who, as Adenauer's economics minister,
wielded state power to reinvigorate free markets while championing moderate welfare-
state provisions. A 1957 CDU publicity picture depicted him comfortably reading his
book, *Prosperity for All*. He incorporated the concept, popularized by non-Socialist
postwar moderates, of the "socially responsible market economy."

In the 1950s, the Deutsche Reichspartei (German Reich Party) represented itself as
successor to pre-1933 rightist conservatism, but with residual loyalties to Hitler's regime
as well (although it differed from the blatantly neo-Nazi Sozialistische Reichspartei,
which the Supreme Court in 1952 ruled unconstitutional and banned). The DRP could
not win the requisite votes to enter the national parliament, but it scored some small
successes regionally. In 1965 it disbanded itself in favor of the emergent right-radical
National Democratic Party (NPD). A hint about its failure emerges from a 1950s DRP
placard, depicting a loyal sailor going down with the (National Socialist) ship, with

(b)

FIGURE 19.3 *(continued)* appeals "never to forget and stay forever true to Germany." Such imagery conjured up painful and humiliating, often deeply traumatic memories and emotions that few wished to re-encounter – one basic reason, doubtless still potent today, why right-radicalism exerts little pull on the German imagination.

Yet the Adenauer years saw prominent ex-National Socialists in high places, including Hans Globke (1898–1973), Chancellor Adenauer's chief of staff and key adviser in the years 1953–1963. Among Globke's other official acts under National Socialism was authorship of the authoritative legal commentary on the anti-Jewish Nuremberg Laws of 1935. In 1956 the liberal weekly *Der Spiegel* publicized Globke's past, to Adenauer's and other conservative Germans' embarrassment. In 1963 the East German regime tried him *in absentia* for abetting National Socialist racism. After 1963 Globke retired, legally undamaged, from politics. Other cases included those of Alfried Krupp von Bohlen und Halbach (1907–1967), heir to the Krupp industrial colossus and NS Party activist, who was condemned to twelve years' imprisonment in 1948 for his family firm's collusion with Hitler and for exploitation of slave labor, but pardoned in 1951 and restored to command of his enterprises in 1953 (he subsequently disbanded the Krupp industrial works). Yet another sensational case was that of Heinrich Lübke, Christian Democratic West German federal president in the decade between 1959 and 1969. Lübke's work under Nazism as building contractor, including constructing penal colonies with slave labor, came to light in 1968 in the West German press through access to East German archival records. The revelation compelled Lübke (who himself had suffered brief imprisonment in the 1930s) to resign the presidency.

Source: (a) Deutsches Bundesarchiv; (b) Bildarchiv Preussischer Kulturbesitz/Art Resource, NY.

TABLE 19.1. *Elections to the Bundestag (National Parliament) in the German Federal Republic, 1949–2009*

PARTY	1949	1953	1957	1961	1965	1969	1972	1976	1980	1983	1987	1990	1994	1998	2002	2005	2009
SOCIAL DEMOCRATS (SPD)	29.2	28.8	31.8	36.2	39.3	42.7	45.8	42.6	42.9	38.2	37.0	33.5	36.4	40.9	38.5	34.2	23.0
CHRISTIAN DEMOCRATS (CDU)	25.2	36.4	39.7	35.8	38.0	36.6	35.2	38.0	34.2	38.2	34.5	36.7	34.2	28.4	29.5	27.8	27.3
CHRISTIAN SOCIAL UNION (CSU) [CDU ALLIES]	5.8	8.8	10.5	9.6	9.6	9.5	9.7	10.6	10.3	10.6	9.8	7.1	7.3	6.7	9.0	7.4	6.5
FREE DEMOCRATS (FDP)	11.9	9.5	7.7	12.8	9.5	5.8	8.4	7.9	10.6	7.0	9.1	11.0	6.9	6.2	7.4	9.8	14.6
GREEN PARTY/ ALLIANCE 90									1.5	5.6	8.3	5.0	7.3	6.7	8.6	8.1	10.7
PARTY OF DEMOCRATIC SOCIALISM/ LEFT PARTY												2.4	4.4	5.1	4.0	8.7	11.9
RIGHTIST PARTIES (NPD, REPUBLIKANER, ET AL.)	1.8	1.1	1.0	0.8	2.0	4.3	0.6	0.3	0.2	0.2	0.7	0.4	0.1	0.4	0.4	1.6	1.4
OTHERS (BELOW 5% BARRIER)	26.1	15.4	9.3	4.8	1.6	1.1	0.3	0.6	0.3	0.2	0.6	3.9	3.4	5.6	2.6	2.4	4.6

Source: http://www.parties-and-elections.de/index.html.
http://de.wikipedia.org/wiki/Ergebnisse_der_Bundestagswahlen.

cyclical recession struck. In 1964 the National Democratic Party (NPD), a radical right-wing party conjuring with neo-Nazi allusions and rhetoric, began showing strength at the federal-state level. Concern arose that, in the next Bundestag election, the NPD might break through the 5 percent barrier and take seats in the national parliament. To block such an eventuality, the Social Democrats agreed in 1966 to enter a "grand coalition" with the Christian Democrats to govern the country under the chancellorship of CDU politician Kurt Kiesinger. From the SPD's angle this represented an opportunity to escape long years in opposition to CDU-dominated governments, and to show a united front against neo-Nazism's threat, widely (and understandably) perceived as intolerable.

From 1961, student radicalism mounted, inspired in part by French, Italian, and American New Left ideologies. These, although they sometimes denounced Soviet-style bureaucratic-authoritarian communism and invoked the ideal of democratic socialism, often verged on anarchism (when they did not succumb to Leninist or Maoist illusions). In the name of third-world national liberation movements they vehemently opposed the Vietnam War and other American-championed Cold War military-diplomatic policies, including support of the repressive regime of the Shah of Iran. Overcrowding of expanding German universities, admissions to which had been democratized through provision of governmental stipends, accelerated leftward radicalization. Many among the older generation of liberal-minded intellectuals worried that the students' vehemence ominously recalled bourgeois youth's rejection, in Nazism's name, of the Weimar Republic.

Heightening leftist and liberal discomfort was the polarizing presence of Franz Josef Strauss, from 1961 the nationally powerful chairman of the Bavarian-based Christian Social Union (CSU). As a belligerently tempered Minister of Defense (1956–1962), Strauss provoked widespread apprehension over resurgence of militarism in anticommunist, Cold War guise. His aggressive confrontation in 1962 with the prominent, liberally oriented weekly newsmagazine, *Der Spiegel*, which he accused of leaking national security secrets, forced his resignation. Although he returned as Finance Minister in 1966–1969, and remained politically formidable to his death in 1988, Strauss's reputation for regressive right-wing impulses blocked his path to the federal chancellorship. Disquieting too was the career of Strauss's ally, CDU Grand Coalition chancellor Kurt Kiesinger. His civil service employment and NSDAP membership from February 1933 to war's end branded him, despite evidence he worked during the dictatorship against implementation of anti-Semitic policies, as a regime conformist. That he could rise to Christian Democratic leadership following Adenauer and Erhard dramatized the dilemmas flowing from the integration of former National Socialists into West German politics.

By the late 1960s street demonstrations multiplied, sometimes eliciting violent police repression. The right-wing anticommunist, widely read "boulevard press," commanded by publishing mogul Axel Springer, hounded and vilified the student left. In May 1968 the Grand Coalition defied bitter protests from trade unions, liberal Free Democrats, dissident Social Democrats, and student organizations in passing "emergency laws" (*Notstandgesetze*) authorizing government restriction of individual freedoms in case of internal crises (including hypothesized revolts). Such laws had long been anticipated, and helped reduce lingering Allied powers in West Germany. Yet their passage amid anti-Vietnam War and university-reform protests, following right-radical gains in the 1966 elections and accompanied by early stirrings of future terrorist leftist sectarianism, recalled "Weimar conditions" and signaled loss of confidence among SPD and CDU/CSU politicians and voters in the Federal Republic's stability. In 1970 clandestine, violence-ready cells emerged on the far left, including the anarchist and anti-capitalist Baader-Meinhof organization, or "Red Army Fraktion," which before federal police agencies suppressed it in 1978 killed 28 victims, took 162 hostages, committed considerable arson and robbery, and inspired widespread anxieties fanned by sensationalist media reports.

In this crisis-ridden and polarized atmosphere, the Social Democrats in 1969 won their first national election. The new chancellor Willy Brandt (1913–1992), previously the charismatic mayor of West Berlin, had risked his life in anti-Hitler resistance, for which some on the nationalist right attacked him. The SPD under his leadership formed a coalition government with the middle-class Free Democrats, who moved from right- to left-center, preserving their federal-level influence. The curtain had risen on a new stage.

The "Social-Liberal" Era, 1969–1982

Brandt, politically wounded by the discovery – unbeknownst to him – of an East German spy in his entourage, retired from the chancellorship in 1974. Succeeding him was the keen-minded and politically gifted Helmut Schmidt (b. 1918), who remained in office until 1982. In these fourteen years the Social Democrats, seconded but also sometimes slowed by their coalition partners among the Free Democrats, undertook a series of controversial reforms. Yet the electorate returned them to office three times.

This was evidence of fundamental change in German political culture, viewed against the background of Weimar and Imperial Germany, when Social Democrats figured as enemies of bourgeois society if not also as "unpatriotic rascals." Nor did the radical-right National Democrats (NPD) in 1969, or any other such extremist party in later years, surmount the 5-percent barrier and enter the federal parliament. Had the pre-1933 "folkish syndrome" still pervaded the post-1945 imagination, the Social-Liberal chapter could not have been written.

In foreign policy, Brandt's government in 1970–1972 negotiated with the Soviet Union, the People's Republic of Poland, and the German Democratic Republic a series of treaties reflecting an *Ostpolitik* or "policy toward the East" that sought peaceful coexistence and improvement of citizen-to-citizen contacts across the "iron curtain" border. Brandt's Federal Republic effectively granted East Germany formal diplomatic recognition, in return for which the

(a)

FIGURE 19.4. TURBULENCES OF THE 1960S

(a) defendant, SS-man Wilhelm Boger, at the first of the three Frankfurt Auschwitz trials (1963–1968). These yielded altogether twenty-two guilty verdicts against SS and police functionaries at Auschwitz, such as Boger (who like most of the defendants denied criminal wrongdoing), and also against German prisoners who collaborated in criminal actions at the infamous camp. The massive testimony and shocking documentation set forth at the trials publicized Holocaust crimes as never before. The impact on high-school and university students, often the children of NSDAP members, fellow travelers, and NS regime conformists, was frequently explosive. 1960s youth, driven to distance themselves from their elders and deeply conflicted over their relation to the national past, streamed into leftist protest.

USSR and its communist satellites accepted the de facto existence of the democratic/capitalist island enclave of West Berlin, liberalizing overland travel to West Germany and West Berliners' access to East Berlin or – as it was officially known (to avoid putting the city's two halves on equal footing) – "the capital city of the German Democratic Republic." Brandt recognized the Oder-Neisse river border between Poland and the communist German Democratic Republic as a legitimate and lasting postwar boundary in the Federal Republic's eyes. These arrangements, although heatedly denounced by CDU politicians and their followers as unwarranted concessions, lowered Cold War tensions and military threats. They opened new channels of contact and western influence

(b)

FIGURE 19.4 *(continued)*
(b) the Congress of Delegates of the Socialist German Student League (SDS), meeting in September 1968 at Frankfurt University. The participants' middle-class identity is evident in dress and self-presentation. Such scenes testified to an intense longing, such as had also been felt in the 1918 revolution and now swept through the universities and rapidly burgeoning big-city counter-cultural scene, for "direct" or "grassroots" democracy (*Basisdemokratie*).
Source: Bildarchiv Preussischer Kulturbesitz/Art Resource, NY.

in the communist East, contributing in the long run to the Soviet system's breakdown in central and eastern Europe.

At home in West Germany the Social-Liberal coalition carried out important reforms in university and secondary education, aiming at greater egalitarianism among students and in society. Notable was the 1971 expansion of public funding to all university students through grants free of repayment obligation ("*BAföG*"). Sums varied with students' parents' incomes while partial repayment schedules and other restrictions were later introduced, but students retain today legal right to adequate financial support.

A 1977 prison reform limited sentences in all but the gravest cases to fifteen years, while proclaiming incarceration's objective to be rehabilitation. The 1949 constitution had already prohibited the death penalty. In 1976–1977, women achieved recognition as equal in law to men, and a conservatively defined right to abortion gained legal sanction. Against these and other liberal measures there stood the 1971 "decree on radicals," which (like the 1968 emergency laws) stirred criticism among civil rights advocates by its empowerment of government to scrutinize political activities of public-sector employees and fire those among them found guilty of supporting leftist extremism. This was an overreaction to the terrorist movement that, in many critical eyes, cast a shadow on West Germany's otherwise progressive approach to civil liberties and human rights.

The Social-Liberal coalition unraveled in 1982 as a result of domestic controversies stirred by the "second cold war." This began in 1979 in U.S.-Soviet relations, inflamed by Middle East crises in Iran and Afghanistan. It soon confronted West Germany with the question of stationing American nuclear-armed missiles on its soil, in opposition to new Soviet weaponry and to what President Ronald Reagan's government and many others in the West perceived as new Soviet aggressiveness. Since 1973 economic conditions had worsened in the Federal Republic, as elsewhere in a western world stricken by 1970s oil crises. West Germans confronted the end of the post-1948 quarter-century of unprecedented growth and prosperity.

Among the heirs of 1960s radicalism, a coalition of peace and antinuclear activists, feminists, environmentalists, and critics of big capital and labor came together to form local social movements that eventually coalesced into a national-level Green Party. They deprived the Social Democrats of support on the left. Meanwhile, the Free Democrats, persuaded that Helmut Schmidt's coalition was foundering, sailed back to the CDU's harbor.

Christian Democrats and the Nation, 1982–1989

In 1983 CDU leader Helmut Kohl (b. 1930) won a mandate in national elections for a Christian Democratic–Free Democratic coalition. The same polling enabled the Green Party, with 6 percent of the vote, to enter the Bundestag. Criticized in conservative quarters as pacifists, neutralists, ecological romantics, and leftist radicals, the Greens embodied, despite various internal programmatic struggles, ideas familiar in America from the post-1960s "new social movements." From these, starting with the U.S. civil rights and anti-Vietnam War movements, they absorbed many ideas and organizational tactics. They drew their support mainly from younger generations of the university-educated West German middle classes, many active in the professions, education, and small enterprises or businesses, especially in the big cities' countercultural communities.

The CDU's return to power signaled a desire among moderates and conservatives to assert a German self-identity more pronounced than the Social-Liberal elites and their followers had been interested in claiming. In part this reflected the conservative turn accompanying the end of the postwar economic boom and the onset of the "second cold war," embodied in American president Reagan and British prime minister Margaret Thatcher. It part it was the CDU's strategy against SPD, Greens, and associated constituencies. But it also represented a resurgence into the public sphere, as National Socialism faded from living memory, of German national sensibility, which in myriad forms

(a)

FIGURE 19.5. *OSTPOLITIK* AND THE "SECOND COLD WAR"
(a) Willy Brandt in Warsaw, Poland, 1970, kneeling before the monument to the martyred Warsaw Ghetto Jews, rickety socialist architecture looming in the background over an urban landscape the National Socialists had ravaged. This dramatic and authentic gesture sought to express German acceptance of responsibility for the Holocaust. Born in 1913, Brandt struggled through an unprivileged Weimar-era youth. As a left-wing Social Democrat, he worked actively in the anti-Hitler resistance, both from abroad (living in Scandinavia) and, dangerously in 1936–1938, as an undercover agent in Germany. His rise from popular mayor of West Berlin to the chancellorship validated within the Federal Republic's emergent political culture a left-leaning anti-nationalist presence at the helm of state. For his part in the 1970–1972 dismantling of east-west tensions Brandt received the 1971 Nobel Peace Prize.

Ostpolitik peaked in the signing of the 1975 Helsinki Accords, pledging the Soviet Union alongside the West to protection of universal human rights. Representing the Federal Republic was Brandt's successor as chancellor, Helmut Schmidt, who signed the accord alongside East German communist party leader Erich Honecker, U.S. President Gerald Ford, and Austrian Social Democratic Prime Minister Bruno Kreisky. Schmidt's expertise and negotiating skills earned him a high and lasting reputation. His cooperation, which he saw no way of refusing, in President Ronald Reagan's anti-Soviet missile policy cost him backing – despite his advocacy of liberal domestic reforms – among young voters and from the left. This hastened the birth of the Green Party, which cut into the Social Democratic Party's electoral base.

(b)

FIGURE 19.5 *(continued)*
(b) Green Party leaders after their 1983 entry into the Bundestag. Petra Kelly (1947–
1992 [center]) was a German-born but partially U.S.-educated feminist and peace
activist. Lawyer Otto Schilly (b. 1932 [on Kelly's right]) came from a leftist background,
having defended several West German revolutionary terrorists in court. German feminism underwent "second-wave" rebirth in the 1960s Federal Republic, as part of the
era's larger youth mobilization, but then made little headway against men's domination
of left-wing leadership positions. The 1970s expansion of the women's movement's
own organizational structure and media presence, advanced by political successes such
as the Bundestag's 1976 qualified legalization of abortion, enabled women and feminist
concerns finally to gain powerful presence in national politics, at first among Greens
but then also among other parties.
Source: (a) Bildarchiv Preussischer Kulturbesitz/Art Resource, NY; (b) Deutsches
Bundesarchiv.

had survived and found expression at the supper table, in pubs and clubs, and
in individual hearts and minds.

Such consciousness had, in consequence of National Socialism, lost precise
political valence, although some on the far right tested the waters of Hitlerite
apologetics, only to be driven back to high ground by the center-left political
elites and media. But national feeling existed, often channeled – as had always
been true of German nationalism – into identification of the local homeland
(*Heimat*) with the nation. Symptomatic was film director Edgar Reitz's masterful eleven-part television series, *Heimat: A German Chronicle*, broadcast in
1984. It dramatized, to a huge audience, twentieth-century German history
as experienced in the rural and small-town Rhineland, intertwining the many

fates – tragic, baleful, loving, faithful, self-delusive, self-destructive, transient – that formed the tapestry of collective life in Hitlerism's darkest days, and also in the preceding and following eras that, in Reitz's depiction, did not merely stand in National Socialism's shadow.

The question was whether consciousness of German identity could be repoliticized in liberal-democratic form so as to psychologically satisfy and politically serve the large segment of society standing behind Kohl and his coalition. The years between 1983 and 1989 years showed that this would not be an easy task. Among other obstacles was the Federal Republic's long-standing commitment, not only to the American-led NATO alliance, but to European union, which Adenauer and fellow Christian Democrats had in the 1950s ardently embraced as a means of German reintegration into western European politics and economy. Membership in the European Economic Community, created in 1957, opened an ever-widening free-trade zone to German industry and entrepreneurship, boosting prosperity despite the considerable financial contribution the government in Bonn rendered to the EEC's common expenses. These included not only agricultural subsidies, but investments in less-developed member states to achieve roughly comparable living standards across the Community, alongside administrative costs of burgeoning parliamentary, legal, and military structures.

Whatever their lingering attachments to German national consciousness and sovereignty, Christian Democrats and Free Democrats – like SPD and Greens, if for differing reasons – unwaveringly backed, even after severe economic recession struck in 2008, the construction of ever stronger European economic and political institutions, housed mainly in Brussels. The idea that European identity should balance German identity was widespread among political elites and the university-educated, whether they leaned right or left.

In 1985 Chancellor Kohl met President Reagan at Bitburg military cemetery, where both American and German soldiers killed in World War II lie buried. On the fortieth anniversary of the war's end, Reagan's presence signaled U.S. esteem for its West German ally, which was cooperating in American escalation of pressure on the Soviet Union, whose own Cold War miscalculations and overreachings would soon lead it into oblivion. Two once-opposed war veterans – U.S. General M. Ridgeway and German air-force pilot J. Steinhoff – were photographed at the cemetery, exchanging a highly symbolical handshake. Yet the previously unremarked presence among the buried German soldiers of Waffen-SS fighters raised strong public protests on many sides, as it seemed that Reagan's intended recognition of ordinary German soldiers' patriotic motives inadvertently implied toleration of National Socialist racism and imperialism.

Defeat of the event's conciliatory purpose marked a further step toward erasing the line conservatives and nationalists wished to draw – as some do even today – between an "honorable" National Socialist army (*Wehrmacht*) and politically and morally repudiated SS and National Socialist police power. In the 1990s critical historians irrefutably documented, in a widely visited traveling exhibit, the *Wehrmacht*'s role as co-perpetrator of the Holocaust and associated crimes (although the question can still provoke indignation and denial).

The debate over Bitburg soon retreated in the shadow of the 1985 "historians' dispute" (*Historikerstreit*). It began with a challenge thrown down by West Germany's preeminent social and political philosopher, Jürgen Habermas, to well-known conservative West Berlin historian Ernst Nolte, and widened to include positions that dozens of prominent German scholars heatedly staked out in high-profile, widely read print media. Habermas (b. 1929) was heir to the tradition of neo-Marxism brilliantly developed by the Frankfurt School (see Figure 19.6). Yet he eventually fashioned an influential defense, rooted in Enlightenment rationalism, of liberal democracy in the Federal Republic. In the "historians' dispute" he rejected Nolte's argument, which stood out among other efforts of the 1980s to formulate a philosophically defensible neoconservatism, that National Socialism had been a reaction to Soviet communism, whose brutalities actually prefigured, and in a sense provoked, those of Hitlerism.

Habermas charged Nolte with seeking, by "relativizing" the National Socialist past through its "historicization," to rehabilitate German nationalist attitudes. But only adherence to universalist democratic liberalism, Habermas insisted, could endow contemporary Germany with an acceptable identity: the sole admissible form of German national pride was, in Habermas's influential formulation, "constitutional patriotism" oriented to the West German political system's virtues. It may be added, however, that – as this book shows – there is no alternative to understanding National Socialism as a historically generated phenomenon whose character can only be grasped through comparison with other national histories. Nor does "historicization" disable moral and philosophical commitment – provided we embrace social and political values we are confident in rationally defending – but enhances it through deeper insight into human possibilities, both for conflict and cooperation. Nevertheless, in most West German readers' eyes, the position in the debate taken by Habermas and similarly inclined historians carried the day. Nolte was certainly at fault, and politically suspect, in misapprehending the sources within German history of National Socialist violence.

The Economy and "Guest Workers"

Before East Germany's collapse in 1989–1990 and the German unification that ensued, chancellor Kohl's government registered few successes in combating economic malaise. In the 1980s, following the economic recession of the preceding decade, the Federal Republic found itself saddled with structural unemployment in roughly the 10 percent range. Those without jobs lived – fairly comfortably, by U.S. standards – from long-term unemployment benefits, sometimes supplemented by gray- or black-market jobs – that is, work offered illegally by employers seeking to evade heavy payroll and social welfare taxes.

FIGURE 19.6. JÜRGEN HABERMAS AND THE FRANKFURT SCHOOL'S POSTWAR LEGACY
Pictured here is Jürgen Habermas (b. 1929), philosopher, social theorist, and internationally respected and honored public intellectual, the most eminent postwar student of Max Horkheimer (1895–1973) and Theodor Adorno (1903–1969), who, as we saw, were leaders of the Frankfurt Institute for Social Research, founded in 1923, before their emigration from Hitler's Germany. This was the seedbed of "Frankfurt School" philosophy, still influential today as a fusion of non-dogmatic Marxism with other social theory, including psychoanalysis, and with literary postmodernism as well. Prominent among Frankfurt School concerns was the legitimization of modern capitalism and democracy by means of the "culture industry," epitomized by the mass media, under whose influence ordinary people commonly fail, according to Frankfurt School analysis, to develop awareness of their subordination to – and continuing exploitation by – the economic and political processes of "late capitalism."

As regrettable consequences, traditional scenarios of left-wing resistance pale and self-alienated mass entertainment overwhelms high culture. Isolated from the larger society are the mainly middle- and upper-middle-class intellectuals who, thanks to education in Frankfurt School-style "Critical Theory," succeed in evading cooptation. Yet alone they cannot bring to a halt the late-capitalist dynamic, encompassing – apart from the culture industry – neo-imperialism and environmental degradation.

As the text above suggests, Habermas, while conceding the historical and sociological force of Frankfurt School analysis, finally took his political philosophical stand on a Kantian liberalism that imposes the obligation to advance rational communal discourse. This, ultimately, is possible only under a democratic constitution, despite the shadows that economic inequality and commercialized culture cast on it. For Germans, the human and moral catastrophe of Hitler's dictatorship only reinforces the ethical imperative of "constitutional patriotism" in defense of liberal freedom and transnational human solidarity.
Source: Wolfram Huke.

Over the years a tripartite labor force had emerged. There were employees holding legally registered jobs, often protected by membership in one or another of the powerful, mostly SPD-connected labor unions. Their pay, working conditions, pensions, and vacation benefits (commonly four to six weeks yearly, apart from public holidays) were and remain among the world's best. There were also, among citizens of the Federal Republic, the aforementioned unemployed. Finally, there were several million non-German "guest workers" (*Gastarbeiter*). These were mainly Turks, Turkish Kurds, and others from the Middle East, mostly Muslims, but also immigrant laborers from elsewhere in the Mediterranean basin – Italians, Spaniards, Greeks, Yugoslavs. It was a condition of residence in the Federal Republic that they hold legal jobs, through which they and their dependents acquired claims to social services, including unemployment benefits, should they suffer layoffs.

The "guest workers" arrived in West Germany as labor bottlenecks developed in the manpower-short 1950s and 1960s, on the understanding their stay would be temporary. Yet, as time passed, many sank roots, married locally or brought wives and relatives from their homelands. Few regarded them as proper candidates for citizenship. They were not Germans in an ethnic sense. Many spoke the language with difficulty. Many others retained civic and cultural – especially religious – ties to their homelands.

As recession and unemployment spread from the mid-1970s, voices arose on the right, and among the German unemployed, demanding an end to further immigration. Economic resentments, laced with cultural prejudices, hardened against the "foreigners" (*Ausländer*). Kohl's government, seeking to consolidate its base, went along with such sentiments in 1983 legislation against new economic immigration. It was widely disputed that many or most of the migrants already settled in the country should be granted citizenship rights (alongside the valuable rights they already possessed, as legally resident tax-paying workers, to social welfare benefits and, to the extent they contributed to them, retirement pensions). Kohl's government's efforts in the 1980s at repatriation had no effect in reducing West Germany's non-citizen population of "guest workers" and their families, which by 1990 stood at nearly six million. By 2010 this number had risen, despite liberalization of German naturalization law, to some seven million, while about sixteen million of the Federal Republic's inhabitants – nearly 20 percent of the country's population – possessed, as a new official terminology attempted non-pejoratively to put it, a "migration background." In 2006, reunited Berlin counted nearly a half-million people (some 14 percent of the city's population) who themselves, and often their children too, held foreign citizenship.

On the eve of the Berlin Wall's fall on November 9, 1989, unemployment, unresolved questions of German national identity, disputes over immigration, and indecisiveness over communism's deepening crisis in the neighboring Soviet empire clouded West German skies. Conflicts between Greens and Social Democrats weakened opposition to chancellor Kohl's CDU-FDP government.

FIGURE 19.7. AUSTRIA'S POSTWAR PATH

Leniently categorized by the victorious powers as Hitler's conquest rather than ally, Austria in 1955 gained internationally recognized state sovereignty on condition of permanent military neutrality. Its postwar political life rested on conflict-avoiding compromise between the conservative Austrian People's Party and the Austrian Social Democrats, counterparts, respectively, of West Germany's CDU/CSU and SPD, although rooted in a pre-1938 Austrian history (of Christian Socials and Austro- German socialists) that these pages earlier sketched. Expressive of Austrian liberalism was the long prime-ministership (1970–1983) of Jewish-born, secular-minded Social Democrat Bruno Kreisky (1911–1990). But indicative of Austria's National Socialist burden was the tenure as United Nations General Secretary in the 1970s, and as Austrian state president (1986–1992), of Kurt Waldheim (1918–2007, above right). Evidence that surfaced during his presidency of his involvement during World War II as a German army officer in Balkan war crimes discredited both him and Austria. In this 1973 picture, he welcomes, as a consequence of post-1970 *Ostpolitik*, the German Democratic Republic's first ambassador to the United Nations: two postwar avatars of earlier German national identity, both now unmourned.

Official Austrian acknowledgment of the Holocaust was more halting and belated than in the Federal Republic (on which see also Chapter 21). In 2008, Franz Vranitzky (b. 1937), who had served from 1986 to 1997 as Social Democratic chancellor, presided at a commemoration in Vienna of the seventieth anniversary of the National Socialist *Anschluss*. Eighty thousand candles were lit for Austria's Jewish Holocaust victims, whose names were projected on screens. Well-known in Austria and beyond was Simon Wiesenthal (1908–2005), a Habsburg-born citizen of interwar Poland, who worked before 1939 as an architect in Prague. He survived Nazi concentration camps to emerge after 1945 as founder and director in Austria of the *Jüdisches Dokumentationszentrum*,

If the center-right parties sometimes posed as "more German" than the moderate left parties, these were not reluctant to pride themselves on their internationalism. To be "citizens of the world" – that is, cosmopolitanism – was a badge of honor. Well-educated young West Germans traveled the world extensively, commonly spoke foreign languages fluently, and scorned narrow provincialism. Perhaps a third of the West German population in the 1980s had experienced formative influences under Hitler's dictatorship, but for the rest of them National Socialism was, though still a burden, one that was historical rather than personal, entailing civic responsibility rather than feelings of personal guilt.

In a 1967 book entitled *The Inability to Mourn*, social psychologists Alexander and Margarete Mitscherlich advanced the most influential postwar analysis of National Socialism's emotional legacy to those who had experienced Hitler's Germany. This consisted, not in incapacity to recognize the dictatorship's murderous assault on German Jews and non-Germans, but rather in the impulse among non-Jewish Germans narcissistically to include themselves among Hitler's victims. This psychological strategy veiled the numbing effect of having lost, in Hitlerism's fall and the tyrannical communal father's death, an object of mass self-identification and love, and at the same time a source of resentment and hate. Until their own sorely disappointed commitment to National Socialism and sense of loss at its demise were frankly acknowledged, Germans' psychological susceptibility to worship of new authoritarian idols would not vanish.

West German public culture lived with awareness of such arguments, however vulnerable they were to rational criticism. The Mitscherlichs certainly overgeneralized about "the Germans" and misjudged the progressive potential of the Federal Republic's political life on the very eve of the Social-Liberal era. But, whatever their merit, interpretations of National Socialism's appeal

---

FIGURE 19.7 *(continued)* devoted to bringing National Socialist criminals, including Austrians, to justice. In this he and his colleagues attained considerable success and international renown, discovering and assisting in the capture, most notably, of Adolf Eichmann, assistant to Himmler and iconic "desk murderer." Disconcerting was the appearance of Jörg Haider (1950–2008), leader from 1986 to 2000 of the right-radical, anti-immigrant Austrian Freedom Party. Its emergence from provincial importance to countrywide power in 1999 illustrated the force of conservative anxieties over Austria's burgeoning multiethnicity. The participation of Haider's party in 2000–2006 in a governing coalition with the mainstream conservative People's Party scandalized liberal and leftist opinion throughout western Europe. Like many inhabitants of the largely German-speaking but culturally and politically distinctive Switzerland, those Austrians backing Haider's party (subsequently named "Alliance for Austria's Future" [BZÖ]) defensively guard the land's once-precarious and still – outside the big cities – provincial identities and high living standards in a demographically mobilized and globalizing world.

Source: Deutsches Bundesarchiv.

and the psychic wounds it inflicted could not easily be emotionally internalized by the post-Hitler generations that populated the land after 1945. They were, despite their parentage, different people.

In 1989, the Federal Republic embodied a new, multiform and conflict-beset German nation. Wherever it was headed on the eve of reunification, Weimar's fate had never threatened it. Nor was it a mere creation and reflection of the United States. Its parliamentary structure, having evolved from the Weimar Republic and the Bismarckian constitution, was and remains fundamentally different from American presidential democracy. Its market economy was and continues to be steered and managed through tripartite powers of state, employers' organizations, and labor unions and buffered by strong social welfare institutions. Sometimes labeled by American social scientists "Rhenish capitalism," it too differs fundamentally from the United States model.

20

"Real Existing Socialism" (*real existierender Sozialismus*)

Soviet-Occupied Germany and the German Democratic Republic, 1945–1990

In western eyes, the German Democratic Republic was a repressive Soviet puppet state, a jailor of its citizens behind the deadly Berlin Wall and the no less murderously fortified (but often unremembered) inner "German-German" (GDR-West German) border. Soviet control was secure under an occupation force of some 380,000 soldiers and 200,000 Russian civilians (and through the GDR's dependence on imported Soviet oil and natural gas). But in its own official eyes and the Soviet Union's, the GDR was a self-governing society of well-educated and politically enlightened industrial workers, communally-minded farmers, and revolutionary intellectuals that had successfully reached mature socialism. The GDR was home to "real existing socialism," in contrast (as pro-Soviet communists thought) to postwar western leftists' utopian imaginings of nonauthoritarian, still-to-be-realized forms of "democratic socialism."

According to Marxist-Leninist theory, post-1945 communist-led social revolution in eastern Germany had removed the bases for any possible resurgence of fascism and imperialism. Hence the GDR was a force for world peace. But West Germany was still trapped in ("monopoly") capitalism. As a well-armed member of the "U.S.-imperialist" power system, the Federal Republic menaced East German socialism's achievements. In self-defense the GDR needed to arm itself against the NATO bloc and prevent its citizens by means of censorship and fortified borders from falling prey to capitalist blandishments. Western threat, in other words, forced the GDR to adopt its repressive apparatus, which would only finally wither away when Soviet-style socialism had been achieved in the West.

In contrast to this highly ideological communist self-understanding, the pre-1989 scholarly literature in western countries focused on much different questions. How legitimate was the GDR in its citizens' hearts and minds? Was the GDR likely to be a lasting product of German history, and if so, how should its emergence and maturation be interpreted? Was it, as GDR advocates claimed, the product of a "better German tradition" of popular rebelliousness, democracy, socialism, and pre-1933 communism? Or did its relative stability and success as a Soviet-type polity and society bear witness to authoritarianism's strength in German history, whether deriving from the National Socialist years only, or earlier epochs too?

Red Army Supreme, 1945–1949

In 1944, the United States, Britain, and France jointly approved the creation of the Soviet occupation zone. In 1945, the U.S. Army liberated part of future GDR territory, but withdrew to honor the earlier agreement. The Soviet administrators' first step taken toward political renewal was the founding in April 1945 of a new German Communist Party (KPD). This was the work of Walter Ulbricht (1893–1973) and other pre-1933 communists who had survived the war in Soviet exile. They figured colloquially as "Muscovites." Publicly, they disavowed the intent to copy the Soviet model, instead advocating a search, within a "people's democracy" cleansed of "fascists" and "reactionaries," for a "German Road to Socialism." The pre-1933 Social Democrats (SPD) reappeared on the public stage, alongside newly baptized democratic parties (conjured up from top down) for the middle classes and villagers. They joined with the KPD in a "Popular Front" that carried out land reform against "Junker" estateowners and "rich peasants" and nationalized large-scale industry and commerce.

Soviet-zone denazification struck ex-functionaries and zealots, while the "laboring masses" – that is, the great majority – were declared Nazism's opponents and meritorious "antifascists." The communist interpretation of National Socialism saw it first and foremost as big capital's dictatorship over the proletariat, exercised by populist front-men. The Communist Party had been Hitlerism's first collective victim. Yet communists had fought back from the German underground and from abroad to defeat Nazism and liberate the oppressed masses. Because working people were the communist movement's natural constituency, they shared "objectively" in the Soviet Union's and allied communist parties' heroic victory, as indeed many working-class communists consciously did, even if they hardly represented all "toilers."

In this way, official ideology encouraged ordinary East Germans to regard themselves as antifascist victors rather than co-bearers with the NSDAP of guilt for Hitlerism. Because National Socialist racism did not fit squarely into this interpretive schema, East German memory of the Holocaust was distorted: Jewish Germans and other Jews perished less for having been racially stigmatized than because fascism scapegoated them to distract naïve minds from its defense of embattled capitalism.

The postwar KPD's popularity suffered from lingering effects of National Socialist anticommunist propaganda and widespread fear of Stalinism. Disenchantment followed also from the Soviet army's earlier mentioned depredations, notably widespread looting and rape, which heavily ravaged future GDR territory. Corrosive too was the impact on east German opinion of Soviet plundering of economic assets, justified by reparations claims, as occurred widely throughout the Soviet zone and in Russian-controlled Berlin (where the dismantling of hundreds of factories reduced industry to one-quarter of its prewar capacity). Contemporary estimates of the value of the raw materials and capital goods that Stalin's agents plundered before 1952 run as high as $20 billion – a huge sum at the time.

In 1946 the Communist Party sought to bolster its popularity by forcing merger on the largely unwilling Social Democratic Party, producing the "Socialist Unity Party" (*Sozialistische Einheitspartei Deutschlands* or SED), the future East German communist party. But even this new enlarged ruling party could not win a majority in the October 1946 multi-party elections in the Soviet zone that previous inter-Allied agreements had mandated. In rival West Berlin the still-autonomous Social Democrats, running independently, proved strongest. Many ordinary people were obviously reluctant to vote for Stalin's friends.

The U.S.-Soviet antagonism escalated in 1947 into the Cold War. The Truman Doctrine vowed support for anticommunist governments in Greece and Turkey, as well as around the world. Stalin founded a new international revolutionary communist organization, the Cominform. The USSR sought to bar the western allies from access to Berlin, leading to the dramatic – and unexpectedly triumphant – 1948–1949 American and British airlift of food and other supplies to the city's three western sectors, ensuring West Berlin's continued existence as an island in the communist sea.

In 1949, after the Federal Republic emerged as a separate state, the German Democratic Republic stepped forth in the Soviet zone, under the sole leadership of the SED, now unapologetically a strictly hierarchical and authoritarian Leninist-Stalinist party. It packed the parliament and in 1949 promulgated a Soviet-type socialist constitution. German division was a cause, but equally, or perhaps more importantly, a consequence of the international Cold War, which was a global struggle for predominance between the Soviet and American power spheres and not in Germany alone.

Before the Wall, 1949–1961

The years between 1949 and 1953 witnessed what might be called the GDR's self-Stalinization, expressed in communist party domination of the bureaucratic-governmental system, launching of a Soviet-style, state-led, high-speed five-year industrialization plan, strengthening of the secret security police and quasi-military armed police formations, and fortification of the inner-German border. Hastening this process was the dramatic workers' revolt that exploded on June 17, 1953, centered in East Berlin and other industrial cities, leaving 21 dead and approximately 1,000 jailed. Seven others were later executed.

This was an outburst of working-class fury at oppressively high state-mandated work norms, unchanged by Stalin's death in March 1953. A split that had opened in the SED between Stalinist dogmatists and communist reformers (who argued for lowering of work norms and improvement of private

FIGURE 20.1. STALINIST EAST GERMANY
Pictured here in 1952, from the podium's left, are Socialist Unity – that is, Communist – Party Secretary Walter Ulbricht, President Wilhelm Pieck, and Otto Grotewohl, prime minister, presiding over a virtually all-male array of communist functionaries. They accept "voluntary" and "self-imposed" heightened work output targets from an organization of coal-miners, whom they in turn honor with applause – the often near-incessant accompaniment of communist gatherings and public display. Lenin's and Stalin's visages adorn the background banners.

A photograph of October 1949 captured young men, meagerly dressed in thin workers' holiday clothing, shouldering massive and intimidating images of the Soviet autocrat in night-time marches celebrating the GDR's founding, while others displayed the politically battle-hardened visage of veteran German communist and GDR president Wilhelm Pieck (born in 1876). Another picture of a 1952 review of the communist youth organization (FDJ) displayed the continuity among SED notables in power and office that was one of the structural features weakening the GDR and other Soviet-empire systems. Rosa Thälmann, widow of the martyr to National Socialist dictatorship and pre-1933 communist leader Ernst Thälmann, flanked President Pieck, accompanied by the young married couple, Margot (b. 1927) and Erich Honecker (1912–1994), youth leaders who were destined, through Erich Honecker's succession to Ulbricht in 1971, to become the GDR's final top power brokers.
Source: Deutsches Bundesarchiv.

FIGURE 20.2. THE FIRST WORKERS' REVOLT IN THE SOVIET BLOC: JUNE 17, 1953
Protests by industrial laborers and other GDR citizens erupted in some 400 localities and
within some 600 socialist enterprises. Soviet tanks came to the assistance of the various
branches of the hard-pressed "people's police" (*Volkspolizei*), brutally suppressing the
uprising. This dramatic picture shows East Berliners fleeing the gunfire-punctured scene
across Potsdamer Platz to safety in the British Sector of West Berlin. Presumably some
remained there, while others returned to family and work in the GDR. The city's still
semi-ruined condition is evident. Not until 1955 did the GDR gain Soviet consent to the
formation of a regular army (the "National People's Army" [*Nationale Volksarmee*]).
    During the revolt, Soviet tanks rolled in Leipzig against the background of the
supreme court of Imperial and Weimar Germany, where in 1933 the National Socialists
staged a show-trial against German communists charged with setting the Reichstag on
fire. Soon similar trials would occur against those "provocateurs" the GDR authorities
accused, as "agents of the capitalist-imperialist West," of igniting the June 17 protests.
Source: Bildarchiv Preussischer Kulturbesitz/Art Resource, NY.

consumption) paralyzed the party, requiring the Soviet Army to intervene and
quell the uprising. In the violence's aftermath, the Soviets favored consolidation of power under the leadership of Moscow-loyal prewar communist Walter
Ulbricht, who purged reformers and critically inclined intellectuals, establishing
his unshakeable control until 1971.
    In the years between 1952 and 1955, the Soviets made several diplomatic
proposals to reunify and neutralize Germany, which – had the West accepted
them – would have dissolved the GDR (showing, seemingly, Moscow's doubts
about the fledgling communist state's long-term viability). These initiatives

were probably only long-shot efforts to prevent the rearmament of a NATO-integrated West Germany. In any case, in 1955 the USSR withdrew its occupation forces from henceforth internationally neutral Austria. It also extended diplomatic recognition to the Federal Republic, despite NATO and rearmament, so ensuring the East German state's survival. Ulbricht subsequently paid lip service to the ideal of German unification, but in reality the free and pluralist elections it would have entailed would certainly have destroyed the SED's power monopoly in the east.

In August 1961 Ulbricht's regime, in a startling surprise move, erected the Berlin Wall, encircling the western Allies' sectors. The aim was both to halt the flow of escapees and refugees via West Berlin from East to West Germany (numbering, as we saw, some three million in the 1950s) and to stabilize the GDR so as to more effectively build socialism. This occasioned severe international crisis and even the threat of nuclear war, but in the end John F. Kennedy's new American administration accepted Ulbricht's bold *fait accompli*.

East Germany's High Noon and Twilight, 1961–1985

In 1962 economic reforms (the "New Economic Mechanism") partially decentralized the GDR's planning system, giving more voice to enterprise managers and what was called the technical intelligentsia. The result was considerable economic growth to the mid-1970s, accompanied by full employment of male and female labor. GDR living standards, on average, were high by Soviet measure, but only lower-middle-class, at best, by western European comparison. Even the GDR's political, technocratic, and cultural elites, although favored with access to superior consumer goods, country cottages, and travel privileges, lived modestly by comparison with the Soviet (and western) governing classes.

The mature political system amounted to a personal dictatorship of the SED's First Secretary, working together with the party's multimember Politburo, which was steered from above (although factional conflicts simmered). The SED party apparatus rested mainly in the hands of the educated middle class (sometimes mocked as a "red bourgeoisie"). There was a large GDR army under Soviet high command and a powerful Security Police (*Staatssicherheit* or *"Stasi"*) linked to its Soviet counterpart, the KGB. The Stasi, nearly 100,000 strong (in a population numbering at most only about 17 million), employed an equal or larger corps of "unofficial informants," frequently police or other state officials, but also ordinary citizens. Some 20,000 among them lived, spy-like, in the Federal Republic and West Berlin. All such agents reported on relatives, neighbors, acquaintances, and work colleagues. Many lives were ruined or embittered by the Stasi's intrusions, intimidations, frame-ups, arrests, imprisonments, and other machinations.

In 1971, Erich Honecker replaced Ulbricht, who had stubbornly opposed the new Soviet-approved treaties with West Germany that Willy Brandt's government initiated. The new *Ostpolitik* paid political and economic dividends to the GDR, which together with the Federal Republic won admittance in 1973 to

FIGURE 20.3. THE BERLIN WALL

The GDR began in 1949 to militarize and fortify its circuitous 900-mile-long western border with the new Federal Republic, eventually fitting it with an impassable no-man's land where intrusions would automatically trigger deadly weapons fire. The Berlin Wall, begun at night on August 12–13, 1961, finally encircled West Berlin along a 100-mile-long perimeter. In this picture, West Berliners hail friends or relatives across the precipitately constructed barrier. No adult men are among them. Eventually the Wall came, on its western face, to be colorfully, humorously, anonymously and disrespectfully ornamented, mostly in comic-book style. East German crews were obliged to collect trash that defiant West Berliners routinely tossed over the wall into the wide and murderous no-man's land on the East Berlin side. The numbers of those killed by GDR armed guards in attempts to clandestinely cross the borders are controversial, but certainly run into the hundreds. Some 75,000 GDR citizens were convicted of attempts at "flight from the republic" (*Republikflucht*), including, apart from tunneling, in homemade conveyances by sea and air.

Source: Bildarchiv Preussischer Kulturbesitz/Art Resource, NY.

the United Nations, gaining widespread international diplomatic recognition, including from the United States. Yet the GDR found itself also drawn into international negotiations on human rights, culminating in the 1975 Helsinki Declaration promising their guarantee also to inhabitants of the Soviet bloc, whose member states, including Honecker's regime, could not avoid signing it.

Recognizing the challenges Brandt's diplomacy posed, both by improving cross-border contacts between east and west Germans and refuting Soviet bloc propaganda claims of West German aggressiveness ("revanchism") toward its eastern neighbors, the GDR subsequently practiced a policy of "self-distancing" (*Abgrenzung*) from the West. From 1976, the regime forced into exile prominent dissident but still pro-socialist intellectuals, notably Rudolf Bahro, and artists such as poet-musician Wolf Biermann, while silencing others. Strenuous effort was devoted to educating GDR youth in loyalty to the "Socialist German Nation," in opposition to what official propaganda stigmatized as decadent, narcissistic, consumer-crazed western capitalism. The regime only reluctantly approved the introduction of "socialist rock music," hoping to offset negative effects through intensified military service among GDR youth.

Until roughly 1980, the GDR was a comparatively successful "development dictatorship." Yet it was increasingly dependent on Soviet energy supplies and – something novel since the new *Ostpolitik* – western bank loans, reinsured by NATO-pact governments. In the decade between 1971 and 1981 these totaled $14 billion. The GDR grew ever more reliant on economic ties with the Federal Republic, and indirectly, through the Federal Republic, with the European Community. In its end-phase, the GDR's economic growth faltered, and regime insiders began to doubt whether a successful transition to new western-pioneered computer-based high-technology industry would (or could) occur.

By 1979 the rising cost of imported Soviet oil and the GDR's flagging capacity to sustain energy production powered by its (pollutant-rich) brown-coal industry called further development even of its established industrial model into question. In 1982–1983 the GDR fell into arrears on servicing western loans. Chancellor Helmut Kohl's new conservative government in the Federal Republic found itself obliged to rescue Honecker's regime with new credits in the then-sizeable sum of 2 billion West German Deutschmarks (about $700 million). In these years the Stasi drew up – as research in its archive after 1989 sensationally revealed – top-secret contingency plans for state bankruptcy and liquidation of the GDR itself in an emergency unification with the Federal Republic.

Yet, as long as the arms-bristling, authoritarian, and imperialistic USSR survived, determined to prop up the GDR, so too would the communist system in East Germany persist. The GDR's population understood this, and many people took refuge in gratifications of private life – family, country cottages, avocations and hobbies, vacations within the far-flung Soviet bloc – and sometimes too in extramarital affairs or reckless drinking, or in furtive but burgeoning subcultures of alienated youth. Many well-educated adults shrugged off the

FIGURE 20.4. GDR CULTURE: SOCIALIST LOYALISTS AND DISSIDENTS
Poet Berthold Brecht (1898–1956 [left center]), with fellow writers at a 1948 meeting of the "Cultural League for German Democratic Renewal," later renamed *Kulturbund der DDR*, an organization that attempted after 1945 to unite throughout Germany communist and liberal antifascist intellectuals, but which eventually split along Cold War lines. Brecht often viewed SED policy critically, and gingerly defended the 1953 rebels, but did not break with the regime, which showered him and his internationally celebrated theater group, the Berliner Ensemble, with its favor.

Famous also among officially patronized artists was the talented novelist of a younger generation, Christa Wolf (b. 1929), in 1964 the recipient from Walter Ulbricht's hands of the GDR's national literature prize. Wolf explored private life and emotion within the bounds of socialist loyalty and activism. In 1989 she made passionate public pleas to transform the GDR into a democratic socialist polity rather than acquiesce in merger with the Federal Republic. Poet Wolf Biermann (b. 1936) was the son of a German Jewish communist father, murdered by the National Socialists. In the late 1960s he figured in a circle of other critically minded DDR intellectuals, including prominent dissident chemist-philosopher Robert Havemann (1910–1982), who escaped a National Socialist death sentence for association with the communist resistance movement only to suffer exclusion from the SED and his profession in 1964–1965 for criticism of the GDR's totalitarian features.

Biermann composed passionate folk songs in the tradition of leftist and bohemian satire directed against power elites and hypocritical conformists. In 1976 the regime, attempting to silence him, revoked his citizenship while he was touring in West Germany. He appeared, following this unexpected blow, at a press conference with 1972 Nobel Prize-winning West German novelist Heinrich Böll (1917–1985) and prominent leftist investigative journalist Günter Wallraff (b. 1942), who protested Biermann's expulsion. In exile he remained a strong critic of both the GDR and the West's democracy deficits.

A fate similar to Biermann's struck dissident Marxist theorist Rudolf Bahro (1935–1997), whose SED loyalty the Russian-led 1968 invasion of reform-seeking communist Czechoslovakia broke. His book, *The Alternative: A Critique of Real Existing Socialism*

Soviet-style ritualism of SED membership. Many people, including intellectuals, tried to find work that was relatively untainted by ideology and propaganda.

Still, many GDR citizens also believed in the idea of a yet-to-be-realized "better socialism" or, as the anti-Stalinist rebels in 1968 Czechoslovakia called it, "socialism with a human face." They were skeptical of western capitalism's accomplishments and disapproving of western military assertiveness. With the Communist Party's reluctant sanction, the GDR's Protestant Church spear-headed, beginning in 1972, antinuclear weapons and disarmament protest campaigns. These proved to be the seedbed of a growing mobilization among disillusioned GDR citizens against more than just Cold War tensions and nuclear threats. Church-shielded dissidents also protested against the one-party police-state, advocating instead one or another form of political pluralism (and, increasingly, environmental protection), although rejection of socialism in favor of a free-market economy seldom found expression. In the 1980s the regime yielded to the temptation to use strong-arm police methods in attempting, unsuccessfully, to stifle such swelling dissent.

The late GDR suffered from high divorce and suicide rates, and from widespread disaffection of the youth (many of whom privately glorified western pop culture). Despite communist preaching against it, West German television, easily receivable nearly everywhere in the GDR, became the preferred source of news and entertainment for many – or perhaps even most – East Germans. A southeastern corner inaccessible to West German television broadcasts was known colloquially as *das Tal der Ahnungslosigkeit* ("the valley of the clue-less").

Downfall, 1985–1990

Mikhail Gorbachev came to power in the USSR in 1985 as self-proclaimed reformer at home and throughout the Soviet bloc. He let it be known to the "fraternal" east European regimes that they would have to pay world mar-ket prices for Soviet energy and could not depend in internal political crises on Soviet tanks' intervention. In East Germany, Gorbachev's message pro-voked opposition and anxiety in the SED leadership, while the population showed appreciation for his program of introducing pluralist, if not demo-cratic, procedures within the single-party communist state, and of encouraging

---

FIGURE 20.4 *(continued)* (1977), written in an anti-bureaucratic, Marxist populist tra-dition tinged with Trotskyism and Maoism, triggered his imprisonment and later expul-sion to the West. Other GDR dissidents gravitated toward subcultures of rock and punk music, sometimes combined with engagement in the Protestant Church–backed peace and antinuclear movement, where covert opposition to SED authoritarianism and mili-tarism found expression alongside officially approved criticism of NATO and American nuclear arms.
Source: Deutsches Bundesarchiv.

FIGURE 20.5. DAILY LIFE: HOUSING, WORK, LEISURE

Here, in a 1985 photograph, looms the East Berlin Marzahn district's huge housing project, begun in 1971 as showcase of socialist well-being. Such vast apartment blocks were an invention of global architectural modernism, but they also came to epitomize Soviet-sphere urban life. The nascent GDR, with no accumulations of investment capital, faced a huge challenge in rebuilding housing lost through bombs and battles under National Socialism. Ordinary people were glad to obtain property in a modest few apartment rooms, outfitted with glass, steel, and wooden furniture in the postwar Scandinavian style, nature-substituting houseplants, and with bookshelves filled with inexpensive editions of state-approved works, both classic and contemporary, and left-leaning world literature. Much sought after, too, despite being the butt of western jokes, was the GDR's signature family car: the feebly powered, sometimes thinly fiberglass-housed, often-cramped Trabant. Housing in the GDR's myriad rural villages was mostly old-fashioned, but regime propaganda highlighted availability there as in the cities of preschool and kindergarten services for all children. The GDR prided itself on these and other social provisions, essential though they also were to its goal of women's maximum work mobilization.

East Germany improved its image in the world through success of its well-funded athletes, but after 1989 the extent of steroid drug use at highest competitive levels, and its ill effects on athletes, came damagingly to light. Yet engagement in amateur sports of all kinds – especially in socialist clubs, including for sailing and mountaineering – was widely popular, as was partisanship for soccer teams.

Source: Deutsches Bundesarchiv.

criticism of past Stalinist methods. Honecker's government found no means – whether reformist or repressive – to deflect the light of Gorbachev's vision, which inspired both the many people throughout the Soviet bloc who still harbored hopes for "socialism with a human face" and the no less numerous throng of those who longed for real electoral democracy and an efficient market economy.

Amid the dissolution in 1989 of the communist regimes in Poland and Hungary and the democratic transitions accompanying them, GDR citizens began fleeing to the West through Hungary into Austria. This stirred East German dissident groups to break into independent public life, advocating democratization of the SED-led system, some in hope of revitalizing socialism, others prepared for the sake of individual freedom and human rights to see it fall. Advocates of a pluralized and post-Soviet GDR coalesced in the New Forum (*Neues Forum*), attractive to many intellectuals. By November 9, 1989, after a month of popular demonstrations against the SED regime in Leipzig and other provincial cities, mass sentiment favoring opening to – or even unification with – the Federal Republic led amid Honecker's government's uncontrollable disintegration to the Berlin Wall's spontaneous fall. The crowds of GDR protesters who had been chanting the slogan, "we are the people" (*wir sind das Volk*), in calling for democratization of East German life, came increasingly also to chant that "we are one people" (*wir sind ein Volk*), signaling the desire for unification with West Germany.

Efforts to establish a reformist but still socialist post-Honecker GDR government collapsed after March 1990 elections returned a majority for the Alliance for Democracy, a pro-CDU, pro-Helmut Kohl coalition favoring immediate merger with the Federal Republic. Its opponents complained that Kohl's government was purchasing East German loyalty with its promise to transform the ill-esteemed and hitherto unconvertible East German currency, colloquially known as the "Ost-Mark," into the prestigious and valuable West German Deutsche Mark.

Opposition to immediate fusion with West Germany was not confined to the New Forum's idealistic pro-socialist reformers. Ex-SED notables Gregor Gysi and Hans Modrow figured in 1990 among the leaders of the newborn Party of Democratic Socialism (PDS), self-proclaimed democratic successor to the SED. Their election banners promised (but too late) "productivity" through a "pro-DDR" policy – rhetoric hinting, among other things, that the new party would seek to protect former SED members against political reprisals. Gysi's father – prominent and influential in the SED – had in 1936 been driven by anti-Semitism into exile, but returned to work clandestinely in National Socialist Germany as a communist activist. His son (b. 1948) remained long after the 1990 reunification a talented and influential leader of the postcommunist left.

The opportunity – miraculous in many GDR eyes – to merge into the western Federal Republic was irresistible. The election victory of Kohl's backers in East Germany introduced a transition period ending in the reunification treaty of October 3, 1990, dissolving the GDR and integrating its territory into the West German constitutional system as the "five new federal states."

The question sometimes arises, in both East and West German minds, of the connection between the vanished German Democratic Republic regime and the National Socialist dictatorship that preceded it. Authoritarian continuity

(a)

FIGURE 20.6. THE GDR'S FALL, 1989–1990

As dissident and reformist groups gathered strength, GDR citizens traveling in Hungary in summer 1989 staged their sensational mass flight to the West, politically crippling to the SED regime. In September and October, large street protests flared across the GDR. Finally the capital city exploded. Demonstrations gathering hundreds of thousands erupted on East Berlin's central square, the Alexanderplatz. Summoned by dissident political and artistic-cultural groups, these assemblies voiced calls for the SED dictatorship's end and a new regime of (variously understood) democracy. Crucial to such sentiment's spread, especially in the capital city, was the New Forum, some of whose leaders appear in the picture above (Jens Reich, center, and Bärbel Bohley, right), taken on November 10, the day after the Wall's fall. Seeking the GDR's democratic transformation (and thus its survival as authentic socialist democracy), they assemble in a church made available by pro-reform Protestant clergy. But they soon found themselves marginalized by those myriad East Germans who, responding to chancellor Kohl's encouragement, sought immediate unification with the Federal Republic.

Characteristic of the Christian Democrats' strategy was a poster for the GDR elections of March 18, 1990, declaring – with Mikhail Gorbachev's image as guarantee – that "the path is free. Unity is coming." Among the leaders of the pro-unification and pro-CDU Alliance for Democracy was Angela Merkel (b. 1954), a dissident GDR physicist and Protestant pastor's daughter, elevated in 2005 to the federal chancellorship.

The second picture displays a common popular celebration of the "fall of the wall": a young and (seemingly) working-class East German couple inch their Trabant automobile across the "German-German" border at Helmstedt, the driver displaying a West Berlin tabloid newspaper blaring that "the wall is gone. Berlin is once again Berlin."

Among skeptics about German unification was the young East German man outfitted in punk-rock, Mohawk-haired style – highly provocative in liberal and leftist eyes – who

(b)

FIGURE 20.6 *(continued)* could be seen in 1990 electioneering on East Berlin's Alexanderplatz, wearing a placard of the radical right-wing German Social Union (DSU) promising "better living" (through a program prominently featuring resentment toward foreign immigrants). Other GDR citizens rallied against the Alliance for Democracy with such slogans as "money makes you bad," *"Kohlonie"* ("Kohl's colony"), and, in English – alluding to Yankee influence in the Federal Republic – "Go Home."

Of low visibility during the GDR's collapse was West Germany's Social Democratic Party, which SED propaganda had long accused of "selling out" to "capitalist democracy" in the Federal Republic. It subsequently gained ground and today, together with the powerful CDU and postcommunist Left Party, vies for power in the former East (although, as we will see, the radical right maintains a visible and belligerent presence, particularly among disadvantaged youth and middle-aged people sidelined by socialism's fall).

Source: (a) Bildarchiv Preussischer Kulturbesitz/Art Resource, NY; (b) Deutsches Bundesarchiv.

is undeniable, as evidenced by the sway in both states of single-party dictatorship, police-state apparatus, militarism, and the population's compulsory mass-mobilization behind highly ideological programs of social utopianism (and also – into the 1970s – by a not inconsiderable continuity of personnel in police, army, and lower party echelons between National Socialist and GDR regimes).

Yet such concepts as "red fascism" obscure more than they illuminate, though present-day theories of totalitarianism cast some clarifying light. The German Democratic Republic owed much more to Stalin than to Hitler.

Moreover, the determination of its well-educated and hard-working population to build something of value in a land they could not (after 1961) escape lent the GDR positive qualities, rooted in Germans traditions of craftsmanship and high culture, which offset, if not altogether neutralized, its Soviet-style defects.

The lifeworld and political culture that emerged during forty years of "real existing socialism" could not disappear overnight. Unified Germany since 1990 has witnessed occasionally dramatic confrontation between values and interests of former East and West. In some ways what is popularly called the "wall in the head" still stands.

21

Mauerfall – Fall of the Wall

The Post-Unification Scene in West and East

Twenty-two years after joyous crowds hammered down the Berlin Wall, reunited Germany, counting eighty-two million inhabitants, was the most populous country in the twenty-seven-member European Union, a structure of mixed and shared sovereignties encompassing half a billion people, reminiscent perhaps of the Holy Roman Empire (though no longer "of the German nation"). The Federal Republic's economy – measured by gross domestic product (GDP) – in 2010 was the world's third largest. It is a world leader – recently pre-eminent, second in 2011 to China – in the value of its foreign trade. Per capita income as shares of GDP amounted in 2007 to some $34,000, compared with the European Union's 2008 average of nearly $31,000, and the United States' $47,000. Income inequality – as measured on social science's widely accepted GINI scale – in the United States is relatively high, at a value of 38. Across the Union it averages near 31. In Germany it is – at 30 – comparatively low, though in Denmark – at 25 – it is lower still.

The political system remains, despite occasional faltering, one of the world's most smooth-functioning and transparent. New parties, if they can surmount the 5-percent barrier, integrate themselves into national life, giving voice to emergent constituencies, if also cutting into older parties' bases. Although the Federal Republic is still home to a European class-based society in which propertied and professional elites command considerable power and prestige, higher education is tuition-free, with living costs defrayed, to those who pass entry examinations – about one-quarter of all secondary-school graduates. This affords considerable upward social mobility, even if children of university graduates qualify for admission in far greater proportion than do inner-city children, and especially those of migrant families with roots outside Europe. Secondary-school students uninterested in university study have good opportunities to train themselves as apprentices, in time-honored tradition reaching back to craft guilds, to become skilled workers, both blue- and white-collar, with not illusory hopes of future small-business ownership.

Welfare state provisions, relative to world scale, are generous: well-funded, state-underwritten health care; defined-benefit retirement pensions; and disability, poverty, and unemployment programs minimizing homelessness and poverty. Germans, on average, spend more income for travel, especially beyond their borders, than any other nation. Public cultural institutions are numerous, well-subsidized, and widely enjoyed. Ecological protection and awareness are relatively very high. The Green Party was a pioneer in large countries of effective national-level environmental parliamentary politics. Germany is one of the few large industrialized countries that are meeting the challenge of reducing carbon dioxide emissions by substituting fossil fuels with nonnuclear, nonpolluting energy, while profiting from home consumption and export of green industry products.

In these and other ways, the present-day Federal Republic figures on the world stage as an exemplary embodiment of liberal-democratic modernity. Its shadow sides – above all, class and generational inequalities, difficulties in integrating disadvantaged and stigmatized groups into the social-political mainstream, youth disaffection, trivialized consumerist and mass-media culture, ethnically framed resentments and aggressions on the social margins – are familiar everywhere in the West, and will not soon vanish. Contemporary German political culture's responses to these problems will emerge in the pages that follow.

We saw that pre-1989 West Germany – the "Bonn Republic" – attained political legitimacy and economic prosperity. The question after 1989 was whether the new united polity – the "Berlin Republic" – could sustain those achievements as it sought to stitch the former German Democratic Republic into its fabric.

The Optimistic View of East German Integration

The German Democratic Republic was a self-styled "socialist internationalist" state. The German Federal Republic was – in its official self-understanding, at any rate – a "post-nationalist" state, its identity invested in liberal freedoms, European integration, and democratic welfare-state more than in *Volk* or *Nation*. Such, in pre-1989 eyes, was the end-station, for foreseeable time, of the German *Sonderweg* or "separate path," which had in 1933 led catastrophically to National Socialism. The existence in post-1945 partitioned Germany of two rival states – and an Austria that only slowly found independent identity – further confirmed German-speaking central Europe's historic "exceptionalism." But now, in the eyes of many optimistic, liberal-minded, and influential people, the unification of October 1990 figures as the *Sonderweg*'s end and attainment instead of that which reigning perspectives on modern history – or theories of modernity and modernization – regard as normal and natural, that is, democratically structured national statehood.

This outcome may, as this interpretation holds, be regarded with calm and benevolence, because chancellor Helmut Kohl's united Germany remained

MAP 21.1. REUNITED GERMANY IN ITS CENTRAL EUROPEAN SETTING

The federal structure established by the 1949 West German constitution, into which East Germany's territorial units were integrated intact, is of fundamental importance. The larger share of public revenues and expenditures rests in the federal states' hands, although the central government's role is crucial in managing national finances, including budget deficits and national debt. The federal states embody – or, in some cases, aggregate – historical regional identities that live on vividly in popular consciousness.

In a cultural-linguistic-historical sense, Germans of the Federal Republic feel affinities with Austrians (and the few Liechtensteiners), and with Germanophone Swiss and South Tyrolians, though gulfs of comfortably accepted mutual unfamiliarity also divide them. In Italy, agreements of 1948 and 1972 negotiated between the government in Rome within the NATO alliance. It joined, together with the European Economic Community's other member states, the politically more tightly integrated EU born in the 1992 Maastricht Treaty. The "2 + 4" reunification treaty of September 12, 1990, signed by the two pre-1990 German states and four allied victor powers of 1945, ended the postwar occupation and restored German sovereignty. The new Germany explicitly accepted its present borders. It agreed to reduce its combined armed forces to 370,000 soldiers (a number that by 2010 fell to 250,000 – on its way to 200,000 or fewer in a post-2011 army wholly recruited from volunteers). It renounced, as the Bonn Republic had done in 1955, possession of nuclear, chemical, and biological weapons.

The German Democratic Republic joined the Federal Republic in the March 1990 elections' aftermath as the "five new federal states" (*neue Bundesländer*). As such mild terminology implies, everyday political discourse minimizes the 1989–1990 events' revolutionary character, commonly referring to them collectively as "the change" or "turn" (*die Wende*). Simultaneously, the former GDR's economy underwent rapid privatization of its socialist enterprises and their integration into the formidable West German capitalist system. As we know, this is – much more than its American counterpart – a governmentally regulated *soziale Marktwirtschaft* ("socially responsible market economy") and, through pre-1989 media exposure and post-unification life experience, familiar to former East Germans.

Most easterners, in the optimistic scenario, have a niche in the private-enterprise system. The German Democratic Republic was far from the Soviet empire's industrial showcase that before 1989 it was often held to be. Still, its population was mostly well educated, self-disciplined, accustomed to urban-industrial routines, and familiar with West German public culture and values. The East Germans themselves threw off communism's shackles in 1989's

---

MAP 21.1 *(continued)* and representatives of the German-speaking inhabitants of South Tyrol established a regime of local autonomy and multilinguality that gained strength through creation in 1998 within the European Union of the "European Region of Tyrol, South Tyrol, and Trentino," spanning the Austrian and Italian borders and encompassing in a community exercising considerable self-governing powers speakers of Italian, German, and Italian-related Ladino.

In contrast to their many disparities in the past, present-day Germany and Poland are roughly similar in size: 357,000 and 313,000 square kilometers, respectively. The state of California, by contrast, encompasses 424,000 square kilometers, while France measures 547,000. As the text below makes clear, contemporary Polish-German economic cooperation is mutually profitable. The Federal Republic has made considerable investments in improving cultural relations with its eastern neighbor, particularly in education and scholarship. Many hundreds of thousands of Poles live and work in Germany. Since 1989 awareness has spread in Poland that anti-German resentments the Polish communist regime occasionally inflamed, even if they might be historically justifiable, are anachronistic, while the benefits of German-Polish cooperation are tangible and both materially and psychologically gratifying.

FIGURE 21.1. WORLD WAR II'S LONG-DELAYED END

Here depicted is the smile-suffused conclusion of the West German-Soviet meeting of July 16, 1990, smoothing the path to the signature in Moscow on September 12 of the international "2 + 4 treaty" framing, in its words, "the Final Settlement with respect to Germany." In a rustic Caucasian mountain retreat Soviet leader Mikhail Gorbachev hosted chancellor Kohl and his able, long-experienced foreign minister, Hans-Dietrich Genscher (leader of the liberal Free Democratic Party). Soviet foreign minister Edvard Shevardnadze stands to Kohl's right, while Raisa Gorbachev stands behind her husband. To her right is Theo Waigel, German federal finance minister and influential representative of the CDU's conservative Bavarian sister-party, the Christian Social Union. Departure ensued in the following several years of the Soviet army from the former East Germany. Many Soviet soldiers, some with families, had lived for decades in the GDR. Having no secure destination in the USSR, the 1990 negotiations offered German funding to resettle them at home. Reunified Germany's successive governments have carefully cultivated good relations with postcommunist Russia, knowing that the dissolution of the Soviet empire – for which in his homeland Gorbachev is often blamed – inflicted a traumatic wound.

Source: Presse- und Informationsamt der Bundesregierung.

peaceful revolution. They suffered forty years of "tank socialism," with its half-million Soviet occupiers and myriad Stasi agents and informers. Optimists hold that the East Germans understand the political and other freedoms they were living without. Now, having acquired them, they aim to enjoy and exercise them.

There were, admittedly, transitional aches and pains, and not a few tragedies. Masses of people lost jobs they held under socialism. Many were politically bankrupted and exposed to ostracism or even punishment as communist party members and police collaborators. Many others, socialized into passivity and dependence on government services and tutelage, did not prove very successful under the new market-economy regime of individual self-assertion and self-determination. But these difficulties are passing. East German youth are gaining different and better educations. West Germany has extended generous aid in reconstructing the east. The result has been comparable to the West German post-1945 political recovery and "economic miracle" of the 1950s, when GNP doubled in ten years.

As for West Germans, they have – so hopeful voices assert – made the necessary sacrifices, mindful that the Federal Republic's 1949 constitution explicitly invoked reunification as a national objective, in the consciousness of being one people. They knew, too, that the painful transition would not last forever, thanks to their own skills and wealth and their eastern brothers' and sisters' industriousness.

Unification's Real Hardships

After 1989 East Germans went through revolutionary upheaval, even if West German capital investments in their lands and social-welfare transfer payments to the east were massive: upward of $100 billion (then-current dollar value) yearly through the 1990s. These figures dwarfed the post-1945 Marshall Plan aid the United States extended to West Germany. Moreover, the federal government invested some 2.5 trillion additional German Marks (roughly $1 trillion) in restarting East German industry on a privatized basis, cleaning up environmental pollution, and rebuilding the transportation system and other infrastructure. The investment rate in the five new federal states (that is, the ratio of investment to local GDP) in 1991–1993 averaged 47 percent – a sky-high figure.

By the end of the 1990s the privatization program, run by the state-supervised Trusteeship Agency (*Treuhandgesellschaft*), had sold or liquidated 95 percent of the roughly 16,000 socialist enterprises it took under control. Most of the four million workers in these firms departed from the public sector, whether into new private-sector jobs (in their formerly socialist firm, or elsewhere) or into early retirement or long-term unemployment. Most of the defunct GDR's middle and higher civil officials suffered dismissal or forced retirement. There was massive reduction in numbers of former GDR academics and scientists, disbanding of the Stasi police network, and a halving or more of the former *Volksarmee*. Of the 20 percent of the adult population who were members of the communist party (SED), a great many lost the jobs they were holding when the Wall came down.

Heeding the anti-SED New Forum's call, a mass of citizens in 1989 broke into the Stasi police's vast archive, comprising many miles of shelf-space. Here were housed, among other records, secret files on persons under observation, including reports on them by the myriad notorious "informal collaborators."

The protesters – a cross-section of GDR society – carried banners with such heartfelt messages as "Down With Stasi and SED, Dictatorship and Nazism. You Stand Accused of Much Injustice and Suffering." Rigorous debate over access to Stasi files eventually opened them to those who had suffered surveillance. Controversy swirled, especially as prominent people objected to revelations about their GDR past.

Between 1989 and 1994, reductions in the East German work forces amounted to 70 percent in agriculture; 60 percent in manufacturing; 39 percent in mining and energy production; 22 percent in services, including in the state sector. In construction work a 10 percent increased occurred. Overall, between 1989 and 1992, one-third of preexisting East German jobs vanished, a figure that would have been higher without temporary public works projects, later largely phased out.

Official unemployment in October 1995 stood at 15 percent in the east and 8.2 percent in the west. In February 2009 it was not much different, at 14 and 7 percent, respectively (nationwide: 8.5 percent), although the trend, as will be seen, was falling – despite the post-2008 recession. For eastern Germany, such unemployment was the highest since the 1930s. Since 1989, far more than half the East German adult population experienced upheaval in the form of job loss, job change, retirement, and/or unemployment – and this in a land where, under the communist regime, lifetime positions were easy to secure and joblessness was unknown.

The East Germans' integration into the West German economy raised their level and range of consumption in comparison with the communist past. For *employed* persons in former GDR lands, wages and benefits are now not far below those of West Germany, which are among the world's highest. From the employer's viewpoint, this makes investing in East Germany expensive. Retired pensioners are better off than before. Still, most of the inhabitants of the new federal states are living in modest or even poor circumstances, measured by West German standards. The communist middle class was a public-sector stratum, with few or none of the assets and other possessions characteristic of a capitalist "bourgeoisie of property" (*Besitzbürgertum*). After 1989 the "red bourgeoisie" turned pale.

The communist-era elites' competence as an often highly educated intelligentsia did not guarantee survival under free-market conditions. Leadership positions in economy, academia, applied science, and the governmental sector in the new federal states initially fell disproportionately to westerners. These newcomers – pejoratively labeled "Wessis" – often appeared to their embittered eastern detractors as conquering figures of a triumphant western "capitalist neo-colonialism." Such resentment and paranoia aside, there long remained a real problem of eastern subordination to western managerial leadership, from construction-work crews up to university rectors and provincial governors. Many asked themselves: What could "Ossis" themselves contribute? What did they learn from forty years of socialism that remained valuable?

FIGURE 21.2. STRUCTURAL UNEMPLOYMENT AND WELFARE BENEFITS DISPUTES

Here, in August 1990, potash miners in the former GDR protest projected closure of their workplace, following the signals of their communist-era trade union, led by the woman miner marching in the foreground to the audience's applause. She was ending a lengthy sit-in protest below ground. In other scenes from the post-1989 period, workers in Leipzig brandished a banner saying "disarmament, yes; unemployment, no" – an expression of their disappointment at finding that unification's cost to them was their job in socialist enterprises that proved uncompetitive, redundant, or too costly to bring up to West German technological and environmental standards. Another banner proclaimed bitterly: "From a Workers' People (*Arbeitervolk*) to a People Without Work (*Volk ohne Arbeit*)."

Discontent over unification's price tag simmers also in former West Germany. In 2005 chancellor Gerhard Schröder's SPD-Green coalition government, under fiscal pressure and in an effort to bring the jobless back into the workforce, scaled down welfare provisions to the long-term unemployed. Although not without some improvements in benefits, this and related reforms, known in shorthand as "Harz IV," squeezed other payments, including housing subsidies and unemployment (as opposed to welfare) stipends,

Many easterners found this situation crushing. Not a few emigrated to the western federal states, as they had already began to do in hundreds of thousands in mid-1989. Some 200,000 left in 1992 alone. Numerous among them were the young and better-educated. They, like easterners who stayed home, faced the challenge of developing self-assertion and competitiveness characteristic of western-style meritocracy and capitalism. Even when they remained employed, and earned more money than under the communist system, many among the young adult and middle-aged population with roots in the vanished GDR had to come to grips with self-questioning and a sense, more or less keenly felt, of having suffered devaluation and delegitimization.

This was especially true of women and the family. In the eastern states in the years between 1989 and 1992 the birthrate fell by 60 percent, the marriage rate by 65 percent, the divorce rate by 81 percent. These were extraordinary crisis symptoms, indicating reluctance to enter into new commitments and make new departures. Women in the east suffered long-term unemployment more often than men. Many jobs disappeared whose female occupants eventually abandoned the goal of working for pay. With post-unification restrictions in the former German Democratic Republic's very permissive abortion laws, loss of child-care facilities and free contraceptives, and under the impact of unemployment, many women abandoned thoughts of family life. This found expression in a rising number during the 1990s of voluntary sterilizations as well as in falling birth and marriage rates.

Such conditions, and widespread unemployment among the less well educated, set the stage for the emergence among East German youth of right-wing violence (whether perpetrated, as the mass media suggested, by skinheads or not). As is still the case today, it was almost entirely the young who committed acts of violence, especially against ethnic outsiders. Yet there was a high degree of complicity among older bystanders, which led, for example, to the posting in the mid-1990s of official notices in Berlin subways and trams warning against passivity among onlookers should racist violence break out.

In politics, East Germans voted strongly in the March 1990 election for the pro-CDU Alliance for Germany, but later only slowly joined the mainstream West German parties in large numbers. The one party rooted almost wholly in East German membership was the postcommunist successor party to the pre-1990 SED ruling party. This was the Party of Democratic Socialism (PDS),

---

FIGURE 21.2 *(continued)* triggering protests and widespread disaffection from the SPD. Schröder's reforms also relaxed laws, to employers' advantage, governing worker layoffs. Reunited Germany faces a huge challenge to deliver a comfortable living standard to all workers while globalized markets confront its high-wage economy with the competition of countries where lower incomes prevail. But its reliance on high-technology exports, especially of advanced machinery produced by a high-skilled labor force, has proved unusually successful.

Source: Deutsches Bundesarchiv.

(a)

FIGURE 21.3. NEO-NAZIS AND THEIR OPPONENTS

(a) A July 2007 neo-Nazi demonstration in West German Gütersloh (a stronghold
of the mainstream political parties). Marching young men display a banner saying
"together against capitalism for a national socialism." They have dressed themselves
as *Autonomen* prepared for street battle, an identity pioneered in post-1968 West Germany by leftist youth who are still today active in big cities fighting neo-Nazis and
police, disrupting peaceful left-wing demonstrations, and staging anonymous attacks
on property – actions that rightist "autonomists" subsequently emulated. Echoes of
Weimar's battling Nazis and Communists are evident.

(b) In Erfurt, in the former GDR, demonstrators support their city council's call for citizenly protest against the local neo-Nazi National Democratic Party (NPD). Their banner
reads: "No Naziion Germany" – (that is, "No Nazi Nation Germany") – "Shut Your
Mouths." In many – perhaps most – present-day German minds, vehement and aggressive nationalism (rarely publicly expressed in the political mainstream) immediately
evokes National Socialism. An antinationalist German identity oriented to Habermas's
"constitutional patriotism," or to leftist progressivism or utopianism, or simply attachment to the charms and virtues of the local or larger *Heimat* ("homeland") is for most
people far the more comfortable choice.

Source: (a) Marek Peters; (b) Deutsches Bundesarchiv.

which gained steadily through the 1990s until it commanded some 20 to 30
percent of the vote in the five eastern federal states, governed some important
cities, and sat in the federal parliament (Bundestag). It appealed especially to
die-hard GDR loyalists and those who saw themselves as unification's victims.

   In 2002 the PDS merged with leftist groups in the western federal states –
old-school Marxists, socialist idealists, opponents of liberal globalization – to

(b)

FIGURE 21.3 *(continued)*

form the new "Left Party" (*Die Linkspartei* or *Die Linke*), which in 2005 broke the 5 percent barrier to gain 8.7 percent of the vote and 54 seats in the 614-seat Bundestag, and in 2009 raised its strength robustly to 11.9 percent and 76 deputies. Crucial to the Left Party's advance was disaffection, particularly in West Germany, with the Social Democratic Party's emergent program of welfare and labor-force reform (see Figure 21.2). In day-to-day politics, the Left Party supports egalitarian and redistributive policies, champions the economically weak and opposes neoliberal globalization and armed engagement in foreign war zones.

Despite the Left Party's presence, the venerable West German mass-based parties – the labor-oriented Social Democrats and the center-right Christian Democrats – gradually became the predominant parties in the east, measured by popular vote, active party membership, and elective office holding. The Greens initially suffered a negative image in many easterners' eyes (as privileged "elitists" prepared to sacrifice jobs to environmentalism). Small right-radical parties – the aforementioned NPD (with roots, as Chapter 20 showed, in the Federal Republic), the German Social Union (DSU), and German People's Union (DVU) – sometimes show modest strength in municipal and federal state elections in the east (as do, in the west, National Democrats and right-radical Republicans [*Republikaner*]). East German rightists play especially on racist opposition to third-world and other immigrants of color, and on resentments

toward "Wessis." But Germany's right-wing parties, often beset by inner turmoil and controversy, have failed to surmount the 5 percent barrier to entry
into the federal parliament and seem unlikely to do so in the foreseeable future.

In the 1990s eastern intellectuals debated the desirability, in a slogan, of
"One State, Two Societies." Many wanted a political forum of their own, and
so joined the post-communist Party of Democratic Socialism. Acculturated in
the GDR, East Germans tended to be sympathetic to plebiscitary or grassroots
politics, and were suspicious of western-style, interest group-oriented parties
and representative democracy. There was some evidence of a specifically East
German inclination toward conflict-avoidance: in a 1994 poll, 58 percent supported the idea that politicians should pull together rather than oppose each
other (compared with 39 percent in the west voicing this opinion); 58 percent
in the east as against 31 percent in the west felt that politicians should give
citizens a feeling of *Geborgenheit* or "protectedness and security."

In the east, a wave of nostalgia is sometimes discernible, not for communism,
but for the cushioned and safe – if lower-middle-class and in various ways
shabby and provincial – pre-1989 society: "*Ostalgie*" (rather than "*Nostal-
gie*"). Deep-rooted regional identities among easterners, paired with a tendency
in the new federal states toward intermarriage among themselves, sometimes
weaken solidarity with West Germans. Yet, twenty years and more after the
fall of the Wall, and despite all embitterment and disappointment, there can be
little doubt that most East Germans prize citizenship in the Federal Republic.

Social Tensions and Multiculturalism in Unified Germany

Many left-leaning West Germans were skeptical about unification, including
such prominent intellectuals as philosopher Jürgen Habermas and Nobel Prize-
winning novelist Günter Grass. This was not because they admired the German
Democratic Republic, which few did. They feared the danger posed to pre-1989
West Germany's "post-national" liberal democracy by what seemed a possible
return to old-fashioned right-wing German nationalism. They worried that, if
the incorporation on liberal-democratic principles of the East German lands
did *not* succeed, then along with the German Democratic Republic the Federal
Republic might also fade and fall.

Such pessimism proved unjustified. But problems and dangers remained,
especially in economic life. Unification cost weaker elements of West German
society a share of their previously relatively good living standards, sacrificed
in rising taxes to finance investments and transfer payments from west to east,
which altogether amounted in the two decades after 1989 to the equivalent
of some $2 trillion (much of it lingering as government debt). Economic and
social conflicts arose in West Germany over distribution of the burden of East
German incorporation. The problem worsened at the turn of the millennium
because of competition facing German exports beyond the EU's boundaries,
and even within it, resulting – according to business management's and the
conservative parties' view – from high labor and social welfare costs.

Adoption in 2002 of the European Union's euro-currency in place of the trusted and internationally esteemed Deutsche Mark seemed, in many ordinary people's eyes, to entail price rises and weakening real incomes. Doubtless membership in the euro-zone exposes the Federal Republic to such internationally generated risks as the new currency may incur. Germany faces too the threat of losses within the Union that result – as was the case after the onset of the 2008 recession – from financial crises in member countries in which German euro-denominated investments are heavy, or where Germany, as the Union's strongest economic power, is expected to contribute to bailouts of indebted governments and failing banks.

Fears arose of competitive "Koreas in Bohemia," that is, of loss of German jobs to cheaper-labor economies in post-Communist eastern Europe, where since 2004 the stabilized and marketized democracies began entering the European Union. German banks and other entrepreneurs invested heavily in capital-short Poland, Hungary, and the Czech Republic – as some argued, to German workers' short-term disadvantage. West German working hours were long among the most advantageous in Europe, vacations among the lengthiest, retirements among the earliest. Publicly well-subsidized German university students were among the slowest to graduate in all of western Europe (although curriculum bottlenecks sometimes blocked students' path). Could these and other worker-friendly features of the West German welfare state long survive the unification with the GDR in an age of neoliberal globalization?

In this setting, anti-immigrant, anti-foreigner hostilities rose troublingly during the 1990s also in West Germany. Right-wing violence led to several alarming cases of arson against immigrants' dwellings and even to deaths. As in East Germany, this was, so far as physical violence went, the work of youth, but with sympathetic adults' tolerance. Far-right voting for the small and divided extremist parties – DSU, DVU, NPD, Republikaner – increased in both East and West Germany, but more in local and federal-state than national elections.

West Germany is a land of unprecedentedly high post-1945 immigration, including its present population of about seven million non-German foreign immigrants and their children. (Few people of immigrant background settled in post-1989 East Germany, though fear of racist hostility began to retreat before the possibility of employment there.) One-third of the entire 1990 West German population of about 60 million were immigrants to the state since 1945 or their children (the majority of them German expellees from east of the Oder-Neisse line and refugees from the German Democratic Republic). No comparable situation exists elsewhere among western nations.

In 2009, most people identified as "migrants" (including the formerly termed "guest workers") were ethnically non-Germans from the 1960s and 1970s and their children, together with political asylum seekers, mainly from third-world countries. Altogether, about 8 percent of the present-day Federal Republic's population are now non-German foreigners or their children; some 11 percent of children born annually have two foreign parents; another 5 percent have one foreign parent. Such is the multiculturalism that has blossomed in a Germany that, a half-century ago, the National Socialists sought so fanatically to reduce to monotone.

In 1993 chancellor Kohl's government imposed new restrictions on political asylum. This was politically unavoidable, because the number of entrants annually seeking refuge (almost exclusively in West Germany) was shooting annually into the hundreds of thousands (vastly more than other European countries admitted), even as similar numbers of East Germans moved westward. Reform of naturalization procedures was also essential, although some 140,000 immigrants were acquiring citizenship each year prior to 1998 reforms carried out by the newly installed SPD-based government of chancellor Gerhard Schröder (1998–2005). These provided for automatic naturalization of children born to foreign immigrants who had resided legally in Germany for eight years or more. As in other advanced industrial societies, the aging native-born population, with a low birthrate at or below the level of demographic reproduction – in 2011 the German fertility rate stood at 1.4 children per woman at the end of her childbearing years – badly needs immigrants to enter the labor force. Otherwise, the ratio of workers to social security pensioners in the advancing twenty-first century is likely to fall from the present 3:1 close to 1:1, putting unmanageable strain on financing of retirement benefits.

Politics and Economics Since the Kohl Era

In the fall of 1998 Gerhard Schröder's SPD-Green alliance's election victory retired Helmut Kohl's Christian Democratic-Free Democrats coalition after fifteen years in power. Kohl had written an enduring page for himself in German history by decisive and skillful intervention in the political crisis of the collapsing German Democratic Republic, leading its population to embrace Christian Democratic formulas for unification. Kohl's diplomacy had also, by adroit arrangements with the Soviet Union and United States, successfully neutralized French and British reluctance to see Germany rise higher, through absorption of the GDR, on the European landscape. Kohl's government also showed strength in investing the huge sums necessary to underpin post-communist social order in the east. Among many critical charges were that West German business profited excessively from the eastern economy's high-speed privatization.

The 1998 transition from Kohl's right-center ("black-yellow") government to Schröder's "red-green" coalition showed that unification's costs and rigors had not driven the electorate to the right. Instead, most voters, including in the east, chose welfare-state liberalism with environmentalist accents. Schröder's government lent military support to the United States-led 1997 and 1999 NATO interventions attempting to shield former Yugoslav Bosnia and Kosovo from ethnic cleansing. This was the first commitment since 1945 of German soldiers to foreign missions that might entail on-the-ground fighting. The move was criticized from the domestic left, but NATO allies welcomed German troops. Schröder's government later declined to support the US-led

(a)

FIGURE 21.4. ANTI-IMMIGRANT SENTIMENT AND VIOLENCE
The deadliest instance of "hostility to foreigners" (*Ausländerfeindlichkeit*) occurred in May 1993, when arsonists set ablaze a house in West German Solingen, killing five Turkish residents. Germany counts some three million inhabitants of Turkish ethnicity, the country's largest minority. About one-fifth possess German citizenship. The rest hold Turkish passports, but they are mostly permanently and legally settled in Germany. They are gaining voice in national politics, as, for example, German-born Cem Özdemir (b. 1965), in 2011 prominent spokesman and national co-chairman of the Green Party. But the Federal Republic's labor needs and (to 1993) liberal asylum-granting policies attracted millions of other immigrants. The number of political refugees admitted before 1993 to West Germany posed an insoluble dilemma between the wish, in National Socialism's aftermath, to honor human rights and the burden reunification placed on public finances and job market.
(a) Turkish residents, joined by German supporters, demonstrate in 1993 at the site of the deadly Solingen blaze. Present at the burial of the victims, whose coffins were draped with Turkish flags, was, among other high dignitaries, German Foreign Minister Klaus Kinkel (FDP), whose attendance was a conciliatory gesture toward Turkey.
(b) right-radical (NPD) protesters, marching in 2007 against the construction of a mosque in former East German Nordhausen. Leading them are youthful men carrying a banner proclaiming "Stop the Islamization of Our Homeland." The GDR was largely isolated from contacts with non-European cultures. In many East German eyes, mass post-1989 unemployment casts immigrant workers in hostile light.
Source: (a) Anonymous. http://commons.wikimedia.org/wiki/File:Brandanschlag_solingen_1993.jpg; (b) Anonymous. http://antinazi.files.wordpress.com/2008/09/npd-hausen-201007.jpg.

(b)

FIGURE 21.4 *(continued)*

2003 war in Iraq, but contributed soldiers to a peacekeeping mission in northern Afghanistan that subsequently entailed battlefield losses.

Fall 2002 elections returned Schröder's SPD-Green coalition to power. The
Social Democrats – reaping 38.5 percent of all votes – suffered minor loss since
1998; the Greens at 8.6 percent gained two points. The Christian Democrats,
like the SPD, polled 38.5 percent, but their former liberal partners, the Free
Democrats, slipped to 7.4 percent. The Party of Democratic Socialism, weakened by leadership crises, fell nationwide below the 5 percent barrier (to 4
percent), although in the east it drew about 15 percent. Leftist dissatisfaction
with Schröder's efforts to bolster Germany's low-growth economy by social
welfare reform and concessions to employers led to secession from the SPD
and creation of the Left Party (*Linkspartei*), which won entry to the Bundestag
in 2005.

Schröder's government fell in the 2005 elections, which brought to power
a CDU-SPD "grand coalition," headed by the Federal Republic's first woman
chancellor, East German Christian Democrat Angela Merkel. The two coalition parties ran head to head (37 and 36 percent of seats, respectively). The
remainder of the electorate comprised liberals, leftists, and Greens in roughly
equal measure. The right-radical NPD reaped some 860,000 votes (1.8 percent). Long-term trends, since the 1950s and 1960s, had weakened the two
large "people's parties" (*Volksparteien*) to the advantage of pro-business liberals and Greens and leftists. Grand coalitions are unwieldy compromises,

whereas, for Social Democrats, "red-red-green" or "red-green-yellow" combinations are fragile undertakings, especially if leftists or pro-business liberals press divisive claims.

Below the level of national politics, right-radical parties, with votes aggregated, constituted a presence in 2009 in roughly the 1-9 percent range in various federal states, both in the west and the east. In state elections since 1998, single parties in this category surpassed the 5 percent barrier to gain seats in local legislatures in four instances (Brandenburg, Mecklenburg-Vorpommern, Sachsen [Saxony], and Sachsen-Anhalt, all in the east). These are protest parties, powered by post-communist hardships and anti-immigrant sentiment, comparable to, if weaker, than similar movements in France (*Front National*), Italy (Northern League), the Netherlands (Freedom Party), and other western European countries.

Survey data in 2009 suggested that some 15 percent of German secondary-school students harbored racist sentiments, while roughly 5 percent were involved to some degree with radical-right organizations or activities, which might include participation in a skinhead subculture. Far-right rock music found an audience. Recent scholarship suggests that radical right-wing or neo-fascist sentiment – racist resentment toward immigrants (particularly from Muslim countries), anti-Semitism, aggressive hostility toward elite-dominated "establishments," contempt for party-based democracy, defense of rightist violence – encompasses in western Europe, including Germany, about one-seventh of the population (whether this attitude finds expression in voting or not).

In 2011, the German federal government's domestic intelligence agency – the *Verfassungsschutz* (Constitutional Defense) – reported the number of right-radical activists nationwide at roughly 25,000, down from 65,000 in 1993. But the number of individuals categorized as prone to commit acts of political violence had risen in the same period from 5,600 to 9,500. It was hypothesized that, as far-right parties weakened, the ranks of potentially dangerous individuals expanded. Whether the Federal Republic – residents of which were among the leaders of Al Qaeda's September 11, 2001 attack on the United States – would suffer new and more extreme acts of terrorism driven by rightist anti-Islamism, or by self-styled Islamic radicalism, was a question increasingly preoccupying the police and political media.

After 2005, resurgent economic growth, propelled by Schröder's business-friendly reforms, buoyed Angela Merkel's government. But in the fall of 2008, global financial crisis and recession struck the Federal Republic as they did other countries. German banks' devalued ("toxic") domestic assets were relatively less massive than in other large western economies, but the security of huge German investments in the less developed European Union countries grew questionable. Germany's traumatic memories of post-1918 and post-1945 currency collapse had long underpinned a public policy of low government deficits and avoidance of ballooning credit-card debt among the consuming public (although unification's costs caused public debt to soar). In 2008–2009 government spending – aimed at rescuing beleaguered banks, subsidizing wages

FIGURE 21.5. POST-UNIFICATION POLITICAL CULTURE

Pictured here is the assembly hall of the federal parliament (Bundestag), housed in the Reichstag building of Bismarck's day. Long a semi-ruin backing onto the Berlin Wall, it underwent architectural renewal when, after reunification, the Bundestag moved from Bonn to Berlin. The glass dome, casting natural light on the debating floor, symbolizes transparency of the democratic process. Nationalist ornamentation, apart from the original (unbelligerent) external sculptures, is – except for the iconic eagle – absent.

Power rivalries tempt the political parties to illegal special-interest contributions and money-raising schemes, resulting in occasional scandals. Yet the channeling of campaigns through publicly owned and controlled television and radio stations lends electioneering a comparatively modest air, reinforced by post-1945 (and post-1989) aversion to nationalist accents and grandiose ideological programs. Although all parties seek embodiment in sympathetic and, if possible, charismatic individuals, emphasis under the parliamentary constitution on parties – voters cast two ballots, one for a Bundestag deputy in their district, and one for a party at the national level – focuses attention on competing platforms.

Only the Free Democrats lean toward free-market libertarianism, so it is sometimes quipped that Germany is a country with four Social Democratic – that is, strongly pro-welfare-state – parties (CDU/CSU, SPD, Greens, Left Party). Significant programmatic choices and differences of discourse among the parties nevertheless tend strongly to determine voter preferences. The 5 percent representation barrier works to stabilize to forestall rising unemployment, and stimulating consumer demand – again generated a budget deficit larger than EU guidelines allow (that is, larger than 3 percent of GDP). German co-responsibility, within the European Union, for assisting debt-stricken member governments to evade crises of bankruptcy inflamed anti-EU sentiment among voters, spurring Merkel's cabinet to redouble its fiscal-conservative hard line.

Chancellor Merkel's education in the GDR taught her Russian, while Russian Prime Minister Vladimir Putin's work in the Soviet secret police (KGB) when stationed in the GDR taught him German. Recognition of the crucial importance of Russian acquiescence in German unification combines with Germany's vital economic interest in Russia's import market and natural gas and petroleum exports to make relations with Moscow hardly less important that those with Washington, D.C. German political self-understanding values the role of mediator and peacemaker with Russia. This has sometimes burdened its relations with Poland and the Czech Republic, whose populations have in any case been slow to abandon resentment over National Socialism's brutal wartime policies, and where Cold War–era West German backing for east European liberation from the Muscovite straitjacket is widely seen to have been subordinated to reluctance to upset the 1970–1972 status quo. Yet the Federal Republic has staunchly advocated its Slavic neighbor countries' integration on favorable terms into the EU. Heavy German investment has helped propel Polish economic growth forward at a fast pace. Coordination of fiscal policies between the two states has worked in Germany to minimize the effect of the post-2008 banking crisis and economic recession and in Poland to avoid financial crisis and maintain a GDP growth rate reckoned for 2011 at over 4 percent.

In the aftermath of the world financial crash of 2008, the chief challenge the Federal Republic faces is to sustain and, so far as possible, raise demand on foreign markets for its industrial goods, which have long enjoyed the highest of reputations. Should exports falter, unemployment and corresponding contraction of domestic consumption would follow, at least until orientation to

---

FIGURE 21.5 *(continued)* government based on parliamentary coalitions. More important still is the 1949 constitution's provision of the "constructive vote of no confidence," barring the Bundestag from removing a sitting government without a new majority party or coalition waiting in the wings to immediately replace it.

The mainstream political culture proscribes racism, right-wing radicalism, and leftist violence. The Bundestag-represented parties advocate, with varying fervor and success, multicultural representation of all German citizens, regardless of ethnicity. They condemn radical rightists and neo-Nazis as disreputable extremists skirting the fringes of the 1949 constitution's and the federal supreme court's banning of antidemocratic movements.
Source: Wolfgang Glock.

new markets occurred. Such a trajectory's political consequences are imponderable, but they would likely be turmoil-stricken. In this uncertain situation, Chancellor Merkel's government's policy favored international cooperation, both in the EU and with the United States, China, and Japan, to recapitalize the banking system under stricter international rules and restore credit flows and investment.

The financial crisis of 2008 did not halt rapid industrialization and economic growth in China, India, Brazil, and other nonwestern economies, where demand for German machine tools, heavy industrial and environmental technology, digital hardware and other sophisticated products buoys employment and profits at home more effectively than elsewhere in the EU or the United States. By 2011 China was the world's largest buyer of Volkswagen vehicles – and poised to play the same role for automobile makers Mercedes-Benz and BMW. While German exports within the EU followed a declining curve (to 41 percent by sales value in 2011), business in Asia surged forward (to 16 percent). France was long Germany's best export market, but in 2009 German capital investments were higher in China than across the Rhine. Such investments boomed after 2006 also in Russia, Brazil, and Japan, and (alone among EU countries) Poland, while they slumped strikingly (in ascending order of magnitude) in Spain, France, the United States, Italy, and Britain. Though embedded in the EU, the German economy is also increasingly an autonomous actor on the global stage.

The fall 2009 national elections registered seismic shifts in German politics. The Left Party surged forward, but the liberal-libertarian Free Democrats scored their history's biggest success with nearly 15 percent of the vote, enabling them to join as sole partners with Merkel's Christian Democrats in a new coalition government. The Green movement also advanced (to nearly 11 percent), but is now the smallest contingent in Germany's five-party system. The Christian Democrats (CDU/CSU) slipped to below 34 percent, but remained in power. It was the Social Democrats, plummeting from 34 percent in 2005 to 23 percent in 2009, who paid the price of their rivals' gains (especially by the Left Party).

Despite the post-2008 economic crisis, the number of unemployed in the fall of 2009 (3.2 million) was lower than the 2005 peak of 5 million – testimony, evidently, to the success of the post-2005 recovery, post-2008 governmental job-shielding policies, and to the German economy's enduring strength on world export markets. Proportional to the work-seeking labor force, unemployment nationwide stood in November 2009 at 8.1 percent (6.9 percent in former West Germany, 12.3 in the former GDR). By July 2010 nationwide unemployment had fallen to 7.6 percent (6.6 percent west, 11.5 percent east). In July 2011 the national figure had reached 7.0 percent, encompassing 2.95 million job-seekers. Absolutely and relatively, fewer Germans were out of work in 2011 than in the mid-1990s or even in 2009.

Among the employed there were in 2011 some 1.4 million whose low earnings qualified them for wage and rent subsidies costing taxpayers some 11 billion euros annually. Although it was long thought that the strong wages secured in German labor union contracts would establish a favorable wage-floor without need for government intervention, critics now hold that only adoption of a national minimum wage will alleviate the plight of the working poor. Conservatives advocate retraining among the marginally skilled for better-paid positions.

In the 1960s, when the "economic miracle" faltered, it was Willy Brandt's Social Democrats who gained the reins of power. In 2009, the electorate preferred center-right government or reinforcement of the environmentalist and leftist camps. Yet subsequent federal-state elections revealed seesawing among the voters to the Social Democrats' advantage and Christian Democrats' and Liberals' consternation. In 2011 Greens and Social Democrats unseated the long-regnant Christian Democrats in the prosperous and economically advanced southwestern state of Baden-Württemberg. In eastern Mecklenburg-Vorpommern the liberal Free Democrats fell under the 5 percent barrier while the Left Party, Greens, and Social Democrats advanced. In Berlin, although the SPD retained mayoral power, the Pirate Party (*Piratenpartei Deutschland*) sailed past the 5-percent barrier – for the first time since its 2006 emergence in Germany – to take seats in the urban parliament, where SPD and Greens were likely to form the majority. Drawing its support from younger citizens engaged professionally and existentially in the dizzily developing digital culture, the Pirate Party, like its counterparts in Scandinavia and elsewhere in Europe, advocates both protection of individual privacy, broadening of the public domain in cyberspace, and transparency of governmental practice.

In 2010-2011, citizens' protest movements multiplied as they had done in left-leaning circles in West Germany of the 1980s. Now more centrist, they targeted Germany's continued reliance on nuclear energy and bureaucratic high-handedness in city planning. The press spoke of "enraged citizens" (*Wutbürger*) seeking to revitalize grassroots democracy and challenge the established parties' pretentions to speak for the nation. One immediate reaction of chancellor Merkel and the Bundestag was to legislate closure of nuclear energy generators by the 2020s.

By mid-2011 a sovereign debt crisis gripped the EU's Mediterranean member states. GDP growth within the EU – including in Germany – slumped toward standstill. The German and French governments pledged leadership in building new centralized institutions to regulate and stabilize EU banking and fiscal policy. In Germany, public opinion bridled at the idea of refunding faltering member states through introduction of euro bonds – new debt in which Germany, with the EU's biggest economy, would unavoidably hold a major share. Unpopular too were further German contributions to emergency funds widely reviled as bailouts for spendthrift neighbor countries and their over-indebted banks.

Yet there was no alternative in German public discourse to upholding and strengthening the EU. Reopening Berlin's wallet would, it seemed, prove unavoidable. At the same time, chancellor Angela Merkel voiced a long German

FIGURE 21.6. JEWISH PRESENCE (AND ABSENCE)

In the first post-1945 years, some half-million Jewish "displaced persons" (DPs) lived in West Germany in Allied-governed camps. Their presence was the Holocaust's painful reminder, eliciting anti-Semitic hostility among Germans still captive to National Socialist ideology. Eventually these refugees migrated to the West or to Israel, leaving but a small remnant of Germany's once numerous and influential Jewish population. While the Federal Republic's relations with Israel slowly crystallized in a positive if memory-tormented pattern, the GDR followed the Soviet Union in relegating post-1956 – and especially post-1967 – Israel to the camp of the "imperialist West."

In West Germany, some cultural figures of Jewish heritage, such as the Polish-born and Berlin-educated literary critic and public intellectual Marcel Reich-Ranicki (b. 1920), or the political publicist and sentinel against anti-Semitism Henryk M. Broder (b. 1946), rose to honors and eminence. West Germany's Jews found representation through the Central Council of Jews in Germany, founded in 1950 as the successor to the 1893-established Central Union of German Citizens of Jewish Faith. This body's postwar name points to fundamental identity changes, as most Jews resident in post-1945 Germany embraced a strong religious or Zionist self-understanding rather than a secular German one. Postcommunist immigration from Russia and eastern Europe roughly doubled the Jewish population, living mainly in Berlin and the former West Germany, to around 100,000.

In recent years the Central Council of German Sinti and Roma has gained recognition, representing the population, formerly known as Gypsies (*Zigeuner*), who faced genocidal policies under Hitlerism. Social outcasts, they faced great postwar difficulties in achieving organization, political voice, and – finally – a small degree of material compensation and acknowledgment of their losses. Meanwhile, German engagement in the Christian churches has weakened. Recent polls show that, in West Germany, only 8 percent of the population regularly attend Sunday church services (but this figure greatly varies regionally); in the "new federal states" just 2 percent do so.

Pictured here is Berlin's "Monument to the Murdered Jews of Europe," designed by U.S.-born architect Peter Eisenman and completed in 2005. It occupies a large space close to the Reichstag building and the Brandenburg Gate – that is, at the heart of historic Berlin. The controversy preceding construction of this imposing Holocaust memorial tradition of state steerage of economic life in saying, in 2011, that "politicians can't and won't simply run after the markets. The markets want to force us to do certain things" – for example, protect international bondholders' or bank creditors' interests above those of German taxpayers. "That we won't do. Politicians have to make sure that we're unassailable, that we can make policy for the people." The future would test such resolve.

Two decades after the Berlin Wall toppled, a many-dimensioned political culture dominates the scene, extending from the resentment-laden, nationalist right-wing fringe across the wide center ground of business-friendly liberals and Christian Democrats and the shifting terrain of the long-mighty, labor-anchored Social Democrats to the environmentalist, feminist, pacifist, grassroots-oriented Greens and the socialist-minded Left Party, while the cyberconscious Pirate Party raises preliminary waves. By contrast, fifteen years after World War I the Weimar Republic disappeared under a social and political tsunami.

Discomfort with multiethnic big-city life and skepticism toward sometimes rosy-lensed multiculturalist idealism continue to erupt on the Federal Republic's political landscape. They did so in 2010, when voices in the left-of-center Social Democratic Party and the right-of-center Christian Social Union, and among chancellor Merkel's Christian Democrats, lamented immigrants' alleged failure, particularly among Muslims, to embrace – in Kohl-era terminology – Germany's "core culture" (*Leitkultur*). This term signified the high German literary and artistic tradition, reaching to Goethe and beyond, and the Federal Republic's foundational political liberalism, harkening back to Kant. Cultural and racial or biological stereotyping dies hard, particularly when economic depression stalks the land. But mainstream politicians' better angels, like those of most other citizens, lead them to resist demagoguery and ethnic-cultural scapegoating. This they do both to affirm long-proclaimed liberal-democratic values, which public intellectuals such as philosopher Jürgen Habermas forcefully reiterate, and to avoid condemnation by world opinion that, especially in the United States and Britain, zealously monitors the possibility of German backsliding.

In eastern Germany's "five new federal states," the better-educated youth, like their elders in middle-aged cohorts, have mostly found work and acceptable

---

FIGURE 21.6 *(continued)* (initially the result of a citizens' initiative) was considerable, but public acceptance of its artistic and historical value followed its completion. While tragic and ominous, it incorporates a variety of heights and depths that are philosophically and historically suggestive. Preceding its construction was that of Berlin's Jewish Museum, completed in 2001. Its design by Polish-born American architect Daniel Libeskind emphasizes linearities, zigzags, breaks, and empty spaces, expressing both the continuities and disruptions in Jewish life in Germany, including, fatally, the Holocaust (represented by an empty tower). The museum's historical display avoids one-dimensionality and inevitabilism.
Source: Chaosdna.

FIGURE 21.7. CONTEMPORARY GERMAN ART
The Federal Republic has been the setting of artistic and literary work that bears comparison with pre-1933 German modernism's heights. The German Democratic Republic witnessed enduring achievements too, especially in prose fiction and – in its early years – in painting and film. But Soviet traditions of Socialist Realism and the propagandistic channeling of art for political effects took a heavy toll. In West Germany, the National Socialist trauma stood near the center of much high art, as here in the 1983 sculptural assembly, entitled *The End of the 20th Century* (1983), by multimedia artist Joseph Beuys (b. 1921), rebellious and ironical exponent of Dada tradition and postmodernism. This work ominously memorializes both war's wreckage and destruction of its victims, who seem to stare through lifeless eyes.

Günther Grass (b. 1927), 1999 Nobel laureate for literature, is perhaps the best known of postwar Germany's many powerful and politically engaged writers. His "Danzig trilogy" of novels, including the celebrated *Tin Drum* (1959), satirically represented National Socialist Germany as a scene of collective narcissism, psychopathology, and ignominious self-seeking. Grass himself repeatedly castigated Hitlerism's postwar survivals, along with other wanderings off the Social Democratic path to post-nationalist liberal democracy's haven. His admission in 2006 that he had served at World War II's end as a Waffen-SS infantryman damaged his reputation. For although his induction into that military branch had defeated his youthful aim to serve in the submarine fleet, and while he fired no shots with intent to kill, his inability to confess to this life episode offered yet another of many sorry spectacles of admirable and estimable Germans burdened by the National Socialist past.

Martin Walser (b. 1927), another towering and prolific West German writer, stood in his early career, like Grass and earlier-mentioned Heinrich Böll, on the political left. Yet in accepting in 1998 the prestigious Peace Prize of the German Book Trade, Walser identities. If nearly all easterners accept unification and the "socially responsible market economy," most are still in search of better and more secure places for themselves and more equal footing with West Germans. This will take time, and strong regional eastern identities will doubtless long prevail, as local identities do in West Germany as well – for example, among Bavarians, Rhinelanders, southwestern Germans ("Swabians"), and North Sea Germans ("Hanseatics").

FIGURE 21.7 *(continued)* sparked a scandal by bemoaning the "instrumentalization" and routinization of German "Auschwitz guilt," a charge he leveled at the domestic media and left-liberal intelligentsia. This provoked protest from the Central Council of Jews in Germany, drawing Walser into self-lacerating polemics both with Council president Ignaz Bubis and literary critic Marcel Reich-Ranicki. Evidently Walser, like many other less eminent Germans, buckled under the psychological and moral pressures of living with the National Socialist memory – a past that, as right-wing historian Ernst Nolte, instigator of the 1985 "Historians' Dispute," said, "does not want to pass away."

Any account of postwar German cultural history would need to appraise many artists and aesthetic orientations. Among them would be Pina Bausch (1940–2009), director and choreographer of the internationally influential Wuppertal Dance Theater. One of many outstanding painters is Anselm Kiefer (b. 1945), whose massive canvasses convey powerful dark visions of history and nature. Trained in East Germany but early exiles to West Germany were painters Gerhard Richter (b. 1932), whose virtuosity in both representative and nonrepresentative media, and evocations of German identity's ambiguities, have won great international acclaim; Sigmar Polke (1941–2010), proponent of "capitalist realism" and, later, pop art; and Neo Rauch (b. 1960), who mysteriously reworks the Expressionist and Surrealist traditions. Among many notable composers are Karlheinz Stockhausen (1928–2007), Hans-Werner Henze (b. 1926), and Wolfgang Rihm (b. 1952), prolific and innovative modernist/postmodernist, serial/post-serial musicians, estimable successors to the great composers of the German past. Internationally influential photographers include Thomas Struth (b. 1954), a large-format specialist, and Beate Gütschow (b. 1970). Many artful and illuminating films, some cataloged in this book's bibliography, issued from East Germany's DEFA Studio, especially in the 1950s and 1960s. Among postwar West Germany's leading film directors are Rainer Werner Fassbinder (1945–1982), Wim Wenders (b. 1945), Völker Schlöndorff (b. 1939), and Werner Herzog (b. 1942).

Notable for popular film successes is Tom Tykwer (b. 1965), director of the internationally successful 1998 film, *Run, Lola, Run*, which conjures, from a young woman's viewpoint, not the German past, but its present and future. Postcommunist films that successfully engaged GDR history included the comedy, *Goodbye, Lenin* (2003), directed by West German Wolfgang Becker (b. 1954), dealing with conflicting generational perspectives on the "fall of the Wall." *Other People's Lives* (2006), directed by Florian Henckel von Donnersmarck (b. 1973), addressed the moral disasters detonated by willing and unwilling involvement with the Stasi, and received Hollywood critics' 2007 Oscar award as best foreign film.

Source: © Artists Rights Society (ARS), New York/VG Bild-Kunst, Bonn/Bildarchiv Preussischer Kulturbesitz/Art Resource, NY.

Germany was never a monolithic country. Integrated into the widening EU, where both complex, transnational European and subnational regional identities are now flourishing, there is no foreseeable prospect it will become one. The mosaic that was once the Holy Roman Empire of the German Nation, although reduced in its colorful components, has not altogether faded away. Yet the dramatic turn of events in 1989-1990 has set in motion the emergence – in these pages' terminology – of a fifth, twenty-first-century nation, now taking shape under globalizing and multicultural skies, more stormy than benign.

Afterword

Germany, and Austria too, emerged from National Socialism's flames and Soviet communism's shadows as societies and political cultures whose genealogy today might plausibly be traced to the eighteenth-century Enlightenment. This is not to say that an enduring, natural (or mystical) entity – "Germany" – has advanced as if by providential evolution or natural law toward this state of affairs. Nor can we appeal to Hegel's "cunning of Reason" (*List der Vernunft*), whose dialectical and ironical twists and turns illuminated the historical process in his mind. As these pages have shown, the political nations that arose from the German-speaking population of central Europe took successively quite varied forms. Each was, in its originality, unpredictable from preceding vantage points.

Progenitors of new national structures and spirits were the great crises and ruptures this book has highlighted: the Thirty Years War, the collapse in Napoleon's day of the Holy Roman Empire, the nineteenth-century civil wars issuing in Bismarck's Empire (with its "friends" and "foes"), the tragic interlocking crises, colossal wars, and mass death of the 1914–1945 years, the Cold War division arising from 1945's profound moral and physical devastation, and 1989's fall of the Wall.

The historian's vision is biased toward discovering continuities and explaining unexpected turns by analyzing the preexisting matrix from which they issued – a procedure that can render itself absurd in infinite regression. We have seen, however, that at each radical juncture in the history of the German lands, certain structures and modalities of national or subcultural identity died away – or were killed off, by German or non-German hands. History is also truly seen as a succession of irrecoverable losses, sweeping away life forms that, in ethical or aesthetic terms, deserved – despite inevitable shortcomings – to endure, as well as those that did not.

Rebirth of a new Germany – for a while, of new Germanies – out of the moral and material catastrophe of National Socialism illustrates not only the recuperative powers of individual and collective humanity. It also shows that the land that fell under modern history's most ruthless and brutal dictatorship – imposed by some Germans on others, as well as on myriads of non-Germans – was a society and culture capable of refashioning its earlier, still vital and constructive forms of civilization to establish a meaningful and ethically higher life after the National Socialist catastrophe. If this challenge was more successfully met in the Federal Republic than in the German Democratic Republic, easterners recognized in National Socialism the ultimate source of their unfreedom, which millions of them yearned to overcome, some through socialism, some against it.

German civilizational structures were in part very old, deriving from the Christianity of medieval and early modern times. They were also creations of the Enlightenment: the rule of law encompassing all citizens, state power directed to technological and material improvement, free markets, civic voice and the Rights of Man. They encompassed too the bourgeois cultures and working-class subcultures of the industrial age. And they embraced the pursuits and promises of modern scholarship and science, which the National Socialists so destructively distorted, but which survive as compasses by whose workings the contemporary world may – and indeed must – find its way forward.

Enlightenment liberalism, born complexly out of Christian and other forms of premodern humanism, has contributed mightily to structuring a world in which countless people today seek their fortune and their cultural fulfillment. But industrialization and scientific technology, lionized by liberalism, have also created a world that may choke on its excesses and exhaust its natural resources, the more so as it is impossible to deny to one sovereign nation what others may possess and enjoy. It is imaginable that, in dialectical self-fulfillment and simultaneous self-contradiction, western society – and with it, perhaps, the world – will plunge into destructive turmoil at the very moment of its highest attainments. Such an outcome would perhaps not surprise Hegel and Marx although as nineteenth-century men, they believed that out of civilizational crisis higher forms of cultural and social life would emerge. Nor would it surprise history's tragic thinkers – among them Thucydides, Hobbes, Nietzsche, Freud, and Weber – and those many theologians, including St. Augustine, who never believed humanity capable of building the New Jerusalem.

In pondering the future of German central Europe, the precariousness of modern liberal civilization must be kept in sight. Capitalism's "creative destruction" – as economist Joseph Schumpeter termed it – may rise to towering proportions. Science has already mixed some fatal cocktails, and there will be more. Global warming may dry up survival's springs. There is no time for complacency about the western world's attainments, to which German civilization has made many contributions. And the German lands' experience under National Socialism shows that a society's catastrophic setbacks and disappointed expectations may be responded to in the cruelest and most self-deluded, self-exalting and self-obliterating ways.

Mass destruction of imagined enemies tempts when national or civilizational scenarios fail. Yet this book has shown that the blueprints a society constructs for itself may be redrawn. Experience has made present-day political culture in the German lands mindful of this potentially saving social power, which can lead humanity away from economic and ecological crisis. Societies need not harbor messianic hopes for the future or counterproductive trust in the past. It is better to ponder history – not to harden identities, but to demystify them – and set sail anew.

Bibliography

Memoirs and Other Primary Sources in Translation,
English-Language Historical Studies,
Subtitled German Films

For more than two hundred years the study of German history has paid homage to
the empirical method. This entails avoiding appeals to religious or other metaphysical
authority while advancing analysis with internally consistent logic and conformity to
relevant known primary sources (that is, those generated by the historical actors in question). Since the birth of historicism or "scientific history," of which this book has briefly
spoken, scholarly publication of research monographs and articles, alongside broader
works of synthesis – not to mention annotated editions of primary-source documents –
has raised up a historical Himalaya that no one can fully traverse. Until the post-1945
decades, the pioneering work was overwhelmingly the product of German-speakers'
pens and minds, so that Anglophone students must eventually learn the language and
gain acquaintance with German historiographical traditions and styles of thought and
expression.

Yet the upheavals and traumas of the world wars greatly swelled the ranks of gifted
and industrious Anglo-American scholars devoting themselves – as a small number had
previously done – to German history in the early modern and modern eras. In many
cases their work has been of pioneering originality, sparking debates into which German historians have energetically plunged. Since the 1960s, the international republic
of letters' subsection devoted to this field has grown to encompass many historians
in western Europe, especially Great Britain but also France and Italy, and in north
America, especially the United States, where German history gained depth and stature
from the arrival after 1933 of eminent émigrés and refugees. As historians in Germany
sometimes wryly observe, the market for works in their field is larger in Britain and the
United States than at home, and they are as interested in having their work translated
into English as their Anglophone colleagues are in German-language versions of their
writings.

The curious reader can, therefore, now widely explore German history by reading
the English-language literature alone. This bibliography points beyond itself to readily
available specialized listings of English-language works, as well as to collections of
historical documents in English translation. It identifies numerous high-quality English-
language research monographs and interpretive syntheses, including translations of
vital works by German historians. It offers too – unusually in books of this sort – a
substantial list of translated personal memoirs and novels in the realist tradition, and of

major landmarks in German philosophy and political thought. Here also the reader will find a guide to readily available, subtitled films depicting German life, psychology, and collective fantasy in one or another historical epoch. Colleagues in the field will know that it is impossible in short compass to report the literature exhaustively. Journal articles, which commonly form the front line in historiographical advance, make no appearance here, although the major English-language journals are identified. Many important books too must be excluded, although the reader who follows the trails marked here will soon discover them.

I. Broad Surveys and Syntheses (With Extensive Bibliographies)

Beller, Steven. *A Concise History of Austria*. Cambridge University Press, 2006.

Blackbourn, David. *History of Germany, 1780–1918: The Long Nineteenth Century*. Blackwell, 2003.

Brady, Thomas A. *German Histories in the Age of Reformations, 1400–1650*. Cambridge University Press, 2009.

Bruford, Walter Horace. *Germany in the Eighteenth Century*. Cambridge University Press, 1968.

Clark, Christopher. *Iron Kingdom: The Rise and Downfall of Prussia, 1600–1947*. Harvard University Press, 2006.

Craig, Gordon. *The Germans*. Meridian, 1991.

Dwyer, Philip G., ed. *The Rise of Prussia: Rethinking Prussian History, 1700–1830*. Longman, 2000.

_____. *Modern Prussian History, 1830–1947*. Longman, 2001.

Evans, R.J.W. *The Making of the Habsburg Monarchy, 1550–1700: An Interpretation*. Oxford University Press, 1979.

Fulbrook, Mary. *A Concise History of Germany*. Cambridge University Press, 2004.

_____. *A History of Germany, 1918–2008: The Divided Nation*. Wiley-Blackwell, 2009.

Gagliardo, John G. *Germany under the Old Regime, 1600–1790*. Longman, 1991.

Gehler, Michael. *Three Germanies: West Germany, East Germany and the Berlin Republic*. Reaktion Books, 2010.

Ingrao, Charles. *The Habsburg Monarchy, 1618–1815*. Cambridge University Press, 2000.

Ingrao, Charles and Franz A.J. Szabo, eds. *The Germans and the East*. Purdue University Press, 2008.

James, Harold. *A German Identity: 1770–1990*. Routledge, 1989.

Jarausch, Konrad H. *After Hitler: Recivilizing Germans, 1945–1995*. Oxford University Press, 2006 (German original: 2004).

Jarausch, Konrad H. and Michael Geyer. *Shattered Past: Reconstructing German Histories*. Princeton University Press, 2003.

Kolinsky, Eva and Wilfried Van Der Will, eds. *The Cambridge Companion to Modern German Culture*. Cambridge University Press, 1998.

Macartney, C.A. *The Habsburg Empire, 1790–1918*. Macmillan, 1969.

Meyer, Michael A. and Michael Brenner et al., eds. *German-Jewish History in Modern Times*, 4 vols. Columbia University Press, 1996.

Nipperdey, Thomas. *Germany from Napoleon to Bismarck, 1800–1866*. Princeton University Press, 1996 (German original: 1984).

O'Dochartaigh, Pol. *Germany since 1945*. Palgrave Macmillan, 2004.

Okey, Robin. *The Habsburg Monarchy, c. 1765–1918: From Enlightenment to Eclipse.* Palgrave Macmillan, 2002.

Ritter, Gerhard. *The Sword and the Scepter: The Problem of Militarism in Germany*, 4 vols. University of Miami Press, 1969–1973 (German original: 1954–1960).

Sagarra, Eda. *A Social History of Germany, 1648–1914.* Holmes & Meier, 1977.

Scribner, Bob, Sheilagh Ogilvie, Richard Overy, eds. *Germany: A New Social and Economic History (1460 to the Present)*, 2 vols. St. Martin's Press/Bloomsbury, 1996–2003.

Sheehan, James J. *German History, 1770–1866.* Oxford University Press, 1989.

Smith, Helmut Walser. *The Continuities of German History: Nation, Religion, and Race across the Long Nineteenth Century.* Cambridge University Press, 2008.

Smith, Helmut Walser (ed.). *The Oxford Handbook of Modern German History.* New York: Oxford University Press, 2011.

Steinberg, Jonathan. *Why Switzerland?* Cambridge University Press, 1996.

Vierhaus, Rudolf. *Germany in the Age of Absolutism (1646–1763).* Cambridge University Press, 1988 (German original: 1984).

Watanabe-O'Kelly, Helen, ed. *The Cambridge History of German Literature.* Cambridge University Press, 1997.

Wehler, Hans-Ulrich. *The German Empire, 1871–1918.* Berg Publishers, 1985 (German original: 1973).

Winkler, Heinrich August. *Germany: The Long Road West.* 2 vols. Oxford University Press, 2006–2007 (German original: 2000).

II. Journals (With Reviews of the Current Literature)

Austrian History Yearbook (USA)
Bulletin of the German Historical Institute (London)
Bulletin of the German Historical Institute (Washington, DC)
Central European History (USA)
German History (UK)
German Politics and Society (USA – contemporary German issues)
German Studies Review (USA)
New German Critique (USA – literary and cultural studies)
http://www.H-GERMAN@H-NET.MSU.EDU

III. Primary Source Collections

German History in Documents and Images – http://germanhistorydocs.ghi-dc.org/index.cfm.
This important project, administered by the German government-sponsored German Historical Institute in Washington DC, offers massive documentation, in the original German together with modern English translations, of a wide set of themes – political, social, economic, cultural – in ten successive periods of German history since 1500. Accompanying the documents are bibliographies and numerous maps and annotated images. All materials are free for non-commercial use.

Gransow, Volker and Konrad H. Jarausch, eds. *Uniting Germany: Documents and Debates, 1944–1993.* Berghahn Books, 1994 (German original: 1991).

Helfferich, Tryntje, ed. *The Thirty Years War: A Documentary History.* Hackett Publishing Company, 2009.

Macartney, C.A., ed. *The Habsburg and Hohenzollern Dynasties in the Seventeenth and Eighteenth Centuries.* Macmillan, 1970.

Noakes, Jeremy and Geoffrey Pridham, eds. *Nazism: A History in Documents and Eyewitness Accounts, 1919–1945.* 2 vols. Schocken, 1983–1984.

Schieder, Theodor et al., eds. *Documents on the Expulsion of the Germans from Eastern-Central-Europe,* 4 vols. Bonn: Federal Ministry for Expellees, Refugees, and War Victims, 1956–1961.

_____. *The Nürnberg Case, as Presented by Robert H. Jackson, Chief of Counsel For the United States, Together With Other Documents.* Knopf, 1947.

_____. *The Trial of German Major War Criminals by the International Military Tribunal Sitting at Nuremberg, Germany,* 4 vols. Hein, 2001 (British original: 1946).

_____. *The Unification of Germany in 1990: A Documentation.* Bonn: The Press and Information Office of the Federal Government, 1991.

IV. Contemporary Memoirs and Novels

These translations, mostly in modern editions, are cited in roughly chronological order of their composition or of their themes. Other English-language versions may exist.

Grimmelshausen, Hans Jacob von. *Adventures of a Simpleton ("Simplicissimus")* (fiction). Continuum, 2002 (German original: 1669–1669). Fuller translations are also available.

Glikl bas Judah Leib (Gluckel of Hameln), *Memoirs.* Schocken, 2002 (Yiddish original: before 1724).

Dietz, Johann. *Surgeon in the Army of the Great Elector, and Barber to the Royal Court: From the Old Manuscript in the Royal Library of Berlin.* Dutton, 1923 (written before 1738).

Boswell, James. *Boswell on the Grand Tour: Germany and Switzerland 1764* (Boswell's journal). McGraw Hill, 1953.

Bräker, Ulrich. *The Life Story and Real Adventures of the Poor Man of Toggenburg.* Edinburgh University Press, 1970 (German original: 1763–1798).

Aldington, Richard, ed. *Letters of Voltaire and Frederick the Great (1750–53).* Brentano's, 1927.

Paret, Peter, ed. *Frederick the Great: A Profile.* Hill and Wang, 1972.

Goethe, Johann Wolfgang von. *The Sorrows of Young Werther* (fiction). Signet, 2005 (among many editions) (German original: 1774–1787).

_____. *Goethe (Life & Times).* Haus Publishing, 2005. One of several versions of Goethe's autobiography of his early life, *Poetry and Truth* (German original: 1808–1831).

Mirabeau, Honoré Gabriel Riquetti. *The Secret History of the Court of Berlin; Or, the Character of the Present King of Prussia.* Barrie, 1900 (first published, London 1789).

Staël, Anne-Louise-Germaine, Madame de. *Germany.* Houghton-Mifflin, 1887 (translation of *De l'Allemagne* [1813]).

Metternich, Clemens Wenzel Lothar. *Metternich: The Autobiography, 1773–1815.* Ravenhall, 2004.

Walter, Jakob. *The Diary of a Napoleonic Foot-Soldier.* Penguin, 1993 (German original: ca. 1840).

Heine, Heinrich. *The Harz Journey and Selected Prose.* Penguin, 1990 (memoirs and fiction, mainly of the 1830s and 1840s).

Freytag, Gustav. *Debit and Credit* (novel of German-Jewish-Polish relations). Howard Fertig, 1990 (German original: 1855).

Fontane, Theodor. *Before the Storm: A Novel of the Winter of 1812–13*. Oxford University Press, 1985 (German original: 1878).

_____. *Effi Briest* (novel of Imperial Germany). Penguin, 2001 (German original: 1885).

Schopenhauer, Johanna. *A Lady Travels: Journeys in England and Scotland from the Diaries of Johanna Schopenhauer*. Routledge, 1988 (German original: 1818).

Lewald, Fanny. *The Education of Fanny Lewald: An Autobiography*. State University of New York Press, 1992 (German original: 1861).

Loring, Charles Brace. *Home-life in Germany*. Scribner, 1853.

Wagner, Richard. *My Life*. Cambridge University Press, 1983 (German original: 1864/1911).

Bismarck, Otto von. *Memoirs, Being the Reflections and Reminiscences of Otto, Prince von Bismarck, Written and Dictated By Himself After His Retirement From Office*. Howard Fertig, 1966.

_____. *Reflections and Reminiscences*, excerpted, with an introduction by Theodore S. Hamerow. Harper and Row, 1968.

Vizetelly, Henry. *Berlin under the New Empire. Its Institutions, Inhabitants, Industry, Monuments, Museums, Social Life, Manners, and Amusements* (a British observer's account), 2 vols. Greenwood, 1968 (originally published in Britain: 1879).

Mann, Thomas. *Buddenbrooks: The Decline of a Family* (fiction). Everyman's Library, 1994 (German original: 1901).

_____. *The Magic Mountain* (fiction). Everyman's Library, 2005 (German original: 1927).

_____. *The Letters of Heinrich and Thomas Mann, 1900–1949*. University of California Press, 1998.

Kelly, Alfred, ed. *The German Worker: Working-Class Autobiographies from the Age of Industrialization*. University of California Press, 1987.

Sidgwick, Cecily (Ullmann). "Mrs. Alfred Sidgwick." *Home Life in Germany*. Macmillan, 1908.

Steed, Henry Wickham. *The Hapsburg Monarchy*. Constable, 1913.

Hesse, Hermann. *Beneath the Wheel* (fiction). Picador, 2003 (German original: 1906).

_____. *Steppenwolf: A Novel*. (fiction). Picador, 2002 (German original: 1927).

Musil, Robert. *The Confusions of Young Torless* (fiction). Penguin, 2001 (German original: 1906).

_____. *The Man Without Qualities* (fiction), 2 vols. Vintage, 1996 (German original: 1931–1932).

Bebel, August. *My Life* (memoir). Cornell University Press, 2009 (German original: 1913).

William II. *The Kaiser's Memoirs, Wilhelm II, Emperor of Germany, 1888–1918*. Harper Brothers, 1922 (German original: 1922).

Kafka, Franz. *Diaries*. Schocken, 1988 (written in 1910–1923; German original: 1949).

Broch, Hermann. *The Sleepwalkers* (fiction). Vintage, 1996 (German original: 1926).

Döblin, Alfred. *Berlin Alexanderplatz. The Story of Franz Biberkopf* (novel of Weimar-era Berlin). Continuum, 2005 (German original: 1929).

Roth, Joseph. *The Radetzky March* (novel of late Habsburg monarchy). Everyman's Library, 1996 (German original: 1932).

Canetti, Elias. *The Tongue Set Free. Remembrance of a European Childhood* (memoirs of a Jewish-born writer from Danubian and Habsburg Europe). Farrar, Strauss and Giroux, 1979 (German original: 1977).

Allen, William Sheridan, ed. *The Infancy of Nazism. The Memoirs of Ex-Gauleiter Albert Krebs, 1923–1933*. Franklin Watts, 1976 (German original: 1959).

Abel, Theodore. *Why Hitler Came into Power* (National Socialist autobiographies collected in the 1930s). Harvard University Press, 1986 (originally published: 1938).

Toller, Ernst. *I Was a German: The Autobiography of a Revolutionary* (émigré memoir). Paragon, 1991 (German original: 1936).

Scholem, Gershon. *Walter Benjamin: The Story of a Friendship* (Weimar-era memoir). NYRB Classics, 2003 (German original: 1981).

Charlotte Beradt, *The Third Reich of Dreams: The Nightmares of a Nation 1933–1939* (compilation of opposition-minded people's dreams, recorded under the dictatorship). Quadrangle, 1968 (German original: 1966).

Sender, Toni. *The Autobiography of a German Rebel* (émigré memoir). Vanguard, 1939.

Plotkin, Abraham. *An American in Hitler's Berlin: Abraham Plotkin's Diary, 1932–33*. University of Illinois Press, 2009.

Lubrich, Oliver, ed. *Travels in the Reich, 1933–1945: Foreign Authors Report from Germany*. The University of Chicago Press, 2010 (German original: 2004).

Shirer, William L. *Berlin Diary: The Journal of a Foreign Correspondent, 1934–1941*. Johns Hopkins University Press, 2002.

Schuschnigg, Kurt. *My Austria*. Knopf, 1938.

Gay, Peter. *My German Question: Growing Up in Nazi Berlin*. Yale University Press, 1999.

Haffner, Sebastian. *Defying Hitler* (1939 German memoir). Picador, 2003.

Reck-Malleczewen, Fritz Percy. *Diary of a Man in Despair* (National Socialist-era journal, published 1947 in Germany). Collier, 1972.

Klemperer, Victor. *I Will Bear Witness. A Diary of the Nazi Years*. 2 vols. Random House, 1998–99 (German original: 1996).

Jarausch, Konrad, ed. *Reluctant Accomplice: A Wehrmacht Soldier's Letters from the Eastern Front*. Princeton University Press, 2010.

Goebbels, Joseph. *Diaries. 1939–1941*: Putnam, 1983; *1942–1943*: Greenwood, 1970; *1945*: Pen and Sword, 2008.

Zweig, Stefan. *The World of Yesterday. An Autobiography* (German émigré memoir, written in 1939–1941). New York, 1943.

Maschmann, Melita. *Account Rendered: A Dossier on My Former Self* (reflections on a National Socialist youth). Abelard-Schuman 1964 (German original: 1963).

Andreas-Friedrich, Ruth. *Berlin Underground 1938–1945* (oppositionist memoir). Paragon House, 1989 (German original: 1947).

Vassiltchikov, Marie. *Berlin Diaries 1940–1945*. Vintage, 1988 (English original: 1985).

[Anonymous]. *A Woman in Berlin. Eight Weeks in the Conquered City. A Diary* (written in 1945). Metropolitan, 2005 (German original: 1953/2003).

Speer, Albert. *Inside the Third Reich* (memoirs). Ishi, 2009 (German original: 1969).

Zassenhaus, Hilgunt. *Walls. Resisting the Third Reich – One Woman's Story* (memoir). Beacon Press, 1993 (German original: 1974).

Johnson, Eric A. and Karl-Heinz Reuband, eds. *What We Knew. Terror, Mass Murder, and Everyday Life in Nazi Germany. An Oral History*. Basic Books, 2005.

Levi, Primo. *Survival in Auschwitz/If This Is a Man*. Touchstone, 1996 (Italian original: 1958).

Sereny, Gita. *Into That Darkness: An Examination of Conscience* (1971 interviews with Treblinka death-camp commandant Franz Stangl). Vintage, 1983.

Gilbert, G.M. *Nuremberg Diary* (American prison psychologist's interviews of the chief Nuremberg Trial defendants). Signet, 1947.

Liddell Hart, Basil. *The German Generals Talk* (postwar interviews with National Socialist commanders). W. Morrow, 1948.

Mayer, Milton. *They Thought They Were Free. The Germans, 1933–45* (postwar interviews with National Socialist supporters). University of Chicago Press, 1955.

Adenauer, Konrad. *Memoirs* (1945–1953). H. Regnery, 1966 (German original: 1965).

Reich-Ranicki, Marcel. *The Author of Himself: The Life of Marcel Reich-Ranicki* (memoir). Princeton University Press, 2001 (German original: 1995).

Grass, Günter. *Peeling the Onion* (memoir). Mariner Books, 2008 (German original: 2006).

_____. *The Danzig Trilogy* (three novels). Pantheon, 1987 (German originals: 1959–63).

_____. *Crabwalk* (novel). Mariner, 2004 (German original: 2002).

Böll, Heinrich. *The Lost Honor of Katherina Blum* (novel). Penguin, 1994 (German original: 1974).

Torberg, Friedrich. *Tante Jolesch, or the Decline of the West in Anecdotes*. Ariadne, 2008 (Austrian original: 1975).

Wolf, Christa. *Patterns of Childhood/A Model Childhood* (East German memoir, 1976). Farrar, Strauss and Giroux, 1980.

Schneider, Peter. *The Wall Jumper: A Berlin Story* (novel) University of Chicago Press, 1998 (German original: 1982).

Bahro, Rudolf. *From Red to Green* (British interviews with East German dissident). Verso, 1984.

Plenzdorf, Ulrich. *The New Sufferings of Young W.* (East German dissident novel, 1976). Waveland Press, 1996.

Brandt, Willy. *My Life in Politics*. Penguin, 1992 (German original: 1982–89).

Schmidt, Helmut. *Men and Power. A Political Retrospective*. Jonathan Cape, 1990 (German original: 1987).

Müller, Herta. *The Land of Green Plums* (fictionalized memoir of a Germanphone novelist of life in communist Romania). Granta, 1999 (German original: 1993)

Hasselbach, Ingo. *Führer-Ex: Memoirs of a Former Neo-Nazi*. Random House, 1996.

Walser, Martin. *The Burden of the Past: Martin Walser on Modern German Identity: Texts, Contexts, Commentary*. Camden House, 2008.

Hensel, Jana. *After the Wall: Confessions from an East German Childhood and the Life that Came Next*. PublicAffairs, 2008 (German original: 2002).

Stern, Fritz. *Five Germanys I Have Known* (memoir of German-born American historian). Farrar, Straus and Giroux, 2006.

V. Significant and Influential Political and Philosophical Texts

These appear here in roughly chronological order.

In many cases these texts may be found in excerpted form in *German History in Documents and Images* – http://germanhistorydocs.ghi-dc.org/index.cfm (heading III, above). Some figure too, among many others, in the translations – invaluable, especially on literary and philosophical themes – published since 1990 under more than one hundred titles by Continuum Press in the series, *The German Library* (http://www.continuumbooks.com).

Lessing, Gotthold Ephraim. *The Education of the Human Race (1777–80)*, in idem, *Philosophical and Theological Writings*. Cambridge University Press, 2005.

Kant, Immanuel. "Idea for a Universal History with a Cosmopolitan Purpose," "An Answer to the Question: 'What is Enlightenment?'" "Perpetual Peace: A Philosophical Sketch," in idem, *Political Writings*. Cambridge University Press, 1991.

Herder, Johann Gottfried. *Reflections on the Philosophy of History of Mankind*. University of Chicago Press, 1968.

Dohm, Christian Wilhelm. *Concerning the Amelioration of the Civil Status of the Jews* (Berlin, 1781). Hebrew Union College-Jewish Institute of Religion, 1957.

Goethe, Johann Wolfgang von. *Faust*. Anchor, 1962, among other editions.

Hardenberg, Friedrich von/"Novalis." "Christendom or Europe," in idem, *Hymns to the Night and Other Selected Writings*. Bobbs-Merrill, 1960.

Schiller, Friedrich. *On the Aesthetic Education of Man*. Routledge, 1954.

Fichte, Johann Gottlieb. *Addresses to the German Nation*. Harper, 1968.

Hegel, Georg Wilhelm Friedrich. Excerpts from *Philosophy of History, Philosophy of Right and Law, and "Political Essays," in The Philosophy of Hegel*, ed. Carl Friedrich. Random House, 1953. See also the excerpts in *Reason in History*, ed. R.S. Hartman. Macmillan, 1953.

Ranke, Leopold von. "A Dialogue on Politics" and "The Great Powers," in Theodore H. Von Laue, *Leopold Ranke. The Formative Years*. Princeton University Press, 1950.

Heine, Heinrich. "Differing Conceptions of History," "On the History of Religion and Philosophy in German," and "Memoirs," in idem, *Selected Prose*. Penguin, 1993.

Feuerbach, Ludwig. Excerpts from *The Essence of Christianity* in Schirmacher, Wolfgang, ed. *German Socialist Philosophy* (New York: Continuum, 1997). See also the selections in this volume from Friedrich Engels's various works.

Marx, Karl. "Critique of Hegel's *Philosophy of Right*" and "On the Jewish Question," and Marx and Engels, *Manifesto of the Communist Party*, pp. 469–500, and idem, "Address of the Central Committee to the Communist League," in Robert C. Tucker, ed., *The Marx-Engels Reader*. Norton, 1978.

Engels, Friedrich. *Germany: Revolution and Counter-Revolution* (on the 1848 revolution), in idem, *The German Revolutions*, Leonard Krieger, ed. University of Chicago, 1967.

Mecklenburg, Frank and Manfred Stassen, eds., *German Essays on Socialism in the Nineteenth Century*. Continuum, 1990. Of particular interest are the selections from Eduard Bernstein, Rosa Luxemburg, and Karl Kautsky, and the sections on women, militarism, and anti-Semitism.

Kautsky, Karl. *The Class Struggle (Erfurt Program)*. Norton, 1971 (German original: 1902).

Nietzsche, Friedrich. Selections from *The Birth of Tragedy, Beyond Good and Evil, The Genealogy of Morals, and The Will to Power* in idem, *Philosophical Writings*, ed. Reinhold Grimm. Continuum, 1995. Good too are the excerpts from *Thoughts Out of Season* published as: Friedrich Nietzsche, *The Use and Abuse of History* (1873–74), ed. Julius Kraft (Bobbs-Merrill, 1949).

Wagner, Richard. *Wagner on Music and Drama*, eds. A. Goldman and E. Sprinchorn, New York, 1964. Note especially the excerpts from "Jews in Music" and "Christian Hypocrisy."

Treitschke, Heinrich von. *Politics* (University of Berlin lectures, 1880s). New York, 1963.

Weber, Max. *Political Writings*, eds. Peter Lassman and Ronald Speirs. Cambridge University Press, 1994. See also Weber's "Science as a Vocation" in *From Max*

Weber: Essays in Sociology, eds. H. Gerth and C.W. Mills. Oxford University Press, 1958.

Mann, Thomas. *Reflections of a Nonpolitical Man*. Ungar, 1987 (German original: 1918).

Kaes, Anton et al. *The Weimar Republic Sourcebook*. University of California Press, 1994.

Hitler, Adolf. *Mein Kampf* (translation by Ralph Manheim). Houghton Mifflin, 2001. This often misunderstood work should be read in connection with a competent scholarly study, such as Werner Maser's *Hitler's Mein Kampf: An Analysis* (Faber, 1970; German original: 1966), or that offered in the secoondary works on Hitler listed below. See also Gerhard L. Weinberg, ed. *Hitler's Second Book: The Unpublished Sequel to Mein Kampf* (Enigma, 2003). From the years of the dictatorship: *Hitler: Speeches and Proclamations, 1932–1945 – The Chronicle of a Dictatorship*, ed. Max Domarus. 4 vols. Bolchazy-Carducci, 2004; and *Hitler's Table Talk, 1941–1944*, ed. H.R. Trevor-Roper. Enigma, 2008.

Mosse, George, ed., *Nazi Culture: Intellectual, Social, and Cultural Life in the Third Reich*. University of Wisconsin Press, 2003.

Horkheimer, Max and Theodor W. Adorno. *Dialectic of Enlightenment*. Continuum, 1999 (German original: 1944).

Meinecke, Friedrich. *The German Catastrophe: Reflections and Recollections*. Harvard University Press, 1950 (German original: 1946).

Jaspers, Karl. *The Question of German Guilt*. Fordham University Press, 2001 (German original: 1947).

Victor Klemperer, *The Language of the Third Reich. LTI–Lingua Tertii Imperii. A Philologist's Notebook*. Continuum, 2006 (German original: 1949).

Heidegger, Martin. *Philosophical and Political Writings*, ed. M. Stassen (Continuum, 2003). Accessible are Heidegger's political writings, including "Only a God Can Save Us: *Der Spiegel*'s Interview (September 23, 1966)," and "The Question Concerning Technology" (1949).

Mitscherlich, Alexander and Margarete. *The Inability to Mourn. Principles of Collective Behavior*. Grove, 1975 (German original: 1967).

Weizsäcker, Richard von, President of the German Federal Republic, "Speech Commemorating the Fortieth Anniversary of the End of the War in Europe and of the National Socialist Regime," May 8, 1985, in Geoffrey Hartman, ed., *Bitburg in Moral and Political Perspective*. Indiana University Press, 1986.

Baldwin, Peter, ed. *Reworking the Past: Hitler, the Holocaust, and the Historians' Debate*. Documentation with commentary. Beacon Press, 1990.

Sebald, W.G. *On the Natural History of Destruction* (on German literature's treatment of the Allied bombing of Germany during World War II, by a wartime survivor and distinguished novelist). Modern Library, 2004 (German original, 1999).

VI. Selected Scholarly Studies

The English-language literature is – as noted earlier – enormous, and the German-language literature is larger still, with its masterpieces only very haphazardly translated into English. Cited here are mainly recent works dealing with the post-1648 period, which are distinguished by past or present influence of argument, empirical depth, and appeal to readers new to the subject. The reader should first consult the works cited in Section I at the beginning of this section. The numerous influential articles published in scholarly journals (notably those cited in Section II) must go unregistered here, as must also be the case with many worthy and interesting research monographs. Citation does not signal advocacy of one or another argument or interpretation. Works with a long chronological coverage are sometimes hard to pigeon-hole. Many studies in one way or another integrate political, social-economic, and intellectual-cultural history.

A. Works Spanning the Post-1648 Era and Age of the French Revolution

1. Political History

Beales, Derek. *Joseph II.* 2 vols. Cambridge University Press, 1987–2009.

Behrens, C.B.A. *Society, Government, and the Enlightenment: The Experiences of Eighteenth-Century France and Prussia.* Thames and Hudson, 1985.

Blanning, T.C.W. *Reform and Revolution in Mainz, 1743–1803.* Cambridge University Press, 1974.

———. *The French Revolution in Germany: Occupation and Resistance in the Rhineland, 1792–1802.* Oxford University Press, 1983.

Brewer, John and Eckhart Hellmuth, eds. *Rethinking Leviathan: The Eighteenth-Century State in Britain and Germany.* Oxford University Press, 1999.

Carsten, F.L. *Princes and Parliaments in Germany, From the Fifteenth to the Eighteenth Century.* Oxford University Press, 1959.

Craig, Gordon. *The Politics of the Prussian Army, 1640–1945.* Oxford University Press, 1955.

Friedrich, Karin. *The Other Prussia: Royal Prussia, Poland and Liberty, 1569–1772.* Cambridge University Press, 2000.

Ingrao, Charles W. *The Hessian Mercenary State: Ideas, Institutions, and Reform Under Frederick II, 1760–1785.* Cambridge University Press, 1987.

Levinger, Matthew. *Enlightened Nationalism: The Transformation of Prussian Political Culture, 1806–1848.* Oxford University Press, 2000.

McNeely, Ian F. *The Emancipation of Writing: German Civil Society in the Making, 1790s–1820s.* University of California Press, 2003.

Meinecke, Friedrich. *The Age of German liberation, 1795–1815* (German original: 1906). University of California Press, 1977.

———. *Machiavellism; The Doctrine of Raison d'État and Its Place in Modern History.* Yale University Press, 1957 (German original: 1924).

Paret, Peter. *Clausewitz and the State: The Man, His Theories, and His Times.* Princeton University Press, 2007.

Schieder, Theodor. *Frederick the Great.* Longman, 2000 (German original: 1983).

Wilson, Peter H. *Europe's Tragedy: A History of the Thirty Years War.* Allen Lane, 2009.

2. Society and Economy

Abrams, Lynn and Elizabeth Harvey, eds. *Gender Relations in German History: Power, Agency and Experience from the Sixteenth to the Twentieth Century.* Duke University Press, 1996.

Behringer, Wolfgang. *Witchcraft Persecutions in Bavaria: Popular Magic, Religious Zealotry, and Reason of State in Early Modern Europe.* Cambridge University Press, 1997 (German original: 1987).

Büsch, Otto. *Military System and Social Life in Old-Regime Prussia, 1713–1807: The Beginnings of the Social Militarization of Prusso-German Society.* Humanities Press, 1997 (German original: 1962).

Duden, Barbara. *The Woman Beneath the Skin: A Doctor's Patients in Eighteenth-Century Germany.* Harvard University Press, 1991 (German original: 1987).

Dülmen, Richard van. *Theatre Of Horror: Crime and Punishment in Early Modern Germany.* Blackwell, 1990 (German original: 1985).

_____. *The Society of the Enlightenment: The Rise of the Middle Class and Enlightenment Culture in Germany.* St. Martin's Press, 1992 (German original: 1986).

Evans, Richard J. and W.R. Lee, eds. *The German Peasantry: Conflict and Community in Rural Society from the Eighteenth to the Twentieth Centuries.* Croom Helm, 1986.

Gagliardo, John G. *From Pariah to Patriot: The Changing Image of the German Peasant, 1770–1840.* University Press of Kentucky, 1969.

Hagen, William W. *Ordinary Prussians: Brandenburg Junkers and Villagers, 1500–1840.* Cambridge University Press, 2002.

Hertz, Deborah. *How Jews Became Germans: The History of Conversion and Assimilation in Berlin.* Yale University Press, 2007.

Hull, Isabel V. *Sexuality, State, and Civil Society in Germany, 1700–1815.* Cornell University Press, 1996.

Lindemann, Mary. *Patriots and Paupers: Hamburg, 1712–1830.* Oxford University Press, 1990.

Luebke, David Martin. *His Majesty's Rebels: Communities, Factions, and Rural Revolt in the Black Forest, 1725–1745.* Cornell University Press, 1997.

Robisheaux, Thomas. *Rural Society and the Search for Order in Early Modern Germany.* Cambrige University Press, 1989.

_____. *The Last Witch of Langenburg: Murder in a German Village.* Norton, 2009.

Roper, Lyndal. *Witch Craze: Terror and Fantasy in Baroque Germany.* Yale University Press, 2006.

Sabean, David. *Power in the Blood: Popular Culture and Village Discourse in Early Modern Germany.* Cambridge University Press, 1984.

_____. *Property, Production, and Family in Neckarhausen, 1700–1870.* Cambridge University Press, 1990.

_____. *Kinship in Neckarhausen, 1700–1870.* Cambridge University Press, 1998.

Stuart, Kathy E. *Defiled Trades and Social Outcasts: Honor and Ritual Pollution in Early Modern Germany.* Cambridge University Press, 2000.

Taylor, Peter K. *Indentured to Liberty: Peasant Life and the Hessian Military State, 1688–1815.* Cornell University Press, 1994.

Walker, Mack. *German Home Towns: Community, State, and General Estate, 1648–1871.* Cornell University Press, 1971.

Wunder, Heide. *He Is the Sun, She Is the Moon: Women in Early Modern Germany.* Harvard University Press, 1998.

3. Intellectual and Cultural History

Beiser, Frederick C. *Enlightenment, Revolution, and Romanticism: The Genesis of Modern German Political Thought, 1790–1800.* Harvard University Press, 1992.

_____. *The Cambridge Companion to Hegel.* Cambridge University Press, 1993.

————. *The Romantic Imperative: The Concept of Early German Romanticism*. Harvard University Press, 2003.

Boyle, Nicholas. *Goethe: The Poet and the Age*. 2 vols. Oxford University Press, 1992–2000.

Brunschwig, Henri. *Enlightenment and Romanticism in Eighteenth-Century Prussia*. University of Chicago Press, 1974 (French original: 1947).

Gawthorp, Richard L. *Pietism and the Making of Eighteenth-Century Prussia*. Cambridge University Press, 1993.

Gray, Marion W. *Productive Men, Reproductive Women: The Agrarian Household and the Emergence of Separate Spheres during the German Enlightenment*. Berghahn Books, 2000.

Head, Randolph C. and Daniel Christensen, eds. *Orthodoxies and Heterodoxies in Early Modern German Culture: Order and Creativity, 1500–1750*. Brill, 2007.

Knudsen, Jonathan B. *Justus Möser and the German Enlightenment*. Cambridge University Press, 1986.

Koselleck, Reinhart. *Critique and Crisis: Enlightenment and the Pathogenesis of Modern Society*. MIT Press, 1988 (German original: 1973).

La Vopa, Anthony. *Grace, Talent, and Merit: Poor Students, Clerical Careers, and Professional Ideology in Eighteenth-Century Germany*. Cambridge University Press, 1988.

Marschke, Benjamin. *Absolutely Pietist: Patronage, Factionalism, and State-Building in the Early Eighteenth-Century Prussian Army Chaplaincy*. Niemeyer, 2005.

Melton, James Van Horn. *Absolutism and the Eighteenth-Century Origins of Compulsory Schooling in Prussia and Austria*. Cambridge University Press, 1988.

Reill, Peter Hanns. *The German Enlightenment and the Rise of Historicism*. University of California Press, 1975.

Saine, Thomas P. *The Problem of Being Modern, or the German Pursuit of Enlightenment from Leibniz to the French Revolution*. Wayne State University Press, 1997.

B. Works on the Long Nineteenth Century (to 1914)

1. Political History, including Austrian and German-Jewish History

Anderson, Margaret Lavinia. *Practicing Democracy: Elections and Political Culture in Imperial Germany*. Princeton University Press, 2000.

Applegate, Celia. *A Nation of Provincials: The German Idea of Heimat*. University of California Press, 1990.

Barclay, David E. and Eric D. Weitz, eds. *Between Reform and Revolution: German Socialism and Communism from 1840 to 1990*. Berghahn Books, 1998.

Berghahn, Volker R. *Germany and the Approach of War in 1914*. St. Martin's Press, 1993.

Blackbourn, David and Geoff Eley. *The Peculiarities of German History: Bourgeois Society and Politics in Nineteenth-Century Germany*. Oxford University Press, 1984.

Boyer, John. *Political Radicalism In Late Imperial Vienna: Origins of the Christian Social Movement, 1848–1897*. University of Chicago Press, 1981.

_____. *Culture and Political Crisis in Vienna: Christian Socialism in Power, 1897–1918*. University of Chicago Press, 1995.

Breuilly, John. *Austria, Prussia and Germany, 1806–1871*. Longman, 2002.

Caron, Vicki. *Between France and Germany: The Jews of Alsace-Lorraine, 1871–1918*. Stanford University Press, 1988.

Chickering, Roger. *We Men Who Feel Most German: A Cultural Study of the Pan-German League, 1886–1914*. Allen & Unwin, 1984.

Cohen, Gary B. *The Politics of Ethnic Survival: Germans in Prague, 1861–1914*. Purdue University Press, 2006.

Gall, Lothar. *Bismarck: The White Revolutionary*. 2 vols. Allen and Unwin, 1986 (German original: 1980).

Green, Abigail. *Fatherland: State-Building and Nationhood in Nineteenth-Century Germany*. Cambridge University Press, 2001.

Hagen, William W. *Germans, Poles, and Jews: The Nationality Conflict in the Prussian East, 1772–1914*. University of Chicago Press, 1980.

Hamerow, Theodore S. *Restoration, Revolution, Reaction: Economics and Politics in Germany, 1815–1871*. Princeton University Press, 1966.

_____. *The Social Foundations of German Unification, 1858–1871*. 2 vols. Princeton University Press, 1969–72.

Hewitson, Mark. *Nationalism in Germany, 1848–1866: Revolutionary Nation*. Palgrave Macmillan, 2010.

Hoffmann, Christhard, Werner Bergmann, and Helmut Walser Smith, eds. *Exclusionary Violence: Antisemitic Riots in Modern German History*. University of Michigan Press, 2002.

Hull, Isabel. V. *The Entourage of Kaiser Wilhelm II, 1888–1918*. Cambridge University Press, 1982.

_____. *Absolute Destruction: Military Culture and the Practices of War in Imperial Germany*. Cornell University Press, 2005.

Jefferies, Matthew. *Contesting the German Empire, 1871–1918*. Wiley-Blackwell, 2008.

Jones, Larry Eugene and James Retallack. *Elections, Mass Politics, and Social Change in Modern Germany*. Cambridge University Press, 1992.

_____, eds. *Between Reform, Reaction, and Resistance: Studies in the History of German Conservatism from 1789 to 1945*. Berg, 1993.

Judson, Pieter M. *Guardians of the Nation: Activists on the Language Frontiers of Imperial Austria*. Harvard University Press, 2006.

King, Jeremy. *Budweisers into Czechs and Germans: A Local History of Bohemian Politics, 1848–1948*. Princeton University Press, 2002.

Krieger, Leonard. *The German Idea of Freedom. History of a Political Tradition*. Beacon, 1957.

Langewiesche, Dieter. *Liberalism in Germany*. Princeton University Press, 2000 (German original: 1988).

Lidtke, Vernon L. *The Alternative Culture: Socialist Labor in Imperial Germany*. Oxford University Press, 1985.

Lüdtke, Alf. *Police and State in Prussia, 1815–1850*. Cambridge University Press, 1989 (German original: 1982).

May, Arthur J. *The Hapsburg Monarchy, 1867–1914*. Norton, 1968.

Mosse, George. *The Crisis of German Ideology: Intellectual Origins of the Third Reich*. Schocken Books, 1964.

Nettl, J.P. *Rosa Luxemburg*. Schocken Books, 1969.

Pflanze, Otto. *Bismarck and the Development of Germany*. 3 vols. Princeton University Press, 1963–1990.

Pulzer, Peter. *The Rise of Political Anti-Semitism in Germany and Austria*. Harvard University Press, 1988.

———. *Jews and the German State: The Political History of a Minority, 1848–1933*. Blackwell, 1992.

Repp, Kevin. *Reformers, Critics, and the Paths of German Modernity: Anti-Politics and the Search for Alternatives, 1890–1914*. Harvard University Press, 2000.

Retallack, James. *The German Right, 1860–1920: Political Limits of the Authoritarian Imagination*. University of Toronto Press, 2006.

Retallack, James, ed. *Saxony in German History: Culture, Society, and Politics, 1830–1933*. University of Michigan Press, 2000.

Schorske, Carl. *Fin-de-Siècle Vienna: Politics and Culture*. Vintage Books, 1981.

Schulze, Hagen. *The Course of German Nationalism. From Frederick the Great to Bismarck, 1763–1867*. Cambridge University Press, 1985.

Sheehan, James J. *German Liberalism in the Nineteenth Century*. Humanities Press, 1995.

Siemann, Wolfram. *The German Revolution of 1848–49*. St. Martin's Press, 1998 (German original: 1985).

Sked, Alan. *Metternich and Austria: An Evaluation*. Palgrave Macmillan, 2008.

Sperber, Jonathan. *Rhineland Radicals: The Democratic Movement and the Revolution of 1848–1849*. Princeton University Press, 1991.

———. *The Kaiser's Voters: Electors and Elections in Imperial Germany*. Cambridge University Press, 1997.

Steenson, Gary P. *Not One Man! Not One Penny!: German Social Democracy, 1863–1914*. University of Pittsburgh Press, 1981.

Stern, Fritz. *The Politics of Cultural Despair: A Study in the Rise of the Germanic Ideology*. University of California Press, 1961.

Verhey, Jeffrey. *The Spirit of 1914: Militarism, Myth and Mobilization in Germany*. Cambridge University Press, 2000.

Volkov, Shulamit. *Germans, Jews, and Antisemites: Trials in Emancipation*. Cambridge University Press, 2006.

2. Society and Economy

Blackbourn, David. *The Conquest of Nature: Water, Landscape, and the Making of Modern Germany*. Norton, 2006.

Brophy, James. *Popular Culture and the Public Sphere in the Rhineland, 1800–1850*. Cambridge University Press, 2007.

Brose, Eric Dorn. *The Politics of Technological Change in Prussia: Out of the Shadow of Antiquity, 1809–1848*. Princeton University Press, 1993.

———. *The Kaiser's Army: The Politics of Military Technology in Germany during the Machine Age, 1870–1918*. Oxford University Press, 2001.

Canning, Kathleen. *Languages of Labor and Gender: Female Factory Work in Germany, 1850–1914*. University of Michigan Press, 2002.

Cioc, Mark. *The Rhine: An Eco-Biography, 1815–2000*. University of Washington Press, 2002.

Dickinson, Edward Ross. *Sex, Freedom, and Power in the German Empire: Debates about Sexual Morality, 1880–1914* (forthcoming).

Evans, Richard J. *Death in Hamburg: Society and Politics in the Cholera Years 1830–1910*. Penguin Books, 1987.

_____. *Rituals of Retribution: Capital Punishment in Germany, 1600–1987*. Oxford University Press, 1996.

Frevert, Ute. *Women in German History: From Bourgeois Emancipation to Sexual Liberation*. Berg, 1989 (German original: 1989).

_____. *A Nation in Barracks: Modern Germany, Military Conscription and Civil Society*. Berg, 2004 (German original: 2001).

Goldberg, Ann. *Sex, Religion, and the Making of Modern Madness: The Eberbach Asylum and German Society, 1815–1849*. Oxford University Press, 1999.

_____.*Honor, Politics and the Law in Imperial Germany, 1871–1914*. Cambridge University Press, 2010.

Hett, Benjamin Carter. *Death in the Tiergarten: Murder and Criminal Justice in the Kaiser's Berlin*. Harvard University Press, 2004.

Kaplan, Marion A. *The Making of the Jewish Middle Class: Women, Family, and Identity in Imperial Germany*. Oxford University Press, 1991.

Kocka, Jürgen. *Industrial Culture and Bourgeois Society: Business, Labor, and Bureaucracy in Modern Germany*. Berghahn Books, 1999.

Kocka, Jürgen and Allan Mitchell, eds. *Bourgeois Society in Nineteenth-Century Europe*. Berg, 1993.

Ledford, Kenneth F. *From General Estate to Special Interest: German Lawyers 1878–1933*. Cambridge University Press, 1996.

Maynes, Mary Jo. *Taking the Hard Road: Life Course in French and German Workers' Autobiographies in the Era of Industrialization*. University of North Carolina Press, 1995.

Pierenkemper, Toni and Richard Tilly. *The German Economy during the Nineteenth Century*. Berghahn Books, 2005.

Quataert, Jean H. *Reluctant Feminists in German Social Democracy, 1885–1917*. Princeton University Press, 1979.

Rosenblum, Warren. *Beyond the Prison Gates: Punishment and Welfare in Germany, 1850–1933*. University of North Carolina Press, 2008.

Sperber, Jonathan. *Property and Civil Society in South-Western Germany, 1820–1914*. Oxford University Press, 2005.

3. *Intellectual and Cultural History*

Aschheim, Steven E. *The Nietzsche Legacy in Germany, 1890–1990*. University of California Press, 1992.

Biale, David. *Gershom Scholem: Kabbalah and Counter-History*. Harvard University Press, 1982.

Blackbourn, David. *Marpingen: Apparitions of the Virgin Mary in a Nineteenth-Century German Village*. Random House, 1995.

Breckmann, Warren. *Marx, the Young Hegelians, and the Origins of Radical Social Theory: Dethroning The Self*. Cambridge University Press, 1999.

Dahlhaus, Carl. *Richard Wagner's Music Dramas*. Cambridge University Press, 1979 (German original: 1971).

Giesen, Bernhard. *Intellectuals and the German Nation: Collective Identity in an Axial Age.* Cambridge University Press, 1998 (German original: 1993).

Iggers, Georg G. *The German Conception of History: The National Tradition of Historical Thought from Herder to the Present.* Wesleyan University Press, 1983.

Jeffries, Matthew. *Imperial Culture in Germany, 1871–1918.* Palgrave Macmillan, 2003.

Löwith, Karl. *From Hegel to Nietzsche: The Revolution in Nineteenth-Century Thought.* Holt, Rinehart and Winston, 1964 (German original: 1941).

Marchand, Suzanne L. *Down from Olympus: Archaeology and Philhellenism in Germany, 1750–1970.* Princeton University Press, 1996.

———. *German Orientalism in the Age of Empire: Religion, Race, and Scholarship.* Cambridge University Press, 2009.

Marchand, Suzanne and David Lindenfeld, eds. *Germany at the Fin-de-Siècle: Culture, Politics, and Ideas.* Louisiana State University Press, 2004.

Mommsen, Wolfgang J. *Max Weber and German Politics, 1890–1920.* University of Chicago Press, 1984 (German original: 1959).

Paret, Peter. *The Berlin Secession: Modernism and Its Enemies in Imperial Germany.* Harvard University Press, 1980.

Ringer, Fritz K. *The Decline of the German Mandarins: The German Academic Community, 1890–1933.* Harvard University Press, 1969.

———. *Max Weber: An Intellectual Biography.* University of Chicago Press, 2004.

Safranski, Rüdiger. *Nietzsche: A Philosophical Biography.* Norton, 2002 (German original: 2000).

Sagarra, Eda. *Germany in the Nineteenth Century: History and Literature.* Peter Lang, 2001.

Sammons, Jeffrey L. *Heinrich Heine: A Modern Biography.* Princeton University Press, 1979.

Sorkin, David. *The Transformation of German Jewry, 1780–1840.* Wayne State University Press, 1999.

Toews, John. *Hegelianism: The Path Toward Dialectical Humanism, 1805–1841.* Cambridge University Press, 1980.

———. *Becoming Historical: Cultural Reformation and Public Memory in Early Nineteenth-Century Berlin.* Cambridge University Press, 2004.

Townsend, Mary Lee. *Forbidden Laughter: Popular Humor and the Limits of Repression in Nineteenth-Century Prussia.* University of Michigan Press, 1992.

Williamson, George S. *The Longing for Myth in Germany: Religion and Aesthetic Culture from Romanticism to Nietzsche.* University of Chicago Press, 2004.

Young, Julian. *Friedrich Nietzsche: A Philosophical Biography.* Cambridge University Press, 2010.

Zimmerman, Andrew. *Anthropology and Antihumanism in Imperial Germany.* University of Chicago Press, 2001.

C. The Twentieth Century and Contemporary Era

1. Political History, including National Socialism and the Holocaust

Allen, William Sheridan. *The Nazi Seizure of Power: The Experience of a Single German Town, 1930–1935.* Quadrangle Books, 1965.

Aly, Götz and Susanne Heim. *Architects of Annihilation: Auschwitz and the Logic of Destruction* (German original: 1991). Princeton University Press, 2002.

Aschheim, Steven E. *Brothers and Strangers: The East European Jew in German and German Jewish Consciousness, 1800–1923*. University of Wisconsin Press, 1982.

Baranowski, Shelley. *Nazi Empire: German Colonialism and Imperialism from Bismarck to Hitler*. Cambridge University Press, 2010.

Bartov, Omer. *Hitler's Army: Soldiers, Nazis, and War in the Third Reich*. Oxford University Press, 1991.

Berger, Stefan. *Social Democracy and the Working Class in the Nineteenth and Twentieth Century Germany*. Longman, 2000.

Biess, Frank. *Homecomings: Returning POWs and the Legacies of Defeat in Postwar Germany*. Princeton University Press, 2006.

Bloxheim, Donald. *The Final Solution: A Genocide*. Oxford University Press, 2009.

Boemeke, Manfred F. with Gerald D. Feldman, and Elisabeth Glaser, eds. *The Treaty of Versailles: A Reassessment after 75 Years*. Cambridge University Press, 1998.

Broszat, Martin. *The Hitler State: The Foundation and Development of the Internal Structure of the Third Reich*. Longman, 1981.

Browning, Christopher R. *Ordinary Men. Reserve Police Battalion 101 and the Final Solution in Poland*. Harper, 1993.

Burleigh, Michael. *Germany Turns Eastwards: A Study of Ostforschung in the Third Reich*. Cambridge University Press, 1988.

Carsten, F.L. *Fascist Movements in Austria: from Schönerer to Hitler*. Sage Publications, 1977.

Chickering, Roger. *Imperial Germany and the Great War, 1914–1918*. Cambridge University Press, 2004.

———. *The Great War and Urban Life in Germany: Freiburg, 1914–1918*. Cambridge University Press, 2007.

Crew, David. *Germans on Welfare: From Weimar to Hitler*. Oxford University Press, 1998.

Earl, Hilary. *The Nuremberg SS-Einsatzgruppen Trial, 1945-1958: Atrocity, Law and History*. Cambridge University Press, 2010.

Epstein, Catherine. *The Last Revolutionaries: German Communists and Their Century*. Harvard University Press, 2003.

———. *Model Nazi: Arthur Greiser and the Occupation of Western Poland*. Oxford University Press, 2010.

Evans, Richard J. *The Coming of the Third Reich*. Penguin, 2004.

———. *The Third Reich in Power, 1933–1939*. Penguin, 2005.

———. *The Third Reich at War*. Penguin, 2009.

Fehrenbach, Heide. *Cinema in Democratizing Germany: Reconstructing National Identity after Hitler*. University of North Carolina Press, 1995.

Feinstein, Margarete Myers. *State Symbols: The Quest for Legitimacy in the Federal Republic of Germany and the German Democratic Republic, 1949–1959*. Brill Academic Publishers, 2001.

———. *Holocaust Survivors in Postwar Germany, 1945–1957*. Cambridge University Press, 2010.

Feldman, Gerald D. *Army, Industry, and Labor in Germany, 1914–1918*. Princeton University Press, 1966.

———. *The Great Disorder: Politics, Economics, and Society in the German Inflation, 1914–1924*. Oxford University Press, 1993.

Friedländer, Saul. *Nazi Germany and the Jews: The Years of Persecution, 1933–1939.* HarperCollins, 1997.

———. *Nazi Germany and the Jews, 1939–1945: The Years of Extermination.* Harper-Collins, 2007.

Fritzsche, Peter. *Life and Death in the Third Reich.* Harvard University Press, 2008.

Fulbrook, Mary. *German National Identity After the Holocaust.* Blackwell, 1999.

———. *The People's State: East German Society from Hitler to Honecker.* Yale University Press, 2005.

Gellately, Robert. *Backing Hitler: Consent and Coercion in Nazi Germany.* Oxford University Press, 2001.

Gerwarth, Robert. *The Bismarck Myth: Weimar Germany and the Legacy of the Iron Chancellor.* Oxford University Press, 2005.

Geyer, Michael and Sheila Fitzpatrick, eds. *Beyond Totalitarianism: Stalinism and Nazism Compared.* Cambridge University Press, 2009.

Gulick, Charles. *Austria from Habsburg to Hitler.* University of California Press, 1948.

Hamerow, Theodore S. *On the Road to the Wolf's Lair: German Resistance to Hitler.* Harvard University Press, 1997.

Herbert, Ulrich, ed. *National Socialist Extermination Policies: Contemporary German Perspectives and Controversies.* Berghahn, 2000 (German original: 1998).

Herf, Jeffrey. *Divided Memory: The Nazi Past in the Two Germanys.* Harvard University Press, 1997.

———. *The Jewish Enemy: Nazi Propaganda During World War II and the Holocaust.* Harvard University Press, 2006.

Hilberg, Raul. *The Destruction of the European Jews.* 3 vols. Yale University Press, 2003 (3rd ed. [1st ed.: 1961]).

James, Harold. *The Deutsche Bank and the Nazi Economic War against the Jews: The Expropriation of Jewish-Owned Property.* Cambridge University Press, 2001.

Kershaw, Ian. *Popular Opinion and Political Dissent in the Third Reich, Bavaria 1933–1945.* Oxford University Press, 1983.

———. *The Nazi Dictatorship. Problems and Perspectives of Interpretation.* Edward Arnold, 1989.

———. *The "Hitler Myth": Image and Reality in the Third Reich.* Oxford University Press, 2001.

———. *Hitler: A Biography.* Norton, 2010. Cf. Kershaw's two-volume scholarly version of this work: Norton, 2000–2001.

Kocka, Jürgen. *Facing Total War: German Society 1914–1918.* Harvard University Press, 1984 (German original: 1978).

———. *Civil Society and Dictatorship in Modern German History.* University Press of New England, 2010.

Kühne, Thomas. *Belonging and Genocide. Hitler's Community, 1918-1945.* Yale University Press, 2010.

Kundnani, Hans. *Utopia or Auschwitz: Germany's 1968 Generation and the Holocaust.* Columbia University Press, 2009.

Liulevicius, Vejas Gabriel. *War Land on the Eastern Front: Culture, National Identity, and German Occupation in World War I.* Cambridge University Press, 2000

Longerich, Peter. *Holocaust: The Nazi Persecution and Murder of the Jews.* Oxford University Press, 2010.

Marcuse, Harold. *Legacies of Dachau: The Uses and Abuses of a Concentration Camp, 1933–2001.* Cambridge University Press, 2001.

Markovits, Andrei and Philip S. Gorski. *The German Left: Red, Green and Beyond.* Oxford University Press, 1993.

Marrus, Michael R. *The Holocaust in History.* Brandeis University Press, 1987.

Mazower, Mark. *Hitler's Empire: Nazi Rule in Occupied Europe.* Penguin, 2008.

Mommsen, Hans. *From Weimar to Auschwitz. Essays on German History.* Polity Press, 1991.

_____. *The Rise and Fall of Weimar Democracy.* University of North Carolina Press, 1996 (German original: 1989).

_____. *Germans Against Hitler: The Stauffenberg Plot and Resistance Under the Third Reich.* MPS/Tauris, 2009 (German original: 2000).

Nolan, Mary. *Visions of Modernity: American Business and the Modernization of Germany.* Oxford University Press, 1994.

Peukert, Detlev J.K. *Inside Nazi Germany: Conformity, Opposition, and Racism in Everyday Life.* Yale University Press, 1987 (German original: 1981).

_____. *The Weimar Republic: The Crisis of Classical Modernity.* Hill and Wang, 1993 (German original: 1987).

Poiger, Uta G. *Jazz, Rock, and Rebels: Cold War Politics and American Culture in a Divided Germany.* University of California Press, 2000.

Rabinbach, Anson. *The Crisis of Austrian Socialism: From Red Vienna to Civil War, 1927–1934.* University of Chicago Press, 1983

Roseman, Mark, ed. *Generations in Conflict: Youth Revolt and Generation Formation in Germany, 1770–1968.* Cambridge University Press, 1995.

Schivelbusch, Wolfgang. *Three New Deals: Reflections on Roosevelt's America, Mussolini's Italy, and Hitler's Germany, 1933–1939.* Metropolitan Books, 2006.

Snyder, Timothy. *Bloodlands: Europe Between Hitler and Stalin.* Basic Books, 2010.

Sofsky, Wolfgang. *The Order of Terror: The Concentration Camp.* Princeton University Press, 1996.

Stahel, David. *Operation Barbarossa and Germany's Defeat in the East.* Cambridge University Press, 2009.

Stern, J.P. *Hitler: The Führer and the People.* University of California Press, 1975.

Stone, Dan, ed. *The Historiography of the Holocaust.* Palgrave Macmillan, 2006.

Vogt, Timothy R. *Denazification in Soviet-Occupied Germany: Brandenburg, 1945–1948.* Harvard University Press, 2000.

Weitz, Eric. *Creating German Communism 1890–1990: From Popular Protests to Socialist State.* Princeton University Press, 1998.

_____. *Weimar Germany: Promise and Tragedy.* Princeton University Press, 2007.

2. Society and Economy

Abraham, David. *The Collapse of the Weimar Republic: Political Economy and Crisis.* Holmes and Meier, 1986.

Balderston, Theo. *Economics and Politics in the Weimar Republic.* Cambridge University Press, 2002.

Baranowski, Shelley. *The Sanctity of Rural Life: Nobility, Protestantism, and Nazism in Weimar Prussia.* Oxford University Press, 1995.

Berghahn, Volker R. *The Americanisation of West German Industry, 1945–1973.* Cambridge University Press, 1986.

Berghahn, Volker R., ed. *Quest for Economic Empire: European Strategies of German Big Business in the Twentieth Century.* Berghahn Books, 1996.

Betts, Paul and Greg Eghigian, eds. *Pain and Prosperity: Reconsidering Twentieth-Century German History*. Stanford Univeristy Press, 2003.

Black, Monica. *Death in Berlin: From Weimar to Divided Germany*. Cambridge University Press, 2010.

Braun, Hans-Joachim. *The German Economy in the Twentieth Century*. Routledge, 2003.

Davis, Belinda J. *Home Fires Burning: Food, Politics, and Everyday Life in World War I Berlin*. University of North Carolina Press, 2000.

Gillerman, Sharon. *Germans into Jews: Remaking the Jewish Social Body in the Weimar Republic*. Stanford University Press, 2009.

Grossmann, Atina. *Reforming Sex: The German Movement For Birth Control and Abortion Reform, 1920–1950*. Oxford University Press, 1995.

_____. *Jews, Germans, and Allies: Close Encounters in Occupied Germany*. Princeton University Press, 2007.

Healy, Maureen. *Vienna and the Fall of the Habsburg Empire: Total War and Everyday Life in World War I*. Cambridge University Press, 2004.

Heineman, Elizabeth D. *What Difference Does a Husband Make? Women and Marital Status in Nazi and Postwar Germany*. University of California Press, 1999.

James, Harold. *The German Slump: Politics and Economics, 1924–1936*.Oxford University Press, 1986.

Kaplan, Marion A. *Between Dignity and Despair: Jewish Life in Nazi Germany*. Oxford University Press, 1998.

Kater, Michael H. *Doctors Under Hitler*. University of North Carolina Press, 1989.

Koonz, Claudia. *The Nazi Conscience*. Harvard University Press, 2003.

Roos, Julia. *Weimar Through the Lens of Gender: Prostitution Reform, Women's Emancipation, and German Democracy, 1919–1933*. University of Michigan Press, 2010.

Tooze, Adam. *The Wages of Destruction: The Making and Breaking of the Nazi Economy*. Viking, 2007.

Turner, Henry Ashby. *German Big Business and the Rise of Hitler*. Oxford University Press, 1985.

Weindling, Paul. *Health, Race, and German Politics between National Unification and Nazism, 1870–1945*. Cambridge University Press, 1989.

3. Intellectual and Cultural History

Breckmann, Warren et al., eds. *The Modernist Imagination: Intellectual History and Critical Theory: Essays in Honor of Martin Jay*. Berghahn Books, 2009.

Eley, Geoff, ed. *The "Goldhagen Effect": History, Memory, Nazism – Facing the German Past*. University of Michigan Press, 2000.

Elger, Dietmar. *Expressionism: A Revolution in German Art*. Taschen 1998.

Finlayson, James G. *Habermas: A Very Short Introduction*. Oxford University Press, 2005.

Gay, Peter. *Weimar Culture: The Outsider as Insider*. Norton, 2001.

Geyer, Michael, ed. *The Power of Intellectuals in Contemporary Germany*. University of Chicago Press, 2001.

Gordon, Peter Eli. *Continental Divide: Heidegger, Cassirer, Davos*. Harvard University Press, 2010.

Isenberg, Noah, ed. *Weimar Cinema: An Essential Guide to Classic Films of the Era.* Columbia University Press, 2009.

Jay, Martin. *The Dialectical Imagination: A History of the Frankfurt School and the Institute of Social Research, 1923–1950.* Little, Brown, 1973.

Jelavich, Peter. *Berlin Alexanderplatz: Radio, Film, and the Death of Weimar Culture.* University of California Press, 2006.

Kaes, Anton. *Shell Shock Cinema: Weimar Culture and the Wounds of War.* Princeton University Press, 2009.

Kater, Michael. *Different Drummers: Jazz in the Culture of Nazi Germany.* Oxford University Press, 1992.

_____. *Composers of the Nazi Era: Eight Portraits.* Oxford University Press, 2000.

Kracauer, Siegfried. *From Caligari to Hitler: A Psychological History of the German Film.* Princeton University Press, 2004 (German original: 1958).

Kurzke, Hermann. *Thomas Mann. Life as a Work of Art: A Biography.* Princeton University Press, 2002 (German original: 1999).

Maier, Charles S. *The Unmasterable Past: History, Holocaust, and German National Identity.* Harvard University Press, 1988.

Moeller, Robert G. *War Stories: The Search for a Usable Past in the Federal Republic of Germany.* University of California Press, 2003.

Moses, Dirk A. *German Intellectuals and the Nazi Past.* Cambridge University Press, 2007.

Müller, Jan-Werner. *Another Country: German Intellectuals, Unification, and National Identity.* Yale University Press, 2000.

_____. *A Dangerous Mind: Carl Schmitt in Post-War European Thought.* Yale University Press, 2003.

_____., ed. *German Ideologies since 1945: Studies in the Political Thought and Culture of the Bonn Republic.* Palgrave, 2003.

_____. *Constitutional Patriotism.* Princeton University Press, 2007.

Olick, Jeffrey K. *In The House of the Hangman: The Agonies of German Defeat, 1943–1949.* University of Chicago Press, 2005.

Rabinbach, Anson. *In The Shadow of Catastrophe: German Intellectuals Between Apocalypse and Enlightenment.* University of California Press, 2000.

Safranski, Rüdiger. *Martin Heidegger: Between Good and Evil.* Harvard University Press, 1998 (German original: 1994).

Schivelbusch, Wolfgang. *In a Cold Crater: Cultural and Intellectual Life in Berlin, 1945–1948.* University of California Press, 1998 (German original: 1995).

_____. *The Culture of Defeat: On National Trauma, Mourning, and Recovery.* Metropolitan Books, 2003 (German original: 2001).

Steinweis, Alan E. *Art, Ideology and Economics in Nazi Germany: The Reich Chambers of Music, Theater, and the Visual Arts.* University of North Carolina Press, 1993.

Welch, David. *Propaganda and the German Cinema, 1933–1945.* St. Martin's Press, 2001.

VII. Selected Films

These historically illuminating films, readily available with English subtitles, appear in roughly chronological order. They are with one exception (Szabó) the work of German- and Austrian-born directors, performed for the most part by German actors and actresses. For an encyclopedic view, see Robert C. Reimer and Carol J. Reimer, *Historical Dictionary of German Cinema* (Scarecrow Press, 2008).

Wiene, Robert. *The Cabinet of Dr. Caligari.* 1919.

Boese, Carl and Paul Wegener, *The Golem: How He Came Into the World.* 1920.

Murnau, F.W. *Nosferatu.* 1922.

————. *The Last Laugh.* 1924.

————. *Faust.* 1926.

Pabst, Georg Wilhelm. *Joyless Street.* 1925.

————. *Pandora's Box.* 1929.

————. *Diary of a Lost Girl.* 1929.

————. *Threepenny Opera.* 1931.

————. *Kameradschaft.* 1931.

Lang, Fritz. *Metropolis.* 1927.

————. *M.* 1931.

Ruttmann, Walter. *Berlin: Symphony of a Metropolis.* 1927.

Sternberg, Joseph von. *The Blue Angel.* 1930.

Riefenstahl, Leni. *Triumph of the Will.* 1934.

————. *Olympia: Festival of Nations & Festival of Beauty.* 1938.

————. See also: Muller, Ray. *Wonderful/Horrible Life: Leni Riefenstahl.* 1993.

Staudte, Wolfgang. *The Murderers Are Among Us.* 1946.

————. *Rotation.* 1949.

————. *The Kaiser's Lackey.* 1951.

Maetzig, Kurt. *Council of the Gods.* 1950.

Klein, Gerhard. *Berlin–Schönhauser Corner.* 1957.

Beyer, Frank. *Carbide and Sorrel.* 1963.

————. *Traces of Stones.* 1966.

————. *Naked Among Wolves.* 1967.

————. *Jacob the Liar.* 1975.

Wolf, Konrad. *Divided Heaven.* 1964.

————. *I Was Nineteen.* 1968.

Kluge, Alexander. *Yesterday Girl.* 1966.

————. *Germany in Autumn.* 1978.

Fassbinder, Rainer Werner. *The Niklashausen Journey.* 1970.

————. *Effi Briest.* 1974.

————. *Ali: Fear Eats the Soul.* 1974.

————. *The Third Generation.* 1979.

————. *The Marriage of Maria Braun.* 1979.

————. *Berlin Alexanderplatz.* 1980.

————. *Lola.* 1981.

Herzog, Werner. *The Enigma of Kaspar Hauser.* 1975.

————. *Woyzeck.* 1976.

————. *Heart of Glass.* 1976.

————. *Nosferatu the Vampyre.* 1979.

Schlöndorff, Volker. *Young Törless.* 1966.

————. *The Tin Drum.* 1979.

Schlöndorff, Volker and Margarethe von Trotta. *The Lost Honor of Katherina Blum.* 1975.

Syberberg, Hans-Jürgen. *Our Hitler: A Film From Germany.* 1977.

Trotta, Margarethe von. *Sisters or the Balance of Happiness.* 1979.

_____. *The German Sisters*. 1981.

_____. *Rosa Luxemburg*. 1986.

_____. *Vision: From the Life of Hildegard von Bingen*. 2009.

Reitz, Edgar. *Heimat 1–3*. 1980, 1992, 2004.

Wenders, Wim. *Wrong Move*. 1975.

_____. *The American Friend*. 1977.

_____. *Wings of Desire*. 1987.

Sanders-Brahms, Helma. *Under the Pavement Lies the Strand*. 1975.

_____. *Germany, Pale Mother*. 1980.

Petersen, Wolfgang. *Das Boot*. 1981.

Szabó, István. *Mephisto*. 1981.

_____. *Colonel Redl*. 1985.

Bickel, Rolf. *Verdict on Auschwitz. The Frankfurt Auschwitz Trial 1963–1965*. 1993.

Tykwer, Tom. *Run, Lola, Run*. 1998.

Schütte, Jan. *The Farewell*. 2000.

Richter, Roland Suso. *The Tunnel*. 2001.

Becker, Wolfgang. *Good Bye, Lenin!* 2003.

Schorr, Michael. *Schultze Gets the Blues*. 2003.

Hirschbiegel, Oliver. *The Downfall: Hitler and the End of the Third Reich*. 2004.

Rothemund, Marc. *Sophie Scholl: The Final Days*. 2005.

Levi, Dani. *Go For Zucker*. 2005.

Wirth, Franz-Peter. *Buddenbrooks*. 2006.

Akin, Fatih. *The Edge of Heaven*. 2007.

Donnersmarck, Florian Henkel von. *The Lives of Others*. 2007.

Edel, Uli. *The Baader-Meinhof Complex*. 2008.

Farberbock, Max. *Aimee and Jaguar*. 1998.

_____. *A Woman in Berlin*. 2008.

Haneke, Michael. *The Castle* (by Franz Kafka). 1997.

_____. *The White Ribbon*. 2009.

Index